JESUS OF NAZARETH

JESUS OF NAZARETH

His Life, Times, and Teaching

by

Joseph Klausner

Translated from the original Hebrew

by

Herbert Danby

With a new foreword
by
Sidney B. Hoenig

BLOCH PUBLISHING COMPANY
NEW YORK

New copyright © Material 1989
BLOCH PUBLISHING COMPANY, INC.

ISBN 0-8197-0565-9 paperback
ISBN 0-8197-0590-X hardcover

Manufactured in the United States of America

Foreword

Joseph Klausner (1874-1958) was one of the most eminent of Jewish historians of the first half of the twentieth century. He was the first to bring to the Jewish world, in a scholarly manner, the place and meaning of Jesus.

Klausner wrote his book in 1922 in the revived modern Hebrew tongue. In this Hebrew milieu, his volume became the best known work on Jesus by a Jew. Because of its popularity, it was translated into many languages. The English translation which is reprinted here was done by Canon Herbert Danby, the outstanding Christian translator of the Mishnah. Through this translation, Klausner's work became known to Christian students interested in the rabbinical sources of the period of the New Testament.

Klausner's work may be initially considered as an expansion of his doctoral thesis, *Jewish Messianic Ideas in the Tannaitic Period,* written in German at the University of Heidelberg in 1897. His deep concern with and immersion in this period led him, over the years, at his residences in Odessa, Heidelberg, and Jerusalem, to write four comprehensive volumes on the *History of Israel of the Second Temple Era.*

In his early twenties, Klausner had also come under the influence of the outstanding philosopher of the early Zionist movement, Ahad Ha-Am (Asher Ginsberg), who stressed the cultural and ethical contributions of Zionism to the world. In 1905, Klausner succeeded Ahad Ha-Am as the editor of the *Ha-Shiloah,* a Hebrew literary, social, and scientific monthly published first in Warsaw and then in Odessa, where he also taught in various schools. In 1920 he emigrated to Palestine where with great enthusiasm he threw himself into the revival of the Jewish National Home and its culture, becoming one of the most ardent of Zionist nationalists and chauvinists. All his works reflect this zeal.

It has been pointed out that Klausner, writing in Hebrew, did not mean to attract Christian readers. Hence, as he himself asserted, his approach to Jesus was not satiric or apologetic, as were many works about Christianity written by Jews in the Middle Ages. In his homeland Klausner did not fear Gentile hostility as would have been the case had he been living in the diaspora. He was thus able to view the events of the New Testament period as being specifically

Jewish. He accepted Jesus as a Jew, as did Wellhausen, but Klausner added that although Jesus was not a Christian, he became one, for his history and his teaching have been severed from Israel (p. 413).

Klausner had said that his book was written to provide "a truer idea of the historic Jesus, not a legendary, exaggerated account or a work of ridicule such as the medieval anonymously written *Toledot Jeshu.*" In his introduction he anticipated "abundant hostile criticism from Jews and Christians alike," which he did indeed receive. If, however, Klausner's volume were of minor significance, it would have been totally ignored, as are many "scholarly" writings. The fact that much vibrant attention had been given to it demonstrates its profound value and ongoing relevance even generations after the author has passed away. One critic, James Luther Adams, Professor of Divinity at Harvard University, wrote, "For the Christian scholar the book poses radical questions regarding the extremism, the lopsidedness, the impracticality of Jesus' ethics. The Christian will not easily dispose of these questions, if indeed he can do so at all."

Klausner's fundamental approach, as he points out in his own introduction, was to solve the great contradiction: "Though he (Jesus) was a Jew, his followers were not Jews." Klausner sought to resolve, as did many others, the anomaly that "Christianity was born within Israel, and Israel as a nation rejected it utterly. Why?" Many sought to explain this riddle in the fact that Christianity absorbed many Greek and heathen elements which stifled the Hebrew element with which Jesus was acquainted. Nevertheless, Klausner maintained that Jesus' teachings "certainly had within them the germs from which there could and must develop in the course of time a non-Jewish and even anti-Jewish teaching." This factor, as Klausner asserted, was the main problem he sought to solve in his book. Hence he studied the Jewish environment as well as what there was in Jesus' charactor per se which was opposed to the Judaism of his own time. Klausner refrained from *apologia* or defining the superiority of one faith above another; he only stressed that the object of his book was to show simply "how Judaism differs and remains distinct from Christianity or Christianity from Judaism." This research is especially relevant today in the face of the growth of missionary movements such as "Jews for Jesus" and similar cults, all seeking to attract Jews to evangelism. Klausner persisted that there was no subjectivity in his research but that "they who continue to establish missionary societies not only for the benefit of the heathen but also for Jews — they are open to the suspicion of subjectivity in all that touches Jews and Christianity, far more than me . . . "

One must always recall Klausner's own statements to comprehend the importance of his books. On the Jewishness of Jesus, he wrote, "Jesus was a Jew and a Jew he remained till his last breath. His one idea was to implant within his nation the idea of the coming of the Messiah and by repentance and good works, hasten the end" (p. 368).

In his discussion of the opposition of Judaism to the teachings of Jesus, he wrote: "The Judaism of that time had no other aim than to save the tiny nation, the guardian of great ideals, from sinking into the broad sea of heathen culture and enable it, slowly and gradually, to realize the moral teachings of the Prophets in *civil life* and in the *present world* of the Jewish state and nation."

Klausner continued, "Hence the nation as a whole could only see in such public ideals as those of Jesus, an abnormal and even dangerous fantasy. This teaching of Jesus became, on the one hand, the negation of everything that had vitalized Judaism, and on the other hand, it brought Judaism to such an extreme that it became in a sense, *non-Judaism*" (p. 376).

One perceives in these statements Klausner's deep nationalism and chauvinism and also his defense of Judaism. Jews and Christians alike will not object to his evaluation of the results of Jesus' teachings. Their objections may be only to his stress of Jesus' morality and ethics which Klausner characterized: "The main strength of Jesus lay in his ethical teachings" (p. 381). Many Jews could not accept this; on the other hand, Christians could not and still cannot accept at all Klausner's negation of Jesus' Messianic role.

Klausner's theses were a continuance of the writing on the historicity and life of Jesus written by Protestant scholars before Schweitzer's monumental contributions to Christian theology. Albert Schweitzer stressed the eschatotogy in the teaching of Jesus, namely that this factor encompassed the entirety of Jesus' life, and he considered this feature as being more historical than even Jesus' existence. Whereas Schweitzer aimed to reject the Jesus of the earlier Protestant liberal scholars, Klausner, continuing the historical perspective, sought the meaning of Jesus from a nationalistic Hebrew standpoint. Klausner emphasized that Jesus could be neither the Messiah nor a prophet; nor did he possess the spirit of "national consolation in the political national sense." Klausner also stressed that Jesus was not a lawgiver or Pharisaic rabbi, for he lacked knowledge of the positive elements in Pharisaic teaching; nor was he fully acquainted with *Halakha* and its legal features. However, Klausner regarded Jesus as a ' great teacher of morality and an artist in parables'' (p. 414), one who was concerned particularly with *Aggada.* Klausner felt that in Jesus' "ethical code there is a sublimity, distinctiveness and originality in form unparalleled in any other Hebrew ethical code . . . If ever the day should come that this ethical code be stripped of its wrappings of miracles and mysticism, the book of the ethics of Jesus will be one of the choicest treasures in the literature of Israel for all time."

Further analysis of the volume displays Klausner's pedagogic methodology. He divides his work into many "books." This exceptional ability is also seen in his *History of the Second Temple Era,* which is well organized and arranged for the student and reader to follow with ease and comprehension. Klausner begins this volume with the sources and the period, then traces the early life of Jesus, his ministry, Jesus' revelation as a Messiah, his presence in Jerusalem, and the trial and crucifixion. It is in the last book (the eighth) entitled "The Teaching of Jesus" that Klausner's special perspective is ascertained. This section deals with the Jewishness of Jesus, the distinctions between Judaism and Jesus' teachings, and Jesus' idea of God, his ethical teachings, the Day of Judgment, and the Kingdom of God.

Reference has been made to the eschatological features of Jesus' teaching which Klausner also discussed. Interestingly, in this vein, a Protestant scholar, Morton S. Enslin in his book *The Prophet from Nazareth* (1962) also emphasized the eschatology of the Christian faith but he held that Jesus never fully explained these pronouncements. Thus, one perceives that Klausner's analysis and evaluation of Jesus' morals and faith and their basis in Judaism are even more relevant now, fifty years after the appearance of Klausner's work.

Criticism of Klausner evolved particularly because of his assertion that the moral teachings of Jesus are superior to those of the Mishnah, the Talmud, and of the Jews of his time. Klausner believed that the teachings of the New Testament are the product of an individual Jesus, while those of the Talmud represent the thinking of many individuals. At times Klausner even aroused resentment when he compared Jesus' ethical ideals with those of Jeremiah, Hillel, and the Talmud, and claimed Jesus' superiority over them in this regard (pp. 389, 390, 397). However, to temper this judgment, he wrote that Jesus gave nothing to his nation and cared not at all for reforming civilization; to adopt the teachings of Jesus, therefore, is to remove oneself from this world. Judaism could not accede to such an ethical ideal which leads to monasticism.

The sections or "books" of Klausner's work dealing with political and religious backgrounds have been severely criticized by rabbinical specialists who claimed that Klausner's writing was a result more of his "imagination than supporting documents." He is characterized also as an amateur Talmudist and a dilettante in the Gospels. To his credit, however, it is to be emphatically asserted that Klausner reviewed much of Gospel scholarship (Sandmel, p. 92). It has also been suggested that if Klausner had drawn from Claude Montefiore's *Synoptic Gospels,* his *Jesus* would have had even greater impact (Sandmel, p. 93). It may be that Klausner, as a disciple of Ahad Ha-Am, did not utilize Montefiore because of his teacher's criticism of that author. Ahad Ha-Am, in his "On Two Threshholds," said that Montefiore's approach to Christianity was a prelude to conversion (Sandmel, *We Jews and Jesus* p. 91).

One of the greatest critiques of Klausner's work, from a Jewish point of view, was written by Arnold Kaminka (*Ha-Toren,* August 1922; see *Harvard Theological Review,* XVI, 1923). Kaminka held that there were academic deficiencies in Klausner's volume and that he was catering to the Christians. To this G. F. Moore (in H.T.R.) added: "Kaminka's criticisms are frequently sound and if the polemic is bitter and sometimes descends to invective, we may be reminded that the Jews have small reason to admire Christian ethics in application, whether ecclesiastical, political, social or individual and judging the tree by the fruit it has borne in 18 centuries of persecution, they not unnaturally resent Christian assertions of its preeminence and still more even the qualified admission of such claims by a Jew."

How correct this assessment was can be seen from the following: When Rabbi Stephen S. Wise, commenting on Klausner's book in

January 1925, publicly reclaimed Jesus for Judaism, he, as a spiritual leader, suffered much personal abuse because of the public and reactionary notice his remarks attracted. Many Jews fanatically rejected Klausner's dream of a reclaimed Jesus.

As the translator Herbert Danby already pointed out, many Christians could not agree with Klausner's thesis of Jesus as a teacher of morality only, not a Messiah. Others asserted that Klausner was arrogant and condescending (Sandmel, *We Jews and Jesus,* p. 92). Yet they accepted his volume because it presented the Jewish background and the Hebraic sources of the Gospels, and Christian scholars relied upon him as a rabbinical and historical authority. Klausner argued that he was objective in his approach. Nevertheless, some Christian scholars saw only subjectivity in his writings, asserting that he reflected his own perspective that Jesus was "undoubtedly a nationalist Jew by instinct and even an extreme nationalist." Klausner backed up his position by reference to Jesus' deprecatory manner of referring to the "heathen and the publicans," and also stressed Jesus' love for Jerusalem and his devotion to the "lost sheep of Israel." Christian scholars, on the other hand, would naturally emphasize Jesus' general humanity, namely that he came as a "light to the gentiles," and they stressed the value of Jesus' teachings from the point of view of universal history.

Jewish scholars, however, felt that Klausner was truckling to the Gentile world, although he wrote for Jews in the Hebrew language, and that his approach was far removed from that of traditional Judaism. Some scholars also disagreed with Klausner's scholarship. While Klausner's book gives to the Christian world the essence of the Jewish background and the various rabbinical references which previously they obtained only from the writings of A. Edersheim and Emil Schurer, many Jewish scholars felt that Klausner simply gave his own individualistic interpretation of the rabbinical materials and often misread the basic point of the rabbinical statements.

One of the greatest and severest critics of Klausner's work was the late Professor Solomon Zeitlin of Dropsie University. In his usual determined manner, he wrote that Klausner was of the opinion that Jesus was an historical person and that in the *Corpus Tannaiticus* mention is made of Jesus. Zeitlin (J.Q.R. July 1923) referred to A. Drews who wrote, in *Witnesses To The Historicity of*

Jesus, that Talmudic passages are no proof of Jesus as an historical person, since it is universally accepted that it was in the beginning of the second century that the Gospels were compiled. Therefore, the Talmudists obtained their knowledge of Jesus from adherents of Christianity who quoted from the Gospels. Zeitlin also disagreed with Klausner who accepted the statement about Jesus in Josephus' work as genuine, asserting that "even the most conservative Christian scholars admit that the passage is not authentic."

In his volume, Klausner supplies many proofs of Jesus' life from the Synoptic Gospels. To this Zeitlin retorted, "Mark is far more a primary authority for the thought of the Apostolic Age than for the life of Jesus." As to the latter, particularly concerning the details of the last Passover meal and Jesus' trial, Zeitlin maintained that Klausner "blindly follows D. Chwolson and others and even sometimes accepts two views which do not harmonize." Chwolson had maintained that the court which tried Jesus was composed of Sadducees, notwithstanding the fact that the procedure outlined in the Mishnah is Pharisaic. W. R. Husband, in his *Prosecution of Jesus* (1916), suggested that Jesus was tried by the Romans and the Jews mentioned in connection with the trial were but a kind of grand jury; therefore, we need not concern ourselves with the laws of the Mishnah prohibiting such trials at night and on the eve of a holiday. Zeitlin insisted that Klausner in his eclectic manner adopted both views as noted in this book on p. 340: "According to Mark (XIV. 54) and Matthew (XXVI. 57) the Sanhedrin held a session that same night, which was illegal since capital cases could be tried by day only (Sanh. IV 11). But, as we have seen, the Sanhedrin was mainly composed of Sadducees and the Sadducees may have recognized no such rule. Furthermore we have assumed that this was not a trial proper, but only a preliminary investigation for which there was no rule that its work should be carried out by day only." Thus, Zeitlin aimed to demolish Klausner's approach. In all fairness, however, the latter part of Klausner's statement in this paragraph best demonstrates the mode of his methodology. Klausner added (*ibid.*), "These explanations are, however, uncalled for, since Luke knows nothing whatever of a night session: according to him there was but one session of the Sanhedrin, and that in the morning" (Luke XXII. 54, 66).

Klausner's book, in addition to his research and views on Jesus, offers important insights into many continuous and pertinent problems that affect the human being and his existence, in general, as well as that of the Jew in particular. Many of these opinions are noteworthy. For example, Klausner says, "Judaism is not only religion and it is not only ethics: it is the sum-total of all the needs of the nation, placed on a religious basis. It is a national world outlook with an ethico-religious basis" (p. 390).

This is still one of the most valuable books for the information of the interested reader and particularly for the student of the New Testamental period. As Klausner points out (p. 125), he has summarized the work of hundreds of scholars of all nations, but he entered into his own study and his own ". . . account of the life of Jesus untrammelled by any need of entering into any controversy on particular points." Thus, Klausner did not seek to make his book a polemical scholarly volume but one that could be comprehended and accepted by every reader eager to know about Jesus.

Klausner also made various judgments pertaining to the Fourth Gospel. He minimized its importance for the historical life of Jesus, saying, "It may well include a few historical fragments handed down by the author (who was certainly not John the disciple) by tradition; but, speaking generally its value is theological rather than historical or biographical." Today, some Christian theologians believe that the Fourth Gospel is of an earlier period, but the point remains unsettled.

Klausner also stressed a very important point that has been repeated by later scholars, although for many reasons they refrained from mentioning Klausner. He stated, ". . . in any case they (Jesus' acts, arguments and parables) cannot be understood without a knowledge of the Oral Law as it was in the days of Hillel and Shammai" (p. 127).

Similarly, Klausner emphasized (p. 131), "It is also of foremost importance not to confuse periods . . . . to adduce evidence from such a late Midrash as the *Pesikta Rabbati,* or the *Midrash Va-Yoshua* about first century Judaism is tantamount to studying the ideas of Jesus in the writings of Thomas Aquinas."

These insights are most significant in that they show Klausner's incisive and penetrating methodology. He did not hesitate to acknowledge Adolf Büchler who repeatedly emphasized the marked difference between the ideas of the Jews before and after the Bar Kokhba revolt. On the other hand, he did not hesitate to criticize (p. 133) even Yitzhaq Isaac Halevy, saying "It is impossible to argue with one who believes that the Oral Law was finally completed in the time of Ezra and Nehemiah; his researches are simply a result of the necessity imposed on our orthodoxy of antedating everything." A careful reading of this volume will be of inestimable value to the student and show him the true meaning and method of scholarly research.

In his notes Klausner also adds many vital points which are still matters of scholarly controversy. He discusses the title "Rabbi," for example, which also occurs in the Gospels. Klausner (p. 256) maintained, "Yet even though, as an official title for a 'disciple of the wise,' "Rabbi" had not become a fixed title in the time of Jesus, it was already in use in current speech as an unofficial title of honor."

Klausner displays a vast knowledge of sources in every realm. His notes reveal an acquaintance with the Talmud, Midrash, and the Church Fathers, as well as a knowledge of the literature of J. Derenbourg, H. P. Chajes, M. Joel, A. Deissmann, G. Dalman, R. Travers Herford, Samuel Krauss, D. Chwolson, Abraham Geiger, W. Bacher, A. Büchler, M. Guedemann, A. Neubauer, Oscar Holtzmann, Wilhelm Bousset, Emil Schürer, Z. Frankel, Adolph Harnack, and even J. J. Rousseau and Albert Schweitzer. We see, therefore, that Klausner in his preparation for his book devoted full attention to all that preceded him. Even if all of Klausner's conclusions are not accepted, his volume is noteworthy because of its encyclopedic scope, reviewing the opinions of the many scholars who labored in this field of intertestamental study. Even in this decade of anthologies and compilations, Klausner's work is of great value for the information it provides about this period, a fact already recognized by many Christian scholars.

Klausner's volume also takes into account the geography of Israel, the synagogues of Capernaum and Chorazin which have recently emerged into prominence in archelology, the parables in the Talmud, Talmudic medicine, correct readings in the Gospels, the place of the Am Haaretz, the Last Supper as a Passover meal, and Messianic signs in Josephus and the Talmud; in addition, a host of other subjects so important to the study of the intertestamental period are weighed and evaluated here. The general index as well as the index of Biblical and Rabbinical passages add a facility for the use of this volume as a constant handbook in the study of the period in every phase of its research. The reprinting of this volume, making available to all that which has been out of print for years, is most commendable. Klausner's work reread may even stimulate further study of the vital period of the Parting of the Ways and the place of Jesus in the Jewish world — past and present.

TRANSLATOR'S PREFACE

Dr. Joseph Klausner, though not widely known among non-Jews (outside the small group of Christian students interested in the Rabbinical sources for the New Testament period) has a high and well-earned reputation as writer, historian and leader of thought in those Jewish circles which are working in the cause of the present Hebrew cultural revival, commonly called Zionism. To this cause he has devoted his whole life. He was born in Russia in 1874. He early came under the influence of "Ahad ha-Am" (Asher Ginsberg), the philosopher of the Zionist movement and editor of the principal Hebrew periodical, "Ha-Shiloach." In 1897 he entered the University of Heidelberg where he studied Philosophy and Semitic languages. For his degree of Ph.D. he wrote the thesis "Die messianischen Vorstellungen des jüdischen Volkes im Zeitalter der Tannaiten" (*i.e.* Jewish Messianic ideas in the *Tannaitic* period), a subject of study at which he has ever since persistently worked and which compelled him to devote an attention, closer and more minute than had yet been given by any Jewish scholar, to the subject of Jesus, his Messianic claims, and the problem of Christian origins. Dr. Klausner's "Die messianischen Vorstellungen" was published (in German) in 1904, and it is by this book that he has hitherto been known in non-Jewish circles. The bulk of his literary output since has been in Hebrew. This output has been considerable. Apart from the present book (published in Jerusalem in the spring of 1922) his most important publications are:

> The Messianic Idea in Israel (3 vols.: vol. i, In the Prophets [Cracow, 1909] ; vol. ii, In the apocalyptic and pseudepigraphic literature [Jerusalem, 1921] ; vol. iii, In the *tannaitic* period, *i.e.,* first two centuries A.D. [Jerusalem, 1923, translated from the German edition of 1904 and revised]) ;
> The History of Israel (4 vols.: vol. i, Till the Maccabæan age [Odessa, 1909, 3rd ed., Odessa, 1919] ; vol. ii, The Maccabæan Age [Jerusalem, 1923] ; vol. iii, The Herodian Age [Jerusalem, 1924] ; vol. iv, The Jewish Revolt and the Destruction of the Temple [Jerusalem, 1924]).

In 1905 Dr. Klausner succeeded "Ahad ha-Am" as editor of "Ha-Shiloach," and he has edited this, the most important Hebrew literary periodical, ever since. From 1904 till 1919 he held various academic posts in Jewish institutions in Odessa. He came to Palestine in 1920 and at once took a leading position, both as writer and public worker, in the new Hebrew life of the "Jewish National Home."

This is not the place to touch upon the merits of Dr. Klausner's "Life of Jesus"; but a few remarks may be offered as to its significance. As the author points out, this is the first time such a work has been attempted in Hebrew with neither satiric nor apologetic bias. The book was intended for "Jewish Hebrew readers," *i.e.* for those Jews with the revived "Hebrew cultural outlook" on life—a life whose spiritual centre is, or is hoped to be, in Palestine, far removed from the distractions, the obstacles, the fears, and the Gentile hostility which (too often) form the dominating features of the "Galuth." The Jewish nationalist historian, resident at last in Palestine, assured of the safety of his national life, feels himself free to scan the whole range of his nation's life in Palestine, and he no longer thinks it a danger to look with open eyes at the persons and events which ushered in the Christian age. He can look upon them as specifically *Jewish* events, and he can bring the historian's craft to bear and, to the best of his ability and without rancour, define the causes which made possible the rise of Christianity and estimate what, to his mind, constitutes the significance of the Founder of Christianity. Or, from another point of view, the Jewish historian, seeking to display the national and cultural achievements of his people, is free to include in his gallery the person and life of Jesus of Nazareth. Dr. Klausner has, therefore, thought it a duty to his people to place this life before them, and to throw such light upon it as he was able by means of his own learning and researches in contemporary Jewish history and literature, and his knowledge of the critical work done by his predecessors, Jews and non-Jews.

The book is not, of course, intended for Christians. They will, and quite rightly, find much in it to dislike. Though the author is conscientiously convinced that he has been quite untouched by subjective influences, the Christian reader will not agree. But apart from this, the Christian reader, and especially the Christian scholar, will be thankful for the material which the book provides for the better understanding of the Jewish mental and historical environment in which our Lord worked and lived. The fact is deserving of considerable emphasis that here, probably for the first time,[1] there is set out a full range of what modern Jewish scholarship has to offer on the subject of the Jewish background of the Gospels. On some minor points Jewish scholars will be found to differ, but the picture as a whole may be taken as representing the best that unimpeachable Jewish learning has to show. The Rabbinical sources are a most formidable subject of study and quite beyond the capacity of all but

---

[1] Mr. Israel Abrahams of Cambridge, the late Dr. S. Schechter, and, earlier, Daniel Chwolsohn have contributed much in this sphere; but they have only touched on isolated points.

the smallest handful of non-Jewish students. Hitherto Christians have depended on such works as A. Edersheim's "Life and Times of Jesus the Messiah," and the collections of Rabbinical illustrative matter by Lightfoot, Schöttgen and Wetstein, in all of which there is no pretence at critical sifting or weighing of the Jewish material. For a critical knowledge of the Jewish background of the Gospels the Christian can never wholly dispense with Jewish scholarship.[2] The present work gives this in a handy, accessible form, and this fact alone seemed to justify its translation into English.

The book was composed in "modern Hebrew" and this is probably the first time that a modern Hebrew book of any considerable size has been translated into English. At the express wish of the author literalness in the translation has been preserved to the very limit of what is endurable in English,[3] though it is hoped that the limit has not been transgressed. The Hebrew vocabulary in use is not extensive, and its adverbs and adjectives are comparatively few and inelastic; this must excuse the somewhat dead-level of the narrative.

Since the work was intended for Hebrew-reading Jews, the references, whenever possible, are to accessible Hebrew books dealing with the subject in question, in spite of the fact that more standard and more authoritative works in other languages were in existence. These references have been preserved (though their practical utility may be small) with the idea of showing something of the scope of modern Hebrew literature and to how great a degree it interests itself in the subject of the present work. The translator regrets that the obviously desirable course was not followed of replacing, by references to English versions (original or translated), references to the same authority (translated or original) in a language other than English. But this would have involved labour for which the leisure was lacking.

Jerusalem,
January 30, 1925.

[2] Good as is Schürer's *Jewish People in the Time of Jesus Christ*, it uses but a small fragment of the available Rabbinical material, and much of his treatment, even of that, is open to criticism.

[3] The author's hope is that many of his fellow-Jews, who are English-speaking, may be helped by this translation to acquire a knowledge of present-day Hebrew.

INTRODUCTION

Voltaire, who was by no means a friend of the Jews, wrote a "Dialogue du douteur et de l'adorateur," [1] in which he makes the rational-minded Believer say many very severe things about the Jews —that they are the "crudest of Asiatics," while their historical traditions are, to his mind, "the most utterly foolish and futile." To this the Doubter replies:

"I agree that the Jewish faith was futile and abominable; but, after all, Jesus, whom you love, was a Jew. He always observed the Jewish religion and adhered to all its customs."

The Believer, obviously perplexed, answers:

"This again is a great contradiction: though he was a Jew, his followers were not Jews."

By these words—which certainly fell from him unintentionally— Voltaire suggested that he too did not attempt either to explain or to ignore this "great contradiction" which is the chief feature in the difficult and complicated central problem in any book dealing with the life of Jesus. The present book is an attempt to solve this problem.

We have before us two facts: (a) Jesus was born, lived and died in Israel and was a Jew in every respect; (b) his disciples, and still more disciples' disciples, removed far away from Israel, or, rather, the more numerous and more powerful of the Jews rejected the teaching of Jesus: they rose up against it during his lifetime and, even when all the world drew nearer and nearer to Christianity, would not become Christians. Christianity was born within Israel, and Israel as a nation rejected it utterly. Why?

Many Jews and Christians would find the reason in the fact that Christianity, from the time of Paul, absorbed many Greek and heathen elements which all but stifled the Hebrew elements which were all that Jesus knew. Yet, when all is said and done, "as is the tree so is the fruit"; and from a man's disciples, and even from his disciples' disciples, it is possible to draw conclusions about the original teacher. Had there not been in Jesus' teaching something contrary to the "world-outlook" of Israel, there could never have arisen out of it a new teaching so irreconcilable with the spirit of Judaism: *ex nihilo nihil fit*. Though Jesus' teaching may not have been deliberately directed against contemporary Judaism, it certainly had within it the germs from which there could and must develop in course of time a non-Jewish and even an anti-Jewish teaching.

[1] *Dialogues satiriques et philosophiques*, XI.

9

This is the most important, though by no means the only, problem which we seek to solve in the present book. Firstly, by a full account of the times of Jesus and of his Jewish environment, and, secondly, by an account of his life and teaching (which in the case of any great pioneer are one and the same thing), we shall get a clear idea of what there was in him of earlier and contemporary Judaism, and likewise of what there was in him which was opposed to the Judaism of his own time as well as to that of the past and the future generations of Israel.

We shall thus ascertain *not* the superiority of Christianity to Judaism (that we leave to Christian apologists and missionaries), and *not* the superiority of Judaism to Christianity (that we leave to Jewish apologists and to those who would prove Israel's world-mission), but simply how Judaism *differs* and *remains distinct* from Christianity or Christianity from Judaism. This alone is the object of the present book; and every effort has been made to keep it within the limits of pure scholarship and to make it as objective as possible, avoiding those subjective religious and nationalist aims which do not come within the purview of scholarship. Should there emerge from the study of this difference and distinctness the right of Judaism to exist, this will be an advantage, but it is not a purpose for which I could permit myself to deviate from scientific truth or to modify facts out of zeal for the Jewish religion or the Jewish race.

I have no wish here to argue for or against Judaism and Christianity, but merely to explain and expound the "great contradiction" spoken of by Voltaire. The fact that Judaism gave birth to Christianity proves that Christianity much resembles Judaism; but the fact that Judaism never became Christianity and always followed its own particular path, is a standing witness that in many ways Judaism is *not* like Christianity. It only remains to show wherein they are alike and wherein they differ, without discussing at all whether the differences are or are not to the advantage of either. Only so can one remain within the limits of pure scholarship and avoid subjectivity. Only by such an attitude to the problem can one keep from becoming a religious or national apologist.

Such an objective attitude the writer has struggled to maintain throughout the entire book. If Christian students suspect it of subjectivity simply because the author is a Jew and because the book was written in Hebrew, I can only say to them: Remove first the beam from your own eye! As Christians they are far more suspect of a leaning towards Jesus the Christian. They whose faith is paramount, conducing to wealth and honour, they who continue to establish missionary societies not only for the benefit of the heathen but also for the Jews—they are open to the suspicion of subjectivity in all that touches Jesus and Christianity, far more than are we, the Jews, whose faith is trodden down to the lowest depths and who neither wish nor are able to practice proselytism among Christians.

But the explanation of Jesus' relation to Judaism and the relation of the Jews to Jesus, is not the sole aim. Above all things, the writer wished to provide in Hebrew for Hebrews a book which shall tell the history of the Founder of Christianity along the lines of modern criticism, without either the exaggeration and legendary accounts of the evangelists, or the exaggeration and the legendary and depreciatory satires of such books as the *Tol'doth Yeshu*, or the *Ma'asēh Talui*. Of the necessity for such a book it is needless to speak at length: it is enough to say that there has never yet been in Hebrew any book on Jesus the Jew which had not either a Christian propagandist aim—to bring Jews to Christianity,[2] or a Jewish religious aim—to render Christianity obnoxious to Jews.

If I can give Hebrew readers a truer idea of the *historic* Jesus, an idea which shall be alike far from that of Christian or Jewish dogma, which shall be objective and scientific in every possible way, which shall also give some conception of a teaching akin to Judaism yet at the same time far removed from it, and some conception of the civil, economic and spiritual environment of the Jews in the days of the Second Temple,[3] an environment which made possible this historical scene and this new teaching—then I shall know that I have filled a blank page (from the point of view of Hebrew writers) in the History of Israel which has so far been written upon almost solely by Christians.

Of the contents and form of this book I need say little: the reader will grasp them by himself. I would only remark that the work is divided into several "books," each complete in itself and of the nature of a short monograph, preceded in each case by a detailed list of the more important books on the subject, supplementing the books of secondary importance noted at the commencement of the sub-sections and in the footnotes. Thus the *First Book* is devoted to a study of the sources for the history of Jesus, the *Second* to a description of the political, economic and spiritual life of his days, while those which follow are devoted to a description of the life and the teaching of Jesus.

The reader who is anxious to know the history of Jesus himself must needs possess himself of a little patience, unless he prefers to pass over the first two books. More especially patience is required from the average reader in the *First Book:* study of sources never makes very easy reading, and so this section may prove tiresome to a reader unaccustomed to Hebrew learning and science in general. But no other course was possible: to lay a firm foundation for any

[2] Such as *Sefer Tol'doth Yeshu*, by Eben Tzohar (Lichtenstein), Leipzig, 1885; and *Ben Adam: the Life of Jesus Christ and his Works*, by P. Levertoff, published by the *Eduth l'Yisrael* [a Jewish Mission in London], London-Cracow, 1905.

[3] "The Second Temple" is the term adopted throughout the book to signify the period of Jewish history from the Return from Exile until the destruction of the Temple by the Romans in 70 C.E.

considerable building one must first clear the foundation of stones and fragments and sand.

I am quite aware that the method of this book will provoke abundant hostile criticism from Jews and Christians alike. But here again I ask for patience: I have strong hopes that either side, once it reads the book without prejudice, will acknowledge that, whether right or wrong, it is at least written with the best intentions. I only beg one thing: the book has been written during a long course of years crammed with work and the search for truth: may its readers peruse it with the same good intentions with which it was written!

[Lausanne, Eve of Sukkoth, 1907—Jerusalem, 16 Marcheswan, 1922.]

CONTENTS

SHORT GLOSSARY OF TECHNICAL HEBREW TERMS OCCURRING IN THE TRANSLATION

Amoraim (sing. *Amora;* adj. *amoraitic*): Authorities, from the third to the fifth centuries, whose comments and disputations form the substance of the *Gemara* (q.v.) in both *Talmud Babli* and *Talmud Verushalmi.*

Baraita: A tradition emanating as a rule from the *Tannaim* (q.v.) or from the *tannaitic* period, and quoted in the later strata of the *Talmuds* and other Rabbinical literature, but not included in the *Mishna,* the authoritative code of the *tannaitic* traditions.

Gemara: The later (and very much the more profuse) *stratum* in the two *Talmuds,* containing the comments, additions and disputations contributed by the *Amoraim* to the subject-matter of the *Mishna,* either by way of explanation or as (more or less) bearing on the points raised in the *Mishna.*

Haggada (adj. *haggadic* or *haggadistic*): A type of scriptural exegesis, homiletic and edifying rather than logical or legalistic in character; it utilizes at will any current beliefs, legends or folklore. It is rarely used in the *Mishna,* but figures largely in *Gemara* and certain other Rabbinical writings.

Halakha (adj. *halakhic*): A legal binding decision derived by Rabbinical logical processes from the written *Torah.*

Midrash (adj. *midrashic*): (a) Interpretation of Scripture, either *haggadic* or *halakhic* in character; (b) a systematic commentary on *"midrashic"* lines, on a portion of the Scriptures (thus Genesis *Rabba* is a *"Midrash"* or Rabbinical commentary on the book of Genesis).

Mishna: The earlier *stratum* of the two *Talmuds* and (with exceptions) identical in each. It is a codification of the "Oral Law" arranged according to subjects and subdivided into sixty-three "tractates." It was completed in its present form by R. Vehuda ha-Nasi at the beginning of the third century.

Shema' ("Hear!"): The most essential portion of a Jewish act of prayer. It is made up of the three passages: Deut. vi. 4-9 (beginning "Hear, O Israel!"), Deut. xi. 13-21, and Numbers xv. 37-41.

Talmud Babli and *Talmud Verushalmi:* Around the *Mishna* arose a mass of comment, expository matter, illustration and debate, known as *Gemara.* Two Jewish centres, in Palestine and Babylonia, produced each an independent *Gemara.* The *Gemara* of the Palestinian centre and that of the Babylonian centre, together with the original *Mishna,* constitute respectively the *Talmud Verushalmi* and the *Talmud Babli.* The former was completed in the fourth century, and the latter about a century later. The *Talmud Verushalmi* is much shorter than the *Babli* and treats only 39 of the 63 divisions of the *Mishna.*

Tannaim (adj. *tannaitic*): The authorities of the first two centuries, from Hillel and Shammai to R. Vehuda ha-Nasi. It is their views, and the traditions they preserved, which are codified in the *Mishna.*

Torah (lit. instruction): (a) The books of "the Law" (of Moses), *i.e.* the Pentateuch; (b) the traditional Jewish "Law" generally, both written and oral (*i.e.* both the written Pentateuch and the "Tradition of the elders").

Tosefta: A compilation of *tannaitic* material similar in scope and arrangement to the *Mishna.* Its relation to the *Mishna* is uncertain: parts of it seem to come from collections of traditions earlier than the present *Mishna,* but its completion, in the form we have it, must be much later. It often gives much fuller treatment and includes matters omitted by the *Mishna.*

(For a fuller explanation of these terms the reader is referred to: *A Short Survey of the Literature of Rabbinical and Mediæval Judaism* by W. O. E. Oesterley and G. H. Box (London, 1920), or *Introduction to the Talmud,* by M. Mielziner (2nd ed., New York, 1903).)

FIRST BOOK:

THE SOURCES

JESUS OF NAZARETH

FIRST BOOK

THE SOURCES

GENERAL REMARKS

[One or more special chapters in almost every book on the Life of Jesus are devoted to the sources for this life. A valuable and scholarly account of these may be found in the second chapter of Holtzmann's "Leben Jesu," Tübingen u. Leipzig, 1901, pp. 6-47. An entirely scholarly though popular account is to be found in Paul Wernle, "Die Quellen des Lebens Jesu" ("Religionsgeschichtliche Volksbücher," I 1), 2nd ed. Tübingen, 1906. See also the more polemical work of Wilhelm Bousset, "Was wissen wir von Jesus?" 2nd ed., Tübingen, 1906. But in none of these works is there any mention of the Hebrew sources, although earlier writers of the Life of Jesus gave much attention to them, *e.g.*, Theodor Keim, "Geschichte Jesu von Nazara," 1867-1872.]

The sources of the Life of Jesus vary as to their origin, language and importance. The primary sources are the Canonical Gospels; but since these were written by men who believed in Jesus as a supernatural being, we are compelled to inquire carefully whether there exist more objective sources for the Life of Jesus, namely secular sources composed by non-believers, Jews or heathen. To these may be added one which is very early, the earliest of all—namely the Epistles of Paul the Apostle, whose ministry began shortly after the death of Jesus; and a later source, containing statements about the life and teachings of Jesus by certain of the earlier Church Fathers, Papias and Justin Martyr, together with a further though questionable source—the Apocryphal and Pseudepigraphical Gospels.

The Hebrew sources must come first, since Jesus lived and died among the Jews. And the Canonical Gospels must come last, since while all the other sources deal with Jesus only incidentally or in the form of legend (*e.g.*, the *Tol'doth Jeshu*), they, the Canonical Gospels, complete and sum up our knowledge of Jesus and his teaching. The remaining sources come in between. Thus, the following are the sources of the Life of Jesus, and they will be dealt with in this

First Book in this order: (a) The Hebrew sources, (b) the Greek and Latin sources, (c) the Epistles of Paul, (d) the early Fathers of the Church, (e) the *Apocryphal and Pseudepigraphical Gospels*, and (f) the Canonical Gospels.

1. THE HEBREW SOURCES

(A) *Talmud and Midrash*

[The accounts of Jesus in *Talmud* and *Midrash* are collected in the pamphlet "Hesronoth ha-Sha's" (Königsberg, 1860; Cracow, 1895), or in "Kuntres l'malloth hesronoth ha-Sha's," of which many copies exist in MS. In these books are to be found all the omissions from the *Talmud* and *Midrash* made by the papal censorship in the Middle Ages. Most of the omissions are also given in the parts of "Dikduke Sof'rim," published by R. Rabinovitz, 1867-1886, giving variant readings (from *Talmud* MSS. in Munich and Oxford, and from various printed editions) in many of the tractates. Almost all of these omissions are given in their Hebrew and Aramaic original by G. Dalman, "Die Thalmudischen Texte (über Jesu)," published as an appendix to Heinrich Laible, "Jesus Christus im Talmud," 2 Aufl. Leipzig, 1900, a pamphlet giving all the *Talmudic* and *Midrashic* texts and sometimes also valuable notes, though these on the whole are not sufficiently scholarly, while their aim is entirely missionary. The same texts, in their original Hebrew and Aramaic, with more scholarly explanations, are given by the English scholar, R. Travers Herford, "Christianity in Talmud and Midrash," London, 1905 (pp. 401-436, the original passages; pp. 35-96, translation and notes; pp. 344-369, summary and estimate of the historical value of the passages). The earlier literature on the subject is detailed in the introduction to the above-mentioned book by Laible, contributed by Hermann Strack, pp. IV-VI; and also in the latter's "Jesus, die Häretiker u. d. Christen," 1910. Valuable comments on the value of these texts occur in: Richard von der Alm (Ghillany), "Die Urteile heidnischer und jüdischer Schriftsteller der vier ersten christlichen Jahrhunderte über Jesus und die ersten Christen," Leipzig, 1865; Daniel Chwolsohn, "Das Letzte Passamahl Christi und der Tag seines Todes," 2 Aufl. Leipzig, 1908, pp. 85-125; Samuel Krauss, "Das Leben Jesu nach jüdischen Quellen," Berlin, 1902, pp. 181-194.]

It might have been supposed that the earliest mention of Jesus and his teaching ought to be found in the *Talmud;* for Jesus lived at the same time which saw Hillel, and Shammai and their "schools" at the height of their influence in Judæa, and when the main foundation of that religious-literary structure known as the *"Talmud"* had already been laid. But such is not the case. The references in the *Talmud* (this applies of course only to the old editions or manuscripts which have escaped the hand of the Christian censorship) to Jesus are very few; and even these have little historical value, since they partake rather of the nature of vituperation and polemic against the founder of a hated party, than of objective accounts of historical value.

There are two reasons for this. Firstly, the *Talmud* authorities on the whole refer rarely to the events of the period of the Second Temple, and do so only when the events are relevant to some halakhic discussion, or else they mention them quite casually in the course of some haggada. What, for example, should we have known of the great Maccabæan struggle against the kings of Syria if the apocryphal books, I and II Maccabees, and the Greek writings of Josephus had not survived, and we had been compelled to derive all our information about this great event in the history of Israel from the *Talmud* alone? We should not have known even the very name of Judas Maccabæus!

Secondly, the appearance of Jesus during the period of disturbance and confusion which befell Judæa under the Herods and the Roman Procurators, was so inconspicuous an event that the contemporaries of Jesus and of his first disciples hardly noticed it; and by the time that Christianity had become a great and powerful sect, the "Sages of the *Talmud*" were already far removed from the time of Jesus, and no longer remembered in their true shape the historical events which had happened to the Christian Messiah: they were satisfied with the popular stories which were current concerning him and his life. (Many of these stories were known to the heathen philosopher, Celsus, and so must have been very widespread.) In the mouths of the Jews and heathen opponents of Christianity, these stories were turned into subjects of ridicule: all the noble qualities of Jesus which the disciples had found in him were twisted into defects, and all the miracles attributed to him, into horrible and unseemly marvels.

It should be noticed that the earliest of these stories, of which we will speak later, date from a time before the latest of the surviving Gospels reached their present form and before they were accepted as of canonical rank; yet these *Talmud* stories seem as though they are deliberately intended to contradict events recorded in the Gospels: the selfsame facts are perverted into bad and blameable acts. For example, the Gospels say that Jesus was born of the Holy Spirit and not of a human father; the *Talmud* stories assert that Jesus was indeed born without a father, yet not of the Holy Spirit but as the result of an irregular union. The Gospels say that he performed signs and wonders through the Holy Spirit and the power of God; the *Talmud* stories allow that he did indeed work signs and wonders, but by means of magic.

In the Gospels Jesus' opposition to the Pharisees and Scribes and their "rote-learned precepts of men," and his own teaching as to what constitutes true religion, are held up for admiration; the *Talmud*, however, avers that he was a "sinner in Israel" and a "scoffer against the words of the wise." And there is much more in the same strain. This proves that before the latest of the existing Gospels received their final shape, many accounts, oral or even written, of the life and teaching of Jesus were current among the first Christians, accounts drawn upon by the evangelists who are known to us.

It therefore follows that the accounts in the first three Gospels are fairly early, and that it is unreasonable to question either the existence of Jesus (as certain scholars have done both in the eighteenth century and in our own time) or his general character as it is depicted in these Gospels. This is the single historical value which we can attribute to the early *Talmudical* accounts of Jesus.

Yet they have another kind of historical importance equally valuable: we can tell from them what the "Sages of Israel" thought of the origin and teaching of Jesus some seventy years after he was crucified, and sometimes we can see the reasons which alienated from him most of the Jews, including the most learned among them.

But can we also seek for historical truth among these *Talmudic* references? Can we find facts there which the Gospels, on religious grounds, have purposely passed over or modified?

Before we answer this, we must first of all differentiate between the statements which were handed down by the *Tannaim* (and which survive in the *Mishnah*, the *Baraitas* and early *Midrashim*), and those handed down by the *Amoraim* (and which survive in the *Gemara* and later *Midrashim*). While the latter can have no objective historical value (since by the time of the *Amoraim* there was certainly no clear recollection of Jesus' life and works) it may yet be possible to attach some historical importance to the accounts coming from the time of the *Tannaim* (though only to such of them as contain no open controversy with Christian opinions or with the accounts given in the Gospels, which, as already pointed out, were well known among Christians before the Gospels reached their present shape). Consequently we shall make no use of the statements from the *Amoraim;* those who wish may read them in the books and pamphlets cited in the Bibliography.

But in this brief study on Jesus in *Talmud* and *Midrash*, not only must we disregard the later references but also all those referring to "Ben Stada," whom the *Amoraim*, and especially Rab Hisda (217-309 C.E.), identified with Ben Pandera and Jesus.[1] The reason for this is simple: there is no proof that the *Tannaim* ever regarded them as identical. Rabbenu Tam (*Shabbath* 104*b*) declared that "this was not Jesus of Nazareth." Even in the *Tol'doth Yeshu* (to be discussed later) Jesus is referred to only as "Ben Pandera," never as "Ben Stada," although it attributes to Jesus the introduction of "spells from Egypt in a cut in his flesh." Therefore as late as the composition of the *Tol'doth Yeshu*, Ben Stada was not looked upon

[1] *Shab.* 104*b; Sanh.* 67*a.*

as an habitual pseudonym of Jesus. Last century, Derenbourg[2] and Joel[3] both discriminated between what was said of Ben Stada and what could be said of Jesus; and recently two scholars, a Jew and a Christian,[4] have both concluded that by "Ben Stada" is intended the Egyptian false prophet mentioned in Josephus ("Antiquities" XX, viii; "Wars" II, xiii) and in the Acts of the Apostles. This false prophet had attracted multitudes to the wilderness and promised that at his command the walls of Jerusalem should fall. Felix, Procurator of Judæa at the time (52-60 C.E.), went out to him with a strong force of cavalry and infantry and killed four thousand and captured two hundred of the false prophet's followers; but the Egyptian himself disappeared.

Among the references by the *Tannaim* to Ben Stada, we find the following:

(a) Rabbi Eliezer said to the Wise: "Did not Ben Stada bring spells from Egypt in a cut in his flesh?" They answered: "He was a madman, and you cannot adduce proof from madmen." (*Shabb.* 104b; *Sanh.* 67a.)

(b) In the case of any one who is liable to death penalties enjoined in the Torah, it is not proper to lie in wait for him except he be a beguiler. How do they lie in wait? Two scholars are stationed in an inner room, while the culprit is in an outer room. A candle is lit and so placed that they can see him as well as hear his voice. And so they did to Ben Stada in Lod. They concealed[5] two scholars, and stoned him. (*T. Sanh.* X 11; *J. Sanh.* VII 16; and in more detail, *B. Sanh.* 67 a.)

It is difficult to suppose that all this applies to Jesus. The *Talmud* authorities did not regard him merely as a *shoteh* (a madman), but as a dangerous beguiler who attracted a large following. They could not say of him that he was stoned by the Jewish court of law (*Beth Din*) when he was really crucified by the Romans.[6] And it was impossible to say of Jesus that he was condemned and executed at Lod when he was really condemned and executed in Jerusalem.

But these objections no longer apply once we conclude that Ben

---

[2] *Essai sur l'histoire de la Palestine*, Paris, 1867, p. 478. In the Hebrew translation, *Massa Eretz Yisrael*, the reference was omitted from fear of the censorship.

[3] *Blicke in die Religionsgeschichte usw*, II 55.

[4] H. P. Chajes in his article *Ben Stada* (Notes on the period before the Destruction of the Second Temple), in S. A. Horodetski's *Ha-Goren*, Berdichev, 1903, IV, pp. 33-37; and R. T. Herford, *Christianity in Talmud and Midrash*, p. 345 n.

[5] Chajes (*op. cit.* p. 35) rightly amends נמנו to הכמינו.

[6] *T. Sanh.* X 11 says "they stoned him," and only the *Babylonian Talmud*, giving opinions of the *Amoraim*, that Ben Stada was Jesus, writes "and hanged him on the eve of Passover."

Stada was not, as the *Amoraim* supposed, Jesus but the Egyptian prophet, who, as a matter of fact, did perform acts of foolishness and madness in promising the crowds that, at his command, the walls of Jerusalem should fall, and who was a "beguiler" and led the people to the wilderness.[7] After he disappeared and escaped from Felix it is possible that he was found later in Lod, which is not far from Jerusalem, and was there stoned by order of the *Beth Din* after concealment of witnesses in the manner prescribed in the above extract from the *Tosefta*. This episode happened near the time of the Destruction (since Felix's rule ended in 60 C.E.) and so could have been known to R. Eliezer, who had seen the Temple while it was yet standing (*Git.* 56a; *Suk.* 27a; *Gen. R.* 421; *Ab. R. N.* VI, 1st vers., XIII 2d vers., ed. Schechter, p. 30), and of whom it was said, "Go . . . after R. Eliezer to Lod" (*Sanh.* 32b).

That Ben Stada is not Jesus may be seen not only from what has already been said about the *Tol'doth Yeshu*, and Rabbenu Tam's dictum, but also from the fact, noticed by Herford,[8] that although we find in the *Talmud* such titles as "Ben Pandera" (or "Ben Pantere") and "Yeshu ben Pandera" (or Pantere), we nowhere find "Yeshu ben Stada."

How thoroughly unreliable are those *Amoraim* who identified Ben Stada with Jesus may be seen from the way they confuse Pappus ben Yehuda with the father of Jesus, and Miriam M'gadd'la N'shaya (the "women's hairdresser") with the mother of Jesus, and even make the name "Stada" a pseudonym of Miriam (Stada = *S'tath da,* i.e. she went astray [from her husband]).[9] As to Pappus ben Yehuda there is a *Baraita:* R. Meir says, "Like opinions on food so are opinions on women. There are some who, if a fly fall into their cup will pour it away and not drink it; and such was the nature of Pappus ben Yehuda who used to shut his wife in the house when he went out" (*Git.* 90a; *T. Sota* V 9). The wife of this Pappus (mentioned in the *Talmud* as a contemporary of Akiba and one of his fellow-disputants,[10] must have committed some offence which made him so jealous that he would not allow her to leave the house;

---

[7] The *Tosefta* lacks the argument between the witness and the beguiler ("How can we leave our God who is in heaven and worship idols?") which occurs in the *Babylonian Talmud,* and is not possible in the case of the Egyptian false prophet.

[8] Herford, *op. cit.* p. 345 n.

[9] For greater clearness the entire passage may be quoted: "Ben Stada— is he not Ben Pandera? R. Hisda said, The husband was Stada, Pandera was the paramour. Was not the husband Pappus ben Yehuda? His mother was Stada. Was not his mother Miriam M'gadd'la N'shaya? As they say in Pumbeditha, '*S'tath da,*' i.e. she went astray from her husband." (*Shab.* 104b; *Sanh.* 67a.)

[10] *Ber.* 61a (= *Midr.* Prov. IX 2); *Mech.* Ex. XIV 29 (= *Can. R.* I 9) and elsewhere; cf. W. Bacher, *Agada der Tannaiten* I 317-320. Against the theory of Derenbourg (*op. cit.* p. 470) that this is Yehuda ben Pappus (*J. Ber.* II 9; *Baba B.* V 1) see J. H. Shor, *Jüdische Zeitschrift,* VI 289-290.

and R. Meir, the pupil of R. Akiba, knew of the episode which may
have happened about his time.

But in the days of the *Amoraim*, when the illegitimate birth of
Jesus was a current idea among the Jews, and, from a Jewish source,
known also to Celsus (c. 150 C.E.),[11] they confused this incident
told of Pappus ben Yehuda with what happened to Joseph, the
father of Jesus. As for Miriam M'gadd'la N'shaya, who, apparently,
was the wife of Pappus,[12] and whose name was somewhat suggestive
of that of Mary Magdalen in the New Testament, they confused her
with Miriam the mother of Jesus. But neither Pappus ben Yehuda
nor Miriam M'gadd'la N'shaya (the latter of whom is mentioned by
the *Amoraim* only) has any connection with Jesus, a fact which has
been rightly pointed out by Samuel Krauss.[13]

It is quite otherwise with the name "Ben Pandera" or "Ben
Pantere." Only the *Amoraim* use the name in connexion with Ben
Stada; but it occurs alone in several *Baraitas* (quoted below) from
the time of R. Eliezer ben Hyrcanus and R. Yishmael (at the end of
the first and beginning of the second Christian century). This
pseudonym is certainly very old, for we learn from Origen[14] that
the heathen Celsus, about the year 178, heard from a Jew a statement
to the effect that Miriam was divorced from her husband, a carpenter
by trade, after it had been proved that she was an adulteress.
Discarded by her husband and wandering about in shame, she
bore Jesus in secret, whose father was a certain soldier, Pantheras (Πανθῆρας). And Origen himself says[15] that James, the
father of Jesus' father, Joseph, was called by the name "Panther."
Origen apparently wished in this way to explain why Jesus the son
of Joseph was called "Ben Pandera" or "Ben Pantere" by the Jews;
according to Origen, Jesus was so called after the name of his
grandfather.

At all events, the name "Ben Pandera" is very early. It is
impossible for us to assume that there really was a Roman soldier
of the name Pandera or Pantheras, who had relations with the
mother of Jesus, since the entire story of the birth of Jesus by a
Roman soldier is only a legend owing its origin to the conviction of
the Christians, from the time of Paul, that Jesus was born without
a natural father; therefore we must seek elsewhere for the source of
this curious name.[16] Of all the explanations so far offered, that of

---

[11] Origen, *Contra Celsum* I ix 1, 32 and 33. See below on "Pandera."

[12] *Hag.* 4b refers to Miriam M'gadd'la N'shaya in the time of Rab Bibi bar
Abayi, an *Amora* of the end of the 3rd century; but the *Talmud* commentators remark there to the effect that "the angel of death told R. Bibi an
event that happened hundreds of years earlier."

[13] *Op. cit.* pp. 186-188, 274-277.

[14] *Contra Celsum* I ix 1. See Laible, *op. cit.* 20-21, Krauss, *op. cit.* 187,
277.

[15] Epiphanius, *Haereses*, 78. See Herford, *op. cit.* 39 n. 2.

[16] Deissmann, in the volume dedicated to Nöldeke, p. 871 *ff.* contributed
an entire article proving that this name was to be found among the Roman

Nietsch and Bleek appears preferable—that "Pantere" is a corrupt travesty of Παρθένος, virgin.[17] The Jews constantly heard that the Christians (the majority of whom spoke Greek from the earliest times) called Jesus by the name "Son of the Virgin," υἱός τῆς Παρθένου; and so, in mockery, they called him "Ben ha-Pantera," i.e. son of the leopard. It was gradually forgotten that Jesus was so called after his mother, and the name "Pantere," or "Pantori," or "Pandera" was thought to be that of his father,[18] and since this is not a Jewish name, there arose the legend that the natural father was a foreigner; and (as in the case of Miriam bath Bilgah, who married the "Sradiot," סרדיוט, the soldier [*T. Suk.* IV 28; *B. Suk* 56b; *J. Suk.* V 7]), it was concluded that Miriam, the mother of Jesus, committed adultery with a soldier, and, of course, with a Roman soldier, since there were Roman legions in Judæa at the time.[19]

If, therefore, we set aside from the *Talmudic* evidence all the statements of the *Amoraim*, and all that refers to Ben Stada, to Pappus ben Yehuda and to Miriam M'gadd'la N'shaya, there remain only the following *Tannaitic* passages:

(a) A certain *Baraita*, the conclusion of which makes Jesus the contemporary of Yehoshua ben Perachya, is, to our mind, doubtful. It runs as follows:

> Let thy left hand ever repel and thy right hand invite. Not like Elisha who repelled Gehazi with both hands, nor like R. Yehoshua ben Perachya who repelled Yeshu [the Nazarene] with both hands.

There follows this explanation, in Aramaic, about Yehoshua ben Perachya and his relations with Yeshu:

> When king Jannæus slew our Rabbis, Yehoshua and Yeshu went to Alexandria of Egypt. When there was peace [between the king and the Pharisees] Shimeon ben Shetah sent to him (as follows): From me, Jerusalem the Holy City, to thee, Alexandria of Egypt, my sister: My husband dwells in thy midst and I sit

soldiers. But that a Roman soldier of this name had relations with the mother of Jesus is manifestly an outcome of the Christian conviction that Jesus was born of the Holy Spirit; and *because* the name "Pantera" was to be found among the Roman soldiers it was applied to the imaginary paramour.

[17] *Studien u. Kritiken*, 1840, p. 116; Laible, p. 25; Herford's objections (p. 39) are not convincing.

[18] There perhaps still survives an indication of this change of the names of mother and father in the reported debate between R. Hisda and his colleagues, who thought that "Ben Stada" was not the name of the father but of the mother, and said, punningly, "*S'tath da*"—she went astray from her husband.

[19] See on this, Gustav Dalman, note to p. 21 of Laible, *op. cit.*; and Krauss, *op. cit.* p. 276, n. 13.

desolate. So they (Yehoshua ben Perachya and Yeshu) came and they chanced on a certain inn where they were treated with much honour. He (R. Yehoshua ben Perachya) said: How fair is the hostess! Yeshu said to him: Rabbi, her eyelashes are too short. Yehoshua ben Perachya said to him: Wretched man, do you occupy yourself with such things? He sent out four hundred trumpets and anathematized him. Yeshu came before him many times and said, Receive me back. But he gave no heed to him. One day Yehoshua ben Perachya was reciting the *Shema'*. Yeshu came before him and Yehoshua ben Perachya was minded to receive him. He made a sign to him with his hand (that he should wait while he recited the *Shema'*, since he did not wish to be interrupted). Yeshu thought that he had repulsed him and went and set up a brick and worshipped it. Yehoshua ben Perachya said to him: "Repent!" Yeshu said to him: Thus did I learn from thee: Everyone that sins and makes many to sin, they give him no opportunity to repent. The *Baraita* says: Yeshu [of Nazareth] practised sorcery and beguiled and led Israel astray.[20]

First of all it should be noticed that whatever is here told in Aramaic does not belong to the *Baraita* but to the *Gemara* of the *Amoraim* period; also that there is absent from the second version (*Sota 47a*), "The *Baraita* says: Yeshu, etc."—A *Baraita* whose presence would serve to prove that the whole story of the return from Egypt is concerned with Yeshu and none other; and finally, that in the third version (*J. Hag.*) the episode is described in general terms, Yeshu is not even mentioned, and the particular incident happened, not to Yehoshua ben Perachya, but to Yehuda ben Tabbai and "one of his disciples."[21] On these grounds Herford[22] supposes that this third version, from the *Jerusalem Talmud*, is the original and that the two *Babylonian Talmud* versions are due to later Babylonian accretions, arising out of the names "Elisha" and "Gehazi"[23] which precede this story about Yehoshua ben Perachya and Yeshu.

[20] *Sanh.* 107b; *Sota* 47b; *J. Hag.* II 2 (p. 74-77).
[21] The *Yerushalmi* version runs: "Yehuda ben Tabbai—the people of Jerusalem wished to appoint him as President (of the Sanhedrin) in Jerusalem. He fled and went to Alexandria. The people of Jerusalem wrote: From Jerusalem the Great to Alexandria the Little: How long doth my espoused dwell with you while I sit mournful for him? He embarked and went on a ship. He said: Debora, the hostess who received us, what was defective in her? One of his disciples said to him: Rabbi, her eyes were bad. He answered: There are two things lacking in you; one, that you suspected me, and other that you inspected her closely. What did I say? that she was handsome to look at? (No), but that she was good in action. (The disciple) was angry and went away."
[22] Herford, *op. cit.* p. 52, 54; see Laible, p. 41.
[23] Herford thinks that Gehazi is used here and in another place as a pseudonym of the apostle Paul; see *op. cit.* pp. 97-103, and pp. 34-71.

The reasons which led to this change of names or to their presence in this passage are, in the present writer's opinion: (a) Yehuda ben Tabbai and Yehoshua ben Perachya lived about the same time, and since Yehuda ben Tabbai formed a "pair" with Shimeon ben Shetah (*Aboth* I 5-9), Shimeon ben Shetah is also mentioned in the *Babli* version; (b) the name Yeshu-Yeshua, resembles the name Yehoshua (ben Perachya); and (c) the story contains suggestions of the Christian traditions found in the Gospel: in the Gospel Jesus escapes with his parents to Egypt because of a cruel king (Herod), and here also Yeshu escapes with his master to Egypt because of a cruel king (Jannæus); and in the Gospel Jesus attracted women toward him and some of them formed his most enthusiastic followers, and among them were even fallen women (John viii. 11), and here too he gives close attention to a woman.[24]   This explains why, in the *Yerushalmi* version, the name "Yeshu" is added, and the story consequently changed and considerably enlarged. In the *Babli* form the story is so transformed and so late that it is needless to waste a single word in proof of its unhistorical nature.[25]

Jesus as a worshipper of a brick—nothing could be more absurd; and Jesus as the disciple of Yehoshua ben Perachya and contemporary with Shimeon ben Shetah and king Jannæus, who reigned in Judæa 103-76, *before* the Christian era, and about the year 88 B.C. overcame the Pharisees who for six years had fought against him, and killed eight hundred of them, and compelled eight thousand others to escape from Judæa (an episode alluded to here in the words "when Jannæus slew our Rabbis")—could there be a grosser anachronism? This glaring contradiction between the *Talmudic* and Gospel accounts moved a certain writer, who remained anonymous (G. R. S. Mead), to put forward the hypothesis that Jesus really lived in the days of Alexander Jannæus and Yehoshua ben Perachya, as the *Talmud* says; but that the Evangelists confused him with one or other false prophets who caused a disturbance and was put to death in the time of Pontius Pilate.[26]

It is obvious that this hypothesis (even its anonymous propounder did not put it forward as absolute truth) which is based solely on a single *Talmudic* passage (from which is derived also everything that the *Amoraim* and the *Tol'doth Yeshu* say on the subject), does not deserve much attention. The present writer is inclined to sup-

---

[24] Laible, p. 42.

[25] That Krauss (pp. 246-257) could suggest that we fill the gap in Jesus' life, from his twelfth to his thirtieth year, with the aid of this *Talmudic* story about Jesus' visit to Egypt (with which he combines also the story of Celsus, that Jesus sold himself to be a slave in Egypt) as an historical fact—was only possible through his supposing that Ben Stada (of whom the early *Tanna* R. Eliezer said that "he brought spells from Egypt in a cut in his flesh") was Jesus of Nazareth.

[26] See *Did Jesus live 100 B.C.?*, Theosophical Publication Society, London and Benares, 1903; A. Schweitzer, *Von Reimarus zu Wrede: Eine Geschichte der Leben-Jesu-Forschung*, Tübingen, 1906, p. 326.

pose that not only is the *Babli Amoraitic* story very late, but that the conclusion of the *Baraita* itself ("Not like Elisha who repelled Gehazi with both hands, nor like Yehoshua ben Perachya who repelled Yeshu [of Nazareth] with both hands") is only a late addition, and that the main point of the *Baraita* is simply the saying: "Let thy right hand ever repel and thy left hand invite," which is certainly very old and, apparently, uttered by R. Eliezer the Great (see *Mech.* Yithro, § *Amalek* 81; ed. Friedmann 55*a* and *b*; see H. P. Chajes in *Ha-Goren* IV 34 end of n. 2).[27]

(b) There is a second *Baraita* of greater historical value. It is as follows:

On the eve of Passover they hanged Yeshu [of Nazareth] and the herald went before him for forty days saying, "[Yeshu of Nazareth] is going forth to be stoned in that he hath practised sorcery and beguiled and led astray Israel. Let everyone knowing aught in his defence come and plead for him." But they found naught in his defence and hanged him on the eve of Passover.[28]

Following this *Baraita* come these remarks of the Amora 'Ulla:

'Ulla said: And do you suppose that for [Yeshu of Nazareth] there was any right of appeal?[29] He was a beguiler, and the Merciful One hath said: Thou shalt not spare neither shalt thou conceal him. It is otherwise with Yeshu, for he was near to the civil authority.

('Ulla was a disciple of R. Yochanan and lived in Palestine at the end of the third century.)

In this *Baraita* attention should be paid to the emphasis given to the statement that Jesus "practised sorcery and beguiled and led astray Israel," and this, apparently, is what "the *Baraita* said" which is quoted at the end of the previous *Talmudic* extract. The *Talmud*

[27] The objections of M. Friedländer ("Die religiösen Bewegungen innerhalb des Judentums in Zeitalter Jesu," Berlin, 1905, p. 233 n) which he urges against those who find anything about Jesus in the *Talmud* (he himself thinks that all such passages are late additions and pure forgeries) thus fall to the ground; he objected that, on the one side, Jesus was a contemporary of Yehoshua ben Perachya, and, on the other, a contemporary of Pappus ben Yehuda, the contemporary of R. Akiba; that is to say, he lived a hundred years previous to the Jesus of the Gospels, and a hundred years after. We have shown that Pappus ben Yehuda has nothing to do with Yeshu, and we here see that there is no value to be attached to the statement that he was a disciple of Yehoshua ben Perachya. The other *Talmudic* statements, such as are early, are not in such opposition to the Gospel accounts.

[28] *Sanh.* 43*a*. The bracketed words are from *Dikduke Sof'rim*, from the Munich MS. In a Florentine MS. is written "On the eve of Passover and the eve of Sabbath"; and this agrees with the explanation of Chwolsohn that Jesus was crucified on a Sabbath eve which fell on the eve of Passover. See Chwolsohn, *op. cit.* pp. 11-55.

[29] Herford, *op. cit.* pp. 89, 349, wrongly translates: "Would it be thought that anything could be said in favour of Jesus, a revolutionary?"

authorities do not deny that Jesus worked signs and wonders, but they look upon them as acts of sorcery.[30] We find the same thing in the Gospels: "And the Scribes which came down from Jerusalem said, He hath Beelzebub, and, By the prince of the devils he casteth out devils" (Mark iii. 22) ; and in Matthew (ix. 34; xii. 24) the Pharisees speak in similar terms.

That it was as a seducer and beguiler that Jesus was put to death was clear to the *Tannaim*, for in their days his disciples had become a separate Jewish sect which denied many of the religious principles of Judaism; therefore their teacher, Jesus, had beguiled them and led them astray from the Jewish faith. But it is noteworthy that the *Baraita* stresses the fact that they made no haste in putting Jesus to death in spite of his being a beguiler, and that they delayed the execution of his sentence for forty days, in case anybody should come to plead in his favour (a matter of surprise to the Amora 'Ulla).

This is the exact opposite to the Gospel accounts, according to which the trial of Jesus before the Sanhedrin was finished very hurriedly and the sentence hastily carried out by the Roman Procurator. In the opinion of the present writer the statement about the herald has an obvious "tendency," and it is difficult to think that it is historical.

Over against this, the *Talmudic* story agrees with the historic fact that Jesus was put to death on the eve of Passover (which fell on the eve of the Sabbath) as recorded in the Fourth Gospel: "On the eve of that Passover" (John xix. 14), with which should be compared the statement in Mark: "At the feast of the killing of the Passover," which contradicts what goes before: "the first day of unleavened bread" (Mark xiv. 12) ; a condition of things which is also proved from the fact that on the first day of the week, after *three* days, he was not found in his tomb. The *Talmud*, however, speaks of hanging in place of crucifixion, since this horrible Roman form of death was only known to Jewish scholars from Roman trials, and not from the Jewish legal system. Even Paul the Apostle (Gal. iii. 13) expounds the passage "for a curse of God is that which is hanged" (Deut. xxi. 23) as applicable to Jesus.[31]

> (c) Immediately after this *Baraita* comes a second (Sanh. 43a) : Jesus had five disciples, Mattai, Naqai, Netser, Buni and Todah.

This is at once followed by a late *Amoraitic* addition, recognizable as such by the Aramaic language and the punning witicisms:

[30] See L. Blau, *Das altjüdische Zauberwesen*, Budapest, 1898, p. 29. Justin Martyr, *Dial. cum Tryphone Judœo*, c. 69, shows that at that time the Jews spoke of Jesus as a sorcerer.

[31] See Laible, *op. cit.* 81-83.

They brought Mattai (to the judges). He said to them, "Shall Mattai be killed?—it is written: *Mattai* (lit. when) shall come and appear before God." They said to him: "Yea, Mattai shall be killed, for it is written: *Mattai* (lit. when) shall die and his name perish."

They brought Naqai. He said to them, "Shall Naqai be killed?—it is written: And *Naqi* (lit. the innocent) and the righteous thou shalt not kill." They said to him, "Yea, Naqai shall be killed, for it is written: In the secret places he killeth *Naqi*" (lit. the innocent).

They brought Netser. He said to them, "Shall Netser be killed?—it is written: And *Netser* (lit. a branch) from his roots shall blossom." They said to him, "Yea, Netser shall be killed, for it is written: And thou wast cast forth from thy grave like an abhorred *Netser*" (lit. branch).

They brought Buni. He said, "Shall Buni be killed?—it is written: *B'ni* (lit. my son), my first-born, Israel." They said to him, "Yea, Buni shall be killed, for it is written: I will slay *Bin'kha* (lit. thy son), thy firstborn."

They brought Todah. He said, "Shall Todah be killed?—it is written: A psalm for *Todah* (lit. thanksgiving)." They said to him, "Yea, Todah shall be killed, for it is written: Whoso sacrificeth *Todah* (lit. thankofferings) honoureth me."

All this scriptural gymnastics cannot possibly belong to the *Baraita*. At all events it cannot be historical, for it is impossible that a court of law should indulge in such "pilpul," verbal quips, with verses of Scripture at the expense of the condemned before leading them out to execution; or that five disciples of Jesus were all killed together.[32] The *Baraita* itself asserts that Jesus had five disciples, while the Gospel speaks of twelve. Since the number in the Gospel corresponds to the number of the Tribes of Israel, it may be that this was so devised by Jesus himself and is therefore historical; but it may also have been devised by the writers of the Gospel and be unhistorical, just as the statement about the Seventy Disciples whom Jesus chose (Luke x. 1)—a number devised to correspond with the "Seventy nations" and the "Seventy tongues"—is likewise unhistorical.[33]

In any case the *Baraita* itself is lacking in accuracy, for although the names are those of real disciples, they include some who were not disciples of Jesus himself, but disciples of the second generation. Thus we have both Mattai and Naqai, who are obviously, as Krauss

---

[32] We certainly find in Christian martyrologies and also in papyri containing reports of cases in Roman times, similar arguments; but it is hard to suppose that such typical *Talmudic* discussion of names ever came before courts of law.

[33] Graetz, *Geschichte der Juden*, III, I⁶, 296, n. 4.

perceived,[34] Matthew and Luke. Netser is either a pun on *Notsrim,* (Christians), (so Krauss),[35] or, maybe, a corruption of Andrai (Andrew), the brother of Simon Peter (Mark iii. 18; Matt. x. 2; Luke vi. 14). Buni is supposed by most Christian scholars to be the Nicodemus mentioned in the Gospel of John (iii. 1-10, xix. 39), since we find in a *Baraita* (*Taanith* 20a) dealing with Nakdimon ben Gorion: "His name is not Nakdimon but Buni. And why is his name called Nakdimon?—because the sun shone (*naq'da*) because of him."[36] The present writer is of the opinion that "Buni" is a corruption of "Yuhanni" or "Yuani," i.e. John the brother of James, the son of Zebedee. The last disciple, Todah, is certainly Thaddæus, also called Lebbæus (Matt. x. 3; Mark iii. 18).[37]

But since this *Baraita* is anonymous, its early date is not decisive. Some [38] suppose that the *Baraita* was uttered in the time of R. Akiba and Bar Kokhbah, when many Christians were punished because they would not renounce the messiahship of Jesus and confess that of Bar Kokhbah; but (a) Christians were not then put to death, but only scourged, as Justin Martyr tells us ("Apology" I 31); and (b) the killing of these disciples is only related in the course of a scriptural "pilpulistic," casuistical, argument, late in date, and forming no part of the *Baraita* proper.

(d) It is questionable whether this following *Talmudic* story is primarily concerned with Jesus:

> "An impudent one:" R. Eliezer holds that this means a bastard, while R. Yehoshua says that it is a "son of uncleanness" [*ben niddah;* see Lev. xv. 32]; R. Akiba holds that it is both the one and the other. The elders were once sitting [at the gate]. Two children passed before them, one covered his head and the other uncovered his head.* The one who uncovered his head, R. Eliezer calls a "bastard," R. Eliezer, "son of uncleanness," and R. Akiba, "bastard and son of uncleanness." They asked R. Akiba, How do you dare to contradict the findings of your colleagues? He said to them, I will prove what I say. He went to the mother of the child and saw her sitting and selling peas in the market. He said to her, My daughter, if you tell me what I ask, I will bring thee to the life of the world to come. She said to him, Swear it to me. R. Akiba swore with his lips but disavowed it in his heart. He said to her, What is the nature of

---

[34] *Op. cit.* 57, n. 3.
[35] *Ibid.* n. 4. See also Laible, p. 71.
[36] See in detail, Laible, pp. 70-71; Graetz, III, I⁵, 303 n.; Herford (p. 93) sees in most of these names some reference to Jesus: he is "the *Naqi*," the innocent, "the *Netser*," branch, from the root of Jesse, and "the Son" (*Buni*).
[37] See Dalman, *Die Worte Jesu,* Leipzig, 1898, p. 40.
[38] Laible, 37-71; cf. Herford, 91-95.
* To uncover the head before a superior is a mark of gross disrespect among Jews, as among other orientals.

this thy son? She answered, When I entered the bridal chamber I was in my uncleanness and my husband remained apart from me and my groomsman came in unto me and I had this son. The child was thus both a bastard and a "son of uncleanness." Then said they, Great was R. Akiba who put his teachers to shame. At the selfsame hour they said, Blessed be the Lord God of Israel, who revealed his secret to R. Akiba ben Yosef.[39]

Jesus is never mentioned explicitly in this story nor is there any ground for supposing that the Christian censor in the Middle Ages deleted the name of the child.[40] Had not Celsus and the *Talmud* preserved the legend of his illegitimacy, a legend which originated solely from the conviction of the Christians that Jesus was born without a human father, then the author of the *Tol'doth Yeshu* would never have used the present *Talmudic* story as a basis for his legend of the "uncleanness" of Miriam, Jesus' mother, and of the unlawful connexion with the groomsman; and, consequently, it would never have occurred to him to suppose that this account treats of Jesus. Certainly the solemn conclusion, "Blessed be the Lord God of Israel who hath revealed his secret to R. Akiba ben Yosef," would suggest that there is here a "hidden" mystery, and that something of great importance has been "revealed," and that the story is not merely concerned with the origin of some street-child.

But this conclusion is unquestionably later than the story itself. There was already one conclusion, and a simpler one, namely, "They said, Great was R. Akiba who put his teachers to shame." The second and more solemn conclusion is therefore a later addition, added at a time when it was thought that the story really referred to Jesus. The passage only occurs in *Masseketh Kallah* and *Kallah Rabbati,* lesser tractates put together at a very late period, and so containing many accretions which were then either new in substance or corrupt in form.

Jesus as a contemporary of R. Akiba is not an idea emanating from the earlier *Talmud* authorities, but a product of the imagination of the later generation which could suppose that Pappus ben Yehuda was the husband of Miriam, the mother of Jesus. The only reason

---

[39] *Tractate Kallah*, ed. Koronel, p. 18*b* (*Hamishshah Kuntresim*, Vienna, 1864, p. 3*b*) ; *Kallah, Talmud*, ed. Ram. p. 51*a; Bâtê Midrashoth*, ed. S. A. Wertheimer, Jerusalem, 1895, III 23; Dalman, appendix to Laible, pp. 7-8.

[40] On this see Laible, p. 34, who comes to the conclusion that the child is meant to be Jesus, because what is here said does not refer to any bastard child in general. This, to the present writer, does not seem to be the case: the story is only intended to show whose opinion is correct about the word "impudent." See also Herford, pp. 49-50, and Krauss, *op. cit.* pp. 262, 278. Jesus might be accounted "impudent" because he "scoffed at the words of the Sages" (see below), on the basis of what is recorded in Luke ii. 41-47, about the child Jesus, who argued with the Scribes when he was twelve years old. On the illegitimacy see below, in the saying of Ben 'Azzai.

for quoting the story here, is that the author of the *Tol'doth Yeshu*—
of which more later—founded an entire book upon it.

(e) From the time of Abraham Geiger, Jewish scholars have
found early references to Jesus in certain *Talmudic* passages where
Balaam is mentioned.[41] According to this view Jesus is referred to
in the two following passages from the *Mishnah:*

> Three kings and four commoners have no share in the world
> to come . . . four commoners: Balaam and Doeg and Ahitophel
> and Gehazi (*Sanh.* X 2.). The disciples of the wicked Balaam
> shall inherit Gehenna and go down to the pit of destruction, as
> it is said: "The men of blood and deceit shall not live out half
> their days" (*Aboth* V 19).

That in these early passages, and in other early and late passages in
Talmud and *Midrash*, Jesus is meant by Balaam, has become among
Jewish scholars one of the accepted things, so patent as no longer
to call for serious proof.[42] Yet, in the opinion of the present writer,
this supposition is not altogether inevitable. Friedländer[43] is perhaps more correct—not so much in his assertion that the antinomians
("who hold by the teaching of Balaam" and who are referred to in
the New Testament [Jude, 11]) are intended—but in denying that
Jesus is ever referred to under the pseudonym of Balaam in any
really early passage.

And on what is the hypothesis based? Why should the *Mishnah*
authorities conceal their intention and call Jesus Balaam? We shall
see later that when the Sages, for any reason, did not wish to mention Jesus by name, they called him "Such-an-one," which is quite
unambiguous. But to call him by the name "Balaam" (a name
familiar in the Torah as that of a man of well-defined character and
an idolator, whereas, on the contrary, the characteristic features of
Jesus as depicted in the *Talmud*, are not in the least clearly outlined,
and he is a Jew as well) would be to give further opportunity for
error, and was neither necessary nor desirable. Furthermore, *were*
"an evil eye and a haughty spirit and a greedy soul," in the time of
the *Mishnah* authorities, the outstanding marks of the disciples of
Jesus and of them only?[44] And why should the Balaam mentioned

[41] See Geiger, *Bileam u. Jesus, Jüdische Zeitschrift*, VI (1868), pp. 31-37.
The literature on the subject is given by Hermann Strack in his introduction to Laible, *op. cit.* p. VI; S. Krauss, *op. cit.* p. 361. See Laible, pp. 57-58,
and the appendix by Dalman, p. 12 (the Hebrew original); Herford, pp.
64-78 and 404-405 (appendix giving Hebrew original).
[42] See e.g. H. P. Chajes, *Am-Haarez e Min, Rivista Israelitica* III (1906)
94 n.
[43] *Der Antichrist*, Göttingen, 1901, p. 190 ff.
[44] Even Chajes, quoted in the last note but one as agreeing with Geiger,
says (*Markus-Studien*, Berlin, 1899, p. 25, n. 2): "The scholars Geiger, Perles
and Schor take a one-sided view in finding Jesus described in the *Talmud*
in the guise of Balaam"; though he sometimes agrees with them and brings
additional proof for their theory from the *Aboth d. Rab. Nathan* (XXI 1st

in *Mishnah Sanhedrin,* in conjunction with Doeg and Ahitophel and Gehazi, necessarily be Jesus and none other? Geiger,[45] and after him Laible [46] and Herford,[47] are convinced that the Balaam in this passage *must* be Jesus, because reference is here made to Israelites who have no share in the world to come, and Balaam was not an Israelite. But neither was Doeg the Edomite an Israelite. Therefore Laible [48] and Herford [49] are forced to the conclusion that Doeg, Ahitophel and Gehazi were likewise pseudonyms, signifying the apostles Peter, James and John, or else Judas Iscariot (Doeg the traitor), Peter (Ahitophel) and Paul (Gehazi). But are not all of these hypotheses "mountains hung on a hair"? Furthermore, as we shall see later, it was still a subject for dispute whether Jesus had in truth no share in the world to come. Quite apart from this, there are two items of evidence which argue against this pseudonymous use of Balaam, namely, two straightforward passages where Jesus is mentioned side by side with Balaam and completely differentiated from him.

(f) The story is told of "Onkelos son of Kalonymos, son of Titus' sister," that he wished to become a proselyte. He first called up Titus by means of spells. Titus advised him not to become a proselyte because Israel had so many commandments and commandments hard to observe; rather would he advise him to oppose them. Onkelos then called up Balaam, who said to him in his rage against Israel, "Seek not their peace nor their good." Not till then did he go and "raise up Jesus by spells and say to him: What is the most important thing in the world? He said to him, Israel. He asked, And how if I should join myself with them? He said to him, Seek their good and do not seek their harm; everyone that hurteth them is as if he hurt the apple of God's eye. He then asked, And what is the fate of that man? he said to him, Boiling filth. A *Baraita* has said: Everyone that scoffeth against the words of the wise is condemned to boiling filth. Come and see what there is between the transgressors in Israel and the prophets of the nations of the world" (*Gitt.* 56*b*-57*a*).

Whether this passage is early or late is hard to decide. Its Aramaic style [50] and the introduction of the formula "a *Baraita* has said," would prove its lateness. Yet it mentions "the son

vers.), he still thinks that "wherever mention is made of the immorality of Balaam, the Nicolaitans are intended."

[45] *Jüdische Zeitschrift,* VI 32-33.
[46] Laible, 52-53.
[47] Herford, p. 66.
[48] *Op. cit.* pp. 54-55.
[49] *Op. cit.* p. 71.
[50] There are actually Aramaic passages older than those in Hebrew, but not passages in dialogue form like the present.

of the sister of Titus" who, according to Graetz [51] was Flavius Clemens (corrupted to Kalonymos or Kalonikos, as in *Aboda Zara* 11a), the nephew of Domitian (and therefore also of Titus, Domitian's brother) who was put to death as an atheist (we know that the heathen regarded belief in a one and invisible God as atheism) about the year 96 C.E. Therefore the chief actor in the story goes back to an early date. Furthermore, the story only charges Jesus with being "a scoffer against the words of the wise" and "a transgressor in Israel," and even makes him say good things about Israel, thereby estimating him as not only higher than Titus, but higher than Balaam the "prophet of the nations of the world." This, to the present writer, is a proof of the earliness of the story.

To the *Talmud* authorities Jesus was always a Jew; he may have been a Jew who was a transgressor and a "scoffer against the words of the wise" (which he certainly was, especially in view of Matthew xxiii, where he pours scorn on the Pharisees and their burdensome interpretations of the *Torah*, and ridicules them for tithing mint and anise and cummin, straining out a gnat and swallowing a camel; and much more to the same effect), yet the "Jewish spark" was still alight in him and he cared for his people's good. From this point of view the passage is important—not, that is to say, for the better understanding of the events of Jesus' life or of his opinions, but for understanding the attitude of the *Talmud* to Jesus the Jew.

The passage is also important since Balaam and Jesus are here not only separated entirely, but even placed in opposition. Geiger [52] and Herford [53] felt this and so had to modify their statements and allow that Balaam is not always Jesus, and the two are not always inseparable. We, however, for our part, do not find a single passage in *Talmud* or *Midrash* where we feel *bound* to say that Balaam is Jesus and no other. There is no adequate reason for such pseudonymity since Jesus is mentioned many times explicitly by name, or by the term "such-an-one" (to be explained by their general unwillingness to refer to him).

(g) We again find Jesus and Balaam clearly kept apart in the following later *Tannaitic* passage:

> R. Eliezer ha-Kappar said: God gave strength to his (Balaam's) voice so that it went from one end of the world to the other, because he looked forth and beheld the nations that bow down to the sun and moon and stars, and to wood and stone, and he looked forth and saw that there was a man, born of a woman, who should rise up and seek to make himself God, and to cause the whole world to go astray. Therefore God gave

[51] *Geschichte* IV, 109, 403-405 n. 12, 411 n. See also Derenbourg, *op. cit.* II 178 (Heb. trans.).
[52] *Jüdische Zeitschr.* VI 36-37.
[53] *Op. cit.* p. 39.

power to the voice of Balaam that all the peoples of the world might hear, and thus he spake: Give heed that ye go not astray after that man, for it is written, "God is not man that he should lie." And if he says that he is God he is a liar; and he will deceive and say that he departeth and cometh again at the end.[54] He saith and he shall not perform. See what is written: And he took up his parable and said, "Alas, who shall live when God doeth this." Balaam said, Alas, who shall live—of that nation which heareth that man who hath made himself God.[55]

R. Eliezer ha-Kappar, the father of Bar Kappara (whose sayings are often attributed to the father owing to the similarity of their names) was a contemporary of R. Yehuda ha-Nasi and lived in the third century,[56] dying about the year 260. So although the present passage is *Tannaitic*, it is comparatively late. And since we know it only from comparatively modern *Midrashim*, such as *Y'lamm'denu* and the *Yalkut Shimeoni*, which consist of earlier fragments expanded by later additions, we cannot regard the present passage as primitive or in its original shape. Also the words concerning Jesus may belong to the Amora R. Abbahu.[57]

In any case the fact comes out clearly that whether at the end of the *Tannaitic* or during the *Amoraitic* period (when there were more important reasons for not mentioning the name of Jesus) the names of Balaam and Jesus were still kept apart. Though it must be granted that the very fact that the names of Jesus and Balaam are twice brought into such close connexion, gives ground for thought.

We come now to earlier *Talmudic* statements, the earliest in Hebrew literature dealing with Jesus:

> (h) R. Shimeon ben 'Azzai said: I found a genealogical roll in Jerusalem wherein was recorded, "Such-an-one is a bastard of an adulteress" (*Yeb.* IV 3; 49a).

Current editions of the *Mishnah* add: "To support the words of R. Yehoshua" (who, in the same *Mishnah,* says: What is a bastard? Everyone whose parents are liable to death by the Beth Din).

That Jesus is here referred to seems to be beyond doubt, although Dalman disputes this.[58] H. P. Chajes [59] says that "the statement must necessarily have referred to someone well-known, and not to some-

---

[54] We have here clear indications of the "Second Coming" (the Parousia) which is bound up with the Millennium (Chiliasm).

[55] *Yalkut Shimeoni* (Salonica) §725 on *wa-yissa m'shalo* (Num. xxiii. 7), according to *Midrash Y'lamm'denu*. Quoted in Yellinek's *Beth Midrash,* V 207 ff; Dalman in appendix to Laible, pp. 10-11; Herford, p. 404. See also David Kahana, *M'bo l'pharashath Bileam,* Lwow, 1883, pp. 13-14.

[56] W. Bacher, *op. cit.* II 496, 500-508; Sokoloff, *He-Asif* III 330.

[57] Cf. Bacher, *op. cit.* II 506, n. 2, and Herford, *op. cit.* 46.

[58] *Die Worte Jesu,* p. 4, n. 2.

[59] *Rivista Isr.* II 94; the same view is held by Derenbourg, *R.E.J.* III 293, and Laible, pp. 31-32. Suidas (under 'Ιησοῦς) says in the name of the

one of no special significance," and Herford [60] rightly urges that unless there had been some strong reason for avoiding his name, the name would have been given, since giving the name would have served to strengthen the case of Ben 'Azzai and "to support the words of R. Yehoshua."

In the time of Ben 'Azzai (and also in that of his elder contemporary R. Eliezer), there was adequate reason for not mentioning Jesus by his name, because, as we shall see, the disciples of Jesus used at that time to heal the sick "in the name of Jesus."

It is also possible that the word "such-an-one" was later introduced into this passage when Christianity was more widespread and they would no longer mention the name openly "by reason of the anger of Minim" (i.e., Jews rightly or wrongly suspected of a leaning towards the new Christian "heresy"). (*Ber.* 12a; *Pes.* 56a.) Ben 'Azzai was the "colleague-disciple of R. Akiba" (Baba Bathra 158b) and flourished before the Bar Kokhbah rebellion, and was, it seems, killed after this rebellion subsided (*Ekha Rabbati* II 2; *Midrash Tehillim* IX 13, ed. Buber, p. 88); his words may, then, have been uttered about the time of Celsus who, as we have seen, reported "in the name of a Jew" that Jesus was illegitimately born, although, according to Celsus, it happened to Miriam when she was still only espoused, while Ben 'Azzai refers to an *esheth ish*, the terminology invariably used to indicate a married woman. But in the time of the *Talmud* espousal was in all respects equivalent to marriage.[61] That there is no historical foundation for the tradition of Jesus' illegitimate birth and that the tradition arises from opposition to the Christian view that Jesus was born without a natural father—all this we have repeatedly seen, and we shall have reason to refer to it again when we come to the actual history of Jesus (see the beginning of the Third Book).

(j) About the same time, R. Eliezer ben Hyrcanus (or R. Eliezer the Great), one of the earliest and greatest of the *Tannaim,* makes use of the same pseudonym "such-an-one." We read in an early *Baraita:*

> They asked R. Eliezer, "What of such-an-one as regards the world to come?" He said to them, "You have only asked me about such-an-one. . . . What of a bastard as touching inheritance?—What of him as touching the levirate duties? What of him as regards whitening his house?—What of him as regards whitening his grave?"—not because he evaded them by words, but because he never said a word which he had not heard from his teacher (*T. Yeb.* III 3; *Yoma* 66b).[62]

Byzantine Jew Theodosius, that the genealogical roll of Jesus was preserved at Tiberias (Krauss, *op. cit.* p. 159); and Ben 'Azzai lived in Tiberias (Bacher's criticism on Herford, *J.Q.R.* XVII, 175).

[60] *Op. cit.* pp. 43-45.

[61] Krauss, *op. cit.* pp. 186-187 (n. 10).

[62] Dalman, who in his appendix to Laible quotes the saying of Ben 'Azzai about "such-an-one" and also two *Amoraitic* stories where *"p'lan"* is used

The *Amoraim* who discussed these passages in *Yoma* did not know to whom the questioners referred, and thought that by the word "such-an-one" King Solomon was meant. But taking into account the above statement of Ben 'Azzai, and the story told in the *Amoraitic* period (*J. Ab. Zar.* II 2 [p. 40, 4]; *J. Shab.* XIV 4 [p. 14, 4]; *Qoh. R.* on *Yesh ra'a*) where the term "such-an-one" (*p'loni* or *p'lan*) refers to Jesus, and taking into consideration also the fact that in the present *Baraita* the various questions about the bastard follow immediately after the question about "such-an-one," it is tolerably certain that the "such-an-one" here is likewise Jesus.[63] Büchler [64] maintains that R. Eliezer's answer to the question whether Jesus had any share in the world to come was, like his answer to the other questions, in the affirmative.

But if, with Chwolsohn,[65] we regard his answer as ambiguous, "neither yes nor no," we can even so conclude (as Chwolsohn rightly does) that since R. Eliezer would not wholly deprive Jesus of his share in the world to come, the *Tannaim*, the successors of the Pharisees, were at the end of the first Christian century, far from regarding Jesus as anything more than "a transgressor in Israel," and were still accustomed to come into close religious touch with the Christians. This last fact we also observe in another early *Baraita*, where we find R. Eliezer again the central figure, and where Jesus is mentioned openly by name—but again, not in utter condemnation.

(k) Our teachers have taught: When R. Eliezer [the Great] was arrested for *Minuth* they brought him to the tribunal for judgment. The Procurator said to him, Does an old man like you busy himself with such idle matters? He answered, I trust him that judges me. So the Procurator thought that he spoke of him, whereas he spoke of his heavenly Father. The Procurator said to him, Since you trust in me you are *dimissus*, acquitted. When he returned home his disciples came in to console him, but he would not accept their consolations. R. Akiba said to him, Suffer me to tell you one thing of what you have taught me. He answered, (Say on). He said, Perhaps [a word of] *minuth* came upon you and pleased you and therefore you were arrested (*Tosefta* reads: Perhaps one of the *Minim* had said to thee a word of *Minuth* and it pleased thee?). He answered, Akiba, you have reminded me! Once I was walking along the upper market (*Tosefta* reads "street") of Sepphoris and found one [of the

as a pseudonym for Jesus, does not quote the present passage by R. Eliezer at all, since Laible also does not quote it. For an explanation of the form of the entire *Baraita* see Graetz IV³ 194 (n. 5).

[63] See *Hame'iri* in *Beth ha-Behirah*, Jerusalem, 1885, p. 60c; R. Brüll's *M'bo ha-Mishnah*, p. 274 (n. 31); C. A. Tottermann, *R. Eliezer ben Hyrcanus*, Leipzig, 1877, p. 17 ff.; D. Chwolsohn, *op. cit.* p. 101 (n. 4).

[64] A. Büchler, *Der Galiläische Amhaarez des zweiten Jahrhunderts*, Vienna, 1906, pp. 292-3 n.

[65] *Op. cit.* 100-102.

disciples of Jesus of Nazareth][66] and Jacob of **Kefar Sekanya**
(*Tosefta* reads "Sakkanin") was his name. He said to me, It is
written in your Law, "Thou shalt not bring the hire of a harlot,
etc." What was to be done with it—a latrine for the High Priest?
But I answered nothing. He said to me, So [Jesus of Nazareth]
taught me (*Tosefta* reads "Yeshu ben Pantere"): "For of the
hire of a harlot hath she gathered them, and unto the hire of a
harlot shall they return;" from the place of filth they come, and
unto the place of filth they shall go. And the saying pleased me,
and because of this I was arrested for *Minuth*. And I transgressed against what is written in the Law: "Keep thy way far
from her"—that is *Minuth*; "and come not nigh the door of her
house"—that is the civil government.[67]

In spite of M. Friedländer's various attempts to persuade us that,
"every *Talmudist* worthy of the name knows that the few *Talmudic*
passages which speak of Jesus are a late addition," [68] and "the
Talmudic sources of the first century and the first quarter of the
second afford not the least evidence of the existence of Jesus or
Christianity," [69]—in spite of this, there can be no doubt that the
words, "one of the disciples of Jesus of Nazareth," and "thus Jesus
of Nazareth taught me," are, in the present passage, both early in
date and fundamental in their bearing on the story; and their
primitive character cannot be disputed on the grounds of the slight
variations in the parallel passages; [70] their variants ("Yeshu ben
Pantere" or "Yeshu ben Pandera," instead of "Yeshu of Nazareth")
are merely due to the fact that, from an early date, the name
"Pantere," or "Pandera," became widely current among the Jews as
the name of the reputed father of Jesus.

We know of R. Eliezer ben Hyrcanus (*Gen. R.* 42; *Ab. d'R.
Nathan* VI 1st vers. XIII 2nd vers., ed. Schechter, p. 30) that until
his twenty-second or twenty-eighth year he had been engaged in
agriculture on his father's estate. He then went up to Jerusalem
and spent many years studying the Law under R. Yochanan ben
Zakkai, with such success that when his father, Hyrcanus, came to
Jerusalem, his son Eliezer expounded in the presence of R. Yochanan
ben Zakkai things "such as ear had never heard." [71]

So we may say that R. Eliezer was born at least thirty or even

[66] The words in square brackets are given in *Dikduke Sof'rim* to *Aboda
Zara*, edited by Dr. Rabinovitz from the Munich MS.
[67] *Ab. Zar.* 16b-17a; *T. Hulin*, II 24. See also *Qoh. R.* on *Kol-ha-D'varim*
and *Yalkut Shimeoni*, Micah 1, and Prov. 5, 5.
[68] See his *Der vorchristliche jüdische Gnosticismus*, Göttingen, 1898, pp.
71-74; *Der Antichrist*, introd. pp. XIX-XX; *Die religiösen Bewegungen*, pp.
191-192; 206-207 n; 215-221.
[69] *Die religiösen Bewegungen*, p. 215.
[70] See what Herford writes against the view of Friedländer, *op. cit.* 11 . n.,
371.
[71] Graetz, *op. cit.* IV³ 40-41.

forty years before the Destruction of the Temple, between 30 and 40 C.E.[72] R. Eliezer cannot have been very young at the time of the Destruction, since his younger contemporary, R. Yehoshua ben Hanania, was one of the Levitical choristers in the Temple (*Sifre* to Numbers 116, ed. Friedmann, p. 53a and b) and hence must have reached maturity by the year 70 C. E.[73] We also gather from the *Talmud* (*Sukkah* 27a) that King Agrippa (the Second) and his steward consulted R. Eliezer on certain religious matters, and even if, with Derenbourg,[74] we assume that such discussion took place after the Destruction, we must yet allow that it must have been between the years 79 and 85 C.E.; for from the year of the Destruction until the accession of Titus (70-79 C.E.) Agrippa was in Rome, and in 85 C. E., during the reign of Domitian, he lost those Jewish territories bestowed on him by Claudius and Nero, and also, perhaps, by Vespasian,[75] and his discussions with R. Eliezer could only have taken place while he was king and in the habit of coming to his capital, Cæsarea Philippi, where R. Eliezer was to be found (Sukkah 27b).

This latter fact is mentioned in *Sukkah* immediately after the questions of Agrippa's steward, showing that the discussion was with R. Eliezer ben Hyrcanus and with him only, and that he was then so well known that it was to him that the king appealed. Therefore about the year 80 C. E. (and probably even before the Destruction) he must have been well advanced in years; and we can safely say that he was born by the year 40 or even 30 C. E., a short time after Jesus was crucified. So it is not impossible that he should have spoken with one of Jesus' actual disciples, and not simply with one of those of the second generation as Laible[76] and Herford[77] felt bound to suppose.

Herford himself holds that R. Eliezer was arrested for heresy (*Minuth*) in the year 109, during Trajan's first persecution of the Christians, when S. Simeon, the aged Bishop of Jerusalem, was killed.[78] But he makes the encounter with Jacob of Kefar Sekanya occur too soon before R. Eliezer's arrest. A long time elapsed between the two, since R. Eliezer had forgotten the meeting and R. Akiba had to remind him of it—an impossibility if, as Herford supposes, only a few months or even a year or two had intervened. At the time of the arrest R. Eliezer was quite old, as is apparent

---

[72] Herford, *op. cit.* p. 143 n. 1.
[73] Derenbourg, *Essai* (Heb. Trans. II 172).
[74] *Ibid.* p. 134. In n. 5 the writer says: "Perhaps King Agrippa only asked these questions of R. Eliezer after the Destruction of the Temple."
[75] Graetz III, 2, 52-53; cf. Schürer, *Geschichte des Jüd. Volkes im Zeitalter Jesu Christi*, I², pp. 587-588, n. 45.
[76] Laible, pp. 60-71.
[77] Herford, pp. 106, 143-145.
[78] *Ibid.* p. 141. H. P. Chajes (*Ha-Goren* IV 34 n.) places the date of his arrest earlier, in the time of Domitian.

from the remark of the Procurator: "Does an old man like you occupy himself in such matters?" If, with Chajes, we conclude that the arrest took place in 95 C.E., the year of Domitian's persecution, and assume that R. Eliezer was then sixty years old, it is easily possible that he encountered Jacob of Kefar Sekanya twenty-five or thirty years earlier, about the year 60 C. E. during his early manhood. By that time Jacob of Kefar Sekanya may have been well advanced in years and in his younger life (about thirty years earlier) have been a disciple of Jesus, from whom he personally heard the interpretation of "the hire of the harlot." It is quite impossible to explain the straightforward words, "thus Jesus of Nazareth taught me," as applicable to a second-hand tradition.

Laible and Herford find it difficult to accept this conclusion (that R. Eliezer encountered an actual disciple of Jesus rather than one of the second generation) owing to another *Baraita* which mentions a certain Jacob who healed the sick in the name of Jesus:

> It happened to R. Eliezer ben Dama [son of R. Ishmael's sister] [79] that a serpent bit him; and Jacob of Kefar Sama [Sekanya] came to heal him in the name of Yeshu ben Pandera. But R. Ishmael forbade him. He said, Ben Dama, you are not permitted! He (R. Eliezer ben Dama) answered, I will bring thee a proof that he may heal me [I will bring thee a verse from the Law showing that it is permitted]. But ere he could bring a proof he died. R. Ishmael said [called to him]: Happy art thou, Ben Dama, that thou hast gone in peace [that thy body is clean and thy soul has gone forth in purity] and hast not broken down the fence of the Wise." [80]

Friedländer [81] argues that the words "in the name of Yeshu ben Pandera," lacking in the version from the *Babylonian Talmud* (*Ab. Zar. 27b*) come from the story of "the grandson of R. Yehoshua ben Levi" (*J. Shab.* end of X, p. 14b), where it follows the story of Ben Dama; but how then could they have come into the *Tosefta* and the *Jerusalem Talmud* (II 5, p. 40d and 41a)? It is more to the point to decide whether "Jacob of Kefar Sama" and "Jacob the Min of Kefar Sekanya" are identical. Herford [82] argues that since Kefar Sekanya (the modern Sukneh) and Kefar Sama (the modern village of Somiah) are only nine miles apart, Jacob the Min may have lived in both and have been called sometimes by the name of one village and sometimes by the name of the other. But if we decide that Jacob the Min, who had dealings with R. Eliezer,

---

[79] Bracketed words are from the version in *Ab. Zar. 27b*; the rest from *T. Hul.* II 22-23.

[80] *T. Hul.* II 22-23; *B. Ab. Zar. 27b; J. Shab* end of xiv (p. 14d) ; *J. Ab. Zar.* II 2 (p. 40d and 41a).

[81] *Relig. Beweg.* pp. 218-220.

[82] *Op. cit.* p. 106.

was one of Jesus' actual disciples and that R. Eliezer met him about
the year 60 C.E., we cannot then identify him with the Jacob the
Min, who wished to cure the nephew of R. Ishmael; because R.
Ishmael was ransomed from the Romans by R. Yehoshua immediately after the Destruction while still a young boy;[83] therefore the
incident of Jacob of Kefar Sekanya and R. Ishmael's nephew could
not have taken place before the year 90; some would even put it as
late as 116[84] or 130.[85] Obviously no disciple of Jesus could have
survived for so long.

But if we suppose that Jacob of Kefar Sekanya and Jacob
of Kefar Soma were two distinct people (the latter not being
introduced as a disciple of Jesus but only as healing the sick "in
the name of Jesus"—a practice of the second generation of disciples[86]) we can then regard the former not simply as a disciple
of Jesus, but even as his *brother,* "James the brother of the Lord"
(Galatians i. 19), or "James the brother of Jesus" ("Antiquities,"
XXIX i), or "James the Righteous" (ὁ δίκαιος). This James
who, as the brother (or near relative) of Jesus, became the chief
of the disciples after the crucifixion, was one of the most ardent
advocates of the Jewish written and oral Law. The disciples of
Jesus were then a small party of Ebionites or "Nazarenes," and
James, their leader, lived an abnormally severe ascetic life. Eusebius,
quoting Hegesippus,[87] tells how he drank no wine nor strong
drink, ate no flesh, never cut his hair, clothed himself in cotton and
never in woollens, possessed only one garment, and spent much
time fasting and praying in the Temple.[88] He and his companions
requested Paul the apostle to give money to the Nazarites to shave
their heads (which they had left uncut while under a vow) and
that he himself should sanctify himself with them and enter the
Temple (Acts xxi. 18-26), all in accordance with the teaching
of the Pharisees. In the presence of the followers of this same
James, Peter and Barnabas were afraid to eat with the Gentiles, and
were forced to keep apart from the uncircumcised and to abstain
from forbidden foods (Galatians ii. 12-13).

James "the righteous," "Brother of the Lord," was, then,
distinguishable from the Pharisees only in regarding the Suffering
Messiah as the Redeemer and Saviour, and in supposing that the
Messiah was already come; whereas the Pharisees still awaited
him and looked for him to appear in both material and moral triumph
and glory. It is not, then, a matter of great surprise that when
Hanan (Annas) the Second, the Bœthusean High Priest (who
held office in the interim between the death of the Procurator Festus

[83] See Bacher, *op. cit.* I 186, 232.
[84] Chwolsohn, *op. cit.* n. 3 to pp. 99-100.
[85] Herford, *op. cit.* 105, 145.
[86] Graetz, *op. cit.* III, I[5], 312-313.
[87] Eusebius, *Historia Ecclesiastica* II, 23.

and the coming of Albinus), condemned to death "James the brother of Jesus which was called Messiah," the Pharisees complained against this perversion of justice on the part of the Sadducæan-Bœthusean High Priest and sent secret messengers to Agrippa II and Albinus, reporting the miscarriage of justice, with the result that he was deposed by Agrippa. Such is the account of Josephus ("Antiq." XX, ix 1).

We show later (p. 59) that there is no foundation for the doubt of Jewish scholars like Graetz [89] and Christians like Schürer [90] as to the historical value of this account so far as it affects James the brother of Jesus. James was, therefore, put to death in the interim between the procuratorships of Festus and Albinus, i.e. 62 C.E. Schürer [90a] considers that this date is not definitely ascertainable, because Hegesippus states that *immediately* after the death of James the war of Vespasian and Titus broke out, so placing the event at a later date. In any case it was not earlier than 62 C.E.; and since we have already seen that R. Eliezer was well known by the year 60 it is quite possible that he had met "James the brother of the Lord" and spoken with him about the interpretation which he had heard from Jesus. They met at Sepphoris in Galilee, whereas James' regular place of residence was Jerusalem; but this need not surprise us since we know that the first Christians used often to go backwards and forwards between Jerusalem and Galilee: they were almost all of them Galilæans. Neither need the discussion with R. Eliezer on the exposition of Scripture, though it now strikes us as unseemly, be a matter of surprise.

There is no attempt in the story to pour contempt on Jesus: on the contrary, the saying reported in the name of Jesus pleases the great Tanna. All this goes to show that we have here a story bearing the stamp of truth. Certainly, at first sight, this exposition dealing with the hire of the harlot and the latrine does not accord with the character of Jesus' teachings as we know them from the Gospels: there we are accustomed to see him preach only about ethics and personal piety. But we should note that the Pharisaic methods of exposition are by no means foreign to him, as may be observed from the way in which he expounds the passage: "The Lord said unto my lord, Sit thou on my right hand," asking "How can David call the Messiah 'Lord,' when the Messiah is David's son?" (Mark xii. 35-37; Luke xx. 41-44; Matthew xxii. 41-45).

The compilers of the Gospels did not, of course, see fit to quote sayings of Jesus dealing with religious rulings and ceremonial laws,

[89] Krauss, *Das Leben Jesu*, pp. 23, 193, 299-300; Schwegler, *Das nach-apostolische Zeitalter*, I 173.

[89] *Op. cit.* III 2³, 444, n. 2.

[90] *Op. cit.* I⁴ 581-583.

[90a] P. 582 and n. 43 to that and following page. Derenbourg, one of the best Jewish scholars, regards the story as true (II 106, 67) and in this he is supported by Chwolsohn, *op. cit.* pp. 101-104.

since they wrote their books at a time when Christianity was endeavouring in every possible way to emphasize the opposition between the teaching of Jesus and Pharisaism—Judaism *par excellence*. But such an Ebionite and observer of the Law as "James the brother of the Lord" could still remember this halakhic exposition by Jesus, the same Jesus who had been hailed by the title "Rabbi" and "Mari" [91] just like any Pharisaic Rabbi; [92] and when the opportunity came, James repeated it to one of the great *Tannaim.*

It is worth while paying attention to these words, improbable though they may at first sight appear, [93] especially to Christian scholars. Two distinguished Christian scholars, W. Brandt [94] and W. Wrede [95] have concluded that Jesus was simply a teacher and a Rabbi, and that his messianic attributes are the creation of the early Christian sect ("Gemeindetheologie"). We are not concerned at the moment with the truth of this, but will come to that question later; yet in any case, this exposition serves to show that Jesus often resembled the Pharisees in his mode of teaching. Friedländer,[96] however, thinks it impossible that Jesus could so "demean himself" ("erniedrigen konnte") as to treat Scripture in such an "unholy" fashion; but let us remember that Jesus, like all Israel's sages, from the Prophets to the *Amoraim,* thought nothing "unholy" which concerned the needs of mankind. It is not only the *Talmud* which expounds Scripture in ways which, to our modern taste, are unseemly, but even Jesus, in the Gospels, speaks of human needs with a freeness unacceptable in these days: "Whatsoever goeth into the mouth passeth into the belly and is cast out into the draught" (εἰς ἀφεδρῶναι) (Matt. xv. 17); "Whatsoever entereth a man from without, cannot defile him; because it goeth not into his heart but into his belly and goeth out thence into the draught" (Mark vii. 18-19).

That it should have been to R. Eliezer ben Hyrcanus in particular that Jacob told the exposition, is not a great matter of surprise.

---

[91] מרי is the Κύριε of the Gospels, as in Syriac. רבי ומורי for רבי ומרי is an old mistake already pointed out by S. D. Luzzatto in *Bethulath bath Yehudah* p. 111; and he mentions in his French article *Editions rares* (Steinschneider *Hamazkir*, i 87) that he had found in *Berachoth,* ed. Sonzino, 1483, the reading שלום עליך רבי ומרי in place of רבי ומורי. See also Dalman, *Die Worte Jesu,* pp. 268, 276.

[92] Graetz (III 2⁵ 759; IV³, n. 9, pp. 399-400) concludes that the name "Rabbi" in the Gospels is an anachronism, since previous to the Destruction no great Pharisee was so called. But, in the mind of the present writer, this is only half true: the official title may not have been "Rabbi," but it may have been used popularly to signify the Scribes.

[93] Laible (*op. cit.* pp. 59-62) agrees with the view that Jesus may have uttered such an exposition, since it was of importance in the time of the Temple.

[94] *Die evangelische Geschichte u. der Ursprung des Christenthums,* Leipzig, 1898.

[95] *Das Messianitätsgeheimniss in den Evangelien,* Göttingen, 1909.

[96] *Op. cit.* p. 220.

We have already seen that R. Eliezer was not able to deny Jesus a share in the world to come; and certain of his sayings survive which bear a resemblance to sayings in the Gospels. For example, his saying, "Everyone who has a morsel of food in his basket and says, What shall I eat tomorrow? is of little faith" (*Sota* 45b), corresponds to the saying in Matthew (vi. 30-34), " . . . how much more you, O ye of little faith; therefore be not anxious saying, What shall we eat and what shall we drink . . . be not anxious therefore for the morrow." The short prayer of R. Eliezer, "Do thy will in heaven above and give comfort to them that fear thee here below and do what is good in thine eyes" (*Berachoth* 29b; *T. Ber.* III, 11), corresponds to the prayer which Jesus taught his disciples; "Our Father in heaven . . . thy will be done, as in heaven so also on earth" (Matt. vi. 9-11; Luke xi. 2); and to the passage in the Gospel, "Glory to God in the highest and peace to the children of men" (Luke ii. 14).

Perhaps such similarity caused his arrest for *Minuth*.[97] R. Eliezer's connexion with Christianity was certainly distasteful to his neighbours, who opposed *Minuth* to their utmost. Evidence of this is forthcoming in the last *Talmudic* extract, which we quote here because it deals with R. Eliezer, and because it explains a further point in Jesus' teaching as it is portrayed in the Gospels:

(1) Imma Shalom was the wife of R. Eliezer and sister of Rabban Gamaliel. There lived near her a *philosoph* who had the reputation of never taking a bribe. They sought to make a mock of him. She sent him a lamp of gold. They came before him. She said to him, "I desire that they give me a share in the family property." He said to them, "From the day when ye were exiled from your land, the Law of Moses has been taken away, and the law of the *Evangelion* has been given, and in it is written, "A son and a daughter shall inherit alike." The next day he (R. Gamaliel), in his turn, sent to him a Lybian ass. He (the *philosoph*) said to them, "I have looked further to the end of the book, and in it is written, 'I am not come to take away from the Law of Moses and I am not come to add to the Law of Moses,' and it is written, 'Where there is a son, a daughter does not inherit.'" She said to him, "Let your light shine as a lamp." R. Gamaliel said to her, "The ass has come and trodden out the lamp." [*i.e.* the Lybian ass, as a bribe, has prevailed over the bribe of the golden lamp] (*Shab.* 116a and b).

This interesting story occurs nowhere else in *Talmud* or *Midrash,* nor is it indicated as being a *Baraita.* Its Aramaic style, recalling the style of the story of Onkelos bar Kalonymos (see above, f, pp. 33-

[97] The point is discussed by H. P. Chajes (*Ha-Goren*, IV 34, n. 2). He thinks that it was perhaps because of this resemblance that "his (R. Eliezer's) companions brought forth weapons to anathematize him."

34) testifies to its lateness, as do the words *"aven gillayon"* or *"avon gillayon,"* names first applied to the Gospel by R. Meir and R. Yochanan (*Shab.* 116a—shortly before the present story). Therefore the present form of the narrative is undoubtedly late, though the fact recorded is not necessarily invented. The figures in the story are: Imma Shalom,[98] wife of R. Eliezer and sister of Rabban Gamaliel, and Rabban Gamaliel himself (i. e. R. Gamaliel of Yabneh, Gamaliel II). Laible [99] offers the hypothesis, worth noticing, that neither the wife nor the father-in-law of R. Eliezer felt easy at the friendly relations existing between R. Eliezer and the *Minim;* and so they sought to hold up to ridicule the Christian *Philosoph* who lived near Rabban Gamaliel, and to show R. Eliezer what sinners and wrongdoers were these *Minim,* who could be perverted by a bribe.

But the present writer would suggest that there is a still subtler intention: it was not requisite only to draw ridicule on the *Philosoph,* but also to show that there was something equivocal in the relation of Jesus and the Christians to the Law. In this case we obviously have before us the Gospel passage: I came not to destroy but to fulfil (οὐκ ἦλθον καταλῦσαι ἄλλα πληρῶσαι Matthew v. 17). Instead of the reading "and I am not (אלו) come to add," etc., there occurs in the *Talmud* version the variant *"but* (אלא) I am come to add," etc.—agreeing entirely with the Gospel form: "I came not to destroy *but* to fulfil." [100] Güdemann [101] argues that the correct version is, "and I am not come to add," whereas Matthew, in writing *"but* to fulfil," has mistaken the Aramaic original from which he drew the saying. In any case we may deduce from Jesus' words that he did not come to set aside the ceremonial laws, although many other verses of the Gospels speak of their annulment by Jesus. The early *Tannaim* perceived this inner contradiction, and Imma Shalom and her brother wished to expose it to R. Eliezer and so alienate him from *Minuth* altogether.[102]

For many reasons the view of Nicholson [103] and Herford [104] is to be accepted—that the episode occurred immediately after the Destruction, about the year 73; and Güdemann [105] and Herford [106] are

---

[98] On the name "Imma Shalom" see Geiger *Yochanan ben Zakkai und Eliezer ben Hyrcanus,* in *Jüdische Zeitschrift,* VI 134 n.

[99] *Op. cit.* p. 63.

[100] Chwolsohn (*op. cit.* p. 99, n. 3) accepts this reading.

[101] *Religionsgeschichtliche Studien,* pp. 69-70. With him agree Graetz (III I ⁵ 292 n. 3) and H. P. Chajes, *Markus-Studien,* Berlin, 1899, p. 39.

[102] See Herford, *op. cit.* pp. 151-155, on further anti-Christian hints in the remarks attributed to Imma Shalom and her brother (*e.g.,* "Let thy light shine"; Matt. v. 15; and the ass as symbol of the Messiah).

[103] For details see E. B. Nicholson, *The Gospel according to the Hebrews,* p. 146 n.

[104] Herford, *op. cit.* p. 148.

[105] Güdemann, *op. cit.* pp. 69-70.

[106] Herford, *op. cit.* pp. 150-151.

to be followed in saying that the *Philosoph* drew the parable: "I came not to take away from the Law of Moses," etc., not from the Gospel of Matthew (since it is very doubtful whether it existed at the time), but from a collection of the Words of Jesus (*Logia*) from which Matthew himself drew.

This brings us to the end of the *early* statements about Jesus in the *Talmud*. They may be summarized as follows:

(a) There are reliable statements to the effect that his name was Yeshu'a (Yeshu) of Nazareth; that he "practised sorcery" (*i. e.* performed miracles, as was usual in those days) and beguiled and led Israel astray; that he mocked at the words of the Wise; that he expounded Scripture in the same manner as the Pharisees; that he had five disciples; that he said that he was not come to take aught away from the Law or to add to it; that he was hanged (crucified) as a false teacher and beguiler on the eve of the Passover which happened on a Sabbath; and that his disciples healed the sick in his name.

(b) There are statements of a tendencious or untrustworthy character to the effect that he was the bastard of an adulteress and that his father was Pandera or Pantere; that for forty days before his crucifixion a herald went out proclaiming why Jesus was to be put to death, so that any might come and plead in his favour, but none was found to do so; that there was doubt whether Jesus had any share in the world to come. Some of these latter statements are important (namely those about the illegitimacy and the name Ben Pandera) since they are to be found in Celsus, while their appearance in the *Talmud* testifies to their early character and to their being very widespread at a very early date.

But these statements quoted from the *Talmud* have a still greater value: we see from them what was the attitude to Jesus and his teaching of the first generation of the *Tannaim* who lived after the Destruction, and who counted among them the most learned and pious of the nation. This attitude does not display the same bitter hatred and hostility which we find later, when the Christian peoples, those who bore aloft the name of Jesus of Nazareth, began to oppress and persecute the Jews with all their might.

Primarily, in the eyes of the sages of Israel, till the time of Trajan and Hadrian (the reader has, without doubt, noticed that the most important and the earliest *Talmudic* notices about Jesus come from R. Eliezer and his contemporaries), Jesus was a true Jew: he may have been "an Israelite who had sinned," or "a transgressor in Israel," yet he remained an Israelite in every respect. He is raised to a rank higher than the "prophets of the Gentiles," and none dare deny him a share in the world to come. More even than this: he is described as one of the Scribes and *Tannaim*, who expounded the Scriptures and who created the *Midrashic Haggada;* and his treatment of the verse about the "hire of the harlot" pleased so severe and demanding a *Tanna* as R. Eliezer the Great; but his attitude to the Law, which, one moment, he emphatically says he came to support, while another time he sets it aside and makes a "mock of the words of the Wise"—this aroused the ire and the severe condemnation of the *Talmud* authorities.

It was because of this that they tried to transform the merits which later, in the Gospels, were held up for admiration (at the end of the first Christian century they were still only current orally), into drawbacks and even grave faults. They never doubted that he worked miracles: they merely looked upon them, as we have already found, as acts of sorcery; while his birth by the Holy Spirit they transformed into an illegitimate birth. Furthermore, it is not in the earlier passages from the *Talmud,* but at the very end of the *Tannaitic* era, some two hundred years after the Crucifixion, that we find a *Tanna* (R. Eliezer ha-Kappar, a contemporary of R. Yehuda ha-Nasi, the editor of the *Mishna*) accusing Jesus of "making himself God."

The early *Tannaim* knew nothing whatever of this. They only knew that his disciples used to heal the sick in his name; and they used to prohibit this method of healing even when there was danger of the illness proving fatal—as was laid down in a *Halakha*: "A man may not be cured by the *Minim* even if it is doubtful whether he will live more than a short time." [107]   In the earlier period they were more averse to the *Minim* than to Jesus himself, since in them they saw a danger to the national existence.[108]   It is this which accounts for the "rite of the Benediction of the *Minim*" [*Ber.* 28b-29a; Herford, *op. cit.* 125-137] at Yabneh at the end of the first century, and the *Halakha* about breaking off all relations with the *Minim*, occurring in the *Tosefta* [*T. Hul.* II 20-21]. But to Jesus, at least until the end of the second century, we find no such aversion.

(B)   THE *TOL'DOTH YESHU*

[The earlier literature dealing with the *Tol'doth Yeshu* or *Ma'aseh Talui* is to be found in Wagenseil, "Tela ignea Satanae," Altdorf, 1681, which gives the *Tol'doth Yeshu* in Hebrew (a revised version giving a good text) with a Latin translation, together with a "Refutation." The entire material necessary for the critical study of the book is carefully amassed in S. Krauss, "Das Leben Jesu nach jüdischen Quellen," Berlin, 1902, giving three Hebrew versions from various types of MSS. together with fragments from MSS. illustrating other types, including fragments

---

[107] *Ab. Zar.* 27b; *T. Hul.* II 20-21. Friedländer (*Die Religiösen Beweg-ungen,* pp. 172-178) tries unsuccessfully to show that this has nothing to do with the Christians, but only with the antinomians among the Jews [i.e., opponents of the ceremonial laws] and pagans. These latter may have been included, but there is no doubt that the passage deals also with the Christians. See Herford, *op. cit.* pp. 177-189.

[108] On this see the sound remarks of Herford, *op. cit.* pp. 392-393.

in Aramaic. Krauss has discussed minutely and expertly everything bearing on the *Tol'doth Yeshu,* and the present and previous chapters have drawn largely from his work. The *Tol'doth Yeshu* was published in Yiddish, in German characters, by E. Bischoff: "Ein jüdisch-deutsches Leben Jesu," Leipzig, 1895. Most of the matter contained in the Hebrew version is to be found in Gershom Bader's "Helqath M'hoqeq"—History of the Christian Lawgiver, Cracow, 1893; the author pretends to draw only from MSS. but he actually reproduces accounts of the life of Jesus from the *Tol'doth Yeshu* and from Christian sources. Useful comments on the legends in the *Tol'doth Yeshu* and on their origin may be found in Richard von der Alm (Ghillany): "Die Urtheile heidnischer und jüdischer Schriftsteller der vier ersten christlichen Jahrhunderte über Jesus und die ersten Christen," Leipzig, 1864.]

This book is not now common, though at one time it had a wide circulation (under various titles, such as *Tol'doth Yeshu, Ma'aseh Talui, Ma'aseh do'otho v'eth b'no,* and the like) in Hebrew and Yiddish among the simpler minded Jews, and even more educated Jews used to study the book during the nights of *Natal* (Christmas). Now, however, readers of Hebrew are rare among the Jewish masses outside of Russia and Poland, and there the book was banned by the censor. Yet the book may still be found in MS, and in print [1] among many educated Jews. Our mothers knew its contents by hearsay—of course with all manner of corruptions, changes, omissions and imaginative additions—and handed them on to their children. Different versions of the book exist in MS., some expanded to greater length and others abbreviated; some following closely the *Talmudic* legends about Ben Stada, Pandera, Pappus ben Yehuda, Miriam M'gadd'la Neshaya and Yeshu, while others differ from them considerably. But though such changes are sometimes great, as a rule they affect only details, especially names; some versions added longer or shorter episodes, while in others certain episodes are omitted. But the general tenor of the story, its general spirit, and the outstanding features remain the same in all.

The contents are roughly as follows:

A certain Yochanan, "who was learned in the Law and who feared God," of the House of David (according to some versions, it is Pappus Ben Yehudah, following the *Talmud*), espoused to himself in Bethlehem Miriam, the daughter of his widowed neighbour, a respectable and humble virgin. But Miriam attracted a handsome villain named Joseph Pandera (or Ben Pandera) who betrayed her at the close of a certain Sabbath. Miriam supposed that it was her espoused husband, Yochanan, and, submitting only against her will, marvelled at the act of her pious betrothed; and when he himself came, she mentioned her astonishment. He suspected Pandera and told his suspicions to Rabban Shimeon ben

---

[1] Recently there appeared an edition of *Ma'aseh Talui* without date or place of publication.

Shetah. When Miriam was with child and Yochanan knew that it was not by him but that he could not prove who was the guilty party, he fled to Babylon.

Miriam brought forth a son and called him Yehoshua after the name of her mother's brother; and this name was corrupted to Yeshu. The child learnt much *Torah* from an able teacher and distinguished scholar; but he proved "an impudent child," and on one occasion he passed in front of the Sages with uncovered head (and, according to another version, delivered an offensive exposition about Moses and Jethro), whereupon the Sages said that he was a bastard and "a son of uncleanness." Miriam confessed to this (the whole account follows the episode told in *Tractate Kallah;* see above, (pp. 30-31) and Shimeon ben Shetah recalled what his disciple Yochanan had told him.

Yeshu then fled to Jerusalem and in the Temple learnt the "Ineffable Name." In order that the brazen dogs, which stood by the gate of the place of sacrifice and barked at all who learned the Name and so made them forget the name [this resembles the legend of the lions of Solomon's throne told in the "Second Targum"]— in order that they should not make him forget the Name, Yeshu wrote it on a piece of leather and sewed it in the flesh of his thigh. He gathered around him in Bethlehem a group of young Jews and proclaimed himself the Messiah and Son of God; and as a retort to those who rejected his claims he said that "they sought their own greatness and were minded to rule in Israel," while to confirm his claims he healed a lame man and a leper by the power of the "Ineffable Name." He was brought before Queen Helena,[2] the ruler of Israel, and she found him guilty of acts of sorcery and beguilement.

But Yeshu restored a dead man to life, and the queen, in her alarm, began to believe in him. He next went to Upper Galilee where he continued his miracles and drew many people after him. The Sages of Israel then saw that it was essential that one of their number, Yehuda Iskarioto (some versions give R. Yehuda the Pious), should learn the "Ineffable Name" just as Yeshu did, and so rival him in signs and wonders. Yehuda and Yeshu came before the queen. Yeshu flew in the air, but Yehuda flew higher and defiled him so that he fell to earth. The queen condemned Yeshu to death and delivered him up to the Sages of Israel. They took him to Tiberias and imprisoned him there. But he had instilled into his disciples the belief that whatever happened to him had been prepared for the Messiah, the Son of God, from the days of

---

[2] It would seem that Helena, queen of Adiabene, mother of King Monobaz, and Helena, the wife of the first Christian emperor, Constantine, have here been confused with Shelom-Zion (Shalminon, Alexandra), the queen who, according to the *Talmud,* was sister of Shimeon ben Shetah (*Berach. 48a; Gen. R.* 91; *Qoh. R.* on the verse *Tobah Hokhmah*).

Creation, and that the Prophets had prophesied it all. So the disciples of Yeshu fought against the Sages of Israel, rescued Yeshu and fled with him to Antioch.

From Antioch Yeshu went to Egypt to fetch spells [as is recorded in the *Talmud* of Ben Stada], but Yehuda (Iskarioto or "the Pious") had mingled among his disciples and robbed him in the meantime of the "Name." Yeshu then went a second time to Jerusalem to learn the "Name." Yehuda reported this intended visit to the Sages of Israel in Jerusalem, and told them that when Yeshu should come to the Temple, he, Yehuda, would bow before him, and thus the Sages would be able to distinguish between Yeshu and his disciples, for he and his disciples all dressed in garments "of one colour" (or, according to another version, because all his disciples had sworn never to say of him, "This is he").

And so it came to pass: the Sages of Israel recognized him and arrested him. They took and hanged him on the eve of Passover (as recorded in several of the *Talmudic* versions) on a cabbage stem—for no other tree would bear him, because Yeshu, during his lifetime, had adjured all trees by the "Ineffable Name" not to receive his body when he was hanged; but he failed so to adjure the cabbage stem since that does not count as a tree. The body was taken down while it was yet the eve of the Sabbath (in order not to violate the prohibition: "His body shall not remain there for the night") and at once buried. But Yehuda the gardener removed the body from the tomb and cast it into a water-channel in the garden, and let the water flow over it as usual.

When the disciples came and did not find the body in the tomb, they announced to the queen that Yeshu had been restored to life. The queen believed this and was minded to put to death the Sages of Israel for having laid their hands upon the Lord's Anointed. All the Jews mourned and wept and fasted because of this dire decree, until at last R. Tanchuma [who lived four hundred years after Jesus!] found the corpse in Yehuda's garden by the help of the Holy Spirit. The Sages of Israel removed it, tied it to the tail of a horse and brought it before the queen in order that she might see how she had been deceived.

We are next told how the disciples of Yeshu fled and mingled among all the nations. Among these disciples were twelve apostles who sorely distressed the Jews. One of the Sages of Israel, Shimeon Kepha [Petros—Peter—"rock," in Greek, of which the Aramaic equivalent is "Kepha"], thereupon undertook to separate the disciples of Yeshu from the Jews and give them religious laws of their own, so that they might no longer affect the Jews.[3] After he had acted in such a way as to feign belief in Yeshu, he went and lived by himself in a tower built in his honour [a reference to the Church

---

[3] Obviously a distant echo of the dispute between Peter and Paul about the keeping of the ceremonial laws, which Peter supported and Paul opposed.

of St. Peter in Rome] where he composed hymns and psalms full
of devotion and piety which he sent to all the scattered communities
of Israel, by whom they are sung in the Synagogues to this day.[4]
The *Tol'doth Yeshu* also gives an account of Nestorius and his
teaching, but that is outside our subject.

The most superficial reading of this book serves to prove that we
have here nothing beyond a piece of folklore, in which are confusedly
woven early and late *Talmudic* and *Midrashic* legends and sayings
concerning Jesus, together with Gospel accounts (which the author
of the *Tol'doth* perverts in a fashion derogatory to Jesus), and other
popular legends, many of which are mentioned by Celsus, and
Tertullian and later Church Fathers, and which Samuel Krauss
labels a "folkloristische Motive." [5] Specially noticeable is the attitude
adopted by the *Tol'doth* to the Gospel accounts. Scarcely ever does
it deny anything: it merely changes evil to good and good to evil.

The Gospels tell how Jesus performed miracles; the author of
the *Tol'doth Yeshu* also tells us so, but while the former say that he
performed them by the help of the Holy Spirit, the latter says that
he performed them through the "Ineffable Name," which he had
learnt for an evil purpose, and through the magic spells which he
had brought from Egypt. The Gospels say that Jesus was born of
the Holy Spirit, while the *Tol'doth* asserts that Jesus was born as a
result of deceit and seduction. The Gospels say that the body was
not found after burial; the *Tol'doth* also says that the body disappeared, but while the Gospels say that the body disappeared because
it had been restored to life, the *Tol'doth* holds that it disappeared
because Yehuda the gardener cast it out of the tomb.

And there is much more similar contradiction. This alone proves
that the book contains no history worth the name. It is possible
that certain accounts, inserted later, were current among the Jews by
the beginning of the second century, as is shown by the relevant
passages in Origen and Tertullian. It is also possible that some book
entitled *Tol'doth Yeshu*—though more or less different in content
and altogether different in form and Hebrew style—was in the hands
of the Jews as early as the fifth century, and that it was the same
book which fell into the hands of Agobard, Bishop of Lyons, (who
refers to it in his book "De judaicis superstitionibus," which he composed in conjunction with others about the year 830), and into the
hands of Hrabanus Maurus, who became Archbishop of Magenta
in 847, and, in his book, "Contra Judæos," referred to Jewish legends
about Jesus which correspond to much of the contents of the surviving *Tol'doth Yeshu*. Certain Aramaic fragments of disparaging
stories about Jesus (published by Krauss in his "Leben Jesu," and
in the "Revue des Etudes Juives," LXII 28-31: "Fragments

---

[4] Clearly a confusion between Simon Peter and the hymn-writer, R.
Shimeon.
[5] See Krauss, *op. cit.* pp. 154-236 and the notes pp. 249-298.

Araméens du Toldot Jéschou") also testify to the existence of such
an early book. But the language of the earliest of the versions which
have been recovered, and most of the stories they contain, stamped
as they are with the marks of a later age, forbid us to suppose with
Krauss [6] that the present book was composed, almost in its entirety,
about the year 500. The episode about the "impudence" of Yeshu,
by which R. Akiba "recognized that he was a bastard and a 'son of
uncleanness'," is unknown to us from sources previous to the *Tractate Kallah*, which itself, as regards many of its contents, and explanations and legends, is as late as 500 C.E.; and even Krauss considers it unlikely ("unwahrscheinlich") that the author of the
Tol'doth Yeshu drew his material direct from Hegesippus, believing
that he obtained it through the medium of Yosippon,[7] though not, so
Krauss believes—from the present Yosippon (which was only published in the tenth century), but from an earlier Yosippon referred
to by an Arab writer, Ibn Hazm (d. 1063), and the author of *The
Chronicles of Yerachmeel*.[8] But Ibn Hazm says of "Yusuf ibn
Quorion" (Joseph ben Gorion) that he makes little mention of
Yoseph ben Miriam,[9] as is actually the case in all the versions of
Yosippon; and so the author of *Tol'doth Yeshu* could not have
derived his many legends from that source. As for the author of
The Chronicles of Yerachmeel, it is more probable that he confused
the original Josephus with Joseph ben Gorion. Some of what *The
Chronicles* quotes in the name of Ben Gorion [10] does occur in
Josephus (who speaks of John the Baptist, of Jesus and of James the
brother of Jesus); and Josephus may have originally contained much
more than we now possess; while what we now possess may have
once existed in a different shape owing to omission and modifications
by Christian copyists (as may be illustrated from the present account
of Jesus in Josephus, which is adapted in several points).[11] Also
the author of *The Chronicles of Yerachmeel* may have added certain
matter from memory to the statements of the Gospels, matter which
he had read in other books. But even if that other source was
Josephus (whom many ancient writers confused with Yoseph ben
Gorion, since this Hebrew name was familiar to them from the
Talmudic "Nakdimon ben Gorion"), he could have read there only
about John and Jesus and James.

But in any case we may not rely on such a doubtful and isolated
item of evidence in order to date Yosippon earlier, and thereby argue
that it was the source of the *Tol'doth*, and that the *Tol'doth* could
therefore be dated in the fifth century. The present Hebrew

[6] *Op. cit.* 246-248.
[7] *Ibid.*, 241.
[8] *Ibid.*, 238-9.
[9] A. Neubauer, *J.Q.R.* XI 356.
[10] A. Neubauer, *Mediæval Jewish Chronicles*, Oxford, 1887, I 190; Krauss, *op. cit.* 239.
[11] For details see next chapter.

Tol'doth Yeshu, even in its earliest form, is not earlier than the present Yosippon, i.e. it was not composed before the tenth century [12] Therefore it cannot possibly possess any historical value nor in any way be used as material for the life of Jesus.

Yet it has another value, which may, in some sense be described as a historical value. We can gather from it what was the view of the Jews on the life and teaching of Jesus, from the fifth to the tenth centuries (for many of the statements must be earlier than the time when they were set down in writing), just as we may gather from the remarks about Jesus in the *Talmud* what were the views of the Jews about Jesus during the first five centuries. Krauss rightly says: "I am far from investigating on the basis of the statements contained in the *Tol'doth Yeshu* such far-reaching questions as the truths of the Christian faith; I do not think the book in the least suitable for this. I do not regard the *Tol'doth Yeshu* as a criterion of the fundamental truths of Christianity, but it can make clear what were the views on Christianity which arose among the Jews. That is to say, it does not contain objective, but subjective truths, for while it does not know what really occurred, it does know how these events looked in the eyes of the Jews." [13]

And if we look into it solely for these subjective truths, its value is great. We see from it that the attitude to Jesus became worse when the Gentiles began to embrace the new faith and to despise Judaism; and that it became still worse when the Christians, of non-Jewish or Jewish origin, began to persecute the Jews and "throw stones into the well whence they had drunk." The Jews, unable to exact physical vengeance from their strong enemies, retaliated in speech and writing. The inventions and legends, compact of hatred and sometimes of penetrating and stinging ridicule against Christianity and its Founder, went on increasing.

Nothing in the Gospels was denied: it was only perverted into a source of ridicule and blame. The Jews of the Middle Ages did not deny that Jesus worked miracles but (and this shows their state of mind at the time) agreed that he really did do so, but it was by use of the "Ineffable Name," by magic and with evil purpose! . . . Nor did they deny the moral good in Jesus' teaching: they asserted that it had been introduced into the new religion by Simon Cephas, Peter—the Jewish Christian against whom Paul quarrelled for retaining the ceremonial observances; and all this moral good he derived from the religion of Israel, to which all his life he secretly remained faithful.

This is the spirit which runs through the *Tol'doth Yeshu*, and which was certainly the spirit which prevailed among all the Jews

[12] It is impossible to draw reliable conclusions from the fragments in Aramaic and the statements by Agobard and Hrabanus Maurus.

[13] *Op. cit.* p. 237.

during the early Middle Ages. Thus, though it is valueless for a knowledge of the historical events affecting Jesus, or of his character and teaching, the book is very important for a knowledge of the spirit which prevailed among the Jews at that particular time.

II. THE GREEK AND LATIN SOURCES

[Virtually every "Life of Jesus," ancient or modern, treats of these sources; cf. Albert Réville, "Jésus de Nazareth," Paris, 1897, I 266-281; P. W. Schmidt, "Die Geschichte Jesu, erläutert," Tübingen u. Leipzig, 1904, pp. 18-21; Oscar Holtzmann, "Leben Jesu," Tübingen u. Leipzig, 1901, pp. 10-13; and, more briefly, in the following: Paul Wernle, "Die Quellen des Lebens Jesu," pp. 3-4; Wilhelm Bousset, "Was wissen wir von Jesu?" pp. 15-17. See also the notes to the two following chapters.]

(A) JOSEPHUS

[See Schürer, "Geschichte des Jüdischen Volkes im Zeitalter Jesu Christi," I³ 544-549 (app. 2); Joseph Salvador, "Jésus-Christ et sa doctrine," Paris, 1838, I 157-158 note; A. Réville, *op. cit.* I 279; Chwolsohn, "Das Letzte Passamahl," pp. 101-102.]

Yoseph ben Mattathiah ha-Cohen, or, as he is usually called, Flavius Josephus, was born in the year 37-38 C.E. In his books, "The Antiquities of the Jews" and "The Wars of the Jews," written a few years after the Destruction of the Temple, he ignored nothing of the political and social events in Judæa, especially those from the time of Herod the First till the Destruction. There is no passing revolt, no temporary tumult, no just or unjust condemnation to death, if it have some social or political interest, but finds a detailed description in his writings. It is, then, natural to suppose that they should contain a detailed account of the movement which arose in Palestine in the time of Pontius Pilate, in consequence of the teaching and death of Jesus.

But in place of such a detailed account we find in the "Antiquities" (written in the last decade of the first century) the fewest possible words, less even than are devoted in the same book to John the Baptist; and, what is still more unsatisfactory, these few words contain what are manifest additions by Christian copyists. The "Antiquities" speaks twice of Jesus. It is the first of the passages in which the additions occur and which is here quoted (italics indicate the suspected additions) :

> Now there was about this time (*i.e.*, about the time of the rising against Pilate who wished to extract money from the Temple for the purpose of bringing water to Jerusalem from a distant spring) Jesus, a wise man, *if it be lawful to call him a man* (σοφὸς ἀνὴρ εἴγε ἄνδρα αὐτὸν λέγειν χρὴ). For he was a doer of

wonderful works, a teacher of such men as receive the truth with pleasure. He drew over to him both many of the Jews and many of the Gentiles. *He was the Messiah* (ὁ Χριστὸς οὗτος ἦν); and when Pilate, at the suggestion of the principal men among us (ἐνδείξει τῶν πρώτων ἀνδρῶν παρ' ἡμῖν), had condemned him to the cross, those that loved him at the first ceased not [so to do], *for he appeared to them alive again* (πάλιν ζῶν) *the third day, as the divine Prophets had foretold these and ten thousand other wonderful things concerning him;* and the race (φῦλον) of Christians, so named from him, are not extinct even now.[1]

No Christian scholar, even, who has any regard for critical methods, allows that the italicised words could have come from Josephus, the Jew and Pharisee. Josephus could never have written of Jesus such words as "he was the Messiah;" and Origen twice states that Josephus did not admit that Jesus was the Messiah.[2] Some scholars throw doubt not only on part, but on the entire passage in Josephus: they hold that everything about Jesus in the "Antiquities" is a late addition by Christian copyists, who found it difficult to accept the fact that a writer of the history of the time should make no mention whatever of Jesus.[3] These same scholars argue that it is incredible that a man like Josephus, who loved to dilate on every petty incident, could be content to dispose of such an event as the life and terrible death of Jesus in the few words which are all that are left, after the obvious interpolations are omitted.

Although none but his disciples could recognize the importance of the event at the time when Jesus was crucified, yet the "Antiquities" was written about the year 93 when the Christians constituted a large, widespread sect in Judæa, Rome, Asia Minor and elsewhere; how, then, could so verbose a historian be content with a few phrases in recounting an important event such as this, from which had sprung a great Jewish sect which even attracted many Greeks? It is, therefore, inadequate to explain, as many Christian and Jewish scholars have done for the last hundred years, this excessive brevity as due to the fact that all the acts of Jesus and his execution seemed at the time to be of small moment.

Most of the scholars who consider the Jesus-passage as an inter-

[1] *Ant.* XVIII iii 3. Salvador (*op. cit.* I p. 157-8 n) already picked out these italicised passages from the genuine elements. Réville (*op. cit.* I 272-280) also regards the phrase "a teacher of such men as receive the truth with pleasure," as an addition. We shall see later that Salvador's view is the more correct; although he attached little importance to *any* of Josephus' statements, even to those which appear to be genuine. Cf. also *J.E.* IV 50.

[2] *Contra Celsum* I 47; *Comm. in Matth.* x. 17.

[3] Schürer, I[4] 544-549. This writer gives the passage in the original and in translation, together with a very full bibliography, divided into (a) those which regard the entire passage as genuine, (b) those who regard it as partly interpolated, and (c) those who regard the whole as an interpolation.

polation, therefore conclude that Josephus deliberately avoided the whole subject, since he could not touch on it without treating of the Messianic ideas of the Jews; and Josephus was obviously chary of dealing with such a topic, political to the core, in pages written for the benefit of the Romans at the very time that the emperor Domitian was persecuting all the descendants of the House of David.[4] Such are the grounds which Schürer finds convincing for supposing that nothing in the passage is genuine.[5]

The present writer believes, however, that there are not sufficient grounds for supposing the *whole* to be spurious. Josephus treats of the life and death of John the Baptist at fair length,[6] and what he says does not at all correspond with the Gospel account, and there is no reason, therefore, to suspect Christian copyists of interpolating this section as well, as does Graetz.[7] According even to Schürer "the genuineness of this passage is only rarely open to suspicion"[8] It is remarkable that Josephus tries his hardest to conceal from his readers that John preached the coming of the Messiah (for reasons which we have mentioned) : in order to make the episode comprehensible to Greek readers he describes John the Baptist as "a good man who commanded the Jews to exercise virtue, both as to righteousness towards one another, and piety towards God, and so to come to baptism."[9] Even the three Jewish parties, the Sadducees, Pharisees and Essenes, Josephus explains in terms of philosophic schools, all with a view of making himself understood by his Gentile readers.

And he did precisely the same with Jesus: he described him as "a wise man," just as he described John the Baptist as "a good man ;" he described Jesus as "a teacher of such men as receive the truth with pleasure," just as he described John the Baptist as one who "called upon the Jews to exercise virtue, etc ;" and he described Jesus as "a doer of wonderful works" (for Josephus himself was a firm believer in miracles).[10] He could say of Jesus that "he drew after him many Jews and also Greeks," because the Church contained many Greeks at the time of writing, 93 C.E., and ancient historians had a habit of judging earlier conditions from later times. It was also Josephus who wrote that, "they who loved him at the first did not cease to do so even after Pilate had condemned him to

[4] See Eusebius, *Eccles. Hist.* III 19-20, quoting Hegesippus.
[5] *Op. cit.* I 547-9.
[6] *Ant.* XVIII v 2.
[7] *Op. cit.* III I [5] 277 n.
[8] *Op. cit.* I [4] 438, n. 24.
[9] For further treatment see the chapter on John the Baptist.
[10] The present writer believes that it was from this sentence that the words were taken which are quoted from Josephus in the *Religious discussion in the court of the Sassan'ds,* published by Bratke (p. 36, lines 3-11) ; and there is no cause to follow Bratke and Schürer in thinking that we have here another Christian forgery in the *Antiquities.*

crucifixion at the suggestion of the principal men among us," and that the "race (or tribe) of Christians, so named from him, are not extinct to this day." Albert Reville [11] rightly urges that no Christian interpolater would speak of Jesus as "a wise man," and so necessitate the further interpolation, "If it be lawful to call him a man." Nor would a Christian interpolator be satisfied to apply to Jesus the general term "wonderful works" (παράδοξα ἔργα), or call his disciples simply "lovers" (ἀγαπήσαντες); nor would he have given the Christians such a name as "race" or "tribe"(φῦλον), with its nuance of contempt.[12]

We must treat as interpolated only the italicised passages. It is difficult to decide whether these passages stand in place of others by Josephus not to the mind of the Christians, or whether they are simply supplementary. But we can almost certainly say that Josephus, writing as a Pharisee and for the sake of the Romans, was chary of saying anything either favourable or detailed about Jesus or about Christians, and was satisfied to make just a few general and superficial remarks, written with great care and containing nothing of much positive value to the Christians, nor much about their Messiah.

This was not at all to the liking of the early Christian copyists, and in the third century they interpolated the spurious passages. We say "in the third century" because Eusebius, who lived in the fourth century, knew the whole paragraph, interpolations and non-interpolations, and used both at need; whereas Origen, who lived during the first half of the third century, does not mention them at all: in its primitive form the passage had no value for the Christianity of his day, for which Jesus was far from being only "a wise man," or one "who did wonderful works and was a teacher of men."

(2) The second mention of Jesus by Josephus is where he tells how Annas, the son of Annas, the High Priest, in the interim between the death of the Procurator Festus and the arrival of his successor Albinus, lost no time in bringing before the Sanhedrin one by name James, "the brother of Jesus who was called the Messiah" (τὸν ἀδελφὸν Ἰησοῦ τοῦ λεγομένου Χριστοῦ Ἰάκωβος ὄνομα αὐτῷ), and others whom he regarded as breakers of the Law, and condemned them to be stoned. The most ardent supporters of the Law protested against this illegal act, and in secret lodged a complaint against the High Priest with Albinus and Agrippa II, with whom lay the appointment of the High Priest. Agrippa immediately deposed Annas and appointed in his place Jesus the son of Damnæus.[13]

These words are also quoted by Eusebius;[14] but several scholars

[11] *Op. cit.* II pp. 272-280.
[12] Contrary to Holtzmann (*Leben Jesu,* p. 13) who holds that this word signifies "a people," and so only comes aptly from a Christian.
[13] *Ant.* XX, ix 1.
[14] *Hist. Eccles.* II 23.

question them on the following grounds: Origen, who is prior to Eusebius, on three occasions [15] quotes the "Antiquities" to the effect that the execution of "James, the brother of Jesus who is called the Messiah," was the cause of the Destruction of the Temple; and the writer of the *Chronicon Paschale* (I 463) quotes the selfsame passage as from "The Wars of the Jews;" and Hegesippus[16] tells how James was thrown down from the roof of the Temple, stoned, and finally killed by a fuller with his felting-stick; and immediately after (εὐθύς), Vespasian laid siege to Jerusalem. Thus Hegesippus also connects the death of James with the siege of Jerusalem.

From this evidence of Origen, the *Chronicon Paschale* and Hegesippus, these same scholars conclude (a) that in place of this present passage in the "Antiquities" there was, prior to the time of Eusebius, a completely different passage about the same event, and (b) that James was most probably put to death later than 62 C.E., near to the time of the siege of Jerusalem; therefore whatever is said about James in the "Antiquities," as we now have it, is a Christian interpolation.[17]

But there is no need here to assume an interpolation.[18] Not only the writer of the *Chronicon Paschale* (who confused the "Antiquities" with the "Wars of the Jews") but also Origen has here gone astray in the matter of names, and confused the accounts of "Josephus" with those of "Hegesippus" (which in Hebrew is also "Joseph"); Origen attributing them to the "Antiquities," and the *Chronicon Paschale* to the "Wars." Hegesippus here only reports Jewish-Christian legendary matter which has nothing to do with the historical statement of Josephus.[19] Anyone reading the remarks of Josephus in the existing "Antiquities" and keeping clear of an exaggeratedly sceptical attitude, will see at once that there was never any reason for any Christian to interpolate such statements: they contain nothing in praise either of James or Jesus; Josephus condemns the hasty sentence: he does not belaud the doings of James (as is done in Origen and Hegesippus), nor defend him against the charge brought against him.

Réville[20] rightly urges that no Christian would write of Jesus "who was called (λεγομένου) the Messiah:" such an interpolation would be subtlety overdone. None could write in such a fashion but a Pharisaic *Jew* like Josephus, who had previously referred to

---

[15] *Comm. in Matth.* xiii. 55; *Contra Celsum* I 47 and II 13 end.

[16] Quoted by Eusebius, *loc. cit.*

[17] For more details (and the relevant literature) see Schürer, *op. cit.* I⁴ 548, 581-3.

[18] Holtzmann, *op. cit.* p. 11, considers that "there is not the slightest room for doubt"; and P. W. Schmidt (*Geschichte Jesu, erläutert*, p. 20) proves that "it is unquestionably genuine" ("*zweifellos echt*").

[19] On Hegesippus as a source of Christian legends, see Krauss, *op. cit.* pp. 238-41.

[20] *Op. cit.* p. 280. Chwolsohn, *op. cit.* pp. 97-98, also considers them genuine.

Jesus and did not wish to say much either in praise or blame of the Christians: he would not praise—because he was a Pharisaic Jew, and he would not blame—because in his days his Greek and Roman readers still confused the Christians with the Jews; nor, as we have seen, was it agreeable to him to make mention of the Messianic beliefs of a certain Jewish sect.

Such are the two references of the "Antiquiti's" to Jesus; the second we consider wholly genuine, and the first only genuine in part. It must be confessed that from neither do we learn much about Jesus; yet even from these fragmentary statements we at least receive confirmation of his and his brother James' existence, of his career as a wonder-worker and teacher, and of his terrible death—his crucifixion at the hands of Pilate with, at least, the consent of the principal Jews.

(B) Tacitus, Suetonius and Pliny the Younger

[Réville, *op. cit.* 269-272; Schmidt, *op. cit.* 18-20. On Suetonius, see Schürer, *op. cit.* III[4] 62-63; Graetz, *op. cit.* III ii[5] 371 and 423; also IV[3] 77. All these extracts are given in E. Preuschen, *Analecta,* Freiburg, 1893.]

So far, we have been dealing with Hebrew and Greek Jewish sources. We come now to Latin non-Jewish sources.

Tacitus clearly refers to Jesus, and so we present him first.

In his "Annales," written about 115-7 C.E., while treating of the burning of Rome in the time of Nero, an act for which the Christians were accused, he speaks of the "Christiani" with open dislike; and in explanation of the name "Christians" he says: "Christus, from whom they derive their name, was condemned to death in the reign of Tiberius by the Procurator Pontius Pilate."[1]

These words would have had considerable value as the spontaneous evidence of a Gentile if they had been written earlier than seventy-five years after the event. But we do not need the evidence of Tacitus to know that at the beginning of the second century the belief was widespread that there had been a "Messiah," or "Christ," who was condemned to death by Pontius Pilate.

Though no earlier, the evidence of Suetonius (65-135), a contemporary of Tacitus, is more important. He speaks of a Messianic movement during the reign of Claudius, who preceded Nero and was emperor from 41 to 54 C.E.

While dealing, in his "The Twelve Cæsars," with Claudius, he says: *"Judæos impulsore Chresto assidue tumultuantes Roma expulit"* (he banished from Rome the Jews who made great tumult because of Chrestus).[2] This entirely agrees with what we find in the

[1] *Annales* XV 44.
[2] *Claudius* 25.

Acts of the Apostles (xviii. 2)—how Aquila of Pontus and his wife Priscilla came from Italy during the time of Paul's missionary work "because of the decree of Claudius that all the Jews should leave Rome." Orosius [3] says that this expulsion took place in Claudius' ninth year as Cæsar, 49 C.E., and it certainly could not have been later than 52.[4] If, with very many scholars, we identify "Chrestus" with "Christus" [5] we have here reliable evidence that, within fifteen or twenty years after the death of Jesus, many Jews, even as far off as Rome, believed that Jesus had existed and that he was the Messiah. Graetz,[6] however, supposes that "Chrestus" is not the same as "Christus," but that "Chrestus" was an apostle or Christian teacher of the same type as Apollos, mentioned in the Acts; Graetz also holds that in I Corinthians, i. 12, "Chrestus" should be read for "Christ" (Χρήστου in place of Χριστοῦ).

Yet even if we suppose with Graetz that Suetonius here refers to a Christian teacher, the fact that, only twenty years after the death of Jesus, there were to be found Christian apostles and teachers, is itself proof not only of his existence but also of the important effect of his personal influence. Others, again, think that "Chrestus" only points to some Jewish Messiah who rose up in Rome; but Bousset [7] rightly points out that "the appearance of a messianic revolutionary in Rome is not only inconceivable in itself, but is unproved by any other source." Suetonius' words are, therefore, to be connected with the movement and internal dissensions which arose within the Jewish community at Rome owing to the spread of the belief in Jesus; and this movement led, in the year 49 (or 52), to the expulsion of all the Jews, or of a portion of them.

It therefore follows that a Christian community was founded in Rome during the fifth decade of the first century, i.e. not later than ten years after the crucifixion. This is an important fact from every point of view.

A like importance attaches to the "Epistle" of Pliny the Younger, which he wrote, in his capacity of Proconsul of the province of Bithynia, to Trajan in the year 111.[8] He describes Christianity as a popular movement; and it may be gathered from his statements that there were at that time members of the Christian community who had been Christians for more than twenty years. He knows nothing of the nature of Christianity and he is only able to say that they sing some sacred hymn in which they appeal to Christus as God ("Carmen Christo quasi deo dicere secum invicem").

This is very valuable from the point of view of Christianity as a

[3] Ed. Zangemeister 1882, VII 6, 15; Schürer, III[4] 62 n. 92.
[4] Schürer, loc. cit.
[5] Schürer, III[4] 63 n. 93. He also believes them to be identical.
[6] III ii[5] 423 n. 3; cf. p. 371 n. 4, and IV[3] 77 n. 1.
[7] Op. cit. pp. 16-17; cf. Schmidt, op. cit. p. 20.
[8] Plinius Secundus, Epistolæ, X 96-97.

movement and as a religion,[9] but less valuable than Tacitus' evidence as to the existence and teaching of Jesus. Pliny is writing some eighty years after the crucifixion, and says nothing about the life or death of Jesus; it only transpires from his evidence that by the beginning of the second century Jesus was deified by the Christians.

Latin and Greek sources, Jewish or pagan, tell us little about Jesus. If we possessed them alone, we should know nothing except that in Judæa there had existed a Jew named Jesus who was called the Christ, the "Anointed;" that he performed miracles and taught the people; that he was killed by Pontius Pilate at the instigation of the Jews; that he had a brother named James, who was put to death by the High Priest Annas, the son of Annas; that owing to Jesus there arose a special sect known as Christians; that a community belonging to this sect existed in Rome fifty years after the birth of Jesus, and that because of this community the Jews were expelled from Rome; and, finally, that from the time of Nero the sect greatly increased, regarded Jesus as virtually divine, and underwent severe persecution.

We pass now to the Christian sources.

[9] Réville, *op. cit.* 269-270.

III. PAUL THE APOSTLE

[There is a work in Hebrew on Paul: P. Levertoff, "Paulus ha-Shaliach o Shaul ish Tarsus," London, 1906; but it has a veiled conversionist tendency. On Paul's relation to Jesus see P. Feine, "Jesus Christus und Paulus," Tübingen, 1902. On the sayings of Jesus quoted by Paul, see A. Resch, "Der Paulinismus und die Logia Jesu," 1904 (*Texte u. Untersuchungen. Neue Folge*, XII) pp. 140-151; 405-464; 597-603; A. Resch, "Agrapha: Aussercanonische Schriftfragmente," 2 Aufl. 1996, pp. 24-34. Against A. Kalthoff ("Die Entstehung des Christentums," Jena 1904, p. 110 ff.) who denies the genuineness of all the Pauline writings, see Bousset, *op. cit.* pp. 17-26. See also P. W. Schmidt, *op. cit.* pp. 65-82; and for a brief account of the importance of Paul for the history of Jesus, see P. Wernle, *op. cit.* pp. 4-5.]

The earliest of all the Christian sources are the Epistles of Paul contained in the New Testament. Not all of them are genuinely attributable to him: most scholars question the genuineness of II Thessalonians, I Timothy, and Titus, and the "Dutch School" of New Testament criticism questions the genuineness of many others. But whoever reads the bulk of the letters attributed to Paul will feel at once that here we have documents dating from the earliest days of Christianity and emanating from the "Apostle to the Gentiles," an expert in combining the *Haggadic* and *Midrashic* methods of the Sages of Israel with the Hellenistic methods of thought as they had been developed during the twenty years before the Destruction.

Romans and Corinthians and certain others, are, therefore, very early and far nearer the time of Jesus than any other Christian or non-Christian literature; for Paul became a Christian about the time 32-33 C.E.[1] No matter how early we place the death of Jesus, only a few years intervened before the conversion of Paul. Paul knew not only of the life of Jesus and his death on the cross, but believed also in his resurrection; he testified to seeing him in a vision on his way to Damascus, and also, what is more important, had dealings with the brother of Jesus and his most intimate disciples. Paul is, therefore, a trustworthy witness as to the existence of Jesus and the powerful influence which the personality of Jesus exercised upon his disciples. But we must immediately add that this witness does not extend *beyond* Jesus' existence and influence. In all Paul's writings we find no reliable historical facts about the life and work

[1] Graetz, III ii[5] 790-7, tries to show that Paul was converted between 43 and 48 C.E., but this is not confirmed by recent research.

of Jesus, beyond the vague hint that he was "the firstborn of many brethren" (Romans viii. 29), the statement that he was crucified, the account of the last supper which Jesus held on the night of his arrest (I Corinthians xi. 23-26), and the questionable statement to the effect that Jesus was of the lineage of the House of David (see below, Book Three).

This might seem a matter for surprise seeing that his writings include so many of Jesus' sayings (e.g. "Let not a woman separate from her husband," I Cor. vii. 10; "Let them that preach the Gospel live by the Gospel," I Cor. ix. 14) in the form of "codicils" by Jesus; and in the Acts (xx. 35) he quotes in the name of Jesus "It is better to give than to receive." But such surprise is uncalled for. Paul consistently aimed at exalting the spiritual Jesus over the material Jesus, the Jesus who rose from the dead over the Jesus who lived a human life and performed human acts. He could not otherwise lay claim to the title of "Apostle:" he was not one of Jesus' disciples nor, apparently, had he ever seen him while he was on earth; in the latter event he must have been subservient to James, the brother of Jesus, to Peter and the other Apostles.

Therefore since Paul believed himself, and impressed the belief on others, that his own teaching was more important than that of James and Peter and that he had authority to set aside the Jewish Law and its ceremonial ordinances and make Christianity entirely spiritual and a matter of personal piety—for this reason he was bound to make little of the earthly life of Jesus. "To Paul's mind, the centre of interest was not the teacher, the worker of miracles, the companion of publicans and sinners, the opponent of the Pharisees; it was the crucified Son of God raised from the dead, and none other." It therefore follows from the character of Paul's teaching that this earliest historical witness is least valuable for our knowledge of the life of Jesus.[2]

[2] See Paul Wernle, *op. cit.* p. 5. What Paul makes known of the views and character of Jesus is briefly summed up in O. Holtzmann, *op. cit.* pp. 6-9; and more fully in P. W. Schmidt, *op. cit.* 68-74.

IV. THE EARLY FATHERS OF THE CHRISTIAN CHURCH

[On Justin and the additional facts he supplies about Jesus, see Holtz-mann, *op. cit.* 14-16. The sayings of Jesus occurring in the three books of Justin have been collected by A. Resch, "Agrapha," 2. Aufl., 98-104; 171-175, etc.]

After Paul, we may take into account those only of the early Fathers of the Christian Church who wrote before the Canonical Gospels became the prevailing standards. There are but two of these: Justin Martyr and Papias.

The first of Justin Martyr's surviving writings, "Dialogus cum Tryphone Judæo," was composed about 135 C.E. It has a further importance for Jews, since, in this dispute with a Jew, are very many of the messianic ideas (though sometimes distorted) such as were current immediately after the Destruction, near the time of the defeat at Bittir. Also it is supposed by some [1] that this "Trypho the Jew" is the Tanna R. Tarphon, who used to engage in contro-versy with R. Akiba. In this book we find a few statements about the life of Jesus, e.g. that Jesus "the son of the carpenter" used to make ox-goads and ploughs (*Dial.* 88); we also find several sayings which Justin Martyr attributes to Jesus.[2] These will be dealt with in their proper place. But they are so few and of such slight value that they add little to the sum-total of our information.

The statements of Papias, who wrote his "Expositions of the Oracles of the Lord" about 140, are of a different type. They sur-vive only in fragments as quoted by Origen and Eusebius. The fragments which Eusebius [3] quotes from Papias as coming from "the Elder" (the Presbyter)—who, it transpires, was John of Asia Minor (and not John the Apostle, the son of Zebedee) who lived in the time of Trajan—deal with the origin of the Gospels, and we will treat of them in detail in the next chapter (see p. 74). But Origen's quotations [4] are concerned with Jesus himself. They de-

---

[1] This is held by so cautious a scholar as Emil Schürer, *op. cit.* II [4] 444-5; 650 n. 98; R. Z. Frankel (*Darke ha-Mishnah*, p. 105 n. 7) opposes it on the grounds of the gross errors in the statements of Trypho the Jew, but these may be placed to the account of Justin, a Christian of pagan origin. For bibliography of the "Apocryphal Sayings" see next chap., p. 67.
[2] On these, see A. Resch, *loc. cit. supra;* Holtzmann, *op. cit.* 14-16.
[3] Eusebius, *Hist. Eccles.* III 39.
[4] See further, J. Klausner, "*Ha-Ra'yon ha-Meshihi b'Yisrael*," pt. 2, Jeru-salem 1921, pp. 55-56; *Die Messianischen Vorstellungen des jüdischen Volkes im Zeitalter der Tannaiten,* Berlin, 1904, pp. 108-111.

scribe the material blessings, such as the abnormal fruitfulness of nature, which will mark the kingdom of the Millennium, a description which in every detail calls to mind the description of the material blessings of the "Days of the Messiah" (the messianic age) contained in the *Book of Baruch* (29, 5-8), in the *Talmud* (*Kethuboth* 111b; *Shab.* 30b; *Kallah R.* 2) and in the *Midrash* (*Sifre to Deuteronomy*, 315 and 317); and these descriptions are repeated as representing the belief of Jesus. Modern Christian theologians, being as a rule pronounced rationalists, are unwilling to allow that Jesus was so "worldly" as to believe in such "material" things as the multiplied fruitfulness of the vine and the "flour of wheat." [5] Yet we shall see later, when we come to describe Jesus' messianic ideas (see Book Eight), that this Papias tradition "in the name of John the Elder" is very important, but that the modernizers of Jesus (intent as they are to transform an eastern Jew of nineteen hundred years ago into a European possessed of the same exalted beliefs as the best of Christian theologians, beliefs compounded of the teachings of the ancient Eastern prophets and Greek and modern philosophy) have neither recognized nor wished to recognize this importance.

Apart from the contents of the canonical and uncanonical Gospels (discussed in the following chapter), the writings of the early Christian Fathers contain certain scattered sayings of Jesus. These go by the name of "Agrapha," or uncanonical sayings.[6] That most of these are not genuine is universally admitted, and some well-known scholars, such as Wellhausen [7] and Jülicher,[8] regard them all as spurious. Resch, however, in the first edition of his "Agrapha" (1889) reckons seventy-four of them as genuine, though in his second edition (1906) he reduced the number to thirty-six. Ropes [9] considers only twelve to be authentic. It is certainly inadvisable to make too great use of them. But even if the presumably genuine sayings contribute little to our knowledge of the character of Jesus, they at least serve to approximate him more nearly to contemporary Judaism and demonstrate the existence of a material element in his messianic ideas; but when, from the time of Paul onwards, Jesus was made more and more divine, the form of his ideas was, intentionally or unintentionally, distorted beyond recognition.

[5] See Resch's characteristic remarks, *op. cit.* 2 Aufl. pp. 166-7, and, on the other side, the cautious words of Holtzmann, *op. cit.* p. 41-2.

[6] Ably and scrupulously collected by A. Resch, *op. cit.;* also in J. H Ropes, *Sprüche Jesu die in den kanonischen Evangelien nicht überliefert sind,* Leipzig, 1896 (*Texte u. Untersuchungen,* Bd. XIV 2). Some of them may be found in Hebrew: J. E. Landsman, *Sefer tol'doth Yeshu'a ha-Mashiah,* London, 1907, pp. 219-220. See further on this book, *infra* pp. 72 n. 2.

[7] Wellhausen, *Einleitung in die ersten drei Evangelien,* Berlin, 1905, p. 85. See also P. W. Schmidt, *op. cit.* pp. 103-106.

[8] See Jülicher's article in *Theologische Litteraturzeitung,* 1905, no. 23.

[9] *Op. cit.*

V. THE APOCRYPHAL AND UNCANONICAL GOSPELS

[The Apocryphal Gospels have been published by E. Hennecke, "Neu-testamentiche Apocryphen in Verbindung mit Fachgelehrten in deutscher Uebersetzung und mit Einleitungen herausgegeben," Tübingen und Leipzig, 1904. On their contents and sources see R. Hoffmann, "Das Leben Jesu nach den Apocryphen," Leipzig, 1861. Fragments of the uncanonical Gospels have been collected by E. Nestle, "Novi Testamenti Graeci Supplementum," Leipzig, 1896; and, with German translation, by E. Preuschen, "Antilegomina: Die Reste der ausserkanonischen Evangelien und urchrist-lichen Ueberlieferungen," Giessen, 1905. See also Baring-Gould, "The Lost and Hostile Gospels," London, 1874. A satisfactory valuation of these may be found in Holtzmann, *op. cit.*, pp. 35-41, 42-43. On the "Sayings of Jesus" in the Apocryphal and Uncanonical Gospels, see Resch, *op. cit.*, pp. 115-267 and 365-380.]

The Apocryphal Gospels exist in large numbers in the Christian literature. They are all later than the Canonical Gospels and are filled with legends (especially about the childhood of Jesus) showing the wonderfully childlike faith of the Christian bodies from the second century onwards. They have virtually no historical value, for even if they should contain a grain of truth, it is impossible to extract it from the thick overgrowth of legend.

But the same does not apply to the "Uncanonical Gospels" (by which we mean those Gospels which were rejected from the Christian Canon and have survived only in a few fragments) such as the *Gospel of Peter,* the *Gospel of the Egyptians,* etc., and especially the *Gospel according to the Hebrews.* This last (called in Greek καθ' 'Εβραίους) existed, according to Resch,[1] in two versions: the first was the *Gospel of the Ebionites,* of which fragments have been handed down in Epiphanius (*Haer.* xxx 13ff.), and which gave no account of the birth and childhood of Jesus because the Ebionites believed that Jesus was born in normal fashion of Joseph and Mary (we may recognize here the influence of James the brother of Jesus, the first leader of early, Ebionite, Christianity); the second version was the *Gospel of the Nazarenes,* of which fragments have been handed down by Jerome (*Adv. Pelag.* III 2; *Comm. in Isaiam* XI 2 and XL 12; *in Ezech.* XVI 13 and XVIII 7, *in Matth.* XII 17, XXIII 35 and XXVII 9; *Proem. in lib. XVIII Esaiae*).

According to Resch both versions were compiled from the Gospel according to Matthew, which was itself compiled for the sake of

[1] *Agrapha* 1906, pp. 363-371.

Jewish Christians—as is apparent from the "proof-passages" which it adduces from the scriptures; and although Jerome saw the *Gospel according to the Hebrews* (apparently in the "Nazarene" version) written in Aramaic and in Hebrew characters, and translated it into Latin and Greek, this Gospel was not originally composed in Aramaic, but, like its source, Matthew, was at first written in Greek and afterwards translated into Aramaic for the sake of the Jews who had accepted Christianity. According to this view, the *Gospel according to the Hebrews* also will be later than the Canonical Gospels, or, at least, than Matthew (and therefore later than Mark which preceded Matthew [see the following chapter]).

Most scholars, however, hold that there is no reason for confusing together the *Gospel of the Hebrews* and the *Gospel of the Ebionites:* the former, according to the evidence of Jerome, is the *Gospel of the Nazarenes,* and was originally written in Hebrew (or Aramaic). According to Harnack [2] this Gospel was written between 65 and 100 C.E., and so is at least no later than Luke and the Fourth Gospel; it therefore ranks with some of the Canonical Gospels and in some respects is superior to them in that it was certainly written in Palestine, the birthplace of Christianity, for the benefit of Jewish Christians who were still akin in spirit to Jesus and his first disciples, including his brother James. Its value is, therefore, considerable.

The new facts which it supplies about the life of Jesus may not be very important since they are mostly legendary; but it is of value, firstly, because of the many sayings of Jesus not included in the present Gospels,[3] and, secondly, because of the Hebrew (or Aramaic) mannerisms of speech which cast light on the existing Greek text. Thus, in connexion with Matthew vi. 11, in the Lord's Prayer, Jerome tells us that in place of ἐπιούσιος ("continual") the *Gospel of the Hebrews* read "mahar" (=מחר, tomorrow, translated by Jerome as "crastinum"); and in another place (*Ep. 20 ad Damasum*) he says that the phrase ὡσαννὰ ἐν τοῖς ὑψίστοις (Matt. xxi. 9) was there written "Osanna barrama, id est Osanna in excelsis" (representing the Hebrew הושענא במרומ, "Hosanna in the highest").

Mention still remains to be made of additions to the Canonical Gospels in certain ancient manuscripts.[4] The principal one is that known as *Codex Bezae* or *Codex Cantabrigiensis* ("D"), so called because it was given by Theodore Bèze, one of the Reformation theologians, in 1581 into the keeping of the University of Cambridge; it is a sixth century manuscript and its archetype dates back as far

---

[2] A. Harnack, *Geschichte der altchristlichen Litteratur,* I 6-10; II 625-651.
[3] Collected and explained at length in Resch, *op. cit.* pp. 215-252, and briefly treated in Holtzmann, *op. cit.* pp. 35-39. Against their genuineness and against the early date of this Gospel generally, see Schmidt, pp. 106-112.
[4] Collected and annotated in *Agrapha,* pp. 36-54; see also Holtzmann, *op. cit.* pp. 45-46.

as the year 140 C.E.[5]   It contains enough additions and differences to show that the present text of the first three Gospels cannot represent the original text unchanged in every detail.

These additions and differences are most important as showing a "Nazarene" tendency—not very extreme, yet a tendency, more or less Jewish, and approaching nearer the messianic belief of Jesus the Jew than do the later tendencies which are markedly influenced by paganism.[6]   Furthermore there are several additions throwing light on Jesus' motives, e.g. the addition to Matthew xx. 28; also worthy of note is the addition to Luke vi. 4: "On the same day, having seen one working on the Sabbath, he said to him, O man, if thou knowest what thou doest, thou art blessed, but if thou knowest not, thou art accursed and a transgressor of the Law (παραβάτης τοῦ νόμου)."   Such a penetrating and semi-Jewish idea is not likely to have been invented after the time of Jesus.

It may here be pointed out that the story of the woman taken in adultery, found now only in the current text of John (vii. 52— viii. 11)—though actually belonging to Mark xii. 18 or xii. 35— is to be found in Codex Bezae; it also occurs in several MSS. in Luke xxi. 38; other Gospels omit it, seeing in it something opposed to current morals (this in itself argues its genuineness: none could have invented it at a later date).   This same Codex lacks the ending to the Gospel of Mark, xvi. 9 to the end, as do also the best manuscripts; the ending was apparently composed, according to an Armenian manuscript, by Aristion, who lived in Asia Minor at the beginning of the second century (hence its historical value, in any case not great, it still more diminished).   All these, together with many papyrus fragments, containing sayings of Jesus, recently found at various places, deserve attention as sources for the life of Jesus; but they must be used with great caution, for since the time that such Gospel material was banished from the Christian Canon, no care was given to it, and it was modified or added to without the reverence that would have been bestowed upon it had it possessed canonical sanctity.   Therefore, in spite of its great mass, the extent of scientifically valuable matter which it contains is small.

*   *   *   *   *   *   *

If, before proceeding to the Canonical Gospels, we sum up what we have so far learnt of the life of Jesus from the Hebrew, Greek, Latin and even Christian sources (excluding the Canonical Gospels), we quickly realize that, apart from a few facts about his life and a few of his sayings, we have acquired but these two things: (a) we

---

[5] On its nature and importance see *Agrapha,* pp. 338-352, where the detailed discussion is deserving of study.

[6] Thus in a very old Syriac manuscript found by two English women in the Monastery on Mt. Sinai, there occurs in Matt. i. 16 the reading: "And Joseph, to whom was espoused Mary the virgin, begat Jesus." See Agnes Lewis Smith, *The Old Syriac Gospels,* London, 1910, p. 2, Syriac text, p. *b.*

learn the period and the environment in which Jesus lived, and the political conditions and the religious and ethical ideals which prevailed; these are so important that we cannot overestimate the value of what we learn from the *Talmud* and *Midrash*, the writings of Joseph, Tacitus, Suetonius and the early Church Fathers; (b) fragmentary though the information is, we can confidently conclude from it that Jesus did indeed exist, that he had an exceptionally remarkable personality, and that he lived and died in Judæa during the Roman occupation.[7]

All this stands out firm and irrefutable, and there is no solid foundation for the doubts raised by Bruno Bauer and more recently by Albert Kalthoff and Arthur Drews (cf. the following section). During the time (fifty years or less) which elapsed between the death of Jesus (at the date approximately recorded by the Canonical Gospels) and the age of Josephus and R. Eliezer ben Hyrcanus, or between Paul and Tacitus, it was quite impossible for a purely fabricated presentment of the figure of Jesus so firmly to have gripped people's imagination, that historians like Josephus and Tacitus, and men like R. Eliezer ben Hyrcanus (who was so cautious in transmitting what he had heard from his teachers), should believe in his existence and all refer to him as one who had lived and worked quite recently and had made for himself friends and disciples; or that Paul should have had such a complete belief in him and never doubt that James was the brother, and Peter and his fellows, disciples of Jesus. That much is clear; and those who would utterly deny not simply the form which Jesus now assumes in the world or that which he assumes according to the Gospels, but even his very existence and the great positive, or negative, importance of his personality—such men simply deny all historic reality.

Joseph Salvador [8] speaks of the same problem, a problem raised (very many years before Bauer) as early as the eighteenth century; and in answer to sceptics, he quotes these words of Rousseau; "In reality this (the denial of Jesus' existence) is only shirking the difficulty (raised by the dissimilarities in the Gospels) and not getting rid of it. It is far more incomprehensible that many men should have agreed to compose this book than that one man alone should have provided it with its subject matter. . . . So impossible of imitation are the characteristics of the Gospels that the man who invented them must needs be greater than his hero" (Emile, "Profession de foi").[9]

This may be taken also as an adequate rejoinder to the conglomeration of pseudo-scientific proofs advanced by Bruno Bauer, Kalthoff and Drews!

[7] The importance of the *Talmudic* statements in this respect was recognized by Herford, *op. cit.* pp. 359-360. For an opposing view see Friedländer, *Die religiösen Bewegungen*, pp. 191-192.

[8] J. Salvador, *Jésus-Christ et sa doctrine*, I 156-159.

[9] On this see further p. 76.

VI. THE CANONICAL GOSPELS AND THE STUDY OF THE LIFE OF JESUS

[A good account of the connexion between the first three Gospels is to be found in P. Wernle, "Die synoptische Frage," Tübingen, 1899; for details see J. Weiss, "Das älteste Evangelium," Göttingen, 1903, and especially J. Wellhausen, "Einleitung in die ersten drei Evangelien," Berlin, 1905. A clear account is also given in F. Godet, "Introduction au Nouveau Testament," Neuchâtel, 1904, II 671-844. On the relation of the Fourth to the first three Gospels, see the brief treatment in P. W. Schmiedel, "Das 4te Evangelium gegenüber den drei ersten" ("Religiongesch. Volksbb." I 8, 10), Tübingen, 1906. On the four Gospels as a whole, see O. Holtzmann, "Leben Jesu," pp. 17-35; W. Wrede, "Die Entstehung der Schriften des Neuen Testaments," Vorträge ("Lebensfragen," herausg. von. H. Weinel) Tübingen, 1907, pp. 36-73; Maurice Vernes, "Evangile" ("Grande Encyclopédie," XVI, 863-874). Brief though adequate accounts are also to be found in P. Wernle, "Die Quellen des Lebens Jesu," pp. 7-87; W. Bousset, "Was wissen wir von Jesu?" pp. 27-62. To illustrate graphically the relations between the narratives of the first three Gospels, synoptical tables, or "Synopses" have been compiled (on the term "Synoptics" see further in the course of the present chapter) giving the material of the Gospels in parallel columns according to the Greek text. Such are: A. Huck, "Synopse der drei ersten Evangelien," 2 Aufl. 1898; in German translation: Koppelmann, "Deutsche Synopse. Zusammenstellung der 3 ersten Evangelien," 1897; E. Morel et G. Chastand, "Concordance des évangiles synoptiques," Lausanne, 1901 [in French, with different colours to aid comparison]. In English: W. Wright, "A Synopsis of the Gospels," London, 1896. A sort of synopsis, or rather "harmony," in Hebrew is: Immanuel Landsman, *Sefer Tol'doth Yeshu'a ha-Mashiach:* containing all the narratives of the acts of Jesus and his teaching as found in the four Gospels in their proper form and language, in the translations of Prof. Franz Delitzsch, edited and arranged in chronological order with references and table of contents, London, 1907. But the work has two marked defects: it gives the contents of the Fourth Gospel without discriminating them from those of the first three, and certain propagandist remarks in the introduction are not in place in a scholarly work; but the notes, the glossary, and the "Uncanonical Sayings" are useful. On the researches devoted to the Life of Jesus see especially H. Weinel, "Jesus im neunzehnten Jahrhundert. Neue Bearbeitung," Tübingen, 1907; A. Schweitzer, "Von Reimarus zu Wrede. Eine Geschichte der Leben-Jesu-Forschung," Tübingen, 1906. On the various problems raised, see H. V. Soden, "Die wichtigsten Fragen im Leben Jesu," Berlin, 1904.]

As a result of our examination of the non-Christian sources, and the scattered sayings and details to be found in the uncanonical

Gospels and the early Fathers, we are forced to conclude that, as the main source of knowledge for the life and teaching of Jesus, we must draw from the Canonical Gospels alone.

But we are quickly faced with the following problem: the objective of the Gospels was not "history" in our sense, but the proclaiming, spreading and confirmation of the new faith; how, then, can we regard them as historical sources suited to scientific biography? Again, was it within the power of the writers of the Gospels to depict the events of Jesus' life in the terms of an ordinary historical, human life? The attempt to answer this fundamental problem has provided a powerful impetus alike to Gospel criticism and the study of the history of Jesus—two subjects so interrelated as to be inseparable. Although it involves a chapter of exceptional length, we are bound to deal with the two subjects together.

The word "Gospel," Evangelion (εὐαγγέλιον), means "good tidings." [1] It still remains a matter of doubt whether the *Talmud* is referring to the Gospels when it says of the "*Gilyonim* and Books of the *Minim*" that they should not be saved from burning, and that (according to R. Ishmael) "they cast enmity and hatred and strife between Israel and their heavenly Father," and that R. Tarphon was prepared to burn them even though they contained the sacred names of God (*Shabb.* 116a).[2] According to M. Friedländer [3] the "*Gilyonim* and Books of the *Minim*" are the same as the "Books of the magicians" referred to in the *Talmud* (*Hul.* 13a) and *Tosefta* (*Hul.* II 20), composed by the Gnostics. H. P. Chajes [4] considers that the *Gilyonim* are the Apocalypses, since the name given to the "Book of Revelation, or Apocalypse of St. John" in Syriac is *Gelyana*. Yet if we accept this view, it should be said that the *Talmud* does not refer to Apocalypses generally, but only to those of the Christians or Gnostics: the *Tannaim* could not possibly have waxed so indignant over such Jewish Apocalypses as that of *Baruch*, or *Fourth Esdras*, so full of moral guidance and devotion.[5]

The four Canonical Gospels are, following the order preserved

---

[1] The *avon-gillayon* (עָוֹן גִּלָּיוֹן, lit. iniquity-table) is referred to by the *Talmud* in the story of Imma Shalom and Rabban Gamaliel, who came to the "Philosoph" (*Shabb.* 116a and b; see above, pp. 37-8); but this spelling in place of אֵיוַנְגֶלִיוֹן is perhaps late and changed with derogatory intent as we find among the late *Tannaim* and early *Amoraim:* "R. Meir calls it אָוֶן גִּלָּיוֹן ; R. Yochanan calls it עָוֹן גִּלָּיוֹן" (*Shab.* 116a in the Amsterdam edition or in the collections of "*Talmud* omissions" given in the note to p. 18). On the non-Jewish origin of the word "Evangelion" see Wellhausen, *op. cit.* pp. 108-112.

[2] As is explained in the *Tractate Yadaim* the proper treatment in such cases is to store the writings away in the "Genizah."

[3] *Op. cit.* 188-202.

[4] See his *La lingua ebraica nel Cristianesimo primitivo*, Firenze, 1905, p. 9.

[5] J. Klausner, *Sefarim Hitsonim* ("Specimen Pages" of an *Otsar ha Yahaduth*, ed. "Ahiasaf," Warsaw, 1906, pp. 95-96.

in the New Testament: the Gospel according to (κατά) Matthew, the Gospel according to Mark, the Gospel according to Luke, and the Gospel according to John.[6] St. Augustine [7] already perceived the very close similarity that existed between the first three; on the other hand, the briefest glance suffices to show how utterly the fourth, "according to John," differs from the others. It is not simply that its contents are different (we shall see shortly that such differences occur also as between the first three Gospels themselves), but that from beginning to end it is distinct from them entirely in its plan and arrangement. It is permeated by a different atmosphere, and the purpose of its author was different.

To distinguish the first three, with their common characteristics, from the fourth "according to John," scholars are accustomed to call the former by the title (first given them by Griesbach in his "Synopsis," 1797) "Synoptic Gospels," i.e. Gospels having a "common aspect," such as can be taken in the same conspectus; while their authors go by the name "Synoptists."

But the Synoptic Gospels are not only markedly different from the Fourth Gospel: though they closely *resemble* one another, they are not *similar* to one another. It is true that they are similar in the wider sense—as regards the narratives they give of Jesus' life and their reports of his sayings and teachings; and sometimes the similarity extends to a complete identity of words, expressions and minutest details.

Yet just as often they differ in details, words and expressions, and, frequently, in complete narratives; this is particularly the case with his sayings and discourses, which are sometimes to be found in one or two Gospels, and are absent in one or both of the others. Thus the account of the supernatural birth, though it occurs in Matthew and Luke, is lacking in Mark. In Luke, between the account of Jesus' ministry in Galilee and his entry into Jerusalem, there is a long passage containing many discourses—usually referred to as "The travel-narrative" or "Peræan section"—occupying nine chapters, almost a third of the whole book (ix. 51—xviii. 14), none of which occurs in Mark or Matthew, although the latter gives, in abbreviated form and usually in the shape of continuous conversation, the sayings and discourses dispersed here and there in Luke's "Peræan section." On the other hand, Luke lacks the whole of Mark vi. 45—viii. 26, and Matthew xiv. 22—xvi. 12.

Again, we find in Matthew the "Sermon on the Mount" (v. 3—vii. 27), in which is concentrated virtually the whole of Jesus' teaching; while in Mark we find, scattered here and there, only a fraction of these teachings contained in the "Sermon on the Mount." In Luke, out of the hundred and seven verses which make up the

---

[6] Attention should be given to the expression "according to." Its meaning and value will be explained later.

[7] *De consensu evangelistarum*, III 4, 13.

"Sermon on the Mount," we find twenty-seven verses in Chapter vi, twelve in Chapter xi, fourteen in Chapter xii, three in Chapter xiii, one in Chapter xiv, three in Chapter xvi; while forty-seven are wholly wanting.

Speaking generally, Mark is more concerned with the doings of Jesus, Matthew prefers long and frequent discourses, while Luke —who aims at a more finished literary form and style—reproduces the same discourses which Matthew gives in disconnected fashion, as though they arose out of certain specific causes or acts. Luke again, more than the other Synoptists, relates many sayings and discourses which are peculiar to him. The order of events in the Synoptists is also varied for no apparent reason; similarly words and phrases have been changed in one or other of the Gospels without our being able to see what could have been the original motive for the change.

To take one example out of many: when Jesus is sending out his twelve disciples to spread his teaching, he tells them, according to Mark (vi. 8), that "they should take naught save a staff," but in Matthew (x. 10) and Luke (ix. 3), it is written that "they should take naught, not even a staff." Again, whereas Matthew writes, Blessed are the poor in spirit (Μακάριοι οἱ πτωχοὶ τῷ πνεύματι), Luke writes, Blessed are the poor (Μακάριοι οἱ πτωχοί). Such cases occur in plenty.

There thus arise two important problems: (a) Which are the better historical records, the Synoptists or the Fourth Gospel? and which of the three Synoptists ranks highest, whether in priority or quality? (b) If we assume that the Synoptists drew from different sources, how explain their remarkable similarities? If from a common source or from one another, how account for their remarkable differences?

There are two things which make the problems still more complicated. First of all, John, the author of the Fourth Gospel, the Church holds to be "the disciple whom Jesus loved," and therefore an eyewitness. And, in the second place, as to Matthew and Mark, the church supposes the former to be Matthew Levi, the publican summoned by Jesus (Matt. ix. 9; Mark ii. 14; Luke v. 27) and one of the twelve Apostles (Matt. x. 2; Mark iii. 18); and the latter John Mark, the son of Mary, mentioned in the Acts of the Apostles as the chief disciple of Peter (Acts xii. 12) and companion of Paul (Acts xii. 25).

Furthermore, Eusebius has preserved the tradition of Papias, an early Christian writer (see above, p. 65), which says: "Matthew wrote the sayings (of Jesus) in Hebrew and each one translated them as he was able" (Ματθαῖος μεν οὖν ἑβραΐδι διαλέκτῳ τὰ λόγια συνεγράψατο, ἡρμήνευσεν δ' αὐτὰ ὡς ἦν δυνατὸς ἕκαστος); and again: "Mark, who became the interpreter of Peter, wrote exactly, but not in order (ἑρμηνευτὴς Πέτρου ἀκριβῶς ἔγραψεν οὐ μεν τῇ τάξει) all whatsoever he remembered of the words and works of Christ, for he (Mark) himself knew him not. . . . He had but one care—not to omit anything that he heard or to set down any false statement therein." [8]

John, Matthew and Mark were, therefore, accounted trustworthy witnesses, and two of them actual eyewitnesses. As for Luke, we find at the beginning of his Gospel the following words: "Forasmuch as many have taken in hand to draw up a narrative (διήγησις) concerning those matters which have been fulfilled among us, which from the beginning were eyewitnesses and ministers of the word, it seemed good to me also, having traced the course of all things accurately (ἀκριβῶς) from the first, to write unto thee in order (καθεξῆς), most excellent Theophilus, that thou mightest know the certainty concerning the things wherein thou wast instructed" (Luke i. 1-4). There were thus many different sources.

When, therefore, a critical spirit became apparent in Christian theology, the following serious questions arose: How explain the fact that the four Gospels contradict each other in certain details? Which of them is earlier and which later? Which of them drew from the others, or what was their common source? On which should one rely more and on which less, and on which should one not rely at all? These and similar questions have occupied the wide range of literature devoted to Gospel criticism and that equally wide range of literature devoted to the study of the life of Jesus.

We propose now to trace the course of these two lines of study, important as they are in marking the stages of human thought.

Neither the question "What is the historical value of the Gospels?" nor its corollary "What was the historical character of Jesus?" (as we understand the problems) were raised in the Middle Ages or in the time of the Reformation. Socin (1525-1562) and Michael Servet (burnt at the instance of Calvin in 1553) both denied the divinity of Jesus and regarded him only as a prophet and the founder of a religion, but they found no problems in the actual life of Jesus, nor had they learnt how to apply methods of historical criticism to the Gospels.

More scientific was the attitude of the English Deists.[9] John *Toland* (1671-1723), Peter *Annet* (d. 1768) and, most of all, Thomas *Woolston* (1669-1731) denied the Gospel miracles and tried to rationalize them, e.g. they held that Jesus did not raise the actual dead but awakened them from a lethargic sleep that had the appearance of death; or that there was a conspiracy between such as were apparently restored to life and between Jesus' disciples, since the

---

[8] Eusebius, *Hist. Eccles.* III 39, 15. Cf. Graetz, *op. cit.* III ii[5] 755-756.
[9] For detailed account see G. v. Lechler, *Der englische Deismus*, Stuttgart, 1841; Leslie Stephen, *History of English Thought in the Eighteenth Century*, vol. 2, 2d ed. London, 1881; J. Klausner, *Ha-Deistim u-biqqoreth ha-Migra*, Ma'abaroth, 1920, I 512-519.

latter, seeing Jesus' faith in his messiahship weakening, wished to revive this faith by means of the miracles which they engineered. Jesus' own resurrection was also regarded by the Deists as based merely on a phantom seen by visionaries and dreamers, or as a deliberate invention.[10]

The Deists anticipated many of the ideas of early nineteenth century writers on the subject. They looked on Jesus as a great prophet and the founder of a religion which was the "natural religion" existing in all men and among all nations, but which was revealed in a fashion more profound and more perfect in the words of Jesus.

The English Deists exercised an influence on the great eighteenth century French writers. Voltaire, for example, insists time after time that Jesus was a great prophet and nothing more. They treated the miracles and the advanced ethical code, which were not to the liking of these rationalists, as the "barefaced inventions" of "artful priests" (hence "priestcraft" and the corresponding French term "prêtres rusés"), who invented them deliberately to take advantage of the ignorance of the people and so secure a hold over them.

The English Deists (likewise Voltaire and his school) frequently touch on such problems as Jesus' messianic claims which are bound up in his title "Christ," his Jewish environment, the contemporary beliefs and ideas of the Jews, and the like, and sometimes deal with them at length; yet they could never see in them problems demanding scholarly research, irrespective of religious or anti-religious bias. Discrepancies in the Gospels were seized upon as evidence of the utter untrustworthiness of the Evangelists. Of the four Gospels preference was given, not to the Synoptists, but to John—because it was more philosophical, contained fewer miracles, and placed more stress on Jesus' religious and ethical teaching than on his messianic claims.

Jean Jacques *Rousseau* (in a letter dated 1769) also ranks the "sage hébreu" (Jesus) with the "sage grec" (Socrates). He holds that Jesus' desire was to relieve the Jews from the Roman yoke and make them free, and that his ethical teachings were intended to revive the enthusiasm for freedom in such a manner as not to arouse the suspicions of the Romans; but that the Jews did not understand him and he was too gentle by nature forcibly to press through a political revolution.

Rousseau speaks generally of Jesus as of a "divine man" who opposed miracles to the utmost;[11] he is strongly opposed to the theory that Jesus never lived and that the Evangelists invented him: "My friend, such things are not invented; the matters told of Socrates—whose existence no one doubts—rest on far slenderer evidence than do those told of Jesus of Nazareth." We have quoted

---

[10] See, *e.g.*, P. Annet. *Supranatural Examined*, London, 1747.
[11] J. J. Rousseau, *Oeuvres complètes*, Paris, 1846, IV 771-2.

already (p. 70) his remarks to the effect that we cannot solve the problems enveloping Jesus by simply denying his existence, and that it is far more difficult to explain how certain Jewish writers (the Evangelists) invented such a wonderful character than it is to admit that they were describing someone who did really exist.[12]

Of the same school of thought as the Deists, though he far surpassed them, was Hermann Samuel *Reimarus*, professor of Oriental Languages at Hamburg (1694-1768). In his epoch-making book, "Vom Zwecke Jesu und seiner Jünger" (published by Lessing ten years after its author's death, 1778, with an appended essay refuting the author's opinions, entitled "Noch ein Fragment des Wolfenbuttelschen Ungenannten"), Reimarus was the first who tried to explain Jesus not as a Son of God or as a prophet or lawgiver, but as a Jewish Messiah. He emphasizes the fact that neither Jesus nor his disciples ever explained what the "Kingdom of heaven" is, for the simple reason that it was a familiar, widely current conception among the Jews of the time, and that we shall, therefore, best comprehend Jesus from a study of contemporary Jewish literature. Reimarus' presentation of Jesus' career may be summarized as follows:

The keynote of Jesus' teaching was "Repent! for the kingdom of heaven is at hand!"—a call which drew to him large numbers of the Jews who were groaning under Roman tyranny and believed in the coming of the Messiah. Jesus never opposed the Mosaic law and, at the most, only emphasized the fact that mere observance of ceremonial laws was not enough to prepare men for the kingdom of heaven, but that a high ethical standard of life was requisite. He bade his disciples to preach the gospel of the kingdom not to the Gentiles but "to the lost sheep of the house of Israel" (Matt. x. 6); and Peter, as we learn from the Acts of the Apostles (chh. x and xi), greatly doubted whether he should admit the Gentile Cornelius to baptism.

Like the rest of the Jews, Jesus observed the Passover without introducing any change, and, in general, the sole difference between the teaching of Jesus and contemporary Judaism, was that while the latter believed in a Messiah still to come, Jesus taught that the Messiah was come already. The miracles recorded in the Gospels were either ordinary cures which Jesus' contemporaries regarded as miraculous, or else marvels interpolated into the story with a view to attributing to Jesus the same things written in the Old Testament of the Prophets and their wonderful works and all that befel them. But the Jews, as a whole, did not believe in him. At first he tried to gain followers by sending his disciples to preach throughout the cities of Israel and he believed that "they should not have gone through the cities of Israel before the Son of Man was come" (Matt.

<hr />

[12] *Op. cit.* II 597.

x. 23) ; but the disciples did not attract many. He then decided to test his powers in Jerusalem, the centre of the Jews.

At first he was so successful as to be acclaimed in the terms: "Hosanna, Son of David !" *i.e.*, Messiah; with the result that he made bold to execute judgment on the traffickers in the Temple. But even in Jerusalem his following was but small and the Sanhedrin and the Romans were able to arrest and crucify him. His cry on the cross, "My God, my God, why hast thou forsaken me !" proves that he neither thought nor wished to die, and that he looked on his death as the end of all his work; he saw that God had abandoned him and not helped him to finish what he had begun, to establish an earthly kingdom and deliver his people from the Romans.

His disciples had expected earthly greatness and that, in the kingdom about to be, they should be appointed by the Messiah rulers and princes; in this they had been encouraged by Jesus' saying, "There are some standing here that shall not taste of death till they see the son of man coming in his kingdom" (Matt. xvi. 28) ; it had never occurred to them that Jesus would be killed: otherwise they would not have shown such cowardice at his trial and crucifixion ;. at first they were wholly perplexed and afraid even to stir from their homes. Later, however, their spirits revived and they remembered the other Jewish messianic belief—a spiritual and not a material hope—found in the Book of Daniel, in the *Hebrew Apocalypses*, in *Talmudic* literature, and in Justin Martyr's "Dialogue with Trypho the Jew."

According to this idea, the Messiah must suffer and die, but he would in the end rise again and, this second time, appear in glory and establish the kingdom of heaven. To make this idea appear true the disciples stole the body of Jesus and hid it; after fifty days—by which time the body must have become unrecognizable even if found, they spread the rumour that he was risen from the dead and that he had shown himself alive to them. Thenceforward they awaited his Second Coming (Parousia), when he should establish his kingdom, the everlasting kingdom of heaven. And this Coming, rather than the ethical teaching of Jesus, became the fundamental hope and basis of early Christianity. All at first believed in his speedy coming; but when there seemed no prospect of an early coming they allocated it to a later age, to the close of a thousand years (the Millennium).

Then the promise that the present generation should see the Son of Man in his majesty, was changed into a new promise—that Jesus should come only after the nation of Israel came to an end; "thus," says Reimarus, "through the art of the commentators, these things were relegated to the far distant future, for the people of Israel do not die." As to the abolition of the ceremonial laws, this did not arise out of the teaching of Jesus but because his disciples, completely severed from the Jews, sought to make adherents to Christianity from among the Gentiles.

It is difficult to overestimate the importance of Reimarus for the better understanding of the Gospels and the life of Jesus. He was the first to prefer the Synoptists to the Fourth Gospel; he ignored the latter almost completely as a source for the life of Jesus. He was the first to set Jesus within the framework of his historical and national environment. He was the first to illustrate the "positive" attitude of Jesus to Judaism. He was the first to emphasize the importance of Jesus' messianic claims in their relation to Jewish eschatology, Jewish teaching on the future life and the kingdom of heaven, instead of looking upon him solely as a prophet or lawgiver.

Finally, he was the first who thoroughly grasped the fact that the Jewish messianic idea had a twofold basis, the one material and political, and the other spiritual and ethical—the former apocalyptic and the latter prophetic; but he erred in attributing only the first of these to Jesus, and only the second to his disciples after his death. He was also wrong in many of his rationalizations of Gospel incidents, rationalizations which were the fruit of his own time and due to Deist and Voltairean influence, and the "enlightenment" of the eighteenth century. In short, Reimarus was scores of years in advance of his contemporaries, and his influence on Gospel criticism did not become apparent until the time of David Friedrich Strauss. Much credit is due to Lessing for appreciating the value of Reimarus and for publishing the work, despite all the opposition of his friends, Moses Mendelssohn and Nicolai.[13]

Lessing also helped towards the development of Gospel research. In the same year in which he published Reimarus' book (1778), he wrote his "Neue Hypothese über die Evangelisten als blosse menschliche Schriftsteller betrachtet," which only appeared after his death, in 1784. As the title shows, Lessing took as his main thesis that we look upon the Gospels not as verbally inspired by the Holy Spirit but as writings of a religious and historical character; also, which is more important, he made the first serious attempt to account for the genesis of the Synoptic Gospels and for the differences between them. According to him, there existed in Palestine, previous to the composition of the present Gospels, an account written in Aramaic known as the Gospel "of the Nazarenes," or "of the Twelve Apostles," or "of Matthew."

This was a collection of short, isolated narratives, which ultimately suffered modifications and additions by readers or copyists possessed of extra material. Matthew, who as a publican and official had a knowledge of writing, translated this Aramaic document into Greek when Christianity began to spread among the Gentiles. Mark later translated it from a more condensed version; and Luke, with his more elegant Greek style, translated it from the same

[13] A. Schweitzer in his *Von Reimarus zu Wrede*, pp. 14-25, gives a good account and estimate of Reimarus' work.

version used by Matthew. According to this view, the Synoptic Gospels have one common source—a primitive Gospel composed in Palestine and written in Aramaic.

Griesbach (already mentioned as the originator of the term "Synopsis") concluded, as early as 1790 (like most scholars of the time), that Mark was only an abbreviator ("Epitomator"), and that his Gospel had no independent value, but was only an abridgment of Matthew and Luke.

Yet previous to this, Koppe ("Marcus non epitomator Matthaei," 1782) and Storr ("Ueber den Zweck der evangelischen Geschichte und der Briefe Johannis," 1786) had tried to adduce proof that not only was Mark not dependent on Matthew, but that it was actually the source used by Matthew and Luke, and was composed of accounts derived from Peter, of whom Mark was one of the earliest disciples. Otherwise it is hard to explain why he should have made so numerous and extensive omissions from Matthew, or why he should have added so little to Matthew and Luke, since he had at hand the accounts of Peter.

Mark wrote for the Syrian churches after the persecutions suffered by the Jerusalem church; Matthew wrote later for the Palestine churches in Aramaic, using Mark and Luke; while Luke was composed in Rome with Mark as the basis, but with supplementary matter derived from eye-witnesses in Jerusalem.

Johannes Gottfried *Herder* was, like Reimarus, before his time. In his two books "Vom Erlöser der Menschen: nach unseren drei ersten Evangelien," 1796, and "Von Gottes Sohn, der Welt Heiland: nach Johannes-Evangelium," 1797, he first put forward the view that while the first three Gospels are Palestinian and historical, describing Jesus as the Jewish Messiah and replete with Palestinian ideas and beliefs, the character of the Fourth Gospel is not historical so much as doctrinal, giving more space to Greek ideas and beliefs, and aiming at depicting Jesus, not as Jewish Messiah but as the Saviour of the World. The Fourth Gospel miracles have only a symbolic value, illustrating religious and philosophical ideas. It was composed after the Synoptic Gospels.

Of these three, Mark is earliest. We have seen that until the time of Herder, Mark was looked upon as the "Epitomator" of Matthew and Luke, because he omits the birth stories and many of Jesus' sayings and discourses. Herder derides the notion of an "Apostolic Committee" ("apostolische Kanzlei") engaged in arbitrary or necessary abridging and supplementing; he tries to show that Mark neither abridged nor omitted, but that Matthew and Luke supplemented from written or oral sources. Herder regards Mark as the corner-stone of all the Gospels because it gives nothing but the simplest unadorned details. The Matthæan and Lukan birth stories are additions arising out of the later needs of the Church.

Similarly the prevailing tone in Mark and his fellow evangelists is explicable from the point of view of current needs: Mark does not deal harshly with the Jews since at the time of its composition the Christians had not separated from the Jews; the tone of Matthew is more bitter because by that time the Jews had begun to persecute the Christians and the latter had become convinced that it was impossible for them to remain within Judaism. The basis of all three Synoptists was a primitive oral Gospel as it was narrated in brief form by the Apostles in Aramaic.

Out of this Mark first developed, from which it is as though we still hear the accounts of Peter, and which made but little change from the primitive Aramaic Gospel; next came Luke, giving such supplementary matter as he had acquired, and, finally, Matthew, who added what he thought necessary. The primitive Gospel being oral only, it is easy to account for the similarities and dissimilarities in the surviving Gospels, since their authors were not historians in the modern sense. Hence we are not to look to them for naked, unadorned history: they are compilations, religious in their nature, seeking to portray the messianic character of Jesus, and so ordering the story of his life as to make it a fulfilment of the prophecies contained in the Old Testament.

In all this, Herder was fifty years in advance of his contemporaries, and a pioneer in the path later followed by Strauss. He is somewhat behindhand only in his attitude towards the miracles which, according to him, are part of the faith of the Church and whose truth it is impossible to examine, but which, within certain limits, cannot be denied. In principle this opinion also approaches closely to that of the best of modern scholars, who see in Jesus' casting out of evil spirits, a healing of serious nervous disorders by means of spiritual influence or "suggestion."

About this same time there were written two "romances" on the life of Jesus, and these have some importance as marking a stage in Gospel criticism.

Karl Friedrich *Bahrdt* (1741-1792) between the years 1784 and 1792 published twelve volumes entitled "Ausführung des Plans und Zwecks Jesu;" and Karl Heinrich *Venturini* (1758-1849) during the years 1800-1802 wrote his "Natürliche Geschichte des grossen Propheten von Nazareth," in four volumes. Both works aimed at the same thing: to find a connecting link between the isolated episodes recorded in the Gospels and to find reasons for what Jesus did and why he suffered, and so account for all the miracles by natural means.

Link and reasons are both found in the Essenes, whom these two authors describe as a secret order, of the type of the present-day Freemasons. The Essenes taught Jesus certain methods of healing by which he worked the supposed miracles, or else Luke, who was a physician, assisted him in many instances of supposed death; such are the acts which Jesus did and which were accounted as miracles by the onlookers and the disciples. So, too, his resurrection was only imaginary: Luke gave him drugs to render him insensible to the acutest pain during the crucifixion, and immediately afterwards, when he was apparently dead and put away in the tomb, Luke and Joseph of Arithmathæa (who also was an Essene) or some other Essenes (who with their white garments looked to the women and the guardians of the tomb like angels) came and restored him out of the trance. Thus all the miracles are explicable by natural causes though they may have seemed to be supernatural to the uninitiated.

This rationalising system in explanation of the miracles reached its extreme pitch of development at the hands of the Heidelberg theologian Heinrich Eberhard *Paulus,* in his "Das Leben Jesu als Grundlage einer reinen Geschichte des Urchristenthums" (1828). According to this, Jesus used drugs or else he worked on the nervous systems of mentally diseased persons. When Jesus is described as walking on the sea as though on dry land, this was only the fruit of the disciples' imagination: when they saw him he was really walking along the sea shore, but owing to the darkness he appeared to them like a phantom hovering over the surface of the water. When Jesus is described as feeding five thousand men with five loaves and two fishes, and four thousand men with seven loaves and a few small fishes—the true facts are plain: after Jesus and the disciples had given the people all the food they had, all the others who had food with them shared it with the crowd, and so the food was sufficient for all and to spare.

Of course, those whom he raised from the dead were only seemingly dead; and he himself only died in appearance—the spear thrust (recorded in John xix. 34) served the purpose of blood-letting and assisted his recovery. Every single miracle in the Gospels is thus susceptible of explanation precisely after the manner by which M. A. Shatzkes (1825-1898) explained the *Talmud* miracles, in his "Ha-Mafteach."

Meanwhile, in 1794, *Eichhorn* had tried to account for the similarities and differences in the Synoptists as due to a primitive Aramaic source, composed and written down by one of the Apostles under the supervision of the others, and furnishing the source of our present first three Gospels. This explains the similarities. The differences are due to the fact that this Aramaic original was rendered into Greek in various versions, and modified by many emendations, additions and omissions; it was from these various versions that the Synoptists drew.

Friedrich *Schleiermacher,* in his "Ueber die Schriften des Lucas" (1817), endeavoured to prove the contrary. According to him there was not a single primitive document, but many short ones, containing separate episodes or discourses; these separate documents were used for the composition of the present Gospels—a state of things indicated in the preface to Luke. Schleiermacher regards Luke as the most reliable of the Synoptists. His hypothesis explains both the differences and the similarities, and it represents a certain step forward in the attempt at solving the Synoptic problem.

Yet in his lectures, delivered in 1832, on the life of Jesus, and published after his death in 1864, we still find the old-fashioned view that the life of Jesus is best comprehended from the Fourth Gospel since it contains fewer miracles, and Jesus is there depicted chiefly as the founder of a religion and as world-redeemer.

As to the miracles, Schleiermacher wavered between advanced rationalism and the more primitive rationalism; and with him dialectics overrides the claims of historical research. Yet he advances the understanding of the Synoptic Problem by showing, in the aforementioned lectures, that the Aramaic *Logia* of Matthew mentioned by Papias, could not have been our present Matthew, since this does not consist of sayings only, and it was originally written not in Aramaic but in Greek.

As opposed to Eichhorn and Schleiermacher who postulated, as the source of the Synoptic Gospels, one or more *written* documents, *Gieseler* ("Historisch-Kritischer Versuch über die Entstehung und die frühesten Schicksale der schriftlichen Evangelien," 1818), like Herder, supposed that they were based on an *oral* source: the very word εὐαγγελίζεσθαι (to preach good tidings, to preach the Gospel) points to oral statements. The simple nature of the Aramaic language as well as the simple nature of the first Christians and the picturesque speech used by Jesus, all combined to fix immutably in the minds of the early Christians the apostolic narratives and the Jesus-sayings: changes were inconsiderable despite the fact that nothing was fixed in writing.

Gieseler shows, from the *Talmudic* literature, the Hindu *Vedas* and early Arabic poetry, how it was possible for the simple orientals with their fresh memories to preserve entire works orally. In this fashion was the early Christian tradition preserved and, in course of time with the conversion of many Greeks, made to assume (about the end of the first century) a Greek form; and this oral tradition it was which served as the groundwork of our present Gospels. In this way Gieseler finds no difficulty in explaining the similarities and differences: the latter were inevitable with an oral tradition.

David Friedrich *Strauss* (1808-1874), whose "Das Leben Jesu" (1835-6) marks a new epoch in this line of study, based his work on the ideas and researches of Gieseler. He first overthrows the rationalism of Paulus, and maintains that the ungarnished Gospel accounts of the miracles form the strongest possible proof against their being simple natural acts. He regards the Gospel discrepancies as proofs that the Gospels are not historical works, but rather historico-religious documents written by men with a deep sense of faith unable to describe actual events without letting their own and their contemporaries' religious feelings and ideas colour their statements.

After showing in lengthy detail how the time when the Gospels were written was an age of belief in miracles, he concludes that we must regard the Gospel miracles in the same way as we regard the miracles described in the historico-religious documents of Greeks or Romans or Jews. The Gospel miracles had their origin in the "legend-creating faith" (mythenbildender Glaube) of the first Christians, and in the natural desire to find in the doings of Jesus a fulfilment of the Hebrew Scripture prophecies, and to rank him higher than the prophets of Israel by showing how he both equalled and surpassed them.

In this way, for example, we must account for the genealogical tables in Matthew and Luke, which make Jesus a descendant of David, as well as for most of the details of his sufferings and death. Satan's temptation of Jesus is a parallel to Satan's temptation of Job; many of the healings and miracles (even according to Strauss some of the healings may really have occurred, only there was nothing miraculous in them), and the raisings from the dead, form a parallel to the like incidents recorded of Elijah and Elisha; the face of Jesus shone when he spoke with Moses and Elijah, just as the Old Testament describes the face of Moses as shining; Jesus ascends into heaven because Elijah went up to heaven in a flame of fire.

And it is possible to draw many similar parallels.

According to Strauss, Jesus at first regarded himself as the forerunner of the Messiah, and subsequently as the actual Messiah and "son of man," who should establish the kingdom of Israel and bring the heathen to Judaism and do away with the ceremonial laws. But these things he was to bring about not by political means, like a Jewish King-Messiah, but by the help of his heavenly Father and legions of angels. Not until the end of his life was it possible for Jesus to think also of his "atoning death" and resurrection and Second Coming, "with the clouds of heaven," at the right hand of God in the kingdom of heaven. Strauss finally broke with the conception of the Fourth Gospel as a historical document, and showed clearly that its interest was solely theological.

On the other hand, he preferred Matthew, and even Luke, to Mark: Mark's simplicity he thought artificial, and its omissions and abridgments late. To him, Mark is still the "epitomator."

Strauss found a supporter in one of the greatest of New Testament critics, Ferdinand Christian *Baur*, the founder of the "Tübingen School" and the author of "Kritische Untersuchung über die kanonischen Evangelien" (1847). Like Strauss he abandoned belief in the historical character of the Fourth Gospel, and regarded Mark as composed on the basis of Matthew and Luke. But he introduced a new criterion for the interpretation of the Synoptic Problem: he first showed the internal struggle which, shortly after the crucifixion, waged between Peter and Paul, between the Apostle of the Jews and the Apostle of the Gentiles; he showed the gulf that lay between "Nazarenism" or Jewish Christianity (Judenchristentum) and Non-

Jewish Christianity (Heidenchristentum) ; and he explained the dispute (owing to the reception of Christianity by the Samaritans and Gentiles) which arose between Simon Peter, supported by James the Lord's brother and the other early Apostles and eyewitnesses and Ebionitic Nazarenes, on the one side, and between Paul and his sympathizers, on the other—a dispute which centred on the observance or non-observance of the ceremonial laws, especially those relating to circumcision and forbidden foods.

Baur (and *Schwegler,* who, to a certain extent, anticipated Baur in his "Das nachapostolische Zeitalter," 1846), and Baur's "Tübingen School" supporters, wished, on the basis of this apostolic dispute, to account for the differences in the Synoptic Gospels. According to this view, Matthew was the "Gospel of the Hebrews," with certain modifications and additions, which was referred to by the early Church Fathers, and which represented the views of the Nazarenes or Jewish Christians; Luke was Marcion's extreme Pauline Gospel (with, of course, certain modifications and additions), referred to by Tertullian and Epiphanius, which represented the views and served the needs of non-Jewish Christians, especially the followers of Paul; while Mark was a colourless Gospel mediating between the two extremes. The Tübingen School thus introduced into the Synoptic Problem the feature of deliberate motive: the Evangelists did not simply compile their books free of *arrière pensée,* but were theologians with a purpose in view.

Gustav *Volkmar,* a pupil of Baur, in his "Der Ursprung unserer Evangelien" (1866), saw also in Mark a Pauline document. He regarded it as the work of the same Mark known to us as the disciple of Peter, and as a retort, in 73 C.E., to the Apocalypse of John, a Nazarene document. Matthew in its primitive form (Proto-Matthäus) was replete with the Nazarene spirit; while Luke was written on behalf of Pauline Christianity and to undermine the influence of the Proto-Matthew. The surviving Gospel of Matthew has been modified, on the basis of Mark and Luke, to effect a compromise between Nazarenism and Paulinism. Matthew and Luke, one after the other, were both composed in the early decades of the second century. Thus Volkmar also failed to grasp the true value of Mark.

This was, in the end, appreciated by C. H. *Weisse* ("Die evangelische Geschichte, kritisch und philosophisch bearbeitet," 1838), and C. H. *Wilke* ("Der Urevangelist," 1838). In the same year they both proved that Mark was not an "epitomator" and that what does not occur in Mark is not an omission but an addition on the part of Matthew or Luke. According to these two scholars Luke first drew from Mark, and afterwards from Matthew, who, according to Wilke, drew also from Luke.

Credner ("Einleitung in das Neue Testament," 1836) and *Reuss* "Geschichte der Heiligen Schriften Neuen Testaments," 1842) argued on behalf of the theory that the present Synoptists are derived from *two* sources—a proto-Marcus (of which Papias speaks), from which were drawn the narrative sections of the Synoptists, and the *Logia* of Matthew (also referred to by Papias) from which Matthew and Luke drew for the discourses of Jesus. The present Mark lacks most of these discourses, but it is the earliest and most original among the Gospels.

A further, though more risky step was taken by Bruno *Bauer* (1809-1882) in his "Kritik der evangelischen Geschichte des Johannes" (1840), and "Kritik der evangelischen Geschichte der Synoptiker" (1841-2). He not only gave a lafe date to John, Matthew and Luke, but even concluded that Mark's account of the life of Jesus contained nothing of real historical value. In the end, Bauer held that everything recorded of Jesus is nothing but the product of Mark's able imagination. . . .

At first Bauer thought that Jesus might have existed, although we do not know who he was or what he did; but later, in his "Christus und die Cäsaren: der Ursprung des Christentums aus dem römischen Griechentum" (1877), he concluded that there never had been such a person: he was only an imaginary being—a combination of the Roman philosopher Seneca and the Jewish Alexandrine philosopher Philo.

The total experiences of the early Church, its persecutions, massacres, disputes with Jews and especially with Pharisees, were all laid to the account of one great personality, who gathered up in his own person all the characteristics and fortunes of the early Church. Furthermore, the contemporary religio-philosophic ideas, the exalted ethics of Seneca and the profound religious ideas of Philo (which, fused together, were adopted by early Christianity), were also ascribed to the same single personality. From all this there emerged Jesus the Messiah, Jesus the religious innovator and the embodiment of a lofty ethical ideal. . . .

Bruno Bauer had removed Christianity from its Jewish, Palestinian setting into an Alexandrian-Jewish and Græco-Roman framework. On the other hand, August Friedrich *Gfrörer* ("Kritische Geschichte des Urchristentums," 1831-38) and Richard *von der Alm*, the pseudonym of Friedrich Wilhelm *Ghillany* ("Theologische Briefe an die Gebildeten der deutschen Nation," 1863), demonstrated the intimate bond between *Talmudic* Judaism and the teaching of Jesus and his disciples.

Gfrörer very carefully brought together the messianic ideas of Judaism during the time of the Second Temple and during later times; and although he did not differentiate early and late ideas, the ideas of the *Mishnah* and early *Baraitas* as distinct from those of the later *Amoraim*, he yet succeeded in showing that none can understand early Christianity who does not first understand the Judaism of Jesus' time.

Richard von der Alm also, in his second book, "Die Urtheile

heidnischer und jüdischer Schriftsteller der vier ersten christlichen Jahrhunderte über Jesus und die ersten Christen" (1864), collected most of the *Talmudic* statements concerning Jesus and the *Minim* and much of what is told in the *Tol'doth Yeshu;* and he tried to prove that the whole content and even the method of Jesus' teaching were identical with those of the early *Tannaim,* and that all his ideas were derived from contemporary Judaism, which can be understood only from the *Talmud* and *Midrashim.*

He was the first to show the importance of "Messiah the son of Joseph" for the understanding of Christianity, and he also tried to show that the Jews, too, recognized a "suffering Messiah." He insisted that the kingdom of heaven has not a political character but that it is a transitory condition, and so Jesus could never have thought of using material means to hasten its coming. Hence Jesus was never an agent, who should hasten by action the coming of the messianic age, but one who was on the alert for the dawn of the kingdom of heaven. But when it failed to come he endeavoured to hasten it by his death.

His death was to be an atonement for the sins of those who, by refraining from repentance and good works, delayed "the end," at the very moment when, according to the belief of Jesus and his companions (a secret sect akin to the Essenes), the kingdom of heaven was at hand.

This latter book, in spite of its great importance for the understanding of many aspects of the life of Jesus, hardly made any impression. On the other hand, Ernest *Renan's* "La vie de Jésus" (1863) had an immense influence, greater perhaps than it deserved. Within the author's lifetime, between the years 1863 and 1892, no fewer than twenty-three editions were published and a complete literature grew up around the book.

The Pope placed it on the "Index" and the Roman Church offered up prayers to counteract its influence. The work owed its influence to its elegant style and its excellent arrangement which lent a unity to the inconsequent fragments of the Gospels—for, after all, the Gospels do not provide a consecutive, chronological biography, but only a collection of unconnected episodes. The psychological illustrations which Renan scattered throughout the book are often important and sometimes light up narratives and facts which at first sight seem to have little value. Still more important—and this alone makes the book worth reading—is the attention devoted to the geography of Palestine and especially the very poetical picture of Gallilee (Renan began the writing of his book in 1861, during the "Canaanitish Expedition" on the summit of Mount Lebanon).

Otherwise "La vie de Jésus" is not important: it is rather a historical novel than a work of scholarship; it is significant that Renan uses the Fourth Gospel as a historical document, preferring it to the Synoptists. Matthew he regards as the nearest approach to the

Syro-Chaldaic Gospel promulgated by the Nazarene communities who had escaped with James, the Lord's brother. Mark, who wrote in Rome the first Greek Gospel, from accounts derived from Peter, was the first of our Gospels, from which Matthew and Luke drew. The "redactor" of Matthew also adapted the Hebrew *Logia*. Luke employed Mark and a Hebrew Gospel, but was not acquainted either with the *Logia* or with our present Matthew into which the *Logia* have been introduced.

So Renan explains the Synoptic Problem—which he did, at least, feel to be a problem: the other difficulties pointed out by Strauss, Bruno Bauer, Weisse and others, Renan never felt at all. Everything was quite simple to him! What the Evangelists left out, this brilliant writer filled in from his own rich imagination. The raising of Lazarus (John xi), for example, was, according to Renan, merely a trick practised on Jesus by his disciples who were anxious to fortify his faith in himself which had begun to waver (precisely the explanation of Thomas Woolston, the English Deist—see above, p. 75).

Talmudic literature and what is to be learnt from it about Jewish life contemporary with Jesus, was known to Renan only at second or third hand, yet he quoted freely from it when it suited his general purpose. It was, none the less, a fine book and well written. The Jesus it depicted was a liberal, a philosopher-poet, one closely akin to the Central European rationalists of the 'sixties! Therefore Renan's book made an immense impression in his time, far greater than the Life of Jesus by Strauss, who had been Renan's teacher and far surpassed him in depth and learning.

Following in Renan's footsteps came many writers of "The Life of Jesus from the liberal point of view" (as Albert Schweitzer labels the type). The first among these was David Friedrich *Strauss* himself, in his "Das Leben Jesu, für das deutsche Volk bearbeitet" (1864). All these "Lives" have the same thing in common: they seek to present to modern people a *modernist* Jesus, because the historic Jesus was too bizarre for the over-enlightened folk of to-day: he was too close to the Jewish ideas of the time of the Second Temple.

Thus Jesus, in these "Liberal Lives," became non-historical. He was not primarily a Messiah but an ethical teacher. All his eschatology, as being unsuited to the "spirit of the age," was softened down or allowed to evaporate. Jesus became more antagonistic to ancient Judaism, more replete with new ethical ideas—and less historical.

Standing somewhat apart from this type is the great work, great alike in quantity and quality, of Theodor *Keim*, "Die Geschichte Jesu von Nazara" (1867-1873). Although a "liberal," the author describes with considerable skill Jesus the Messiah, Jesus the Jew. Keim was acquainted (though not always at first hand) with Jewish history and literature of the Second Temple period and later, and at every turn saw the Jew in Jesus. The Fourth Gospel he regarded as late and unhistorical; but he preferred Matthew to Mark, while, in his opinion, Papias made reference to the *Gospel* of Matthew (written not in Greek but in Hebrew) and not simply to a collection of *discourses* arranged by Matthew. Luke drew on an Ebionite and Nazarene Gospel, while Mark drew from both Matthew and Luke and from an oral tradition.

Keim was also the first, after Renan and Heinrich Julius Holtzmann (see below), to perceive two stages in the career of Jesus: the period of success ("the Galilæan Spring," as he calls it) and the period of failure. He perceived also a gradual development in Jesus' consciousness: at first the kingdom of heaven seemed to be something for the future, just as it did to John the Baptist; afterwards more and more he felt himself to be the Messiah—an idea which, though it retained something of its material, Jewish features, was from the beginning mainly spiritual. At Cæsarea Philippi Simon Peter recognized in him such a Messiah, and to this Jesus offered no disavowal; and as Messiah Jesus entered the gates of Jerusalem.

Afterwards his messianic ideals became more spiritual as his popular success became less, so that by the time of his trial he looked upon his kingdom as "not of this world." Keim depicts the stages of this development well and clearly.

Heinrich Julius *Holtzmann*, in his "Die synoptischen Evangelien" (1863), explains this development in greater detail: he finds seven stages in Jesus' Galilæan ministry, during which Jesus' success, at first great, gradually diminished. Solely on account of this lack of success did he decide to go to Jerusalem and there try his fortune. After failing to attract the Jewish people, owing to his refusal to work on their hopes of a political Messiah, he saw no other way open before him except to go up to Jerusalem and there be put to death.

Indeed, in Holtzmann's opinion, Jesus never at any time had in his mind a Messianic kingdom—only an inner change in the moral and religious consciousness. As for his own bodily resurrection from the dead and the Second Coming as the "Son of Man," "with the clouds of heaven," to inherit the kingdom of heaven which was to be established on earth—of this he never even dreamed. Holtzmann supported the priority of Mark and also the "two-source hypothesis" —the theory of an "Urmarkus" as the source of the narrative passages in the three Synoptists and the *Logia* as the source of the discourses in Matthew and Luke. This hypothesis is now accepted by most scholars and is the general basis of most of the literature on the Synoptic Problem, though Holtzmann himself subsequently rejected it in favor of a hypothesis put forward by *Simons* in his "Hat der dritte Evangelist den kanonischen Matthäus benutzt?" (1880), maintaining that there is no necessity for an "Urmarkus" and that Luke used Matthew.

We may mention further the extensive works by Bernhard *Weiss* (1882) and Wilibald *Beyschlag* (1885-6) which have found many readers. The former is a dialectical compromise between the scientific view of Jesus and the religious view of "Christ;" while the latter combines the accounts of the Synoptists and the Fourth Gospel, with by no means commendable results. Like Keim and Holtzmann, Beyschlag also notes several stages in the life of Jesus. According to him they are three in number. At first Jesus thought that the kingdom of heaven was something for the future, and his preaching aimed at hastening its coming. The people were aroused by this teaching and Jesus inclined to the belief that the kingdom had already come. But in the end came failure, and Jesus transferred the coming of the kingdom of heaven to a time yet to come after his death. Beyschlag thus emphasized the importance of the eschatological factor in the life of Jesus.

*   *   *   *   *   *   *

After the "eighties" of last century we find fewer books on the general criticism of the Gospels and on the life of Jesus, but an increase of special studies on individual problems. We will deal later on with the question of what language Jesus spoke and in what language the primitive Gospel was written.

Weiffenbach, in his "Der Wiederkunftsgedanke Jesu" (1873), tried to throw light on the question of the Second Coming, or "Parousia"—whether Jesus himself expected to come back to life and reveal himself to the world, and promised this to his disciples during his lifetime, or whether this expectation arose among his disciples only afterwards—after he was crucified and dead—when his followers could not consent to the idea that he was finally gone from the world, especially in view of the fact that belief in the resurrection from the dead was widespread in Judæa at the time. Weiffenbach is inclined to believe that Jesus himself was responsible for such a promise, otherwise we cannot find any link that will join up Jewish with Christian eschatology.

Wilhelm *Baldensperger,* in his "Das Selbstbewusstsein Jesu in Lichte der messianischen Hoffnungen seiner Zeit" (1888),[14] a book remarkably well informed about Jewish literature during and after the period of the Second Temple, sought to prove that, in his own consciousness, Jesus was the Messiah in the same sense as that of the "Son of Man" in the Book of Daniel and the "Similitudes of Enoch" (37-71), with, of course, no political projects of any kind, but only such as were messianic in the spiritual sense; while, to all this, was added a new ethical and religious content.

The full importance of eschatology in the life, the consciousness and the teaching of Jesus is explained by Johannes *Weiss* in his "Die Predigt Jesu vom Reiche Gottes" (1892; a new and enlarged

---

[14] In the 3rd edition, 1903, the section bearing on our subject is entitled *Die messianisch-apocalyptischen Hoffnungen des Judentums.*

edition in 1900). He showed how seriously Jesus' teaching had been misconstrued owing to those new ideas which had been read into it by modernist theologians, and how, in consequence, we no longer recognized the true Jesus, the historic Jesus, who, at the outset, was neither teacher, nor religious innovator, nor even the founder of the kingdom of heaven, nor really Messiah, but only one who preached the coming of the kingdom and the Messiah. Only when he became convinced that the kingdom was not yet at hand and that the people did not repent, did he begin to realize that he himself must play the rôle of Messiah and that his death must stand in place of repentance—that his life must be an atonement for the sins of the people.

So, after a temporary doubt, he died of his own will on behalf of the people, in the expectation that he should return to life and come "with the clouds of heaven" as "Son of Man" (*i.e.*, as a spiritual Messiah) sitting on the right hand of "the ancient of days;" and this, he anticipated, should come about during the lifetime of the generation whom he had taught, following the "Day of Judgment" as currently believed. All this was to happen not by force nor by human aid, but by the grace of God, for the kingdom of heaven is wholly spiritual: "The righteous shall sit with crowns on their heads having joy in the splendour of the divine presence." [14a]

This same question, whether or not Jesus' consciousness worked along these eschatological lines, was treated, from opposing points of view, by W. *Wrede* ("Das Messiasgeheimniss in den Evangelien, zugleich ein Beitrag zum Verständness des Marcusevangeliums," 1901) and Albert *Schweitzer* ("Das Messianitäts und Leidensgeheimniss: eine Skizze des Lebens Jesu" [Das Abendmahl im Zusammenhang mit dem Leben Jesu und der Geschichte des Urchristentums] Heft 2, 1901).

Wrede again threw doubt on the originality of Mark: he argued that this Gospel, too, was the offspring of the religious conviction of the early Church; that it could not persist with the belief in the messiahship of the crucified Jesus. He urged also that Mark, like the other Gospels, is not a historical document wherein the recorded events follow in chronological and logical order, but a collection of episodes with a late messianic colouring.

Actually Jesus was not a Messiah but a "Rab," a teacher from Galilee and a combination of preacher and prophet. He instructed the people who followed him, and especially his disciples, and performed miracles (mainly driving out evil spirits) after the custom of most of the great men of the time; Josephus records miracles in connection with every man of note, as does the *Talmud* in connection with Onias the "circle-maker" and others. In his teaching, Jesus endeavoured to stress the inner significance of the laws of Scripture, of which the ceremonial laws were but a cloak.

[14a] *Ber. 17a.*

Hence he stood in opposition to the majority of the Pharisees and their followers who made the external act the main object and the underlying intention only a secondary matter; and he did not reject even the publicans and sinners if only he found in them whole-hearted faith and penitence. This aroused the indignation of the Pharisees and Jewish leaders, and when he came to Jerusalem to promulgate this same kind of teaching they arrested him and condemned him to death.

The sentence was carried out by the Romans, who opposed every Jew who acquired influence over the masses, lest he use his power to undermine their authority. Not till after Jesus' crucifixion and after his disciples had perceived a hidden secret in his life and conduct, did his followers account for this secret by crediting him with messianic claims.

Much the same line of thought is followed by Wilhelm *Brandt* in his "Die evangelische Geschichte und der Ursprung des Christentums" (1893), eight years earlier than Wrede's work; the only difference is that Brandt supposed that the messianic consciousness was developed out of the simple "Rab-consciousness" after Jesus, the "Rab" and reformer, came to Jerusalem.

*   *   *   *   *   *   *

The first two decades of the twentieth century mark a noticeable change, not so much in the study of the Gospels as in the study of the character and teachings of Jesus and, especially, in the study of his Jewish environment. We no more encounter the portraiture of Jesus, the "meek and gentle," the "liberal" or the "romantic;" nor a picture of Jesus unconnected with Judaism or Palestine.

The first, and also the most extreme, effort to change our conception of the spiritual character of Jesus is from Albert *Schweitzer*, in his "Das Messianitäts- und Leidensgeheimniss" (1901), and "Von Reimarus zu Wrede" (1906), pp. 348-395. Like Johannes Weiss, he rebels against the modernist interpretations of Jesus and stresses the importance of eschatology for the better understanding of Jesus' messianic consciousness: for Schweitzer, eschatology explains everything that Jesus ever said or did, from first to last. To prove his point Schweitzer draws not only from Mark, but, when necessary, from Matthew also, since even Mark, as Wrede showed, was influenced by Christian Church ideas which arose after the time of Jesus.

According to Schweitzer, Jesus is not a "Weltbejaher" but a "Weltverneiner:" he dissociates himself completely from the life and civilization of this world: his teaching aimed solely to prepare his people to meet the future, the kingdom of heaven, which, as interpreted by Jesus, meant the life to come. He therefore sends out his disciples to summon the nation to repentance; but when their preaching met with negligible success, and the "pangs of the Messiah" (the trials and sufferings which must befall the world *before* the coming of the Messiah—ἀρχὴ ὠδίνων) delayed their coming, and when the "Day of Judgment," which was to herald the final redemption, was brought no nearer by national penitence, then Jesus realized that it must rest on *him*, through his own sufferings and death, the death of the Messiah himself, to hasten the "pangs of the Messiah" and the day of judgment. From the very beginning of his career, *i.e.*, his baptism by John, Jesus regarded himself as the Messiah in the eschatological sense, "Son of Man" in the spiritual sense, who was destined to come in the future.

At Cæsarea Philippi he drew forth from Simon Peter an acknowledgment of his messiahship and this event counts as the central point of Jesus' life. The Galilæan incidents, up to the resolve to go to Jerusalem, all lead up to it, and from it resulted the Jerusalem resolution itself which aimed, through the death of the Messiah, at bringing about the period of "the pangs of the Messiah," and so hastening the coming of the Kingdom and the resurrection of the Son of Man and his appearance at the right hand of God "with the clouds of heaven," in all his pomp and glory; and all this was to be during his disciples' lifetime.

It followed from this that the peculiar characteristic of Jesus' moral teaching was a negative attitude to all that concerned this present earthly life, the family, the state and property; his teaching was only an "Interimsethik," a moral code applicable only to the short intervening period, between this "present world" and the world to come—the "Days of the Messiah," when family, state and property cease to have any value. Thus Jesus was and remained, according to Schweitzer, not a "modernist" or "liberal," but a historical though mystical personality, bound up almost entirely with the beliefs of his own people and time and country.

Very different are the views of Wilhelm *Bousset*. In his two books, "Jesu Predigt in ihrem Gegensatz zum Judentum" (1892), and "Die Religion des Judentums in neutestamentlichen Zeitalter" (1903), he tries to show the presence of two streams of Jewish thought in Jesus' time: the one material, political, national and particularistic, unable to rise to the height of true universalism and spirituality; and the other more spiritual, more universal and profound.

Jesus' final purpose was not to foster nationalism and separatism, but the idea that men are "sons of God." This brought him joy in life: he felt himself living in the midst of a long-drawn festival; the nearness of the kingdom of heaven filled him with joy; he saw himself as a bridegroom, and so he did not fast as did the disciples of John and the Pharisees, but shared in festivities to such a degree that the Pharisees regarded him as "a glutton and a wine-bibber" (φάγος καὶ οἰνοπότης).

Jesus felt in himself that he was the Messiah and he believed that the kingdom of heaven had already begun; therefore he could not act the part of the Nazarite, the ascetic and the recluse; all that the Gospels say of his terrible visions of his end and the end of the world are the product of the thought of a later age. He came to root out the last remnants of Jewish nationalism and exclusiveness; therefore—without putting this forward as a new teaching—he abolished the ceremonial laws which had stereotyped this nationalism and exclusiveness.

In this sense Jesus' messianic ideas approximated to the spiritual aspect of the Messianic hope as it was held by most of the ancient prophets, by "the humble and meek" of the Psalms, the *Psalms of Solomon*, the *Book of Enoch*, and the *Apocalypses of Baruch* and *Fourth Esdras*. Thus, according to Bousset, Jesus perfected Judaism by raising himself above it, *i.e.*, above the views of most Jews, of the nation's leaders and writers and spiritual guides. Furthermore, Jesus was not a "Weltverneiner" but a "Weltbejaher," he assumed not a negative, but a positive attitude to the world—that world which was now, with him and through him, entering into a new epoch, the kingdom of heaven. "The Gospel develops hidden tendencies of the Old Testament, but protests against prevailing ideas in Judaism."

Therefore Jesus was in strong antagonism with the Pharisaic Judaism of the time. Such is Bousset's conclusion in his first book. But in his second (see p. 52), he admits that "he was wrong in stressing so strongly the antithesis between Jewish piety and the teaching of the Gospels;" and in his excellent conspectus "Jesus" (Religionsgesch: Volksbücher, herausg. v. F. M. Schiele, Tübingen, 1907), he recognized the extremist character of Jesus' ethical teaching as well as, historically, the essentially Jewish basis of his career.

Julius *Wellhausen*, in his "Israelitische und Jüdische Geschichte" (1894), devoted a final chapter to the Gospels, and he, too, wavers between a Jesus who maintains and a Jesus who destroys Judaism. This chapter underwent modification from one edition to another. In his fourth edition (Berlin, 1901, pp. 389-390, n. 1) he still insists that Jesus introduced nothing new, and that "Micah vi. 6-8 and Psalm lxxiii. 23-28 give us the complete Gospel." In his fifth edition those words were deleted . . . but, even so, he still allowed that the Pharisaic teaching comprised all that of Jesus: "the Pharisaic teaching contains *all, and very much more* (Wellhausen's own italics): πλέον ἥμισυ παντός" (the half is more than the whole).

"The originality of Jesus was shown in his perception of what was true and enduring in the confused mass (of Pharisaic Judaism), and it was on this that he placed the utmost emphasis" (5th edition, p. 390 n. 1). In the 7th and last edition (1914) these words also are deleted, and in a note to "Das Evangelium," the last chapter of the book (p. 358), he says: "I have left this chapter as it stands, though I agree only with part of what is there said." . . .

And in this chapter we find that Jesus "did not desire thoroughgoing changes, neither did he reverse anything nor lay any new foundation" (Kein Woller, kein Umstürzer und Gründer, p. 366);

"he had no thought whatever of breaking down the Jewish Church and setting up the Christian Church in its stead" (p. 366); "his ministry was primarily concerned with instruction" (p. 360); and "like the Pharisees he based his teaching on the Old Testament and did not deny Judaism" (p. 360); "his discourse was not the stormy discourse of the Prophets, but such as would be listened to peacefully as from a Jewish sage. He expressed only what any honest soul was bound to feel. What he said was not startling, but it was plain and explicit; and according to his innermost conviction it was the same as was laid down in the Law of Moses and in the Prophets" (p. 367).

But in spite of this, Jesus was the antithesis of Judaism: he ranged above the teaching of ceremonial laws in his ethical teaching, and from this high ethical standpoint the material and political ideals of the Jews lose their importance: mankind as a whole and not the nation is the central point in religious thought and in "the world to come." Jesus' teaching becomes thus the contrary not alone of Pharisaic Judaism but also of Scriptural Judaism: it is therefore the negation of Judaism.

From 1903 to 1905 Wellhausen engaged in the criticism of the Synoptic Gospels, devoting a separate book to each. The results of his labours (labours which did not meet with such entire approval of fellow scholars as did his work on the Old Testament which brought him most of his fame) he summed up in "Einleitung in die drei ersten Evangelien" (1905). It is here that we find the remarkable but shrewd conclusion: "Jesus was not a Christian: he was a Jew. He did not proclaim a new faith, but taught men to do the will of God. According to Jesus, as to the Jews generally, this will of God is to be found in the Law and the other canonical Scriptures" (p. 113).

But he taught a new way by which to fulfil this divine will and opposed the Pharisees who, in his opinion, choked the faith by their accretions and their exaggerated respect for the ceremonial laws. He thus unwittingly broke down the Jewish faith although he never intentionally rebelled against it. In the same way he broke down Jewish nationality since he saw no importance in the Temple and the sacrificial system (which, according to Wellhausen, constitutes "Jewish nationality"!), in spite of the fact that he wished to remain and did remain within Judaism (pp. 113-115).

Until Peter's avowal at Cæsarea Philippi, Jesus, like any other great Pharisee, was simply a teacher (p. 94); not till after this avowal did he come to regard himself as the Messiah, and even then did not so style himself. As Messiah he wished to reform Judaism through the medium of personal piety and to restore it to the primitive character which it wears in the Scriptures; but he never dreamed of reviving the kingdom of the House of David, nor did he anticipate his untimely death or his resurrection as the "Son of Man."

In his literary criticism of the Gospels Wellhausen shows minutely that all the Synoptists had an oral Aramaic source and perhaps also a written one (p. 35). The first of the Synoptists was Mark. Matthew and Luke drew from the present Mark and not from an earlier source; but they also drew from a second, slightly later, source (called "Q") containing many sayings of Jesus (*Logia*) but not confined to his discourses. Matthew is later than Mark but earlier than Luke, which already tends in the direction of the Fourth Gospel (p. 65). Mark and Matthew were written in Palestine, but not Luke. Mark may have been composed before the Destruction of the Second Temple, and the sections apparently referring to the Destruction are a later addition; both Matthew and Luke were written after the Destruction and embody beliefs and tendencies characteristic of the early Christian Church. The Gospels do not provide suitable or adequate material for systematic biography, since they disregard chronological order and contain later ideas.

In Wellhausen's description of Jesus' relation to Judaism there is much indecision and ambiguity. But his emphatic words "Jesus was not a Christian: he was a Jew," do not lose their force in spite of what he adds with the object of weakening their impression. Never before did such a statement escape the pen of a Christian scholar, and such a scholar, and such an enemy of Jews and Judaism, as was Wellhausen!

Adolf *Harnack*'s most famous book, "Das Wesen des Christentums," was published in 1900, shortly before Wellhausen's last work. There, the historical Jew, Jesus, disappears totally: virtually every word he taught is made to be of permanent and universal humanitarian interest. The messianic features are abolished entirely and virtually no importance is attached to Judaism in its capacity of Jesus' environment: Jesus arose independently and so towered above contemporary Judaism as to be untouched by it. It was not without cause that Harnack devoted his last book to that extremist of early Christian opponents of Judaism, Marcion ("Marcion," 1921). Harnack's Jesus is altogether a modernist and philosopher, the Jesus of the liberal and anti-Jewish Germany of the early twentieth century.

Extremes meet! The philosopher Edward *von Hartmann*, in his "Das Christentum des Neuen Testaments" (1905), opposed this modernist interpretation of Jesus and advocated the portrayal of him in his primitive aspect. This book is a new and revised edition of his "Briefe über die christliche Religion" (1871), which he published under the pseudonym of Müller.

As opposed to Harnack and his school, Jesus is to von Hartmann a true Jew, a Semite with all the Semite's defects. Jesus is a "quiet zealot" who hates the world and its life and civilization, and despises labour and property and family life; his teaching is fundamentally plebeian ("grundplebejischer Natur") since he hated those of high degree, the wealthy, those who had acquired possessions by their own efforts, and also the intellectually great. And all this is attributed to Jesus because he was a Jew and a Semite! Hartmann acknowledged that "the family instinct and the devotion to the family are one of the best features of the ordinary Jewish character"—and this also was entirely lacking in Jesus. But the root defect in Jesus was his Semitism.

The most liberal of Aryans can never come to terms with Jesus the Semite, Jesus the Jew, nor make any compromise with Christianity's rejection of the things of daily life, which (so such critics erroneously suppose) is a Jewish characteristic.[15]

Edward von Hartmann was a pupil of Schopenhauer, whose system he supported and continued: Friedrich *Nietzsche* was also a pupil of Schopenhauer but became his greatest opponent. But they are at one in their idea of Jesus. Nietzsche's "Antichrist" emphasizes Jesus' remoteness from daily life and the facts of existence: "culture is unknown to Jesus even by hearsay; he feels no need for opposing it—he does not dispute it;" that is to say, he does not even adopt a negative attitude towards it since for him it does not exist at all.

"So, too, with what concerns the state, civil order and the society, labour and war; he never had any grounds for denying the world, for he never even realized the existence of the 'world' in its ecclesiastical connotation." For him, nothing existed except heaven and the future life. "He died as he had lived and as he had taught —not so as 'to redeem mankind,' but so as to show how one should live," for to him, true life was—death.

So he went to meet it willingly; he wished for it and sought for it in Jerusalem. Therefore he did not defend himself at his trial nor appeal for the justice which his judges deprived him. Hence he loved them that hated him and murdered him: for they benefited him by killing him as they did by hating him. In this sense Jesus was for Nietzsche "the most interesting decadent." For, to Nietzsche, "decadence" is the total denial of life, that life which was fashioned to be near to nature and to develop with it and follow it in all respects so as, in the future, to create the type of the "laughing lion," the "blonde beast" in the likeness of the "superman."

According to Nietzsche, the Gospels also represent "decadence" as opposed to the Hebrew Scriptures, of which Nietzsche speaks in terms of veneration such as have been uttered by no other author: "Glory and honour to the Old Testament! There we find great men, an environment of heroes and, what is rarest on earth, the incomparable simplicity of the stout heart; still more, we find a *nation*. But, on the other hand, in the New Testament, we find nothing but petty party dealings, only 'rococo' of the soul, fondlings, flourishes, only an atmosphere of secret meetings, an occasional unforgettable

[15] On the "German Jesus" see the excellent comments of Schweitzer, in his *Von Reimarus zu Wrede,* pp. 305-310, 400.

flavour of bucolic sweetness peculiar to the age (as *also* to the Roman state), which is not so much Jewish as Hellenistic. The juxtaposition of meekness and pride; sentimental babblings which almost deafen the ears; petty longings in place of passion; a wearying game of grimaces. Clearly we here have an utter absence of sound education. How can worlds be stirred by petty blemishes, as was done by these small mannikins! A mere creature would pay no attention, let alone God! And, in the end, they even expect a 'crown of eternal life'—all these little villagers! And why? It would be difficult to be more lacking in humility. . . . The New Testament raises the more manly persons' gorge: the foolishnesses, the worries and troubles of street-loungers—as though the essence of all essences (God) were bound to care for such things; it never wearies nor tires of dragging God himself into the pettiest care into which these people are plunged." [16]

Whereas, on the other hand, "in the Jewish Old Testament, the book of divine righteousness, there are men, affairs and discourses on so magnificent a scale as to surpass the Greek and Hindu literatures. We stand in awe and reverence before these titanic relics of what man once was, and we are distressed when we think of Asia, and of its small excrescence Europe which is so confident that it represents human progress as compared with Asia.

"Of a surety, he who is himself only a meagre, domesticated animal with only the needs of a domesticated animal (like our present-day intellectuals and the adherents of 'enlightened' Christianity), will not be amazed or even distressed at those ruins (the criterion is their appreciation of what constitutes 'greatness' or 'littleness' in the Old Testament) ; and such a man may prefer the New Testament, that book of 'lovingkindness' (which contains much of the real, vapid, musty reek of brother-devotees and little minds). To take this New Testament, so altogether 'rococo' in taste, and bind it together artificially with the Old Testament, and make them into a single, complete Bible, is perhaps the greatest piece of effrontery and the worst kind of 'sin against the Holy Spirit' with which literary Europe has ever burdened its conscience." [17]

The absolute antithesis to Nietzsche is Leo *Tolstoy*. But even so, Tolstoy's Jesus, "Jesus the spiritual anarchist," is not far removed from the Jesus of Nietzsche. The Jesus of Tolstoy, like the Jesus of Nietzsche, adopts a completely negative attitude to the state and society, the only difference being that he does so not because he is unaware of them, but because there is no need for them in "the kingdom of heaven that is within us."

The Tolstoyan Jesus does not resist evil even in self-defence nor

[16] Fr. Nietzsche, *Zur Genealogie der Moral*, Werke, Leipzig, 1902, VII 462-3.
[17] See *Jenseits von Gut und Böse*, III Hauptstück, 52. Werke, I Abteilung. Leipzig, 1902, VII, 77.

demand the justice that is denied him nor try to raise the level of culture, and he ordains that a man "resist not evil by violence;" but all this, which Nietzsche holds up to ridicule, Tolstoy holds up for admiration. What cannot be done by *culture*, since it merely increases the world's egotism, can be accomplished by this *love* of one's fellow man: other things can only harm and not help.

The Tolstoyan Jesus, any more than the Nietzschean Jesus, is not the result of research, but is "made in the image of his creator." And just like Nietzsche, Tolstoy bases his ideas of Jesus on the Fourth Gospel and not on the Synoptists, since the former is more abstract and spiritual, and less profuse in miracles and descriptions of human frailties in Jesus. For to Tolstoy's mind the miracles in this and the other Gospels are only parables and symbols. According to Tolstoy, Jesus' conception of God is pantheism mingled with Schopenhauer's philosophy of the will, for Tolstoy, like Nietzsche, was a disciple of Schopenhauer.

Naturally, with Tolstoy, scarcely anything of the historical Jesus was left; Tolstoy tears him forcibly from his Jewish surroundings since these same surroundings see in the kingdom of heaven not the antithesis of national and political welfare, but its highest point. Also in his attitude to Judaism Tolstoy remained the disciple of Schopenhauer who was unable to endure "Jewish optimism" and placed Jesus in the same rank as Buddha.[18]

Friedrich *Naumann* (once a Protestant pastor and later the founder of the "Socialist-Nationalist" party), in his "Briefe über die Religion" (1903), accuses Jesus of being a hater of culture. A journey which he made in Palestine aroused in him the thought: What did Jesus do towards raising the level of civilization and improving the economic condition of this poor country? Did he give any care towards improving its roads, building bridges, bettering the economic and educational condition of the inhabitants of Galilee and Judæa? He loved the poor, but did he really do anything to help them? And did he think, by the performing of miracles, to hold out to them any tangible help?

In this book Naumann departs somewhat from what he had said of Jesus in his earlier "Jesus als Volksmann" (1894), where he speaks of Jesus as the *saviour of the poor*. This book is part of a series dealing with "Jesus the Socialist" (Lublinski, Lozinski, Kautsky and others); nothing much need be said of them here since they are not written on a scientific basis, and because their authors, amateurs in the field of Gospel study and Jewish history, found in Jesus nothing but their own ideals.[19]

---

[18] On Jesus and Buddha see R. Seydel, *Das Evangelium von Jesu in seinen Verhältnissen zur Buddha-Sage und Buddha-Lehre* (1882); H. Weinel, *Jesus im neunzehnten Jahrhundert*, Neue Bearbeitung, Tübingen, 1907, pp. 240-260; E. Grimm, *Die Ethik Jesu*, 2 Aufl. Leipzig, 1917, pp. 302-312.

[19] On these see the chapter "Jesus im Lichte der sozialen Frage," in H. Weinel, *op. cit.* pp. 159-212.

Of the same character is what Houston Stuart *Chamberlain* says of Jesus in his "Die Grundlagen des neunzehnten Jahrhunderts" (1899). His Jesus is the complete German and modernist. Chamberlain's attitude to Judaism has nothing in it of the scientific, but is crudely antisemitic. His knowledge of the Jewish environment and the spirit of the age is derived at second and third hand.

The "startling" innovation in his book is this—that the father of Jesus was an Aryan and not a Semite (this is the Jewish legend about Pandera), an innovation, the doubtful honour of the discovery of which Chamberlain must share with Ernst *Häckel* ("Die Welträthsel") and Ernst *Bosc* ("La vie ésotérique de Jésus Christ et les origines orientales du Christianisme," 1902) and Dr. Aaron *Kaminka* (who anticipated all of them) and Professor Paul *Haupt* ("The Aryan Ancestry of Jesus," 1909).

The object of all these authors was not the same, but (with the exception of the Jewish writer Kaminka [20]) their common feature is to "justify" the Aryan nations' acceptance of Christianity. For how, indeed, was it possible that a faith which came to embrace the half of mankind, could issue from that "tiny, feeble nation," which is made great only when these authors come to describe the great *loss*, which accrued to the Aryan nations because of it?

Otto *Pfleiderer* ("Urchristentum," 1887; "Die Entstehung des Christentums," 1905) argued that all the early Christian beliefs about Jesus' birth and resurrection originated from eastern pagan cults which spread widely throughout the Roman Empire. Basing his ideas on these books, Albert *Kalthoff* ("Das Christusproblem, Grundlinien einer Sozialtheologie," 1902; "Die Entstehung des Christentums," 1903) went to the length of utterly denying the existence of Jesus. According to him, Christianity originated not in Jerusalem but in Rome, and not from the teaching of any Jesus of Nazareth, but from the economic and social conditions prevalent in the first century. Slavery and the bad economic conditions in Rome aroused in the masses the desire for world reform, for a communistic movement, and combined with this were the messianic and apocalyptic hopes of the Jewish proletariat, hopes in the greatest measure worldly and material, as we may see from the *Apocalypse of Baruch, Fourth Esdras*, the *Book of Enoch* and the early *Sibylline Oracles*, as well as from the *Talmud* and *Midrash*.

Communistic corporations were thus formed uniting the Roman socialistic movement with the messianic and religio-philosophic beliefs of Judaism. Out of this arose Christianity, whose mystical beliefs (the resurrection from the dead, the Sacrament of the Saviour's .Body and Blood, and the like) were taken from the religious beliefs of the orientals who were accepted as members of these corporations (θιασοί).

The origin of Christianity is thus explained according to the

[20] A. Kaminka, *Studien zur Geschichte Galiläas*, Berlin, 1889.

principles of "materialistic history." Jesus became the "saint" and "hero" of the communistic societies, just as all the oriental mystical societies had their semi-divine heroes. The recorded doings of Jesus, especially his sufferings and death, were derived from the events which befell the Church, which, in the reigns of Nero and Trajan, endured terrible persecutions; and these events were, by the writers of the Gospels, attributed to a single individuality which, even if it had existed (and there may have lived in Judæa some political Messiah, Jesus by name, who rebelled against Roman rule), had scarcely any connexion with Christianity.[21]

Kalthoff thus repeats Bruno Bauer's attempt.[22] But whereas the latter accounted for the existence of Christianity and the story of Jesus by a combination of Græco-Roman philosophy and Jewish religion (in its Alexandrine form) with its messianic ideas (as was appropriate to Bauer's age that of Hegelian philosophy), Kalthoff explained it from a combination of Roman economic conditions and Jewish and pagan religious and messianic hopes (as was appropriate to *his* time, that of the preaching of socialism with its materialistic history.)

Another denial of the existence of Jesus is forthcoming from an American writer, B. *Smith,* in "The Pre-Christian Jesus" (1906). He thinks that there never was such a town as Nazareth and that Jesus was an object of worship to a sect of Nazarites who existed at the time when Christianity came into being, and whom the Christian father Epiphanius mentions at great length. Hence the name "Nazarenos, Nazaræos;" for Matthew (ii. 3) says: "And he (Joseph together with Jesus) came and dwelt in a city called Nazareth, to fulfil what was spoken by the Prophet, For he shall be called a Nazarite (Ναζωραῖος)." We thus see how the Gospels already confuse "Nazareth" and "Nazarite."[23]

Yet another disbeliever in Jesus' existence is Arthur *Drews,* "Die Christusmythe" (1909), whose views, as we shall see later, were refuted by a Jewish scholar and another of Jewish origin.[24]

More positive and conservative in its attitude to Jesus and the events of his life is R. W. *Husband's* "The Prosecution of Jesus" (1916), in which the author tries to show that the trial of Jesus took place on the eve of a Sabbath, the fourteenth of Nisan, 33 C.E., because the eve of Passover fell on a Sabbath during the procurator-

---

[21] A detailed account and defence—inadequate in the present writer's opinion—of Kalthoff's teaching (which has as an ultimate aim to deprive Palestinian Judaism of its chief share in the creation of the new world faith and so lessen the value of Judaism) is given in B. Kellermann's *Kritische Beiträge zur Entstehungsgeschichte des Christentums,* Berlin, 1906. See the present writer's review of this book in *Sulle origine del Cristianesimo* (*Rivista Israelitica,* 1906, III 218-220).

[22] See above, p. 86.

[23] See below, p. 230.

[24] See later, pp. 115 and 123.

ship of Pontius Pilate only in this year 33; and because Jesus began his ministry in the fifteenth year of Tiberius, i.e. the year 29-30; therefore his ministry lasted, as in the Johannine tradition, three years (pp. 34-69).

More important is what Husband proves from the numerous recently discovered papyri—that in Egypt the local authorities had the right of arresting those suspected of smaller or greater crimes and to conduct a preliminary investigation as to the gravity of the crime; only if it were discovered to be a capital offence was the prisoner handed over to the Roman authorities, who then tried the culprit afresh and either condemned him to death or released him.

And this, the author thinks, was the case also with Jesus' trial: the Sanhedrin, the local authority in Judæa, arrested Jesus through the medium of the Temple police and carried out only a preliminary enquiry; therefore this enquiry does not conform with the normal judicial procedure required of every court of law established for the conduct of actual trials (pp. 70-181). From this point of view the writer shows that the Sanhedrin's judicial enquiry was legal and constituted no injustice (pp. 181-208); furthermore, that the crime alleged against Jesus was completely proved and that he was condemned to death according to the *lex Juliana* for treason, promulgated in the time of Augustus (pp. 281-2, 209-233).

This is the exact opposite of the conclusion arrived at by G. *Rosadi*, "Il Processo di Jesù" (1904), who sees in Jesus' trial a "judicial murder" and a travesty of all the claims of justice.[25]

Gustav *Dalman*, who had published at the end of the nineteenth century a work which is very important for the understanding of the sayings of Jesus ("Die Worte Jesu," 1898), issued in 1909 his "Orte und Wege Jesu," invaluable for the study of the Palestinian environment of Jesus; the author pays attention to the Hebrew sources in the *Talmud* and *Midrash* but he does not exhaust them.

Finally there has recently appeared ("Ursprung und Anfänge des Christentums" I-II, Stuttgart and Berlin, 1921) two volumes by the great student of ancient history and the period of the Second Temple, Eduard *Meyer* (the third volume does not bear on our subject). The first volume deals with the Gospels and the second with "the development of Judaism, and Jesus of Nazareth."

In the main, Meyer follows Wellhausen, though he is more conservative and accepts the genuineness of many details denied by Wellhausen. And in this he is mostly right. But, on the other hand, it is difficult to suppose that he is right in his conclusion about the *Testaments of the Twelve Patriarchs* and the *Book of Jubilees*— that the earlier portions of them were composed in the last decades of the third pre-Christian century, and their later parts in the time of Jason, 179-171 B.C. (See vol. II, pp. 11-12, 44-45, 167-170, on the

[25] Against him, see H. P. Chajes, *Il Processo di Gesù di Rosadi: Note Marginali: Rivista Israelitica*, 1904, I 41-57, 105-106.

Testaments of the Twelve Patriarchs; II 45-47, 170-172, on the "Book of Jubilees").

Also it is difficult to agree with him about the *Book of Damascus,* which is, he thinks, like the *Book of Enoch* and the later parts of the *Testaments of the Twelve Patriarchs* and the *Book of Jubilees,* to be dated in the time of Jason, before the persecuting edicts of Antiochus Epiphanes (II 47-49, 172-174; see also the same author's "Die Gemeinde des Neues Bundes im Lande Damaskus," 1919).

In everything dealing with the history of the Maccabæan period, he relies on II *Maccabees,* thus following the footsteps of Niese, Laqueur, Wilcken and others, although he does not go to such extremes as Niese and still pays attention to I *Maccabees.* But in his outlook on the Maccabæan dynasty and the Jews generally in Palestine during the period of the Second Temple, he is influenced by the opinions of Wellhausen and Wilcken, who, in their turn, had been influenced by Mommsen and Renan. When speaking of Joseph ben Tobias and his son Hyrcanus he finds it hard to refrain from a crude attack on modern Judaism, quite out of place in a scholarly work; and this same attack occurs twice in his book (II 32 and 129).

Needless to say, the Maccabees and their supporters were gloomy bigots, while truth and enlightenment were the possession of the Hellenists, whom he calls "Reform Judaism," the Judaism which wished to bring the Jewish people out into the open and to endow it with enlightenment and love of its fellow races. The author is regardless of the fact which transpires from his own remarks that these "reformers" had no root within the nation, and that if they had succeeded it would have meant the end of Judaism (and so no Christianity could have arisen in Palestine).

But despite this, there is in these ideas an objective scientific value apart from subjective attitudes to Judaism in general. Still, he cannot keep himself from passing caustic remarks even about this so-called "Reform Judaism." "At all times enlightened and reformed Judaism has revealed an instinctive feeling to be drawn after the dominant stream and after what it can turn to profitable business" (II 146). If such be the case, then everything good that the author has said of "Reform Judaism" crumbles away; but in the prejudice which spoils his judgment, the author is oblivious of all this. . . .

He quotes with great glee the gibes of the early antisemites— Poseidonius, Tacitus, Cicero and the rest; and for him as to most of his ilk, the Maccabæan kingdom was a "robber-state" (Raubstaat), and by destroying it Rome did a kindness to humanity; once the Jews were made independent and granted a certain control, they could do nothing but damage and destroy. And the cause of this was, "the spirit of the book of Deuteronomy!" (II 279-828)—neither more nor less. What wonder, then, if to him Philo of Alexandria is "not a great spirit," and "his aims, though proper, are narrow" (II 366).

But in spite of all this, Eduard Meyer has much to say that is new about what the Greek and Roman sources teach and emphasize concerning the period of the Second Temple, and also a certain amount about Persian influence on the Jews and Jewish literature. But he has made scant use of the Hebrew sources, even of those written in or translated into German. His single source for Jewish learning is the antiquated work of Weber, "Jüdische Theologie" (in its equally antiquated second edition).

It is not, therefore, a matter of surprise if he blunders over the fact, well enough known, that the Jews conclude with the *Hallel* (Psalms 113-118) only after one domestic meal in the year, *i.e.*, the "Seder," the first meal of the night on which Passover begins, and supposes that the "Last Supper" of Jesus with his disciples was just an ordinary meal which "as is well known" is concluded by the singing of the *Hallel* (I 177).[26]

The last chapter of his second volume is devoted to Jesus of Nazareth (II 420-453). It constitutes a summary of all his Gospel criticism. Normally he relies on Mark except when it deals with eschatology and the "suffering Messiah;" and in a lesser degree he relies on the source "Q," the discourses in Matthew and Luke. He is driven to the conclusion that "the religious complexion of Jesus' world is exactly that of the Pharisees" (II 425). Jesus was not, like the Prophets, interested in the political and social events of the day, but only in the kingdom of heaven; "he did not, like many others, found a new school or sect, still less a new religion—this came about only after his death with the development of Christianity" (II 445).

This is identical with Wellhausen's view, and, as with Wellhausen so with Ed. Meyer, there here begins a "but" which contradicts what goes before. The Pharisees possessed "a law taught of men," they were immersed in the ceremonial laws and neglected those laws which affected a man's relations to his fellowmen. This tendency was opposed by Jesus, for whom the main issue was personal piety and love of humankind; and Jesus' opposition went the length (though it was not done deliberately) even of assuming a free attitude with regard to the precepts contained in the "Law of Moses;" and thus "Judaism, in its very essence, was overcome" (II 432).

In Judaism God is regarded as "Father" even in the sense of begetter and creator of the Jewish nation; and so the Jews use "Father" and "King" in the same breath ("Abinu Malkenu") Jesus deprived this of its "nationalist motif" (II 437). He made use of the title "Son of Man" (as against Lietzmann and Wellhausen, who deny altogether its use by Jesus) purely because of its ambiguity and because in itself it did not, before Peter's avowal at Cæsarea

[26] See later, p. 329 n. 32.

Philippi, disclose his messianic claims (II 345). His baptism by John the Baptist is of doubtful authenticity since it is bound up with Satan's temptation in the wilderness, which is only a legend or a vision (I 83-84; II 425).

Jesus' "sending forth of the Apostles" is derived from the doings of the early members of the Christian Church twenty years after the crucifixion: Jesus himself never sent out any apostles (I 278-280). There was nothing fraudulent in Jesus' miracles, but they were in all respects like those performed by contemporary Jewish sorcerers and the Mormons of the present time (II 359).

When Jesus was on his way to Jerusalem he supposed that he should suffer there as did the ancient prophets and John the Baptist, but he knew nothing of the Christian teachings of a Suffering Messiah who was to rise from the dead (II 449-450). He hoped to attract the people and receive from them a recognition of his messianic claims by some striking demonstration; but having been bred in the primitive conditions of Galilee, Jesus did not know the condition of a great town like Jerusalem nor the power of those in authority, and the result was inevitable (II 451).

The Synoptic Gospels (as distinct from the Fourth Gospel) were wrong in describing the popular leaders in Jerusalem as mere "hypocrites" who betrayed Jesus to Pilate because they wanted to be rid of a dangerous opponent, and not because of any anxiety about the welfare of the country and nation: there really was a political danger involved in Jesus' appearance: such popular movements, in times of stress and excitement, automatically become popular rebellions; and this might have been the case also with the popular movement aroused by Jesus, even against his will (II 451, I 164-5).

Paul had been grounded in Pharisaic ideas and made use of all the Rabbis' casuistical devices (II 349, 365 and elsewhere). Because Christianity made its appeal to the unlettered, the "Am-haaretz," and rejoiced over the "little ones" and "babes" ($\nu\acute{\eta}\pi\iota o\iota$), the result was mental darkness in the world for many centuries; the Christians began, at an early date, to prefer emotionalism and blind faith to intellect and knowledge; and thus there followed in the footsteps of Christianity the prolonged reign of ignorance of the Middle Ages (I 289-291).

Such is the way that the last great work to appear in recent times looks upon the Gospels, Jesus and Christianity.

And when we look afresh into all that has been said of these three during the first twenty years of this century, we come to the conclusion that nearly all the many Christian scholars, and even the best of them, who have studied the subject deeply, have tried their hardest to find in the historic Jesus something which is not Judaism; but in his actual history they have found nothing of this whatever, since this history is reduced almost to zero. It is therefore no wonder that at the beginning of this century there has been a revival of the eighteenth and nineteenth century view that Jesus never existed.

As to his teaching, the most they have found is the opposition of a Pharisee to other Pharisees—Pharisees who failed to fulfil the duties which they had assumed. The best of the Christian scholars have so generalized this opposition as to make the opposition extend to the *whole of Judaism;* and thus there remains to them of Christianity nothing but—hatred of Judaism. . . .

* * * * * * *

It still remains to give a brief account of complete works written in recent times by Jewish scholars concerning Jesus.[27] "Complete works" is emphasized, since there is scarcely a single Jewish scholar, especially among those who have treated of the period of the Second Temple, who, in his writings on Judaism, has not dealt with the nature and importance of Jesus and his teaching.

The books of A. *Büchler* ("Die Priester und der Cultus im letzten Jahrzehnt des Jerusalemischen Tempels," Wien, 1895; "Der galiläische Am-Haarez des zweiten Jahrhunderts," Wien, 1906; "The Political and the Social Leaders of the Jewish Community of Sepphoris in the Second and Third Centuries" [London 1909] ; "The Economic Conditions of Judæa after the Destruction of the Second Temple," London, 1912), of M. *Güdemann* ("Jüdische Apologetik," Glogau, 1906, and several other works), of J. *Derenbourg* ("Essai sur l'histoire de la Paléstine," Paris, 1867 [also in a Hebrew translation: "Massa Eretz Yisrael," trans. Mibshan, Petrograd, 1896]), of M. *Joel* ("Blicke in die Religionsgeschichte zu Anfang des 2. christlichen Jahrhunderts," Breslau 1889), of H. P. *Chajes* ("Marcus-Studien," Berlin, 1899, and many articles in Hebrew, German and Italian) ; also the works of Israel *Levi, Bacher, Krauss, Perles* and others, are a valuable treasury for all who would comprehend the social and political environment from which Jesus arose, on which he based his teaching, and to which he appealed.

But complete works by Jewish writers in any language, devoted solely to Christianity and its Founder, are few ; and even to these few, Christian scholars have not paid proper attention.

The most important of such works is the famous book by one who was a Jew on his father's side and a Roman Catholic on his mother's side, and who remained faithful to the Jewish people all his life—Joseph *Salvador.* "Jésus Christ et sa doctrine: histoire de la naissance de l'église, de son organisation et de ses progrès pendant le premier siècle," 2 vols. Paris, 1838.[28] Although Schweitzer, in his

[27] An important work still remaining to be done is a book on all that has been written about Jesus in Jewish literature from the close of the *Talmud* period until Jacob Emden. At present we have only the important article by J. Broydé: *Polemics and Polemical Literature* (*Jewish Encyclopedia,* X 102-109).

[28] For an account of the man and his writings, see the book written by a kinsman, Gabriel Salvador, *Joseph Salvador, sa vie, ses oeuvres et ses*

"Von Reimarus zu Wrede," often treats at great length of very many works of most doubtful value, he was not able to devote more than a short note to this important book,[29] and even so, a note which is only one long error: instead of "Salvador" he calls him "Salvator;" he makes him "one of the cleverest of Venturini's successors," whereas there is scarcely a single resemblance between the two; he says that "Salvator expected the spiritual and mystical Mosaic system to overcome Christianity"—an idea which could never have passed through Salvador's mind since he regarded the Mosaic Law as the very antithesis of mysticism.

It would seem that Schweitzer had either never seen or never read the book, either because it was written in French (and he only treats in detail books written in German, referring only briefly to others), or because it was written by a Jew, and books about Jesus composed by Jews were antecedently suspect (only so can we account for his not referring even to Graetz's "Sinaï et Golgotha" and the chapter on Jesus in Graetz's third volume of the "History of the Jews," while he devotes far more space than it is worth to the queer book by De Jonge, a Jewish convert (see Schweitzer, *op. cit.* pp. 319-320 English translation, "The Quest of the Historical Jesus," 321-2).

Had Schweitzer read "Salvator" carefully he would have found there (especially in the last chapter of the first volume) strong support of his, Schweitzer's, main conclusion—that Jesus' teaching was that of a "Lebensverneiner."

Salvador often [30] stresses the idea enunciated later by Abraham Geiger (see later, p. 115 f.), that Jesus never laid down a single ethical precept not to be found in the Prophets or in contemporary Jewish sages. He finds the whole of the "Sermon on the Mount" in Ben Sira,[31] so anticipating Kalthoff. Yet at the same time he finds a great difference between the general tone of Pharisaic Judaism and the teaching of Jesus. In the first place, he shows that Pharisaic Judaism endeavoured to secure men earthly happiness so far as this is possible without damage to their spiritual life, and so it occupied itself with everyday life and its reform: it was a law of life intended for a people living on the earth, and so it tried to reform earthly life by the "fear of God" and by the inculcation of such good qualities as are requisite for the reformed life of society—and no more.

Whereas Jesus, who cared not at all for the social life, and for whom the religious and ethical life of the individual was the one aim and object of his teaching, despised the civilized life of this

critiques, Paris, 1881. A fine character sketch of Salvador, the man and the scholar, is given by James Darmesteter, *Les prophètes d'Israël,* Paris, 1895, pp. 279-387; especially with reference to the book under discussion see pp. 323-342.
[29] *Op. cit.* p. 161, n. 1.
[30] See especially, *op. cit.* I 355-6.
[31] *Op. cit.* I 357, 401 ff.

world, and in his reaching forward to the future life, adopted a negative attitude to the life of this present world as did all the priests of the Oriental nations (the Egyptians, the Hindus, etc.), who, caring only for the life of the soul after death, disregarded the existing social order and abandoned themselves to asceticism and despair of the present world.

Secondly, Salvador shows that Pharisaic Judaism felt itself compelled, by interpretations derived from the Law, to lay down rules regulating every human act and to pay special attention to the prescribed ceremonial laws in order by such means to ensure national persistence; this "réglement" embracing the whole life, moral or social, matters of faith or matters of religious practice, served as a buttress against the danger of assimilation and the obliteration of the peculiar Jewish national features which must needs be preserved in order that the Law of Israel might itself be preserved till such time as redemption should come to the whole world.

Jesus, on the other hand, caring only for the religious and moral life of the individual, gave no thought to the possible importance of the social and ceremonial laws of the *Torah* in their capacity of a defensive hedge guarding Jewish nationalism. This constitutes the difference between the teaching of Jesus and contemporary traditional Judaism; and just because of this difference the decisive majority of the Jews rejected his teaching. [32]

Permeating the whole of Salvador's book is the theme that Christianity arose out of a compromise between Judaism and paganism. In Jesus' time Paganism was in extremis, since its moral life was rotten to the core; the pagan nations needed, therefore, a new rule of life, yet one that should be adaptable to their ancient principles, since paganism which had originated with them had become ingrained in them. But Judaism had preserved its moral life intact and so needed no change or transformation or compromise. The Jews therefore rejected Christianity, and the pagans, in accepting it, made it semi-pagan.

As the reader will observe, these ideas are profound and important and still by no means antiquated. We shall have reason to return to them again and again in the course of these pages.

But since Salvador, as he himself acknowledges,[33] was unable to utilize Strauss's recently published work, and since he had concerned himself but little in Old Testament and Gospel criticism (for which he is rightly blamed by Renan), his views frequently lack scientific value. None the less, he instinctively arrived at many of Strauss's views. Thus, for example, he perceived that much of what was recorded of Jesus was inserted out of an impulse to fulfil what had been written in the Holy Scriptures; he explained that much of what was told of the birth death and resurrection of Jesus was

[32] *Op. cit.* pp. 356-414.
[33] *Op. cit.* Preface XV-XX.

derived not from the Old Testament but from oriental and contemporary Greek mythology.[34] In this, and also in explaining the genesis of Christianity from the pagan religious corporations (θίασοι) Salvador anticipated the celebrated writings of Pfleiderer, from which Kalthoff drew most of his ideas.

From every point of view Salvador's book is in advance of almost all the works on the life of Jesus till the advent of Strauss, with the exception of Reimarus. As Darmesteter well says, he wrote "not the human history of God," but "the divine history of man." [35] Salvador's views of the trial of Jesus were very original and caused a great outcry at the time and even brought him to the criminal dock.

Apart from Salvador's writings, the present writer knows only of three other complete works about Jesus written by Jews, one in French and two in English.[36] Only one of these lays serious claims to scholarship—that of *Graetz*. It was originally written in German but never appeared in its original form, since it was almost all embodied in his "History of the Jews" (III⁵ Leipzig, 1905, pp. 271-313). The French translator and editor was Moses Hess, the author of "Rome and Jerusalem." Its French title is: H. Graetz, "Sinaï et Golgotha, ou les origines du judaïsme et du christianisme, suivi d'un examen critique des Evangiles anciens et modernes. Traduit et mis en ordre par Maurice Hess." Paris, 1867. It (as also the corresponding part of the "History") is, both in form and style, the work of an artist; and in many respects it is not yet antiquated.

Most of the book (to p. 270) is devoted to a detailed and very clear survey of the history of the Jews till the time of Jesus, special attention being given to the period from Maccabæan times to the rule of the Roman Procurators. The remainder (pp. 270-362) deals with the life of Jesus and his teaching, the history of subsequent Christianity being touched upon briefly. As an appendix we are given a short critical account of the four "ancient" Gospels and a more detailed criticism of the two "modern" Gospels (as Graetz facetiously puts it) "according to Renan," and "according to Strauss" (the latter's "Popular History of Jesus," published, 1864). According to Graetz, neither Renan's nor Strauss's "Life of Jesus" is a piece of scientific work, but a "New Gospel."

Graetz regards Matthew, and not Mark, as the earliest of the ancient Gospels, and holds that even that was not written until the time of Bar Kokhbah (c. 136); this, he thinks. is clearly evident from

---

[34] Darmesteter, *op. cit.* pp. 331-340.
[35] *Op. cit.* 332.
[36] The author was unfortunately unable to secure Hippolite Rodriguez', and Michael Kolischer's books in spite of all his efforts. He may also have overlooked other like books. Harris Weinstock's *Jesus the Jew* (3rd ed. New York, 1907) is merely a publicistic essay on the value of Jesus to the Jews of to-day. There has recently appeared a work by E. Pappeport, *Das Buch Jeschua,* Wien, 1920, the aim of which is to depict Jesus as a Jew. But it has no scientific value.

Matthew xxiv and Mark xiii, where "the abomination that maketh desolate" referred to is the image of Jupiter which Hadrian erected on the site of the Temple after Jerusalem had been destroyed and rebuilt under the name Aelia Capitolina. Mark was written shortly after Matthew; Luke (and the Acts of the Apostles) was not composed before 150; and John, which according to Graetz has no historical value whatever, was composed between 170 and 180. The Gospel of the Nazarenes was written in Aramaic as early as 100-130, since it is mentioned in the *Talmud*,[37] but it is not the Gospel of Matthew.[38]

In the light of this very late date of all the Gospels Graetz "frankly acknowledges that even what seems most certain in the study of the life of Jesus has only the value of a hypothesis. The sole historical fact we possess is that Christianity arose out of Essenism" (p. 376). On this point—the Essenic origin of Christianity—Graetz has a great deal to say both in the course of his book and in the "Appendix" (pp. 407-415), and he is so obsessed by the idea as to call Christianity "Essenism mixed with foreign elements."

Apart from certain well-known passages in the Gospels to which he attaches but small importance, Graetz' main evidence consists in the facts that John the Baptist, who paved the way for Jesus' manifestation, was an Essene in all his manner of life, and that James the Lord's brother, who led the early Church after the crucifixion, had all the habits of an Essene, and that even the entire Church, while it yet consisted of those who had known Jesus personally, behaved in all respects like an Essene community.

But it was, furthermore, apparent to Graetz that Jesus "assumed nothing more than the principal features of the Essenes, particularly the love of poverty, community of goods, dislike of oaths, power to heal those possessed with devils, lunatics and the like; though, to all appearances, he did not observe the less fundamental points ('points accessoires') of Essenism, such as the scrupulous avoidance of everything unclean, wearing the 'apron,' and the like. Nor does he seem to have attached importance to the lustrations, since it is never recorded that he himself carried out the rule or urged it upon others" (p. 305).

Still another matter is apparent to Graetz—that Jesus never proposed to abolish the ceremonial laws; and that whatever the Gospels say of this is but a later addition by the followers of Paul; otherwise James the Lord's brother and Peter, Jesus' most intimate disciple, and all their party, could never have observed these same ceremonial laws; and Paul, who abolished them, would have justified his action by the words of Jesus; and we actually see the contrary in the Epistle to the Galatians, which Graetz regards as the

---

[37] See above pp. 35-38.
[38] *Sinaï et Golgotha*, pp. 380-381.

earliest Christian document and the one genuinely Pauline epistle.[39] The Sermon on the Mount (absent in both Mark and John, and occurring only in isolated sayings in Luke) never, according to Graetz, had any existence in fact. The question whether "the founder of Christianity introduced any conception of God or any moral law differing from or surpassing those in Judaism" is answered by Graetz with a most definite negative.[40]

And if any would protest: Is it possible that a universally accepted religion could arise out of nothing? or, Do not the intense feelings of enthusiasm which the first disciples of Jesus felt towards their teacher, and which they passed on to their disciples, and which dominated the entire world—do not they constitute irrefutable evidence that Jesus was an altogether exceptional being?—Graetz would point to Shabbathai Zevi who, during his lifetime secured far more followers than did Jesus, including many Christians and Moslems, and who, even at the time when Graetz wrote, still had followers in Poland and Turkey.[41]

The deaf, the blind and the sick whom Jesus healed, and those whom he raised from the dead, were, in actual fact, simply the ungodly and sinful, the publicans and harlots, to whom he preached the living words of God and showed a new way of life which should cure their spiritual defects and revive their dead souls by this loftier moral code. But Graetz would not deny that Jesus did, literally, engage in healing: he healed such as were afflicted with nervous illnesses and hysterical women, and such as, in those days, were supposed to be possessed by an evil spirit; and this he did through his spiritual influence.[42] The proof of this is to be found in the fact that his disciples also practised the driving out of evil spirits and uttering incantations over a snake-bite.[43]

This spiritual healing was the one thing in Jesus that was new; in all other respects Jesus was "a teacher honoured in his own circle just as Hillel was in his circle; his 'sayings' or *Logia* were impressed upon the memories of his disciples and they tried to hand down what he taught to the coming generation."[44] In his religious beliefs Jesus approached closer to Hillel than to Shammai—e.g. in permitting the sick to be healed on the Sabbath; and it was from Hillel that he inherited the great saying: What is hateful to thyself,

[39] *Sinaï et Golgotha*, pp. 314-318; 400-402; 416-417.

[40] *Op. cit.* 392-407.

[41] *Op. cit.* pp. 376-377. It never, however, occurred to Graetz to maintain that Shabbathai Zevi also was a great man; but only that the time and the means did not fall out well, and because of a certain flaw in his character—his love of power and pleasure—he was unfitted to give a new teaching suited to his contemporaries; and such was not Shabbathai Zevi's main purpose, but only to gain an earthly kingdom which was just as impossible then as in the time of the Romans in Judæa.

[42] Cf. 312-3 and 321-2.

[43] See above, p. 40.

[44] *Op. cit.* p. 383.

do not unto thy neighbour; this is the whole of the Law. But Hillel never expelled evil spirits and no miracles are recorded in connexion with him.

Such are the opinions of Graetz as given in his French book. In his "History of the Jews" (III ch. 11) he puts forward the same views in briefer form, so that chapter need not be dealt with here. Worth notice, however, is the accurate sense of proportion and the excellent "tact" shown there in his estimate of Jesus: he did not multiply words unnecessarily, but offered his readers a *multum in parvo*. Neither did he forget that whoever depreciates Jesus thereby depreciates Judaism itself, since that was the source of Jesus' teaching.

Furthermore, Graetz could not see in Jesus' sayings or in his whole ministry any protest against contemporary Judaism, nor, on the whole, did he perceive any strong intention or desire to alter any of its fundamental principles. Hence, according to this chapter of the "History," as far as the ceremonial laws are concerned, Christianity arose out of nothing at all: it arose solely in consequence of the political oppression under the Romans, ably described by Graetz, and as a result of the messianic hopes which grew stronger at that time owing to that oppression.

The second book solely concerned with Jesus and written by a Jew is "As Others Saw Him: A Retrospect: A.D. 54," London, 1895.[45] It is in the shape of a narrative written down for the sake of a Greek physician in Corinth by a Jewish scribe in Alexandria, Meshullam ben Zadok, who had lived in Jerusalem throughout the whole of Jesus' ministry and had seen personally what Jesus did and what was done to him in Jerusalem, although he knew nothing of the Galilæan period. After relating the incident of the driving out of the money-changers from the Temple, and giving briefly the rumours of Jesus' origin and early life, the writer reports a discourse which Jesus gave in a Jerusalem synagogue, a discourse founded almost entirely on the uncanonical sayings known as *Agrapha*;[46] and he offers this teaching as drawn from the Hebrew book entitled "The Two Ways," which contains the ethical teaching of Hillel (pp. 51-56). He then gives the story of the woman taken in adultery[47] and that of the rich young ruler; he quotes Jesus' teaching about the greatest commandment, which is, in the author's opinion, Hillel's.

And then he gives a second discourse likewise based on uncanonical sayings, which the author employs in such a way as to show the difference between Jesus and the Prophets: they gave their message

[45] The book was published anonymously, but in the bibliography to the article *Jesus of Nazareth* in *J.E.* VII 160-166, the author is stated to be Joseph Jacobs. The views of the book under discussion form the basis of this article, and so that article need not be specially dealt with here.

[46] See above, pp. 65-66.

[47] See above, p. 69.

in the form "Thus saith the Lord," whereas he spoke in his own name (pp. 85-9; see also p. 202).[48] At a "Bar Mitzvah" feast (the occasion when a Jewish boy reaches the age of thirteen and a day, and is of an age to assume the responsibility of observing the Law), Jesus makes his harsh remarks about the "hypocrite Pharisees," found in Matthew xxiii.

But his host argues that hypocrisy and insincerity are not the outstanding characteristics of the Pharisees, that Hillel the Pharisee was very far indeed from preferring the outward observance of the ceremonial laws to purity of heart and love of mankind, and that the Pharisees themselves expressed great dislike of hypocritical Pharisees, including the type whose axiom was "What am I bound to do and I will do it," and those who were Pharisees only "out of fear," and that even among the Ebionites, with whom Jesus was so closely akin, there were many "who did not practise what they preached." To this Jesus replies that his strictures were aimed not at the true Pharisees but at the insincere among them (pp. 95-105).

Very many were induced to follow Jesus because they saw in him a saviour from the Romans whose yoke was pressing so hardly upon them and because they saw in this bondage an insult to the God of Israel, "the great, the mighty and the terrible;" but when Jesus bade them "give to Cæsar that which was Cæsar's" he entirely lost his popularity (pp. 157-160). For such a reason must we explain the crowd's demanding from Pilate to release to them not Jesus "bar Amma" (*i.e.*, son of the mother, hinting at the popular scandal about his origin), but Jesus "bar Abba" (*i.e.*, son of the father) who had rebelled against Rome and was therefore popular (pp. 192-195).

Jesus was a Jew in all his sayings and ways: he observed all the ceremonial laws; as a true Jew he looked upon God as his heavenly Father; he had compassion on the poor, helped the fallen, and rated the repentant more highly than the scrupulously pious. He even had the Jewish national defects: he never observed beauty in nature; he never smiled. He taught by tears, threats and reproofs.

In all this Jesus was most Jewish of Jews. But in two respects he differed from his nation and especially from the prophets: in the first place he did not speak as a messenger sent from God but as one who had power to command and teach his own views (see above); and, in the second place, he lacked patriotic feelings. He was a stranger to the nation in everything affecting their longings for freedom from Roman subjection. "Did he feel himself in some way as not of our nation? I know not; but in all ways we failed to know him." "In all his teaching he dealt with us as men, not as Jews." And this was the reason for his rejection and death: the soul of the people abhorred the "Son of Man" who felt no sorrow at the national sorrow (pp. 200-2, 210).

[48] See "Ahad ha-Am," Collected Works, IV 42-44.

The third book is Rabbi H. G. *Enelow*'s "A Jewish View of Jesus." New York, 1920. We get here Jesus the "Liberal." Jesus gave nothing that was not already to be found in Judaism, but he presented the old material in more striking fashion than did the sages of Israel, and in all his sayings he left the impress of a unique personality which moved him to embody his teaching in actual practice.

Therefore although the Jews cannot see in him anything divine (which would contradict the whole idea of Judaism), or even the Messiah (since the Jewish expectations were not fulfilled in him nor by his coming to the world), they should still look upon him as a great and exceptional Rabbi and teacher, who gave a new aspect to Jewish ideas and thereby influenced humanity more than any other great man among the Jews. This presentation of Jesus is virtually "Unitarianism."

There are three similar books on Christianity (and not solely on Jesus): one in German and two in English. The German work is that by Rabbi J. *Eschelbacher*, "Das Judentum und das Wesen des Christentums" (also translated into Hebrew: "Ha-Yahaduth u-Mahuth ha-Natsruth," ed. "Ha-Zeman," Wilna, 1911), a polemical work in defence of Judaism in retort to Bousset's book.

The second is that by C. G. *Montefiore*, "The Synoptic Gospels," 2 vols., London, 1909, a Jewish commentary on the Gospels which attempts to show, on the one hand, that much of what is in the Gospels comes also in the *Talmudic* literature, and, on the other hand, that the Gospels are generally superior to the *Talmud* and are Hebrew works which should be acceptable to Jews.[48a] It was this work which stirred up "Ahad ha-Am" to write the celebrated article "Al shte ha-s'ippim" (Collected Works, IV 38-58 [= *Ha-Shiloach* XXIII 97-111]), in which that distinguished author points out the distinctive features of Judaism and Christianity—how (a) Judaism is not bound up with any tangible personality, (b) the religious and ethical purpose of Judaism is directed towards society generally, and (c) the moral basis of Judaism is absolute justice and not compromise or asceticism.

Another rejoinder to Montefiore's book is G. *Friedlander's* "The Jewish Sources of the Sermon on the Mount," London, 1911. The writer shows with much learning that not only the Sermon on the Mount, but the entire Christian system (excluding its asceticism) is borrowed from the Old Testament, the *Book of Ben Sira*, the *Testaments of the Twelve Patriarchs*, *Philo of Alexandria* and the earlier portions of the *Talmud* and *Midrash*.

He shows further that Jesus himself was not consistent: he taught that men should not make long prayers, but himself prayed the whole night through; he taught that men should love their

---

[48a] See also his *Some Elements of the Religious Teaching of Jesus*, London, 1910.

enemies, and himself spoke in hatred of the Pharisees; he said "Judge not that ye be not judged," and himself judged all his opponents harshly; and other such examples might be adduced. The writer also argues that society and the state must collapse if men lived in accordance with the teaching of Jesus; but that Judaism was given to such as belonged to civilization, to nations and societies and states, that through it they might live and not die.

After Drews' "Die Christusmythe," (Berlin, 1909), which like Kalthoff's "Entstehung des Christentums" (1903), denied Jesus' existence, came G. *Klein's* "Ist Jesus eine historische Persönlichkeit?" Leipzig, 1910, showing that all ancient Jewish literature proves that Jesus was a real individual, though his portraiture had been more or less obscured by the Evangelists.

We have still to notice books by Jewish scholars which, though not exclusively devoted to Jesus and his teaching, give special attention to the subject.

Abraham *Geiger* devoted three lectures to Jesus and his disciples (Lectures 9-11) in his Lectures on the History of Israel, published in 1864 under the title "Das Judentum und seine Geschichte" (I. Abteilung: bis zur Zerstörung des zweiten Tempels. 2 Aufl., 1865, pp. 108-148), and like Graetz added a long appendix criticizing the works of Strauss and Renan (pp. 162-187). He agrees with Graetz in thinking that in Jesus' teaching "there is either nothing new or that what is new is put before us in a somewhat enervated form just as it originated during an enervated period" (p. 119).

But, unlike Graetz, he does not think that Jesus was an Essene or something approaching an Essene, but "a Jew, a Pharisaic Jew of Galilæan type, one who looked forward to the hopes held at the time and who believed that those hopes would be fulfilled in himself. He propounded nothing whatever that was new,[49] nor did he transcend the national limitations" (p. 117). Although, if our sources are to be believed, he was compelled to belittle this or that ceremonial observance if he found it a hindrance, yet he never doubted his earlier conception that the commandments were from God and that no jot nor tittle of the Law, of which they were part, should ever pass away (pp. 117-118).

But "as distinct from the Pharisees, he praised poverty and con-

[49] This, together with Geiger's remark (which Franz Delitzsch wrongly attributed to one of the assistants of Geiger's *Jüdische Zeitschrift*) that "when all was said and done Jesus did nothing at all" (*Jüd. Zeit.* X 1872, p. 156), aroused Delitzsch's indignation against Geiger and his associates for so grossly disparaging one whom hundreds of millions of every age had revered "and whose advent had unquestionably formed the dividing line between the two divisions of universal history" (*op. cit.* pp. 308-9). Geiger's reply (pp. 309-311) was that Christians had still more disparaged the sanctity of Judaism—a satisfactory enough retort to the social-religious side of Delitzsch's charge, but not to the scholarly historical side, *i.e.*, to the problem: How can a belief accepted by hundreds of millions of mankind arise from nothing?

tempt of this world, a contempt of all that material life had called forth, and he disliked sharing in the joy of this world's affairs" (p. 119). But this in itself did not constitute opposition to the teaching of the Pharisees nor a tendency towards Essenism—it was only the result of the bad conditions of the Jews under the harsh rule of the Procurators. The riddle—how a new faith was created by one who "propounded no new idea of any kind"—Geiger explained by the fact that Jesus during his lifetime had told his disciples that he was the Messiah, and that with him had begun the era of "the world to come" or the "new world."

He found men who believed this. After his death this belief was preserved and his disciples looked, from day to day, for the beginning of this new world. They were thus spiritually convinced that Jesus had risen again and would soon appear a second time. He may himself have believed that this new world, a wonderful world, should begin before he died; but after his death the belief was modified to the form just described. And this is the one certain thing that we know of him, a thing quite sufficient to account not only for his appearance but also for its consequences.

This historic fact can neither be denied nor weakened; but nothing more may be added to it, since apart from it we know nothing for certain (pp. 180-181). Geiger differs from Graetz in thinking that Mark's Gospel approaches nearest the truth, though each of the Gospels is full of late tendencies (p. 118). Geiger's criticism of the lives of Jesus by Renan and Strauss is very shrewd and convincing, and more profound than that of Graetz.

Almost diametrically opposite to the views of Graetz and Geiger are those put forward by M. *Friedländer* in the long chapter devoted to the subject in "Die religiösen Bewegungen innerhalb des Judentums im Zeitalter Jesu" (Berlin, 1905), pp. 314-341. Both here and in his other books ("Zur Entstehungsgechichte des Christentums," Wien, 1894; "Das Judentum in der vorchristlichen griechischen Welt," 1897; "Der vorchristliche jüdische Gnostizismus," 1898; "Der Antichrist," 1902), he puts forward the opinion that the teaching of the Pharisees was narrow-minded, superficial and atrophied as compared with Alexandrine Judaism, which was broad, universal and freed from the shackles of the ceremonial laws.

In Palestine itself there was an opposition to the Pharisees, maintained by such men as the writers of apocalypses like the *Book of Enoch*, who carried on the tradition of the Wisdom Literature (Job, Ecclesiastes, the *Wisdom of Solomon*, etc.), and in their beliefs about the Messiah and his adversary Azazel, Belial-Samael (the new culture), were influenced by Hellenistic literature and especially the Sibylline Oracles (see especially pp. 289-314). These apocalyptists filled the rôle of popular prophets ("Volkspropheten"), prophets of the "Am-haaretz," the unlettered class, who were hated and neglected by the Pharisees (pp. 22-77, 78-113); both John the

Baptist and Jesus were of this same type of popular prophets (pp. 98-113).

Friedländer finds two stages of development in Jesus' views on the ceremonial laws and in his personal consciousness. At first he favoured the ceremonial laws if only they were observed with a proper intention; then he rose in opposition only against insincere Pharisees, the "street-corner Pharisees," the more disreputable among them, whom the *Talmud* itself blames and dubs, "the plague of Pharisees;" not till later times did the Evangelists generalize Jesus' strictures and repeat them as though they were aimed at the Pharisees as a whole (pp. 227-230; 316-320).

In the later period, however, of Jesus' ministry he tended to set aside the ceremonial laws, because he had become influenced by Hellenistic Judaism through the medium of the Palestinian apocalypses. And since he perceived more and more clearly the harm caused by Pharisaic literalism, there grew up in him, quite unwittingly and without any break in the unity of his own personality, the tendency to replace the system of the ceremonial laws by a more ethical system—the antithesis of the Pharisaic system and more akin to that of the Palestinian apocalyptists, the popular prophets, akin also to the systems of Philo and of the Essenes, the same Essenes who, according to Friedländer, had been materially influenced by Jewish-Hellenistic philosophy, and who, in their turn, exercised a certain influence on John the Baptist, Jesus and the Nazarenes (pp. 114-168; 321-2, 332).

A similar development, still leaving his personality intact, is also recognizable in Jesus' personal consciousness: at first he only thought of himself as continuing the work of John the Baptist, and only later felt within himself that he was the Messiah, the religious reformer and saviour of the world (pp. 322-323). He was unable to preach to the Gentiles and so restricted his teaching to the Jews. But his terrible death acted as a stimulus which resulted in his teaching being spread by Paul among all the Gentiles, and in himself being accepted as the saviour of the world (pp. 326-327).

In any case Jesus perfected the prophets' universalistic teaching, ridding their expectations of all that savoured of "national limitations and political hopes" and wholly spiritualising them (p. 335). The love of God, as taught by him, was personal in the sense that it was a cleaving to the living God, and impersonal in the sense that it was not bound up with personal inclinations (pp. 334-336). He did not insist on asceticism but only allowed it to those who could choose it in the proper spirit (pp. 336-338). The primary importance of his teaching lies in his directing his chiefest care to individual piety and combining it with the universal faith in a universal Godhead (pp. 338-339).

In his use of the Gospels Friedländer makes no distinction as a rule between the three Synoptists; if he has any preference it is for Matthew, or even Luke, rather than Mark, since those two are more akin in spirit to Hellenism, so favoured by him. For this reason he sometimes even uses the Fourth Gospel. Speaking generally he places no pedantic stress on the criticism of the ancient sources, particularly of the Gospels; he considers that "every branch of Judaism until the period after the Apostles, was remarkable for the reverence which it paid to tradition," and no matter how much the sages of Israel might wish to get rid of certain books, as a rule they dared not do so, and so they would certainly not dare to make changes in them, or additions or omissions (*Vorwort*, p. xxiv).

In conclusion four other books may be passed in review, written by converted Jews, and possessing some originality in contents or language.

Alfred *Edersheim,* who became a Christian in 1846 at the age of twenty-one, and acted for some time as a missionary in Jassy, Roumania,[50] wrote (besides other books bearing on our subject, such as "Sketches of Jewish Social Life in the Days of Christ," "The Temple: its Ministry and its Services," London, 1874), "The Life and Times of Jesus the Messiah," 2 vols. London, 1883. This large work, consisting of more than fifteen hundred pages, passed through five editions during its author's lifetime, and a twelfth edition (London, 1906) now lies before the present writer. It is in the highest degree conservative: all the miracles, even the raisings from the dead, are accepted by him as trustworthy facts.[51]

Whatever the Gospels record, he accepts as historical, though he gives unscientific reasons for some of the stranger stories.[52] He makes no use whatever of Gospel criticism: he prefers no single Synoptist to another, and treats the Fourth Gospel as wholly historical and in no way differentiates it from the Synoptists. He says in his introduction that it was not his intention to write a Life of Jesus, since the material in the Gospels was not enough for a biography in the true sense, nor, indeed, did the Evangelists write their Gospels as essays in biography;[53] his book is, rather, more or less a commentary on the four Gospels.[54] Yet he gives in detail all the events of Jesus' life as recorded in the Gospels, and he does this in the most naïve way: what is lacking in Mark he fills in from Matthew, Matthew he supplements from Luke, and Luke he supplements from the Fourth Gospel, and vice versa.

It is a curious "harmony of the Gospels"—the heaping up of narrative and legend. Occasionally he finds a "reasonable" cause why one Evangelist omits something recorded by another, but usually he refrains from searching for such reason, since he holds that we

[50] An account of his life may be found in his posthumous autobiography, *Tohu va-Bohu,* London, 1890. It is given briefly in *J.E.* V 39.
[51] *Op. cit.* I 138-143, 150-159, 558-560, 627-634, II 308-326, 623-629, etc.
[52] *E.g.,* the coming of the Magi, I 202-216.
[53] Preface to First Edition, p. vii.
[54] *Ibid.,* p. xiv.

cannot know the real reason why any particular Gospel was composed, and such reason may well have induced the omission in one Gospel of what actually occurred and is recorded in another Gospel whose object was different (II 312). Thus Edersheim's treatment of the events in Jesus' life has no scientific value, in spite of his close acquaintance with the labours of his predecessors and his "reasonable" objections to their arguments.

Yet it has a value of another sort, for we find in it (and also in his other book, "Sketches of Jewish Social Life") reliable pictures of the social life (and, to a certain extent, of the economic life) of the Jews of the time of Jesus.

Here Edersheim's intimate knowledge of Jewish literature stood him in good stead. The reader who wishes to know what was the condition of the family, the society, the village, the town, the state, child-education, labour, agriculture, dress, etc., may learn about them from Edersheim; the detail may be insufficient, but the information is there to a far greater extent than in any other "Life of Jesus." For this reason the book repays attention.

But, on the other hand, there are many things which detract from the value of his description of the spiritual life of contemporary Judaism. The main reason is that Edersheim could not forget his former avocation of missionary, and he finds himself incessantly bound to emphasize the superiority of Jesus' teaching over that of the Pharisees (which he calls "traditionalism").

With this purpose before him he paints the teaching of the Pharisees in the blackest possible colours. Occasionally he lets fall words in praise of Judaism, but even then he tries to bring out the fact that the teaching of Jesus surpassed it in every respect.[55] He is, for example, well aware that without the ceremonial laws of the written *Torah* monotheism could not have survived, and that in order that Israel should not become sunk in the degraded state of the ancient world it was essential to mark out the distinctions between Israel and the Gentiles (I 3) ; but he will not extend the same comprehension to the ceremonial laws of the unwritten *Torah*.

Yet that is not the only drawback of the book. It contains three crude errors into which virtually all Christian scholars have fallen, though their ignorance is more pardonable than is his.

In the first place he disregards the fact that the *Talmud* in its Halakhistic portions is not only a religious but a legal code ; and in a legal code legislators are compelled to deal carefully with the tiniest details. Therefore the traditional laws about Sabbath observance (which he gives in a special appendix, II 777-787, in the greatest detail to show how petty and narrow were the religious ideas of the "Rabbis"), were not so terrible ; they were religious *laws*, and it is the nature of laws to go into detail ; and here, as in all that has to do with jurisprudence, formality and "casuistry" are unavoidable.

[55] See, *e.g.*, what he says about Hillel, I 128-129.

In the second place he disregards the fact that the *Talmud* in its Haggadistic portions is not only a religious book but also, and primarily, a romantic and poetic book, a collection of folklore where curious and extravagant legends are sure to find place. To quote the curious legend in *Baba Metzia* 80a (about the dispute which Rabba bar Nahmani decides between God and the heavenly beings, I 409-410), and the Haggadistic fancy that the God of Israel studies the Scriptures by day and the *Mishna* by night, and wears the praying-shawl and phylacteries—as proving the pretentiousness of the Rabbis, is futile (II 15-16, I 144n).

In the preface to the Second and Third Editions (pp. xvii-xx) he is at pains to defend himself against suspicion of antisemitism, and he insists that nothing which he quotes from the *Talmud* or *Midrash* can supply the antisemites with material for attacking the Jews, for three reasons: (a) the tirades in the *Talmud* and *Midrash* against foreigners have no bearing on Christians, but only on heathen persecutors of the Jews whom the Jews naturally hated; [56] (b) the age, the place and the causes should be borne in mind, and as modern Calvinists are not to be blamed because their founder, Calvin, burnt Michael Servet, so modern Jews are not to be blamed for the bitterness of Jews many hundreds of years ago against foreigners; and (c) modern Jews do not abide by the antiquated ideas of the *Talmud*, but their ethical standard is high. As to the claim that every foolish remark in the *Talmud* is counterbalanced by a wise one, he replies that his object was not to submit stray remarks and ideas of the Rabbis but their general teaching and ideals (p. xix).

But it is precisely his own offence that he does *not* bear in mind "the age and the place," and the "general teaching and ideals" of the Rabbis, of Pharisaic Judaism. Had he done so, so many of the laws and definitions and foolish legends would not have struck him as so ridiculous, just as he is far from finding cause for ridicule in the Gospel story of the driving out of the unclean spirits and their entering into the swine. "Stray remarks and ideas" out of the *Talmud* are precisely the things which he is able to regard as foolish and even gross, and it is just "the general teaching and ideals" of the *Talmud* which created the spiritual environment in which could be born a man of such moral calibre and religious feeling as Hillel.

But from the standpoint of pure scholarship, worse than the preceding two errors is the third error, common to all Christian scholars who have written on the period, and also to nearly all Jewish scholars as well: namely, that they make no distinction between the really ancient sources for Pharisaic Judaism and those which are relatively late.

Any one adducing arguments about the views of Jews con-

---

[56] This case for the defence of the ancient Jews he refers to again at the end of his seventh chapter (I 89-92), where he describes the animosity which the *Talmud* authorities bore to the Gentiles.

temporary with Jesus from the sayings of the *Amoraim* or from a late *Midrash* like *Pirqe d'Rabbi Eliezer* (as does Edersheim in describing the Messianic ideas of the Jews, *Appendix* IX, II 710-741, and also I 160-171), might just as well adduce proofs from Sophocles or Euripides as to the beliefs prevalent in the time of the Homeric epics, or even from the early Christian Scholastics as to the beliefs of Jesus. This serious defect—to which we shall find reason to refer constantly—detracts from the worth of Edersheim's work in spite of all its care and detailed knowledge.

The reverse of Edersheim's book in all that concerns the estimate of Judaism in the time of Jesus is Daniel *Chwolsohn's* "Das letzte Passamahl Christi und der Tag seines Todes," St. Petersburg, 1892 (2nd edition, unchanged, but with much additional matter at the close of the book, Leipzig, 1908). The book is mainly devoted to a single problem in the history of Jesus: how to harmonize John's statement—that Jesus was crucified on the eve of Passover which fell on the eve of a Sabbath, and that he ate the Passover on the thirteenth of Nisan—with that of the Synoptists, that Jesus was crucified on the first day of Passover, also falling on the eve of a Sabbath, and that he ate the Passover on the fourteenth of Nisan.

But in the course of his argument the author touches on many important questions bearing on Jesus' connection with the Pharisees, and the connection of the Sadducees with Jesus and the part played by the Sadducees and Pharisees in his death; [57] he also touches on the value of the *Talmudic* literature towards the understanding of the Gospels.[58] In Chwolsohn's opinion, Jesus throughout behaved as a true Pharisee and observed all the ceremonial laws in accordance with Pharisaic teaching. It was not the Pharisees but the Sadducees and Boethuseans who were debased (Annas and Caiaphas, as we know, were of the House of Bœthus).

"Jesus said and taught nothing to which the true Pharisees could not have subscribed, and did nothing with which they could find fault" (note 2, pp. 95-96). "If cast in such a form that their creator was not discernible, the collection of Jesus' sayings and teachings would be regarded by every pious Jew as an excellent manual of morals" (p. 88). The Jew was accustomed to the expressions "Our Father, our King" (אבינו מלכנו), "Our Heavenly Father" (אבינו שבשמים), and "Ye are the sons of the Lord your God" (בנים אתם לה' אלהיכם), which is an expression occurring in the *Torah* and of a piece with "Sons of God" (בנים למקום) employed in the *Talmud*.

If Jesus complains against insincere Pharisees (Matthew xxiii),

[57] Chwolsohn's excellent notes (p. 73-74) about the *Talmud* tirades against the unlettered "Am-haaretz" deserve attention; they are a satisfactory reply to the attacks and arguments of Friedländer in his *Die religiösen Bewegungen*, pp. 78-113.

[58] *Ibid. Appendix*, pp. 67-125.

so also does the Talmud (R. Yehoshua ben Hanania, c. 130-150 C.E., in *Sota* III 4) when it speaks of "the plagues of Pharisees," and in the well-known *Baraita* (*Sota* 22b and parallel passages), when it mentions the seven kinds of Pharisee (supposed by Chwolsohn to be very early since the popular names there used are not understood by the *Amoraim:* p. 117), and in *Pesikta Rabbati* (§22), which refers to insincere Pharisees who cloaked themselves in praying-shawls and phylacteries only to practise deception; Jesus, too, only spoke against the more degraded and insincere among them.

The transcriber of the Gospels in many instances confused the word γραμματίςε (scribes), replacing it by Φαρισαῖοι (Pharisees) or adding this word after it, when actually the former word was intended to denote the "scribes" of the Sadducees (p. 113). "The just shall live by his faith" is in the *Talmud* (*Makk.* 23b-24a), also the foundation of the whole Law, and "what is hateful to thyself do not unto thy neighbour," or "thou shalt love thy neighbour as thyself," is the whole of the Law also according to the view of Hillel (*Shab.* 31a).

In his practical manner of life Jesus also conducted himself like a Pharisee: in breaking of bread, in careful observance of the blessing of the bread and wine, and even in the matter of the Sabbath day's journey; he eats the Passover and says the "Great *Hallel*." When he allowed his disciples to pluck ears of corn on the Sabbath, he defends it by proofs drawn from David's eating of the altar-bread, and from the offering of sacrifices in the Temple on the Sabbath, and said that "the Sabbath was given for man and not man for the Sabbath" (Matt. xii. 1-5, Mark ii. 23-27); and in exactly the same way the Pharisees also proved by this *a fortiori* argument, from the Temple and David's eating of the altar-bread (in *Y'lamm'denu*, Yalkut II §130), that the needs of life override the Sabbath restrictions (פקוח נפש דוחה שבת); and they also said (the early Tanna R. Shimeon ben Menassia, in *Mechilta* on Exodus 31, 14, beginning of §1): "The Sabbath was given for you: ye were not given for the Sabbath" (p. 92).

In matters of divorce Jesus is nearer to the School of Shammai than to that of Hillel, which made divorce easier. His prohibition of swearing, even on the truth, agrees with the *Talmud's* "a righteous yea and a righteous nay" (*Sifra*, "Qedoshim" 8, 7 and parallels). His disciples attached little importance to the washing of hands; but this was not such a serious offence and, it would appear, the Jews generally in the time of Jesus acted in the same way, since at first the proviso applied only to the eating of sacrificial offerings. What Jesus says against the Pharisees about the "tradition of the elders" and vows (Mark vii. 11, Matt. xv. 5) is directly contrary to the injunctions of the *Talmud*, and his remarks can certainly only apply to some single *Tanna* and his disciples, whose view, as being that of a single individual only, is not preserved in the *Talmud*. His views on forbidden foods (Matt. xv. 11-20; Mark vii. 15-23) cannot be taken literally, for if so, Paul would have relied on them when he did away with the ceremonial laws (so Graetz; see above, p. 110).

Thus Jesus' teachings and doings agree, almost entirely, with those of the Pharisees; and we actually see the Pharisees allowing him to teach in their synagogues and inviting him to their feasts, and he himself praises the words of one of them.

Why, then, could the Pharisees condemn him to death? A "beguiler," or "one who leads astray," or "a false prophet," is not guilty of death until he pervert someone to the extent of worshipping an idol, a thing impossible in Jesus (p. 88 n. 1).

His trial with all its injustice did not conform with the regulations of the Pharisees; and, in fact, there was not then a majority of Pharisees in the Sanhedrin. It was only the Sadducees—whose sentences were severe compared with those of the Pharisees ("Ant." XIII x 6; XXX ix 1; "Wars" II viii 14) and whose judges, because of their excessive harshness, were popularly called "robber judges" (dayyanē g'zēloth) and not "law-giving judges" (dayyane g'zēroth)— who, unaware of the spiritual character of his teaching, feared that Jesus as a Messiah might be a rebel and conspirator.

Therefore they condemned him to death by their severe laws during a hasty night sitting and even hired some of the crowd to clamour for his crucifixion (pp. 118-120, 124-125).

Chwolsohn believes that an Aramaic Gospel was the common source of the Synoptists (pp. 11-12). Since he considers that John and Luke still knew the Jewish Passover customs he concludes that there is no reason to date them later than 50-55 C.E. (p. 66); but elsewhere (p. 98) he hints that John is later than the others and that all were influenced by the development of early Christianity. Mark must have used earlier sources since he attributes to Jesus matters not far removed from the Pharisaic customs and from the spirit of contemporary Judaism.

Chwolsohn makes a specially noteworthy point that, rightly to understand Pauline and post-Pauline Christianity, a knowledge of the *Sibylline Oracles,* Philo and Greek literature generally, is most important; but to understand Jesus, far more important are the Prophets and the *Talmudic Haggada* which are even more valuable than the early *Palestinian Apocrypha* and *Pseudepigrapha,* for Jesus was not affected by Greek literature and hardly at all by the uncanonical books. We will return later to these important points.

Chwolsohn also wrote "Ueber die Frage, ob Jesus gelebt hat," Leipzig, 1910, in reply to Drews' "Die Christusmythe," and defended Jesus' existence by proofs drawn from early Jewish literature and the Gospels, and the Jewish and Palestinian spirit which pervades the latter.

Entirely bereft of scientific worth is *De Jonge's* "Jeschua, der klassische jüdischen Mann: Zerstörung des kirchlichen, Enthüllung des jüdischen Jesus-Bildes," Berlin, 1904. De Jonge was a converted German Jew who, after three years, tried to return to Judaism, but with "evangelical reservations" (mit evangelischen Vorbehalten); the Berlin Rabbis refused him. He tries to prove that Jesus and his disciples were true, proper Jews.

He holds that Jesus was a pupil of Hillel and did not hate worldly life or culture or even rightly acquired riches. Jesus was not the Messiah, but more than the Messiah. De Jonge is independent of scientific proof: whatever contradicts his view is an early Christian forgery; he prefers the Fourth Gospel to the Synoptists, though only where it is more in accord with his purpose of describing Jesus as almost divine.

The last book is by Paul *Levertoff*, in Hebrew,[59] "Ben ha-Adam: hayye Yeshu ha-Mashiach u-po'alâv," ed. *Eduth l'Yisrael* (a missionary society), London, 1905 [Cracow]. The author is a converted Russian Jew who became a missionary. In his introduction he indulges in argument against "Ahad ha-Am," Dr. Neumark, S. J. Horowitz, Dr. Bernfeld and the present writer, because in their articles in *Ha-Shiloach* on the "Nature of Judaism" they did not perceive the advantages of Christianity.

The plain purpose of the writer (in spite of what he says to the contrary in his Preface, p. xxi) is to win adherents to Christianity from among Russian Jews who read Hebrew; and such a book is not to be relied upon for objective and single-minded scholarship. The author skilfully refrains from imposing upon us most of the unacceptable miracles; he follows (as he tells us in his preface) P. W. Schmidt's excellent "Die Geschichte Jesu, erzählt [without "erläutert"], save that he conceals a few miracles and some missionary teaching in an account of natural facts (obviously not always explained as they should be) and a presentation of the ethical teachings of Jesus. . . . And this has been the *only* work about Jesus in modern Hebrew literature!

---

[59] There is another work in Hebrew: *Helqat m'hoqêq*, Cracow, 1893, by Gershom Bader, who pretends to publish it from some manuscript; but it is really based on the old *Tol'doth Yeshu*, supplemented by a few mangled statements from the Gospels. It has no scientific and very small literary value.

VII. SUMMARY OF CONCLUSIONS

The last section has been deliberately, and, it might seem at first sight, unnecessarily prolonged. But apart from the urgent need of giving Hebrew readers (who have in their language no scholarly book on the subject) a true idea of the far-reaching and difficult work carried out by hundreds of scholars of all nations in the last hundred years and more, in an effort to dissipate the most of religious prejudice which had obscured the earliest sources of Christianity and the life of its Founder,—apart from this, only after an account of the main ideas about the Gospels and Jesus could we lay down what we think to be the right conclusions arrived at by that wide research, and start our account of the life of Jesus untrammelled by any need of entering into any controversy on particular points. The points of view which we have accepted and which will receive further confirmation in the course of the book, are as follows:

The Fourth Gospel is not a religio-historical but a religio-philosophical book. It was not composed until about the middle of the second Christian century, at a time when Christians were already distinct from Jews (at least as a special party) with no dealings with official Judaism, and after many pagans had been converted. The object of the Fourth Gospel is to interpret Jesus as the *Logos*, the "Word of God," in the extreme Philonic sense, and it therefore passes over such details in the life and death of Jesus as would appear too human. It may well include a few historical fragments handed down to the author (who was certainly not John the disciple) by tradition; but, speaking generally, its value is theological rather than historical or biographical.

Of the Synoptic Gospels, the earliest is Mark, composed near the time of the Destruction of the Temple (c. 66-68), possibly by one of the disciples of Mark, the disciple of Peter. He drew from an early Aramaic (or Hebrew) source of which the author (according to Papias: see above, p. 74) was the real Mark, the disciple of Peter, and which contained both narratives and discourses, though few of the latter. These Aramaic (or Hebrew) sources were written and not oral, thus accounting for the many similarities: the important differences are to be accounted for by a difference of source, and the slighter differences by the fact that ancient writers were not pedantically exact in quoting from other books or even from their own. Slight differences in figures and words exist, for example, in abundance in Josephus' writings, even where we see plainly that the author had only one source. From such Aramaic sources is derived the Aramaic passage occurring in the story of Imma Shalom and the neighbouring "philosoph"—a story of an event which happened immediately after the destruction of the Temple (see above, p. 44).

Following Mark came Matthew, founded on the present Mark and an Aramaic (or Hebrew) collection of sayings (*Lógia*) which, according to Papias, were written down by Matthew the Publican, the most educated of the disciples; it also contained further oral traditions current among the first and second generations of the disciples. It was composed after the Destruction and near the end of the century by a disciple of Matthew for the sake of Jewish Christians, whose one interest was to find scriptural warrant for all the doings of Jesus and to accentuate his divine origin, because the attitude of the Jews to Jesus was contempt rather than hatred.

Hence this Gospel reveals a strong dislike of the Jews and especially of the Pharisees: for sects of the same religion which still exist in close relations with each other, regard each other with a hatred and jealousy far greater than is the case with sects which have severed all bonds of union.

The last of the Synoptists is Luke, the physician, the disciple of Paul. By his time many accounts of the life of Jesus had been written and his object was to pick out what was most acceptable and to retell it in orderly fashion (as he himself explains in his preface). He had had a Greek education and he tried to give a historical cast to the narratives and even to the legends, and to this end he associates discourses with events, and to the events he tries to apply a chronological framework.

By this time, Christianity was farther removed from Judaism than in the time of Mark and Matthew; hence he does not display the same bitterness towards Jews and Pharisees. A Greek atmosphere pervades the book and it forms a sort of bridge to the Fourth Gospel. It was written at the beginning of the second Christian century.

According to Papias (see p. 75) Mark, the disciple of Peter, wrote "accurately all that he remembered of the words and deeds of Christ, but not in order." This lack of order survives in all the Gospels which used this early source. Therefore it is difficult to give a complete life of Jesus, not so much because of scarcity or credibility of material, but because we do not know the chronological order of his sayings or actions. The material was handed down by the Apostles as they recalled it at the moment, and this material was arranged later by their disciples, the Evangelists, according to their (the Evangelists') liking and religious aims (not, of course, deliberately, but because to them the chief object in writing was not historical or biographical, but religious).

But to cast wholesale doubt on the historicity of the Synoptic Gospels becomes more impossible the more widely we study all the branches of Judaism during the period of the Second Temple. Notwithstanding all the efforts of the authors of the Gospels to stress the great opposition between Jesus and Pharisaic Judaism, every step he took, everything he did, every word he spoke, all recall to us—chiefly by confirmation though sometimes by contradiction—the Palestine of his time and contemporary Jewish life and Pharisaic teaching.

It is no matter whether his acts, his parables or his arguments support or do not support some *Halakha, Haggada* or *Midrash:* in any case they cannot be understood without a knowledge of the Oral Law as it was in the days of Hillel and Shammai.

In consequence of the results of Gospel literary criticism, of study of the life of Jesus and of knowledge of contemporary Judaism, the mystical and dogmatic atmosphere which enveloped Jesus is removed, and we now know what in the Gospels to accept and what to reject, what is early and what is late, what the Evangelists unconsciously attributed to Jesus owing to their living under the influence of the post-Pauline Church, and what, still unconsciously, they have preserved of Jesus' national Jewish features.

Only after such a process of selection can we come to recognize the *historical* Jesus, the Jewish Jesus, the Jesus who could have arisen out of none other than Jewish surroundings, but whom the Jews, from certain historical and personal reasons which we shall understand later, could not receive as their Messiah nor his teaching as the way of redemption.

SECOND BOOK

THE PERIOD

GENERAL REMARKS

[Virtually all the books so far cited touch on the political, economic and religious conditions in the time of Jesus. We give here only the more important works which give special attention to the subject: (In Hebrew): Yitzhaq Isaac Halevy, "Doroth ha-Rishonim," III 1 (from the end of the Maccabæan period till the Roman Procurators), Frankfurt-a.-Main, 1906; Z'eb Yaabetz, *Tol'doth Yisrael*, pt. 5 (from Herod to the Destruction of the Temple), Cracow, 1904. (In German): H. Graetz, "Geschichte der Juden," III 1⁶, Leipzig, 1905; E. Schürer, "Geschichte des jüdischen Volkes im Zeitalter Jesu Christi," Bd. I-III, 4 Aufl. Leipzig, 1901-07; A. Schlatter, "Israels Geschichte von Alexander dem Grossen bis Hadrian," Stuttgart, 1900; J. Wellhausen, "Israelitische und jüdische Geschichte," 5 Aufl. Berlin, 1905. (In French): J. Salvador, "Histoire de la domination Romaine en Judée," Paris, 1847; E. Renan, "Histoire du peuple d'Israel," T. 5, Paris, 1893; J. Juster, "Les Juifs dans l'Empire Romain," T. 1-2, Paris, 1914.]

Before proceeding to the life of Jesus, a general idea must first be given of the period in which he was born and in which he lived and laboured, that is to say, the political, economic and religious conditions of Palestine and the Jews in the days of Jesus.

Some preliminary remarks are further called for:

(1) It is only possible here to give a *general* idea of contemporary conditions: to go into details would demand more space than is devoted to the entire life of Jesus. Also it would then have been frequently necessary to return to the same things in the course of the detailed events of Jesus' life and teachings, involving tedious repetition; conditions are treated in detail only when this is called for in Jesus' personal history.

(2) Without presuming to settle the vexed question: what is the foundation of history and what its superstructure, whether economic conditions are fundamental and the political and spiritual life merely matters built thereon (as the school of materialistic historians suppose), or whether, on the contrary, the essence of history is the political and spiritual life for which economic conditions are but a preparation—we think it right here to speak first of the political life and afterwards of the economic and spiritual conditions.

The political conditions of Palestine in Jesus' time were occasioned not so much by internal facts as by *external*, .e., by the forces of the Roman legions. Besides Judæa Rome had conquered innumerable other states having entirely different economic conditions; therefore economic conditions arising out of internal development were not the deciding factors in creating the political position which resulted from the intrusion of an external power. So a description of the political life precedes that of the economic and spiritual life.

(3) Those who write on the life of Jesus, or the history of Christianity, or what Christian scholars call "The History of New Testament Times," usually begin with the war of Antiochus, the dawn of the Maccabæan period, and end with the war of Hadrian, the revolt of Bar Kokhbah; and, certainly, for the right understanding of Christianity, to account for the internal development of Jesus' teaching and its external expansion from the time of Paul, a knowledge of the complete history of the Jews from Judas Maccabæus to Bar Kokhbah, is important.

But to understand the rise of Jesus and his teaching it is enough to have a thorough knowledge of the Herodian age, or at most of the period from Pompey's conquest till the Destruction of the Temple. It was not the might of the Maccabees nor their wars and victories which caused the appearance of the suffering Messiah, but the political collapse which began with Pompey's conquest and continued until the Destruction, a collapse which, in Herod's time, was masked with a veneer of pomp and splendour, but which, in the days of his sons and the Roman Procurators, was unmasked in all its dreadful reality.

Therefore we are here concerned merely with a general conspectus of the events immediately following the death of Salome-Alexandra (the queen Shelom-Zion), events which inevitably brought in their train an utter despair of political ambitions. We shall only make passing reference to the Maccabæan victories in the time of John Hyrcanus, Judas Aristobulus and Alexander Jannæus.

(4) In speaking of economic conditions we shall endeavour to restrict ourselves to facts bearing on the period between Pompey and the Destruction, and if facts are adduced from an earlier or later period these will only be those which, by their nature, are not subject to rapid variations (such as geography, climate and natural products). Unlike political conditions, which are influenced by external factors, economic conditions change but slowly; and in ancient times—and generally in the East—economic conditions are a more stable and persistent factor than in modern times and in European countries.

(5) In dealing with spiritual conditions we ignore those of the Hellenistic Jews, whether outside Palestine or within its borders, whether in Egypt or in Hellenized Palestinian towns. To understand Christianity, *i.e.*, the teachings of Paul and his successors, and to understand the victory and growth of Christianity during its first two hundred years, a knowledge of Hellenistic Judaism is very necessary since it, alone, accounts for the origin of the Trinity and

the "Word" as Son of God, and the introduction of Greek elements into the Jewish Nazarene system, as well as the wonderful expansion of the new faith. This last, especially, could never have been possible but for the adherence of large numbers of Hellenized Jews who had become far removed from their original Hebrew manner of life and knew nothing of the Hebrew language and its original literature.

But, on the other hand, the person of Jesus, his entire teaching and his works and life àre, from their advantageous or disadvantageous sides, wholly explicable by means of Hebrew, Palestinian Judaism alone—by the Judaism of the Scriptures and by the Judaism of the Pharisees and early *Tannaim*, together with the *Palestinian Apocrypha* and *Pseudepigrapha* (excluding the *Hellenistic Pseudepigrapha*). This will appear in the account which we give of Jesus. This same fact was recognized by Chwolsohn, who, however, goes too far and excludes even the *Palestinian Apocrypha* and *Pseudepigrapha*.[1] Nothing whatever, therefore, will be said of Hellenistic Judaism since our concern is the history of Jesus, not of Christianity.

(6) It is also of paramount importance not to confuse periods. Christian scholars and also most Jewish scholars [2] are accustomed to describe the spiritual condition of the Jews in the time of Jesus not only on the basis of the writings of Josephus, but also on the basis of the Apocrypha and *Pseudepigrapha* and the *Talmudic* and *Midrashic* literature. And, indeed, it is not possible to avoid doing so. But at the same time it should not be forgotten that between Ben Sira and the *Midrash Ve-Yoshua* there is an interval of at least twelve hundred years, and that even from the time of Jesus and the completion of the *Talmud* there is an interval of seven hundred years.

It is impossible for ideas to remain stationary all that length of time. How could the religious and moral life rest unchanged for a thousand, or even five hundred years? To adduce evidence from the sayings of some Babylonian Amora as to the views of the Pharisees of Jesus' day is as valid as to adduce evidence from St. Augustine as to the views of Jesus; and to adduce evidence from such a late *Midrash* as the *Pesikta Rabbati*, or the *Midrash Va-Yoshua* about first century Judaism is tantamount to studying the ideas of Jesus in the writings of Thomas Aquinas.

It should be further borne in mind that the Destruction of the Temple, and especially the collapse of the Bar Kokhba rebellion, tore the very soul of the Jews and effected a complete breach in their religious and moral consciousness.

---

[1] See above, p. 123.
[2] An exception is the Jewish scholar, A. Büchler, who, in his writings which we have already cited (p. 106) repeatedly emphasises the marked difference between the ideas of the Jews before and after the Bar Kokhba revolt.

Yet another change came about owing to the transferring of the religious centre from Palestine to Babylon (after the time of Rab Yochanan). There we must, at all costs, avoid the error of depicting the spiritual conditions of Jesus' day in colours derived from late *Talmudic* literature.

Even the *Book of Ben Sira* should be employed with caution; for, in the first place, it is not consonant with the Pharisaic spirit, and, in the second, it is two hundred years too early (or even three hundred years, if, as some suppose, the book describes Simon the First); and in that interval there occurred such portentous events as the persecution of Antiochus Epiphanes, the Maccabæan War, the struggles between the Sadducees and Pharisees, the conquest of Palestine by Pompey, the rule of the Herods, the Procurators in Judæa, and such men as Simeon ben Shetah, Hillel and Shammai.

Yet we should avoid the other extreme which would ignore altogether such earlier sources as *Ben Sira*, or such later sources as the *Talmud*. After all, beliefs in ancient times never changed completely or easily gave place to new beliefs. *Ben Sira* was still in popular use as late as the tenth century, since it is often quoted in the *Talmud* and other Jewish literature and in Hebrew manuscripts unearthed from the Cairo Geniza; therefore his moral axioms must have been traditionally current among the people of Jesus' time and must have influenced him too.

As for the *Talmud*, it is possible to distinguish early ideas from late. Special attention must be paid to the teachings prior to Jesus and contemporary with him (such as the sayings of Simeon ben Shetah, Shemaiah and Abtalion, Hillel and Shammai); and it is also possible to take into account the teachings of the *Tannaim* who flourished immediately after the Destruction and until the time of Bar Kokhba: the majority of them had seen the Temple and were almost contemporary with Jesus.

Such were R. Yochanan ben Zakkai, R. Eliezer ben Hyrcanus, R. Yehoshua ben Hananiah, R. Eliezer ben Zadok, R. Ishmael ben Elisha, and even R. Akiba ben Yoseph. But the sayings of the *Tannaim* who had never seen the Temple, and of those who taught after the fall of Bar Kokhbah and after the transference of the religious centre from Judæa to Galilee—these may only be utilised when there is a probability that the late *Tanna* is quoting a religious opinion or tradition which he had received from his early teacher or which had been preserved by popular tradition from a distant past. Still greater care must be taken with the *Amoraim* (though they, too, make occasional use of earlier opinions). But as for the very late *Midrashim* it is always possible that they have been indirectly influenced by Christianity.[3]

The same applies not only to ideas and beliefs but also to religious

[3] See David Castelli, "Il Messia secondo gli Ebrei," Firenze, 1874, pp. 222-4.

customs and even to many of the rulings which we find in the *Mishnah* (and, needless to say, in the later literature as well). Many of these were not observed at all in the time of Jesus, and those which were in force were not then hedged about with the same precautions and restrictions, and so did not bear so heavily on the people. So long as the life of the state persisted it was not possible endlessly to increase the burdensomeness of the *Torah*.

This applies to the rulings relating to the uncleanness of the ordinary people (טומאת עם־הארץ),[4] and the laws dealing with capital punishment.[5] From among the undisputed capital sentences referred to in the *Talmud*, one only conforms to the rules laid down in the *Mishna* (the death-sentence on the son of Simeon ben Shetah), and that one itself is of doubtful historicity. It is, of course, easy to argue that in all the instances given it was a Sadducæan court of law which was responsible or (as when Yehudah ben Tabbai killed a false witness, or when Simeon ben Shetah hanged eighty women in Ashkelon) that they were temporary measures.[6] But while the Second Temple stood, the Sanhedrin which put to death one man in seventy years was not yet called "bloodthirsty" (חובלנית),[7] nor were the numerous and complicated rules (even those given in *Tractate Sanhedrin* alone) about capital punishment yet carried out in practice.

To take one example: according to this *Mishna*,[8] "even if the prisoner say, 'I have something to plead in my own defence,' they take him back to the Court—it may be even four or five times, if only there be some ground for his assertions." Obviously the meaning of the passage is that they may keep on bringing the prisoner back again till the very last moment.

Yet, side by side with this, we find a saying of R. Hisda, supported by an ancient *Baraita*, that "when a man is going out to be killed they suffer him to drink a grain of frankincense in a cup of wine to deaden his senses." . . . the *Baraita* adds, "Wealthy women of Jerusalem used to contribute these things and bring them."[9] This *Baraita* bears every sign of an early date in so far as it is describing a historic fact. If, however, the rule that the condemned man could return four or even five times to plead fresh points in his

---

[4] See Büchler, *Der galiläische Am-Haarez des zweiten Jahrhunderts*, Vienna, 1906, pp. 41-46.

[5] See *Haqiroth Talmudiyoth* by M. L. Lilienblum (Collected works, I 259-292).

[6] As does Yitzhaq Halevy in his *Doroth-ha-Rishonim*, I ii (Frankfurt-a.-Main, 1906). Thus he decides in every instance where it is impossible to explain away outstanding examples by abundant quotation or by crude attacks on the best Jewish and non-Jewish scholars. But it is impossible to argue with one who believes that the complete oral Law was finally complete in the time of Ezra and Nehemiah; his researches are simply a result of the necessity imposed on our orthodoxy of antedating everything.

[7] *Makkoth* I 10.

[8] *Sanh.* VI 1.

[9] *Sanh.* 43a.

defence, was in force at the time when the Jews could conduct capital cases, how was it possible to carry out the custom of giving him "a grain of frankincense to deaden his senses?"

The general conclusion to be drawn from the account of Josephus is that many of the regulations about the Sabbath, the behaviour of kings, the Sanhedrin, and the like, which occupy so many of the *Talmudic* tractates, were never in force such time as the Jews lived a more or less normal life, in their own land, and with a certain autonomy, at least in internal matters.[10]

The above points will be borne in mind in the following three sections. Every effort will be made to keep distinct early and late evidence, and also to distinguish between what was actually in force and what was only later enjoined by the *Talmud*, when independence was no longer possible, and when it did not matter if they ignored reality so long as they could fence in the Law and find support for their rulings from the Scriptures.

[10] This same idea—that we may not deduce from the *Mishnah* what were the legal punishments and judicial procedure of the law courts contemporary with Jesus—has recently been put forward also by a Christian scholar: H. Danby, *The Bearing of the Rabbinicial Criminal Code on the Jewish Trial Narratives in the Gospels* (*Journal of Theological Studies,* XXI 8, October, 1919, pp. 51-76).

I. POLITICAL CONDITIONS [1]

The Maccabæans built up a Jewish Palestine : the Herodian kings destroyed it.

Those Jews who had returned in the time of Cyrus and Darius and, later, in the time of Artaxerxes, only built up Judæa, a tiny Judæa which never equalled in extent or importance the pre-Exilic kingdom of Judæa. The coast towns were all of them Hellenic and developed into independent republics; even Ekron and Gezer only became part of Judæa in the Maccabæan period; the towns of Transjordania and Samaria were independent; Galilee ("Galilee of the Gentiles") was wholly separated from Judæa and its Jewish inhabitants were so few that, according to the *Book of Maccabees,* Judas Maccabæus transferred all the Galilæan Jews, their wives, children and belongings, to Judæa to save them from their foes.[2]

So insignificant a state was Judæa that it was indistinguishable within the great Persian Empire and even within the satrapy of Transpotamia (Syria). Those Greek writers who were contemporary with the Maccabees scarcely knew of the existence of Judæa : Syria they knew and Philistia they knew, but not Judæa. Herodotus, painstaking though he was, never mentions it and only refers to "the Syrians of Palestine" (οἱ Σύροι τῆς Παλαιστίνης).

Thus for three hundred and seventy-six years, from Zerubbabel to Jonathan Maccabæus (537-161 B.C.E.), Judæa remained a negligible state.[3] But after that, the Maccabees not only raised the small Persian province into an independent kingdom, but, out of Judæa, fashioned the Jewish Palestine. Jonathan annexed Ekron and the three Samaritan districts (νόμοι), Ephraim, Lydd and Ramathaim, while his brother Simon annexed Jaffa, Gezer and Beth-Zur; but those who were mainly responsible for extending Judæa into a Jewish Palestine were the three Maccabæans, John Hyrcanus, Judas Aristobulus and Alexander Jannæus. Jewish history has been written by Christians or by Jews who admired "culture" rather than politics, and they could not forgive the "lay" character of John Hyrcanus (at the

[1] For relevant literature see p. 129.
[2] I *Mac.* 5 23; see Schürer *op. cit.* 1⁴ 183-184. He, however, exaggerates the trustworthiness of the literal statements of the *Book of Maccabees;* there certainly were still many Jews in Galilee, and from them (and not from foreigners only) originated the populous Jewish settlement in Galilee (see B. Meistermann, *Capharnaüm et Bethsaïde,* Paris, 1921, pp. 256-7 n.). But the account has a certain value.
[3] On the state of Judæa throughout this protracted period see J. Klausner, *Historia Israelit,* I 130-300.

end of his reign), or of Judas Aristobulus, and specially of Alexander Jannæus; consequently Jewish history has never yet rightly appraised the importance of the victories of these three Maccabæans for the history of the Second Temple or the history of Israel as a whole—and perhaps for the entire history of humanity.

But for these victories a Jewish Palestine could never have come into being: the Jewish state must have remained a tiny district called "Judæa," lost within the greater expanse of Syria or the smaller expanse of "Palestine."

It was through these Maccabæans alone that the borders of Judæa were enlarged and "Philistia" became the "Land of Israel." John Hyrcanus conquered Samaria, Edom and part of Moab, and also, perhaps, Lower Galilee; he converted the Edomites to Judaism and settled Jews in Samaria and Moab. Judas Aristobulus, who assumed the crown but reigned only one year (conjointly with his brother Antigonus), succeeded during his brief reign in conquering and Judaising a part of Galilee—apparently Upper Galilee,[4] while Alexander Jannæus completed what his father John Hyhcanus, and his brother Judas Aristobulus, had begun. He conquered Gadara, Amathus, Pella, Dium, Hippos, Gerasa, Gaulana, Seleucia, the fortified city of Gamala across Jordan, and the towns of Philistia which had been completely Hellenised: Rafia,[5] Anthedon and Gaza.

Thenceforward Palestine ("Philistia") ceased to exist; it was called "Judæa" by non-Jews and "Eretz Israel" (the Land of Israel) by the Jews. But this did not content Alexander Jannæus: he subdued such parts of Moab as had not been conquered by his father, Gilead, and, before he died, laid siege to the town of Ragaba across Jordan, which place was captured immediately after his death. He thus enlarged the insignificant Judæa until its boundaries were virtually identical with those of David and Solomon.

These defeated cities were all compulsorily Judaised or repopulated by Jews, and those few places which refused to accept Judaism were mercilessly destroyed. From the moral side, needless to say, it is impossible to justify such forcible conversion at the hands of kings and rulers whose forefathers had endured such religious persecution, persecution which itself had compelled the Maccabæans to resort to arms. But only by such methods were the Jews able to secure their position beyond the confines of Judæa and lay the foundation of a considerable kingdom such as should stand in no fear of the heathen who surrounded these believers in the unity of God, and these who preserved the moral teaching of the Prophets. But for the heroism

---

[4] It is difficult to conclude from Josephus' remarks (*Ant.* XIII xi 3) referring to the conquest and conversion of "a part of the Ituræans" (quoting Strabo), that Judas Aristobulus, during his short and tragic reign, was able to conquer and convert the whole of Galilee, as Schürer supposes (I 275-6). But he certainly did this to part of Galilee (see last note but one).

[5] Written רפיח (with *heth*) and not רפיה (with *he*) as is customary on the ground of the Greek Ραφια. See Schürer II⁴ 108.

of the Maccabees the heathen must, finally, have swallowed up the Jews.

Only by such conquests and forced conversions could Judaism be established in its ancestral home and become a power, strong politically and socially, so that even the Romans, great conquerors though they were, were forced to take them seriously; otherwise the Jews must have remained a negligible quantity both in religion and civilization. Such, then, constitutes what the great Maccabæan conquerors accomplished for Judaism, and, therefore, for the whole of humanity as well!

But all that the Maccabæans built up was destroyed by the Romans and by Herod "the Great," who, by the help of the Romans, sat on the throne of Judæa.

The wife of Alexander Jannæus, Queen Shelom-Zion,[6] did not enlarge the Maccabæan realm, but neither did she cause it to decrease. In her reign matters remained stationary instead of advancing as they did, without exception, during the reign of all the Maccabæans who had gone before her.[7]

But the period of deterioration set in quickly. The sons of Alexander Jannæus and Shelom-Zion, Hyrcanus II and Aristobulus II, were rivals for the throne. When Hyrcanus the elder would have given way and remained content with the high priesthood, Antipater the Edomite, the father of Herod, appeared on the scene and persuaded him to withdraw from his conciliatory attitude. The king of Arabia, Aretas, first intervened and afterwards, the Roman Pompey. That year (65 B.C.E.), when Pompey's legate Scaurus intervened in the civil war, marked the beginning of the destruction of the Land of Israel.

For the next thirty years, until Herod sat on the throne of the Maccabees, we witness a series of long, sanguinary wars (65-37 B.C.E.). These wars, combined with Herod's tyranny and, after his death, the absolute power assumed in Judæa by the Romans, were instrumental in destroying the best powers of the Jewish nation, weakening it as a state, and stirring up both political Messiahs and that conception of a Messiahship "not of this world," which played on the popular mental confusion in Judæa and, as we shall see later, also affected the mind of Jesus in the earlier part of his career.

These wars are almost too many to enumerate; but each one entailed the death, in numbers great or small, of part of the nation.

In 65 B.C.E. Aristobulus was defeated by Aretas, king of Arabia.

---

[6] In *Talmudic* and later literature: Shelzion, Shelomzah, Shelomtu, Shalminon, Shelomith Alexandra. Cf. Derenbourg, *Massu Eretz Yisrael*, p. 51 n. 1, and Chwolsohn, *op. cit.* p. 14 n. 3; Schürer, I⁴ 287 n. 2.

[7] All the devious arguments alleged against this by Halevy, *Doroth Rishonim*, I iii pp. 505-646, are of no avail in face of this outstanding fact that in the time of Shelom-Zion the country of Judæa was in no way enlarged, whereas it was continually being increased during the time of her predecessors.

In this war Jews fell on either side since with Aretas were found Jews who championed the cause of Hyrcanus.[8] In 63 B.C.E. Aristobulus was obliged to accompany the army of Pompey in the latter's expedition against the Nabatæan Arabs, after which Pompey immediately attacked Jerusalem. The party of Hyrcanus opened the gates of Jerusalem to Pompey, but the followers of Aristobulus fortified themselves within the Temple Mount. Pompey besieged the Temple for three months, during which time more than a thousand Jews fell in its defence and in defence of such other parts of the city as had not been delivered up to him.

When Jerusalem was at last conquered (apparently on the Day of Atonement, or on one of the Sabbaths in the winter of 63), there began an orgy of slaughter. The fall of the Temple was signalized by the death of twelve thousand Jews.[9] The Romans thereupon commenced to "cut Judah in pieces:" they took from Judæa all that the Maccabæans had conquered. The latter had augmented Judæa into the Land of Israel: the Romans endeavoured to reduce the Land of Israel once more to Judæa. They took from the Jews all the coast towns from Rafia to Dor ($\Delta\tilde{\omega}\rho\alpha$) and the Hellenistic cities of Transjordania—Gadara, Dium, etc. They also tore away from Judæa Samaria and Beth-Shean (Scythopolis). They made Hyrcanus ruler of the remnant, depriving him of the title "king" and leaving him the high priesthood only. Of political rights nothing but a vague memory was left.

In 57 B.C.E., Alexander, the son of Aristobulus, who was being taken captive to Rome, escaped on the way and returned to Palestine. There still remained an affection towards the Maccabæans in the hearts of the healthier-minded among the people who still had a longing for freedom, and the fugitive quickly found a following of ten thousand armed footmen and fifteen thousand horsemen. With this army he captured the forts built by his predecessors, Alexandrion, Hyrcania and Machærus. He lost six thousand men in the battle against Gabinius' army (which contained Jews of Hyrcanus' party and Jewish adherents to Rome), and a large number of Jews in the Roman army must also have been killed.[10]

Again, when Alexander later escaped to the fortress of Alexandrion and was besieged by Gabinius, many Jews were killed.[11]

Finally, to wipe out all memory alike of the Jewish kingdom and of the remnants of Jewish political rights (which had dwindled down to the central organization of the single Higher Upper Sanhedrin in Jerusalem), Gabinius divided Judæa into five Sanhedrins, each to control a part of Judæa, namely, Jerusalem, Gezer, Hamath, Jericho

---

[8] *Antiq.* XIV ii 1.
[9] *Antiq.* XIV ii 4; *Wars* I vii 5.
[10] *Wars* I viii 3. *Antiq.* XIV v 2 states that 3,000 were killed and as many captured.
[11] *Wars* I viii 4.

and Sepphoris. Thus Jerusalem ceased to be the principal city and political centre, and became simply a chief provincial town. The government of the country was broken up into five fragments, according to the Roman axiom: *Divide et impera.*

But the wretched country had not seen the end of disturbances: the Maccabæans fought like wild beasts for their throne. In the year 56 Aristobulus—who had graced Pompey's triumphal procession—escaped from Rome to Judæa, and so great was the love of the Judæans for this heroic family that he at once found thousands of supporters. It is true that he also found opponents among the Pharisees, as is apparent from the *Psalms of Solomon* and from the fact that when the followers of Hyrcanus and Aristobulus came to settle their dispute before Pompey there also came "ambassadors from the people" asking that the powers of the High Priest be restored together with the theocratic order of pre-Maccabæan times.

But these "ambassadors from the people" were but the delegates of the priests and elders (חבר היהודים "The Association of the Jews") and the wealthy class: the mass of the people longed for the Maccabæan dynasty, and any scion of this family found thousands of followers prepared to die for him. So Jews in their thousands attached themselves both to Alexander, the son of Aristobulus, and to Aristobulus himself. So numerous were they that Aristobulus was compelled to dismiss thousands owing to his inability to arm them. Eight thousand only did he retain and with these went out to meet the Romans.[12] Five thousand fell before the Roman attack and a thousand more were killed when Aristobulus took up a fortified position in Machærus.

His son, Alexander, despite these heavy defeats, again revolted and collected a still greater army, so great, indeed, that even after part of them had deserted through the enticements of Antipater the Edomite, thirty thousand still remained with him, and of these no less than ten thousand fell in the battle against Gabinius near Mount Tabor.[13] Then Gabinius again changed the manner of government in accordance with the desires of Antipater.[14]

Even after Aristobulus had again been taken captive to Rome it was enough for a certain general named Pitholaus to summon the people in the name of Aristobulus, and there straightway gathered under his banner thirty thousand Jews. Thereupon Cassius, after defeating the Parthians, turned aside to Judæa, captured Tarichæa, killed Pitholaus and carried thirty thousand Jews into slavery (53-51 B.C.E.).

The civil war broke out in Italy in 49 and lasted about twenty years, from the day Julius Cæsar crossed the Rubicon until the death of Antonius (49-30). Within this period Palestine four times

[12] *Antiq.* XIV vi 1; *Wars* I viii 6.
[13] *Antiq.* XIV vi 2-3; *Wars* I viii 7.
[14] *Wars* I viii 7.

changed masters. Owing to the quarrel between Pompey and Julius Cæsar, Aristobulus was poisoned and his son, Alexander, put to death. After the battle of Pharsalis and Pompey's death (48) Hyrcanus (or rather Antipater, since Hyrcanus was but his tool) went over to the winning party, Julius Cæsar.

Antipater was ever one of those who support the stronger side, and now, to show his devotion to his new master, he did not spare his Jewish soldiers. In the year 47 he sent three thousand Jews to help Julius Cæsar, and in 45 provided a Jewish troop to support Cæsar's general, Antistius Vetus. For this Jewish blood he was well rewarded: Cæsar made him "Epitropos" (*i.e.*, Procurator or Vice-regent, a post to which, after Herod Roman officials were appointed), and Hyrcanus "Ethnarch" (Chief of the People, in Hebrew שַׂר־עַם־אֵל). But this latter was only for appearance' sake: the real government was in Antipator's hands and he appointed his son Phasael [15] Governor of Jerusalem and district, and his son Herod Governor of Galilee.

The father and his two sons governed tyranically. First they tried to free themselves from the danger which threatened them from the mass of the people who longed for Maccabæan rule. After the violent deaths of Aristobulus and his son Alexander the people no longer possessed strong Maccabæan leadership under which to rise up against the Romans and their Edomite minions; so they formed themselves into guerilla bands in the Jerusalem and Galilee districts, hiding in the mountains, and avenged the blood of the people that had been shed and the wounded national honour, on the Romans and their supporters who had betrayed Israel—the confederates of Antipater and his sons.[16]

Such patriotic "terrorists" are always forthcoming when a nation's sufferings reach the highest pitch and when this nation is unable forcibly to recover its freedom by open and decisive warfare. Such bitter-minded warriors are always extreme nationalists whose feelings overcome their intelligence, and who are prepared to accept martyrdom at all times on the national altar, their hearts burning with a sacred fire—the fire of national love—but who have no clear plan of rebellion. "Council and heroism for war:" "heroism" they have and to spare, but "council" they have none.

After long, sanguinary wars and disorders in the entire political life, desperation sets in under its two unhappy aspects: a feeble,

---

[15] Not "Phazael" (with *zain*) as it is usually written in Hebrew. In a Nabatæan inscription a son of Aretas, king of Arabia, is called "Phatsael" (see Schürer, I [4] p. 739 and n. 34). The meaning of Phatsael is "God has redeemed and brought relief" (like Padiel, Pedaiah), as in Ps. 144, 10: "Who freeth (הפוצה) David his servant from the evil sword." The *tsade* is transliterated by sigma in Greek, following the pronunciation of *tsad in* Arabic; hence the transliteration "Phasael."

[16] For greater detail see Graetz, III I [5] in many places.

passive despair ending in abject slavery and a mute acceptance of the new condition; and an active, bitter-minded despair, the despair of those who have nothing to lose, the despair of nervously disordered, excited fanatics, who put their confidence in a hoped-for miracle and are capable of the utmost cruelty in their bitterness of desperation. "Let my soul die with the Philistines," is their feeling as they carry out their atrocities, killing every stranger and every suspect they encounter, moved only by the fiery vengeance blazing within them, plundering and ravaging suspected villages and caravans to find themselves means of maintenance.

The foreign tyrants who hold by force the reins of government could only see, in these zealous patriots, brigands and bandits (like the *Boxers* in China, or the *Combitadjis* in Macedonia and Albania before the last war), and sometimes not without reason, for in their excessive lust for revenge they did not always distinguish the innocent from the guilty. Having no organization nor official status they were not soldiers of a regular army; they had no fixed control above them and often indulged in brigandage. Yet they were essentially the true defenders of the country, fighting a guerilla warfare for national freedom against the foreign conquerors and against the traitors from among their own countrymen who were subject to these foreigners and helped them.

The troops of Judas Maccabæus and his brother Jonathan were at first made up of such "sicarii." Of the same type were the "brigands" and "bandits" who, especially in Galilee, combined together in large numbers and, under the leadership of Hezekiah the Galilæan, became a "mighty host." This same Hezekiah and most of his band were killed out of hand by Herod without any trial, and this aroused against him the indignation of the people of Jerusalem who compelled the feeble Hyrcanus to summon Herod to stand for judgment before the Sanhedrin.

Herod came, supported by a large body of soldiers, and in all his behaviour during the trial showed himself not the culprit but the prince and ruler. The elders of the Sanhedrin were afraid of him and dared not condemn him to the death to which he was rightfully liable. One only among them, Shemayah or Shammai (Σαμέας),[17] dared to tell the truth openly to Herod, Hyrcanus and the Sanhedrin, with the result that Herod was compelled to escape lest the Sanhedrin, in the end, should take courage and pass the sentence which he had incurred (47-46 B.C.E.). This shows what was the actual nature of Hezekiah's "brigands" and what was the attitude adopted towards them by the people as a whole and also the leading people in Jerusalem.

It is important for our subject to take special note of the fact

---

[17] Scholars are still uncertain whether Σαμέας and Πωλλίων are Shemayah and Abtalion or Shammai and Hillel (see *Doroth Rishonim*, I iii 40-49), but the difference in the present instance is not material.

that these "brigand" bands were very numerous in Galilee, which was far removed from the political and religious centre, and that ignorance, disorder and injustice were there most frequent. Galilee was far more suited than Judæa for the nurturing of unruly, unbalanced zealots. This affords an explanation why Jesus (who, as we shall see later, regarded himself for a time as a Messiah of the usual type) should arise in Galilee rather than elsewhere, and especially in Galilee find disciples and admirers.

When Julius Cæsar was killed in 44 B.C.E., Judæa fell into the hands of Cassius who exploited it to the utmost. When he left, in the year 42, fighting broke out in the neighbourhood of Jerusalem which cost Phasael, the governor of Jerusalem and brother of Herod, the loss of many men. Mattathias (as he is called in his coins) Antigonus II, the second son of Aristobulus II and son-in-law of Ptolemy Menæus of Chalcis, then with the help of the latter and Marion, governor of Tyre, endeavoured to regain the throne of his fathers. He, too, immediately found himself surrounded by Jewish supporters. Herod went out to meet him and defeated him, and, naturally, not without bloodshed.

This defeat of a member of the Maccabæan family did not greatly please the people. They had wearied of the harsh rule of the sons of Antipater, and after Antonius and Octavius had defeated Brutus and Cassius (in the year 42), a Jewish delegation presented itself before Antonius at Bithynia in 41, and complained against Herod and Phasael. But Herod placated Antonius with a bribe and the delegation was unsuccessful.

In the same year the Jews sent a second delegation, numbering a hundred men, to Antonius at Daphne, near Antioch. They also complained against the two brothers. This again had no effect: Hyrcanus was afraid to say anything disparaging about Herod and Phasael, and the result of the good things which he told about them in Antonius' presence was that Antonius appointed them Tetrarchs, and Hyrcanus lost even the shadow of power that he once had.

Still the Jews did not rest content: the iron yoke of the Edomites was intolerable. They sent yet a third delegation to Antonius at Tyre, comprising no less than a thousand men who, in the name of the entire people, protested against the rule of Herod and Phasael. But Antonius was again heavily bribed by the brothers, and commanded the members of the delegation to be put to death! The delegates were aware of this terrible order, yet, even so, were unwilling to return before lodging their petition. The Romans then attacked them and many were killed, wounded or imprisoned, and the rest escaped home. On the people's protesting against this unheard of atrocity Antonius ordered the death of the prisoners! [18]

The following year the Parthians attacked Syria and Mattathias Antigonus tried to gain their help in restoring to him his ancestral

[18] *Antiq.* XIV xiii 2; *Wars* I xii 6-7.

throne with the promise (which either he did not fulfil or which his enemies invented against him) of a thousand talents of gold and five hundred women. The Parthians agreed for political reasons (since the Parthians were ever the enemies of Rome and its allies) and sent a large army to help him. But before this army arrived, Mattathias Antigonus found, as did all the Maccabæans, supporters from among the Jews.

These formed a formidable army and laid siege to Jerusalem. The followers of Herod and Phasael went to meet them, but most of the people within the city were on the side of the Maccabæans, and the fighting was carried on in the streets of Jerusalem itself. Those who favoured Antigonus burnt the supporters of Phasael and Herod in their houses, for which Herod took dire vengeance and put many of them to death. It was near the feast of Pentecost and crowds of people had come to Jerusalem and all joined themselves to the army of Antigonus. The Galilæans, too, supported Antigonus against Herod.[19]

When Phasael and Hyrcanus II were captured and Herod was forced to escape out of Jerusalem, so great was the Jews' hatred of him that, according to Josephus, "the Jews, more even than the Parthians, harassed him in his flight and fought against him for a distance of sixty-nine stadia from the city." [20]

Mattathias Antigonus was made king of Judæa—the last king of pure Maccabæan stock (40-37). Then began the fierce war between him and Herod which ended in the latter being made king. This war between the Jewish Maccabæan king supported by the Parthians and the Jewish Edomite king supported by the Romans, drenched the Land of Israel in blood and enfeebled it to an extreme limit. The Parthians looted Jerusalem and its neighbourhood as well as many other cities of Palestine, and Herod also plundered wherever he saw fit.[21]

Not only did Herod fight against the troops of Antigonus that were found in Galilee, but he also began to kill at sight those "brigands" and "sicarii," i.e., the zealot patriots who were hidden away in the caves and mountains. Even Josephus, despite the fact that he labels them as "brigands," thus describes their great moral courage: "A certain aged Galilæan, one of the fanatics, had seven sons, and when they would have obeyed Herod's command and left their cave, he stood at the mouth of the cave and killed them all one by one; and when Herod held out his hand and promised not to punish him, the old man only reviled the king for his Edomite origin and threw himself over the precipice." [22] So great was the hatred

[19] *Wars* I xiii 4.
[20] *Wars* I xiii 8.
[21] *Wars* I xv 6.
[22] *Antiq.* XIV xv 4-5; *Wars* I xvi 4. The present writer considers this hero to be identical with "Taxo and his seven sons" who "came to a cave in the country and preferred to die" referred to in the *Assumption of Moses*,

of the zealots against the Edomite slave, and so great their faith in
the Maccabæan house! Shortly afterwards we find the Galilæans
drowning Herod's sympathisers in the lake of Galilee.[23]

Such were the Galilæans near the time of Jesus, and such the
state of Galilee forty years before his birth! There could not have
been better material for a messianic movement.

In the course of these wars an incalculable number of Jews were
killed, especially in Galilee.[24] Later, the war broke out again in
Samaria against Pappus, the general of Antigonous. Even Josephus
is moved by Herod's cruelty in this war.[25] Following these bloody
victories Herod besieged Jerusalem; but so strongly did he realize the
Maccabæan popularity that, in the course of the war itself, he found
it incumbent upon him to marry one of the Maccabæan family and
so attach to himself some of their royal prestige. In the year 37 he
interrupted the siege of Jerusalem, went to Samaria and there married
Mariamne, the daughter of Hyrcanus II's daughter and Aristobulus
II's son.

He then resumed the siege. Large numbers were killed in the
course of it, and the long siege culminated in a final attack, the terrible
nature of which appalled even Herod's stony heart. When the
Romans entered the city they spared none, men, women and children,
old and young, tender girls and aged women; in the houses, markets,
streets and even in the Temple they slaughtered human beings like
sheep. A blind murderous fury overcame the Romans and the soldiers of Herod. Josephus tells us that "Herod's soldiers did their
utmost that not a man from the other side be left alive." [26]

It is needless to dilate on the pillage and violence carried out in
the city; it reached such a pitch that Herod intervened and asked
Sosius, the Roman general: "Would the Romans deprive the city of
all its inhabitants and possessions and leave me a king of the
wilderness?"

Such was indeed the case. By the time that Herod "the Great"
came to the throne (37 B.C.E.) not only the royal city, Jerusalem,
but the entire Land of Israel, was a wilderness. During the thirty
years which had elapsed from the death of the queen Shelom-Zion
till Herod became all-powerful (67-37) far more than a hundred
thousand Jews were killed. And these were the pick of the nation,
the healthiest, mainly the young men, and the most enthusiastic, who
had refused to suffer the foreign yoke.

Thus the nation was enfeebled to the last degree. It no longer
contained men of bold courage for whom political freedom was more
precious than life; there remained only those whom we have described

ix 1-7 (see also *Assumption of Moses* by A. S. Kaminetsky, *Hashiloach*, XV
47-48).
[23] *Antiq.* XIV xv 10; *Wars* I xvii 2.
[24] *Antiq.* XIV xv 6-7 and 11-12.
[25] *Antiq.* XIV xv 12.
[26] *Wars* I xviii 2.

—the bitter-minded and the fervid of faith who did not shrink from martyrdom for the sake of the Law. And even these, ere long, Herod had crushed by force.

There remained no longer the possibility of a great, popular rising which should venture forth, sword in hand, to meet the usurper, a foreigner by birth and depending upon foreigners for support. Josephus refers to the same fact: "Owing to perpetual wars the Jews were no longer capable of revolting against anybody." [27] None remained save companies of lurking patriot-terrorists who had fire in their hearts but no clear plan in their minds; and those others who would fight for the faith, but, while their purpose was clear, could not rise to the level of political activity because "their kingdom was not of this world."

Both alike were a danger to Herod in that they were inflammable material which, when the time was ripe, "would also be added to his enemies," although in themselves they did not constitute a political factor. But such was the best material for messianic movements, whether political or religio-spiritual; and such also was the material out of which was formed the party which supported Jesus.

Of Herod "the Great" a certain historian has remarked: "He stole along to his throne like a fox, he ruled like a tiger and died like a dog." And how true this epigram is! We have seen how Herod possessed himself of the throne after hedging about with deceit the weak Hyrcanus. And when he came to play the king he began to ravage and tear like a wild beast.

First he tried to wipe out all memory of the Maccabæan house and the noble families which supported it. So very strong was the widespread popularity of the Maccabæans that, according to the spontaneous evidence of Strabo, "it was impossible to compel the Jews to recognize Herod as king after he had been proclaimed in place of Antigonus; torture could not move the Jews to hail him as king; so highly did they value the former king (Antigonus)." [28] This popularity must, therefore, be forcibly suppressed. So Herod persuaded Antonius to behead Antigonus—a thing which the Romans had never done before to any king. By this means he wished to prove that Antigonus II, a king, the son of a king, and the grandson of a king, was reckoned in the eyes of the Romans as a simple brigand.

We shall see later how, one after another, Herod destroyed every member of the Maccabæan royal family and all their kindred.

After he came to the throne, Herod was not the cause of much bloodshed in war. Despite his lust for blood and his military skill, he did not, from fear of the Romans, organize any wars except those with the Arabs in the years 32-31 B.C.E. and at the end of his life, about the year 9. At least, during his reign Jewish blood was not

[27] *Antiq.* XVIII i 1.
[28] Josephus quotes this statement by the famous Greek writer in *Antiq.* XV i 2.

shed to the same degree as in the thirty preceding years of warfare.
Yet his efforts to choke the national spirit and the remnant of internal
freedom effected a loss to the nation greater far than that effected
by all the wars in the world.

Yitzhaq Isaac Halevy, the author of "Doroth ha-Rishonim," has
devoted a volume of many hundred pages to the period of Herod and
his sons.[29] He does his best to depict Herod as one who, all his life,
aimed at being a "king of the Gentiles" and not a "king of the
Jews." His arguments are not very new and are somewhat per-
spicuous. Herod's many activities for the benefit of the Hellenistic
cities, the magnificent buildings which he set up there, the many
donations he gave them, the immense sums which he expended on
the Greek games—these easily create the impression that Herod was
minded to be a "king of the Gentiles," especially when we set over
against them the objections of the Jews to such actions.

But in spite of this, and perhaps even precisely because of this,
the impression is not correct. Josephus had the same idea: he, too,
was astonished that Herod laboured more for the good of the Gentiles
than for the good of his Jewish subjects.

Yet Josephus gives a clear reason for this. Herod's most con-
spicuous trait was his appetite for fame. He knew that whatever
he might do for the good of his subjects would be a thing taken for
granted and for which no fame would accrue. He knew, too, that
the Jews would never forgive his foreign origin, his filching the crown
from the Maccabees, his unjustifiable bloodshed, his slavelike subservience to the Romans and his disregard of many of the laws of
Israel. There remained but one means of satisfying his appetite for
fame, namely, a magnificent open-handedness to the Greek cities and
to those, generally, who were not his own subjects; he was under
no obligation to benefit them and he could count on their gratitude.

And so well was he served by the flattery prevalent in the Greek
cities and the multitude of professional rhetoricians, that his fame
became widespread and he obtained abroad what he could not obtain
in his own country. His calculations proved correct: it was his Greek
flatterers who hailed him as "Herod the Great;" and all that we find
in Josephus concerning "all the works of his might and majesty"
is derived from the writings of the Hellenist Nicholas of Damascus;
whereas the people of Israel dubbed him "the Edomite slave." To
his account of Herod's conceit Josephus adds the further explanatory
fact that "the Jews were not able to flatter his vanity by statues or
palaces, and the like;" therefore he had no liking for this people and
turned to the Greeks who had all these means of honouring him.[30]

We find elsewhere in Josephus remarks which seem to be deliberately aimed against the view held by the author of "Doroth ha-
Rishonim," e.g., "On the whole, Herod's munificence could arouse no

[29] *Doroth ha-Rishonim* Pt. I vol. 3. Frankfurt-a.-Main, 1906.
[30] *Antiq.* XVI v 4.

suspicion that, in his generosity towards the Greek cities, which was greater than that of their own rulers, he was moved by hidden motives." [31]

The most outstanding proof that he wished also to secure the esteem of the Jews and to secure it in a place where he knew that some such great act would most redound to his credit among the Jews, regardless of the huge cost that it would entail, is the building of the Temple, that "Herod's Building" so famed in Jewish literature. This great and sacred building was the one edifice which he might set up in the Land of Israel and gain thereby glory and honour from among the Jews; and upon this building he lavished enormous sums. He also looked upon himself as a Jew and king of the Jews in all that bore on the protection of the Jews outside Palestine.

When, in the year 22, he came to meet Agrippa in the Greek islands, Mitylene and Lesbos, the Jews living there came to complain about their neighbours and officials who oppressed them and hindered them in the practice of their religion; and Herod came forward as their advocate and did all in his power on their behalf, while the spokesman of these Jews on several occasions hailed Herod as "our king." [32] It would also seem that the edicts issued by Augustus in favour of the Jews of Asia and of Cyrene in Libya, though of different dates, were also published through the efforts of Herod since Josephus includes them amongst the events of Herod's reign. [33]

Again, when the Arab Syllæus, chief minister of Obodas, king of the Arabs, sought from Herod his sister Salome to wife, he whom Halevy would call "the king of the Gentiles" required him first to become converted to Judaism (ἐγγραφῆναι τοῖς τῶν Ἰουδαίων ἔθεσι); and when the Arab prince refused these terms his request was rejected. [34] These facts are sufficient to contradict the idea that Herod wished only to become a "king of the Gentiles."

And why should he have been so wroth with those who opposed him in Judæa if he had no wish at all to be a "king of the Jews?" [35]

All that can truthfully be said is that he sought honour and fame wherever he might get it; and since he knew it was more easily obtained abroad than at home, from the Greeks rather than from the Jews; and since he required abundant wealth for the buildings and statues and munificent acts wh'ch alone could ensure his fame and spread his reputation, for this reason he forcibly raised the means from his Jewish subjects and gave it to strangers, since the Romans would never have allowed him to collect the money from those who were not his subjects.

[31] *Wars* I xxi 12.
[32] *Antiq.* XVI ii 3-5.
[33] *Ibid.*, vi 1-7. All that is alleged in this connexion by the author of *Doroth ha-Rishonim* (I iii 25-86) is pure casuistry.
[34] *Antiq.* XVI vii 6. See also Schürer I⁴ 397, 406.
[35] Réville, *Jésus de Nazareth*, 2 ed. Paris, 1906, pp. 210-211.

But however this may be, his friendliness to the Gentiles and his oppression of his Jewish subjects embittered the people and aroused their antagonism towards this half-Jew who ruled by virtue of Roman favour. See, for example, how he is described by the Jewish delegation which went to complain before Augustus against Archelaus immediately after Herod's death: "He (Herod) committed acts of tyranny which might have made an end of the Jews, and also devised new things according to his own mind which were contrary to the spirit of the Jews; and he killed many men with a cruelty unparalleled in history.

"Worse still was the lot of those who still remained alive, for not only did he oppress them but also threatened to confiscate their property. The cities which were near by the Land of Israel he bedecked and adorned without end at the expense of his plundered subjects. He reduced the people to abject poverty though he had found it, apart from exceptional cases, in a condition of wealth. The property of the higher families—whom he had condemned to death on the slightest pretext—he confiscated, and those whom he suffered to remain alive he deprived of their wealth. Not only were the taxes levied on all the inhabitants year by year exacted mercilessly and by force, but it was impossible to live without bribes to himself, and to his domestics, and his friends and officers who were entrusted with the gathering of the taxes.

"It was impossible to speak of his corruption of virgins and wives; after he had done these wicked things when drunk and without witnesses, those who had suffered preferred to remain silent as though nothing had happened rather than publish such things abroad. And so Herod had behaved to the Jews with a cruelty as great as though a wild beast had been given rule over mankind. Though the Jews had before suffered many hardships and oppressions, their history had never known so great an affliction as they had suffered at the hands of Herod." [36]

Such is the history of the works of Herod "the Great:" bloodshed, confiscation of property, harsh taxation, debauchery and contempt of the law. The loss of the best cultural elements, stern political oppression, deprivation of freedom, suspicion, espionage, flattery of the great, increase of want and poverty—these are the marks of Herod's government which lasted close on to the time of the birth

---

[36] *Antiq.* XVII xi 2. *Wars* II vi 2 repeats almost the same words but in briefer and stronger form: "He was not a king but the most barbarous of tyrants who had ever sat on a throne. He had slain men innumerable, but the lot of those which survived made them envy those that were slain. He not only tortured his subjects individually but oppressed entire cities. Foreign cities he adorned but his own he destroyed; foreign peoples he enriched with the blood of the Jews. So, in place of the former wealth and good laws, there came utter poverty and bad laws. In short, the Jews suffered more in a few years from Herod than their fathers had suffered since they left Babylon and returned in the reign of Xerxes."

of Jesus. Drop by drop Herod had drained the blood of the Jews in the course of his thirty-three years' rule (37-4B.C.E.). Scarce a day passed but someone was put to death.

In the year 37 when he had just ascended the throne, he killed forty-five of the noblest in Jerusalem who belonged to the Maccabæan family; their property he confiscated to his own use: it was the "year of release" (Deut. 15, 1) and he needed money.[37]

At the close of the year 35, Aristobulus III, brother of the queen Mariamne and Herod's brother-in-law, was by Herod's order drowned when bathing at Jericho.[38]

In the year 34, Joseph the husband of Salome, Herod's sister, was put to death.[39]

In the year 30, Hyrcanus II was killed when he was eighty-two years old, although, apart from his great age, he was possessed of a physical defect and so ineligible for the high priesthood, and therefore not dangerous to Herod (the self-same Hyrcanus who had raised Antipater and his sons to power, saved Herod from death at the hands of the Sanhedrin, and who was grandfather of Herod's beloved wife Mariamne!).[40]

At the close of the year 29, Sohœmus of Ituræa, Herod's wife Mariamne, and shortly afterwards Alexandra, mother of Mariamne and mother-in-law of Herod, were put to death.[41]

The year 25 saw the murder of Costobarus (Kauzgeber), Salome's second husband, and the sons of Baba, of Maccabæan descent, who belonged to the Antigonus party and whom Costobarus had concealed from Herod; with them were also killed Lysimachus Gadius, known as Antipater, and Dositheus. Shortly afterwards when the populace had become enraged at the athletic games, the theatre and the amphitheatre conducted in Jerusalem by Herod, ten men conspired to kill Herod, and among them was a blind man who urged them on; and although he could take no part in the assassination owing to his defect he was prepared to share the penalty should they fail.

The conspirators were caught owing to information lodged by a spy, and they boldly confessed that they had intended to kill Herod, or at least those near to him, in order that their death might prove to men how dangerous it was to treat lightly what the nation held sacred. They were all put to death with atrocious cruelty, but the people tore in pieces the spy who had betrayed them and threw his body to the dogs. None would disclose the names of those who had killed the traitor since all held him deserving of death. Herod

[37] *Antiq.* XV i 2; *Wars* I xviii 4.
[38] *Ant.* XV iii 3; *Wars* I xxii 2.
[39] *Ant.* XV iii 9; see *Wars* I xxii 4-5.
[40] *Ant.* XV vii 1-4; *Wars* I xxii 1.
[41] *Ant.* XV vii 4-6, 8; *Wars* I xxii 3-5.

thereupon ordered certain women to be scourged and under torture they divulged various names. All the suspects were immediately put to death and their families as well.[42]

About the year 7 B.C.E., Alexander and Aristobulus, the sons of Herod by his wife Mariamne, were strangled at Sebaste (Samaria) by order of their father, together with three hundred men who were, or were suspected of being, their supporters.[43]

In the same or following year many Pharisees were put to death for refusing to swear the oath of allegiance to the Emperor and to Herod, having first been heavily fined. These fines had been paid for them by the wife of Pherora, Herod's brother, and in return for this benefit they had prophesied that Pherora or his sons should sit on the throne of Herod. (It may be, however, that this "prophecy" was invented by the calumnious-minded princess Salome.) The eunuch Bagoas, the slave Carus, and all Herod's courtiers who gave credence to this forecast were killed together with the Pharisees.[44]

In the year of Herod's death, 4 B.C.E., two sages, Yehuda ben Tzarifa (or Ben Sepphorai) and Mattathias ben Margaloth, incited their many disciples to tear down, at the risk of their lives, the golden eagle which Herod had set up on the Temple gate. The captain of the army captured forty of the disciples and their two teachers. They heroically confessed their act and that they did not regret it. Whereupon Herod ordered them to be burnt alive after a mock trial which he arranged in Jericho at a time when he was already mortally sick and could not stand upright.[45]

The same year, five days before his death, he ordered the death of his son Antipater; and in the course of the few days which preceded his loathesome end he was able to imprison in the hippodrome many of the chief people, one from every family of importance, with instructions to his sister Salome and Alexas her husband that as soon as he expired the army should put to death all the arrested men, so that at his own death the mourning should be great and every family from among the people of Jerusalem should mourn its dead.[46]

Even if this order is not to be believed owing to its extraordinary

[42] *Ant.* XV vii 10, viii 3-4. It would seem that the *Talmudic* legend about Baba ben Buta (that when Herod killed the sages he allowed him to survive and only bored out his eyes: *Bab. Bath.* 3b-4a) is in some way connected with the sons of Baba and also with the blind man who shared in the conspiracy; they are distant and indistinct echoes of what happened in the time of Herod and so names and facts are confused. Also all that is told in the *Talmud* (*Bab. Bath.* 3b-4a) of Mariamne and her attitude to Herod, is also only a late and vague echo. See Z'eb Ya'betz, *Tol'doth Yisrael* V, Cracow, 1904, p. 58 n. 1.
[43] *Ant.* XVI xi 2-7; *Wars* I xxvii 2-6.
[44] *Ant.* XVII ii 4.
[45] *Ant.* XVII vi 2-4; *Wars* I xxxiii 1-4.
[46] *Ant.* XVII vii 1, vi 5; *Wars* I xxxiii 6-7.

barbarity [47] just as doubt is cast on his order to kill the children of Bethlehem [48]—and we regard both alike as legendary—still the very existence of the legends is proof enough of how great was the "Edomite slave's" cruelty and how strong was the fear of death which this cruelty spread over the people during his life and even after his death. We cannot wonder that, in early Jewish literature, it is said: "Now the day on which Herod died was made a festival." [49]

But worse even than the effect of this interminable bloodshed was the effect of the political terror which Herod exercised on Judæa. Here Herod rivals the terrorists of the French Revolution and of Bolshevism. Josephus tells how "Herod watched most carefully over his subjects that they should have no opportunity of voicing their dissatisfaction against his rule." Citizens were forbidden to assemble together or walk together or hold public meetings. Offenders were heavily punished. Many were brought openly or secretly to the citadel of Hyrcania and there put to death. Numerous spies patrolled the city and the roads.

It is said that Herod himself did not despise this means of spying and often disguised himself in simple clothes and mixed with the crowds at night to know what they thought about his government. "Those who entirely opposed his innovations were persecuted by various methods, and the rest he compelled to swear an oath of allegiance to him and to be subservient to all the acts of the government. A great number obeyed these demands either to please him or because they feared him, but all those who were dissatisfied or complained at these abominations, he made away with by all possible devices." [50]

The Sanhedrin, the true supreme authority of the people, was in Herod's time virtually non-existent: it was suffered to deal only with unimportant religious matters, whereas in civil matters it was compelled to submit to the dictation of the tyrant. The High Priests he changed as he might change his clothes. After the death of Mattathias-Antigonus II, he appointed as High Priest "Ananelus the Babylonian" (according to Josephus) [51] or (according to the *Mishnah*) "Hanamel the Egyptian." [52] Soon after, he appointed

[47] *Meg. Taanith* (scholion), §9, relates this of Herod. But §11 says the same thing of Jannæus, clearly wrongly. The truth may be as Salome and her husband stated, that Herod ordered the release of these notables who may have been imprisoned a short time prior to his death for political reasons, and not just to raise a lamentation. The legend, however, explains the arrest in a way consonant with the spirit of Herod. (The statements of Salome and her husband are quoted in Josephus, *Ant.* XVII viii 2; *Wars* I xxxiii 8.)

[48] Matthew ii. 1-18.

[49] *Meg. Taanith* (scholion) §9.

[50] *Ant.* XV x 4.

[51] *Ant.* XV ii 4, iii 1.

[52] *Para* III 5.

Aristobulus whom, the same year, he ordered to be drowned in Jericho.

Then he reappointed Hanamel, after whom followed a long succession of High Priests raised and deposed at will by Herod: Yeshua ben Fiabi, Shimeon ben Bœthus, Mattathias ben Theophilus, Joseph ben Ellem, Yoezer ben Bœthus. To carry out his tyranny Herod depended on an army of mercenaries: Thracians, Germans and Gauls, as if, says Josephus, "he needed such protection against his subjects."[53] His principal officers were Greeks. The Greek Ptolemy was, for example, the chief of the national treasury. And there were three foreign eunuchs "who exercised a powerful influence over affairs of state."[55]

It is easy to imagine how hateful and detestable was such a rule to people like the Jews, and what terror and fear such tyranny cast upon them. The people gnashed their teeth in secret at the "Edomite slave" who had risen over them; and this impotent rage festered and infected the youth and the pick of the nation, manifesting itself in a conspiracy during his lifetime and in complete revolt immediately after his death.

The more it becomes necessary to conceal dislike of any political government, the deeper it penetrates and the more likely it is to produce potential rebels who do but wait for a favourable moment to raise the flag of open rebellion. Since the people saw in Herod nothing but a Roman emissary, this same hatred attached itself both to the "kingdom of Edom" and to the "wicked kingdom of Rome," the two titles becoming synonymous terms, so that in the *Talmud* and *Midrash* "Edom" is used in the place of "Rome" (except in places where the change has been made from fear of the censor).

To the afflictions which the people endured from a cruel king were added many hardships from natural causes. In 31 B.C.E. occurred an earthquake in Judæa killing about thirty thousand people and a great number of cattle.[55] And this calamity befell the Jews at a time when they had suffered heavy losses in men in a defeat at the hands of the Arabs. The years 25-24 were years of famine which, in conjunction with the resulting starvation, brought in its train plague and pestilence.[56] And these appeared to the people to be the veritable "pangs of the Messiah" which presaged the advent of the redeemer.

Consequently there were aroused among the people of this time strong messianic longings which found expression in many *Apocryphal Books* filled with messianic fantasies and apocalyptic visions. The Sadducees, like the wealthy and aristocratic of all ages and nations, were thorough realists and saw that there was no hope of

[53] *Ant.* XV ix 5.
[54] *Ant.* XVI viii 1.
[55] *Ant.* XV v 2; Wars I xix 3.
[56] *Ant.* XV ix 1.

freeing themselves from Roman rule, and that their own position was not so bad as to be unendurable; and even the Pharisees were wise enough to recognize that "vain is the help of man" and that all that they could look forward to was the mercy of heaven when in its good time it should see fit to send the righteous redeemer to Israel.

But very different were the younger people, the hot-blooded and enthusiastic, who collected together in parties of "zealots" whose object was to hasten the redemption and "bring near the end." From one end to the other Palestine was filled with malcontents and the rebellious-minded, and especially was this the case in Galilee, the cradle of "zealotism." This is a fact which should not go unobserved in the history of Jesus. Also in Judæa and Jerusalem the great majority were weary of the heavy burden of the "kingdom of Edom" —in both of its meanings. And once a people is "weary of enduring" we can expect considerable political changes, for in those conditions the restless multitudes seize the first suitable moment for uprooting the existing order.

Scarcely, indeed, had Herod closed his eyes than there immediately broke out such tumults and riots as the Jewish nation had never before witnessed. Before Archelaus could mount his father's throne, the people, who could not forget the horrible murder by Herod of the heroic Yehuda ben Tzarifa and Mattathias ben Margaloth, gathered themselves together and, instead of lamenting the dead king, proclaimed a lamentation over those whom he had wrongfully put to death. They demanded from Archelaus that he exact vengeance for those martyrs—still unburied—from the advisers at whose instigation the dying king had inflicted the sentences, and that, first of all, he dismiss Joezer the Bœthusean, the last High Priest appointed by Herod.

Not having yet been confirmed as king by the Romans, Archelaus did not wish to do this and tried to persuade the people not to press their demands. But they were now beyond control and incapable of listening to reason. Archelaus despatched a body of soldiers against the people who had gathered together in the Temple courtyard, but the people stoned them and put them to flight. Then Archelaus, though he dared not punish Herod's advisers without the Emperor's sanction, yet allowed himself to send his entire army against those who had assembled in the Temple, and in one day killed three thousand men.[57] The people were killed like sheep side by side with their Temple offerings, and the Temple was filled with the dead.[58]

This revealed the true character of Archelaus: he was a true son of Herod; so far as cruelty and injustice were concerned, it was "like father like son;" even while he was still being educated at

---

[57] *Ant.* XVII ix 1-3; *Wars* II i 2-3.
[58] *Ant.* XVII ix 5; *Wars* II ii 5. Perhaps Luke (xiii. 1), in speaking of the "Galilæans whose blood mingled with their sacrifices," confused Archelaus with Pilate. See below, p. 164, n. 86.

Rome, the Roman Jews had complained against him for seducing their daughters and wives.[59]

The people could no longer expect any good from him; and fifty Jewish elders, joined and supported in Rome by more than eight thousand Jews, formed a delegation to the Emperor Augustus and petitioned to be set free from that "kingdom" which had been governed* by such monsters as Herod and Archelaus. They and those who sent them preferred to return to conditions as they were in the pre-Maccabæan times, under the Persian and Greek empires, before Antiochus came with his decrees; let them be governed by the representative of the Roman Empire, the Syrian procurator, rather than by a king from among themselves—if only they might have autonomy in internal affairs.[60]   Not only was this the petition of the people's delegates but even of the relatives of Archelaus themselves, who saw clearly that their only hope of remaining in peace was that one of the house of Herod should not hold the reins of government.[61]   How great must have been the sufferings endured by the people to make them see freedom rather in the rule of a foreign power than in the rule of one of their own faith! It was only because they had drained the cup of suffering to the dregs and their power of endurance had failed.

That their power of endurance had failed is amply proved by what happened in Judæa immediately after Herod's death, when the outspoken protestations against the terrible villainy of the house of Herod, protestations which had been choked down during Herod's lifetime from fear of the Edomite, burst out like a flood and did not shrink even in face of greater danger.

Having quenched the flames of the first rebellion with the blood of three thousand men, Archelaus went to Rome to have his father's last testament (which made Archelaus king of Judæa, Samaria and Edom) confirmed by Augustus; but while he was still occupied in Rome, fresh outbreaks occurred in Judæa. Varus, governor of Syria (the same Varus who afterwards in the year 9 C.E. fell at the hands of Arminius Cheruscus in the forest of Teutoburg, and whom Augustus apostrophized in the saying: "Varus, Varus, give me back my legions!"), arrived and heavily punished the rebels, and returned to Antioch leaving Sabinus and a legion behind in Jerusalem.

This Sabinus deliberately oppressed the people in order to provoke it to further revolt that he might have the opportunity of crushing it with the help of the army and so remove the reproach of the charge alleged against him in Rome that, in his avarice, he had tampered with the royal money-chests in the fortresses. The episode occurred in the feast of Pentecost when Jerusalem was thronged by

* A. Berliner, *History of the Jews in Rome* (Hebrew trans. published in *Bibleotheca* ed. Ha-Zeman, Jan. 1913, Vol. 8, Wilna, 1913, p. 29).
[60] *Ant.* XVII xi 1-2; *Wars* II vi 1-2.
[61] *Ant. ibid.; Wars ibid.;* cf. *Ant.* XVII ix 4.

pilgrims from Judæa and elsewhere, Edomites, people of Jericho and from beyond Jordan, and especially Galilæans.

These all joined with the Jerusalem Jews in exacting vengeance from the tyrant Sabinus. They attacked the Romans simultaneously from three quarters: from the north (by the Temple), from the south (by the hippodrome), and from the west (by the royal palaces). Fighting was severest in the Temple quarters. The Jews climbed on the roofs of the galleries surrounding the Temple and, with slings or by hand, hurled stones at the soldiers. The Romans adopted the terrible plan of secretly setting fire to the galleries. . . .

The fine buildings were reduced to ruins and those fighting on the roofs fell down and were burned in the fire or were buried alive in the débris, while many put an end to their own lives so as not to fall into the enemy's hands. Still worse, the Roman soldiery even penetrated the Temple itself and looted all they found. Not only did Sabinus not prevent them but openly went himself and stole four hundred talents from the Temple treasury.[62]

Such deeds simply served to enrage the people the more, and some even of Herod's own soldiers deserted to the side of the rebels, and together they laid siege to the Palace of Herod, in which Sabinus and his troops had fortified themselves, and demanded that the Romans should leave the town. But because of the Jews Sabinus was afraid to leave the palace, and waited for help from Varus. The Great Rebellion, which was to end with the destruction of the Second Temple, began immediately after the death of Herod: these riots and revolts were the "beginning of the end."

All Judæa was, indeed, out of control. There was no ruler whose position was confirmed and who was accepted by the people; the smouldering hatred against the Edomite-Roman rule burst out like a volcano, and from one end of the country to the other were riots and disorders, tumult and confusion. Two of Herod's generals who had completed their service with the army returned home to Edom and there fought against those who had remained faithful to Herod, and against Herod's kinsman, the governor Ahiab, who was compelled to take refuge in the mountains.

Simeon of Transjordania, one of Herod's officers, a man of great height, courage and comeliness, seized the throne and robbed the royal palace in Jericho and burnt down many other palaces in the country, until Gratus met him in battle and captured and beheaded him. Again, at Beth-Ramtha[63] on the Jordan, one of the royal palaces, was burnt by a crowd of rebels.

A certain shepherd, Athronges, whose only claim to distinction was his height and courage, and four brothers similar to himself, tall and strong, was minded to sit on the throne of Herod, and even he,

[62] *Ant.* XVII x 1-2; *Wars* II iii 1-3.
[63] So the town is called in *Wars* II iv 2; in *Ant.* XVII x 6 it is called "Hamath."

at this abandoned time, found a crowd of supporters; they attacked the Romans, to whom they bore a deadly hatred because of the abominations done in Judæa, and those soldiers of Herod who were in league with the Romans; but—as is usual with insurgents who depend only on the support of the mob—Athronges and his following attacked also such of their fellow-Jews as they suspected of a leaning towards the Romans or simply of a preference for peace. . . .

Josephus tells us that "in those days Judæa was filled with bands of marauders; wherever a malcontent crowd assembled they elected them a king, to the harm of the entire nation. Indeed, these kings inflicted but slight loss on the Romans, but they went about among their own people like a pestilence that walketh in darkness." [64]

But the most dangerous rebel of all, whose great strength lay in his being inspired by a feeling of nationalism, was Judah the Galilæan, son of that same Hezekiah of Galilee whom Herod had put to death before he became king and because of whose death Herod was arraigned by the Sanhedrin.[65] The father, the great nationalist and zealot, whom Herod and Josephus try to depict as a mere freebooter, bequeathed to his son a bitter and undying hatred against those who had enslaved and oppressed his people—Romans and Edomites alike. By the son's efforts Galilee's mountains and fastnesses became the centre for those who fanned into flame the fanaticism of the nation and for the nationalist rebels and idealists.

Near Sepphoris, only an hour's journey from Jesus' birthplace, Nazareth, Judah the Galilæan collected a large body of desperate nationalists, attacked the king's armoury, seized the weapons and with these armed his followers, and took away all the money he found. Then the warrior-zealot fought against all those, Gentiles or Jews, who opposed the idea of freedom; and, as is usual in such campaigns, he made little distinction between actual enemies and traitors, and those who were merely peace-loving Jews. He put the fear of himself on the whole of Galilee.

Such was the state of Judæa, and especially Galilee, immediately after the death of Herod. The revolt spread throughout all the provinces, Judæa, Idumæa, Galilee and beyond Jordan; no quarter was given to any Roman legion or to any Herodian soldiers or to anybody who did not enroll himself as a member of some nationalist party—complete anarchy prevailed: "In those days there was no king in Israel; every man did that which was right in his own eyes." And all this, it should be emphasized, happened only three or four years before the birth of Jesus.

Finally, after much effort, the tumults and rebellions were crushed. Varus, with a strong Roman army, reinforced by divisions from Beyrout and Arabia, came a second time against the Land of Israel. He first despatched some portions of his army against Sep-

[64] *Ant.* XVII x 8.
[65] See above, p. 141.

phoris. He burnt Sepphoris and sold its inhabitants into slavery. He himself marched against Samaria and burnt the neighbouring Emmaus. In the regions round about Samaria and Emmaus the Arabs burned villages and looted everything in their hatred for Herod and his friends the Romans. It was as though everyone had united to destroy the Land of Israel and its inhabitants.

Varus next went up to Jerusalem, and when the Jews, who were besieging the Romans who had fortified themselves within Herod's castle, saw his large army, they raised the siege and began to excuse themselves by saying that it was only the crowd of pilgrims, and Sabinus, who had provoked them, that were guilty of the riots.

Sabinus saw fit to leave the town, and Varus sent his army in pursuit of the rebels outside Jerusalem, and having commanded the crucifixion of no less than two thousand men he returned to Antioch. Those who had headed the revolt in Idumæa Varus sent to Rome. There they were tried before the Emperor Augustus, and he, too, commanded large numbers of them to be put to death.[66]

But even this did not mark the end. In times of political anarchy there arise another type of self-appointed rulers, different from Simeon of Transjordania or Athronges the shepherd, namely, such as pretend to be kings or princes who, it was supposed, had died or been killed. Such pretenders endeavour to secure a following from among those who adhered to the cause of those now dead; and the affection for the Maccabæans was so strong and deeply rooted in the hearts of the Jews that it only required the appearance of a comely young man resembling the Alexander, son of Herod and Mariamne the Maccabæan, who had been put to death, to spread the rumour that he had been miraculously saved from death (he asserted that the executioner had taken pity on him and his brother Aristobulus and strangled in their stead two others who resembled them), and all the Jews were stirred and accorded him royal honours and ample wealth.

The Jews of Crete and Melos provided him generously with money, and the Jews of Rome went out to greet him, and when "he travelled abroad in a chariot they burst into tumultuous joy, more especially because he was the son of Mariamne the Maccabæan."[67] He adopted a wholly regal manner of life and crowds of people used to surround him and raise joyful cheers in his honour. To such a degree could even a doubtful descendant of the Maccabæans inspire the nation!

But it all came to nought: a servant of Augustus and Augustus himself recognised that he was not of royal descent and persuaded him to admit his fraud. He confessed to save his life. But to what a state of confusion and excitement must the people have been reduced for such frauds to have obtained a hearing!

[66] *Ant.* XVII x 8-10; *Wars* II i 4.
[67] *Ant.* XVII xii; *Wars* II vii 1-2 (with slight differences).

Then the kingdom of Herod was divided up into its component parts. Many scholars have justly observed that there were, *mutatis mutandis*, certain resemblances between the kingdom of Solomon and the kingdom of Herod. As with the kingdom of Solomon, so with the kingdom of Herod: it was glorious without and rotten within. Like the kingdom of Solomon it seemed, in comparison with its small neighbours, to be wealthy and powerful, yet the mass of its population was ground down by taxation and harsh government, and changes innumerable were introduced with a complete disregard to the historical character of the nation.

Again, as in the days of Solomon, the small neighbouring states were either subject to Judæa or feared it, while the great empires— the Egypt of Psusennes II and Shishak in Solomon's time and the Rome of Antonius and Augustus in Herod's time—were well disposed to the ruler of Judæa, permitting him a certain freedom of government so long as he was a "faithful ally," *i.e.*, such time as he was subservient to them.

Thus the glory and liberty were only apparent, a fact which the people realized; they were able to estimate at their true valuation all the honour and glory and wealth and success accorded at the court of the Pharaoh or the reigning Cæsar. Like Solomon, Herod, too, was addicted to glorious buildings, and like Solomon he built the Temple. Even in his multiplicity of wives Herod bore some resemblance to Solomon. The political fortune of the Land of Israel after the death of Solomon was markedly like its political fortune after the death of Herod.

As in the closing days of Solomon and immediately after his death there broke out the revolts of Hadad the Edomite, Rezon the son of Eliyada of Damascus, and Jeroboam the son of Nebat the Ephraimite, so too in the closing days of Herod, and more especially immediately after his death, there broke out riots and revolts. Just as the "glorious" kingdom of Solomon was divided and Edom and Syria severed from it, so too Herod's kingdom was divided and the Palestinian Greek cities (Gaza, Gadara and Hyppos) severed from it. And just as the breaking up of Solomon's kingdom marked the beginning of the process which culminated in the destruction of the First Temple, so too the breaking up of Herod's kingdom began the series of events which ended in the destruction of the Second Temple.

Augustus did, indeed, confirm Herod's testamentary wishes but with many alterations. Archelaus was granted Judæa, Samaria and Idumæa, but not the title "king" bequeathed to him by Herod; he was granted instead the title "Ethnarch" (leader of the people); the Palestinian Greek cities already referred to were attached by the Emperor to Syria. Furthermore, according to the will of Herod, the towns of Jamnia, Ashdod and Phasaelis went to Salome.

Archelaus thus inherited only the half, or even less, of Herod's kingdom. The rest was apportioned to Herod's other sons: Antipas received Galilee and Peræa, while Batanæa, Argob (Trachonitis) and the Hauran (including the eastern shore of the Sea of Galilee) went to Philip. These both were granted the title of "Tetrarch" (*lit*. the chief of four—*sc*. cities or states, though later the term became the title of a ruling noble, like the German "Herzog" or English "Baron," one who is less than a king but, within his own domain, has all the privileges of a king).

For ten years (4 B.C.E.-6 C.E.) Archelaus ruled over Judæa, Samaria and Idumæa. The same tyranny which he had shown immediately after his father's death, he still showed after he had been appointed Ethnarch. Like his father he made constant changes in the High Priests: in the place of Joezer ben Bœthus he appointed his brother, Eliezer ben Bœthus, who in his turn was replaced by Jeshua ben Sie.

Archelaus, after divorcing his wife Mariamne, married the daughter of Archelaus king of Cappadocia, Glaphyra, who had been the wife of Alexander, his step-brother (by his father), and who, after Alexander had been killed by his father, became the wife of Juba king of Lybia, whom she survived.[68] This marriage of Archelaus with Glaphyra the people considered wrong since it was not a fulfilling of the levirate law, Glaphyra having had children by Alexander and having been also married in the meantime to another. Archelaus also put up magnificent buildings. He rebuilt the palace in Jericho which had been burnt down during the riots; he built the town Archelais and laid down aqueducts to provide water for the palm forest which he planted near Na'aran, north of Jericho (a site where there has recently been discovered the remains of an ancient synagogue).

All this he carried out with the money drawn from a people who had already been greatly impoverished by the past disturbances. There is no doubt that he was guilty of atrocities against both Jews and Samaritans, for emissaries of both races, in spite of their mutual animosity, united in complaining against Archelaus before Augustus. So enraged was the Emperor at his conduct that he summoned him to Rome and exiled him to Gaul and confiscated all his possessions.[69] Judæa, Samaria and Idumæa were attached to Syria and put in charge of a Roman governor or commissioner (Procurator), thus fulfilling the desire of the Jewish delegation which waited on Augustus immediately after Herod's death.

But those who had asked for such a change certainly regretted it before long. The era of the Persian and Ptolemaic empires did not return. The days were for ever gone when Judæa could remain a negligible quantity, hidden away in such a remote corner of Asia that Herodotus could pass it by without any mention. Greater Palestine

---

[68] It is truer to say that she was divorced by him. See *Ant*. XVII xiii 4; *Wars* IV vii 4, where the statements are disputed by Schürer I⁴ 451-2.
[69] *Ant*. XVII xiii 1-2; *Wars* II vii 3.

had become a very important part of Syria, which abutted on the frontier of the Parthian empire, a foe with whom Rome was ever at war but could never subdue. Again, Palestine had acquired an increased importance as the religious and national centre of a widespread and peculiar people, a people which was scattered throughout the whole of the civilized world and which everywhere exercised considerable influence, and, in Egypt and Babylon, almost a predominating influence.

Such a country Rome could not leave in the hands of a High Priest only nominally supervised by the Governor of Syria, as in the time of the Persian and Greek empires. Hence, over the territory formerly ruled by Archelaus was appointed a special governor (styled *Epitropos* in Greek and *Procurator* in Latin; the Hebrew equivalent would be משניח, to distinguish him from the Governor [נציב] of Syria). The High Priests were, apparently, still the leaders of the people (τὴν δὲ προστασίαν τοῦ ἔθνους οἱ ἀρχιερεῖς ἐπεπιστεύοντο —a remark which Josephus puts in the mouth of the Romans), and a certain measure of autonomy was left to the Jews and administered through the channel of the more important families.[70]

In practice, however, no important step could be taken in Palestine apart from the consent of the Roman Governor. Judæa lost the right of conducting war, and only copper money could be minted in Palestine. The Procurator resided in Cæsarea but exercised a close surveillance over Jerusalem, where a permanent Roman army was stationed and where the Roman governor stayed at the time of the three Great Feasts, especially during Passover, when Jerusalem was crowded and when the people were most inclined to display their dislike of foreign rule. At such a time the Romans placed sentinels by the galleries surrounding the Temple.[71]

Cæsarea thus came to rival Jerusalem in importance; in the words of the *Talmud*, "Cæsarea came not to fulness save only through the destruction of Jerusalem." [72] Jewish judges might still decide in cases relating to property, and the Sanhedrin still held jurisdiction in religious matters and might even pass judgment in capital cases; but the Sanhedrin was only competent to pass sentence of death as the result of its findings in a preliminary investigation: it could not actually carry out the sentence; every trial involving capital punishment must come before the Roman Governor and the sentence must be confirmed by him. He had unrestricted powers of life and death (the *jus gladii* or *potestas gladii*).

Customs and taxes were collected by "publicans" or "tax-farmers" (גבאי טמיון),[73] lit. tax-collectors to the royal treasury—ταμεῖον, locally recruited. These men levied their dues by force, and so the

[70] *Ant.* XX x (end).
[71] *Ant.* XX v 3, and viii 11; *Wars* XII ii 1 and V v 8.
[72] *Megilla* 6a; *Pesahim* 42b; *Lam. R.* s.v. *Hayu tsareha.*
[73] *Gen. R.* §42; *Lev. R.* §11.

name מוכם "tax-gatherer" came almost to be synonymous with robber and brigand,[74] and the name נבאי sometimes synonymous with thief.[75] These men transmitted all taxes, customs and dues to the Procurator in whose charge were all the state finances. How such taxes were collected and how the state finances were conducted is well seen from Tiberius' epigram: "The officials of the Roman provinces are like flies on a sore; but those already sated with blood do not suck so hard as the new-comers." [76]

Also the Procurator exercised the same right that had been assumed by Herod—of deposing and appointing the High Priests. The high-priestly robes were under the Procurator's charge and deposited in the care of the captain commanding the Fort of Antonia, being sealed up by the High Priest and the Procurator and handed over to the High Priest only on the occasions of the Day of Atonement and the three Great Festivals. This was a most galling insult to the people: a more marked symbol of subservience could scarcely be found!

With such rights exercised by the Procurator, what was left of internal autonomy? These "rights" were all backed by force, by five cohorts and a squadron (ala) of cavalry, sometimes reinforced by local troops recruited not from the Jews but from foreigners resident in Palestine.[77] A people like the Jews, believing in the power of the spirit, could not but see in such a government, exercised by the "godless kingdom" and dependent on force, the harsh visitation of God which (popularly described as "the pangs of the Messiah" or "the footmarks of the Messiah") was to precede the imminent redemption. In the mind of the Jew the "Kingdom of Heaven" and the "Kingdom of Edom" were two great opposing conceptions, each of which called up the picture of the other.

The visitation was the more severe since the ideas and beliefs of the Jews were so completely different from those of the Romans. The first Procurator was Coponius (c. 6-9 C.E.). Owing to the fact that Judæa now passed from Jewish to Roman control, the governor of Syria, Quirinius, Coponius's superior, saw fit to carry out a census of the people of Judæa and their property, with a view to fixing the taxation levied by Rome on the Jews (6 C.E.). The Jews, however, looked upon such a census as contrary to the will of God, for when David numbered the people a plague broke out (II Sam. 24); they also saw in this census the clearest mark of their servitude, in that it enabled the tax-gatherers to oppress them to an unlimited extent. They raised the strongest opposition and almost rose in rebellion.

[74] *Nedarim* III 4; *Baba Qama* X 1 and 2.
[75] *Hagiga* III 6; *Tos. Toharoth* VIII 5-6.
[76] *Ant.* XVIII vi 5.
[77] For details of the political condition of Judæa under the Procurators, see Schürer I⁴ 454-485.

From that time onwards the Greek word χῆνσος became in Hebrew synonymous with fine or punishment (קנם, קונסין) Although the High Priest, Joezer ben Bœthus, succeeded in appeasing the people, and although the census was actually carried out, one great result followed: it had the effect of uniting all the more extreme nationalists, who, as we have frequently noticed, had existed since the time of Pompey, and made of them a new sect, the Zealots (הקנאים). Judah the Galilæan, who hailed from Gamala in the Jaulan (and who was probably the same Judah ben Hezekiah mentioned in connexion with the riots after Herod's death),[78] and Zadok the Pharisee (apparently also a native of Galilee) founded the sect of the Zealots, a body of men zealous for the Jewish Law and the national honour, men who, in their zeal, were regardless of the political state of country and people and demanded but the one thing—that the people rise up in solid revolt against the Romans. It was, they held, an unheard of indignity that the Jews should be enslaved by flesh and blood; the King of Israel could be none other than God himself, and not an idolatrous Roman Emperor. Thousands and tens of thousands followed Judah the Galilæan and joined the Zealots. Right up to the Destruction of the Temple it was they who everywhere led the riots and revolts.[79]

Coponius was succeeded in turn by Marcus Ambibulus (c. 9-12 C.E.) and Annius Rufus (c. 12-15). Their period of office was too short for them to accomplish much; they may have been in fear of Augustus and not have dared to do too much harm to the Jews. Augustus died in the year 15, and his successor, the emperor Tiberius, appointed Valerius Gratus Procurator of Judæa (15-26 C.E.).

Gratus was mainly noteworthy for the innumerable changes he made in the holders of the high priesthood. He first deposed Ananus ben Seth who had been appointed by Quirinius in place of Joezer ben Bœthus (the same Ananus [Annas] who receives unfavorable mention in the Gospels), and set up in his stead Ishmael ben Phiabi. Shortly afterwards the latter also was deposed and replaced by Eliezer ben Anan. Only a year later the Procurator appointed Simeon ben Kamhith, who also did not hold office for more than a year. He was succeeded by Joseph Kaïaphas (or Ben ha-Kayyaf),[80] who also receives unfavourable mention in the Gospels.

It is easy to imagine the dominating character of such a Roman

---

[78] See above, p. 156.
[79] On the character of the Zealots see the two articles of K. Kohler: *Wer waren die Zeloten oder Kannaim?* (Memorial Volume to A. A. Harkavy, Petersburg, 1909; German section pp. 6-18) ; and *Zealots, J. E.* XII 639-643.
[80] On this see Derenbourg *Massa Eretz Yisrael* (trans. Mibshan, Petersburg, 1896, p. 112. The *Tosefta* (*Yeb.* I 10) refers to the family of the house of Kayyafa, and in the *Talmud* (*Yeb.* 15b) mention is made of the "house of Kophai" some "of whom were High Priests" (see S. L. Rapaport in A. M. Luncz's *Ha-Me'amar* II 560).

Procurator who could play about with the High Priests as a child might play about with a ball; he must also have been of a very mercenary character, too; for the aspirants to office could only contrive their appointments by means of bribes.[81]

Worse than Gratus, however, was Pontius Pilate (26-36), who governed Judæa for ten years and in whose time Jesus was crucified. Philo of Alexandria quotes the shrewd judgment which Agrippa I passed on Pilate: "He was cruel by nature and in his hard-heartedness entirely lacking in remorse." The Judæa of his day was marked by "bribes, vainglorious and insolent conduct (ὕβρεις), robbery, oppression, humiliations (ἐπηρεῖαι), men often sent to death untried, and incessant and unmitigated cruelty." [82]

The moment he became Procurator he showed how he despised the Jews and their religious laws. It was an accepted usage that Roman troops never entered Jerusalem carrying standards or symbols containing the image of the Emperor, out of respect for the Jewish observance of "Thou shalt not make any graven image or likeness." Yet Pilate ordered his troops to enter Jerusalem equipped with such standards. At this the people flocked in crowds to Cæsarea, where the Procurator resided at a convenient distance from Jerusalem, and begged him to have these emblems removed from the Holy City. But he refused: he interpreted it as an insult to the honour of the Emperor.

Then for five days and nights without a pause the Jewish crowds stood before the tyrant's residence, weeping and beseeching him to withdraw his order. Pilate found this wearying and the sixth day he ordered the people to go away to the hippodrome where he had placed troops in ambush. The people went there and still continued their petitions that he take pity on the people and remove the images. Pilate thereupon tried to frighten them. He bade the soldiers draw swords while he raged at the crowd with a loud voice: "Whoever will not cease his begging and does not return to his home, shall be put to the sword!" But he was ignorant of the Jewish character. As one man the multitudes fell on their faces, bared their necks and announced that they were prepared for death rather than suffer their laws to be broken.

At last the tyrant was abashed at their display of moral courage and gave way.[83] Yet even this episode did not deter him from putting up ensigns (*signa*) dedicated to the Emperor and bearing the

---

[81] The *Talmud* refers to this period in the following terms: "And since they gave him money for the post of High Priest they used to change him (the High Priest) every twelve months," etc. (*Yoma* 8b). And Josephus also tells how Eliezer ben Anan and Simeon ben Kamhith only held office for a year. That "they gave money for the post" needs no proof, for had not the Roman rulers received money from the would-be High Priests they would not have changed them so often.

[82] *Embassy to Caius* §38.

[83] *Ant.* XVIII iii 1; *Wars* II ix 2-3.

Emperor's name, but without his image; only at Tiberius' order were they removed from Jerusalem to Cæsarea.[84]

Pilate again aroused popular indignation by bringing aqueducts to Jerusalem made at the expense of "the treasure of the Temple known as 'Qorban.' " [85] When he came, at the same time, to Jerusalem the people gathered together and began to complain that Pilate had touched sacred funds. Apparently, however, he had spies who warned him of the turbulent feeling among the people. He commanded his soldiers to disguise themselves in civilian clothes and arm themselves with whips and if they heard protests to beat the unarmed protesters till they died. The soldiers actually did this and killed many.[86]

But an atrocious act against the Samaritans finally brought about his downfall. A Samaritan false prophet had promised his followers to show them the sacred vessels (most probably those belonging to the Tabernacle) which Moses had hidden in Mount Gerizim. Great crowds assembled and there would seem to have been some messianic feeling connected with the movement since, according to Josephus, the Samaritans were armed.[87]

Pilate promptly sent an army, mounted and on foot, who killed a great number and captured many others, and the more important among them he condemned to death. The Samaritans complained to Vitellius, the governor of Syria, who ordered Pilate to go to Rome and there justify his actions. In the meantime Vitellius appointed another Procurator.

This was the condition of Judæa (and of Samaria and Idumæa also) at the time of Jesus. Conditions elsewhere in Palestine were better, since the government was in the hands of a Jew, even though he was not altogether independent. Of Philip, the son of Herod (4 B.C.E. to 34 C.E.), nothing much needs to be said. In the first place, his domain (Batanæa, Trachonitis, the Hauran, Gaulanitis, Panias and Ituræa) was not solely inhabited by Jews, but contained many Greeks, Syrians and Arabs. And, in the second place, his

---

[84] *Embassy to Caius* §38.

[85] So *Wars* II ix 4. Apparently this was a special fund which it was forbidden to touch, for there is an explicit *Mishna* to the effect that it is permitted to use Temple funds for such public needs a saqueducts: "Waterways and city walls and towers and all municipal needs are to be supplied from the funds of the Temple office" (*Shek.* IV 2). This is opposed by Ya'betz, *Tol'doth Yisrael* V 83. It is difficult to suppose that such a thing was forbidden at a time earlier than the *Mishna*.

[86] Luke xiii. 1: "Now there were some present at that season which told him of the Galilæans whose blood Pilate had mingled with their sacrifices," confuses Pilate with Archelaus who had killed three thousand men, including many Galilæans (*Ant.* XVII x 2) in the Temple; the delegation which complained against him to the Emperor Augustus emphasized the fact that "they had been slaughtered like sacrificial beasts." A similar confusion survives in Luke in connexion with the census of Quirinius. And also in the *Talmud* it is very common. (See above, p. 153 n. 58).

[87] *Ant.* XVIII iv 1

realm remained peaceful and his rule was in no way remarkable either for good or for evil, except for the building of the town Kesarion, or Cæsarea-Philippi (to distinguish it from Cæsarea-Palestinæ built on the seacoast by Herod) on the site of the ancient Panias, near the source of the Jordan; and the building of the town Beth Saida where the Jordan enters the Sea of Galilee: the same city was called "Julias" in honour of the daughter of Augustus and is not to be confused with the other Julias, south of the Valley of the Jordan ("Beth-haram" in the Old Testament, "Beth-haramtha" in the *Talmud* and Josephus, the present Tel er-Ramah). [88]

The Tetrarch Philip was a just man and a man of peace, but a friend of the Romans and an imitator of the Greeks. In this, as also in his fondness for magnificent buildings, he was a true son of Herod. In one thing he even surpassed his father and brothers: he was the first to engrave on his copper coinage the image of the Emperors Augustus and Tiberius; such a thing neither Herod his father, nor Archelaus and Antipas his brothers had dared to do. He may have done this because, as we have said, many if not the majority of his subjects were Gentiles. But the fact that he tried to hide his Jewishness from his foreign subjects sufficiently proves that, although as a man and a ruler he was the most placable among the brothers, as a Jew he was no better than they.

We have still to treat of Herod Antipas (4 B.C.E. to 39 C.E.) who ruled Galilee and Transjordania and had, among his subjects, Jesus of Nazareth. He was a clever, subtle man and not without reason did Jesus refer to him as "that fox" (Luke xiii. 32). There were many Gentiles in Galilee as is attested by its name "Galilee of the Gentiles;" yet from the time of John Hyrcanus and his son Aristobulus I, many of these Gentiles had been compulsorily converted to Judaism and more and more Jews had settled there.[89] Antipas knew how to lend an importance to Galilee.

Sepphoris, destroyed by Varus in order to crush the rebellion of Judah the Galilæan,[90] he fortified and surrounded with a great wall, and, for the protection of Transjordania, he built Beth-haramtha, which he at first named Livias, in honour of the wife of Augustus, and afterwards Julias, after the name of the Emperor's daughter.[91] His special title to fame is the building of Tiberias, so called in honour of the Emperor Tiberius.[92]

---

[88] On Beth Saida and its situation see B. Meistermann, *Capharnaüm et Bethsaïde,* Paris, 1921, and see below, p. 260 ff.

[89] What Dr. A. Kaminka (*Studien zur Geschichte Galiläas,* Berlin, 1889, pp. 29-38) says on this subject is in part true but contains much that is exaggerated. See above, p. 135 n. 2.

[90] See above, p. 156.

[91] On this town see Ya'betz, *Tol'doth Yisrael* V 80-81 n. 6; Schürer II⁴ 213-216.

[92] This was known to the *Midrash:* "Tiberias after the name of Tiberius," *Gen. R.* §23.

But here again we notice the son of Herod: he paid no attention to the fact of the city's being built on the site of an ancient cemetery (probably that of Hamath or Rakkath), with the result that such Jews as were scrupulous about the rules of clean and unclean, and especially the priests, would not live in it; he was therefore compelled to people it with Gentiles, beggars and Jewish vagabonds, building houses for them and granting them many privileges.[93]

Similarly he had no hesitation in building a theatre and a royal palace containing pictures of animals (for which reason it was destroyed at the time of the great Jewish revolt) and conducting the municipality along the lines of Greek cities. None the less he shared in the Jewish protest against the ensigns dedicated to the Emperor which Pilate set up in Jerusalem, and he never went so far as to engrave the Emperor's image on his coinage. Here too we see how closely allied in spirit was Antipas to his father, who while following the ways of the Greeks and Romans still kept a hold on Judaism. Antipas, again, in everything to do with the love of building, was a true son of his father.

And just as he inherited from his father this love of building, so too did he inherit his love for women. While in Rome Antipas became enamoured of Herodias, the wife of his step-brother Herod (son of king Herod and Miriam the daughter of the High Priest Simeon ben Bœthus), the daughter of the murdered Aristobulus, and mother of the Salome mentioned in the Gospels in connexion with John the Baptist. But Antipas had already married the daughter of Aretas king of Arabia. Her he decided to divorce and to take Herodias, his brother's wife, contrary to the religious law. To avenge his daughter, the king of Arabia made war on Antipas and heavily defeated him. Antipas appealed to Tiberius who ordered Vitellius, the governor of Syria, to punish Aretas.

But in the meantime Tiberius died [94] (37 C.E.). Antipas interfered in the negotiations between the Romans and Parthians, and this was one of the causes of his downfall. The principal reason was that when Agrippa I received the throne of Judæa from Caius Caligula, Antipas' wife, Herodias, incited him also to try to secure the title of king. Agrippa, however, sent a special emissary to Rome to prevent this, lest there should be two kings claiming the same crown; and the same emissary accused Antipas of having dealings with the enemies of Rome, the Parthians, and with Sejanus, the object of Galigula's special hatred, and also of preparing a large stock of arms.

Caligula was angry with Antipas, exiled him to Gaul and bestowed his tetrarchy upon Agrippa. Caligula would have left Herodias her

---

[93] Dr. A. Kaminka, *op. cit.* pp. 17 ff. tries to prove that this is only a legend, but *Ant.* XVIII ii 3 ἐπὶ μνήμασιν, ἃ πολλὰ τῇδε ἦν is quite clear and not easy to contradict; Tiberias was built almost in Josephus' own days.

[94] In the next section of the present volume, in the chapter dealing with John the Baptist, this subject will be dealt with in more detail.

private heritage, since she was the sister of his friend Agrippa; but she possessed a Maccabæan strain in her blood, and with a pride in keeping with a grand-daughter of Mariamne she refused the Emperor's kindness and preferred to follow her husband into exile. She and her daughter Salome were instrumental in the death of John the Baptist at the hands of Antipas; but this complicated matter will be explained in the following section.

* * * * * * * * *

Such was the political condition of affairs during Jesus' lifetime and during the generation that preceded him, from the outbreak of the war between the brothers Hyrcanus and Aristobulus to the close of the procuratorship of Pontius Pilate in Judæa and of the reign of Herod Antipas in Galilee (from 67 B.C.E. to 39 C.E.). Scarcely a year went by during this century without wars or other disturbances: wars, rebellions, outbreaks and riots, and all of them with their concomitant of incessant bloodshed; and this state of things prevailed in the Land of Israel throughout the whole epoch which preceded Jesus and prevailed also during his lifetime, a period which can be styled "the Edomite epoch"—from the rise of Antipater, the father of Herod, till the rise of Agrippa I, the grandson of Herod.

Were we to count up one by one those who fell in the wars and rebellions and those murdered by Herod and the Procurators during this dreadful century, we should reach a total of not less than two hundred thousand men—an appalling number for such a comparatively small country; and it is even more terrible when we recall that those who died in war were the pick of the nation physically, and those murdered by Herod were the pick of the nation intellectually and culturally.

Most of the survivors were of the weaker and more vapid type, those "not of this world," those who turned their eyes away from current state events and occupied themselves only in religious matters or in abstract speculation and mystical visions. Still more, the Roman Procurators and Herod, by their cruelty and harshly applied justice had sapped the courage of the Jews and laid their terror upon the people. This is aptly described by the *Talmud* when it records how Herod came disguised to Baba ben Buta and, with malicious intent, began to speak ill of the government, while Baba ben Buta feared to utter a word, for "the fowls of the air would spread abroad whatever he might say." [95]

At this time, therefore, near to the time when Jesus was born, none dare take part in political matters or adopt a definite attitude towards the fortunes of his miserable but beloved fatherland: he might not even utter his ideas aloud. Spies were everywhere and police held the population in subjection: all alike were downtrodden and overcome by fear.

[95] *Baba Bathra* 3b, 4a. Cf. *Eccles.* x. 20.

Such a condition, especially when accompanied by wars, endless tumults, and even earthquakes and famine, ever begets vast numbers of unbalanced men. Oppression, danger and fear, all combined, upset the nerves, and added to the ranks of the excited and hysterical. Those possessed of any strength and vitality joined the party of the Zealots, whole-hearted antagonists of the government whether with the tongue or with the sword, antagonists alike of the foreign enemies and the Jewish traitors.

The half-hearted and the moderates became the "stay-at-homes," who studied *"Torah* for its own sake," a *Torah* which had no direct connexion with political life, and comforted themselves by spreading among the people the "knowledge of God," a higher moral and ethical standard. The more weak and downtrodden and passive among them cultivated secret, mystic doctrines which had but little to do with this world and were given up entirely to the heavenly life. From such soil as this sprang up the various sects prevalent in Palestine in the time of Jesus.

All alike were dissatisfied with existing political conditions, with perhaps the one exception of the Sadducees. These had more or less come to terms with things as they were, firstly, because they were "practical politicians" and saw that nothing could avail against the Roman government which dominated nearly the entire known world; and, secondly, because they themselves were wealthy and so dreaded any change which might disturb their peace and their enjoyment of the pleasures of this life.

But the rest of the people could not so come to terms. Every country which had fallen under Rome's iron yoke groaned under the harsh bondage; but none felt it so bitterly as did the Jews. Of the nations subdued by Rome none was so peculiar and exceptional as the Jews. The Romans failed utterly to comprehend them. Other conquered peoples, too, had their own special ideas and habits, but they all, in the end, came to an understanding with Roman usage, while Rome, on her part, was tolerant in all matters affecting beliefs and ideas.

But the Jews no more understood the spirit of the Romans than did the Romans understand the spirit of those Jews who showed themselves capable of rising in solid revolt over what, to the Romans, seemed matters of the most trivial importance. Images of the Emperor, for example, were not religious but only political emblems, yet the Jews deafened the whole world with their protests against them. The Olympian games and wrestling contests, again, had nothing to do with religion, and were good in themselves, yet the Jews raved against these also. And what had theatres and circuses to do with religion? Yet the Jews would bar them in Judæa. And in the case of so useful a matter as aqueducts, why could not the Temple "Qorban" funds be used to provide them? Yet the Jews nearly raised a rebellion over it. It could be nothing but sheer obstinacy and an innate rebellious nature.

Such was the conclusion arrived at by the Roman Procurators who had not, nor could have, any clear conception of the singular characteristics of the Jewish faith (we have a present-day parallel in the Palestinian English officials). So they "behaved themselves deviously with the perverse:" in every popular outburst of protest, unpolitical in character, the Roman officials saw preliminaries to revolt and therefore crushed the outburst without mercy. This but served the more to enrage the people, who well knew how far they were from revolt, and to strengthen their complaints anew and so lead on to a further measure of suppression by the Roman executioner who only saw a second attempt at rebellion.

And so the misunderstanding continued.

The effect of this condition of things was to beget either utterly fanatical seekers after freedom who turned into actual rebels, or utterly despairing visionaries, extreme moralists and mystics, who waited for nothing less than the mercy of heaven, for a freedom which should come by miraculous means, a salvation which could be hastened only by deep faith and good works, by a patient watching for the "end" in a humble and lowly spirit, which forgave insults and could forego material possessions: "hoping and quietly waiting for the salvation of the Lord" (Lam. iii. 26).

To these two types of men can be traced, on the one hand, the destruction of the state and, on the other hand, the rise of Christianity—the destruction of the national religion; they were the two sides of the same medal.

But these effects arose out of a still more fundamental reason— the chasm that lay between the messianic ideal and the facts of reality.

Those who returned from the Babylonian Exile brought with them the promises of Jeremiah and Isaiah, especially those of the Second Isaiah, who foretold for them such great things: "the riches of the Gentiles" were to come to the new Judæa; "kings should be their nursing fathers;" all nations "should bow down to them with their faces to the ground;" all nations "should lick the dust of their feet;" Jerusalem's "foundations" should be "sapphires" and its "windows carbuncles;" its "enemies should be cut off and great should be the welfare of its children." Such was the Second Isaiah's promise.

But what was the actual fact? Slavery to foreign governments, wars, tumults and torrents of blood. Instead of all nations being subject to Judah, Judah was subject to the nations. Instead of the "riches of the Gentiles," godless Rome exacted taxes and tribute. Instead of "kings being her nursing fathers," there comes Pompey and his army. Instead of the Gentiles "bowing down with their faces to the ground" and "licking the dust of their feet," comes a petty

Roman official with unlimited power over Judæa. Instead of Messiah the son of David, comes Herod the Edomite. . . .

It was all beyond endurance. Josephus,[95a] Tacitus,[95b] and Suetonius [95c] reach the like conclusion that the chief cause of the great revolt which culminated in the destruction of the Second Temple (and the same applies to the other Jewish rebellions) was "an ambiguous oracle found in their sacred writings to the effect that in those days one of their race should rule over the whole world" (χρησμὸς ἀμφίβολος ὁμοίως ἐν τοῖς ἱερεῖς εὑρημένοις γράμμασιν, ὡς κατὰ τὸν καιρὸν ἐκεῖνον ἀπὸ τῆς χώρας τις αὐτῶν ἄρξει τῆς οἰκουμένης).

Not even Herod himself, strange though this sounds at first, was innocent of this belief. There is no truth in what the author of "Doroth Rishonim" says of Herod's preference to be a "King of Gentiles" rather than a "King of Jews," as we have already seen; yet with some measure of restatement the idea is quite true. Herod wished to be both "King of Gentiles" and "King of Jews," king, in fact, over the whole world.

Herod, the Edomite Jew, with his craving for endless glory, was, despite his "healthy" understanding and ability to cope with facts, none the less, replete with superstition. In his inmost heart he hoped to be that universal ruler whose coming the Jews awaited and whom they styled "King Messiah." His ideas about this may have been vague but it ever appeared to him through the mists of the future as a distant hope for which he must prepare the ground. Tyrants of Herod's gloomy cast of mind are, at the same time, most "practical politicians" and visionaries obsessed by dark, hidden hopes, hopes which play just as great a part as their pursuit after glory, and which are just as deep as their burning ambitions.

Only in such a sense as this can one agree with Albert Réville [96] that Herod hoped to become a supreme ruler once Rome had become enfeebled through the collisions of its rulers. That such a thing was not impossible he saw from the example of the Parthian Empire which never became subject to Rome. A proof that Herod meditated a kingdom as universal as that of King Messiah may be found in Josephus' story about the eunuch Bagoas.[97] Bagoas was assured by the Pharisees that "the king who was to come," i.e. King Messiah, would make him a father and benefactor, and restore to him the ability to marry and beget children.[98] In his indignation Herod killed this eunuch Bagoas, for he himself expected to be the "king who was to come."

But if Herod desired a worldly kingdom only, the people looked

[95a] *Wars, VI*, v, 4.
[95b] *Hist., V*, 13.
[95c] *Vespasianus*, 4.
[96] See his *Jésus de Nazareth*, 2d ed. Paris, 1906, I 203-204, 209, 211-212.
[97] *Ant.* XVII ii end of 4.
[98] See Schürer, II ⁴ 599 and n. 18; he rightly corrects the faulty translation here given by all translators of Josephus.

forward both to a kingdom of this world and also to a kingdom of heaven; for a political stronghold and sovereignty over the Gentiles, together with the recognition of the truth of Israel's religion. But, as we have seen, political reality was a direct contradiction of this hope; and the complete antithesis between the dark political reality and the bright prophetic ideal, which lived in the heart of the people, had a twofold effect.

On the one side, the antithesis provoked the healthy and courageous younger generation—especially those of simple Galilee, far removed from the more sophisticated society of Jerusalem—to fight for their nation, their country and their God: the ardour of the Zealots recognized no sovereignty of flesh and blood: God alone was King in Israel; and (as is invariably the case with extreme enthusiasts) they found it necessary to add to their zeal a tyranny and violence which only served to augment the prevailing confusion. They failed to discriminate between actual traitors and Roman sympathizers, and those who were simply peaceful-minded—who had no love for Rome and remained faithful to their people, but were not by nature men of war.

On the other side, the same antithesis between political reality and the prophetic ideal moved most of the Pharisees, devotees of the *Torah*, to abandon all interest in temporal things, in the uncertainties of politics and the incidents and changes of daily life: they gave themselves up entirely to the "life eternal," to the explication of the *Torah* in its minutest detail. It was not that the Pharisees opposed political action on principle: they did not find the moment propitious; they fulfilled in themselves the injunction "Go, my people, into your inner chambers . . . hide thyself for a little moment, until the indignation be overpast" (Is. xxvi. 20).

Such was the party of the "quietist Pharisees" who confined themselves within the narrow limits of *Torah* interpretation and made "submission" the basis of their lives. Like Archimedes of Syracuse their chief desire was that the Romans touch not their "zig-zags."

Quite distinct were the "Zealot Pharisees" (in essentials the Zealots were but extremist and active Pharisees: one of their founders was Zadok "the Pharisee;" and Josephus [99] tells us that, apart from their excessive devotion to freedom "they were in all things akin to the Pharisees"). The Zealot Pharisees added to their devotion to the *Torah* an obligation to defend it with the sword.

Distinct again were the "moderate Pharisees," men who did not oppose intervention in political affairs but who realized that "there was a time for all things" (Eccles. iii. 1). When Shemaiah and Abtalion (or Hillel and Shammai) saw that the times favoured Herod, they tried to persuade the people to open the gates of Jerusalem to Herod; [100] and when Rabban Yochanan ben Zakkai saw

[99] *Ant.* XVIII i 6.
[100] *Ant.* XIV ix 4; XV i 1.

that the times favoured the Romans he recommended that peace be made with them and that they should be tolerated "till indignation be overpast." To the attitude of the "quietist Pharisees" conformed "those that feared the Lord," "the meek upon earth," such as belonged to no party and who wholeheartedly loathed force, and were unable to fight against the high-handed empire: the earth was given into the hands of sinful men—therefore these lifted up their eyes to heaven, waiting for the kingdom of heaven, for the coming of the Messiah, for the time when God alone should be king of all the earth and righteousness prevail throughout the world, when ungodliness should be consumed like smoke and that proud kingdom should pass away and the people of Israel be exalted above all the Gentiles.

Such people as these were the creators of a great part of the "Pseudepigraphical Literature" (the *Book of Enoch,* the *Book of Jubilees,* the *Assumption of Moses,* and the like). which is full to repletion of the messianic hope in its widest sense. More will be said of these books later.

This same antithesis between ideals and facts created yet other parties. It increased the number of those visionaries and day-dreamers who, because of the evil of present things, allowed their minds to wander in a world "where all was good," in the shining spheres far removed from actualities. Such men became mystics and forecasters of the future. The sect of the Essenes, which was far removed from political life, was largely comprised of such as knew the future and performed miracles; such as Menahem the Essene who had prophesied to Herod that he should be king.[101]

Such wonder-workers were not, however, to be found only among the Essenes: Shemayah (or Shammai) the Pharisee also foresaw, when Herod stood on trial before the Sanhedrin accused of the murder of Hezekiah the Galilæan, that Herod would be king.[102] These visionaries altogether despaired of things as they were, because political life was full of godlessness, violence and every abomination, and present conditions were the utter antithesis of the political ideal of the prophets.

Since, however, they were too feeble and spiritually-minded to fight against present evils and so effect tangible reforms, they turned away and immersed themselves in problems of ethics and visions of

---

[101] *Ant.* XV x 5. It is very probable that Menahem the Essene was the same as Menahem the colleague of Hillel who "went forth in the service of the king" (*Hagiga* 16b; but see *J. Hag.* II 2); for the Essenes were not. like the Sadducees, direct opponents of the Pharisees, and an Essene might well be a "quietist Pharisee" who at first mingled in politics as "Father of the Beth Din" in the Sanhedrin and afterwards gave this up to become an Essene hermit. To the *Talmud* the rumour that he prophesied good things of Herod was sufficient to make them conclude that he "went forth in the service of the king." The *Mishna* (*Hag.* II 2) says only "Menahem went forth." See Graetz (Heb. trans.) I 495; and Derenbourg, *Massa Eretz Yisrael,* pp. 243-244.
[102] *Ant.* XIV ix 4.

the future; they turned towards the "meek upon earth," to the poor and destitute, to the small and feeble, to the lost and the outcast, to the miserable and penitent. To them they preached comfort and for them they spun the golden threads of the messianic idea in its more spiritual and less political form, namely, the kingdom of heaven: a glorious future life must needs be the reward for the present gloomy life; they that now were little would then be great in the days of the Messiah, and they that now were lowly would be exalted in the kingdom of heaven. Thus did they save themselves from desperation and God from the charge of injustice.

In Galilee Gentiles were numerous, and it had never been a centre of the Law [103] or a place of resort for High Priests or the richer classes; it had no cities approaching the scale of Jerusalem nor, till the time of Antipas, even towns of the scale of Jericho. In Galilee were to be found neither Pharisees learned in the Law nor Sadduceans or Bœthuseans, nor any of the richer and more powerful classes who acquiesced in Roman domination; there remained only the two dissimilar types: Zealots of the party founded by Judah the Galilæan and Zadok the Pharisee, numerous in Galilee (though not as a sect) from the time of Hezekiah the Galilæan; and the "meek upon earth" and the many varieties of the mystic, visionary type—"quietist Pharisees," Essenes, and the like. All who had strength enough to take up the sword joined themselves with the Zealots; the rest were more or less akin in spirit to the "meek upon earth" who abandoned interest in temporal things to dream of a future life, a life based on the ethics of the Prophets and the messianic idea. The Zealots, too, as well as every type of Pharisee and the Essenes, held most strongly to those same conceptions, but in the thoughts of the "meek" they assumed a more imaginative and mystic form.

It was from these circles of the "meek" that Jesus and his new teaching sprang.

[103] Cf. the saying of Rabban Yochanan ben Zakkai: "O Galilee, Galilee! thou hast hated the Law: thou wilt in the end beget oppressors" (*J. Shabb.* xvi 8, near end of section); and these "oppressors" were found in the marauding zealots (see *Baba Qama* 116b).

II. ECONOMIC CONDITIONS

[Literature: in *Hebrew:* Joseph Klausner, *"Biy'me Bayith Sheni,"* Berlin, 1923, pp. 9-88; Abner, *"Ha-Gor'mim ha-Kalkaliyim ha-Chebruthiyim shel M'ridath ha-Chasmonäim"* (*Ha-Shiloach* xxiv 40-44, 141-149, 243-251); Joseph Klausner, *"Historiya Yisraelith,"* I 130-287, II 51-53, 76-77, 137-139, 144-145; III 44-89; S. Krauss, *"Qadmoniyoth ha-Talmud,"* I pt. i, Odessa, 1914; Zadok Kahn, *"Ha-'Abduth al-pi ha-Torah v'ha-Talmud"* (trans. S. Fuchs), Cracow, 1892.

In *German:* Frants Buhl, "Die Sozialen Verhältnisse der Israeliten," Berlin, 1899; L. Herzfeld, "Handelsgeschichte der Juden des Altertums," 2 Aufl. Braunschweig, 1894; S. Krauss, "Talmudische Archäologie," I-III Leipzig, 1910-1912; E. Schürer, "Geschichte d. Jüd. Volkes im Zeitalter Jesu Christi," II⁴ 67-82; D. Farbstein, "Das Recht der unfreien und freien Arbeiter nach Jüdisch-Talmudischem Recht," Frankfurt a. Main, 1896; H. Weinheimer, "Geschichte des Volkes Israel," Vol. II, Berlin, 1911.

In *French:* R. P. Schwalm, "La vie privée du peuple juif à l'époque de Jésus-Christ," Paris, 1910; E. Stapfer, "La Palestine au temps de Jésus-Christ," 8 ed.

In *English:* A. Edersheim, "The Life and Times of Jesus the Messiah," 12th ed. London, 1906; "Sketches of Jewish Social Life in the Days of Christ," London, 1896; A. Büchler, "The Economic Conditions of Judæa after the Destruction of the Second Temple," London, 1912.]

(1) Though the Jews, in the time of Jesus, were no longer *solely* an agricultural people, they were still *essentially* an agricultural people; especially was this the case in Galilee where Jesus was born and where he began his ministry: Josephus [1] tells us that Galilee "was wholly under cultivation and seemed to be one great garden." Particularly famous was the wheat from Galilee, from the valley of Arbel and from Chorazim and Capernaum (places mentioned in conjunction with each other both in the Gospels and in the *Talmud*). [2] A good quality of wheat was also grown in Samaria (in the valley of Ain Sokher) and in Judæa, at Michmash and Zanochah, and also at Apharaim, famous for its large ears of corn and the abundance of straw obtained after the threshing.

In the period of the Second Temple the Jew proved himself a skilful agriculturalist; he knew how to prepare the soil, manure it and clear it of stones and thorns. He was accustomed to terrace the

---

[1] *Wars* III iii 2.

[2] Matt. xi. 21-23; see *Menahoth* 55a where, for "Chorazim and Kefar-Ahim," should be read "Chorazim and Kefarnahum" (or Kefar Tanhum), the modern Korazi and Tel-Hum in Lower Galilee near the Sea of Galilee.

hills and valleys ³ so that the "sweeping rains" (Prov. xxviii. 3), so violent in the Palestinian winter, should not wash away the thin layer of soil off the rocks, and he knew how to practise irrigation by means of cisterns, wells and canals.

In a normal season the Judæan farmer reaped fivefold from a normal soil, while with good seasons and from fruitful soil he reaped as much as a hundredfold; and Galilee was even more fruitful than Judæa. In ordinary years, if we take no account of droughts, Palestine produced bread enough not only for its population but even for exportation.

Besides grain crops (wheat, barley, spelt, oats, rye, millet and even rice, which had been brought from the east and acclimatised), the country was rich in vegetables (cabbages, carrots, cucumbers, gourds, onions, garlic, radishes, rape-seed, lettuce, lentils, beans, peas, and acclimatised vegetables like melons, artichokes, orach, lupine, asparagus, Egyptian beans, Egyptian and Greek gourd-fruit), which provided the bulk of the ordinary food for the poorer classes; while Palestine was especially rich in fruit (grapes, olives, figs, pomegranates, charobs, citrons, cherries, plums, nuts, almonds, dates, mulberries, apples, pears, apricots, quinces, and acclimatised fruits like crustumenian pears, peaches and medlars).

The wine of Judæa and Samaria was plentiful and good; the grapes were so plentiful that they were used for raisins, and so sweet that they were used to make honey (dibs). From the sour wine, vinegar was obtained. Oil too was plentiful and good, especially in Galilee. The best came from Gush Halab, the very name of which testifies to its luscious olives; we can comprehend why it should be just Yochanan of Gush Halab who, about the time of the Destruction, received the monopoly for selling Galilæan oil to the merchants of Cæsarea or to the Syrian Jews.⁴

Likewise famous for oil were the districts Netopha, Meron and Thekoa in Galilee, and Shiphkon and Beth Shean in Samaria.⁵ In Judæa too the olive was plentiful as is evident from the names "Mount of Olives," "Gethsemane," and the like. Palestinian olive oil was exported to Tyre and Sidon and Syria and Egypt. Another source of wealth was the date-palm which produced "date palm oil" and "date honey;" according to Pliny ⁶ Judæa was as famous for dates as Egypt for spices, and he enumerates five varieties of Jericho dates, famous for their fine flavour and delicate odour. He also extols the balm of Ain Gedi which, according to him, was sold for twice its weight in gold.⁷

The Jews were also shepherds, cowherds and cattlemen, and

³ Shebi'ith III 8.
⁴ Wars II xxi 2; Life of Josephus §13.
⁵ Peah VII 1 and 2.
⁶ See Hist. Nat. XIII 4. 44; and Wars IV viii 3.
⁷ Hist. Nat. XII 111, and Strabo, Geographica, XVII, 1, 15.

Jerusalem had a special "cattle-market." [8] The name "Tyropæan" (cheese-market) proves that they were dairymen too. The Jews of Transjordania trafficked in wool, and in the new portion of Jerusalem was a "Woollen-merchants' market," to the north of the city adjoining the markets of the ironworkers and carpenters, and the shops of the dealers in cotton and clothes.[9] As for poultry, the Jews had, from very early times, reared doves and pigeons; other species which they began to breed at a later stage were those which bear a foreign name: cocks and hens (תרנגול and תרנגולת which ousted the Hebrew terms נבר, and, apparently פרניה, respectively), geese (avis אווז) and ducks (בן האווז).

Hunters were few, but fishermen were numerous, especially in Galilee. The Sea of Galilee contained all manner of fish, including certain very choice varieties.[10] Countless fishing-boats filled the lake which was surrounded with villages inhabited wholly by fishermen. So plentiful were the fish that they were salted and sold in Palestine and abroad; this accounts for the fact that a town on the lakeshore, which apparently bore the Hebrew name Migdal or Migdal-Nunaya,[11] was in Greek called by the name "Tarichæa," from the word τάριχος salted fish.[12] The newly built Tiberias became the fishing centre and fish market of Galilee.

Galilæan fishermen who became attached to Jesus play a prominent part in the Gospels, and two of them, Simon Peter and Andrew his brother, after having been fishers in the Sea of Galilee, were called by Jesus to become "fishers of men." [13] In the Jordan and the Mediterranean Sea fish were also plentiful, and as early as the time of Nehemiah, when the Tyrians used to bring fish, probably salted, to sell in Jerusalem (the coast-towns were then in the hands of the Phœnicians and Philistines) there was a special gate called "the fishgate." [14]

From the Dead Sea ("the sea of Sodom") came salt, bitumen,

---

[8] *Erubin* VIII 9. That the reference is not to incense dealers appears from the words of R. Yose (*ibid.*) that "it was the woollen market," and not, as S. L. Rappoport supposed, the market of the pharmacists and spice-dealers (see his article in *Ha-Maggid*, 1874, no. 17, reprinted in *Ha-Me'ammer* ed. Luncz, II 556).

[9] *Erubin ibid.; Wars* V viii 1.

[10] *Wars* III x 8.

[11] *Pesahim* 46a; *J. Ma'as'roth* III 1; *Sanh.* II 1; such is the conclusion of Klein, "Beitr. z. Geographie u. Geschichte Galiläas," Leipzig, 1909, pp. 76-84. 89-93, and Dalman, *Orte und Wege Jesu*, 2 Aufl. Gütersloh, 1921, pp. 114-116; "Beth Yerah" or "Ariah" is the modern Hirbet el Kerakh, near the colony Kinnereth. According to N. Slousch (*Qobetz* I, Tel Aviv, 1921, p. 66 note 2 to the article *Hor'both Tarichaia* by R. Ashbel) Tarichæa was in Hebrew called *"M'laha"* since, corresponding with the Greek name, the Arabs call Kinnereth "Malaha."

[12] See Strabo, *Geographica* XVI. He also commends the muries, the brine of preserved fish. from Tarichæa, *ibid. 2*.

[13] Matt. iv. 18-20 and parallels.

[14] Cf. Nehem. iii. 3 and xiii. 16.

varieties of phosphorus and tar, for home-consumption or export.[15] Pliny [16] tells us that "Judæan pitch" was world-famous, and to this day bitumen is known by the name of "Jewish pitch" (Judenpech, Judenharz). 'The country also contained "Antipatris nitre." The henna-flower (Song of Songs, I, 14) produced a dye employed in the female toilet, and from roses, to which entire gardens were devoted, was made a precious "attar of roses." [17] Iron-mines were to be found in the Lebanon and in the north of Edom, near the town Pinon or Punon, and Josephus [18] mentions "the hill of iron" which "extended as far as the land of Moab." There were certainly such mines in Transjordania since Ibrahim Pasha still used to quarry iron near Jebel Ma'rad, about an hour and a half north of the Jabbok (Wadi Zeraqa).[19]

(2) The Jews were equally alert and practised in handicrafts. Even though we were to regard the many *Talmudic* passages in praise of handicrafts, and the dictum that a man must teach his son a trade,[20] as nothing more than abstract, academic ideas, it is still apparent from the actual lives of the greatest of the *Tannaim* at the close of the period of the Second Temple and after the Destruction that the Jews of that time were skilled in handicrafts: Hillel the Elder was, for some time, employed as a wood-cutter; R. Yehoshua ben Hananya was a smith; R. Nehunya, in the latter days of the Second Temple, was a well-digger. We hear too of R. Yehudah "the baker," of R. Yochanan "the shoemaker," of R. Yehudah the "apothecary," of R. Yehoshua the "miller," and so forth.[21] Jesus of Nazareth was a carpenter and maker of cattle-yokes,[22] and Saul of Tarsus, Paul the Apostle, was a tent-cloth weaver or tapestry-worker.

We find, almost contemporary with Jesus, mention of no less than forty kinds of craftsmen in the Jewish literature: Tailors, shoemakers, builders, masons, carpenters, millers, bakers, tanners, spice-merchants, apothecaries, cattlemen, butchers, slaughterers, dairymen, cheesemakers, physicians and bloodletters, barbers, hairdressers, laundrymen, jewellers, smiths, weavers, dyers, embroiderers, workers in gold brocade, carpet makers, matting makers, well-diggers, fishermen, bee-keepers, potters and platemakers (who were also pottery dealers), pitcher makers, coopers, pitch-refiners and glaze-makers, makers of glass and glassware, armourers, copyists, painters and engravers.

Handicrafts were passed on from father to son, a fact indicated by the expression in the *Talmud:* "a carpenter and son of a carpen-

---

[15] *Wars* IV viii 4.
[16] *Hist. Nat.* XIV 25. "Gardens of roses," *Ma'as'roth* II 5.
[17] *Shabbath* XIV 4.
[18] *Wars* IV viii 2.
[19] See Frants Buhl, *Die sozialen Verhältnisse der Israeliten*, Berlin, p. 72; G. Dalman, *Palästina-Jahrbuch* IX (1913), p. 68, on this iron mine.
[20] *Aboth* I 9 (Shemayah); *Kiddushin* IV 14.
[21] See Büchler, *Economic Conditions*, p. 50.
[22] Justin Martyr, *Dial. cum Tryphone*, §88.

ter," or "of carpenters," [23] or "Hananya the son of apothecaries," and, in the Old Testament, "Malkhiya the son of metal-refiners." [24] And Christian-Jewish tradition tells that both Jesus and his father Joseph were carpenters. There were entire families, especially skilled in some craft, who would not reveal their secret outside the family.[25]

Whole cities were famous for one class of work: e.g. in Magd'la (Migdal Sabo'aya in Transjordania) were numerous dyers, Beth Saida had numerous fishermen (דיינים, and not ציידים, hunters), in Kefar Hananya and Kefar Sihin were jarmakers, and "to bring jars to Kefar Hananya" was like "bringing straw to Apharaim;" [26] Sepphoris had its weavers,[27] and the finest cotton came from Beth Shean, while the commoner sort came from Arbel.[28] Nazareth was apparently a town of carpenters and wood-sawyers.[29]

At the time of R. Hoshayah the Great (first half of third century) there were towns in the south where the people were mainly occupied in purple dyeing,[39] and in the fourth century the author of *Totius Orbis Descriptio* mentions Lydda, Samaria, Cæsarea and Sarepta ("which pertaineth to Sidon") as "noted for purple."[31] Although this is very much later than the time of Jesus we know that in the East, and especially in earlier times, craftsmen did not so readily change their trades as in present-day Europe.

Before, and most probably during, Jesus' time the Jews had something like factories giving employment to whole families, *e.g.*, "the families of the fine linen workship of the house of Ashbe'a," and "the inhabitants of Netaim . . . which were potters." [32] There were smaller workshops where a man worked by himself or with his sons or one or two apprentices: "Beth kaddad" (house of the jar-maker) and "Beth tsabba' " (house of the dyer) ;[33] but "Beth y'tsirah,"[34] with the abstract "y'tsira" and not "Beth ha-yotser" (house of the potter, as in the Old Testament),[35] refers apparently to an entire factory, employing a larger or smaller number of hands.

(3) But in spite of the comparatively large number of artisans

[23] *Ab. Zar. 3b* (beginning); *J. Yeb.* VIII 2.
[24] Nehem. iii. 8 and 31.
[25] *Yoma* III 11.
[26] *Gen. R.* §86.
[27] *J. B. Bathra* III 3.
[28] *J. Kiddushin* II 5; *J. Kethuboth* VII, 8; *Gen. R.* §19; *Qoh. R.* on *Ki b'robh hokhma; Mid. Tanhuma Bereshith* §24, ed. Buber p. 9; *Mid. Shemuel* VII 3, ed. Buber, p. 66. On this see Munk, *Palästina* (Hebrew trans. M. Rabinson, Vilna, 1909) ; S. Klein, *Beiträge*, p. 53 n. 1.
[29] See Joseph Halevy, *Shemoth 'Arê Eretz Yisrael* (in *Yerushalayim* ed. Luncz, IV 11-20).
[30] *Tanhuma, Naso* §8; ed. Buber p. 32 n. 70.
[31] See Büchler, *Economic Conditions*, p. 50 n. 1.
[32] I Chron. iv. 21 and 23.
[33] *Mo'ed Qatan 13b; Pesahim 55b.*
[34] *T. Kelim: B. Qama* III 8; *Siphre Zutta* 35, 11 (ed. Horowitz, *Qobetz Ma'aseh ha-Tannaim*, III 331 n. 3).
[35] Jerem. xviii. 2-3.

and the many and various handicrafts in Palestine, the bulk of the people were not artisans but peasants possessed of small holdings. The *Mishna*, the *Baraitas* and the Gospels have alike much to say of the life of the peasant and comparatively little of that of the Hebrew artisan. The reason for this is perhaps to be found in the fact that Jewish craftsmen were not able to compete with foreign goods; the foreign names borne even by such common articles as stools (ספסל—"subsellium"), handkerchief (סודר—"sudarium"), sandals (סנדל —σανδάλιον) and felt-hats (פיליון—πίλιον), show that these things were imported from abroad.[36] Therefore the part played by native artisans was not so prominent.

It was quite otherwise, however, with the peasant class, and especially with what we now call the "small-holder." He is the "ba'al ha-bait," the "householder," of the *Mishna*. the exact Greek translation of which is given in the Gospels (οἰκοδεσπότης). These middle-class peasants, whose land provided them with an adequate though limited subsistence, were the bulk and the mainstay of the nation. They populated most of the villages (of which there were, especially in Galilee, hundreds) and also the small and medium sized towns, such as retained the title "Kefar," village, even after they had ceased to be villages in the ordinary sense (*e.g.*, Kefar-Nahum, Kefar-Saba, which were real towns).

These "small-holders" lived by the labour of their hands. They, their wives and children, did their own ploughing and sowing, reaping and sheaf-binding, threshing and winnowing. Most of their produce they reserved for their own household needs, and the rest was brought to the town and either bartered or sold for money to procure absolute necessaries. Such a peasant was not able to lay by any wealth, and one or two years of bad seasons or illness would be enough to deprive him of his property and reduce him to the status of a hireling or labourer, or even cause him to be sold into slavery to a richer land-owner because of his debts. In any case some of his children would be forced to become hirelings or labourers since the small-holding sufficed only for the eldest son who received "a double share" of their inheritance. The other sons, not having land enough for their needs, were, in spite of themselves, turned into members of the "proletariat," the class which owns nothing but its powers of work. When no work is forthcoming they are reduced to the level of "unemployed labourers," and become beggars or—robbers and brigands.

In Judæa, however, and in a lesser degree also in Galilee, was a class of wealthier peasants whose land earned for them more than enough for their needs; it was they who would lend money or seed to the impoverished small-holders on the security of the latter's property, and this property sometimes passed into the possession of the lenders to enlarge still further their holdings.

[36] See in detail R. P. Schwalm, *La vie privée du peuple juif à l'époque de Jésus-Christ,* Paris, 1910, pp. 262-272.

These "wealthy proprietors" laid the foundation of a produce market and of Hebrew trade generally. The middle-class landowner traded with the money gained by the sale of such of his produce— vegetables and fruit—as was left on his hands after satisfying the needs of his own household. This class was fairly numerous compared with the class of really wealthy landowners, of whom there were but few.

There were "men of property" (עתירי נכסין or בעלי נכסין) even in the time of the Macabees and especially in Herodian times; they were mostly connections of the royal family and of the high-priestly families, but the same class was to be found among the merchants already in the time of Joseph ben Tobias. "Latifundiæ," large landed estates such as were to be found in Italy and which brought about the downfall of Rome, were not a prominent feature of Palestine; but they did exist. The Gospels speak of the *Oikonomos* and the *Epitropos,* the "steward" who supervised the numerous servants of a great property while the wealthy owner lived in the city or was absent travelling in pursuit of business.[37] The *Mishna* refers to the fact that Rabban Gamaliel II ("of Yabneh") had workmen who tilled his land,[38] and that he used to let his fields.[39]

Palestine thus possessed both the artisan and the hireling class. The hireling hired himself out for a definite period, not exceeding six years; he could also hire out his services for a single day (hence the term "daily hireling" (שכיר יום). He was either an impoverished small-holder or the son of a small-holder who, not having inherited land enough to support him, allowed himself to be hired by a rich land-owner for a certain length of time until he could improve his position. His relations with the wealthier proprietor were those of the "client" with the "patron" in Rome.[40]

There were, again, in Judæa and Galilee peasants who had no land and spent all their life in the position of hired workmen to rich peasants and others; such were known as *l'qutoth,* and an entire village in Palestine, "Kefar-L'qutaia" was named after them.[41] The hireling lent himself for any kind of labour and was the counterpart of the English "unskilled labourer." The artisan, *po'el,* on the contrary, was hired only for some definite craft or crafts.

The *Talmud* refers to the "unemployed *Po'el,*" and the Gospels contain a parable about a householder who went out to hire workmen and found "workmen who had been idle all the day" because "no man had hired them."[42] The householder or employer used to enter into an agreement with the workman, usually by word of mouth

[37] Luke xvi. 1-8; Matt. xx. 8, etc.
[38] *Demai* III 1.
[39] *B. Metzia* V 8. On Rabban Gamaliel's wealth see Büchler, *op. cit.* pp. 37-38.
[40] Krauss, *Talmudische Archäologie,* II 102.
[41] *Lam. R.* on 'al eleh.
[42] Matt. xx. 1-7.

though sometimes also in writing, and whoever should break the agreement (חוזר בו) had to pay a fine, whether employer or employed. The sympathy shown in the *Mishna* and the *Tosefta* [43] in favour of the labourer redounds to the *Talmud's* credit; but this sympathy dates from a period later than the Second Temple and is mainly no more than an academic view never widely held in real life.

Yet the position of the Hebrew labourer was better than that of the Roman, Egyptian or Babylonian labourer, both by reason of the simpler conditions and fewness of men of great wealth, and also because of the democratic spirit infused into daily life by the Scribes and their successors, the Pharisees and *Tannaim*.

The labourers mostly worked on the land, but the craftsmen also employed labourers who were called חניכים or שוליות, apprentices. [44] They worked ten hours a day and were paid anything from an *as* to a *sela*, though the average was a *drachma* [45] or a *dinar* [46] a day (about eightpence). This was the rate in Macabbæan times, about the time of writing of the *Book of Tobit*, and in the reign of Domitian when the Gospel of Matthew was written. [47]

Besides the peasant pure and simple, there were to be found in the Palestine of Jesus' time varieties of the same class: (a) the contractor or middle-man (קבלן), who undertook to carry out the required work and pay all taxes and, in return, received a half, third or quarter of the produce.

(b) The tenant farmer (אריס), corresponding to the Roman "colonus," who received seed, implements and beasts of burden from the owner of the land, but tilled the ground himself and, as pay, received a half, third or quarter of the produce. Such "tenant farmers" were numerous in Italy in the time of Jesus, and it was they who, on the expropriation of this "foreign" land, brought about the downfall of the Roman Empire. In Palestine they were not so common since the "householder" and "small holder" predominated. But even there the tenant farmers played an important part and, as may be seen from the Gospel parable of the "Wicked husbandmen," [48] there prevailed strife and enmity between them and the propertied class.

(c) There was also the "lessee" who did not receive but *gave* a fixed portion of the produce in lieu of rent, so that if the land produced less than this portion the lessee was the loser, and if more he stood to gain.

(d) Finally there was the hirer, who differed from the lessee in

[43] See Farbstein, *op. cit.*
[44] *Pesahim* 108a; *B. Qama* 32b; *Shabb.* 96b (in the latter passage see the reading of the "Aruch").
[45] *Tobit* 5, 4.
[46] Matt. xx. 2, 9, 10, 13.
[47] See L. Herzfeld, *op. cit.* pp. 195-196.
[48] Matt. xxi. 33-42.

that he paid in money and not in produce, but was in other respects identical with the lessee.

Besides the unattached labourers there were the "children of the household," corresponding to the male and female domestics of today, and the "ministers" (שמשים ושמשות or משמשים ומשמשים), usually personal attendants, especially of aged people and students requiring personal assistance and service, the valet and lady's maid of today.[49]

Thus, apart from the comparatively few large landowners with great estates ("fathers' houses"; בתי אבות is the Hebrew term),[50] and the more numerous well-to-do peasant class, we find a multitude of small-holders and a complete "proletariat" of every kind: hirelings, artisans, landless peasants, tenants, lessees, renters (and, to a certain extent, contractors), household servants and personal attendants.   These were all men and women who had no means of subsistence beyond their ability to work. So long as they could secure work, all was well with them; but if not, they were reduced to want and beggary—the passive victims of grievances and the dreamers of dreams, or else imbued with violent rage and the spirit of revolt.

All the proletariat so far enumerated were, however, independent —at least from the legal standpoint: their labour might be sold to others, but their bodies were not enslaved by strangers. But there were, in Palestine, also slaves. It is true that the slave did not lack work and so did not lack bread; but he was not free: he could not choose his work or his master. The Hebrew slave was a hireling for six years, but he differed from the hireling in not having the right to change his master or choose his work. It might be true from the humanitarian standpoint of the *Talmud* that the body of the Hebrew slave is not "a thing that can be bought," [51] and that "whoso getteth a Hebrew slave is as he that getteth himself a master," [52] but such humanitarian laws [53] were, so far as the time of Jesus was concerned, merely academic expressions of opinion.

The Hebrew slave in his master's house was then an *actual* slave, enslaved in body and mind to his master and feeding from the crumbs off his master's table; he was, however, spared the consciousness of perpetual slavery and so his spirit was not wholly crushed. The primitive relationship prevailing between master and slave in a country where the simple life was the rule and the democratic Pharisaic spirit was much in evidence, largely removed the possibility of cruelty

[49] Krauss, *Talmudische Archäologie*, II 101-102.
[50] *T. Terumoth* II 11; *B. Bathra* 46b.
[51] See *Arakhim* VIII 5 against the opinion of Rabba in *Qiddushin* 16a and 25a and *Baba Qama* 113b.
[52] *Qiddushin* 20a, 21b.
[53] Collected in Zadok Kahn's *Ha-Abduth al-pi ha-Torah v'ha-Talmud*, translated into Hebrew from the French by J. S. Fuchs, with added notes, Cracow, 1892.

and persecution; none the less, a master could scourge an idle or disobedient slave and treat him altogether as an inferior being.

It is true that Hebrew slaves were not so numerous in Palestine as, for example, in contemporary Rome, and so could not play the same decisive rôle, culturally and economically, as they did in Rome (though Eduard Meyer combats the prevalent view of their evil influence in the Roman Empire).[54] But they were, none the less, an important factor in the political and spiritual upheavals in the time of Jesus.

Without them we cannot account for the frequent rebellions and the many religious movements from the time of Pompey till after the time of Pontius Pilate. Where there are no crowds of destitute men and impoverished small-property owners, it is not popular revolts that mature but only political conspiracies among the army and the ruling powers. The same holds good with regard to extremist religious movements: their leading figures are invariably the discontented crowds seeking fresh paths to happiness because the present is evil and affords no justification to the accepted religious beliefs.

Again, neither numerous nor an important social element in Palestine were the "Canaanitish slaves" (so called because they came from Tyre and Sidon, or because of the verse: "Cursed be Canaan, a slave of slaves shall he be to his brethren . . . and Canaan shall be their slave")[55] A hundred francs in present money was the average price of a Canaanite slave (male or female; the expression "Cushite female slave" is also common); but the price might be as high as a hundred *mânë* or as low as a gold *dinar*.[56] The slaves acted as tailors or barbers, bakers, butchers, pearl-stringers, and even tutors and teachers; female slaves were also hairdressers, singers, dancers and the like.

Their sale was completed by a written contract as though they had been goods or cattle; they were "marked" so that in case of escape they might be everywhere recognized: a seal was stamped on them or else a bell was hung upon them, round their necks or on their clothes, as is done with camels in the East or with cattle in the Swiss mountains; or they wore a special cap (כביל): and sometimes their flesh was branded just like cattle. Legally the Canaanite slave was his master's chattel: he could have no private property ("what a slave has acquired, his master has acquired"); the work of his hands, his finds, and even money accruing to him as compensation for harm incurred, belonged not to himself but to his master. But in spite of all this "the hand of a slave is as the hand of his master"[57] and

[54] See his excellent *Die Sklaverei im Altertum* and *Wirtschaftliche Entwickelung im Altertum*, Jena, 1895.
[55] Gen. ix. 25-27. On slave traffic in Tyre and Sidon see II *Macc.* viii. 11.
[56] *B. Qama* IV 5.
[57] *Ma'aser Sheni* IV 4; *Gittin* 77b.

"a man's slave is as his own body" [58]—which was hardly the case with the Roman slaves.

Canaanite slaves were not so well fed as Hebrew slaves,[59] and the former were deemed idle, dissolute, shameless and lewd: so little respect did their masters feel for their presence that "some performed the most private actions in front of them."[60] And there were some masters and their sons who "considered all things lawful with the female slaves."[61] The owners held their slaves in complete subjection, scourging them with whips and thongs, with the "fargel" (*flagellum*) and "magleb" (some kind of knout, with a knob of metal at the end), and inflicted on them "forty stripes save one," or "sixty strokes" (*pulsim*). Only if the slaves suffered in consequence some manner of deformity they used to be freed; and if they died as a result of their injuries inflicted by their master, the master was put to death (thus removing the slave from the category of a chattel or mere animal).

In all other respects they were treated like cattle: they had legally no family relationships, no rights of marriage, divorce or widowhood, and the incest laws did not hold in their case. In actual fact, however, it was different; if Herod's brother, Pherora, had a slave-girl as paramour and the all-powerful Herod could not separate them,[62] and if Rabban Gamaliel ha-Nasi suffered his slave Tabi to fulfil the injunctions of the Law and mourned over him and received consolation at his death (as enjoined in the Law),[63] and if in the Nasi's house the eldest slave was styled (though this was at a late period) *Abba*, father, and the eldest female slave, *Amma*, mother—then the same human conditions probably held good in the time of Jesus.

But in any case, "Canaanitish slavery" was then a horrible plague affecting the national body of Israel as was also the case with other nations in those early days. Even if the Canaanitish slaves took no part in the subversive political and religious movements in Palestine, by their very existence they unwittingly helped to bring them about. Harsh slavery invariably produces a body of malcontents, and there is no more readily available fuel for such movements than those men who have been crushed and reduced to the level of brute beasts.

(4) Besides agriculture and handicrafts, commerce also flourished in Palestine at the time of Jesus. During the time of the First Temple and the beginning of the Second, in the Persian period, the merchants were mainly Canaanites, and it was from them and in company with them that the Jews learned the business of the mer-

[58] *B. Qama* 27a.
[59] *Gittin* I 6.
[60] *Niddah* 17a.
[61] *Lev. R.* §9; see also *Yeb.* II 5.
[62] *Wars* I xxiv 5.
[63] See *Sukka* II 1; *Berakhoth* 16b; *B. Qama* 74b; *J. Erubin* X 1; *J. Sukka* II 1; *J. Kethuboth* III 10.

chant and pedlar (לסחור and לרכול *i.e.,* to go round from place to place "on foot" with the object of bartering various commodities), and, later, to practise salesmanship in one fixed place (חנות shop, חנוני shopkeeper), to bargain and trade, and, finally, to practise commerce (מקחה). [64]

From the time of Alexander the Great, however, when Jerusalem began to be surrounded by Greek cities, mainly trade-centres, the Jews learnt commerce from the Greeks. This is apparent from the many Greek mercantile terms: "Siton" (סיטון-σιτώνης) is the general dealer in corn produce; the dealer in only one variety of corn or other goods is a "monopol" (מנפול-μονοπώλης); and he who deals in various articles, and especially in bread, is called "p'latar" (πρατήρ according to Schürer and Krauss; πωλητήριον according to Herzfeld). Even the shopkeeper's account-book (הפטיף) had a Greek name, "pinaks" (πίναξ). The Hebrew word for mirror (מראה) was changed for the Latin *aspeclaria* (speculum); the cobbler (רצען) became the *sandalar* (sandularius); the table (שלחן) was called *tabla* (tabula); the seat (כסא) became *safsal* (subsellium); the salver (קערה שטוחה) became *escutela* (scutella), and the curtain (יריעה) became *vilon* (velum). A robe of honour was given a specifically Greek name *astala* (στολή), and even the cover of a sacred volume had a Greek name *tik* (θήκη).

When Hillel introduced an important reform in the interests of Palestinian commerce, he gave it a Greek name *prozbol* (προσβολή). Scores of other Greek and Latin words became naturalized in Hebrew literature and are only accountable through the influence of Latin and Greek commerce. [65] Such foreign words do not, however, prove that Greeks only, and not Jews, practised trade in Palestine: they prove only that the first impetus to trade came from the Greeks. "These borrowings (from Greek)," says Schwalm, "do not indicate that the articles in question came to the Jews from the Greeks: it was, simply, that the language of national trade was filled with neologisms because the language of trade was Greek.

It was precisely the same in the sixteenth century when the Florentines, going through and about France, brought with them Tuscan words which have now become naturalized: *agio, bilan, banqueroute, banque.*" [66] The Jews had, in fact, practised trade in Palestine from the time of Simon Maccabæus, when the coast towns gradually became subject to him and his son, John Hyrcanus, and his grandson, Alexander Jannæus. Palestine was greatly benefited by the economic policy of the Maccabæans. Simon Maccabæus took measures to improve agricultural conditions. His many efforts to secure an outlet to the sea [67] and his harsh insistence that the coast dwellers should either

[64] Nehem. x. 32.
[65] Collected in Schürer, *op. cit.* II⁴ 67-82; Krauss, *op. cit.* II 355-356; Klausner, *Biy'mê Bayith Sheni,* Berlin, 1923, pp. 42-43.
[66] Schwalm, *La vie privée du peuple juif,* pp. 325-326.
[67] Clearly shown in I *Macc.* xiv. 5.

turn Jews or leave, are best explained as the outcome of an economic rather than a national policy or religious zeal. His example was followed by his son and grandson who enlarged the Land of Israel till it embraced the whole of Palestine.

The taxation of exports and imports brought the Maccabæans, from John Hyrcanus to Hyrcanus the Second, into important negotiations with the Senate of Rome.[68] The Maccabæan monument at Modin gives a picture of ships, and the anchor (together with ears of corn, grape-clusters and pomegranates) is a symbol on the Jewish coinage from Alexander Jannæus till the Herods.

Internal trade, too, was also well developed. "Market-days (ימי כניסה) had long been in existence, and to these were added permanent markets (שווקים) [or streets devoted solely to trade], an old Jewish institution, as opposed to the ירידים "goings down" (i.e., to the coast towns, in the lowlands by the sea: cf. "they that go down to the sea," [68a] and the Aramaic (נחותי ימא), markets instituted by non-Jews.[69] The regular pilgrimages to Jerusalem at the great festivals served also to develop internal trade. The Palestinian towns exchanged their agricultural produce. Sharon in Judæa sold its wines and bought bread. Jericho and the Jordan valley sold their famous fruits for bread and wine. The Judæan Shefela had a superabundance of bread and oil, and Galilee of corn and vegetables. Palestine also exported its surplus of oil, wine, wheat and fruit, while it imported a considerable number of commodities.

Of the two hundred and forty articles of commerce mentioned in the *Talmud* and *Midrash* in connexion with Palestine, enumerated by Herzfeld,[70] one hundred and thirty, or more than a half, came from abroad. Trade routes within the country were numerous, and many important routes radiated towards neighbouring states.[71] Jewish sailors were just as numerous as Jewish donkey-drivers and camel-drivers, the companies of which brought into use the collective nouns חמרת a donkey-caravan, and גמלת a camel-caravan.

So prevalent was trade within the country that we actually find in the High Priests' prayers on the Day of Atonement, a prayer for "a year of trade."[72] Alike in Jerusalem and every considerable Judæan and Galilæan town (Tiberias, Sepphoris, etc.), the merchants and craftsmen had their markets and booths: the booth of the cobblers, of the dyers, of the flax-dealers, of the spice-merchant, of the cotton-dealers and of the clothiers; the market of the bakers, of the weavers, of the metal-workers, of the glass-makers, of the car-

[68] *Ant.* XIII ix 2; XIV viii 5, x 6.

[68a] Ps. cvii. 23.

[69] See *Gen. R.* 67: "Esau has ירידים, and Jacob שווקים."

[70] See his *Handelsgeschichte*, pp. 129-130.

[71] Krauss, *Qadmoniyoth ha-Talmud*, Odessa, 1914. I 158-159; Herzfeld, *op. cit.* 22-23, 141-142; Klausner, *Biy'mê Bayith Sheni* pp. 50-53; Buhl, *op. cit.* pp. 7-8.

[72] *J. Yoma* V 3.

penters, of the wool-merchants, of the cattle-breeders—the cattle market, and so on.

There were also the *maqolin* (macellum), or meat-market; the *atliz* (אטליז‎ קטלין‎ - κατάλυσις) for the sale of meat, cattle and wine; the *nahtomar* and *p'latar* (see above) sold baked bread and sometimes vegetables also. The קבע‎ and תרים‎ were the stalls for the market-women. The סטיו‎ (στόα) was a hall of pillars, surmounted by a dome, corresponding to the French "depôt" or the German "Markthallen;" and the "dome of accounts" (כפת־החשבונות‎) was, apparently, the "stock-exchange" of those days. Pedlars (רוכלים‎) went about in the smaller towns selling their wares to the country folk, and also spices and embroidery to the town women; and the "clothes dealers" (מוכרי‎ כסות‎) used to "fold on a rod behind them" the garments which they carried about for sale.[73]

Export and import dues were levied on merchandise, and paid to tax-gatherers (נובים‎, נבאים‎) בלשים‎, excise-officers and publicans (מוכסים‎), who farmed the tax from the Government or from other publicans. We are not aware of the extent of taxation at the time of the Maccabees but we know that the Seleucids took from the Jews a poll-tax, a salt tax, a "crown" tax (crowns of the bride and bride-groom), a land tax, a cattle tax, and a tax on fruit trees.[74] We may assume that, most probably, the Maccabees did not add to these taxes but may even have reduced them, since we hear no complaints against their method of taxation (*e.g.*, from the popular delegates who came to complain to Pompey against Hyrcanus and Aristo-bulus).[75]

On the other hand, the moment Herod died we hear an emphatic demand from the nation to abolish the "annual tax" and the "tax which was levied indiscriminately on everything bought and sold in the market."[76] The inference is that Herod increased the burden of taxes and duties (what the Romans called "tributum" and also "vec-tigalia") beyond endurance. It was, apparently from that time—that of the Romans and their agent Herod—that the name "publican" became synonymous with robber, brigand, ruffian, murderer, and reprobate;[77] one whose evidence was invalid, whose money could not be accepted as alms for the poor nor used in exchange, since it was suspected of having been acquired by robbery.[78]

In this the Gospels are in complete agreement with the *Talmud*, and the collocation "publicans and sinners" (τελῶναι καὶ ἁμαρτωλοί commonly occurs.[79] The Procurators taxed far more heavily even

[73] *Kelaim* IX 5; *Shab.* 29b; *Pesahim* 26b.
[74] I *Macc.* x. 28 and 33; xi. 34-36.
[75] *Ant.* XIV iii 2.
[76] *Ant.* XVII viii 4.
[77] *Sifra, Kiddushim,* ed. Weiss, 91b; *Shebuoth* 39a; *Hagiga* III 6; *T. Tohar.* VIII 5; *Nedarim* III 4; *J. Nedarim* III 5; *B. Qama* 113a.
[78] *Sanh.* 25b; *B. Qama* X 1.
[79] *Matt.* ix. 10-11; *Mark* ii. 6-7; *Luke* v. 30.

than Herod. The Romans exacted from the Palestinians (to the same extent as from the natives of other countries subject to Rome) a water-tax, a city-tax, a tax on such necessities of life as meat and salt, a road-tax and a house-tax.[80]

The frontier-taxes proved a special hardship: every city was a frontier in itself and Pliny tells how "that at every stopping place, by land or sea, some tax was levied," [81] with the result that goods were sold in the Roman market at a hundred times higher cost than at the place of their origin or manufacture, in spite of the fact that the fixed duty imposed by the general Roman administration in, for example, the province of Asia (in which Palestine was included) was only two and a half per cent of the value of the goods. Such taxes impoverished the people and made them full of impotent rage against the "despotic kingdom" which, through its many minions, drained their blood.

When at last all power of endurance failed them, a part, the healthiest and strongest, utterly rebelled against this government; but another part waited, in its helplessness, for the kingdom of heaven which should make an end of this "kingdom of wickedness"—for the King-Messiah and all his wondrous works.

But notwithstanding the many heavy taxes and customs dues, home and foreign trade enriched a portion of the Jews. As we have seen, they were much concerned in shipping and for this reason often resorted to the "cities of the sea." This fact is apparent from the innumerable names to be found in *Talmudic* and *Midrashic* literature for the ship and all its fittings,[82] and also from the figures of ships and the anchor inscribed on the Maccabæan and Herodian coins, and yet again from the coin, struck by Titus in commemoration of the Fall of Jerusalem, on which are engraved a date-palm and the symbolic figure of "Judæa" seated on the ground surrounded by discarded shields, while on the reverse is the head of Titus with the Latin words "Judæa Navalis"! [83]

Jewish ships, manned by Jewish crews and laden with Jewish merchandise, sailed the Jordan, the Dead Sea, the Sea of Galilee, the Mediterranean, the Black sea, the Nile and the Euphrates, and travelled as far as France, Spain, Cyrene, Carthage and even India. As the result of this commerce and the great industry of the Jewish peasantry, part of the Jews became wealthy. From the time of Alex-

[80] *Ant.* XIX vi 3.
[81] *Hist. Nat.* XII 63-65.
[82] Collected in Krauss, *op. cit.* I 338-349.
[83] S. Raffaeli, *Matbe'oth ha-Yehudim*, p. 147 and Tab. 21, fig. 147. Josephus seems to refer to this in *Wars* VII v 5, when he says that Titus issued at the time of his triumphal procession "figures of ships in great number." On the pirates of Aristobulus see *Ant.* XIV iii 2, and on the Jewish pirates of Jaffa during the great revolt, who infested the whole northern coast of the Mediterranean Sea, see *Wars* III ix 2-4. See also A. Zifroni, *Pompeius be'Eretz-Yisrael* in the Hebrew weekly *Ha-Tor*, Vol. I, no. 31.

ander Jannæus, Palestine contained not only retailers and ordinary merchants (תגרי־לוד, תגרי־ירושלם), but merchants on a considerable scale.

Besides the greater land proprietors we find rich bankers who did business not with the *dinar* merely, but with the *talent* (worth about 9,500 francs), *i.e.,* with very large sums in comparison with the financial conditions of the time. Such bankers were not only occupied with the business of exchange connected with the conversion of local and foreign money, but also acted as money-lenders to the small-holder, the shopkeeper, corn-merchant and caravan master.[84]

"The notable men of Jerusalem "[85] and "the notable women that were in Jerusalem "[86] were not only important, but wealthy people. Kalba Shabua, Nicodemus ben Gorion, Tsitsith ha-Kassaf,[87] Eleazar ben Harsum and Martha bath Bœthus are famous in the *Talmud* for their vast wealth, which reached fabulous proportions.[88] Even by the end of the Maccabæan and beginning of the Herodian period the number of noted wealthy men, whom Herod accused of rebellion and whose possessions he confiscated, reached many scores.[89]

The people of Jerusalem are described as being vainglorious folk (אנשי שחץ),[90] given up to pleasure, finicking in their speech and, like the wealthy of every age and place, priding themselves in their excesses. The source of such wealth was most probably commerce, but it was just as probably acquired through the gradual accumulation by the wealthier peasant class of the small holdings of the poorer peasants in payment of debts.

Palestine thus came to possess a class of poor, destitute and unemployed, and landless peasants, side by side with a class of wealthy farmers, great landed proprietors and rich bankers. The former waxed poorer and poorer, sinking into mendicancy, crushed and depressed, hoping for miracles, filling the streets of town and village with beggary and piety or (in the case of the more robust) with brigandage, highway-robbery and revolt; outcasts, haunting the caves and desert places and the rocks and crevices of the mountains.[91]

Both alike sought a release from poverty and want. Some sought it by natural means, civil and social, urging revolt against Rome and social revolution with all that came in its train—murder and rapine against the richer and upper class, which the poorer, exploited class looked upon as its social, political and national enemy. The others sought release by means of prayer, repentance, and submission to

---

[84] As against Krauss II pp. 352-355, see Schwalm, *op. cit.* pp. 376-408.
[85] *Yoma* VI 3; *Sukka* 37a.
[86] *Sanh.* 43a.
[87] Thus J. N. Epstein reads in place of הכסת "Monatsschrift," 1919 262-3.
[88] Büchler, *op. cit.* 34-41.
[89] *Ant.* XV i 2.
[90] *Shab.* 62b.
[91] Büchler, *op. cit.* 55-7.

the will of God. And these brought into being the spiritual messianic movements, the pedantically severe observance of the commandments, separatism and asceticism; and certain of this latter type, for whom the fulfilling of the commandments brought no spiritual satisfaction, were induced to look forward to a mystic redemption "not of this world," a desire later embodied in Christianity. . . .

Why should it have been just after the death of Herod "the Great" that there arose, contemporaneously, a most terrible rebellion and a new sect—Christianity—which endeavoured to separate itself from Israel?

The answer is that already given in the preceding section: the Maccabæans built up Palestine on a sound economic foundation, while Herod destroyed it in the economic sense, for, like Solomon, he placed too heavy a burden on the country and thereby hastened the end.

With all their efforts to find a sea-outlet, to conquer the southern ports and, as far as possible, the northern ones too, the Maccabæans still exercised a wise moderation in their economic demands. They, too, constructed magnificent buildings: forts like the Citadel in Jerusalem, and Hyrcania, Alexandrion, Machærus and Masada, buildings of such artistic pretensions as the Palace of the Maccabees and the Cave of Machpelah, and all the wonderful mausoleums in the Kidron Valley near Jerusalem which, in the present writer's view, are certainly Maccabæan in origin. And it is possible that they, too, were responsible for the fine tombs near the Bocharan Quarter north of Jerusalem, and the tomb of "Simon the Just." [92] But all these things they did gradually, in the course of some eighty years or more, and from spoil derived from their enemies.

Herod, on the other hand, placed no limit to his ambition, and where he failed to satisfy it owing to his subjection to Rome, he found other means of acquiring fame and glory. Not only did he bedeck his own country with magnificent buildings, but even Tyre and Sidon, Greece and Asia Minor, Rhodes and Antioch, Athens, Lacedæmonia and Pergamon.

Money was required for all this. Furthermore he was obliged to placate the Romans, to give many presents to their politicians and bribes to their generals. He also kept a brilliant court, a great palace and an army of mercenaries and spies and innumerable detectives: there was no end to his expenses. The necessary funds could be got only by confiscation of property, unbearable taxation, and an economic policy beyond the powers of such a small country and contrary to the inclinations of the Jewish farming class who, after all, were the backbone of the nation in those days. The remark of Josephus that "the Jews showed no tendency towards commerce or international trade" [93] may not be literally true but intended as a de-

* Klausner, *Biy'mê Bayith Sheni*, pp. 67-76, 117-149.
** *Contra Apionem* I 12.

fence only against the Greeks,[94] but it is partially true so far as the time when it was written is concerned.

The present writer has elsewhere [95] tried to show that a fixed economic policy dictated Herod's doings—his buildings outside Palestine and even his solicitude for the Jews abroad and his great works in Transjordania—though this policy was an outcome of his pursuit after wealth which should establish his political position as king by the grace of Rome, and satisfy his boundless lust for fame and glory. And it was with this object in view that he instituted a reign of terror hitherto unexampled in Jewish history. This is plainly indicated in Josephus: "When he could no more refrain from his oppressions since this would diminish his income, he made use of the people's very hatred for his private enrichment." [96] Josephus frequently emphasizes the fact [97] that Herod's disbursements were beyond the scale proper to so small a state.

To increase his income he sought to establish in Palestine Greek trade (and the Greek culture which was bound up with it) beyond the present capacity of the Jews. And side by side with this went an unendurable increase in taxation, precisely as in the days of Solomon, who served as a model to Herod for the spreading of commerce, for erecting great buildings, and for encouraging a foreign culture. The same results followed in both cases: rebellion and the disintegration of the state. Just as, after the death of Solomon, the people desired of Rehoboam that he would "make light the grievous service of his father and his heavy yoke," so, immediately after the death of Herod, the people demanded of his son Archelaus that he "lighten the annual taxes and abolish the duties that were exacted mercilessly on everything bought and sold in the markets."

But Solomon—at least in appearance—was an independent monarch, whereas Herod was subject to the Roman Emperor. Hence the elders of Israel complained against Herod not only before his son but also before the Roman rulers. Among other charges they alleged the outstanding fact that "He brought the people to a state of complete poverty, though he had found it, with certain exceptions, in a state of prosperity." [98] Or, differently expressed, "thus, in place of the prosperity and virtue of the past, came complete poverty and vice." [99]

This is strong proof of economic welfare under the Maccabees and of deterioration under Herod. This material deterioration brought with it also a spiritual deterioration. As with every case of bad economic conditions which multiply the number of the unemployed and the "Lumpenproletariat," Herod increased the number of malcontents,

[94] Klausner, *op. cit.* p. 9.
[95] *Ibid.* pp. 77-88; *Historia Yisraelith*, III 81-89.
[96] *Ant.* XVI v 4.
[97] See for example *Ant.* XVII xi 2.
[98] *Wars* V vi 2.
[99] On the moral decay see *Ant.* XV viii 1; *Sotah* IX 9.

both rebels and idealists. These two types effected, on the one hand, the civil eruptions that began with Archelaus and reached a climax in the revolt in the time of Nero and the consequent Destruction; and, on the other, spiritual and messianic eruptions, which, receiving a strong impetus in the time of Herod, came to a head with the rise of Christianity.

Herod's economic policy, which hastened the natural process of decay and led to the ultimate catastrophe, was followed by Archelaus and, in a measure, by his other sons, Antipas and Philip, and also attracted the Roman Procurators. All alike practised the policy of Herod with all his defects but without any of his glamour.

Two results followed this policy: (a) by taking the Jews out of their proper economic sphere and turning them into a cosmopolitan rather than a national people, it served to create within Judaism a desire for a world religion, a desire which later became embodied in the shape of Christianity; and (b) by destroying nation and state, through constant rebellions resulting from the unnumerable class of malcontents brought into being through Herod's civil and economic policy, this same policy brought about the rise of Christianity and its adoption in certain Jewish circles. The Jews no longer possessed a national-civil vitality, rooted in their own territory, enabling them to stand firm in the face of the new denationalizing Creed.

None is so conservative or tenacious of ancient customs as the peasant associated with the soil; and Herod's policy, which increased both the number of traders and of destitute, increased also the class which had no stake in the country. Such a class, with no stable position and nothing to lose, served as the foundation of the enthusiasm for the new political and religious movements. It was not specially from this class that Jesus and his disciples arose (they were all artisans and fishermen living by the labours of their hands); but if Jesus successfully taught of the kingdom of heaven, it was simply and solely because of the disordered condition of life in the country, and the bad economic conditions generally. The humble and simple and the downtrodden from among the uprooted and discontented class sought a release from their sufferings and a firmer basis of life, both in the material and spiritual sense; and this they found in the "kingdom of heaven" (in its moral and abstract sense) as taught by the carpenter and son of a carpenter from Galilee.

III. RELIGIOUS AND INTELLECTUAL CONDITIONS

[The literature on the religious and intellectual conditions in the time of the Second Temple is boundless: an entire volume would be taken up by their titles alone. Here it will be enough to refer to the books mentioned in the note to page 129. Graetz (5th ed. vol. III pt. 1) and Schürer (4th ed. vols. 2 and 3) give most of the literature. We would only add Weiss, "Dor Dor v'Dor'shav," pt. 1; Frankel, "Dar'kê ha-Mishna"; Chwolsohn, "Das Letzte Passamahl," Leipzig, 1908; J. Elbogen, "Die Religionsanschauungen der Pharisäer," Berlin, 1904; W. Bousset, "Die Religion des Judentums im neutestamentlichen Zeitalter," Berlin, 1903; M. Friedländer, "Die religiösen Bewegungen innerhalb des Judentums in Zeitalter Jesu," Berlin, 1905; H. Graetz, "Sinai et Golgotha," Paris, 1867.]

The centuries of work carried out by the "Scribes," and the Pharisees who succeeded them, were not without effect. There was gradually created in Palestine an educated class, comprising not only the priestly families and the upper classes but the common people as well. Those able to read and write became more numerous, especially from the time of Shimeon ben Shetah, since it was he, and not Yehoshua ben Gamala, who laid the foundation of the Hebrew school system.[1] Josephus, a contemporary of Yehoshua ben Gamala, mentions as a generally known fact that the *Torah* makes it incumbent to teach children to read and write ($\gamma\rho\acute{\alpha}\mu\mu\alpha\tau\alpha$), that they should know the laws ($\nu\acute{o}\mu o\upsilon\varsigma$) and be told of the deeds of their forefathers, "that they might follow in their ways and, having been brought up on the laws, become accustomed to observe them and have no excuse for not knowing them." [2]

According to him, Moses had already enjoined "that they teach

[1] So *J. Kethuboth* VIII 11: "Shimeon ben Shetah ordained . . . that children go to the *Beth ha-Sefer* (school)." But the *Talmud Babli* (*B. Bathra* 21a) says that Yehoshua ben Gamala "decreed that they station teachers of children in every city and town." Derenbourg has already observed (*op. cit.* p. 132 n. 1) that "it is difficult to suppose that at the time of this High Priest the Jews were able to attend to such matters." It may be added that Yehoshua ben Gamala was High Priest near to the time of the Destruction and held the office hardly more than a year (63-65 C.E.). It would seem that Shimeon ben Shetah founded the school system in Jerusalem and that Yehoshua ben Gamala ordained that there be teachers in every town. The term "Beth ha-Sefer" is not found in the Old Testament and was certainly the creation of the Maccabæan period, when the Hebrew language was revived in its entirety (Graetz, Hebr. trans. I 419-425; E. Ben Yehudah *'Ad emathai dibb'ru 'Ibrith,* New York, 1919, pp. 60-71, 108-124).

[2] *Con. Apion.* 2, 25.

the children first of all the laws, the most seemly knowledge and the source of happiness." [3]   Elsewhere Josephus emphatically says: "Most of all we are mindful of the education of children (παιδοτροφία); [4] so that if anyone ask us concerning the laws, we can tell them all more easily than our own name. Having learnt them straightway with our earliest perception (ἀπὸ τῆς πρώτης εὐθὺς αἰσθήσεως), they become engraven in our souls." [5]

Such words, even though they be somewhat exaggerated, indicate the wide extent of the school system by the time of Jesus, some fifty years before Josephus wrote. Philo also, the exact contemporary of Jesus, testifies how the Jews learn the laws "from their earliest youth" (ἐκ πρώτης ἡλικίας). [6] Such a result could be secured only by the school system: fathers, according to the *Torah,* were bound by the precept "thou shalt teach them diligently to thy children;" but they themselves were too busy to do this at the close of the period of the Second Temple, when the old, simple patriarchal life had grown into one more complicated and hard.

Besides the elementary school (*beth ha-sefer*) there was the more advanced school or college (*beth ha-Midrash*). Such colleges, intended for the expounding of *Torah* to specially selected students (תלמידי חכמים), certainly existed in the time of the "Scribes" previous to the Maccabæan period; and from the Maccabæan period, and specially from the time of Hillel and Shammai, the colleges assumed a more popular guise. There they read the *Torah,* and where the people no longer spoke Hebrew they translated into Aramaic, and as a rule they expounded (דורשים) it to the common people on the Sabbaths, and also, possibly, on the market-days, [7] so that the villagers (*i.e.,* the bulk of the people) when they came to town acquired some notion of the *Torah*

In spite of this, however, most of the village peasants were *Ammē ha-aretz* (ignorant of the *Torah*), as were also the innumerable proselytes, voluntary and involuntary, who embraced Judaism in the time of John Hyrcanus, Judas Aristobulus and Alexander Jannæus. But in the larger and smaller towns, and specially in Jerusalem, there could be found many who were instructed in the *Torah* among the artisans, merchants, priests and officials; and though the "sages" (חכמים) were as yet few, the "students of the sages" (תלמידי החכמים) were numerous. [8]

It is, however, a mistake to suppose that the learning of the time was confined to the *Torah.* There was secular learning also in Israel. The poetical and narrative literatures which have been preserved as

[3] *Ant.* IV viii 12.
[4] *Con. Apion.* I, 12.
[5] *Ib.* 2, 18.
[6] *Del. ad Caium* 31 (ed. Mangey II 577).
[7] Though such may not have been the case until a later period.
[8] Perhaps for this reason the phrase "student of the wise" came in course of time to be used instead of simply "the wise."

Apocrypha and *Pseudepigraphas* in foreign languages, and which possess a wonderful beauty and variety, mostly emanated from a time a little earlier and a little later than the time of Jesus. And contemporary Jewish art, especially architecture, the mausoleums and ceramic ware, has a notable beauty and grandeur, and exhibits considerable national peculiarity.[9]

In the *Book of Enoch,* the *Book of Jubilees* and, later, in the *Mishna* and *Baraita,* we find much knowledge of the calendar, of astronomy in general (combined with much superstition), of geography, general and Hebrew history (mingled with many strange legends), physiology, human and animal, geometry and land-surveying and the like.

Such studies could not, of course, be compared in importance with the religious study of the *Torah.* But the "Jewish religion" has a wide scope: it comprises all the "wisdom of life," all the knowledge that satisfies the needs of an entire nation; it does not isolate religion from learning and life. In essence it is not so much a religion as a national world-outlook based on religion. It includes philosophy, jurisprudence, science, and rules of seemly behaviour to the same extent as matters of belief and ceremonial practice such as are usually classed under religion.

The crucial test of a nation's civilization at any specified epoch, is the position of its women. And this position from the Maccabæan period is a tolerably high one. The *Kethubah,* the text of the marriage contract, was certainly earlier than the time of Simeon ben Shetah since similar contracts occur in the Aramaic documents of Elephantine dating from the time of Ezra;[10] it is not, therefore, drawn up in Hebrew as would have been more proper during the Maccabæan revival.

But all the amendments introduced by Simeon ben Shetah were in favour of the woman. And there is strong ground for supposing that the technical terms נכסי מלוג (usufruct, lit. "property of plucking") and נכסי צאן ברזל (mortmain, lit. "property of the sheep of iron") used in the contract, which are so original and so stamped with the features of a living language, have also come down to us from the Maccabæan period, a period near the time of Jesus when the Hebrew language was still prevalent in the free or semi-free Hebrew state.

The story of Hanna and her seven sons and that of Judith, where the woman holds the most important possible place as defender of the faith and saviour of her country and nation, both show the high status of the women of the time. The pious and wise queen

[9] For details see Klausner, *Biy'mê Bayith Sheni,* pp. 115-149 and illustrations.

[10] See S. Daiches, *K'thaboth Aramiyoth miy'mê Ezra, Ha-Shiloach* XVII 511-5; and E. Ben Yehudah, *op. cit.* pp. 121-124, where further proof is given that the *Kethubah* was earlier than Simeon ben Shetah.

Shelom-Zion is highly venerated among the Pharisees; while the
wicked Shelomith, sister of Herod, holds a position in the story of
that great tyrant possible only in a condition of things in which
women had the freest rights. Such a status for women in Judæa
shows that Hebrew civilization had, by the time of Jesus, reached a
considerably high general level.

As in most countries of some degree of culture where many of
the inhabitants have attained to means and even to wealth, so also
in Palestine there were the superior "breakers of the yoke," scoffers
and doubters, seeking only after pleasure and dissipation. Of such
a type especially were the great landed proprietors, the rich men and
merchants, certain members of the high priestly families, and most of
the royal families who were in contact with the Greeks and Romans.

It was in Jerusalem, the centre of culture and the home of the
richer and ruling classes, where were to be found the greatest number
of these "wicked" and "ungodly," who "kicked" owing to excessive
prosperity and oppressed the poorer and weaker classes. They were
called by the apt title of שחץ אנשי, the insolent and vainglorious.[11]
Likewise among the *Am ha-aretz* were to be found "breakers of the
yoke" who were such owing to their boorishness, ignorance and disso-
luteness, and these were known by the name עברינים "transgressors." [12] But the majority—the peasants on the one side and the
"students of the wise" (who were also occupied with some handi-
craft) on the other, were pious, God-fearing people.

There was a lofty and noble conception of God. In Jesus' time a
pure form of belief in the divine unity was everywhere current. The
Jews had even ceased to pronounce the "Honourable Name" or the
"Express Name" (שם המפורש), and it was pronounced by none except the High Priest and by him on the Day of Atonement only.
Where "Jehovah" was written, they read אדני, "my Lord;" and they
soon made sparing use even of this name. "Heaven" took the place
of "Jehovah" and even of "Adonai" and "Elohim" (compare the use
of "the kingdom of *heaven*"—which induced the strange plural in
Greek βασιλεία τῶν οὐρανῶν, "the fear of *heaven*," "to sanctify the
name of *heaven*," and similar expressions), which induced the Romans to call the Jews *coelicolae*, worshippers of heaven.[13]

A more abstract title for the Godhead was "the Holy One," to
which was invariably added "Blessed be He." This is found as early
as the *Book of Enoch.*[14] More abstract, even philosophical, is the
designation "The Place" (המקום); its meaning according to the *Mid-*

[11] *Shabbath 62b;* see the *Talmudic* sentence (*J. Shek.* IV 3): "There was
great arrogance (שחצית) among the members of the high-priestly families."
[12] *Shabbath 40a;* the name, the present writer holds, seems to be earlier
than might be supposed from its place in the *Talmud.* Cf. παραβάτης τοῦ,
νόμου quoted above, p. 69, from an early Gospel gloss, Luke vi. 4.
[13] See Wellhausen, *Israelitische u. Jüdische Geschichte,* 7 Aufl., Berlin,
1914, p. 212.
[14] See especially the Ethiopic *Book of Enoch,* XXV 3.

rash is "because the Holy One, blessed be He, is the 'place' of the world." [15] But this is certainly a later explanation, and that of Philo is to be preferred, that the divine essence is in every place. [16] Another early title is "power" (נבורה), and Onkelos translates "the hand of the Lord" as "the power of God." In the Gospels also we find "And ye shall see the son of man sitting on the right hand of power" (ἐκ δεξιῶν τῆς δυνάμεως). [17]

More distinctive and imaginative is the title "Shekina," or divine presence; a title apparently borrowed from the Temple where the Lord chose "to cause his name to dwell" (cf. משכן, ושכנתי בתוכם, Ex. xxv.8). The Shekina was, as it were, a light reflected from the Godhead; it had no existence apart from the Godhead yet could be seen of man apart from the Godhead, like the sun which itself cannot be seen but only the light poured from it for the benefit of mankind. So though the Godhead cannot approach man, the Shekina may approach him, shed its rays over him, just as its rays are shed over the Temple (בית המקדש is transplated in Aramaic by בית שכינתא).

The Shekina even goes into exile with the nation. Though this is a late conception it could not have developed except for the earlier conception of the Shekina. The Shekina is the first "hypostasis" of the Godhead: it is not yet thought of as an emanation, but the Godhead itself revealed in such a form as is seemly for it to be revealed. In spite of its complete abstractness the idea became possible owing to the poetic grace and tenderness inherent in it—it was a first step towards an incarnation.

A further stage is reached with "the voice of God," such as is heard by man and more than which even the prophets did not hear: for material speech cannot be imagined in connexion with God. The phrase כביכול "as if such a thing were possible," must, as its linguistic form shows, be ancient, although we first find it in a saying of R. Yochanan ben Zakkai (*T. Bab. Qama,* VII, 2). Closely resembling the "voice" (to which must also be added the *bath qol,* echo, or voice from heaven, parallel in thought to the "reflected light" of the Shekina), is the conception of the "word" (מאמר, Aramaic מימרא) by which the world was created.

The "Ma'mar" has something in common with the Greek "Logos" as taught by Heraclitus and Philo; but while for Heraclitus the "Logos" means "the idea of the world" and for Philo "the intelligence of the world," and for both of them it includes the notion of an emanation from the Godhead (such is the Philonic idea of "the first-born of God" rather than the more involved Christian idea)— the "Ma'mar," on the other hand, is only as it were the "working instrument" of the Deity, and serves only to mediate between the wholly spiritual and the sensual, material world. God needed not to

[15] *Gen. R.* §68 (quoted by the *Amora* R. Huna in the name of R. Ammi).

[16] See Philo *On the Confusion of Tongues* §27, *On the Offspring of Cain* §5.

[17] Matt. xxvi. 64 and parallels.

make the world and its fulness, it was enough for him to *say* the word, and through the "Ma'mar" all things came into existence.

The angels, too, are a medium between the spiritual and material worlds. Though themselves wholly spiritual they are not an original, independent power; in this they resemble men, but they differ in that they have neither the semblance nor the needs of the body, and, therefore, possess neither desires nor vices. It is they who carry out the "word" of the Godhead: they are his emissaries (*la'aka,* the root of *mal'ak,* angel, means in Ethiopic "to send"). The angels are divided into "ministering angels" and "destroying angels." Both ideas are comparatively old and are mentioned as early as the *Book of Enoch* and the *Book of Jubilees,* before the period of the *Talmud.*

Among the "ministering angels" are included the "angels of the presence," which, seven in number, are referred to in the *Book of Tobit* (xii.15), a work apparently written in the Maccabæan period. In the *Talmud,* and especially in the earlier *Book of Enoch,* occur innumerable names of angels—and names of strange formation. It may be that most of these names were known to a select few, such as the Essenes (see below). Of those mentioned in the *Talmud* may be noted: Metatron and Suriel, the prince of the Presence,[18] Michael, Gabriel, Uriel (perhaps identical with Suriel) and Raphael, the first two of which are mentioned in the Book of Daniel. Later we hear of Sandalfon,[19] Domah the angel of the winds,[20] and Yurqami the prince of hail;[21] popular imaginative creations of various periods; while "Rahab" prince of the sea,[22] and "Laila" the angel of conception,[23] are only academic creations based on some Scriptural passage. Among the "angels of destruction" an important place is held by Ashmodai (an old Persian name) and Samael, the personal name of Satan, which in post-Biblical times became his general title, and Lilith, the flying night-demon,[24] taken from the name of a terrifying night-bird (Isaiah xxxiv.14).

Belief in harmful spirits is ancient and widespread: primitive heathen gods later became devils and evil spirits; and so real were they supposed to be even by the most enlightened of that time that even the *Mishna* takes them into account, although it is in general free from superstitions and even makes no mention of angels. Even Josephus, a learned Pharisee with a Greek education, has strange things to say about a familiar spirit, about Eliezer who drove out unclean demons in the time of Vespasian, and about the root of rue

[18] *Sanh.* 35b; *Berachoth* 51a.
[19] *Hagiga* 13b.
[20] *Sanh.* 94b.
[21] *Pes.* 118a.
[22] *B. Bath.* 74b (though there are Biblical passages mentioning Rahab these may be an echo of the fight between the Babylonian Marduk and Tiamat).
[23] *Niddah* 15b.
[24] *Shabb.* 121b; *Niddah* 24a.

which has supernatural qualities ("if one but touch a sick man therewith it drives away the demons, namely the evil spirits which enter living men and kill all who continue without help").[25]

The Gospels also speak much of devils and evil spirits which Jesus expelled from the sick; and one of the reasons for his success was certainly a widespread belief in devils and harmful spirits which a holy man and miracle-worker could drive away and so heal diseases brought about by such "possession." As in Babylon the antidote to evil spirits was whisperings, conjurations and all manner of sorceries and incantations.

Sorceries and incantations were forbidden by the *Torah,* but the people (and especially women) paid no regard to such prohibition; and although the *Mishna* rose up against these "whisperings over a wound," [26] even the "sages" sometimes practised such conjurations, whisperings and spittings. Men, however, such as Eliyahu and Mashiach could cure simply by prayer or a touch of the hand; and Jesus was regarded as such a one as these by his disciples, and especially by his women followers.

From the time of the Book of Daniel most of the people, taught by the Pharisees, more and more believed in the Divine Providence, in rewards and punishment after death and in the resurrection of the dead. These were not fundamental articles of faith, yet we find them in most of the *Apocrypha* and *Pseudepigrapha* dating from the close of the Second Temple period.

The older belief of Scripture—that prosperity should befall the righteous and misfortune the ungodly in this present world, however belated—still prevailed, mingled with a confusion of newer ideas, and the more recent beliefs in the survival of the soul, and in Paradise, and Gehenna, had already spread, though not in its later and more developed form. The *individual* had already a place in the Jewish religion of this time, as well as the nation. The individual had greater need for individual reward and punishment, and when he saw that this did not come to him during his lifetime he was compelled to look for it after death.

But the individual did not oust the nation. The nation had its own "survival of the soul," its own reward and punishment. This is the belief in the persistence of the nation, in the day of judgment or the days of the "pangs of the Messiah," and in the messianic age. The Prophet Jeremiah taught that the nation should not die (xxxi. 35-6), a belief of necessity enforced by the belief in the day of judgment (the "pangs of the Messiah") and the "Day of the Lord," also preached by the Prophets, a day when the nations who had oppressed and persecuted Israel and who had not known God and his moral law and had filled the world with violence, should suffer the punishment due to them.

[25] *Ant.* VIII ii 5; *Wars* VII vi 3.
[26] *Sanh.* X 1. See L. Blau, *Das altjüdische Zauberwesen,* Strassburg, 1898.

This punishment was to be universal: on that day the whole world would be judged; there would be an increase of drought, famine and war, of individual moral corruption, and of the punishments which should befall the people individually or as a whole. This is the view of the *Mishna* or an ancient *Baraita*[27] containing a very old conception found also both in the Gospels and in the writings of the early Christian fathers.[28] The Destruction of the Second Temple, the fall of Bittir and the defeat of Bar-Kokhbah unquestionably influenced the terrible pictures of the "pangs of the Messiah,"[29] though most of these pictures are to be found in the *Book of Enoch* and the *Assumption of Moses* which were written before the Destruction, and in the *Book of Baruch* and in *Fourth Esdras,* before the defeat of Bar-Kokhba.[30]

The "pangs of the Messiah" introduce the messianic age when there shall be a gathering together of the dispersed Jews after Elijah shall have appeared. Of him Ben Sira wrote that "he is ready for the time" not only to "turn the hearts of the fathers to the children" but also "to restore the tribes of Israel."[31] Elijah shall blow the trumpet of the Messiah and the scattered Jews shall be assembled together from the four corners of the earth.

Then shall come the Messiah, the "Saviour" full of the spirit of God, who shall overwhelm the heathen and restore the kingdom of Israel to its full power, rebuild Jerusalem and the Temple, and make them a spiritual centre for the whole world. Such nations as have not been destroyed, since they did not oppress Israel, shall become proselytes, and the world shall be reformed by the "kingdom of heaven," or, "the kingdom of the Almighty:" the Lord shall be the God of the whole earth, and righteousness, justice and brotherliness shall prevail. The Messiah will be the son of David.

This was not, however, altogether taken for granted at the time, since the Book of Daniel makes no mention of a human Messiah and Bar Kokhbah was not of the lineage of David—in spite of which, Rabbi Akiba saw in him the actual Messiah. But we find, from the *Psalms of Solomon* (composed soon after the death of Pompey, c.45 B.C.E.), that most of the Pharisees thought of the Messiah as the son of David, and so rejected even the Maccabæan royal house, which was of the seed of Aaron. Also in the Gospels the regular title of the Messiah is "Son of David" (as in the *Talmudic* Messianic *Baraita*) together with "Son of Man."

Such are the outstanding ideas in the messianic belief as it had grown out of the visions of the Prophets and the Book of Daniel. It had reached this form as early as the *"Shemoneh Esreh"* blessings,

[27] *Sotah* (end of *Mishna*) and *Sanh.* 97a.
[28] See J. Klausner, *Die messianischen Vorstellungen,* pp. 49-50.
[29] *Ibid.* 8-12.
[30] See Klausner, *Ha-Ra'yon ha-Meshihi,* pt. 2, Jerusalem, 1921.
[31] *Ben Sira* 48, 10; cf. Malachi iii. 23-24.

and, judging from the Hebrew text of the *Book of Ben Sira* (ch.51), these blessings contained the main features of the messianic belief prior to the Maccabæan revolt (Praise be to the Saviour of Israel," "praise be to him that gathereth the dispersed of Israel," "praise be to him that buildeth his city and his Temple," "praise be to him that maketh to spring up a horn for the house of David," "praise be to him that hath made choice of Zion").

Such ideas as we find elsewhere (e.g. Messiah ben Joseph, the suffering Messiah, etc.) are popular accretions dating after the Destruction of the Temple and the fall of Bittir, when the sore afflictions and the defeat of Bar Kokhbah served to provide the colouring for the lurid descriptions or visions of vengeance, together with the vivid and multicoloured pictures of redemption. But by the time of Jesus the content of the messianic belief was no more than what has here been described. Yet even that sufficed to stir popular imagination with the hope of release from the foreign yoke and of dominion over those nations which now enslaved Israel; and having been brought up on the "popular prophets" (the authors of those *Pseudepigrapha,* replete with Messianic apocalypses), the popular masses were accustomed to see in every wonder-worker and preacher a prospective saviour and ruler, a king and messiah, a supernatural political saviour and a spiritual saviour filled with the divine spirit.

And such a king-messiah, a saviour both political and spiritual, the people at first saw also in Jesus, till such time as it became manifest to them that the kingdom was "not of this world."

*　　*　　*　　*　　*　　*　　*

The whole nation looked forward to the coming of the Messiah: but the degree of expectation was not the same with all.

The sect of the Zealots was the most enthusiastic: they even tried to hasten his coming by force.

Least bound up with the belief were the Sadducees. They did not go so far as to deny belief in the Messiah altogether since such a belief was found in Scripture, whose sanctity the Sadducees acknowledged. But they disbelieved in all the post-Biblical accretions and took pains to belittle an idea which was politically dangerous.

For the Essenes the idea of the Messiah had become an entirely mystical idea: it was bound up with a supernatural idea of social equality, of purity, of righteousness and of perfect worship.

A central position was held by the sect of the Pharisees who represented the bulk of the people; they did not allow belief in the Messiah to evaporate into a species of visionariness far removed from practical possibilities; yet they believed in it with all their heart and made it a political and a spiritual ideal. To them and their followers its fulfilment was unquestionable; none the less they taught that it was not their part "to hasten the end" nor to abandon themselves to any miracle-worker, whereby they might bring disaster upon the nation.

Of these four parties the mystical and moral messianic belief of the Essenes was nearest that of Jesus, who, in the end, abolished its political aspect and made it purely mystical and ethical. Farthest removed from him were the Sadducees for whom the messianic idea was hardly more than an empty name. As we shall see later the more definitely political messianic idea of the Zealots was nearer the heart of Jesus at the beginning of his ministry. But, on the whole he rather favoured the political-spiritual messianism of the Pharisees despite its lack of mysticism and its being too much "of this world" for his liking during the later period of his career, when his "kingdom" became definitely "not of this world."

Properly to understand the reason of Jesus' success and his crucifixion, a clear idea of the general teaching of these four sects is necessary, for it was these sects which influenced the political and spiritual life of the Jews in the time of Jesus. Much has been written about them, and the present writer has dealt with them at length in the second volume of his "History of Israel" (*Historiya Israelith*, Vol. II, Jerusalem, 1924, pp. 89-118). Here it is possible to give only a brief summary and the final conclusions.

First of all it should be observed that all four sects originated, in the time of the Maccabæans, from two parties which existed prior to the Maccabæan revolt: the "Hasidim," Assidæans ("the pious" or "saints"), and the Hellenists. From the Hasidim sprang the Essenes, who were, in fact, the actual "Hasidim" (חֲסִין, חֲסִיאָ in Syriac,

חֲסִידִים in Hebrew, and Ἐσσαῖοι Ἐσσηνοί in Greek); hence they are only referred to in the *Talmud* by the name "the first *Hasidim*," and are not specially mentioned in the Gospels. Only Josephus, Philo and Pliny have preserved any mention of them.

The Essenes were the extreme *Hasidim* who would not consent to fight together with Judas Maccabæus on behalf of political freedom once religious freedom had been secured, and so were prevented from taking part in the political life in the time of the Maccabæans and Herod. Only in the moment of danger, in the days of the great revolt, do we find their warriors fighting in the rebels' camp against ungodly Rome.

The Pharisees likewise owed their origin to the pre-Maccabæan *Hasidim:* they are the *Hasidim* who supported the Maccabæans in all their wars, whether for religion or for the State, and they sided with them from the days of Jonathan the son of Mattathias till the end of the time of John Hyrcanus. They fought in the fiercest possible way against the Sadducæan king Alexander Jannæus, but again supported the Maccabæan house in the time of Shelom-Zion. From the time of the conquest by Pompey, through the Herodian period and the rule of the Procurators, they played the part of a popular party adopting a policy of passive resistance towards the Herods and the Romans.

The Zealots also were derived from the same *Hasidim:* they were the *Hasidim* for whom politics became an actual religion—"whoso marries an Aramæan woman, the Zealots lynch him." [32]   In Maccabæan times this *Mishna* was modified to "the Maccabæan court of law issued decrees against any who had connexion with a heathen woman." [33]   Josephus [34] attributes the founding of the sect to Judah the Galilæan (the Gaulanite) from the town of Gamala in the Jaulan, and to Zadok the Pharisee, at the time of the Census of Quirinius (c.6 B.C.E.).. But the whole of Josephus's description of Judah's father, Hezekiah, whom Herod, when governor of Galilee, had put to death with his followers—a deed which resulted in Herod's being summoned by Hyrcanus II for trial before the Sanhedrin [35]—shows clearly that we have here not simply the chief of a band of murderers but the leader of an important national party. [36]

The sect of the Zealots must, therefore, have had its origin as early as the Maccabæan period, but it only became a powerful political force at the beginning of the Roman-Edomite rule (in the time of Hyrcanus II). It was they who opposed Herod by conspiracies and revolts, and, immediately after Herod's death, in the time of Quirinius, they were joined by the Pharisees, headed by Zadok, the disciple of Shammai. [37]

The fourth of these parties, the Sadducees, came from the pre-Maccabæan Hellenists and their leaders were the highly born priests of the Sons of Zadok (hence the name Zadokites). After the destruction of the Hellenists, and after the *Hasidim* (and their successors, the Pharisees) had been reconciled to the Maccabees, the Zadokite aristocracy was from the first wholly opposed to the Maccabæan rulers. But this condition of things did not endure for long. The new dynasty found itself compelled to negotiate with foreign rulers, the Seleucids and Romans, and it began to hanker after power and glory and the good things of life which were not always in accord with the religious restrictions of Pharisaic Judaism. Hence their sympathies tended towards the old ruling body, the house of Zadok, especially now that the Zadokites had given up hopes of securing the high-priesthood.

It needed only the Pharisaic opposition to John Hyrcanus (or Jannæus) [38] for the Maccabæan dynasty to pass over to the Sadducees and extend the highest favour to the Zadokite aristocracy. To

[32] *Sanh.* IX 6.

[33] *Sanh.* 82a; *Ab. Zar.* 36a.

[34] *Ant.* XVIII i 1 and 6; *Wars* II viii 1, cf. II iv 1.

[35] *Ant.* XIV ix 2-5; xv 5; *Wars* I x 5-7; xvi 4. Cf. Graetz, III I⁵ 178-9.

[36] On the Zealots see K. Kohler, *J.E.* "Zealots" XII 639-43; "Wer waren die Zeloten oder Kannaim?" (German section of the Memorial Volume to A. A. Harkavy, Petersburg, 1909, pp. 6-18).

[37] Graetz III I⁵ 258; Weiss, *"Dor Dor v'Dor'shav,"* I 168; Kohler, *J.E.* XII 642.

[38] Such is the view of I. Friedländer—that the breach was between king Jannæus and the Pharisees as recorded in the *Talmud* (*Kidd.* 66a), and not between them and John Hyrcanus, and that Josephus (*Ant.* XIII x 5-6) erred in attributing the breach to John Hyrcanus (See *J.Q.R.* IV 443-448).

these latter, in the time of Herod, were added the priests of the house of Bœthus; so that "the Sadducees and Bœthusæans" became synonymous terms in the *Talmudic* literature, though the Gospels speak only of the Sadducees.

What did these four parties teach?

(a) The *Zealots*: These were the young enthusiasts who were unable to endure the yoke of the "kingdom of Edom" (the rule of Herod the Edomite) which with them was synonymous with the "kingdom of Rome:" for both alike they had a deadly hatred. In speaking of the Zealots Josephus [39] explicitly mentions "the young men" τοῖς νεοῖς and in the time of Hezekiah the Galilæan, father of the Zealots, the women came crying, and wailing, and seeking vengeance for the blood of their children shed by the young Herod when governor of Galilee.[40] It was these young people, therefore, whose mothers bewailed them, who were the "licentious ones," the "outlaws" and "sicarii" at the time of the Destruction—the "Bolsheviki" of the time, who hated the rich, powerful and ruling classes.

And yet they were the finest patriots Israel knew from the rise of the Maccabæans to the defeat of Bar Kokhba. The times proved favourable for the Maccabæans and they achieved success, but the Zealots found themselves arrayed against a power which was not only stronger than they, but stronger than the whole of the rest of the world: so they fell in battle. Their one crime was that they acted according to their conscience. They were ready to lay down their lives for national freedom and with such a goal they never hesitated to measure their own forces against those of the Herods or the Roman emperors.

They rebelled against Herod the Edomite when he was not yet king, and they rebelled against him in the worse days after he had become king. During the Census of Quirinius, realizing that its motive was to enslave them and drain fresh taxation out of them for the good of the Roman leech, they appealed to the Jews to rise unanimously against the Romans. How could a Jew serve flesh and blood! God alone was king of Israel and not any idolatrous Roman Emperor.

It would certainly seem to be of one of these that we read in the *Mishna*: "A Galilæan sectary said, 'I protest against you, O Pharisees, that ye write the name of the Governor together with that of Moses on the divorce decree.' The Pharisees answered, 'We protest against thee, O Galilæan sectary, that ye write the name of the Governor together with the Sacred Name on a [single] page; and what is worse, ye write the name of the Governor above and the Sacred Name below, as it is written, And Pharaoh said, Who is the Lord that I should hearken to his voice?'"[41] But there is no explicit reference to them by name (with the exception of the *Mishna, Sanh.*

[39] *Ant.* XVII vi 3.
[40] *Ant.* XIV ix 4.
[41] *Yadaim* IV 8.

IX.6, quoted above) except in *Aboth d'Rabbi Nathan:* [42] "And when the Emperor Vespasian came to destroy Jerusalem, the Zealots tried to burn the whole of that good thing with fire."

The Zealots were, in fact, simply active and extremist Pharisees (who like them had their origin in the *Hasidim*). One of their founders was the Pharisee Zadok, of the School of Shammai, and Josephus says of them that save only for their excessive love for freedom "they tend in all other things to the Pharisees." [43] They merely added to their love for the written and oral law of God the duty of protecting it with the sword. Thousands and tens of thousands followed Judah of Galilee and joined the Zealots, and right up to the Destruction of the Temple it was the family of Hezekiah the Galilæan (Judah and his three sons, Jacob, Shimeon and Menahem, and their kinsman Eliezer ben Jair of Masada) who everywhere headed the insurgents and rebels.

Through their zeal for the ideals of freedom and equality they became extremists, and treated the peaceful and wealthy among the nation as did the fanatics of the French Revolution the aristocrats and Royalists, and as the present-day Bolsheviki have treated the "counter-revolutionists" and the bourgeoisie. Therefore the best of the *Tannaim* and the enlightened of that generation opposed them and dubbed them "sicarii" and "licentious," and Josephus loads them with all manner of derogatory epithets.

Yet for all this the *Midrash* [44] still retains some words of commendation for "the *Hasidim* and sons of the *Torah*, like Judah the son (ב"ר) of Hezekiah," of whom it is said, "in the time to come, the Holy One, blessed be He, shall appoint for him a company of his own righteous ones and seat them by him in a great congregation." And Josephus, although he cannot blame them sufficiently for their cruelty, cannot praise them sufficiently for their heroism, courage and devotion for all that the nation held sacred: "They possess unbounded love for liberty and look upon God as their only leader and ruler; it was a light thing for them to go forth to meet death, nor did they regard the death of their companions and kinsfolk, if only they might save themselves from the burden of a human ruler. Since all may find proof of this by the facts themselves I do not find it necessary to say more. It is not that I fear that credence will not be given to my words: on the contrary, what I have said has not told all the greatness of their soul and their readiness to endure sufferings." [45]

These were the most wonderful warriors of Israel, inflamed alike by a political and religious idea, and even by a great social-economic idea; but they arrived at an extremist position and wished to realize

---

[42] *Aboth d'R. Nathan,* §6 near end, Version I (in version II "sicarii" comes instead of "Zealots"). See Schechter's edition, p. 32 (p. xvi).

[43] *Ant.* XVIII i 6.

[44] *Qoh. R.* on *En zikkaron la-rishonim.*

[45] *Ant.* XVIII end of i.

what was not yet possible for that generation: the time was not fitting for them that they should go forth as conquerors in a war against mighty Rome.

It is almost certain that they are referred to in the Gospels in the following passages: "And from the days of John the Baptist (when the Zealots were most numerous) and till now, the kingdom of heaven suffereth violence (is seized by a strong hand, βιάζεται) and the violent (βιασταί) take it by force." [46] This is an expression of opposition to the political fanaticism which recognized only a divine sovereignty (the kingdom of heaven) and sought to bring it forcibly into effect by the sword. But being fundamentally Pharisees, the Zealots preserved the messianic idea and gave their enthusiastic adherence to any wonder-worker who might "hasten the end."

Thus it was possible for a Zealot to be a disciple of Jesus, for during the earlier stage of his ministry it seemed as if he, too, were a political-spiritual messiah like the other messiahs of the same age; and we find among his disciples one "Simon the Zealot" [47] whose name was later (when the kingdom of Jesus became "not of this world" and it was difficult to understand why a Zealot, a Jewish nationalist, and a fighting patriot, was numbered among the disciples) corrupted to "the Canaanite." [48]

(b) The *Essenes:* These formed a society which, in the time of Philo and Josephus, contained about four thousand members. They lived only in Palestine, mostly in villages but also, to a certain extent, in the towns, since we find in Jerusalem a "Gate of the Essenes;" [49] in Pliny's time they were to be found chiefly in the wilderness of En Gedi, by the Dead Sea. In their villages they had common dwelling places and, in any case, ate their meals at the same table. None was received into the community until he had undergone a year's probation, after which he was allowed to perform the lustrations.

There followed two more years of probation, and only then was he received as a full member after taking a solemn oath to conceal nothing from his fellow Essenes, to reveal no secrets of the community to non-Essenes, and also not to reveal the names of the angels. A member could be dismissed by the authority of a court consisting of a hundred other members if that member had transgressed community laws, and such dismissal, if he held to his oath, amounted to *Kareth,* a species of social death. In charge of each community was a "treasurer" whom the members must obey unhesitatingly. There was a common fund, the treasurers supervised the common property brought in by the new members, and any new income or agricultural produce was handed over to special officials.

All shared alike in the fruit of their labours. Besides food, even

[46] Matt. xi. 12.
[47] Luke vi. 16; Acts i. 13.
[48] Matt. x. 4; Mark iii. 18.
[49] *Wars* V iv 2.

their clothes were possessed in common, summer clothes and winter clothes; and in their travels from town to town some member of the community was appointed to see to the needs of the travellers. Every Essene might give alms from the common fund, but he must have the permission of the superintendent to assist a poor kinsman. Trade was altogether barred as a harmful occupation. The majority were occupied in agriculture and so lived in the villages; they also practised handicrafts but never engaged in the making of harmful weapons.

Their fundamental rule was to live on the results of their own labours, to live in peace and to abjure all things that might injure others. Their needs were small and they refrained from all the joys of the flesh and the pleasures of life; they ate and drank sufficient only to keep them alive; they never anointed themselves with oil; they wore but simple clothing and only discarded it when it was worn out. These clothes were white, and a white garment was bestowed on every new member, together with an apron with which he girt himself when bathing or washing, for decency's sake. He received also a kind of hoe (ἀξινάριον) with which to dig a hole in the ground when satisfying the needs of nature, being at the same time covered by his cloak "that he shame not the glory of the sun" (cf. the *Talmudic* expressions, "dull the orb of the sun," "restrict the goings of the Shekinah," and the like, where there is no Persian or Pythagorean influence). This is a fulfilment of the plain rule of the *Torah*, "and thou shalt have a trowel on thy girdle, etc." (Deut. xxiii.14-15). On the Sabbath, when it was not allowable to dig a hole, they used not to satisfy their needs.[50]

They held no possessions in gold, silver, or slaves, nor were they slaves to any one. They did not take oaths, even on the truth, but held that yea is yea, and nay nay. The majority did not marry that they might be kept free from uncleanness and undisturbed in the worship of God. Some of them, however, married, but held no connexion with their wives once they were pregnant, since they married only to maintain the numbers of their sect and not for their private gratification—just as Tolstoy has required in modern times. That the abstention from marriage should not too seriously reduce their numbers they also brought up children of parents sympathetic to Essenism, or orphans, and trained them according to their system.

They sent gifts to the Temple (what Josephus says in this connexion perhaps means that they brought the *Minhah*, the meal-offering of flour mingled with oil), but not offerings of beasts or birds; in other words, they recognized the importance of the Temple

[50] This is the simple reason for the non-performance of natural needs on the Sabbath, and it is not necessary to deduce from this that the Essenes were akin to the Parsis or sun-worshippers. Josephus' words may also mean (see Derenbourg, *op. cit.* p. 90) that no man left his place on the Sabbath, according to Scripture, and thus has nothing to do with the non-performance of natural needs.

but not the efficacy of blood-offerings. This same tendency was also apparent in other Jewish circles and sprang from the aversion of the Prophets and Psalmists to sacrifices; otherwise the Jews would not have accepted so readily the cessation of the sacrifices after the Destruction of the Second Temple.

The Essenes observed a fixed daily routine. They began with prayer before dawn (קודם הנץ החמה, which is the Hebrew rendering of the Greek πρὶν ἀνασχεῖν τὸν ἥλιον,[51] to which Josephus adds "as though they were asking the sun to rise," a pleasant poetic fancy to appeal to Greek taste). Following this prayer they proceeded to their work. They first of all bathed together, and then began the common meal. This was prepared by selected priests (obviously in order that the food should be ritually clean). No stranger shared this meal. The priest began by blessing the bread. Before each Essene was placed a single piece of bread and only a single dish. The meal was carried through in silence, or the elders of the community engaged in conversation on the *Torah*. The meal finished, they all returned to their work.

At evening they had a second and last meal of the day. They bathed before this also. It is highly probable that in this washing before meals we have nothing more than the usual ritual "washing of hands," which Josephus and Philo have called "lustrations" or "bathings" just to impress the Greeks. Even if we allow that the "washing" referred to is a washing of the whole body, it need be no more than an act of supererogation, an aiming at a higher ritual holiness than was incumbent (אכילת חולין על טהרת-הקודש), just as after the Destruction there were Pharisees who, like these Essenes, aimed at the same ritual standard of purity as the priests and avoided all defilement.

The Essenes did no more than pay excessive observance to the custom of washing: "They that wash at dawn (obviously an epithet applied to the Essenes) say: We protest against you, O Pharisees, that ye mention the Name at dawn without washing. The Pharisees say: We protest against you, O washers at dawn, that ye mention the Name out of a body wherein is defilement." [52]

Besides the name of God, the Essenes reverenced the name of Moses also, and whoever cursed him was put to death.[53] They believed in unrestricted divine providence, *i.e.,* in predestination, limiting the power of free choice, a belief in keeping with solitaries and semi-monastics. They believed, too, in the survival of the soul but not in the resurrection of our actual bodies. They held a theory that

[51] *Wars* II viii 5. Derenbourg has pointed out that this is the repetition of the *Shema,* of which a *Baraita* (*Berach.* 9b) says, "and the worthy ones finished it עם הנץ החמה with the rising of the sun" (*op. cit.* p. 88 n. 5).

[52] *Tosefta,* end of *Yadaim* (following the corrected version of the *Mishna* text).

[53] See S. Krauss (quoting Graetz) in *Ha-Qesar Hadrianos, ha-rishon l'hôq'rê ha-Aretz* (*Ha-Shiloach,* XXXIX 429-430).

souls were attracted by sensual love from the thin ether to this lower world where they were shut up as in a prison; on leaving the body, their place of captivity, they rejoiced greatly and were raised on high.

Good souls lived beyond the eternal ocean, where was no snow, rain nor excessive heat, and where only a light, pleasing breeze blew. Evil souls were tormented in a dark, cold corner. Josephus certainly "adapted" this belief in Paradise and Hell to suit the taste and spirit of the Greeks, and the same reason may account for his statement about the Essene's belief that the body is but a prison of the soul.

According to the Pharisees this world is but an antechamber to the world to come, a distinctly ascetic view. The Essenes carried this belief much further and Josephus supplemented it with a view to approximate Jewish ideas to the Greek mind habituated to Pythagoræan and Platonic ideas.

The Essenes likewise had their own sacred writings (τά τε τῆς αἱρέσεως βιβλία) [54] and "from the books of the ancients they learned the medicinal power of roots and the quality of stones." [55] Whoever entered their community must swear not to divulge the writings of the sect nor the names of the angels.[56] By means of their piety, exclusiveness and extreme purity, and by means of the concentrated study of the sacred writings and angelic names, the Essenes were vouchsafed the vision of the Shekinah and, like the prophets, were enabled to see into the future—as Josephus records of Judah the Essene (in the days of Aristobulus I), Menahem the Essene (in the days of Herod) and Shimeon the Essene (in the time of Archelaus).

There is, therefore, some foundation for the theory that the whole or part of the *Book of Enoch*, which has so much to say about angels, secret remedies and hidden wisdom, is of Essene origin.[57] At all events they were the source of the "secrets of the Law," and the ultimate source of both "Practical" and "Theoretical Kabbala," which, as "hidden wisdom," has left traces in the Pharisaic *Talmud*.

If, however, we remove from the teaching of the Essenes the philosophic veneer with which it was overlaid by Philo and Josephus in their attempts to approximate it to Greek ideas, there is nothing in it, so far as we know, to force us to the conclusion that it contains anything derived from the Pythagorean philosophy, as Joseph indicates and as Eduard Zeller, in his history of Greek Philosophy, tries to insist; nor is there much point in the elaborate arguments put forward by Schürer,[58] who found it difficult to arrive at any definite conclusion. What there is in Essenism of Persian teaching was, at an

[54] *Wars* VIII ii 7.
[55] *Ibid.* viii 6.
[56] *Ibid.* viii 7.
[57] See E. Renan, *Histoire du peuple d'Israel,* V 64-65.
[58] See Schürer II⁴ 675-680.

earlier stage, accepted in considerable measure by Pharisaic Judaism: the Essenes merely exaggerated it.

Joseph Derenbourg [59] has shown that there is nothing in Essenism which cannot be paralleled among the stricter Pharisees (*Haberim*); and even Schürer and Renan hold the same view that "Essenism is primarily nothing but a more emphatic Pharisaism" (*Der Essenismus ist also zunächst der Pharisaismus im Superlativ,*"—so Schürer; Renan's words are *"L'essenisme est ainsi le superlativ du Pharisaïsme*).[60]

Such would be perfectly true if we were to say that Pharisaism and Essenism both sprang from a common source, the teaching of the first *Hasidim* (of the time of the Maccabæans, Mattathias and Judas, and the early days of Jonathan); but whereas Pharisaism was *Hasidism* living at large among the people, trying to subjugate politics to religion and adapting religion to life, Essenism was *Hasidism* isolated, set apart from the world.

Essenism might be described as a great human-national vision. It embodied in a remarkable way the moral socialism of the Prophets: it was the first social Utopia. Whereas the system of the Zealots was a socialism imposed by violence, a species of Bolshevism on its negative sides, Essenism embraced all the positive characteristics of socialism: equality, community of possessions, opposition to bloodshed even in sacrifices, and, above all, labour and manual work. They taught a Tolstoyan morality, yet it was a Tolstoyism Jewish and not Christian. They taught an asceticism, but it was not exaggerated, and they practised monasticism, but did not go to extremes.

Though the Essene monasteries may have provided the model for the Christian monasteries, Essenism still remained so far nationalist and Jewish that those who practised it were never able altogether to separate themselves from ordinary life nor shut themselves up altogether in their cells as did the Christian monks. They at times took part in the ordinary life of the time and took an interest in national affairs; thus they never became complete "universalists" but continued to be Jews and nationalists.

Josephus, as though quite forgetting what he had previously said about their isolation from the world and their absence of nationalist feelings, suddenly says: "The war with the Romans demonstrated of what manner of spirit they were. They (the Romans) stretched and lacerated their bodies and cut and broke their limbs, tormented them with all manner of instruments of torture in order to compel them to revile the Lawgiver or eat forbidden foods; but it was impossible to force them to do either." [61]

[59] *Op. cit.* 86-92.
[60] Compare Schürer II⁴ 673 with Renan V 69, though Schürer may have anticipated Renan in his first edition of *Lehrbuch der Neutestamentlichen Zeitgeschichte* (Leipzig, 1874). The fifth volume of Renan's history was published in 1891.
[61] *Wars* II viii 10.

The Essenes, therefore, took part in the Jewish wars with the Romans, which would have been impossible if they were a party of philosophers or a company of monks. And not only did they take a part but they stood in the van of the fighters: when officers were chosen to lead the rebellion against Vespasian we find that, for the district of Timnah, Jonathan the Essene was appointed, and all Ludd, Jaffa and Emmaus were placed under him.[62] If, therefore, such important places like Jaffa and Ludd were put under the command of an Essene officer, there can be no doubt that this Jewish community of Essenes was in truth Jewish.

They suffered with the nation and shared its deeds, and, despite their repugnance, they were perfectly prepared to shed blood for the sake of country and nation if the times demanded it—as in the struggle with the Romans—just as was the case with the "early *Hasidim*" in the wars with the Syrians.

Many scholars, and especially Graetz, have wished to see in Christianity a purely Essene movement. This is not true. Jesus' object was not to form a community of solitaries, nor, as we shall see later, did he consistently practise monasticism and asceticism. Furthermore, even the early Nazarenes were no Jewish nationalists as were the Essenes, for whereas the latter played their part in the war between Judæa and Rome, the former fled from Jerusalem to Pella, beyond Jordan.

The Christians seek to save the soul of the individual: the Essenes sought to save the community by social means. Yet there is in Christianity much of Essenism: John the Baptist, the forerunner of Jesus, approached far more than did Jesus the Essenes in his whole manner of life; and James "the brother of the Lord," the closest kinsman to Jesus, lived, like a veritable Essene, the life of a monk and ascetic. Christianity, therefore, drew from Essenism for a short time before Jesus and immediately after the death of Jesus.

And, in a certain measure, Jesus had points of resemblance with Essenism. The effort to save the soul by complete abnegation, something of asceticism (less than among the Essenes), abstention from political and national affairs (more than among the Essenes), the obsession of mysticism and eschatology, Paradise and Gehenna, the "pangs of the Messiah," and the messianic age, and the personality of the Messiah (forcibly recalling the Essene portions of the *Book of Enoch*), and, above all, the far-reaching sociological ideals which attracted the people to Jesus and created the idea of the Millennium —all these are, more or less, an inheritance from the Essenes which Jesus drew from them directly or indirectly, bequeathing them to his disciples who developed or modified them to fashion a complete system—Christianity.

We may almost go to the length of saying, with some confidence,

[62] *Ibid.* x 4.

that whatever of primitive Christianity is not derivable from Pharisaism may be sought for in Essenism.

(c) The *Pharisees:* These were the popular party, the representatives of the middle classes in the towns and to some extent in the villages as well (though the majority of the village folk were *'ammê ha-aretz*), and of the enlightened nationalists whose education consisted of the national *Torah* and its interpretations, and of the numerous "disciples of the wise," whose object was to develop and enlarge the national *Torah* and adapt it to the needs of everyday life; they represented the national democracy ir. Maccabæan times and in the time of Jesus, a fact often pointed out by Josephus.[63] Josephus gives the following account of the fundamental precepts of the Pharisees:

Contrary to the Essenes the Pharisees held that all was not predestined: though divine providence governed all things man still had freedom of choice in which also might be seen a divine decree. And this is the view to which R. Akiba, the heir of the Pharisees, gave permanence at a later stage in his apophthegm, "All is foreseen but the right (of choice) is permitted." [64] The Pharisees preserved and developed the tradition of the Fathers, and with this tradition as their basis they gave many rules to the nation not to be found in the Law of Moses. They followed the more stringent interpretations of the rules of the *Torah,* but adopted more lenient interpretations in all pertaining to punishments.

They were remarkable also for their high ethical standards and their aloofness from the pleasures of life, and for this reason Josephus likens them to the Greek Stoics.[65] They believed in the survival of the soul, in post-mortem rewards and punishments, that the souls of the righteous are transferred to other bodies and that the souls of the wicked are reserved for perpetual tortures (in Gehenna).

This is all that Josephus, himself a Pharisee, tells us of the beliefs of the Pharisees; but brief as are his words, they comprise all the views of the Pharisees as they may be perceived in the *Mishna* and the earliest *Talmud Baraitas.* The *Tannaim* and *Amoraim* and Jews as a whole are all of them no more than the successive generations of the disciples of the Pharisees who perpetuated the work of the "Scribes" and laid the foundation of the *Talmud* and all later Jewish literature.[66]

---

[63] See, e.g., *Ant.* XIII x 5-6; XVII ii 4; XVIII i 3 and elsewhere.

[64] *Aboth* III 12. See also *Sifre,* on Deut. §53, ed. Friedmann 86*a* and *b*.

[65] Josephus, *Vita* §2.

[66] Their beliefs are given by Dr. Isaac Moses (*Ismar*) Elbogen in his Hebrew article *P'rushim,* in *Otzar ha-Yahaduth,* specimen volume, Warsaw, 1906, pp. 85-94, and in his German pamphlet *Die Religionsanschauungen der Pharisäer,* Berlin, 1904; but in the latter there is too much apologetic, and both works utilize passages too late for the period under discussion. The most objective studies by Christians on the Pharisees are O. Holtzmann, *Jüdische Schriftgelehrsamkeit zur Zeit Jesu,* Giessen, 1901; T. Herford, *Pharisaism,* London, 1912; *The Pharisees,* London, 1924.

Much of what Josephus and the *Talmud* tell us of the Pharisees is to be found also in the New Testament. But the Gospels are also a severe attack on the Pharisees. Jesus included them together with the Scribes, rightly, and condemned them for preaching the good but not practising it, for priding themselves in the carrying out of the commandments, for enlarging their phylacteries and wearing long tassels, for seeking after honour, sitting in the chief places at table and seizing the chief seats in the synagogue, loving to be styled "rabbi."

He charged them with being hypocrites, tithing mint and anise and cummin, cleansing the cup and platter, such time as they swallowed up widows' houses and left undone the graver commands of the Law—justice and mercy and faith. He described them as "blind leaders of the blind," "straining out the gnat and swallowing the camel," as "whited sepulchres," fair without but full of rottenness and uncleanness within. Though they adorned the tombs of the dead prophets, if prophets like them were to come to life they would stone them.[67]

It is not worth while to deny all these things and, like most Jewish scholars with an apologetic bias, assert that they are nothing but inventions. One of the principal passages in Josephus says of the Pharisees that "they take a pride in the scrupulous observance (ἐξακριβώσει) of the religion of the Fathers and think to themselves that God loves them more than others." [68] But it should not be forgotten that such charges may be urged against the world's best and most honest sectaries. It never yet happened that there were parties and teachings or systems where in course of time they did not deteriorate, and their teachings become corrupted by certain of their adherents, who had no higher motive than honour, power or gain.

In every system, as time goes on, the secondary comes to be regarded as primary and the primary as secondary; the most exalted idea has associated with it disciples who distort it and transform it, and so there is aroused the indignation of the better against the worse disciples and the dispute is not with the system or the teaching but with fellow partisans who have greatly damaged the system to which they adhere. This happened to the Law of Moses in the time of Jeremiah, to Christianity not long after Jesus, and to the teaching of the Buddha two hundred years after its promulgation.

And the same certainly happened to the teaching of the Pharisees. The *Mishna* and the *Baraita* say hard things about the many types of hypocritical or extremist Pharisees. "A stupid *hasid*, and a cunning knave, and a female devotee, and the plagues of the Pharisees" are they who (in the opinion of the *Tannaim*, themselves the heirs

---

[67] Matt. xxiii, and parallels.

[68] *Ant.* XVII ii 4; according to Derenbourg, *op. cit.* 92 n. 1, Josephus is here quoting Nikolaus of Damascus, since he himself could never praise the Pharisees sufficiently.

of the Pharisees) "destroy the world." [69]   When one of the disciples
of R. Yehudah ha-Nasi had been victimized by some sharper, Rabbi
sorrowfully replied, "As for this man, he is afflicted by the Pharisaic
plague." [70]

Furthermore, in an ancient *Baraita*, so ancient that the interpretation of most of its epithets has been lost, the *Talmud* enumerates
seven types of Pharisee, of which only two (and perhaps only one)
find favour in the eyes of the *Tannaim:* "There are seven kinds of
Pharisee:—the *"shikhmi"* (hunchback) Pharisee, the *"qizzai"*
(bookkeeping) Pharisee, the *"niqpi"* (knocker or borrower) Pharisee, the *"m'dokhya"* (pestle-like) Pharisee, the "what is my obligation and I will do it" Pharisee, the Pharisee who is one from fear,
and the Pharisee who is one from love." [71]

It is difficult to know the exact meaning of these ancient and popular epithets *"shikhmi," "nikpi," "qizzai" and "m'dokhya,"* since there
is already a marked difference between the explanations given in the
Talmud Babli and those of the *Talmud Yerushalmi;* but it is obvious
that we have here extremist Pharisees and ascetics who carry out
their piety to such an excessive extent as to become deformed. The
"what is my obligation and I will do it" Pharisee is the type who
prides himself in the keeping of the commandments, and who says "I
have already fulfilled all of the commandments, but perhaps you know
of some commandment which I have not fulfilled: I will fulfil it at
once" (like the young man in Matt. xix. 20 who says, "All these
things have I performed from my youth up; what lack I yet?").
Other Pharisees there are who serve God only out of fear.

The *Talmud* dislikes them all (with perhaps the one exception of
the "Pharisee who is one from love" who may have overdone his
Pharisaic piety with a perfectly good intention), and dubs their extremist, ascetic and self-complacent ways "the Pharisaic plague." It
regards their extreme Pharisaism as the conduct of "a stupid *hasid*,"
and their hypocrisy and pride as that of "a cunning knave," and "a
female devotee;" and their cant and pietisticism as that of "a fasting
virgin or a giddy widow." [72]

That the Pharisees lauded it over the common people is due to
the bad relations between the *"haber"* (Pharisee) or "disciple of the
wise" and the *"am ha-aretz;"* [73] but the *Talmud* allows that every

[69] *Mishna Sota* III 4; see also *J. Peah* VIII 8.

[70] *J. Sota* III 4. There is a similar story told by R. Eliezer worth noticing: "And the plague of the Pharisees—that is he who gives advice to
orphans to compel maintenance from the widow," closely corresponding to
Mark xii. 40, Luke xx. 47.

[71] *Sota* 22b; also *J. Sota* V 7, *J. Berachoth* IX 7, where, for *"Parush
m'dokhya"* is read *"Parush m'nakhaya"* or *"Ma ha-n'khiya,"* and for "what
is my obligation and I will fulfil it," "I know my obligation and I fulfil it."

[72] *Sota* 22a (*J. Sota* III end of 4: "*Bethulah tzaimanith*," fasting girl,
where the expression is Hebrew and not Aramaic).

[73] See A. Büchler, *Der Galiläische Am-haaretz des zeiten Jahrhunderts,*
Wien, 1906, pp. 180-185, who holds that all the passages in the *Baraita* about

"*am ha-aretz*" may become a "disciple of the wise," a "*haber*" and a Pharisee, once he learns *Torah* and scrupulously observes the commandments (R. Eliezer ben Hyrcanus, R. Akiba). Even Jesus, like the *Talmud,* becomes indignant at the spoiling of the teaching of the Pharisees by cant and hypocrisy, by the pursuing of honour, power and gain, such as was certainly often the case in the Pharisaic party; but it does not follow that Pharisaism as a whole was made up of such defects. That this was not the case may be shown from an ancient passage attributing to Alexander Jannæus—the great enemy of the Pharisees, who embittered his life and struggled against him for many years—the following: "King Jannæus said to his wife, Fear not the Pharisees nor them that are not Pharisees, but fear rather the hypocrites which are like unto the Pharisees, whose deeds are as the deeds of Zimri and who seek the reward like Phineas;" [74] —showing that Pharisaism and hypocrisy were not the same thing, but that there were hypocrites among the Pharisees and also among the Sadducees, just as there were, and are, and will be, in every religion and sect and party the world over.

What would be thought by Christian scholars were we to judge Christianity not by its Founder, nor its early fathers and saints who died a martyr's death, but by the many hypocritical and canting Christians who have flourished in every generation? A religion and a sect should be judged by the principles it expounds and by the best of its teachers rather than by its unworthy members: it should be judged by the best that it contains and not by the worst.

It must, however, be admitted that Pharisaism did, in truth, contain one serious defect which enabled the more hypocritical to pride themselves in the mere performance of the commandments, and which justified Jesus' fighting against it *quâ* Jew, and even *quâ* Pharisee; for though Jesus may not have been wholly a Pharisee he was, like any "Rab" or teacher of those days, much more of a Pharisee than a Sadducee (the Essenes and Zealots were, as we have seen, but the exponents of certain extreme aspects of Pharisaism).

This defect was that the Pharisees attached almost as much importance to those commandments dealing with the relations between man and God as to those dealing with the relations between man and his fellow-man (though they insisted that nothing could atone for the breach of the latter, and that if a man had not performed good deeds, his observance of *Torah* would not avail him nor would ample observance of the ceremonial laws). Hence the Pharisees were far more concerned with the discussion of *Halakha,* with those commandments dealing with man's relations to God, than with the

the "*am ha-aretz*" (*Pesahim* 49b) come from the Usha Academy, after the destruction of Bittir. See on the contrary H. P. Chajes, *Am ha-Aretz e Min,* Rivista Israelitica, III 83-96.

[74] *Sota* 22b.

others, because the latter seemed to them far more self-evident and simple.

Yet the casuistry and immense theoretical care devoted to every one of the slightest religious ordinances left them open to the misconception that the ceremonial laws were the main principle and the ethical laws only secondary. To the orthodox Pharisee (and to the modern orthodox Jew) the violation of the Sabbath and the oppression of the hireling were alike crimes deserving of death (and to the average Jew of all times the former seems the worse crime); and it almost inevitably followed from such an attitude that, despite the efforts of the best Pharisees, the common people of that day should assume that the value of morality was less than that of religion— just as in the time of the Prophets the people assumed that the Temple and sacrifices were more important than "to do judgment and to love mercy."

This it was which stirred up Jesus, the Pharisee, to war with Pharisaism, just as it was this also which stirred up Saul (though he could say of himself that he was a Pharisee and son of a Pharisee)[75] to abrogate the ceremonial laws. How far such a struggle was opportune and restricted within suitable bounds will become clear when we deal with this particular aspect of Jesus' ministry; here it is sufficient to say that without Pharisaism the career of Jesus is incomprehensible and even impossible, and that despite all the Christian antagonism to the Pharisees, the teaching of the Pharisees remained the basis of early Christian teaching until such time as it gathered within itself elements from non-Jewish sources.

(d) The *Sadducees:* These were the priestly party, the Zadokite families, to whom were allied the Bœthuseans and other well-born families and those with priestly connexions, the wealthy and official classes. This party was the spiritual heir of the Hellenists. They at first opposed the Maccabæans who took from them the high-priestly office, but by the end of the reign of John Hyrcanus they became reconciled to the ruling house which, more or less unconsciously, became Hellenised. In the time of Antigonus Mattathias, the Sadducees were in good odour with the Maccabæan claimants and were therefore the object of Herod's persecution; but once the Bœthuseans, through Herod's favour, secured the high-priesthood, the Bœthuseans and Sadducæans (now identical) became more friendly with Herod's court and even accepted peacefully the Roman Procurators; and such internal autonomy as was permitted the Jews was exercised by the Sadducees.

Whatever information we have of them comes from their opponents—Josephus, himself a Pharisee, the *Talmud,* the literary offspring of the Pharisaic spirit, and the New Testament, which, if not Pharisaic, is still less Sadducæan. But the very fact that no indu-

[75] Acts xxiii. 6.

bitably Sadducæan document survives in Judaism [76] is proof enough that this party had no deep roots in the nation : a party deeply rooted in the life of the nation cannot but leave behind it deep traces.

The single Sadducæan document of any note (surviving in a Greek translation) is, apparently, the *First Book of Maccabees* (and even this is not wholly Sadducæan). It redounds to the praise and glory of the Sadducees. The document found in the Geniza and entitled by its discoverer, S. Schechter, "The Book of the House of Zadok," [77] (a Zadokite and not a "Sadducæan" work), is most probably the product of some sect akin to the Sadducees but not an actual Sadducæan document. But for all that, even this book indicates that what our early authorities have said of the Sadducees needs some revision and modification.

We learn from Josephus that the Sadducees denied predestination and any divine influence on men's doings, good or bad ; everything is in man's hands and he is responsible for his happiness or misfortune. That they denied the tradition of the Fathers (the Oral Law) and recognized the Written Law alone. That they taught that the soul died with the body and so there was no survival of the soul, no resurrection of the dead and no rewards and punishments after death. That in the administration of justice they were noted for their harsh punishments. That, unlike the Pharisees who lived on friendly and brotherly terms one with another, they treated even their own partisans as strangers, while their manners were severe and crude. And, finally, that the teaching of the Sadducees was accepted only among the few, though these were found among the principal officials (πρῶτοι τοῖς ἀξιώμασι) and the wealthy (εὔποροι).

Yet they were never responsible for any outstandingly important action since, on acquiring office, they acted (certainly not of their own will) according to the ideas of the Pharisees in everything : otherwise the mind of the crowd would not suffer them.[78]

With the exception of the first point, the disbelief in divine providence, all that is alleged by Josephus (who, it should be noted, manifests the true partisan hatred) is confirmed by the *Talmud* and *Midrash*. The *Talmudic* literature tells us that "the Sadducees used vessels of silver and gold; not because their spirit was gross; but they used to say, It is a tradition among the Pharisees to deprive themselves in this life though in the world to come they shall have noth-

---

[76] Rudolf Leszynsky (*Die Sadduzäer*, Berlin, 1912) regards as Sadducæan the books of *Qoheleth, Ben Sira, I Maccabees*, the *Book of Enoch*, the *Book of Jubilees*, the *Testaments of the Twelve Patriarchs*, the *Assumption of Moses*, and the *Book of the House of Zadok*. Against him see B. Revel, *J.Q.R.* (New Series) VII 429-438.

[77] Charles, *Apocrypha and Pseudepigrapha*, Oxford, 1913, II 785-834 (*Fragments of a Zadokite Work*). It is published with a commentary in Hebrew by M. H. Segal under the title *The Book of the Covenant of Damascus* in *Ha-Shiloach* XXVI 399, 406, 483-506.

[78] *Ant.* XIII v 9, x 6; XVIII i 4; XX ix 1; *Wars* II v 14.

ing." [79]   And a *Haggada* tells how Zadok and Bœthus learnt from the words of their Rabbi, Antigonus Ish Sokho ("Be not like slaves who serve their master for the sake of a reward"), to deny rewards and punishments in the world to come.[80]

The New Testament also tells of this denial of the resurrection of the dead and of the existence of angels and spirits.[81]   Again, the *Scroll of Taanith* (or at least the later *"scholion"*) reports the harsh judgments of the Sadducees: "On the 14th of Tammuz was issued a decree not to mourn," on which comment of the *"scholion"* is: "because the Sadducees had drawn up and decreed a book of laws how these are to be burnt, these beheaded, these stoned and these choked; and when they were decreeing (sentence) a man would consult this book, etc."   Yet again we find in the *Tosefta* that a certain Bœthusean High Priest said to his father after the service in the Temple: "All your days have you been preaching and not practising until I stood up and practised (according to your preaching)."   The father said to him: "Although we preach we do not practise, and we are obedient (in practice) to the words of the wise." [82]

The one thing that provokes doubt is Josephus' assertion that the Sadducees disbelieved in divine providence.   If the Sadducees acknowledged the authority of nothing beyond the Pentateuch (though they certainly acknowledged also the Prophets and Hagiographa), how could they deny divine providence, since the Scriptures are full of it?   It would seem rather that the remark of Josephus should be understood in the following manner:

The Scriptures strongly emphasize God's guidance of the world and rewards and punishments to the *nation* and *society;* but the *private individual* is not so definitely the object of divine providence. Therefore the Sadducees denied divine providence so far as it concerned the individual, just as it was denied by some in the Middle Ages; but they did not deny a *general providence*—that God supervises his world and his people.   Such a view was natural: if they denied post-mortem reward and punishment, they must also deny individual providence, else how could they account for "the righteous that suffer evil and the godless that prosper?"

If there is no recompense in the world to come, there remains but one of three solutions.   That of the Book of Job, that man can understand nothing and must trust that God is surely just.   Or that of Qoheleth (emanating from the same source from which came the Sadducees), that "one event happens alike to the righteous and the ungodly, to the clean and the unclean."   Or, finally, that man governs his own destiny, that if he is happy his happiness comes from his own acts, and that if he is miserable he alone is responsible for his misery.

[79] *Aboth d'R. Nathan* §5 (Vers. I, ed. Schechter p. 26).
[80] *Idem* (in both versions).
[81] Matt. xxii. 23 and parallels; Acts xxiii. 8.
[82] *T. Yom ha-Kippurim* I 8 ed. Zuckermandel, p. 181; see also *J. Yomah* I, 5, *B. Yoma* 19a.

According to Josephus the Sadducees adopted the last solution, which is the most "practical" and the most "political." Yet God guides the nation and humanity and rewards them according to their deeds. The First Book of Maccabees is permeated by this spirit and this idea. The casuistical arguments brought by Derenbourg [83] and Schürer [84] to bear on the subject have no sound basis.

Both the *Mishna* and *Baraita* preserve details of decisions wherein Pharisees and Sadducees differed. They deal with cases of clean and unclean, with Temple ritual, the dating of festivals and with capital and non-capital cases in law. We need only touch briefly on these.

The Pharisees were more stringent than the Sadducees in the matter of the purity of the High Priest who burnt the Red Heifer,[85] the purity of the Temple vessels [86] and the "uncleanness" of the Scriptures.[87] The Sadducees, on the other hand, were the more stringent in the question of *"Nitstsoq"* (the pouring of liquid from an unclean into a clean vessel),[88] the uncleanness of a woman in childbirth, and the *Halitsah* ceremony (requiring actual spitting in the face and not spitting in front) ; but they were less stringent as to the Levirate laws (which, according to the Sadducees applied only to the affianced bride of the dead brother and not to his actual wife), the proofs of virginity (that they should spread out the garment and show the actual blood, instead of the clearer proofs required by the Pharisees).

The Pharisees held that the *Tamid* sacrifice should be offered at the public cost; the Sadducees, by private payment. The former held that the meal-offering should be wholly sacrificed; but according to the latter, it should be consumed by the priest. According to the Pharisees, the High Priest should arrange the incense within the Holy of Holies on the Day of Atonement and burn it outside ; whereas the Sadducees held to a contrary ruling. The Sadducees were against the beating of the willow and the water libations at Sukkoth ; whereupon the Pharisees gave much publicity to this practice and made the "Joy of the Water Drawing" a great popular festival. In the matter of the "Sanctifying the New Moon" there was also a divergence of opinion, the Sadducees and Bœthuseans trying to lead the Sanhedrin into error by false witnesses.

Specially marked was the dispute as to the fixing of the time for the Feast of Pentecost which is not precisely laid down in the Scriptures. The Pharisees expounded "on the morrow of the Sabbath" (Lev. xxiii. 21) as "on the morrow of the feast when

[83] *Op. cit.* p. 33.
[84] *Op. cit.* II ¹ 460-463.
[85] *Parah* III 7.
[86] *J. Hagiga* III 8; *T. Hag.* III 35, ed. Zuckermandel p. 128 (a smart gibe of the Sadducees as against the Pharisees).
[87] *Yadaim* IV 6.
[88] *Ibid.* IV 7.

men ceased from work," *i.e.*, on the second day of Passover. Whereas the Sadducees ruled that "on the morrow of the Sabbath" referred to the actual Sabbath (*"Sabbath B'reshith,"* the Sabbath of the Creation) ; therefore, like the Samaritans and the Karaites, the Sadducees observed the Feast of Pentecost on the first day of the week.[89]

To us these differences seem trivial, but they were not so regarded in the time of the Second Temple. Because Alexander Jannæus showed his contempt for the custom of the Water Libation and poured it over his feet, the nation rebelled against their king, and the outbreak lasted several years. The dispute as to whether or not the "Laying on of Hands" (upon the sacrificial victim as a mark of ownership, or, it may be, as some hold, in reference to the ordination of disciples of the wise!) could be practised on a Festival, was prolonged for generations—throughout the age of the *"Zugoth"* and the *"Eshkoloth,"* from Yose ben Yoezer and Yose ben Yochanan, till Hillel and Shammai, and even longer.

Perhaps nothing could have so aroused the opposition of Jesus toward the Pharisees as this importance attached to such trivial religious details which to the Pharisees and Sadducees had come to be the primary elements of the religious life.

Of more importance were the disputes which the two parties waged over capital and non-capital cases. According to the Pharisees, if an ox or an ass have done any damage the owner is liable, though if a slave have done any damage the owner is not liable. According to the Sadducees, the owner is liable in both cases. In the mind of the Pharisees slaves are not to be treated like cattle since "they possess knowledge." [90] In cases of personal injuries the Sadducees enjoined "eye for eye" in the most literal sense as laid down in the Law. Whereas the Pharisees laid down "eye for eye" in money value, lest there be "both eye and life for the eye." There is no need to point out that the latter is the more humane view. On the other hand, it might appear that the Pharisees held more stringent views in the matter of "false witnesses" (עדים זוממים). They held that "false witnesses are not put to death until the trial is completed and the sentence carried into effect," so that if the accused is put to death, the false witnesses are not put to death. Only if the case is actually *decided* and the accused *not* yet put to death can the witnesses be put to death. Whereas the Sadducees held that "false witnesses are not put to death until the accused is put to death" (the Pharisees expounded "in accordance with the evil that they had intended" and not "in accordance with what they had performed").

[89] Since the Samaritans (the *"Cuthites"*), like the later *Karaim*, in many respects resembled the Sadducees, we often find *"Cuthite"* in place of Sadducee, and *vice versa*. From fear of the Censor, *"Saddoki"* sometimes occurs instead of *"Min"* (*e.g.*, "Galilæan Sadducee" for "Galilæan *Min*," at the close the *Tractate Yadaim*, where *Kannaite* is meant; or *Sanh.* 93a "to the Sadducæan teaching" for "to Minuth").

[90] *Yadaim* IV 7.

They held further that false witnesses must be two, and not one in number. Schürer [91] supposes that in this the Pharisees showed themselves the more stringent. Actually, however, even here the Pharisees are the less stringent. Just as their treatment of the "eye for eye" law came from their fear lest there be two blemished people instead of one (or even "an eye and a life for an eye," *B. Bathra* 84a), so here they do not wish two (or even three) to suffer death instead of the one who is put to death. So also they required that the false witnesses be actually two, so as to make such cases less frequent: it was easier to find one false witness than to find two whose testimony agreed in all points.

Thus even here the words of Josephus are confirmed, that "the Pharisees were by nature more lenient in all that concerned punishments" [92] and that the "Sadducees were the harshest of all the Jews in their judgments." [93]

The Pharisees tried to adapt religion to life: it was immaterial whether this induced new stringencies. or new leniencies. For both Pharisee and Sadducee the Law was most holy and all must decide matters of everyday life in accordance with the Law: but while the Sadducees insisted on the letter of the Law, the Pharisees interpreted the words of the Law in accordance with the needs of daily life. In this consisted the merit of the Pharisees: they thus introduced the spirit of development into the Jewish religion.

The Sadducees also had their merits: where the Law was silent they allowed themselves freedom, and so could be liberated from stringencies just as the Pharisees permitted themselves leniencies. Wherever the Law did not lay down a definite ruling, the Sadducees permitted scope for private inclinations. In this they approached closer to the attitude of "Let us become like all the nations, O house of Israel" (Ezek. xx. 32). Thus their political life was less shackled by religion and they could more easily serve as leaders for the more prominent members of the state, for the aristocracy and governing classes, the more powerful and wealthy element.

Hence it came about that when the Maccabæans became more secularized and the high-priesthood became of secondary importance compared with the crown and civil rule, they were compelled to desert their former supporters, the Pharisees (in the same way as their earliest supporters, the *Hasidim,* had deserted the Maccabæans) ; and from the death of John Hyrcanus till the reign of Shelom Zion the Sadducees were the country's rulers. The same held good in the reign of Herod—so far, that is, as he could share his rulership with anybody—and the reign of his sons and the age of the Procurators. The Sadducees were not popular leaders but they consorted

[91] See Schürer II [4] 482.
[92] *Ant.* XIII x 6.
[93] *Ant.* XX ix 1.

with "the great ones of this world" and so, to some extent, themselves became "great ones."

Jesus and his disciples, who came not from the ruling and wealthy classes but from the common people, were but slightly affected by the Sadducees. There is a theory [94] that much of the opposition shown in the Gospels to Pharisaism and Judaism generally, was directed against the Sadducees; while another theory holds that Jesus himself was a Sadducee.[95]

Though there may be some truth in the first theory so far as it concerns some isolated passages, the second is quite baseless. The Galilæan carpenter and son of a carpenter, and the simple fishermen who accompanied him, may, from the stress of the cares of everyday life or from their superficial knowledge of Pharisaic teaching, have lightly regarded the regulations of the Pharisees; but they were as far removed from Sadducæanism as were the highly connected priests from the simple-minded common people.

The bare fact that the Sadducees denied the resurrection of the dead and did not develop the messianic idea must have alienated Jesus and his disciples. What had, unconsciously, the strongest influence on Jesus was Essenism, while the most conscious influence was that same Pharisaism through opposition to which Christianity came into being. Those we struggle with must be nearest to us; and though the struggle estranges us it is the best evidence of the affinity between the recent combatants.

The Zealots were a party of hot-headed enthusiasts; the Essenes were a group of semi-anchorites, while the Sadducees were only an aristocratic minority. The ordinary people, the average citizen, and a fair proportion of the village-folk (though among these the *"ammê ha-aretz"* predominated) were Pharisees. And to what an extent these were capable of being moved by a living faith, by a devotion to their sacred beliefs, may be seen from what happened but a few years after the crucifixion, when Caius Caligula wished to set up an image in the Temple (39-40 C.E.).

Jews from towns and villages, in thousands and tens of thousands, flocked to the plain of Acre where the Legatus Petronius and his army were stationed; they fell down before him, with their faces to the ground in all humility, and, with a courage unparalleled in history informed him that he must do one of two things: either refrain from setting up the image or destroy the Jews to the last man. When the Legatus left for Tiberias thousands and ten thousands of Jews followed him there, forsaking their fields even in the seed-time, and remaining out in the open for forty or fifty days regardless of rain and dew, regardless of the famine which threatened them from neglecting their fields. After they had told Petronius, "Better for us

[94] Chwolsohn, *op. cit.* 118-120; 124-125.
[95] Leszynsky, *op. cit.* 228, 291.

to die than to transgress our Law," they fell to the ground, bared their necks and declared themselves prepared to die at once.[96]

Such was the religious feeling which moved the people of Judæa and Galilee but a few years after the time of Jesus, when, according to Christian scholars, Judaism was petrified and Pharisaic hypocrisy prevailed, when the Jewish religion was nothing but the observance of the ceremonial laws in hope of future reward. Humanity has never known the like of such moral heroism and devotion. Every monotheistic religion has had its isolated heroes who accepted martyrdom; but the Jews alone have played that rôle as an entire people, and precisely in the days of Jesus.

Such a people moved by such magnificent heroism could not but raise up great men, religious and moral heroes, in whom the nation's faith found its strongest expression. And such a great man, comprising in himself the national characteristics in their most potent form, was the Elder Hillel, an earlier contemporary of Jesus.

This is not the place to treat in detail the biography and principal labours of this greatest of Pharisees; we must be content here with general characteristics based on researches published elsewhere by the present writer (see his "Historia Israelith," Vol. III). Hillel was not a great reproving or pugnacious prophet, nor a political revolutionary. He lived in the reign of Herod and therefore held aloof from politics, which was a dangerous pursuit in the time of that great tyrant. He did not possess the sweeping vision nor the wide perspective demanded in one who would accomplish a world-wide work. His interests did not embrace general humanity nor did he declare war on political evils.

Yet he was an original force in the world of ethics and in the inner life of the Jews. The saying "what is hateful to thyself do not unto thy neighbour" may not have been his own invention: it was current in Palestine from the time of the *Book of Tobit;* but Hillel proclaimed it and promulgated it in the language of the day, and from him it came to Jesus who transformed it into its positive form.

But that is not the main point. The main point is, rather, the popular and delicate impression of his entire mental and intellectual outlook: a moral optimism which became the main support of Judaism in bitter exile, a deep faith in divine justice and a complete trust in divine providence, an amiability to his fellow creatures, an affinity with his nation and a belief in it, humility, unfailing kind-heartedness, a joy in life, a confidence in the power of the individual, and, above all things, tenderness, simplicity and love of mankind—these constitute a crown of noble qualities not often paralleled among the highest specimens of mankind, among the greatest preachers and reformers. In him, it would seem, all the power of popular appeal of the Scribes and Pharisees was concentrated and became a life-giving system.

[96] See J. Klausner, *Rega' gadol b'hayye-ha-Ummah* (*Ha-Shiloach,* XXI 108-114).

For him Judaism was the Law of life and not the Law of death, it was the Law of the people and not the Law of the "disciples of the wise" alone. All could, and must, learn: all must be brought near to the Law; strangers, even, must not be turned away from Israel and the simplest labouring classes should draw near to the Law.[97] There is nothing to be gained by bad temper and rage, nor by contemptuousness, nor by gloominess. To do well to mankind is the main thing; yet man must also do well to himself. Man must not cultivate the joys of the flesh, for if he multiply luxury, riches, women and slaves, he injures himself; yet it is a charitable act to care for the bodily needs and a religious duty to have resort to the bath, for the body of man was made in the image of God and man must needs preserve this image in cleanliness and purity.[98]

In all this we have a post-Biblical Jewish ethic together with all Judaism's easy popular appeal, its popular affinity, right-mindedness and cheerfulness. This appeal is very different from that of the Prophets; the Prophets protected the nation and saved it from oppressors, but the Prophets were too exalted in ideals to live a common life with the people whose defects provoked them to anger and rebuke. The peculiarity of Hillel's appeal is that it is not so exacting: he was in all things the sympathetic friend of human kind and a fellow-man. The Prophet played the rôle of apologist and mighty defender of his nation: Hillel is simply the elder brother who shares the nation's life and struggles.

But for the popular appeal of this model, with its amiability and tenderness, Judaism could not, bereft of leadership, survive as it did the exile with its terrible persecutions. Only a people who had, consciously or unconsciously, inherited the same attitude of life as was exemplified in Hillel, could have borne through the ages the Jewish faith, torn from its own land, and preserved it alive; for this faith was to become to the bulk of the nation bone of its bone and flesh of its flesh.

We may see from this how far Hillel and Jesus resembled each other and how far they differed.[99] Jesus, so far as he held aloof from politics and laid the main stress on love to mankind and on well-doing, followed in the steps of Hillel. But Jesus, more even than the Prophets, made exacting claims on the people in general. He required of men that they should strip themselves of themselves and abjure all personal possessions, since the poor and oppressed alone might enter the kingdom of heaven; and he went even so far as to abrogate the importance of those religious customs, for which the

[97] See the attractive story in *Aboth d'R. Nathan,* 2nd vers., §26 end. ed. Schechter, p. 54.

[98] *Lev. R.* §34.

[99] Franz Delitzsch (*Jesus und Hillel,* 3rd ed. Leipzig, 1879) has attempted to deal with the fundamental differences between them, but for him, a Christian believer, an unbiassed attitude was impossible.

nation lived, in favour of abstract morality and good works. By such means Jesus, though he attracted many, repelled still more.

Hillel drew around him the simple folk, the pious and the unsophisticated, but repelled the boorish *"am ha-aretz"* who remained obstinate in his boorishness, and such as indulged in exaggerated piety and foolish pietisticism. Jesus, on the other hand, took pleasure in the boorish and every type of the *"am ha-aretz."* Jesus also lacked Hillel's joy in life and his optimistic ethical outlook. "Serve the nation with gladness" was a sentiment with which Hillel could wholeheartedly agree, though Jesus would have doubted it. "And when I am for myself, what am I?" might have been said by Hillel but not by Jesus: the rest of mankind was everything to Jesus, but his own people, the national group, was nothing at all to him.

There is yet another fundamental difference which is, again, in a sense the same difference as between Hillel and the Prophets. Hillel, like all the redactors of the Pentateuch and all the Scribes and Pharisees from the time of Ezra, and like their many generations of disciples up to the present day, draws no distinction between ethics and religion on the one side, and between theory and practice on the other. For him all is religion, be it "And thou shalt love thy neighbour as thyself," or the problem about laying on of hands, or devotion to the welfare of the righteous poor, or rules about *Nidda* and *Halla*, or reservoirs or diseases. The same Hillel who popularised the principle "what is hateful to thyself do not to thy neighbour" was likewise the author of the "Seven rules of hermeneutics" (*"a fortiori," "gezera shawa,"* etc.)[100] by which he laid the basis for the whole of Pharisaic Judaism.

He was the first to practise this lack of distinction. Just as the *Torah* gives us decrees about sacrifices and prohibited foods side by side with decrees about kindness to strangers, the law "thou shalt not avenge thyself or retain anger," the return of the pledge and the rule that a man help his enemy's ass that is fallen under its load— so also we find in the traditions of the Scribes and Pharisees rules about morals and justice all mixed up with rules about "diseases" and "tents."

And though there is reason for supposing that, till Maccabæan times, the Pentateuch only concerned judges and lawyers, while the Psalms, Proverbs, Job, *Qoheleth* and Daniel, the literary products of the early Scribes, were concerned only with theoretical matters and had no bearing on legal affairs, most of them (Proverbs, Job and *Qoheleth*) having a general human interest and the rest (Psalms and Daniel) being concerned with Jewish problems—yet, from the time of the Maccabees onwards, there began, as a reaction against the

---

[100] *Baraita* of R. Ishmael §7 (at the beginning of the book according to the text given by R. Abraham Ibn Daud) ; *T. Sanh.* VII 11 (see A. Schwarz, *Die hermeneutische Induction in der talmudischen Litteratur*, Vienna, 1909, p. 5 n. 2).

Hellenizing decrees, this confusion of morality and religion, of which we already find traces in the *Book of Jubilees*.

The tyranny of Herod and the Procurators in forcibly preventing the nation from taking a part in politics, still further increased this tendency. But none went so far as Hillel in placing both religious rulings and ceremonial laws in the first rank of importance. In his mind there was no difference between them. "What is hateful to thyself do not to thy neighbour: this is the whole Law, the rest is commentary: go and learn it." The *Torah* includes matters bearing on the relations between God and Man, also cases of "diseases" and "reservoirs" and rules as to the Passover sacrifice, and it gives them equal importance with matters of the highest morality: all alike came forth from the mouth of the Almighty and there was no difference between them.

This fact, already felt by the disciples of Ezra, from the earliest days of the Second Temple, reached its most emphatic expression with the Elder Hillel and became an unbreakable rule for the whole of Judaism. The Scribes, the Pharisees, the *Tannaim* and *Amoraim*, men like Maimonides and the Jewish Rabbi of the present day, have all been alike teachers, lawmakers, judges, scribes, physicians (as to unclean food and *Nidda*), lawyers (divorce decrees and marriage contracts), priests and preachers instructing their congregations in righteousness. The one man included all these things in himself in that he was conversant with *Torah*, for *Torah* is not solely concerned with matters of faith but also with matters of law and justice and science and every aspect of civil life. Religion and state, religious and civil life are not held apart but gathered together in one. Hillel could both be the teacher of "thou shalt love thy neighbour as thyself: this is the whole Torah," as well as the reformer who introduced the *"Prozbol"* and determined the measure of "the drawn water."

Herein lay the weakness of Judaism and the reason why it did not develop civil science, scientific jurisprudence and secular learning as independent subjects. Hence it was difficult for the Jewish political government to persist side by side with the strong religious government: the priest-kings of the Maccabæan dynasty necessarily became Sadducees, and the Arabian, Abyssinian and Cuzarite kings, who embraced Judaism in the Middle Ages, found themselves unable to survive. Yet it has also proved the strength of Judaism: it thus became "of a single piece" with all that concerns the moral and intellectual life and penetrated into every corner of the workaday life. By this means it broke down the dividing wall between religion and daily life, making daily life an essential part of religion, and religion an essential part of daily life. That which was holy was not thereby profaned but was brought down to earth, while the secular life was transformed into the sacredness of a religious duty.

This served to make Judaism at once national and popular: the daily life of the whole nation was permeated by Judaism and the people saw it both as a heritage from their fathers and a popular system of daily life. Hence the Jewish people have fought desperately and heroically for their existence, cultivated carefully the corporate life, and promulgated their knowledge and the manner of life consequent on this knowledge among every class of the people.

*   *   *   *   *   *   *

At a time when popular national enthusiasm could rise to such heights, as at the attempt to set up an image in the Temple, and at such a time of economic weakness and political decay, there must needs have been among the crowds of people many men, with a hot and living sense of faith, who were not able to appreciate the two sides of Pharisaism. They were revolted by the fact that there were many Pharisees who could attach more importance to the ceremonial than to the moral laws.

The *Talmud* itself refers to the "Pharisaic plague" and to the "what is my duty and I will fulfil it" type of Pharisee; and a Pharisaic document (or if not Pharisaic, at least Essene or Zealot, i.e. extreme Pharisaic) such as the *Assumption of Moses* speaks of hypocrites and canting men who ruled over the people, swallowing up the inheritance of the poor by pretending to do them a kindness, men whose "hands and hearts were busy with uncleanness and whose mouth did speak proud things, and who said, Draw not nigh me lest ye defile me!" [101] It is even told of Shammai, the founder of the great *Beth ha-Midrash* in Israel, that when his daughter-in-law bore a son during or near the Feast of Tabernacles, and while she was still in bed (and, being a woman, not bound by the Tabernacle laws), "he broke the roof and built a booth over the bed for the sake of the child," i.e. so that the child, though but a few days old, might keep the Law and sit (or lie) in a tabernacle. [102]

It was such extremism as this which evoked the idea that such pedantry in important or unimportant religious duties swallowed up the purer faith and true morality. And just as the Prophets, though they never opposed the ceremonial laws in themselves, cried out, "What are the multitude of your sacrifices to me, if ye judge not a righteous judgment for the orphan and plead not the cause of the widow?"—so too the more ardent in Jesus' time could not but see in the excessive devotion to the ceremonial laws a danger to puremindedness and spirituality.

These men found their leaders not only in the early Prophets of the nation but in the "popular prophets," the writers of the *Pseudepigrapha*, Pharisees and Essenes who concerned themselves comparatively little with the ceremonial laws and gave most of their attention to moral problems, questions about the world to come, future

---

[101] *Assumption of Moses* VIII 9-10. Cf. Klausner, *I Farisei nella Assumptio Mosis, Rivista Israelitica* III 222-223 (and the notes of H. P. Chajes).
[102] *Sota* II 8.

recompense, Paradise and Gehenna, the day of judgment, the "pangs of the Messiah," the gathering together of the dispersed Jews, and the messianic age. These "meek upon earth" could not fight for their country's freedom against the might of Rome, but the messianic promise served them instead. The popular imagination found its satisfaction in these promises: it looked for their fulfilment at the hands of some great human figure who should work marvels and redeem the Jews and the entire world from slavery and misfortune by his supernatural power. This imaginative nationalism was all that survived in the hearts of these simple people, the "meek upon earth," great in faith but small in deed.

The degraded political conditions, slavery at home, dispersion abroad, made a breach in the messianic hope (a hope which was essentially nationalistic) : the morality which was bound up with it ("the kingdom of heaven" in the sense of the decisive rule of right) acquired, on the one hand, a universalistic tendency, and, on the other, an individualistic tendency—in the direction of the human hope that the individual should, in the world to come, receive a recompense for his good or evil deeds. Such recompense for the nation in this world was an idea which, unconsciously and gradually, became more and more distant, and almost disappeared into the realm of vision and mysticism.

From this circle of "the meek upon earth" came Jesus of Nazareth, and in him all this confused ferment of views received powerful and unique expression.

THIRD BOOK

THE EARLY LIFE OF JESUS: JOHN THE BAPTIST

I. THE CHILDHOOD AND YOUTH OF JESUS

Jesus (יהושע, ישוע or, in its abbreviated form ישו)[1] was born in the reign of Augustus two to four years *before* the Christian era[2] in the small town of Galilee called Nazareth (נצרת). The *Talmud* only mentions this place in an adjectival form נוצרי or נצרי applied (as also in Arabic *Nasrāni*, pl. *Nasāri*)[3] to the disciples of Jesus; but the name itself is mentioned in an ancient "Lament" for the Ninth of Ab, composed by R. Eliezer ha-Kalir (who flourished, according to recent authorities, in the 7th century),[4] entitled איכה ישבה חבצלת השרון, and based on an ancient *Baraita* treating of the "Twenty-four Courses of the Priests,"[5] and going back as far as the third century.

Verse 18 reads: "And in the uttermost parts of the earth Natzrâth was scattered (נזרית ; a variant reading gives נזירת). The vocalization "Natzrâth" is demanded by the rhyme of the verse and also occurs in the Peshitta. According to this *Baraita* there was in Nazareth a "course" of priests of the House of Happitzetz (1 Chron.

---

[1] The common idea that "Yeshu" is a nickname used instead of ישוע or יהושע, and made up of the initials of ימח שמו וזכרו ("May his name and memory be blotted out") is wrong, and arises from such attempts at "Gematria" as are found in the later versions of the *Tol'doth Yeshu*, according to which ישו (adopting the German pronunciation of Jesus!) is derived from the initials of ימח זכרו ויּמח שמו (see S. Krauss, *The Name Yeshu among the Hebrews*, *R.E.J.* LX, and the additional note by Poznanski, p. 160). Compare the names Ruth רעית=רעות, Simon שמעון=שמעון, Shammai (שמעיה = שמאי), and the like (Derenbourg, *op. cit.* 46 n. 2); Oshaia (אושעיה = אושיא), in J. Mann, *The Jews in Egypt and in Palestine*, Oxford, 1920, I 15 n. 4. A similar abbreviation is Yose (יוסי) from Joseph (יוסף).

[2] The calculation of this era is not absolutely accurate and was not fixed until the sixth century by Dionysius Exiguus. See R. W. Husband, *The Prosecution of Jesus*, Princeton, 1916, pp. 34-69.

[3] The theory put forward by Graetz (*M.G.W.J.* XXIX 483) and Neubauer (*Géographie de Talmud*, pp. 189-190) that "Beth-Lehem Tzarayah" (in *J. Megillah* I 1) stands for "Bethlehem Natzaraya" (= of Nazareth), is refuted by S. Klein, *Beiträge zur Geographie und Geschichte Galiläas*, 48-9.

[4] Since his teacher Rabbi Yannai flourished "not later than the second half of the seventh century" (Israel Davidson, *Mahzor Yannai*, New York, 1919, English introduction, p. xii).

[5] Klein, *op. cit.* 8-20.

24, 15).[6] Some have held that there was no such place as Nazareth and that Jesus was a god worshipped by the Nazarite sect—hence the name "Nazarenos, Naziraios," for Matthew (ii. 3) says, "And he (Joseph with Jesus) came and dwelt in a city called Nazareth to fulfil the word spoken by the Prophet, For he shall be called a Nazarene (Ναζωραῖος)." Thus it is assumed that the Gospels have already confused "Nazareth" with "Nazir." [7]

But such a theory is contradicted by the "Lament" of Ha-Kalir containing the name "Natzrāth" and based on an ancient *Baraita*, and the adjectival form *Notzri* and *Natzari* in the *Talmud* and in Arabic. Dalman [8] maintains that the Hebrew name was "Notzereth" and not "Natzrāth"—hence the adjective "Notzri;" and that the Aramaic name was "Natzira" (as in modern Arabic) or "Natzirath" —hence "Naziraios" and not "Nazoraios." But to the present writer it would seem that the evangelist was laying no pedantic stress on the fact that he could derive the word "Nazir" from "Nazareth" (Natzrath) or from "Natzirah;" the point for him was that there was a certain similarity in sound between the two words, just as we find the authorities of the *Talmud* basing derivations on like similarities.

"Nazir" had a double importance for the evangelist: (1) Samson the Nazirite was a saviour of Israel, just as Jesus was a saviour, and (2) Jesus, as נְזִיר אֶחָיו ("the prince among his brethren"), was to bear the נֵזֶר, crown, and so was King-Messiah. It may also be that "Nazoraios" comes from נֵצֶר, branch, and so Matthew ii. 23 is a reference to "And a branch from his roots shall blossom." [9]

The present Nazareth does not stand on the precise site of ancient Nazareth which was destroyed at an early date and, in the 12th or 13th century, rebuilt on a site below the old town. Its wonderful beauty has already been described by many scholars and writers [10] and the present writer was deeply impressed by it when he visited the town one May night in 1912.[11] Jerome long ago described it as "the flower of Galilee," [12] and though he supports this title from the passage "A branch from his roots shall blossom," occurring in the

[6] *Ibid.* pp. 74, 95, 102, 107.

[7] See Cheyne, *Encyclopedia Biblica, s.v. Nazareth;* Smith, *The Pre-Christian Jesus,* 1906; Brückner, *Nazareth als Heimath Jesu, Palästina-Jahrbuch,* VII, 1911, 74-84.

[8] See his *Grammatik des Jüdisch-Palästinischen Aramäisch,* 2 Aufl. p. 162; *Orte und Wege Jesu,* 2 Aufl. Gütesloh, 1921, pp. 50-52; E. Meyer, *Ursprung und Anfänge des Christentums,* 1921, II 423-5; G. F. Moore, *Nazarene and Nazareth (The Beginnings of Christianity,* ed. Foakes-Jackson and Kirsopp Lake, London, 1920, I 426-432).

[9] Isa. xi. 1.

[10] See E. Renan, *La vie de Jésus,* Paris, 1863, pp. 25-29; C. Furrer, *Leben Jesu Christi,* 3 Aufl. 1905, pp. 27-29; Dalman, *Orte und Wege Jesu,* pp. 57, 73-4.

[11] J. Klausner, *Olam Mithhaveh,* Odessa, 1915, pp. 174-178.

[12] *Epistola* XLVI, *Ad Marcellam.*

description of the "Shoot from the stock of Jesse,"[13] the natural beauty of the spot itself must also have called forth the title.

Nazareth, like Jerusalem, is surrounded by hills; but unlike the Judæan mountains which overawe by their majesty, the hills of Lower Galilee, the hills of Zebulum and Naphtali, have an indescribably tender beauty. Around Nazareth there still grow forests of palm-trees, fig-trees and pomegranates, and fields of high-growing though thin-eared crops of wheat and barley; and this must have been also the case in older times to an even greater and more prepossessing extent. The view from the crest of the hill on which Nazareth rests is one of the finest in the world. The town was cut off from the rest of the world, far removed from the great "highway to the sea" and the caravan routes.

It was a peaceful Galilæan town, cultivating its own fields and orchards, busying itself in all manner of handicrafts; it was, as it were, sunk into its own self, seeing visions and dreaming dreams. This was indeed a fitting place for the birthplace of the moralist and world-reformer, and for his childish visions and youthful dreams.

Until the fourth century Nazareth was exclusively Jewish,[14] and as late as the 6th century, Antoninus (570) extols the beauty of the Jewesses of Nazareth who were remarkable for their peaceful relations with the Christians.[15] According to other accounts, the town had a bad reputation and a common saying was "Can anything good come out of Nazareth?"[16]

But it is a common habit in small countries to pour scorn on every small town and to ascribe some general drawback to its people; and we hear in the *Talmud* how the Galilæans as a whole were regarded by Judæans as deficient in their knowledge of *Torah*, stupid, having a curious pronunciation and given to uncouth habits.[17] It may be that the author of the late Fourth Gospel argued from the general to the particular and did not reproduce the report accurately.

The statements in Matthew and Luke to the effect that Jesus was born in Bethlehem, have their origin in the theory that, as the Messiah, Jesus must be a son of David and a Bethlehemite and must fulfil the prophecy of Micah, "And thou, Bethlehem Ephratah . . . from thee shall come forth a ruler over Israel."[18] The Bethlehem of Galilee, referred to in the Old Testament,[19] and explained in the *Talmud* as

[13] Is. xi. 1.

[14] So Epiphanius, *Adv. Haereses* 30. That there were Jews in Nazareth in the 3rd century is apparent from the Hebrew inscription found there: סועם בר מנחם נוח נפש (Klein, *Jüdisch-Paläst. Corpus Inscriptionum*, Vienna, 1920, pp. 56-57).

[15] Dalman, *Orte u. Wege*, 64.

[16] John i. 47.

[17] *Erubin* 53a and b; *Shab.* 153a; *Megillah* 24b; *Nedarim* 18b, 48a; *Pes.* IV 5, 55a; *Kethuboth* 12a; J. *Shab.* XVI 5 (near end of section); J. *Sanh.* I 2; J. *Kethuboth* I 1; T. *Kethuboth* I 4 and elsewhere.

[18] Micah v. 1.

[19] Joshua xix. 15.

being "Bethlehem Tsaraya," [20] which Graetz and Neubauer supposed to be "Bethlehem of (= near) Nazareth," and Klein supposes to mean "Bethlehem the Less," [21] has by many scholars been identified with the Bethlehem of the Gospels.[22]

This Bethlehem of Galilee (a German colony in pre-war times) is in the Valley of Esdraelon, two hours' journey from Nazareth. According to these scholars, Jesus was born there and not in Bethlehem of Judæa; the writers of the Gospels placed the event in the latter Bethlehem as being the better known. But there is no sound basis for such a hypothesis. The evangelists were compelled to prove that Jesus, whom they called "Christ," Messiah, and "Son of David," hailed from the same Bethlehem in which David was born.

The two Gospels, Matthew and Luke, which give Bethlehem as the birthplace of Jesus, state that his mother, Mary, conceived by the Holy Spirit. If therefore he had no human father what connexion could he have with the house of David? According both to the *Talmud* and the Gospels, the Messiah is the Son of David; hence Jesus must at least be born in Bethlehem, the home of the house of David.

Jesus' father was Joseph and his mother Mary. Such is the explicit statement in an old Syriac manuscript of the Gospels found in the monastery of Mount Sinai by Mrs. Lewis and Mrs. Gibson. It is there written (Matt. i. 16), "And Joseph, to whom was espoused the virgin Mary, begot Jesus who was called the Messiah." [23] The accounts in Matthew and Luke about the birth of Jesus by the Holy Spirit are lacking in Mark; they stand on the same footing as the stories of Celsus' Jew, and of the *Tol'doth Yeshu* and the *Talmud*, which regard Jesus as illegitimate and the son of Pandera or Pantera, and both alike came into existence only after Christian dogma had determined that not only was Jesus the Messiah but also the Son of God. So long as Jesus was regarded only as the Messiah it was necessary to show that his father, Joseph, was of the stock of Jesse; but as Son of God it was not possible for him to have a human father: therefore he was born of the Holy Spirit by whom his mother conceived in a fashion incomprehensible to mortal beings. This became a matter of dispute amongst the earliest Christian sects. And the Jews, who also lacked the critical faculty and the historic sense (but remained strictly monotheistic), confirmed the fact that Jesus had not a legitimate father, but, instead of the Holy Spirit, introduced into their legends the notion of an illicit union. The truth is that Jesus was as legitimate as any other Jewish child in Galilee, where strict

[20] *J. Megillah* I i.

[21] See above, p. 229 n. 3.

[22] See A. Réville, *Jésus de Nazareth*, I [2] 330.

[23] See Agnes Smith Lewis, *The Old Syriac Gospels*, London, 1910, p. 2 (Syriac Text, p. B). See above, p. 69 n. 6,

supervision was exercised over espoused maidens, though perhaps to a less degree than in Judæa.[24]

So too there is scant support for the theory of Haupt, Chamberlain and Kaminka, that Jesus may have been of Gentile origin[25] because Galilee was a "Galilee of the Gentiles" and, such a short time back as early Maccabæan days, contained only a minority of Jews:

(1) There were numerous Jews in Galilee as early as Jonathan Maccabæus, since Demetrius remitted the taxes of the Jews of Galilee;[26] (2) the *Talmud* (which, as we saw, indulges in frequent gibes against the Galilæans) never charges them with being proselytes and of non-Israelitish stock;[27] (3) there is not the slightest hint in the Gospels that Gentile blood flowed in Jesus' veins, which, for Luke and Paul, would not have been regarded as a defect. It is, therefore, manifest that Jesus was a true Jew of Jewish family, for Galilee was, in his time, mainly populated by Jews; while there could be no stronger proof of his Jewishness than his essentially Jewish character and manner of life.[28]

Jesus' father, Joseph, was an artisan, a carpenter (נגר or חרש in the language of the Old Testament); and, as was the custom then and in much later times in Palestine and the universal rule even in the Middle Ages, the son learnt the father's trade. A happy chance has preserved the *Talmudic* expression, "a carpenter and son of a carpenter."[29] Justin Martyr records how Joseph and Jesus made goads and ploughs which were still extant in his day.[30] Jesus thus came from the ranks of the simple classes, from among those who laboured with the sweat of their brow: he had experienced their troubles, their poverty and their labour.

He had at least four brothers: James, Jose, Judah and Simeon. We have further information of certain of these. Josephus[31] mentions James as "the brother of Jesus who is called the Messiah;" James is also referred to in the Acts of the Apostles and the Epistle

---

[24] See *Kethuboth* 12a; *T. Kethuboth* I 4; *J. Kethuboth* I 1; A. S. Hirschberg, *Minhagē ha-Erusin v'ha-Nissu'in biz'man ha-Talmud, He-Atid*, V, 95-96; H. J. Nordin, *Die eheliche Ethik der Juden zur Zeit Jesu (Beiwerke zum Studium der Anthropophyteia*, Band IV), Ethnologischer Verlag, Leipzig, 1911, p. 47.

[25] A. Müller, *Jesus ein Arier*, Leipzig, 1904.

[26] 1 *Macc.* 10, 30 (Kautzsch wrongly considers "of Galilee" a gloss; the words are found in all the MSS. of 1 *Macc.*). See Kautzsch, *Apocryphen und Pseudepigraphen des Alten Testaments*, I 62, Anm. g.

[27] See B. Meistermann, *Capharnaüm et Bethsaïde*, Paris, 1921, pp. 256-257 n.; see also above, p. 133, n. 4, p. 135, n. 1.

[28] See also L. Sofer, *Welcher Rasse gehörte Jesus an? (Zeitschr. für Demographie u. Statistik der Juden*, 1909, pp. 81-87).

[29] *Ab. Zar.* 3b (beginning); *J. Yebam.* VIII 2.

[30] *Dialogus cum Tryphone Judæo*, §88. J. Halevy (Luncz's *Jerusalem*, 4th year, 1892, 11-20) holds that "Natzrath" is simply the word נסרת, while נניסר is "גיא נסר", and refers to the carpentry and "wood-sawing" there practised.

[31] *Ant.* XX ix 1; see above, pp. 58 ff.

to the Galatians [32] as "the brother of the Lord," and according to Clement of Alexandria, was known as "James the Righteous," [33] and was an orthodox follower of Judaism, observed the ceremonial laws and was also a member of the party of Ebionites and ascetics.

It would seem that he was not at first a believer in Jesus; only after the crucifixion and the success of the early Christian Church did he join the Church and become its leader; but he still remained an orthodox Jew, and when he, together with his fellow Nazarenes, was put to death by the Sadducæan High Priest, Annas ben Annas, charged with deserting the faith, the Pharisees and their followers, knowing James' piety, protested.[34] As for Jesus' brother Judah, we know that his grandsons were persecuted by Domitian, who had heard that the Messiah would remove the yoke of Rome from the neck of Israel and that the Messiah was to be of the house of David.

The Christians at the close of the first century regarded Jesus as the Son of David, therefore all members of his family must be members of the house of David.[35] As is apparent from one passage in the Gospels [36] and another in St. Paul,[37] Jesus was "the firstborn among many brethren." He had, furthermore, at least two sisters who, it would seem, were married to natives of Nazareth.[38]

Following the custom of the time, in fulfilment of the command "And thou shalt teach them to thy children," Joseph would, in addition to craftsmanship, teach his son *Torah*. In Jerusalem there had been a boys' school since the time of Simeon ben Shetah, but it was not till thirty years after the crucifixion that a system of schools in every town was organised by the High Priest, Jehoshua ben Gamala.[39] It may be that Joseph, a Galilæan workingman, was one of those "deficient in the *Torah*" and unable to teach his son, and that Jesus learnt from the minister of the synagogue whose incidental duty it was, even before the organization set up by Jehoshua ben Gamala, to teach children.

Jesus certainly knew the Law and the Prophets and the Book of Psalms, and had, also, some knowledge of the Book of Daniel and also, perhaps, of the *Book of Enoch*. It may be, however, that he had only heard the Law read in Hebrew and translated into Aramaic, his spoken language, in the synagogue of Nazareth (there was then

[32] Acts xii. 17; xxi. 18; Galatians i. 19; ii, 9, 12.
[33] Eusebius, *Hist. Eccl.* II 1.
[34] The theory that James was but a step-brother or relative is due to the supposed difficulty that Mary, having once been accounted worthy of bearing a son by the Holy Spirit, should have given birth naturally to other sons. ἀδελφός in the language of Jewish writers of Greek at that period meant brother in the literal sense.
[35] So Eusebius, *Hist. Eccl.* III 19-20, quoting Hegesippus (2nd century).
[36] Luke ii. 7 (and in a variant form Matt. i. 25).
[37] Romans viii. 29.
[38] Mk. vi. 3.
[39] See above, p. 193, n. 1.

practically no Jewish town without its synagogue), for all the sayings of Jesus which have been preserved in the Gospels in his actual language are in Aramaic; e.g. *"Talitha kumi," "Ephphatha," "Reka," "Rabboni,"* etc.; and during his crucifixion he expresses his agony by a verse from the Psalms in Aramaic, *"Elohi, Elohi, lama sabachtani"* (אלהי אלהי למא שבקתני).[40] and not the Hebrew אלי אלי למה עזבתני. Both the *Talmud* [41] and the Gospels [42] tell us that, in Judæa, Galilæans were recognizable by their language (Aramaic).

It would seem that Jesus' father died while Jesus was still young, for though his mother, Mary, is mentioned in connexion with various incidents during his life and even after the crucifixion, and his brothers and sisters are also referred to alone or in conjunction with her, the only reference to the father is at the time of Jesus' birth. It is difficult to suppose that the father is deliberately ignored as a stumbling-block in the way of the story of Jesus' birth by the Holy Spirit, since (though to a smaller extent) the reference to the brothers and sisters is a similar stumbling-block; so we must conclude that Joseph died while Jesus was still young.

On the other hand he has much to say of a father's love for his children, but nothing of a mother's love. It is true that the father in question is God, but even the "prodigal son" is not welcomed by his mother. We must conclude, therefore, that his father's memory was more precious to him than his living mother, who did not understand him and whom he turned away when she and his brothers came to take possession of him (see later). Being the eldest child he was compelled to support his widowed mother and his younger orphaned brothers and sisters by means of manual labour, carpentry.[43]

So labouring and studying he passed his childhood and youth in that small town hidden away in the Galilæan hills. He was unconsciously influenced by the natural beauty of Nazareth. In after-life he speaks of the "lilies of the field" with their gorgeous garb, and how Solomon in all his glory was not arrayed like one of them.[44] Most of his charming parables turn on such subjects as sowers and planters, the fig-tree and mustard-tree, the wheat and the tares; and all this proves how devoted he was to the pleasant fields and vineyards and the beautiful natural scenery with its wealth of many-coloured flowers which characterized his home country.

Certainly, the sight that unfolds itself to-day as one climbs the

[40] Ps. xxii. 2 = Mark xv. 34. On this subject see Arnold Meyer, *Jesu Muttersprache*, Leipzig, 1896; Schulthess, *Problem der Sprache Jesu*, 1913; G. Dalman, *Jesus-Yeschua*, Leipzig, 1922, pp. 6-15.
[41] *Erubin* 53b.
[42] Mark xiv. 70; Matt. xxvi. 73.
[43] See Mark vi. 3, where Jesus is called "the carpenter"; and Matt. xiii. 55, where he is called "the son of the carpenter."
[44] Matt. vi. 28-29. On the "lilies of the field," see Dalman, *Orte und Wege Jesu*, pp. 139-140, 208.

hills around Nazareth is one of the most wonderful in Palestine. To the west are the low-lying hills stretching towards the Mediterranean, whose blue waters turn to silver under the bright sunlight. To the south is seen the Valley of Jezreel, framed in bare mountains, with its profusion of fresh vegetation and trees looking like a sea of green bordered by yellow shores, the whole valley being crowned by the hill of Moreh, the battle-field of Gideon, and the mountains of Gilboa, where king Saul was slain. To the east is the rounded Mount Tabor, green with sparse forests. To the southwest is the thickly wooded Carmel falling away to the Mediterranean. Further east, in Transjordania, are seen the steep, yellow mountains of Gilead, ploughed it would seem into furrows, owing to the deluges of sand blown by the desert winds. To the north are the mountains of Napthali, the mountains of Upper Galilee; while on the northern horizon is the hoary peak of Hermon, and in the far distance the peaks of Lebanon.

Its majestic beauty was an awe-inspiring sight and must, even without his knowledge, have exerted an influence on Jesus. The ancients, and particularly the Jews, did not, as we do, deliberately contemplate nature in order to enjoy its beauty: but later accounts tell how Jesus remained alone in the mountains, under the star-strewn canopy of heaven, spending the night in prayer, prayer certainly accompanied by self-examination and meditations on the world and mankind.[45] It was then that his young mind, searching his heavenly Father, fashioned itself.

There, cut off by mountains from the great world, wrapped up in natural beauty, a beauty tender and peaceful, sorrowful in its peacefulness, surrounded by peasants who tilled the soil, with few necessities in life—there, Jesus could not help being a dreamer, a visionary, whose thoughts turned not on his people's future (he was far removed from their political conflicts), nor on the heavy Roman yoke (which had scarcely touched him); his thoughts turned, rather, on the sorrows of the individual soul and on the "Kingdom of Heaven," a kingdom not of this world. . . .

The mountains of Judæa, overwhelming in their magnificence, the bare, terrible surroundings of Jerusalem—these might beget the prophet-dreamer, the man of might, who could oppose his will against the will of the entire world and rage against the perversion of justice in the *social* sphere, preaching vengeance against the nations and reproving the peoples of the world. But the attractive and charming hills of Galilee, the surroundings of Nazareth, which, with all their glory, are still stamped with a tenderness, beauty and peace —this Nazareth, tightly enclosed within its hills, hearing but a faint, distant echo of wars and conflicts, a charming corner, hidden away and forgotten, could create only the dreamer, one who would reform the world not by revolt against the power of Rome, not by national

45 Luke vi. 12.

insurrection, but by the kingdom of heaven, by the inner reformation of the *individual*.[46]

Besides this natural influence, Jesus was moved by two other powerful factors, the *Law* and *life*. His was an active mind and a fervid imagination, and the study (by his own reading or from the lips of others) of the books of the Prophets set his spirit aflame. The stern reproofs of the "First Isaiah," the divine consolations of the "Second Isaiah," the sorrows of Jeremiah, the soaring vision and stern wrath of Ezekiel, the sighs and laments of the Psalms, the promises foreseen in Daniel (and, perhaps, the *Book of Enoch*), together with those portions of the Pentateuch, full of the love of God and the love of man—all moved him to rapture and enthusiasm, penetrated his soul and enriched his spirit.

During Jesus' earlier years, soon after the outbreaks which followed the death of Herod, and about the time of the Census of Quirinius (which called into being, or rather renewed, the party of the Zealots founded by Judah the Galilæan), the whole of Galilee was a boiling cauldron of rebels, malcontents and ardent "seekers after God." The worst storms may not have reached the little town of Nazareth, but echoes of them were constantly heard. Heavy taxation had made life hard, and disease and destitution, widowed and bereaved women, orphaned children, and forsaken fields—all these abounded in consequence of wars and rebellions.

The majority groaned in silence under the heavy burden. They had but one hope: yet a little while and the "day of consolation" (whether in a political, economic or spiritual sense) would come; the messianic age would draw near and King-Messiah would appear in all the might of his sovereignty and moral grandeur and make an end of all sorrows and pains, all servitude and ungodliness. Jesus, who was one of the people and lived among them, knew their distress and believed too in the prophetic promises and consolations, certainly meditated much on present conditions, and his imagination pictured for him in glowing colours the redemption, both political and spiritual.

As one of the "meek upon earth," the prevailing element with him was the spiritual side of the messianic idea, that of redemption. There may already have flashed through his mind faint glimmerings of the thought that even he (like many other Galilæans) was capable of being the redeemer of Israel, a spiritual redeemer who, by such spiritual redemption, should automatically effect the political redemption. Such an assumption is likely in view of what happened later when Jesus was thirty years old, though we have no exact knowledge of his life and doings until John the Baptist revealed himself. Luke's story [47] that Jesus, when twelve years old, went with his parents to Jerusalem and disputed in the Temple with the Pharisees who marvelled at his wisdom, is confined to Luke's Gospel. Luke may have

[46] See J. Klausner, *Olam Mithhaveh*, p. 174.
[47] Luke ii. 41-52.

heard something about the Jewish *Bar-Mitzvah* rite, applicable to boys of thirteen and girls of twelve, and thought that Jesus must have distinguished himself on such an occasion. Mark tells nothing about the life of Jesus until his baptism by John.

Such a silence is of a piece with the usage of the early Jews. They were interested in a great man's life only *after* he had appeared on the stage of history: the earlier years did not matter, he was then simply an individual no different from others, and the details of his life were not any concern of others. At the most the Bible takes an interest only in a hero's birth and earliest days; *e.g.*, the story of Moses. Legend tells many pleasant stories of the great man's birth, and then leaves him altogether till he has reached maturity; another story is then told, and again he is left till the day when he mounts the stage of history and his life becomes wrapped up with the life of his people, and then only does his history become detailed.

It may be urged that Moses is a legendary figure; yet what do we know of Isaiah before he intervened in the wars of Ahaz and Hezekiah? And what do we know of his later life when he no longer influenced the state? And what do we know of his death beyond a few legends? The same applies to Jeremiah and Ezekiel, Ezra and Nehemiah.

It is even the same with Hillel the Elder, almost a contemporary of Jesus: we know nothing of his birth, his early life in Babylon or his life in Jerusalem until he became famous by his disputations with the Sons of Bethira and took his place in the spiritual history of his nation. And so it is with Jesus. The Jews, even when they became Nazarenes and Christians ("Messianists" in the newly acquired sense), were interested in Jesus' life only after he became an active factor in history, after his meeting with John the Baptist, and when he gathered together disciples.

With what went before neither the Jews nor Jesus himself were interested; for what had a man's private life and family and home to do with sacred history which, for the Jews (and also the early Christians) was purely an aspect of religion and but served to manifest the workings of God in the life of mankind! In this we notice the greatness of Judaism from the philosophic and social side, but its insignificance from the scientific side; for the latter regards theoretical knowledge as the foundation and argues from cause to effect, finding an importance in every detail, and regarding the child as "father of the man."

II. JOHN THE BAPTIST

As with Jesus, so with John the Baptist: history showed no interest in his origin or his life before he came to the front and became an historic figure. What Luke [1] tells of his birth and origin is peculiar to Luke and purely legendary; in substance it is in part an imitation of the Bible stories of the births of Isaac, Samson and Samuel,[2] and the rest is derived from a patent wish to prove that Jesus was greater than John.[3] The utmost that we can draw from Luke is that John's father was called Zechariah and his mother Elisabeth.

Besides the record of the work of John the Baptist given in the four Gospels, which agree in the main, we have also an account from a certain historical source, the principal work of Josephus.[4] This account, however, deals only with the close of John the Baptist's life. Josephus, for obvious reasons, says nothing of the earlier stages: he was chary of speaking of Messianic movements for fear of Roman disapproval; thus he generally refers to messianic movements as simple revolts, or else ignores them. Consequently he says but little of Jesus and deals very briefly with John the Baptist. There is, therefore, no ground for suspecting the evangelists of deliberately inventing facts: in the story of Salome alone is there a legendary element.

After recounting the victory of Aretas IV, king of Arabia, over Herod Antipas in the war arising from the latter's desire to divorce his first wife, Aretas' daughter,[5] Josephus adds: "But many Jews saw in the destruction of Herod's army a just punishment from God for the killing of John who was called 'the Baptist' ('Ιωάννου τοῦ ἐπικαλουμένου Βαπτιστοῦ); Herod had slain this just man (ἀγαθόν) who had called upon the Jews to follow the way of righteousness, for every man to deal equitably with his neighbour, to walk in piety before God and to come for baptism; for baptism only availed in his (God's) sight if it were done not to free from sins but for bodily purity (ἐφ' ἁγνείᾳ τοῦ σώματος) after the soul had been already cleansed by righteousness. And when many others also turned towards John [6] (for at the hearing of his words their souls were

[1] Luke i. 5-25, 55-80.
[2] The *Magnificat* (Luke i. 46-54) contains whole verses from the prayer of Hannah, the mother of Samuel (1 Sam. ii. 1-10).
[3] *E.g.*, the passage relating how John leapt in the womb of his mother before Jesus, who was not yet born (Luke i. 41-44).
[4] *Ant.* XVIII v 2.
[5] Above, p. 166.
[6] In addition to his earlier and more intimate disciples.

uplifted) Herod feared lest his great influence over men cause them
to rebel, for it seemed as though they would do anything in accordance with his advice.   Wherefore he found it better to anticipate anything new which might come to his mind (πρίν τι νεώτερον ἐξ αὐτοῦ
γενέσθαι) and to kill him, rather than endure regret for the change
(μεταβολή) when once it had happened.   So John was sent bound
in fetters to the fortress of Machærus, already mentioned, and there
put to death." [7]

This paragraph like that on Jesus is also regarded as spurious;
Graetz especially is quite convinced of this and dubs everything said
of John the Baptist in the "Antiquities" as a "shameless interpolation:" how, in the first place, could Josephus, writing for Greeks,
have written the word "Baptist" (Βαπτιστής) without any explanation? and, secondly, since the death of John occurred after the appearance of Jesus (c.29-30), and Herod's war with Aretas only
happened six years later (c.36), how could Josephus connect Antipas's defeat with the execution which happened many years earlier? [8]

Yet it is difficult to support this view. Firstly, Josephus explains
the word "Baptist" a few lines later, telling how John summoned the
people to baptism and explaining the kind of baptism which John
intended. And secondly, while the early Christian Father Origen
did not know (or, rather, attached no importance to) the paragraph
about Jesus, he knew of this paragraph about John.[9]   Thirdly, no
Christian interpolator would have forgotten to associate the death
of John with his rebuke to Herod Antipas about his wife Herodias.[10]
And fourthly, Josephus, who says of himself [11] that he served three
years Banus the Nazarite who "lived in the wilderness, was clothed
with leaves of a tree and ate only wild fruits, and baptized night and
day many times in cold water for the sake of purity" (πρὸς ἁγνείαν
—the identical word which he employs for the baptism of John),
may well have been friendly to John and, with "many Jews," have regarded the defeat of Antipas as a divine punishment for killing a
recluse who was moved by no selfish motive.

And, finally, all that Josephus says of John the Baptist is in
accordance with Josephus' principle of not emphasizing anything to
do with the messianic idea and messianic movements, but referring
to them only lightly in such a way that they would be understood by
his Jewish readers but not by Roman and Greek readers, to whom
such statements would be both strange and objectionable as implying
a desire for earthly sovereignty at the hands of the "king-messiah"
—a world kingdom already held by the Romans on the political side
and by the Greeks on the cultural side.

[7] *Ant.* XVIII v 2.
[8] Graetz, *op. cit.* III, I [5] 277 n.
[9] *Contra Celsum* I 47.
[10] See A. Réville, *Jésus de Nazareth,* I [2] 251-259.
[11] *Vita* §2.

Josephus simply makes John a philosopher in search of justice and piety, just as Jesus is made a "wise man," and the politico-religious sects of the Pharisees, Sadducees and Essenes, were made into philosophical sects. Josephus was chary of referring to John's main idea just as he was chary of mentioning the central position held by the messianic idea in the minds of the Pharisees and Essenes. Yet he hints at the main point of John's ministry in the words, "the new things which he thought," and "the change" which he was about to make. And he also stresses the idea of the baptism as "purification of the body" after that the "soul was already purified by righteousness," *i.e.*, by repentance. In the present writer's opinion, therefore, the entire paragraph (with, perhaps, the exception of isolated words coloured by Christianity) is genuine.

Furthermore, there is no contradiction between the Gospels and the Josephus paragraph: they supplement one another. The *Antiquities* still preserves a trace of the politico-national side in the Baptist's preaching which alarmed Herod, while the Gospels preserve a trace of the politico-religious side. As for Josephus' connecting the death of John with the defeat of Herod, which did not happen till the year 36, even this need cause no difficulty. John the Baptist may have been killed in the year 29 (as we shall shortly see) and the people would still be able to recall the slaying of the "popular prophet" and attribute the defeat to a divine punishment for the death of a righteous man whose only fault was that he drew the multitude after him and so excited a fear of a popular outbreak; or Josephus himself may, some time afterwards, have conceived this process of historical cause and effect.

In the Gospels the death of John is connected with Herodias, who was unable to forgive him for rebuking Antipas, obviously publicly, for marrying the wife of his brother, Philip. This is an error. Herodias was not the wife of Philip [12] but of his step-brother, Herod, son of the second Mariamne, the daughter of the High Priest, Simon ben Boethus. By this husband she had a daughter named Salome. Such is the evidence of Josephus. This Salome, as Guttschmidt has shown, was born in 10 C.E., married (about 37-30) the Tetrarch Philip (who was twenty years her senior), and, after Philip's death in the year 34, married again to Aristobulus, son of Herod (the second), king of Chalcis and grandson of Herod "the Great." Nero gave to this same Aristobulus the kingdom of Lesser Armenia, and a coin still survives on which are engraved the heads of Aristobulus and his wife Salome, and containing on the reverse the inscription: ΒΑΣΙΛΕΩΣ ΑΡΙΣΤΟ ΒΟΥΛΟΥ ΒΑΣΙΛΙΣΣΗΣ ΣΑΛΩΜΗΣ ("Of the king Aristobulus: of the queen Salome").

Therefore, in the years 28-29, when John was killed, Salome could still be a "damsel" (χοράσιον),[13] *i.e.*, a young girl and not yet

[12] See above, p. 166.
[13] Mark vi. 22-28.

married to Philip.[14] If Antipas' first wife, the Arab king's daughter, demanded that she be sent to the fortress of Machærus (built by Alexander Jannæus on the Jordan frontier, east of the Dead Sea, Greek Μαχαιροῦς, Hebrew מְכַוֵּר or מַחְבָר, the modern Mekawar),[15] this is not because the fortress belonged to her father[16] (for it would be very difficult to imagine how Herod could imprison John there), but simply because it was near the frontier of Arabia, her native country; the idea that Machærus belonged to Aretas arises from a faulty reading in the *Antiquities*.[17] Thus the Gospels do not contradict Josephus nor contain any historical improbability; and the remarks about John in Josephus are not a Christian interpolation. But there is a definitely legendary colour about the Gospel story which tells how, at a feast given by Herod Antipas on his birthday to his captains and officers, Salome danced so well that Herod vowed that he would give whatever she should ask up to "the half of his kingdom" (vividly recalling Ahasuerus and his words to Esther at the drinking banquet), and she, advised by her mother, asked for the head of John the Baptist on a charger, and this Herod gave her against his will but feeling bound by the oath which he had sworn to her.[18] It is most improbable that Josephus, who knew Salome and enjoyed recounting court intrigues, would have refrained from telling such a wonderful event if it had any historical foundation.

It is worth adding that in the Slavonic translation of the *Wars of the Jews* (the Moscow MS.) containing many passages not in the present Greek text (but whose primitive character is apparent from their Hebrew style still perceptible through the double translation—since the Slavonic version is obviously translated from the Greek), it is stated that Herodias was not married to Antipas until after the death of her first husband; and that the reproof provoked by her marriage was due to the fact that she had a daughter by this husband. This second marriage was, therefore, from the Pharisaic point of view, "a levirate marriage not according to the Law," since the Pharisees expounded "having no son" (in Deuteronomy xxv.5) as referring not to an actual "son," but to offspring of either sex; and in this case there was a child born by the first marriage, viz., the daughter Salome.

[14] See in detail, Schürer I, 441-445; 723-725, n. 64.
[15] *Tamid* III 8; *J.R.ha-Sh.* II 2; *Yoma* 39b ("Mikhmar" for מכוור or מכמר); *R.ha-Sh.* 23b; *T.R.ha-Sh.* 2 (1), 2 חרים וכייר ונדר instead of הרי מכוור); *Wars* VII vi 2; *Ant.* XVIII v 2. The Jews used to light fires on the hill of Machærus to announce the first of the month (*J.R.ha-Sh. ibid.*). On Machærus see S. Krauss, *M'sudath Mikhwar v'divre Nifleötheha* ("Jerusalem," ed. Luncz, VII 1894, pp. 287-292); A. Musil, *Arabia Petræa*, Vienna, 1907, I 237-239; Dalman, *Orte u. Wege*, pp. 16-17; J. Klausner, *Biy'me bayit Sheni*, p. 127.
[16] See below 247-8; *Ant.* XVIII v 1-2.
[17] See Schürer, I⁴, 436 n. 20.
[18] Mark vi. 17-29.

Like Josephus, John was, as we shall see shortly, a thoroughgoing Pharisee with Nazarite and Essæan tendencies; therefore he, too, regarded the marriage as contrary to the Law, and reproved Antipas Yet the reason for his death was not, as the Gospels tell us, the wish of Salome, but, as stated by Josephus, Antipas' fear of rebellion.[19]

What was John's mission in life? What did he teach and what was his aim?

In the 15th year of Tiberius,[20] the year 28-29 C.E., in southern Transjordania (hence John's arrest by Antipas and not by Philip or Pilate) near the border of Antipas' realm (where was the fortress Machærus) not far from Judæa, in the steppe-country along the side of the Jordan (ἔρεμος is not quite the same as מדבר "wilderness"), close to the place where, according to the Old Testament story, Elijah concealed himself, south of Jericho,[21] and probably at the place which still retains a reference to the Jews—the modern "Kasr el-Yahud" (now a Greek monastery)—at this time and place there appeared a remarkable man, clothed in a cloak of camel's hair, with a leathern girdle about his loins, who fed only on clean locusts[22] and honey-combs.[23] A late Gospel preserves the name of the place as "Beth Abara" (another reading is "Beth Araba," "Beth Anya,")[24] but this is simply a ford of the Jordan.

The name of this man was John, and, according to legend, he was the son of Zechariah. Because of his chief activity the people styled him "the Baptist." From his clothing of camel's hair it would seem that he looked upon himself as a prophet, for it is said of the prophets that they "wore camel's hair;"[25] and, from his wearing a leathern girdle, that he supposed himself to be Elijah.[26] Furthermore, the "mantle of Elijah" plays a great part in the legend and this, appar-

---

[19] On this see Simon Bernfeld, *Shelomith bath Herodias*, in *Ha-Boker*, ed. D. Frischman, Warsaw, 1899, No. 121 (Siwan 21). See also Ed. Meyer, *Ursprung u. Anfänge des Christentums*, 1921, I 208 n. 1.

[20] See the laboured detail in Luke iii. 1-2, and cf. Husband, *The Prosecution of Jesus*, pp. 34-69.

[21] 2 Kings ii. 13-21. For detailed discussion on the site of John's solitary sojourning and of the place where he baptised and where Jesus was baptised, see Dalman, *Orte u. wege*, pp. 75-87.

[22] "Unclean locusts pickled with clean locusts" (*Terumoth* X 9); the beginning of *Lam. R.* on the verse "Al he-Harim" makes the exaggerated statement: "There are 800 species of clean locusts" (in Palestine before the First Destruction). Dalman, *op. cit.* p. 78, tells how the Bedouin boil or roast the locusts and eat them with salt; and during the last plague of locusts in Palestine (1917) the Yemenites caught and ate the locusts. See Joseph Schwartz, *Tebhuoth ha-Aretz*, ed. Luncz, p. 379, and the monograph "*Ha-Arbeh*" of A. Aharoni, ed. Zionist Commission, Jaffa 1920.

[23] Such (יערות דבש), in the present writer's opinion, was the Hebrew original in the Gospels; this became דבש היער, and so μέλι ἄγριον (Mark i. 6).

[24] John i. 28. Mrs. Lewis put forward the theory that this is "Beth Aniah" (House of the Ship).

[25] Zech. xiii. 4.

[26] 2 Kings i. 8.

ently, was also a "cloak of hair." [27] John, therefore, thought of himself as Elijah; and as Elijah hid himself in the wilderness [28] by the banks of the Jordan, near Jericho,[29] so John also lived in the Arabah (the wilderness) near the Jordan, not far from Jericho.

Also what John taught was what was, in his time, attributed to the Prophet Elijah. The last of the books of the Prophets is "Malachi," whose very name is strange, and, in early times, was regarded as synonymous with Elijah, because it is said in that book: "Behold I send 'my messenger' ("Malachi") who shall prepare the way before me, and suddenly shall the Lord whom ye seek come unto his temple, and the 'messenger of the covenant' whom ye desire, behold he cometh." [30] "The Lord whom ye (*i.e.* the people of Israel) seek" who "shall come suddenly," was then supposed to be the "king-messiah," who should come unexpectedly, and "my messenger" who was to prepare the way before "the Lord," and who was "the messenger of the covenant" (hence the connexion of Elijah with the covenant of Abraham: cf. "the throne of Elijah" in the circumcision rite, in Hebrew בריתו של אברהם אבינו "the Covenant of Abraham our father"), was Elijah, for, at the end of the book of Malachi it is explicitly recorded: "Behold I send to you Elijah the prophet before the coming of the day of the Lord (the "pangs of the Messiah"), the great and terrible day." [31]

Elijah, who went alive to heaven and did not taste of death, is, therefore, the forerunner of the Messiah. He was so regarded by Ben Sira.[32] And in those hard times, when Palestine was so oppressed and disturbances were so rife, and when false messiahs (the Samaritan Messiah, Theudas, the Egyptian Messiah) arose one after the other, Israel, in spite of disappointments, awaited the Messiah in the near future. The Apocalypses of the "popular prophets" written then, and shortly before and after that time (viz. the *Book of Enoch,* the *Ascension of Moses, Fourth Esdras, Baruch* and the like), are filled with descriptions of the Messiah and the messianic age.

If the Messiah was, indeed, soon to come, then his great forerunner, the Prophet Elijah, must come before him; and so a certain enthusiast saw himself as the Forerunner, and revealed himself as Elijah by his clothing and much of his manner of life.

John was a Nazarite and ascetic, as he imagined Elijah to have been, who hid himself from men in the wildernesses and in caves. Herein John resembled the Essenes who, as we have seen, avoided the company of mankind and supported themselves on scanty supplies

[27] Cf. 2 Kings i. 8 and 1 Kings xix. 13 and 19, 2 Kings ii. 2, 8. 13, 14.
[28] 1 Kings xix. 4; Josephus (*Ant.* XX viii 6; *Wars* II xiii 4; cf. *Wars* VII xi 1) points out that "deceivers and magicians" (false prophets) used to summon the people to the wilderness.
[29] 2 Kings ii. 4-15.
[30] Malachi iii. 1.
[31] Mal. iii. 33.
[32] *Ben Sira* 48, 10-11.

of food and drink. Banus the Essene, the teacher of Josephus, lived in the wilderness, clothed himself in a garment made of leaves, ate only wild fruit, and bathed often day and night in cold water "for the purpose of purification." John also bathed and baptized in the Jordan, and so got the name "John the Baptist."

But there is a great difference between John and the Essenes. The latter were a society of Nazarites, accepting as "brethren" only a few men tested and chosen after a period of probation. John, however, summoned all alike to baptism. The Essenes lived apart in their desert places and abjured the work-a-day outside world: they looked for the coming of the Messiah apart from any efforts of theirs. John gathered around him large numbers, apart from his own disciples, and taught them to "bring nearer" the coming of the Messiah. The Essenes did not mix in political matters except as revealers of the future (Judah the Essene in the time of Aristobulus I, and Menahem the Essene in the time of Herod), and not till the great revolt did they take sword in hand. John the Baptist rose up against Antipas, like Elijah against Ahab, as a preacher and reprover.

Hence we may not regard John as altogether an Essene, as did Graetz, who compared the "Baptist" with the "bathers at dawn," mentioned in the Jerusalem *Talmud*. John thought of himself as Elijah, even though he did not openly proclaim this; and since Elijah was allied in spirit with the Sons of the Rechabites, who abjured town-life, so John the Baptist was akin, in his manner of life, to the Essenes, the successors of the Rechabites. Since he did not eat bread nor drink wine he was regarded by the ordinary people as a holy man; but the Pharisees and Scribes, and the educated classes generally, thought him mad.[33]

John, as the Messiah's forerunner, must prepare the way for him by teaching the need for repentance and good works. So he proclaimed his great message: "Repent ye, for the kingdom of heaven is at hand!"

The expression "kingdom of heaven" (מלכות שמים) is typically Hebrew, and this Hebrew character is apparent in its Greek form which employs the plural (Βασιλεία τῶν οὐρανῶν) to translate the Hebrew dual form in שמים. The Jews of the time habitually used "heaven" to avoid having to pronounce the name of God; so "the kingdom of heaven" meant "the kingdom of God," or "the kingdom of the Almighty," *i.e.*, the messianic age.[34] There is a common idea in the *Talmud* that King-Messiah's kingdom would come, or be hastened, as a result of repentance: "If Israel were to repent, they would straightway be redeemed," and "Great is repentance which hastens

---

[33] Matt. xi. 18; Luke vii. 33.

[34] *Berachoth* II 2 and 5 (the Law and the Commandments); *Sifre* on Deut. 323 ed. Friedmann 139*b*; *Pesiqta d'Rab Kahana*, § *Ha-Hodesh*, ed. Buber 3*a*; *Gen. R.* §9; *Cant. R.* on *"ha-Te'enah han'ta pageha"* (the "days of the Messiah").

the redemption." [35]   From the Book of Malachi (the source of the idea of Elijah as the messianic forerunner) John drew the powerful descriptions of the Day of Judgment and the lot of those who will not repent.

Malachi says, "Behold the day cometh, burning like a furnace, and all the proud and they that do wickedly are stubble and the day shall come shall set them aflame, said the Lord of Hosts, and shall not leave them root or branch;" [36] and John announces, "The axe is already laid to the root of the tree and every tree that bringeth not forth good fruit is hewn down and cast into the midst of the fire . . . and his fan is in his hand and he shall winnow his threshing-floor and gather his wheat into his garner and the chaff he shall burn with unquenchable fire." [37]   Yet John supplements the words of the prophets: to them [37a] who would maintain that they have nothing to fear from the Day of Judgment since they are the children of Abraham, Isaac and Jacob, John retorts (with a play on words), "Think not in yourselves saying, We have Abraham to our father; for I say unto you that God is able from these stones (abanim) to raise up children (banim) unto Abraham." [38]   This is an anti-nationalist touch omitted by Mark, yet it is, none the less, genuine: had not the movement from the very beginning been impregnated with some seed, no matter how minute, of anti-Jewish nationalism, there never could have arisen the religion which so definitely tears away national barriers. Ex nihilo nihil fit.

Yet there is no reason to suppose that John thought of himself as preaching a new faith or teaching the Jews to turn away from their Torah; he sought but the one thing—repentance; and as a symbol of repentance he baptised in the Jordan. Baptism which had before been the symbol of purity of body now also became the symbol of purity of soul, of a new birth in a certain sense. This symbolic sense was especially prevalent among the Essenes. But the same sense was also to be found among the Pharisees in so far as they required proselytes to be baptised as well as circumcised; and there is a statement from an early Tanna that baptism is more important than circumcision. [39]

Baptism alone sufficed with female proselytes. The circumcised and baptised male proselyte, and the baptised female proselyte, were

[35] Sanh. 97b-98a; Yoma 86b, etc.
[36] Malachi iv. 1.
[37] Matt. iii. 10 and 12. Luke iii. 9 and 17.
[37a] Matthew says that they were "Pharisees and Sadducees who came to be baptized, and John called them "offspring of vipers," but Luke says that they were "the multitude of people who came to be baptized by him," which is more likely to be true.
[38] Matt. iii. 10, 12; Luke iii. 9, 17; see H. P. Chajes, La lingua ebraica nel Christianesimo primitivo, Firenze, 1905, p. 11; C. Furrer, Leben Jesu Christi, p. 63.
[39] See Yebamoth 46a and b.

"as children newly born;" [40] thus baptism was, as it were, a new birth and wiped out pre-baptismal sins. The statement quoted above from Josephus to the effect that John employed baptism for purifying both body and soul, can be accepted as true. Mark, of course, lays stress only on the spiritual aspect: "John was baptising in the wilderness and preaching the baptism of repentance for the remission of sins," and adds that those who were baptised in Jordan by John the Baptist "confessed their sins." [41]

The inference is that John held that an essential condition for the coming of the shortly-expected Messiah was *individual* repentance and confession (ודוי as in present-day Judaism and, to a certain extent, in the Judaism of the Second Temple and the *Talmud* period); whereas the Prophets (and the *Talmud,* as a rule) regarded *national* and *social* repentance as the essential principle, considering that this also covered individual conduct.

John did not regard himself as the Messiah. He believed that after him "one mightier than he" should come, and that he himself was not worthy to stoop down and loose the latchet of his shoes" (or, to use the more Hebraic form, he was too small to carry his shoes after him (from the Aramaic metaphor מאניה אבתריה מוביליָנא);[42] and that if he, John, baptised with water, he that was mightier than John (the Messiah), should baptise with fire (such is the correct reading, and not "baptise with the Holy Spirit," which is not a Hebrew form of expression).[43]

This idea again is taken from the Book of Malachi where, of "the Lord who shall come suddenly," it is said; "And who may abide the day of his coming? and who can stand when he appeareth? for he is like a *refiner's fire."* [44] This was a very pregnant saying and greatly influenced John the Baptist. Since "the Lord" should refine by fire, then he, the forerunner, the "messenger" who was to prepare the way before "the Lord," must refine by water. Furthermore John, the incarnation of Elijah, must warn Israel that "the day of the Lord" (the Day of Judgment, the "pangs of the Messiah") was near at hand, the time that was to precede the coming of the Messiah, *i.e.,* the kingdom of heaven. They must by no means trust that because they were descended from Abraham, Abraham would stand up for them on the Day of Judgment (at New Year, the "Day of Judgment" for the individual, the Jews make mention of the Cove-

[40] *Ibid.* 22a.
[41] Mark i. 4-5.
[42] *Erubin. 27b; Baba Metzia* 41a; *Sanh.* 62b; *J. Baba Metzia* VII 9 מאן דמר לי הרא מלחא, אנא נסיב בנדייתא.
[43] But S. Schechter (*Studies in Judaism,* 2nd series, Philadelphia, 1908, pp. 109-110) supports it by the Amoraitic expression, "Who draw the Holy Spirit (שואבין רוח הקודש) *J. Sukka* V 1). Cf. *Gen. R.* §90; Joel iii. 2; Ezek. xlix. 29.
[44] Mal. iii. 2.

nant of Abraham and the Sacrifice of Isaac), but they themselves must make repentance.

This constitutes the whole function and mission of John and his new teaching in the desert of Jericho. As for the rest, he observed the ceremonial laws precisely like the Pharisees and Essenes. Like the disciples of the Pharisees, the disciples of John also fasted much,[45] but Jesus, who neither himself fasted nor his disciples, when rebuked on this point, answered that "you cannot sew a piece of new cloth on an old garment" nor "put new wine in old bottles," but "new wine must be put in new bottles." [46] In other words, John the Baptist, like the Pharisees, thought it possible to keep the old "bottle" in its old form and even fill it with new wine, repentance and good works, and so hasten the coming of the Messiah. But this is not possible: the new wine will burst the old bottles and the wine will be spilled on the ground. A new teaching, the preparation for the coming of the Messiah by means of baptism and repentance, demands the breaking up of the old external forms; otherwise the new teaching itself will be lost.

We shall see later that although Jesus never ventured wholly to contradict the Law of Moses and the teaching of the Pharisees, there yet was in his teaching the nucleus of such a contradiction. But in the teaching of John there was no trace whatever of such a contradiction: at the most there was only some opposition to Jewish nationalism. Luke [47] still preserves sayings which confirm this. When the multitude asked, "What shall we do to escape the 'pangs of the Messiah' "? John answered, "Let him that hath two coats give to him that hath none, and let him that hath food do in like manner."

Here again we have a hint of Essene teaching—on the community of goods; but the rest of his answer is not at all Essenic. When the publicans ask the same question he answers, "Take not more than is your due," and to the mercenary soldiers he says, "Do violence to no man, neither exact anything wrongfully, but be content with your wages." That is to say, John did not require that men forsake their ordinary occupation and go out into the wilderness as he and the Essenes had done; like a true Jew he recommended them to remain in the social world and continue their daily work, but to abstain from wrong and violence. So John continued a true Jew, imitating the Prophets and showing himself akin to them in spirit.

John the Baptist exercised a great influence upon the people. Both Josephus and the Gospels show that Herod Antipas feared him lest he stir up rebellion like the many messiahs who came to the fore about that time. John did not hesitate to rebuke him for unlawfully marrying Herodias, for John, imitating Elijah in all things, imitated

[45] Mark ii. 18.
[46] Mark ii. 21-22.
[47] Luke iii. 10-14.

him also in this that he, too, entered into political matters; as Elijah reproved Ahab and Jezebel for Baal worship and their conduct in the matter of Naboth's vineyard, so John rebuked Antipas and Herodias for their unlawful levirate union.

The two things, fear of rebellion and John's rebuke, caused Herod to arrest him and imprison him in the fortress nearest the scene of his preaching—the fortress of Machærus, and there put him to death. This last was most probably through the instigation of his wife, Herodias, whom we know to have been proud and ambitious (a quality which ultimately brought about her husband's downfall); she could not rest quiet under the revilings of this Transjordanian Nazarite who was stirring up the people against her and against her husband.

So great was John's influence that even his death did not see the end of the movement stirred up by the "voice crying in the wilderness." Josephus tells how, nearly seven years later, the people attributed Antipas's defeat to his murder of John. Again, as we saw, in the time of Jesus there were disciples of John who differed in their customs from the disciples of Jesus. Yet again, even in the time of the Apostles, considerably after the crucifixion, there were to be found some who accepted John's teaching in such fashion as not to acknowledge Jesus' messiahship (and still less his divinity), and thought that that generation still needed preparation for the Messiah who was not yet come. Such a one was Apollos of Alexandria who came to Ephesus in the time of Paul and "knew only the baptism of John;"[48] and Paul found there at the same time twelve other disciples of John who had been baptised "by the baptism of John" only— purely Jewish baptism—and it remained for Paul to teach them to believe in Jesus as the Messiah.[49] It is obvious, therefore, that John had no personal acquaintance with Jesus and did not recognize his messiahship; hence there can be no historical foundation for the account, given by Matthew and Luke[50] but absent in Mark, which tells how John heard in prison (at Machærus) of the wonderful works of Jesus, and sent to ask him whether he was the Messiah or not, and, in reply, Jesus pointed to the wonders that he was doing as a genuine proof of his messiahship. It can be accepted as a historical fact that Jesus was baptised by John, and also that Jesus, speaking to his disciples after the death of John the Baptist, said of him that he was a prophet and greater even than a prophet, that he was Elijah, the greatest of the prophets, and, therefore, the precurser of the Messiah, since contemporary Judaism could not conceive of the Messiah without Elijah the Forerunner.[51] Yet to this, Jesus added that

---

[48] Acts xviii. 24-25.

[49] *Ibid.* xix. 1-7.

[50] Matt. xi. 2-15; Luke vii, 18-35.

[51] J. Klausner, *Die Messianischen Vorstellungen des Jüdischen Volkes im Zeitalter der Tannaiten*, pp. 58-63.

"the least in the kingdom of God is greater than he (Elijah)"; for John was still but "a reed shaken by the wind," i.e., a man who had not sufficient power to break away from what was outworn, who saw himself not as an independent force but as one who served a greater power that was to come after him. Jesus opposed those who continued to follow the teaching of John the Baptist after he, Jesus, had manifested himself, since "the least in the kingdom of heaven" was greater than John,[52] and Jesus was the greatest in the kingdom of heaven, the Messiah himself, and so immeasurably greater than was John the Baptist.

It was, however, only after the Baptist's death, after Jesus himself was become a "Rab" with a large following, that Jesus thus spoke and thought of John. When the Baptist first came on the scene, Jesus saw in him the opener of the kingdom of heaven to all men, including Jesus himself.

[53] Matt. xi. 7-15; Luke vii. 24-28.

III. THE BAPTISM OF JESUS: HIS TEMPTATIONS
AND HIS FIRST MANIFESTATION

According to the four Gospels the ministry of Jesus began with his baptism by John. Luke [1] definitely says that John began to preach in the fifteenth year of Tiberius, and that Jesus, when he came to be baptised of John, was "about thirty years old" (and so must have been born about the year 2 to 4 B.C.). According to the Canonical Gospels Jesus came of his own will to be baptised; but the Gospel to the Hebrews (of which only fragments survive) [2] asserts that he was urged by his mother and brethren.

In any case Jesus of Nazareth came with multitudes from other towns to be baptised by John in the Jordan. John did not recognize him nor pay any regard to his presence: what Matthew has to say [3] about John's not wishing to baptise him and saying that he, John, needed rather to be baptised by Jesus, and how Jesus answered, "Suffer it to be so now, for thus it behoves us both to fulfil all righteousness" (*i.e.*, all the religious duties)—all this is lacking in Mark and Luke, and it only comes as an attempt to explain the anomaly that Jesus, who was greater than John, should yet have been baptised by him, and why Jesus, who was sinless, should have been baptised for the remission of sins.

Yet, on the other hand, all the Synoptists tell how, as Jesus arose from the water, "he looked and beheld the heavens opened and the Spirit like a dove descending upon him and a voice from heaven: "Thou art my beloved son *in whom I shall be blessed*" (so we ought to translate ἐν ᾧ εὐδόχησα, generally rendered "in whom I am well pleased"), or, according to the more exact form given in Luke, "This day have I begotten thee." [4] Although the actual words are legendary, an important historical fact underlies them. Jesus' baptism in the presence of John was the most decisive event in his life. Gifted with a strong imagination, given up to day-dreams about the redemption of his people during his early life in Nazareth (which, like all Galilee, contained many who looked to the advent of the Messiah and were ready to hasten his coming by the sword, such as

---

[1] Luke iii. 1 and 23.

[2] Collected in Nestle's *Novi Testamenti Graeci Supplementum*, Leipzig, 1896.

[3] Matt. iii. 13-15.

[4] Ps. ii. 7; such is the reading in Luke iii. 22, according to Codex D and the Old Latin, supported by many of the ancient Fathers (see Resch, *Agrapha*, pp. 223, 344-347).

the zealots of Galilee), well versed in the prophetic literature and the Psalms (already attributed to David, and explained in many cases as referring to the Messiah), filled with the spirit of the visions of Daniel (and also, perhaps, of the Apocalyptic literature, the fruit of the spirit of the popular prophets)—Jesus came before the Forerunner of the Messiah, the new Elijah, who had now appeared and who preached that the kingdom of the Messiah was at hand, and that nothing now was wanting except baptism and good works. This rite of baptism Jesus now observed.

But if the kingdom of the Messiah was "at hand," then the Messiah must be in the world: and was there any reason why he, great and imaginative dreamer that he was, he who felt himself so near to God, he who was so filled with the spirit of the prophets, he who felt with his every instinct that what above all things was wanted was repentance and good works—was there any reason why *he* should not be the imminent Messiah? Perhaps his very name "Jesus"(יהושע - ישוע - ישו), "he shall save," may have moved this simple villager to believe that he was the redeemer, just as Shabbethai Zvi was influenced by the fact that he was born on the 9th of Ab, the day when, according to a legend, the Messiah was to be born. Dazzled by the blinding light of the Judæan sun, it seemed to him as though the heavens were opened and that the Shekinah shed its light upon him.

An indication is preserved in the Gospel to the Hebrews that by the descent of the Holy Spirit is meant the radiance of the Shekinah; that Gospel treats it as a *bath qol,* a voice from heaven, which said that the Spirit had awaited the coming of Jesus "that it might shine upon him." This *bath qol* is the same phenomenon familiar to us in the *Talmud,* and the "dove," the form taken by the Holy Spirit, reminds us both of the dove which Noah sent from the ark and which fluttered on the face of the waters (in that case the waters of the flood, and in the present case, the waters of the Jordan), and of the *Talmudic* exposition of: "And the spirit of God moved on the face of the waters" [5]—like a dove that flutters over her young without touching them.[6] Suddenly there flashed through Jesus' mind, like blinding lightning, the idea that *he* was the hoped-for Messiah. This was the voice which he heard within him and for which he had been prepared by his thirty years of rich, cloistered, inner life at Nazareth. His dream acquired its utmost realization at this great moment in his life, the solemn moment of his baptism.

John the Baptist was the Prophet Elijah, the Forerunner of the Messiah, the "angel of the covenant," who should "prepare the way" before "the Lord," the "voice crying in the wilderness, Make ready

---

[5] Genesis i. 2.

[6] *Hagiga* 15a; T. *Hagiga* II 5 (where "eagle" occurs instead of "dove"). See S. Schechter, *Studies in Judaism,* 2nd series, 110-116; cf. also *Berachoth* 3a, *Bath-qol* "which coos like a dove."

the way, make straight in the desert a highway for our God;" and the newly baptised Jesus was the Messiah himself.

Men nourish in secret their greatest and loftiest ideas, and so Jesus preserved his great idea sealed tightly within the treasure-chamber of his heart. For who would believe him if he were to reveal it? Would he not be a subject of ridicule? A carpenter and son of a carpenter from Nazareth, the Messiah and Son of David! Could anything sound more foolish? So Jesus hides away his great idea; he begins to doubt it even himself and goes away for a period of solitude in the same deserted place where John the Baptist was preaching. From Moses in Mount Horeb to R. Israel "Besht" in the Carpathian Mountains, such a period of privacy with the object of reaching conviction about some great idea which hovers between the regions of the possible and the impossible, has often been the prelude to public manifestation.

Mark [7] gives a brief record of such a time of solitude immediately after Jesus' baptism: "And straightway the spirit sent him forth into the wilderness and he was there in the wilderness forty days tempted of Satan." Matthew [8] and Luke [9] treat the devil's temptation at great length. They would seem to have preserved a tradition, derived from Peter or some other disciple, in which Jesus describes this temptation parabolically, in a metaphorical and cryptic fashion. From this wonder-story we may deduce the following historical features:

Obsessed by his idea that he was the Messiah, Jesus meditated on the three methods by which, according to the current view, the Messiah would declare himself (the order is here taken from the Gospel to the Hebrews and not from the Synoptic Gospels). Primarily the Messiah is the *King*-Messiah who overcomes the Gentiles by force and rules over them and their kingdoms ("from a high mountain Satan showed him all the kingdoms of the earth and the glory of them").

But there is but one way to reach such an end: rebellion against the Romans. Jesus the Galilæan, nursed in the cradle of the revolutionary ideas of the Zealots, must, like every Jewish messiah, have had such thoughts. But, in the end, he rejected such an idea: his dreamy, spiritual nature was not fitted for such methods; the contemporary conditions rendered them impossible: had he not witnessed the fate of John the Baptist? Secondly, the Jewish Messiah must be mighty in the *Torah*, since there rested upon him "the spirit of wisdom and understanding, the spirit of council and might, the spirit of knowledge and the fear of the Lord" [10] ("the devil bringeth him

[7] Mark i. 12-13.
[8] Matt. iv. 1-11.
[9] Luke iv. 1-13.
[10] Isaiah xi. 2.

to Jerusalem and setteth him on a pinnacle of the Temple"—the site of the Hewn Chamber, where the Law was expounded by the priests and scribes) ; and, as we shall see shortly, Jesus was, for a short space, a "Rab" and teacher akin in spirit to the Pharisees and Scribes.

But, in the end, Jesus rejected this idea also: he saw the defects of the Pharisees and Scribes and, later, found fault with them, sometimes rightly and sometimes wrongly; and what, again, could a Galilæan carpenter do towards introducing anything new into the substance of the Law and of knowledge generally?

Lastly, the Jewish Messiah must bestow upon his people material welfare ("He afterward hungered, and the devil came and said unto him, If thou art the son of God command that these stones become bread"). We have already seen,[11] and shall refer later to the subject in more detail, that Jesus promised a wonderful fruitfulness for the world in the millennium, a statement preserved in the tradition recorded by Papias, and agreeing almost word for word with the material descriptions given in the *Book of Baruch,* in an early *Tannaitic Midrash (Sifre),* and in several *Talmudic Baraitoth.* But, in the end, Jesus rejected this also as a principle of his Messiahship, since it seemed to him too gross: was it not written, "Man shall not live by bread alone?"

What then was left of the messianic idea? How was his messiahship to be disclosed?

Nothing was left but to conceal his claim, and until John the Baptist was arrested finally by Herod Antipas Jesus did nothing. But once the "Forerunner" had been put in prison Jesus thought that the time had come for him to take his place and "to preach the gospel of the kingdom of heaven." His message closely resembled that of John the Baptist; there was in it only one small addition from which none but the most discerning could perceive any change of principle. Instead of "Repent! for the kingdom of heaven is at hand," Jesus proclaimed, *"The days are fulfilled,* and the kingdom of heaven is at hand; repent and *believe in the Gospel."* "The days are fulfilled," i.e., the kingdom of heaven must needs come, no matter what befall; and "believe in the Gospels," *i.e.,* believe that the forerunner of the Messiah has already come, and therefore the Messiah himself has come.

Who or where was the Messiah, Jesus did not say. He did not proclaim himself nor allow himself to be proclaimed as Messiah till comparatively much later. Even to his disciples he did not at first divulge the fact; and when they had realized it for themselves he did not deny it, yet desired them not to make the matter known. He resisted the temptation and only disclosed himself as a "Rab" and simple Galilæan preacher, as nothing more than one of the Pharisees or Scribes. A wandering Galilæan "Rab" and preacher was a common

[11] See above, p. 66.

sight and specially known by the title of "Galilæan itinerant" (עובר גלילאה).[12]

Yet between him and the usual Pharisees, Rabbis and homilists there were certain fundamental differences. (a) The main purport of his teaching was the near approach of the Messiah and, in consequence, of the kingdom of heaven. Though the Pharisees and Scribes also taught this, it was, with them, only secondary. (b) The ordinary Pharisees and homilists taught the observance of the ceremonial laws side by side with the moral law, whereas Jesus taught scarcely anything beyond the moral law: though he did not abolish the ceremonial laws he laid but little stress on them. (c) For all the teaching of the Scribes and Pharisees the one basic principle was exposition of Scripture and the derivative teaching of the *Torah*, whereas Jesus relied but slightly on Scripture, wrapping up his teaching altogether in *parable* form. This, again, was a practice of the Pharisees and it was from them that Jesus learnt the practice; but they never used it to the same extent.[13] (d) Jesus was a worker of miracles. He healed the sick and drove out evil spirits, for it was impossible that the Messiah should not work miracles. Even in this Jesus did not differ from the Scribes and sages of the time except in degree. The early *Tannaim* were also miracle-workers, and Jesus grants [14] that the Pharisees could perform miracles and that, therefore, miracles afforded no clear proof of Jesus' messianic claims in the eyes of the Galilæans: though the Messiah must work miracles not every one who worked miracles was the Messiah.

But here again Jesus differed from the Pharisees. With them the teaching was primary and the miracles only secondary, while with Jesus teaching and miracles possessed equal importance. He was aware that through the working of miracles he could attract the people, yet he knew, as we shall see later, of the danger inherent in a faith based on miracles and often avoided those "who sought for signs."

A theory has been put forward [15] that Jesus never regarded himself as the Messiah and only after his death was he acclaimed as Messiah by his disciples. But had this been true it would never have occurred to his disciples (simple-minded Jews) that one who had suffered crucifixion ("a curse of God is he that is hanged") could be the Messiah; and the messianic idea meant nothing whatever to the Gentile converts. *Ex nihilo nihil fit:* when we see that Jesus' messianic claims became a fundamental principle of Christianity soon after his crucifixion, this is a standing proof that even in his lifetime

[12] *Sanh. 70a; Hulin 27b* (דרש עובר גלילאה).
[13] See P. Fiebig, *Altjüdische Gleichnisse und die Gleichnisse Jesu,* Tübingen, 1904.
[14] Matt. xii. 27.
[15] See W. Wrede, *Das Messiasgeheimniss in den Evangelien,* Göttingen, 1901.

Jesus regarded himself as the Messiah. Yet in the earlier stages he did not make this claim: he was, at first, only a "Rab" and preacher, a "Galilæan itinerant," differing from others of that type only in certain peculiarities.

Like every other "Rab" or preacher he had a following of regular and casual disciples: the regular ones were those who had left all and followed him and remained constantly with him; the casual ones were the ordinary folk who, from time to time, came to listen to him and to be healed by him. They styled him "Rabbi" [16] or, according to the later Aramaic form, "Rabboni" (ῥαββοῦνι, cf. רבונו של עולם) Jesus always called himself "the Son of man" (בן אדם), i.e., simple flesh and blood. This usage survived in Hebrew till a much later period: "Son of man" signifies mere "man" ("sons of men," בני אדם, is the plural of אדם "man"), and has the same implication as איש in the Old Testament. Such, too, is the usage of בר־אנש (pronounced בר־נש, by the elision of א) in Aramaic and the *Talmud;* it signifies "man" as distinct from brute beasts, and as distinct from the angels (cf. לית דין בר־נש).[17]

But in the *Book of Daniel,* in the vision of the four beasts,[18] Israel is likened to a בר־אנש, who comes "with the clouds of heaven," while the other nations are likened to beasts. From an early period it was supposed that this "Son of man" was a title of the King-Messiah since the Book of Daniel says: "He came near to the Ancient of days and was brought nigh unto him, and to him was given might and honour and authority, and all peoples, nations and tongues shall serve him, and his sovereignty is an everlasting sovereignty which shall not pass away, and his kingdom shall not be cast down." Whole chapters of the *Book of Enoch* [19] prove beyond doubt that *walda b'esi, bar-nasha,* "Son of Man," or, in its Hebrew guise, בן אדם was a regular title given to the Messiah before the time of Jesus.[20] Jesus, who spoke Aramaic, made much use of this word. It occurs eighty-one times in the Gospels. The writers of the Gospels (especially Matthew) have introduced it on many occasions into the actual sayings of Jesus. He did not, however, use it in its *technical sense*

---

[16] A word which also occurs in the Gospels and induced Graetz (III, 2⁵, n. 20, p. 759; IV³, note 9, pp. 399-400) to date them late, since Hillel and Shammai and Yonathan ben Uzziel were known by their bare names without prefix. Yet even though, as an official title for a "disciple of the wise," "Rabbi" had not become a fixed title in the time of Jesus, it was already in use in current speech as an unofficial title of honour (see above, p. 43 n. 92). See also *T. Eduyoth,* end.

[17] *Shabbath* 112b.

[18] Daniel vii 2-14.

[19] The Ethiopic *Enoch,* 46, 1-6; 66, 1-16; 99, 5-35. See also 9, 10; 68, 2; 60, 27; 67, 6; 71, 14.

[20] In the *Talmud* and the *Targum* there are also hints as to the messianic significance of "son of man"; e.g., *Sanh.* 98b; *Targum* to 1 Chron. iii. 24; but these passages are considerably later than the time of Jesus.

but instead of "I." Its significance is often simply "man," without any qualification or specific intention.[21]

But even after passing over all the passages where it means "I" or "man," there still remain many instances where Jesus used the word deliberately; and he used it expressly for the reason that while in Aramaic, which Jesus spoke, it had no exceptional meaning in the ears of the ordinary people, it had, for the more enlightened hearers, an added significance, as in Ezekiel and Daniel. By means of this title he partially divulged his messiahship but more frequently concealed it. On the one hand, he hinted that he was a simple, ordinary man (the sense conveyed by the word in everyday Aramaic speech); and on the other hand, he hinted that he too was a prophet like Ezekiel, who also had used the word. And, still further, he hinted that he was the "Son of man" in the sense in which his contemporaries understood the expression in the Book of Daniel, and as it was explained in the *Book of Enoch*—the "Son of Man" who was to come "with the clouds of heaven" and approach "the Ancient of days," and who was to possess the kingdom of the King-Messiah, the everlasting kingdom.

Thus, by such hints, he prepared the minds of his regular disciples to accept his messianic claims, while as for the simple multitude, they saw nothing peculiar in the expression and went after the "Galilæan itinerant" because he taught a high ideal of ethics through the medium of attractive parables, and because he performed miracles and healed the sick.

[21] See H. Lietzmann, *Der Menschensohn*, Leipzig, 1896, who denies altogether the messianic significance in "Son of man." See on the other side P. Fiebig, *Der Menschensohn*, Tübingen, 1901; G. Dalman, *Die Worte Jesu*, 1898, 191-219; W. Bousset, *Die Religion des Judentums in Neutestamentlichen Zeitalter*, pp. 248-255.

FOURTH BOOK

THE BEGINNING OF JESUS' MINISTRY

I. JESUS' EARLY MINISTRY:

THE PREACHER OF PARABLES AND THE PERFORMER OF MIRACLES

The writers of the first Gospels were Jews in spirit. As Jews they aimed not at writing a history of Christianity or a biography of Jesus, but at showing how the will of God showed itself in certain events. Hence we must not expect a chronological account of the ministry of Jesus in Mark or Matthew, or even in Luke (whose aim was to connect the life of Jesus with historical personages and events), and we cannot, therefore, compose a scientific biography of Jesus according to modern methods. We have defined for us only the *opening* point of his ministry (his baptism by John in the Jordan), and the *closing* point (his crucifixion by Pontius Pilate at Jerusalem).

There is a difficulty in fixing the intervening points. Mark's purpose being religious and not historical or biographical, he strings events together according to the parables and sayings of Jesus, and places together in conjunction events (and even sayings and parables), however distant in time, if only they possess an inner, logical connexion.

But between the baptism and the crucifixion it is possible to fix a few points which provide, more or less, a correct guide to the course of Jesus' life. It is scarcely necessary to do more than this, since, according to the Synoptic Gospels, his ministry was not prolonged more than a single year (29-30 C.E.). The Fourth Gospel makes it last three years, and this was the opinion of the early Fathers, Origen, Irenæus, Eusebius and Epiphanius; but Clement of Alexandria and Julius Africanus considered that it lasted one year only, and Irenæus, contrary to the rest of his writings, says in one place [1] that the ministry of Jesus lasted "only one year and a few months," and this is the view of most modern scholars.[2] In so short a period it would be difficult to find a gradual development in activities and teaching: a few landmarks here and there are all we may expect.

[1] See Irenæus, *De Principiis*, IV 5.
[2] Husband, *Prosecution of Jesus*, Princeton, 1916, pp. 34-69, denies this.

259

After the baptism, the first landmark is found in Jesus' resolve, after the Temptation and after John's imprisonment and after Jesus' return to Galilee, to do no more than take the place of John the Baptist and preach repentance in connexion with the approach of the kingdom of heaven. He finally abandoned his work as carpenter, by which he had earned his living, and his family which he had hitherto supported. For his first audience he had four men, two pairs of brothers whose ardent faith he must have known in earlier times when he laboured as a carpenter in Nazareth.[3]

The first pair were Simon and Andrew (Netzer?—it is curious that a simple Galilæan fisherman should have a Greek name),[4] the sons of Jonas. Jesus encountered them as they were spreading their nets in the Sea of Galilee, near their home town, Capernaum: he summoned them to follow him, saying that he would make them into "fishers of men." Near by he saw other fishermen, James and John the sons of Zebedee, sitting in a boat with their father and hired servants, mending their nets.[5] James and John were energetic and passionate men, and Jesus styled them "Boanerges" (from the Aramaic בני רעש or בני רגש), "sons of wrath."[6] He must have known them also previously and considered them fit to form part of his following.

All four forsook their work, and, later, their families, and, without looking back, followed Jesus as Elisha followed Elijah. Afterwards, Simon, James and John became his chief disciples, "pillars" of the new "church" or community; and Simon, their leader, became the "rock" on which the "church" was founded.

Simon, who was married, had a home in Capernaum where he lived with his wife's mother; therefore in Capernaum Jesus began his ministry.

Capernaum was, as we have seen, a town of moderate size noted for its wheat.[7] References to it may be found in the *Tosefta* and *Talmud*, in the *Midrash*[8] and in writings of Jewish travellers, by the name of "Kefar Tanhum,"[9] and also in Josephus ("a most fertile fountain" called by the inhabitants Καφαρναούμ, also Κεφαρνωμών

[3] According to John i. 41-43, Jesus already knew Simon and Andrew when he was with John the Baptist.
[4] But in the Jerusalem *Talmud* (*Berachoth* I 1) it occurs as the name of the father of an Amora.
[5] On the fishing industry of Galilee and the fish found there, see Dalman, *Orte und Wege Jesu*, 1921, pp. 122-124.
[6] On this name see H. P. Chajes, *Marcus-Studien*, Berlin, 1899, pp. 21-22.
[7] *Menahoth* 85a; T. *Menahoth* IX 2: "Chorazim and Kefar-Ahim" (where "Kefar-Nahum" should be read), "Barchaim and Kefar-Ahus" (read Chorazim and Kefar Nahum"). See Dalman, *op. cit.* pp. 121-135; Graetz III 1², 290 n. 2. See above p. 174 n. 2.
[8] *Qoh. R.* on *"U-motze ani"*; and, perhaps, also *Cant. R.* on *"Yonathi"*; *J. Terumoth* XI 7; *J. Taanith* I 7 (beginning); *J. Shabbath* II 1 (כפר־תנחום תחומין, תחמין).
[9] Ishtori ha-Parhi's *Kaphtor wa-Perah*, ed. Luncz, p. 286.

or Κεφαρνωκών, "pertaining to the people of Kefar Nahum").[10]
The town was stretched along the western shore of the lake near
where the Jordan enters, and is most probably represented today by
"Tel-Hum" (corrupted from Tel-Nahum or Tanhum), a ruin near
Hirbet Chorazi (the Chorazin mentioned side by side with Kefar-
naum both in the Gospels and *Talmud*) ; in both sites are remains of
ancient synagogues remarkable for massive stonework and fine carv-
ings and ornamentation.[11] On the shore, not far away, was Migdal
(Migdal-Nunaya [12] or Magdala,[13] the Greek Ταριχέαι—and not "Hir-
bet-el-Kerak," on the site of the Jewish colony Kinnereth, the ancient
Beth-Yerah and Greek Philoteria, which was conquered in 218 B.C.
by Antiochus the Great and apparently reached its zenith during the
reign of Alexander Jannæus).[14] This was the native town of Mary
Magdalene, as also of the early Amora R. Yitzhaq Magdala'ah [15]
and R. Judan (Yehuda) Magdala'ah.[16]

As was to be expected in a town on the banks of a sea well stocked
with fish, the inhabitants of Capernaum were mostly fishermen. But
before Tiberias (founded about 18 C.E.) came to be important,
Capernaum was also a great commercial city with its own customs
station,[17] and this was the reason, according to Meistermann, why
it was also called "Kefar Tehumim [lit. border village],)[18] since,
on the other side of the lake was Decapolis and the realm of Philip.
The name "Kefar-Nahum" dated back to the time when it was actually still a village.

Josephus [19] cannot find words strong enough to describe the
beauty, fertility, wealth and numerous population of the district adjoining the lake of Galilee (the Sea of Kinnereth or Genesareth,[20] or,
as it was also called, the Lake of Tiberias), the district known to the
Talmud as "the lowland (or vale) of Genesar" (the modern el-
Ghuayr) or the "Valley of Galilee" [21] or, simply, "the Valley." [22]
The *Midrash* explains the name "Genesar" fancifully as meaning

[10] *Wars* III x 8; *Vita* §72, and Dalman's emendation, *op. cit.,* p. 133, n. 3.
[11] On Capernaum and Chorazin and their synagogues, see Kohl and Watzinger, *Antike Synagogen in Galilæa*, Leipzig, 1915; B. Meistermann, *Capharnaüm et Bethsaïde*, Paris, 1921; Dalman, *op. cit.*, 2 Aufl. pp. 121-137; Y.
Schwartz, *T'buoth ha-Aretz*, ed. Luncz, p. 226; J. Klausner, *Olam Mithhaveh*,
Odessa, 1915, pp. 198-200.
[12] *Pesahim* 46a.
[13] *J. Maaseroth* III 1; *J. Sanh.* II 1.
[14] See Dalman, pp. 114-116, 160; S. Klein, *Beiträge*, pp. 76, 84.
[15] *Sanh.* 98a; *Baba Metzia* 25b; *Gen. R.* §5, 9 etc.
[16] *J. Taanith* I 3; *J. Berachoth* IX 2; *Gen. R.* §13.
[17] Mark ii. 14; Luke v. 27.
[18] Meistermann, *op. cit.*
[19] *Wars* III x 7-8.
[20] Written with *yodh* and not גינוסר, with *waw;* see Dalman, p. 109-110.
[21] See *Berachoth* 44a; *Erubin* 30a; *Gen. R.* §99 end, and elsewhere.
[22] *Shebiith* IX 2.

"the gardens of princes," [23] and curiously enough Jerome translates it in the same way, *Hortus principis*.[24]

The "fruits of Genesar" were famous.[25] Capernaum traded in fish and fruit, and through it passed the trade of the Jaulan and Bashan, the Greek Decapolis and Galilee. "And thou, Capernaum, which art exalted [or, which hast exalted thyself] to heaven," [26] may be the exaggerated expression of a simple villager for whom every petty town is a great city compared to his own village; yet, compared to Nazareth, Capernaum was really "exalted to heaven."

Of all the towns of Lower Galilee in the neighbourhood of Nazareth, Capernaum was best suited for Jesus' ministry. It may not have been so great a city as Sepphoris, which was, before the building of Tiberias, the chief city of Galilee. But in the greater cities people were too sceptical and, what was dangerous for Jesus, the Government kept a careful supervision. Still, Jesus' object was to make himself known and to propagate his teaching, and, therefore, he must not make choice of too small a town or village: hence this medium-sized town of Capernaum became his centre in Galilee. His choice may also have been determined by the fact that his first followers Simon and Andrew lived there and that he was warmly received as a guest in the house of Simon. He made preaching tours through the towns of Galilee, always returning to Capernaum.

His labours were not extended over a very large area—between Chorazin and Migdal (Nunaia) on the west, and between Beth Saida (Julias) and Gadara on the east shore of the Sea of Galilee and the Jordan; while apart from some cities of the "Decapolis" and the unknown Dalmanutha a Magordan (see below), only Nazareth, Capernaum, Beth-Saida, Migdal, Nain and Kefar-Cana (in the Fourth Gospel only) are referred to, all of them being in the neighbourhood of Nazareth. The more distant regions—Tyre and Sidon and Cæsarea Philippi in the north, and Jericho and Jerusalem in the south—are only mentioned towards the close of his life.

He made his first public appearance in Capernaum, when, on a certain Sabbath, he came and preached in the synagogue. Meistermann [27] may be incorrect in thinking that the fine ruins of a synagogue recently found in Capernaum are those of the synagogue of Jesus' time, but there have been found still more recently (by Père Orfali) the remains of an older synagogue on the foundations of which the present ruined synagogue was built. The present custom

---

[23] *Gen. R.* §98.
[24] Dalman, pp. 109-110; and, for a good description of the surroundings of Genesar, see pp. 110-114.
[25] *Pesahim* 8b; *Berachoth* 44a; cf. "'Full of the blessing of the Lord'—this is the vale of Genesar" (*Sifre* on Deut. §355, ed. Friedmann 147b); *Ruth R.* on *Lini poh ha-laylah*.
[26] Matt. xi. 23; Luke x. 14.
[27] Meistermann, *Capharnaüm et Bethsaïde, suivi d'une étude sur l'age de la Synagogue de Tell-Hum*, Paris, 1921.

of preaching in the synagogues on the Sabbath was in vogue nineteen hundred years ago, as may be seen from the *Talmud* and *Midrash* and also from a remarkable passage in the New Testament: "For from generations of old Moses hath in every city them that preach him, being read in the synagogues every Sabbath.[28]

From this it follows both that there were readers of the Law of Moses in the synagogues in every city and on every Sabbath, and that this reading was regarded as an ancient rite even at the end of the first or the beginning of the second Christian century (when the Acts of the Apostles was composed).

The reading of the Law followed a known order; it was not our present order, according to which the Law is divided into fifty-four sections, the number of the Sabbaths in the year (two sections being combined in an ordinary year and read separately in an intercalated year), but, until the beginning of the Middle Ages, the Jews of Palestine (as opposed to the use in Babylon) read through the Law in three and a half years.[29] After the reading of the Pentateuch they "concluded" (מפטירין) with the reading of the Prophets (though the *Haphtarah* as a fixed use and in its present form is also late), translating (orally and not from a written version) to the people in Aramaic (this was specially the case in Galilee where the unlearned were more than in Judæa, and where few people spoke Hebrew), and expounding the subject matter of all that was read on that Sabbath.

The readers and expounders were almost always Pharisees and Scribes. Judaism in those days was democratic enough to allow anyone to read and expound the Scriptures, but those who could read well enough to do this were not many in number, particularly in Galilee, and were confined to the Scribes and Pharisees, the representatives of the democracy and the opponents of the aristocratic, ruling priesthood. Jesus, in the Capernaum synagogue, read from the Prophets and expounded, and so conducted himself like a Scribe or Pharisee and was regarded as such by the people. He behaved similarly until he came to Jerusalem where, as we shall see later, he revealed himself as the Messiah. His earlier methods enabled him to draw around him disciples and hearers and saved him from persecution almost to the last.

It was a common sight then in Palestine to see teachers ("Rabbis") attracting disciples in large numbers and publicly expounding the Law, and all who were so minded, be they "disciples of the wise" or ordinary people, listened to them, treating them with honour and regarding them as holy men and near to God and his Law, and, in consequence, able to perform miracles. Those responsi-

---

[28] Acts of the Apostles xv. 21.
[29] See S. Asaf, *Babel v'Eretz-Yisrael bi-t'qufath ha-G'onim* (*Hashiloach*, XXXIV 291, n. 3); A. Büchler, *The Reading of the Law and the Prophets in a Triennial Cycle, J.Q.R.* 1893, V 420-468; VI 1 ff.

ble for public order—Herod Antipas's officials or the chief men of the city—would not pay any attention to this new Galilæan "Rabbi"; and although, as we shall soon see, the Pharisees began to realize after a time that Jesus did not altogether follow the beaten track of Pharisaic teachings, it seemed at first only a case of one Pharisee differing from others in certain details, just as a follower of the Shammai School differed from a follower of the Hillel School. The same thing happened to Jesus at the *beginning* of his career as happened to Socrates at the *end* of his career: Socrates who had fought against the Sophists was, in the end, condemned to death as a Sophist; and Jesus, who fought against the Pharisees, was at the outset of his career regarded as a Pharisee in every respect.

But the people saw instinctively that there was in him a certain difference from the Pharisees. The three Synoptics all preserve one noteworthy saying: "And they were all amazed at his teaching, for he taught them as one that had authority and not as the Scribes."[30] The words "as one that had authority" (ὡς ἐξουσίαν ἔχων, in Luke ἐν ἐξουσίᾳ) show clearly that Jesus differed from the Scribes in that they taught nothing of themselves but based themselves wholly on Scripture, while he uttered just what arose out of his own heart without this constant reference to the Scriptures.

We shall see shortly that Jesus, too, could expound Scripture like a veritable Pharisee, but this he did less frequently than the Scribes and Pharisees; as a rule he spoke like the Prophets of old— not basing himself on any "it is said," or "it is written." But while the Prophets proclaimed "Thus saith the Lord," instilling upon the people that what was spoken came from God himself and that they, the prophets, were but the channel and instrument of the Deity, Jesus, on the other hand, made no such qualification and even emphasized his own personality: "But I say unto you"—as opposed to all who had spoken before him.[31]

This seems to constitute the difference between the methods of the Scribes and that of Jesus and to be the import of the remark: "for he taught them as one having authority." Worth noting, however, is the theory offered by H. P. Chajes, that the words ὡς ἐξουσία ἔχων or ἐν ἐξουσίᾳ are due to the more ordinary sense of the Hebrew מושל, used in the primitive Hebrew version of the Gospels. The meaning of מושל was "a preacher in parable," as in על כן יאמרו המושלים ("wherefore they which use parables say—")[32] or אנשי לצון מושלי העם הזה ("ye scornful men which speak parables about this people")[33] or; כל המושל עליך ימשול לאמר כאמה בתה ("Every one that useth parables shall utter this parable against thee, As is the mother so is the daughter").[34]

---

[30] Mark i. 22; Matt. vii. 29; Luke iv. 32.
[31] See Ahad ha-Am, *Al sh'tē ha-s'ippim* (Collected Works, IV 42-44).
[32] Num. xxi. 27.
[33] Isaiah xxviii. 15.
[34] Ezek. xvi. 44.

Therefore the actual meaning of the remark recorded in the Gospels is: "For he taught them as a מושל, one using parables (or, according to Luke, במשל, by a parable) and not as the Scribes," but the Greek translator (or someone using Hebrew material for an oral statement in Greek) changed the sense of מושל, "one who preaches in parable," to מושל, "one having rule or authority," thus giving in his translation (or oral statement) an expression difficult to understand.[35]

However this may be, Jesus was, in popular opinion, different from the Pharisees and Scribes in that he used allegory and parable instead of Scriptural exposition. Yet the *Tannaim* and their successors, the *Amoraim*, also made much use of the parable. Compare the formulæ משל למה הדבר דומה...משלו משל...משל למלך, etc.; [36] so in this respect, also, Jesus was a Pharisee and followed the usage of the Scribes and early *Tannaim*. But while they mainly practised Scriptural exposition and made comparatively little use of parables, the reverse was the case with Jesus. His parables had a double object.

In the first place, he wished to interest the simpler-minded folk who formed his usual audience, and, like every teacher of a new ethical system and every creator of new ideas, Jesus was a poet and skilful story-teller and, therefore, he made use of poetical descriptions drawn from every-day life, and, like the best story-tellers and moral preachers of all times and races, he unconsciously raised such descriptions to the level of ethical symbolism.

In the second place, he often endeavoured, by these parables and metaphorical sayings, to wrap up an esoteric significance which could not yet be openly proclaimed or which men could not yet comprehend, and which he revealed only to the more discreet; as he explicitly stated: "to you (the inner circle of the disciples) it is given to know the secret of the kingdom (of heaven), but for them that are without, everything is told in parable." [37] A further instance of the same idea is contained in: "Give not that which is holy to the dogs and cast not your pearls before swine, lest they trample them underfoot and turn and rend you." [38] He taught in parable because he feared that the people could not understand the inner significance of his message.

But he knew that, in the end, both himself and his teachings would be openly known and that the parabolic wrapping would and must

[35] See H. P. Chajes, *Markus-Studien*, pp. 10-12; but see also Schechter, *Studies in Judaism*, 2nd series, 117, 123.

[36] On the parables in the *Talmud* and *Midrash*, see Giuseppe Levi, *Parabeln, Legenden und Gedanken aus Talmud und Midrasch*, übertragen von L. Seligmann, 4 Aufl. Wien, 1921; P. Fiebig, *Altjüdische Gleichnisse und die Gleichnisse Jesu*, Tübingen, 1904; *Die Gleichnissreden Jesu im Lichte der rabbinischen Gleichnisse*, 1912; T. Ziegler, *Die Königsgleichnisse des Midrasch*, Breslau, 1903; Israel Abrahams, *Studies in Pharisaism*, First Series, Cambridge, 1917, pp. 90-107; H. Weinel, *Die Gleichnisse Jesu*, 4 Aufl., 1918.

[37] Mark iv. 11-12.

[38] Matt. vii. 6.

be removed: the lamp cannot remain "under the bushel or under the bed," but is ultimately placed upon the bushel or upon the bed (*i.e.*, that kind of bed which was and still is used in the East instead of a table); there is nothing hidden which shall not be revealed for "nothing is concealed except that it may be brought to the light." [39]

Jesus, as we have already pointed out, was notable in another matter: he healed many that were sick. The people looked upon the Pharisees and Scribes as holy men and therefore miracle-workers. Both the *Talmud* and *Midrash* give accounts of miracles performed by Rabban Yochanan ben Zakkai and R. Eliezer ben Hyrcanus his disciple, who lived in the time of Jesus.[40] But with the Pharisees miracles were only a secondary interest. The *Talmud* says almost nothing about them in connexion with Hillel and Shammai (it is Josephus alone who records that Shammai, or Shemayah, forecasted Herod's future). With Jesus, however, miracles were a primary factor since, without them, he could not have attracted the simple folk of Galilee.

We have seen how, owing to protracted wars and tumults and the terrible oppression of Herod and the Romans, Palestine, and especially Galilee, was filled with the sick and suffering and with those pathological types which we now label neurasthenics and psychasthenics. The disturbances had multiplied the poor, the impoverished and the unemployed, with the result that in Palestine and, again, particularly in Galilee (since it was far removed both from the centre of civil rule and from saner spiritual influences), such neurasthenics, and especially hysterical women and all manner of "nerve cases"—dumb, epileptics, and the semi-insane—were numerous.[41] At that time even educated people and those who had imbibed Greek culture (such as Josephus) regarded such nerve cases and cases of insanity as cases of "possession" by some devil or evil or unclean spirit, and believed in "cures," and that certain men could perform miracles. And even in the earlier portions of the *Talmud* there are many accounts of illnesses attributed to the influence of devils and "harmful spirits" (מזיקים).

This last, and very apt, title is found in the *Mishnah*,[42] and cases of miraculous healing commonly occur in the early *Baraitoth*.[43] It is, therefore, no matter of surprise that Jesus should practise miraculous cures like a Pharisee, or to an even greater extent than the ordinary Pharisee, since, in his inmost thoughts, he regarded himself as the Messiah, and contemporary belief endowed the Messiah with super-

[39] Matt. iv. 21-23.
[40] *Yoma* 39b; *Hagiga* 17b; *Taanith* 25b; *Baba Metzia* 59b.
[41] See above, p. 152 and elsewhere.
[42] *Aboth* V 8.
[43] The most recent and fullest treatment of *Talmudic* medicine is J. Preuss, *Biblisch-Talmudische Medicin*, Berlin, 1911; see also W. Ebstein, *Die Medizin im Neuen Testament und im Talmud*, Stuttgart, 1903; L. Blau, *Das Altjüdische Zauberwesen*, Strassburg, 1898.

natural powers. All four Gospels are filled with such miracles, and so numerous are they that they almost hide the actual teaching of Jesus; this is especially the case in Mark who gives but little space to the sayings of Jesus.

The problem of miracles in Jesus' ministry is difficult and complicated, and every treatment of the Life of Jesus, from Reimarus by way of Friedrich Strauss to the most recent writers, devotes considerable space to the subject.[44] Since modern science cannot imagine an effect without an external or internal cause, it is unable to rest content with the simple answers offered in the age of the Encyclopædists—that all the miracles attributed to Jesus, as well as to other great men in the world, are mere inventions deliberately contrived by "cunning priests." The miracles of Jesus can be divided into five types:

(1) *Miracles due to a wish to fulfil some statement in the Old Testament or to imitate some Prophet:*

Jesus took the place of John the Baptist, who was regarded as Elijah: Jesus must needs, therefore, perform miracles as did Elijah and his disciple Elisha. He must resemble Elijah not only in being the forerunner of the Messiah (for so many supposed him until Cæsarea Philippi), but also in his miracles. Excepting Moses (who was, primarily, the dispenser of the Law), Elijah and Elisha were the only Hebrew Prophets whose power was manifested by miracles alone and who left us no written prophecy. Most of their miracles were performed for the benefit of individuals and had no value for the people as a whole. If Elijah and Elisha raised children from the dead, then Jesus must raise the daughter of Jairus (Mark knows but this single case of raising from the dead;[45] Luke adds that of the young man of Nain[46] and the Fourth Gospel describes at length the raising of Lazarus [Eleazer] who, in the Gospel of Luke, is a poor man depicted as dead and mentioned in a parable where it is said that, after his death, he was taken to Paradise).[47]

Again, if Elisha, the disciple of Elijah, increased the oil of the cruse so as to fill many vessels and so pay off the debt of the wife of one of the "sons of the prophets," and, with *twenty* loaves of barley, satisfy a *hundred* men with bread to spare,[48] then Jesus must satisfy *five thousand* men with *five* barley loaves and two fishes, with *twelve* baskets-full to spare, according to the number of the tribes of Israel: for Jesus was greater than Elisha.

This episode is even duplicated through the imagination of the disciples of the first or second generation: in the second occurrence Jesus satisfies *four thousand* men with *seven* loaves and a few fishes

[44] For details see Fr. Nippold, *Die Psychiatrische Seite der Heilstätigkeit Jesu*, 1899; H. Schäfer, *Jesus in psychiatrischer Beleuchtung*, 1910.
[45] Mark v. 22-43; see Matt. ix. 18-26.
[46] Luke vii. 11-17; Nain (Naim) is mentioned in *Gen. R.* §98.
[47] Cf. Luke xvi. 19-31 with John xi. 1-46.
[48] 1 Kings iv. 1-37, 42-44.

and *seven* baskets of fragments remained over.[49] We have obviously here an imitation of the greatest of the wonder-working prophets. Jesus, who was, in the opinion of his disciples, the greatest of the prophets or even greater than a prophet (as was John the Baptist, according to Jesus), must do wonders like them and also surpass them.

But it is not only a case of imitating the deeds of the prophets: whatever of the marvellous was comprised in their sayings was, in the time of Jesus, understood to refer to the Messianic Age. When, therefore, it had been said of the Messianic Age: "then shall the eyes of the blind see, and the ears of the deaf be opened; then shall the lame man leap as a hart and the tongue of the dumb sing" [50] — it behoved Jesus to heal the blind and the dumb, to strengthen the lame, give hearing to the deaf and heal every kind of sickness. For he taught the people that "the kingdom of heaven is at hand," and the "signs of the Messiah" must, therefore, come upon the earth and be seen of men.

(2) *Poetical descriptions which, in the minds of the disciples, were transformed into miracles:*

Jesus' disciples were mainly simple folk drawn from the humble classes; their imagination was strong and miracles had a powerful attraction for them. Such men, quite unintentionally and unconsciously, transformed an imaginative description into an actual deed which stirred the imagination. We have a clear case of this preserved for us. Mark and Matthew [51] record the following strange incident:

When Jesus was in Jerusalem, during the week preceding Passover, he was hungry, and, passing by a fig-tree, looked for fruit to satisfy his hunger. He did not find any *because it was not the season for figs.* Mark clearly emphasizes this fact, and, indeed, the episode occurred, according to Mark and Matthew, before the feast of Passover when figs are not in season. Yet despite the natural fact that there were no figs on the tree at a time when no figs could be expected, Jesus curses the tree and condemned it to perpetual fruitlessness: and the fig-tree withered at once, or by the following day!

Luke, however, makes no reference to this curious event; he simply records a typical parable by Jesus: "And he spake a parable and said, There was a man who had a fig-tree planted in his vineyard and he went to seek fruit in it and found it not. And he said unto the keeper of his vineyard, Lo, these three years have I come seeking fruit in this fig-tree and have found it not; cut it down." [52]

It is clear that the subject of the parable is the people of Israel (or else the party of the Pharisees or Sadducees) who would not listen to Jesus' teachings and, therefore, ought rightly to be cut down

[49] Mark vi. 34-44; viii. 1-9.
[50] Isa. xxxv. 5-6.
[51] Mk. xi. 13-14, 20, 21; Matt. xxi. 19-21.
[52] Luke xiii. 6-9.

or withered. And Mark himself actually quotes elsewhere [53] these words: "And from the fig-tree learn this parable," where Luke has: "See now the fig-tree and all the trees, when ye see them bringing forth their blossom (not their fruit, since the fig-tree was not in fruit at that season), do ye not know that summer is nigh at hand? So ye also . . . know that the kingdom of God is nigh at hand." [54] This apt parable was, therefore, transformed in the circle of the disciples or by the evangelists into a strange miracle inflicting a gross injustice on a tree which was guilty of no wrong and had but performed its natural function.

(3) *Illusions:*

The next type of miracles recorded of Jesus were imaginary visions, "hallucinations" of simple, oriental village-folk and fishermen, for whom the whole world was full of marvels. Such a case is the account of how the disciples were on the Sea of Galilee by night, in a small boat, while Jesus was left alone on shore; the wind was against them and they found it difficult to row. In the fourth watch of the night (when they would be weary and overpowered by sleep) they suddenly saw Jesus walking on the sea as though it were dry land.[55] Mark actually says [56] that they thought that it was "an apparition" (ἔδοξαν φάντασμα εἶναι), which is what it really was. But the appetite for miracles gradually implanted within them the belief that they had really seen Jesus and rowed together with him in the boat. And this is one example out of many.

(4) *Acts only apparently miraculous:*

Under this head come events which happen in fact, but which have in them nothing of the miraculous and only appear so to the disciples. Such, for example, is the story of the storm [57] which fell upon the Sea of Galilee while Jesus and his disciples were in a boat; the waves broke over them and the disciples grew afraid, but Jesus was peacefully sleeping in the stern. Owing to their fear they awakened him, but he appeased them, telling them to trust in God and not to be "of little faith;" and the wind fell and the sea became calm. This is unquestionably what happened: the Sea of Galilee frequently becomes rough suddenly and as suddenly becomes calm again. The present writer witnessed such a change while sailing on the Sea in the spring of 1912. Yet for the Galilæan fishermen, with their craving for marvels, it was a miracle which Jesus had performed.

Such has ever been the way with simple-minded people. Fanatical piety knows many such miracles, and this was commonly the case in the days of Besht and his early disciples; it is not possible to treat as fraudulent all the accounts of miracles attributed to the "Saints" of the *Hasidim*, since many of them were truly honest and devout. On a similar basis of unquestioning faith rest the miracles of the

[53] Mark xiii. 28-29.
[54] Luke xxi. 29-31.
[55] Mark vi. 47-51.
[56] Mark vi. 49.
[57] Mark iv. 35-41.

other founders of religions and the saints pertaining to the various faiths. And how many miracles does the author of "Aliyath-Eliyahu" attribute to the Gaon of Wilna, who flourished but 150 years ago, and who held the *Hasidim* in the profoundest contempt!

(5) *The curing of numerous "nerve-cases":*

The fifth and last type of miracles were the wonderful cures effected in many kinds of nervous disorders. Jesus obviously had a power of "suggestion," of influencing others, to an unusual extent. Had not this been the case his disciples could never have held him in such veneration, remembering and teaching every word he spoke; nor could his memory have so persisted and so influenced their spiritual and earthly life; nor could they, in their turn, have so influenced thousands and tens of thousands by the power which they had derived from him. This force which Jesus had, comprises some secret, some mystical element, still not properly studied by the ordinary psychologists and physicians and scientists, who are conversant only with the laws of nature so far determined by science.

It is the same gift, differing, however, in degree, in form and tendency, which was possessed by Mohammed the Arabian Prophet, and by Napoleon.[58] The enlightened Roman, Tacitus, records a similar case of how Vespasian healed a blind man at Alexandria.[59] Certain men, gifted with a peculiar will-power and an inner life of especial strength, can, by their exceptionally penetrating or tender glance or by their inner faith in their own spiritual power, influence many kinds of nervous cases and even cases of complete insanity. Whether such influence effects a complete or only temporary cure is a question which cannot be answered offhand.

Among the many parables recorded by Matthew occur three verses [60] which speak of an unclean spirit which having left a man afterwards returned to him, and his condition became worse than at the first; and may not Jesus have come to know this from his own experience, and turned this experience into a cryptic parable?

Yet it is clear that many nervous cases and hysterical women were completely cured through Jesus' amazing, hypnotic personal influence; [61] though it is noteworthy how Mark points out again and again that Jesus disliked his miracles to be made public. After his effective sermon in the Capernaum synagogue Jesus began to heal the sick with much success, and among them he cured of fever Peter's wife's mother, with whom he was lodging. More and more sick people, and especially "those that were possessed of devils"

[58] O. Holtzman, *War Jesus Ekstatiker?* Tübingen, 1903. An extreme view is taken by Binet-Sanglé, *La folie de Jésus*, 3me ed. 4 vols. Paris, 1911-1915.
[59] See Tacitus, *Historia* IV 81, *Caeco reluxit (Vespasianus) dies.*
[60] Matt. xii. 43-5.
[61] See P. W. Schmidt, *Die Geschichte Jesu, erläutert*, Tübingen, 1904, pp. 258-265; Ed. Meyer, *Ursprung und Anfänge des Christentums*, 1921, I 153-155.

(*i.e.*, nervous and hysterical cases) were brought to Jesus, and he healed many of them; but instead of rejoicing at his success and making use of it, "he would not suffer the devils to speak" (*i.e.*, he would not allow the nervous cases whom he had cured to publish the fact).

The first night after these cures he escaped from Capernaum and went to a desert place "to pray," that is to say, to take thought with himself as to his doings and to seek help from God. When Simon and his fellow-disciples followed him and tried to bring him back to the sick people, Jesus refused to return: he preferred to go to the "villages (κωμοπόλεις) that were round about." [62] The leper whom he healed, he commands to tell no man. [63] The same command he lays upon the blind man, [64] and upon the deaf and dumb. [65] On another occasion he will not permit the unclean spirits to praise him. [66] Only in the Decapolis, in a foreign country and among strangers, where he was an exile and a fugitive, does he allow his wonders to be published. [67]

When the Pharisees demanded from him a convincing sign he refuses to give such a sign to that generation. [68] Matthew and Luke [69] supplement this by saying, "except the sign of Jonah," which Matthew expounds by the resurrection of Jesus after three days, just as Jonah was three days within the whale. But the real object of the words is as told in Luke, that the men of Nineveh repented although the prophet Jonah wrought no miracles and gave no signs; they responded to his appeal only.

In Nazareth, his native town, Jesus failed to perform any miracles, because he did not find there any faith. It follows from all this that his successful cures (most of which were, perhaps, only temporary) were those effected on neurasthenics and the like, where a man with special powers of suggestion can really instil a revived bodily and spiritual sensibility. Jesus knew this when he said to one woman whom he healed, "My daughter, thy faith hath made thee whole"; [70] in other words, this was a case of auto-suggestion. Jesus often tried to make his acts seem less marvellous to the surrounding people, all agog for "wonders." In the case of the daughter of Jairus, which may have been a fainting attack though all thought her dead, he says, "Why make ye this ado and weep? The child is not dead but sleepeth;" [71] and when she was recovered he bids them "give her to eat," and again requires "that no man should know this." [72] Again, after the miracle of the "transfiguration" at Cæsarea Philippi

[62] Mark i. 34-39.
[63] Mark i. 44.
[64] Mark viii. 26.
[65] Mark vii. 30.
[66] Mark iii. 12.
[67] Mark v. 19-20.

[68] Mark viii. 11.
[69] Matt. xii. 39-40; Luke xi. 29.
[70] Mark v. 34.
[71] Mark v. 39.
[72] Mark v. 43.

(which we shall refer to later) "he charged them that they should tell no man what things they had seen." [73]

This dislike of publicity (so strongly emphasized in Mark and undoubtedly historical) is, by the majority of Christian scholars, accounted for by Jesus' unwillingness to be looked upon as a mere "wonder-worker," whose works counted for more than his teaching and ethical injunctions. But a simpler explanation is possible: his miracles were not always successful and he was afraid to attempt them too often; he even disliked publicity for the successful miracles lest the people insist on more. On one occasion when a member of the crowd brought a son who "had a dumb spirit" (*i.e.*, a madman who raved but was incapable of coherent speech),[74] Jesus was angry with them that brought him and rebuked them. Although, therefore, he found some difficulty in working these cures, it was incumbent upon him to practise them since he wished to influence the people and be reckoned as at least a prophet, or as Elijah, the forerunner of the Messiah. The Scribes never denied that he performed miracles: they simply attributed them to an unclean spirit,[75] precisely as did the *Talmud* ("he practised sorcery") and the *Tol'doth Yeshu*, or else they asserted that "he hath Beelzebub and by the prince of the devils casteth he out devils." [76]

This "Beelzebub" was not, as most Christian scholars suppose,[77] a god of the Upper World, who among the Jews had become a demon like other heathen deities, such as "Ba'al Me'on" (the god of the dwelling); because "Zebul," in the *Talmudic* literature, is either the Temple ("who sent forth their hands against Zebul")[78] or one of the seven heavens.[79] The theory, that "Baal Zebul" is used as a derogatory title in place of "Baal-Zebub" and that "Zebul" is derived from "zebel," "dung," is unnecessary.[80] It is easier to suppose that "Beelzebub" is a corrupt reading of "Baalzebub," just as "Beliar" (in the *Sibylline Oracles* and elsewhere) comes from Belial." Since the miracles and behaviour of Jesus, during the interval between the arrest of John the Baptist and Cæsarea Philippi, all conform with the details told of the prophet Elijah, we are forced to conclude that "Beelzebub" referred to in the Gospels is to be identified with the same "Beelzebub" mentioned in connexion with Elijah.[81]

[73] Mark ix. 9.
[74] Mark ix. 19.
[75] Mark iii. 30.
[76] Mark iii. 22.
[77] Especially Movers, *Die Phönizier*, Bonn 1841, I 266.
[78] *Rosh ha-Shanah* 17a.
[79] *Hagigah* 12b.
[80] On this see H. P. Chajes, *Markus-Studien*, pp. 24-26.
[81] 2 Kings i. 2, 6, 16.

II. JESUS AT THE HEIGHT OF HIS SUCCESS:

HIS ENCOUNTER WITH THE PHARISEES

After his first success, Jesus all but fled from Capernaum for fear of fresh demands for miracles, and passed "through the villages that were round about." He would then have taught in Chorazin (whose traces survive in the ruins of Choraze), a village near the Jordan, an hour's journey north of Capernaum,[1] and preached in the synagogue (fine ruins of a later synagogue built on the same site still survive),[2] and healed the sick with the same success as before. But here, again, he found a danger in the large numbers who still followed after him and was afraid lest he draw too much attention to himself.

The earliest of the Synoptic Gospels says that "he went out and began to publish it much and to spread abroad the matter [the kingdom of heaven], insomuch that he could no more openly enter into a city, but was without in desert places."[3] The fate of John the Baptist hovered before his eyes; but outside the larger towns, in desert places, away from the civil authorities, government officials and the more important town notables, the danger was not so great.

From these adjacent villages Jesus returned to Capernaum, where, for reasons already given, he had fixed his home. Capernaum was a frontier town with a customs-house. The customs-official was a Jew, Levi ben Halphai by name. Being a tax-gatherer he was, for that time, comparatively well educated. He would seem to have had an additional name, Matthew (abbreviated from Mattathiyahu), the name by which he is known in the Gospel According to Matthew;[4] or his name may have been Matthew (Mattithiah) ben Halphai and he himself of Levitic descent, which name was, in Mark and Luke, changed from "Mattithiah ben Halphai the Levite" to "Levi ben Halphai (Alphæus)."

It was this disciple who, according to Papias, made a record of the "discourses" (*Logia*) of Jesus which form the groundwork of all three Gospels, but which are more particularly collected together in orderly fashion in the Gospel called (for this very reason) after his name: "The Gospel According to Matthew."[5] Jesus became

---

[1] Dalman, *op. cit.* pp. 135-7; see above p. 260 ff.
[2] Kohl u. Watzinger, *Antike Synagogen in Galiläa*, pp. 198-202; Meistermann, *Capharnaüm et Bethsaïde*, p. 268.
[3] Mark i. 45.
[4] Matt. ix. 9.
[5] See above p. 74.

friendly with this tax-gatherer and visited his house; and in the house of this tax-gatherer (whom, as we have seen, the whole nation, from the "sages" downwards, loathed as representing the Roman-Edomite government, so intensely as to place the tax-gatherer in the same category as thieves, murderers and brigands) Jesus and his disciples consorted with "publicans [= taxgatherers] and sinners," the friends of Matthew.

Matthew was affected by Græco-Roman culture and was, therefore, lax in his attitude towards the Jewish Law (like the Jewish "Aczisniks," tax-officials, in the time of Nicholas I in Russia). The Pharisees were indignant: Jesus was himself regarded as a Pharisee, so what had he to do with publicans and robbers and ignorant sinners? Jesus defended his conduct by a shrewd proverb: "They that are whole have no need of the physician, but they that are sick." [6]

He recognized that the publicans and sinners were "sick," *i.e.,* their conduct was unseemly; but this was the very reason why he must become intimate with them. This answer must have satisfied the Pharisees since the Gospels nowhere hint that they were angry at the retort; still, in the opinion of the stricter Pharisees, it was improper that this wonderful "Rabbi," with his ethical teaching and miracles, should have anything to do with these dregs of Jewish society.

There was another point which they disliked. Jesus preached the advent of the Messiah, in whose footsteps were to follow the "pangs of the Messiah," sorrows and afflictions, affecting (not the Messiah himself, according to the later belief, but) the entire nation and the entire world. Hence one must intercede for the nation and the world, one must fast and abstain from the pleasures of this life. Hence the Pharisees, who prayed for the coming of the Messiah, and the disciples of John the Baptist, who awaited the Messiah whose forerunner he was, all practised fasting and abstention from earthly joys.

But it was otherwise with Jesus and his disciples: they followed the example neither of the Pharisees nor of John and his disciples; they did not fast, nor go out into the wilderness, nor feed on pure locusts and honey-combs, nor abstain from wine; they even frequented the banquets of the publicans. The Pharisees and John's followers were indignant: they called Jesus "glutton and wine-bibber" (φάγος καὶ οἰνοπότης),[7] and asked why it was that he and his disciples so conducted themselves. He defended himself in the cryptic reply, "How can the children of the bride-chamber (υἱοὶ τοῦ νυμφῶνος) fast while the bridegroom is with them?" [8] This defence is entirely in accord with the Pharisaic ruling: "The companions of the bridegroom and all the 'children of the bridechamber' are exempt from

[6] Mark ii. 15-17.
[7] Matt. xi. 19; Luke vii. 34.
[8] Mark ii. 19.

the obligation of prayer and the use of phylacteries (still more of fasting) during the seven days (of the wedding feast). R. Shila (an individual opinion) held: "The bridegroom is exempt but not the children of the bridechamber." [9]

Jesus also hints at his messianic claim: "The bridegroom is like unto a king" [10] —and *he* was the King-Messiah; but it is a very slight hint. The words that follow [11] are patently a later addition since at that time Jesus had not, even to his disciples, revealed himself as the Messiah, and had not, at that time, any idea of affliction and the death on the cross. The exact point of his remark is that the kingdom of heaven is at hand, a time of joy and gladness, like a wedding-feast; the bridegroom is the king-messiah, who is already come (but who he is he does not yet divulge); hence the present is no time for fasting; the seven days of the feast exempt from many of the religious obligations, fasting included.

He likewise hints that, like all their religious observances, the fasting of the disciples of John is but the grafting of the new upon the old, the sewing of new cloth on an old, outworn garment, the putting of new wine in old, out-worn bottles: [12] a new content requires a new garb: Pharisaic Judaism must be transformed from the root, and, to the Pharisaic ceremonial laws, one should not add yet another in the guise of repentance and good works to hasten the coming of the Messiah.

Though we have here a hint towards abolishing the ceremonial laws, it was not a hint understood by his disciples, still less by the disciples of John and the Pharisees. Jesus himself would never, during his lifetime, have dared to explain his metaphor of "the piece of new cloth" and "the old bottles" as pointing to the need for a *new Torah*—although it is probable that the saying, "The commandments shall be abrogated in the time to come," [13] is earlier than the *Amora* Rab Joseph (through whom the saying is transmitted) and does *not* refer merely to life in the next world, as may be seen from the *Gemara* where the saying is quoted.

Jesus remained steadfast to the old *Torah:* till his dying day he continued to observe the ceremonial laws like a true Pharisaic Jew. Even Wellhausen is forced to admit that "Jesus was not a Christian: he was a Jew." Were this not the case we could never understand why James, the brother of Jesus, and Simon Peter, the leading disciple, should have argued in favour of retaining the ceremonial laws as against Paul (who had never seen Jesus), who determined to abrogate the ceremonial laws in order that non-Jews might be accepted within the Christian faith. Yet, on the other hand, had not Jesus'

[9] *T. Berachoth* II 10; cf. *Berachoth* 11a, 16a; *Sukkah* 25b-26a; *J. Sukkah* II 5.

[10] *Pirke d'R. Eliezer*, §16 end; see also *J. Bikkurim* III 3.

[11] Mark ii. 19-20.

[12] Mark ii. 21-22; Matt. ix. 16-17; Luke v. 36-39.

[13] *Niddah* 61b.

teaching contained suggestions of such a line of action, the idea would never have occurred to "Saul the Pharisee," nor would he have succeeded in making it a rule of Christianity. But to this question we shall return later.

Hitherto there had been no open breach between Jesus and the Pharisees. The people flocked after the Pharisaic "Rabbi" whose parables were so attractive and who did not insist that men observe *all* the laws in every detail. Here was a "Rabbi" whose "yoke was easy and whose burden was light." [14] Multitudes followed after him from all the surrounding towns and villages. They consisted of the class of "untaught Jew," the *Am-ha-aretz*, simple fisherfolk and peasants and, perhaps, inferior tax-gatherers and officials, labourers and journeymen. There were certainly many "unemployed," whom Jesus refers to in one of his parables.[15] Here and there a rich man was to be found and sometimes a Pharisee or student of the Law. One of Jesus' disciples was a Zealot who, as we have seen,[16] was nothing more than a Pharisee minded to "hasten the end," Messiah's coming, by an active display of force.

The majority, however, were "ignorant of the Law," *Ammê ha-aretz* in the *Talmudic* sense, yet, at the same time, seekers after God, humble in character and ardent in faith. They were not deliberate "sinners," heretics or dissolute, but they failed in that they did not observe the minutiæ of the religious laws as did the Pharisees (compare the case of the *Am-ha-aretz* and tithable property, when the *Am-ha-aretz* is suspect not because of evil intent but through ignorance; and Hillel's axiom: "No *Am-ha-aretz* can be a pious man").[17]

There were women also, both old and young, women hysterically inclined and women kind-hearted, women who craved after both miracles and good works. Among these was Mary Magdalen, Mary from Migdal, out of whom Jesus had expelled "seven devils." In other words, she was a woman who had suffered from nerve trouble to the extent of madness. Others were Susanna, Mary, the mother of James the Less and of Joses, Salome,[18] a woman of the name of Johanna (the feminine form of Yochanan and identical with the name "Yachne," still preserved among the Lithuanian and Polish Jews but with no knowledge of its Hebrew origin), and Chuza, the wife of Herod's steward (*i.e.*, the wife of one of Herod Antipas's treasury officials and, therefore, a well-to-do woman). And Luke tells us that these women "and many others supported him out of their possessions." [19] Not only Jesus but his disciples also must have been supported by such means; this may have formed a certain attraction (like the "tables" of the *Hasidic "Tzaddikim"* in these days), but, needless to say, it was not the chief attraction for the disciples.

Apart from these more intimate disciples of both sexes, there also

[14] Matt. xi. 30.
[15] Matt. xx. 2-7.
[16] See above p. 206.

[17] *Aboth* II 5.
[18] Mark xv. 41.
[19] Luke viii. 2-3.

followed him "much people from Galilee." [20]   Of this there can be
no doubt; and though the words which follow ("and from Judæa,
and from Jerusalem, and Idumæa, and beyond Jordan, and the neighbourhood of Tyre and Sidon")[21] obviously constitute a later addition,
it is obvious that his followers (who must have included individuals
from outside Galilee since the disciple Judas Iscariot [Ish Kerioth]
came from Judæa) formed a considerable body and that there was
always a throng in his vicinity.

To escape them, Jesus used to put off from shore in a boat, and
the people stood at a distance to listen to his parables and his teachings.   Or sometimes, when a string of boats was crossing the Sea of
Galilee, Jesus, with his more intimate disciples, would be in one boat
while the rest of his disciples and others sat in other boats, Jesus
teaching them by apt parables and shrewd sayings out in the sea
itself, surrounded by the charming blue water in sight of the flowery
shores of Lower Galilee.   It would be an exaggeration to say that
his hearers reached a total of four, and even five, thousand (as
implied in the tale of the five thousand and the seven loaves),[22] but
there can be no question that, in the early days of his ministry in
Galilee, the thronging crowds were so great that "there was no longer
room for them, even about the door,"[23] and that the crowds
"thronged" the "Rabbi;" [24] and (as now happens to the *Hasidic*
"Rabbis") so persistent were the people with their requests that
"they (Jesus and his disciples) had no leisure so much as to eat." [25]
Sometimes in trying to avoid the multitude they used to go by boat
to some deserted spot where they could sit down and rest in private;
but the people followed after them.[26]   This was the most successful
period in his ministry, if a few weeks, or at most two or three months,
can be called a period.   He then reached the height of popularity:
then he really was like a bridegroom during the seven days of the
wedding feast; and it was the pleasant memory which the disciples
retained of these few but prosperous days that knit them to Jesus,
so that when the evil days came they still kept closely to him.

*   *   *   *   *   *   *

Gradually the clouds gathered.   The Pharisees and the local authorities were already displeased by his consorting with "publicans
and sinners," and by his disciples' abstention from fasting and their
frequenting the publicans' banquets.   On the other hand, most of
the common people, though generally the devoted followers of the
Pharisees, preferred this "Rabbi," who made the yoke of the Law
so light.   Jesus and the Pharisees became more and more estranged:
once he told a paralyzed man that his sins were forgiven (obviously
owing to his sufferings, since "sufferings cleanse a man from all

[20] Mark iii. 7.
[21] Mark iii. 8.
[22] Mark vi. 45; viii. 9.
[23] Mark ii. 2,

[24] Mark iii. 9; v. 24 and 31.
[25] Mark iii. 20; vi. 31.
[26] Mark vi. 31-33.

his sins"),[27] and this was, by the Pharisees, looked upon as blasphemy, "for who can forgive sins but God alone?"[28] The details that follow (the miraculous healing of the sick of the palsy, and his carrying away his bed) are legendary accretions to the actual incident, which was primarily a contest between Jesus and the Pharisees.

On another occasion his disciples were passing through a field (according to Luke[29] this happened on the second Sabbath after Passover and, therefore, about a year before the crucifixion and shortly after the beginning of Jesus' ministry), and, as they went, they plucked the ears of corn, either to clear themselves a path through the standing corn or else to satisfy their hunger with the raw wheat (according to Jesus' answer the latter was the real reason). The Pharisees (or the priests) reproved Jesus for his disciples' act, but, like a true Pharisee, he retorts by a defence based on Scripture, on the account of David and his men who, at Nob, ate of the altar-bread (which was permitted only to the priests) because they were hungry. Incidentally, Jesus (or rather the authors of the Gospel) here confuses Ahimelech with Abiathar, just as words and phrases are sometimes confused in the verses which quote (apparently orally) Scripture.[30] It was on this occasion that Jesus made use of the striking utterance: "The Sabbath was made for man, and not man for the Sabbath."[31]

This is quite in accordance with the Pharisaic point of view. One of the *Tannaim*, R. Jonathan ben Yoseph, a disciple of R. Akiba, says: "The Sabbath was given into your hand, and ye were not given into its hand:"[32] and R. Shimeon ben Menassia, the disciple of R. Akiba's disciple, R. Meir, says: "The Sabbath is delivered to you, and ye are not delivered to the Sabbath."[33] Yet no Pharisee would consent to the conclusion that it was permissible to pluck corn on the Sabbath.

What, however, mainly aroused the indignation of the Pharisees was that Jesus should, on the Sabbath, heal a man suffering from a withered hand. The *Talmud*, it is true, concludes that not only "the saving of human life sets aside the laws of the Sabbath," but that the same applied in cases where doubt arises as to imminent danger to life; and R. Shimeon ben Menassia who said that "the Sabbath is delivered to you, and ye are not delivered to the Sabbath," also laid down the reasonable rule: "A man may profane one Sabbath in order that he may observe many Sabbaths."[34]

[27] *Berachoth* 5a.
[28] Mark ii. 3-7.
[29] Luke vi. 1.
[30] See D. Chwolsohn, *Das letzte Passamahl Christi*, pp. 64-67; I. Abrahams, *Studies in Pharisaism*, Cambridge, 1917, pp. 133-134.
[31] Mark ii. 23-28.
[32] *Yoma* VIII 6; *Yoma* 85b; *J. Yoma* VIII 5.
[33] *Mechilta, Ki tissa*, §1, ed. Friedmann 103b.
[34] *Yoma* 85b.

But it is wholly forbidden to heal an illness which is in no sense dangerous; and the *Mishna* lays it down that if, for example, "a man is suffering from toothache, he may not soak them in vinegar, but may dip them in the usual way, and if he is cured—then he is cured." [35] There was no reason for Jesus (or the author of the Gospel) to ask the Pharisees, "Is it lawful on the Sabbath to save life or to destroy it ?" [36] since the saving of life most certainly abrogates the Sabbath laws, as we have seen; but the reason for the Pharisees' indignation was, undoubtedly, that Jesus healed on the Sabbath regardless of the nature of the illness, whether it was dangerous or not. From this stage they began to see that the man whom they had so far considered as nothing more than a Pharisaic "Rab," with his own views on certain religious questions (not a remarkable thing in the time of the Hillel and Shammai controversies), was, in real truth, a danger to religion and to ancestral tradition. The local authorities also began to look upon him with disfavour.

Mark records how, after the argument about healing on the Sabbath, "the Pharisees went out and hastened to take council with the Herodians (μετὰ τῶν Ἡρωδιανῶν) how they might destroy him." [37] Capernaum was quite close to Herod's capital, Tiberias, and, since religion and politics in those days were not separate entities, the currently accepted idea was that whatever was opposed to the accepted opinion of the nation was, therefore, opposed also to the civil order: if a man opposed the "tradition of the elders" he must, in the end, incite people against the ruling authority; and particularly was this the case in Lower Galilee, then a hotbed of political and religious factions.

This furnishes an important landmark in Jesus' career. Not only was he viewed with disfavour by the Pharisees and the civil authorities, but the people, also, began to cool towards him. The people venerated the Pharisees, the leaders of Jewish democracy, and it was as a Pharisee that they had venerated Jesus also (howbeit a Pharisaic "Rabbi" who interpreted the obligations of the Law leniently, a preacher of parables and a healer of the sick, and one who appealed to the popular taste).

The Pharisees instilled into the people a dislike of Jesus: they said that he was a transgressor and a friend of transgressors—publicans, sinners, hysterical women—and that his cures were due to unholy powers; that he was possessed by Beelzebub the prince of devils, and was therefore able to heal the sick—by the same Beelzebub on account of whom Elijah so bitterly rebuked Ahaziah, king of Judah, when the latter sought to be healed by him. These comments by the Pharisees influenced the mother and brethren of Jesus (his father, apparently, was already dead). They heard all that was said

[35] *Shabbath* XIV 4.
[36] ·Mark iii. 4.
[37] Mark iii. 6.

of this member of their family and decided that he must be prevented from leading this curious life. Perhaps they may have suffered through Jesus forsaking his work as carpenter, by which he had hitherto lived and supported them; or it may have been unpleasant for them to hear all his enemies scoff at him and describe him as mad. Mark preserves a brief but most important passage: "And his kindred (οἱ παρ' αὐτοῦ) heard and went out to lay hold on him (κρατῆσαι αὐτόν) for they said, He is beside himself (ὅτι ἐξέστη)." [38] This throws a flood of light on Jesus' conduct and the attitude of his closest relations. His miracles did not inspire them with a belief in him: they simply looked upon them as the tricks of an eccentric and "wonder-worker," familiar to the Galilee of that time and in the East generally. His behaviour in the matter of the publicans, the more ignorant class of Jews, and women, seemed to them extraordinary and not far removed from madness, as also did the fact that this simple carpenter should oppose the accepted view of the most learned men of the nation.

Hence his mother and his brethren were minded to take him back home, if necessary by force; they wanted to get him back again to his ordinary business and to his family circle: let him forget his "foolishness" and be again a good son and brother and a capable craftsman, supporting himself and his family. But because of the thronging and seething crowds, his family could not get near him; so they remained at a distance and sent to summon him. Respect for his mother (a prominent trait among the Jews, ranked in the Ten Commandments on the same level as respect for the father) required that he should go to her at once; but he seems to have understood the feelings of his family and why they had come. He refused, therefore, to go to them and, with a brusqueness unlike the tenderness normally attributed to him by the Evangelists and especially in relation to his mother—he pointed to those before him and said, "Behold my mother and my brethren! for everyone that doeth the will of God, the same is my brother and sister and mother." [39]

This saying, harsh and brusque from one aspect, great and sublime from another, is found in the Old Testament. In the "Blessing of Moses" it is said of the tribe of Levi: "Who saith of his father and his mother, I have seen them not! and he regarded not his brethren and knew not his children, for they have preserved thy commandment and kept thy covenant." [40] Jesus does not show any particular tenderness to his mother. We have already pointed out that Jesus had much to say of a father's love, but never once refers to a mother's love. However this may be, Jesus parted with his family for ever: the Fourth Gospel alone refers to the mother at the time of the crucifixion; but the Synoptics, from this point on-

[38] Mark iii. 21.
[39] Mark iii. 21-35.
[40] Deut. xxxiii. 9.

wards, never again make any reference to dealings between Jesus and his family. Not until the "Church" had been founded, some time after the crucifixion, did they come forward, and two of them, James and Simon, were among the first heads of the Church. We may here repeat the fact that the "brethren of Jesus" were actual brothers and not cousins or step-brothers, as many Christian scholars have tried to maintain out of a desire, conscious or unconscious, to avoid the fact, unpalatable to the early Church, that after the miraculous birth of Jesus Mary bore other children in normal fashion.

After this, from fear of the Pharisees and "Herodians," Jesus left for the Sea of Galilee. He no more taught by the sea-shore but from the sea itself, from a boat, making it difficult for the police of the time to capture him. The crowds listened to him from the shore.[41] He remained outside towns, in some deserted spot or quiet district, where he was not likely to be observed. Those who heard of his fame still resorted to him in considerable numbers, but no longer so numerous as at first; he taught them in parables, but carefully, well knowing that it was still dangerous openly to refer to the Messiah, and, still more, to his own messianic claims. Yet he persisted, strong in the hope that, at last, the lamp would not remain "under the bushel or under the bed," but would be set up on the stand and give light to the whole house, and that, ere long, the hidden things would be revealed and understood of all.

Then he attempts a bold experiment. He goes to Nazareth, his native town (εἰς τὴν πατρίδα αὐτοῦ),[42] where, it would seem, he had never been since he went away to be baptised by John. After his family had tried to "lay hold on him," thinking that he "was beside himself," he was minded to demonstrate his powers over the people of his native town; or, it may be, he hoped to strengthen his influence (which, after his encounter with the Pharisees, had somewhat waned) in a place where he possessed relations and friends; or, yet again, he may have found it impossible to avoid Nazareth in his tour through the villages around Capernaum. It is difficult to determine the order of events as recorded in the Gospels, and Jesus may have been in Nazareth *before* his family tried to restrain him. It is, however, clear that he went to Nazareth after he had opened his ministry in Capernaum, a fact confirmed by Luke, who recounts the visit to Capernaum at the very outset of the ministry.[43]

Jesus preached one Sabbath in the synagogue of Nazareth. According to Luke [44] he read from Isaiah, chapter 61: "The spirit of God is upon me, because he hath anointed me to preach the gospel to the poor, he hath sent me to bind up the broken-hearted, to preach deliverance to the captives . . . to proclaim the acceptable year of the

[41] Mark iv. 1.
[42] Mark vi. 1.
[43] Luke iv. 16-30; and especially verse 33.
[44] Luke iv. 17-21.

Lord." These verses are admirably suited to the forerunner of the Messiah: he "proclaims the acceptable year of the Lord"[45] and preaches redemption to the common people (to the "meek" and the "broken-hearted").

But the people of Nazareth, who had known him as a simple carpenter, who had known his father and mother, his brothers and sisters (who, as is the way with relations in a small town given to backbiting and scandal, would certainly have told disagreeable things about each other), could not imagine how one from their town could be so wise and capable as to perform miracles or, still more, preach the coming of the Messiah! "Is not this the carpenter [Matt. xiii. 54 reads "the son of the carpenter"], the son of Mary [Luke iv. 22 reads "the son of Joseph"] and the brother of James and Joses and Judah and Simeon, and are not his sisters here with us?"[46] Luke[47] reports that they said to him, "Physician, heal thyself!" (or, rather, that Jesus said that his native townsfolk would certainly say this of him).[48] The two older Gospels add, "And he was a cause of offence to them."[49] This is further explained in the following verses: "And Jesus said to them, There is no prophet without honour *save in his own country and among his own kin and in his own house*. And he could there do no mighty work" (*i.e.*, miracles)—further explained by "because of their unbelief."[50] This last fact is one the importance of which it is impossible to exaggerate: from it we recognize the nature of his miracles and the attitude towards him of those who had known him from childhood and during his ordinary life. They did not perceive the transformation that had been effected in him, and he could not give them signs and proofs testifying to the fundamental change in his spiritual powers. He left Nazareth in despair never to return.

[45] It was on the basis of this passage that the early Christian Fathers concluded that the ministry lasted only a single year: but the contrary is possible—that for such a single year's ministry they found a proof-text in Scripture.
[46] Mark vi. 3.
[47] Luke iv. 23.
[48] Cf. *Gen. R.* §23.
[49] Mark vi. 4; Matt. xiii. 57.
[50] Compare Mark vi. 5-6 and Matt. xiii. 57-58.

III. THE TWELVE APOSTLES: FRESH ENCOUNTERS WITH THE PHARISEES

After his failure in Nazareth, Jesus went out to teach in the villages where the easily impressed peasants and simple-minded fishermen were more numerous. But this alone was not enough: he required permanent disciples who should assist him and spread his teaching. He saw that the ordinary people who came to listen to him were like a funnel, taking in at one and letting out at the other, with him one day and with the Pharisees the next. Hence he found it better to choose out from among his many hearers a few who should be more closely attached to him and more sympathetic. The Gospel tradition tells how he chose twelve men, according to the number of the twelve tribes of Israel; Luke adds seventy more,[1] according to the number of the nations of the world (as given in the "table of nations" in Genesis, chapter 10, and in the *Talmud* and *Midrash*).

It is difficult to determine whether Jesus himself chose the number twelve, or whether it was fixed at a later time, since the list of the "Apostles" (as the chosen disciples were called, because they were "sent" [*apostello*] forth among the Jews) is given four times differently.[2] The probability is that, despite such differences, Jesus himself determined on this number.

In the first place, the differences are almost entirely differences in order only, the names in all four lists being identical with but one exception (for Thaddæus or Lebbæus, Luke and the Acts read "Judah ben Jacob," and in Matthew's Gospel the tax-gatherer Levi is called "Matthew." It has already been suggested that his name was "Matthew the Levite").[3]

In the second place, the names, in all four lists, are mostly those of men who were not afterwards remarkable, and there would have been no point in inventing them.

Thirdly, Jesus himself promised his Apostles that "in the new creation when the son of man should sit on his throne in glory, they too should sit on twelve thrones judging the twelve tribes of Israel."[4] There is no reason to suppose that this is a later accretion in Matthew, since Jesus must have believed that, as "son of man," he would come "with the clouds of heaven" and draw near to "the

[1] Luke x. 1.
[2] Mark iii. 16-19; Matt. x. 2-4; Luke vi. 14-16; Acts i. 13.
[3] See above, p. 273.
[4] Matt. xix. 28.

ancient of days" at the Day of Judgment, and, in reference to his messianic claims, Jesus bore in mind the twelve tribes of Israel and therefore made choice of the number twelve. In the course of time, however, one of them, Thaddæus or Lebbæus [5] (Aramaic terms of kindred meaning, the former meaning "breasts" and the second "heart"), was replaced by another, Judah ben Jacob, either because he had not proved a success or because his name was forgotten; or, again, it may be that Judah ben Jacob was the genuine name and "Thaddæus" or "Lebbæus" a nickname (*scil. "ben Thaddai,"* which, being deemed unseemly for the Apostle, was later changed to *"Leb,"* heart).

The principal disciple, and one who was to play a foremost rôle in the history of Christianity, was Simon bar Jonah (later called "Kepha" or "Petros"). The Gospels no more spare him than the Books of Samuel spare David, the nation's beloved hero. Immediately after hailing him as the "rock" (*kepha* in Aramaic = *petros*, rock, in Greek) on which belief in Jesus' messianic claim was to be founded (see later), Jesus calls him "Satan;" and at the time of the crucifixion Simon-Peter denied knowledge of Jesus to save himself. Paul also attacked him, accusing him of hypocrisy and weakness and dubbing him a "lying brother." [6]

He seems to have been enthusiastic and imaginative, energetic and warm-hearted, but thoughtless and not profound, lacking the stamina of a real reformer and one who must endure to the end; he and John are expressly described as "ignorant and of no understanding." [7] The other Apostles were similar in type. James and John, the sons of Zebedee, were passionate by nature, and Jesus styled them "sons of wrath" or "sons of thunder" (בני רגש or בני רעש). They once wished to burn down a Samaritan village which had refused to receive Jesus; but he forbade them: [8] on another occasion John was minded to forbid one who drove out devils in the name of Jesus; but again Jesus forbade him, saying that "he that is not against us is for us" [9] (contradicting what Jesus says elsewhere: "He that is not with me is against me").[10]

Of the other Apostles, mention may be made of Simon the Zealot who, in various versions of Mark and Luke, is wrongly called "Simon the Canaanite."[11] As we have seen, a Zealot might well attach himself to a forerunner of the Messiah, since the Zealots only differed from the Pharisees in believing in the possibility of hasten-

---

[5] A Galilæan Hebrew name: "This question asked R. Jose, son of Thaddai of Tiberias, from Rabban Gamaliel" (*Derekh Eretz Rabbah* §1).
[6] Galatians ii. 4, 11-14.
[7] Acts iv. 13.
[8] Luke ix. 51-56.
[9] Luke ix. 49-50.
[10] Matt. xii. 30; Luke xi. 23.
[11] The correct version Καναναῖος may come from קנאני in Hebrew, קנאניא in Aramaic; cf. קנאניות (נשים) (*Gen. R.* §45).

ing the end by force. Another Apostle worthy of note is Thomas (תומא or תימא‎), in Greek "Didymus," the twin, who afterwards became a type of unbelief. Matthew the Levite has already been referred to. We shall deal later with Judas Iscariot, though it may be observed here that he was, apparently, the only disciple-Apostle who came from Judæa, namely from Kerioth, south of Hebron (the present Karyeten or Kratiyah, east of Gaza), all the others being Galilæans.[12] Legend gives to Jesus a foreknowledge of what Judas Iscariot was to do, though it is clear that had Jesus known that he was capable of betraying him, he would never have given him a place among the disciples. Jesus, therefore, in spite of his keen perception, could not have been a "discerner of hearts" in the highest sense. Judas came to Jesus from a distant part of the country, a proof that he was an exceptional man and attracted strongly by the new teaching. This alone persuaded Jesus to receive him as one of his most intimate Apostle-disciples; not till the very last did Jesus recognize in him that base character which made him a traitor.

Jesus felt the fatigue of constant teaching, and after his enemies had become numerous, he sent out these twelve disciples that they, too, might preach the speedy coming of the kingdom of heaven and the need for repentance and good works. He expressly tells them, "Go not the way of the Gentiles, nor to any city of the Samaritans! Go only unto the lost sheep of the house of Israel."[13] Nowhere else is Jesus' Judaism so strongly shown as here: like every other Jew he was a Jewish nationalist; the kingdom of heaven was for Israel alone; only afterwards should the Gentiles "be added to the house of Jacob" and "proselytes pressing forward in the days of the Messiah." [14]

He sent out his Apostles in pairs to the villages. They must take with them for the journey "neither scrip nor bread nor money ($\chi\alpha\lambda\kappa\acute{o}\nu$= small bronze coins) in their girdle" (i.e., in their purse; cf. הרי מאתים זוז קשורים באפונדתי‎): [15] they must carry a staff only.[16] They might not even carry two cloaks. Into whatever place they went they must enquire who was worthy to receive them, and where they were not hospitably received they must not linger: "shake off its dust from the soles of your feet," i.e., leave it and get away as from a perverted city.

[12] As against the theory of Schulthess (*Problem der Sprache Jesu*, p. 54) that "Iskariota" in the Syriac translation (סכריוטא‎, וכריוטא‎) is "Sicarius," brigand, see Dalman, *Orte und Wege Jesu*, p. 265, n. 3. See also S. Krauss, *Judas Iskariot, J.Q.R.* IV, 199-207, London, 1913.

[13] Matt. x. 5-6.

[14] Ab. Zar. 3b.

[15] J. Rosh ha-Shana II 1.

[16] Matt. x. 10 reads "and not" for Mark's (vi. 8) "only" and Luke ix. 3 gives "nor staves." The correct text is that given in Mark: the two later Gospels wished to magnify the confidence which the Apostles had in Jesus: they needed not even a staff, for, even from far, Jesus was their helper and defender.

Matthew further adds to Jesus' words, that "since they were as sheep among wolves" they must be "both subtle as serpents and simple as doves."[17]   Here we have a trait in Jesus' character that should not be ignored: we shall see later, and more than once, that Jesus was by no means the tender, placable, unworldly character which his apologists, even among the "Liberal" Christians, describe.

So, two by two, the Apostles preached repentance throughout the neighbouring small towns and villages.   They were successful and overjoyed to find that they, too, could "expel spirits," i.e., that they, too, could exercise suggestion in nervous cases; and the Talmudic literature informs us that, at the end of the first or the beginning of the second century, one Jacob of Kefar-Sekanya (or Kefar Sama) wished to heal of snake-bite Ben Dama, nephew of the Tanna R. Ishmael, "by the name of Jesus."[18]   But the Apostles cured also by natural means: "they anointed with oil many that were sick and healed them," as the Evangelist simply puts it.[19]

Jesus rejoiced at their success,[20] but this success caused Jesus and his disciples to be much discussed.   Some thought he was "a prophet" or "one of the prophets" (ὡς εἷς τῶν προφετῶν), that is, not an actual prophet, but like a prophet (much as the Hasidim look upon their Tzaddikim); others thought that he was the Prophet Elijah, the Messiah's forerunner.   The latter idea led Herod Antipas to think that here was John the Baptist again, in a new guise: just as the latter attracted large crowds by proclaiming the nearness of the "end," and so constituted a danger to the Roman-Edomite government, so it was with Jesus.

It is this idea which the evangelist conveys in the words: "And Herod heard and said, It is John whom I beheaded: he is risen from the dead."[21]   That so clever and enlightened an Hellenist as Herod Antipas, whom Jesus dubbed "that fox," did not mean this literally, is obvious: his remark was meant metaphorically, just as in these days any violent antisemite is called "Eisenmenger redivivus" (an Eisenmenger risen from the dead), because his efforts resemble those of

[17] Matt. x. 16; the many efforts of Christian scholars to translate φρόνιμοι as something less pungent than "subtle," do not take into account the plain simile "like serpents" ὡς οἱ ὄφεις, and the antithesis implied by "simple as doves." See Cant. R. on "Yonathi bi-hag'we ha-sela'."
[18] T. Hulin II 22-23; Ab. Zar. 27b; J. Shabbath, near end of IV; J. Ab. Zar. II 2; see above, p. 40.
[19] Mark vi. 13.
[20] Most critics conclude that though Jesus chose twelve disciples he did not send them as "Apostles" to other towns, and that the account of the "Apostles" is but a reflection of the doings of the leaders of the Christian Church, and not of Jesus' Apostles (see Ed. Meyer, Ursprung und Anfänge des Christentums I 278-280); but in that case we should have to ignore such sayings as "the way of the Gentiles" and "ye shall not have gone through the cities of Israel," etc. Critics cannot have it both ways; and since the influence of Jesus was so great it is absurd to reduce his recorded actions to nothing.
[21] Mark vi. 16.

Eisenmenger. Jesus became aware of Herod's suspicion and "hastened with his disciples to embark and cross the sea to Beth-Saïda." [22]

"The village of Bethsaida by Genesareth" was (about the year 3 B.C.) transformed by Herod Philip into a "city of very many inhabitants" and "called Julias after the name of the emperor's daughter." [23] (There was another Julias further south in the Jordan valley, the Beth Haram of the Bible, the Beth Haramta of Josephus and the *Talmud,* and the modern *Tel-er-Rama*).[24] Philip made this Bethsaida his capital, since it was near important roads from Cilicia in the northeast and from Gamala in the south-east. It was four kilometres distance by sea from Capernaum, according to Dalman,[25] if we identify Capernaum with the site of the present "Hirbet Arija" or "el-Araj." Southeast of these ruins is a site, resembling a fortress, still known as "el-Yehudiya." [26]

Since it stood on the seashore and on important trade routes, Bethsaida served as the customs-town for the east of Jordan, just as Capernaum served as the customs-town for the west. Its Hebrew name was Saidan (צַיירָן) [27] or, less correctly, Sidan (צידן) or Sidon (צִידוֹן); [28] this name provides the adjectival form רבי צַיידְתייה "the Saidan Rabbi," "R. Jose the Saidanite," [29] or, inaccurately, "R. Joseph the Sidonian." [30] It is possible that this is the צַיירְתה which the Jerusalem *Talmud* [31] describes as being near הנקב of the Bible, near Yabniel-Yamma.[32] Because of Antipas's hostility, Jesus turned to the frontier of the territory belonging to Antipas's brother, Philip making for the town nearest to Capernaum and Nazareth and not belonging to Antipas. This Bethsaida may be the native town of Jesus' disciple Philip, even if it is not that of Peter and Andrew.[33] The

---

[22] Mark vi. 45.

[23] *Ant.* XVIII ii 1; cf. *Wars* II ix 1.

[24] *Ant.* XX viii 4; *Wars* II ix 1. On the passages in the *Talmud* and *Midrash* see the *Arukh ha-Shalem* of A. Kohut, II 87-88, s.v. Beth Rametha.

[25] Dalman, *op. cit.* 142-148.

[26] *Op. cit.* 146-147.

[27] *T. Ab. Zar.* I 8; J. (Mishnah) *Kiddushin* IV 11 (*Kidd.* IV 14: צריין, and also in *Babli Kidd.* 52a); *Gittin* IV 7 (*Gittin* IV 17 צידון); *J. Ab. Zar.* V 5 (אסטרטיא דציידן); *Qoh. R.* on *Konasti li* (פוסיאנין מן ציידן); *Semahoth* (*Abel Rabbati*) IV 26 (ר. יוסי בציידין).

[28] *J. Berachoth* III 1; *Erubin* 47b; *Ab. Zar.* 13a; *Esther R.* §9 (אבא אורויון אבא); צידון—*J. Shek.* VI 2. See also *Midrash of Abba Gorion,* ed. Buber (*Aggadic Books* on *Meg. Esther,* Wilna, 1886), n. 1 at the beginning of the book. Wellhausen (*Einleitung,* 1905, pp. 37-8) may be right in saying that in Mark vii. 31, "Saidan" has been changed to "Sidon."

[29] *J. Nazir* VII 3, and near end of section (twice): *J. Kethuboth* XII 7 (ר. יוסי צידונייא).

[30] *Kethuboth* 46a (see A. Hyman, *Tol'doth Tannaim w'Amoraim,* London, 1910, p. 741). S. Klein, *Monatschrift,* LIX (1915) 167-168.

[31] *J. Meg.* I 1 (see J. Schwartz, *T'buoth ha-aretz,* ed. Luncz, p. 219).

[32] Josh. xix. 33; *J. Meg. loc. cit.*

[33] John i. 45; xii. 21-24.

name Julias was still new and not yet naturalized, and the Galilæan
Jews continued to call the town by its earlier Hebrew-Aramaic name
"Bethsaida" or "Saidan," as is the habit with the lower classes,
especially among the Jews, in towns whose names are changed by the
whim of some king or ruler.

It may be, however, that Jesus and his disciples did not come to
the new Greek city, but to the older Hebrew village.[34] The notion
that Galilee and Transjordania contained two cities of the name Bethsaida, arises from the mistake of the Fourth Gospel [35] which instead
of "Bethsaida beyond Jordan," says, inadvertently, "Bethsaida
that is in the land of Galilee." [36] Jesus did not allow the people to
accompany him but sent them away.[37] Since the ruler of Galilee,
the Tetrarch Antipas, suspected him, it was preferable that many
people should not come with him into the district of the new ruler.
Jesus did not stay long in Bethsaida, it was too important a city
and there were too many observant eyes. The inference from the
reproach and curse which Jesus levelled at this city in conjunction
with Chorazim and Capernaum,[38] is that he was not too successful
even there.

Jesus went about "the land of Genesareth" ($\dot{\epsilon}\pi\dot{\iota}$ $\tau\dot{\eta}\nu$ $\gamma\tilde{\eta}\nu$ $\Gamma\epsilon\nu\eta\sigma\alpha\rho\dot{\epsilon}\tau$),
i.e. "the valley of Genesar." [39] There many people believed in
him. This displeased the Pharisees who regarded him as a "sinner."
To the Galilæan Pharisees were now added Scribes from Jerusalem
who either came to Galilee by chance or were specially summoned
thither by the less learned Galilæan Pharisees, in order to discuss
the position of this unorthodox Galilæan "Rab." These Scribes at
once see something wrong in Jesus and his disciples. These Ammē
ha-aretz were lacking in orthodox piety. They ate with "unwashen
hands," i.e., they neglected the religious obligations of washing of
hands. The Scribes and Pharisees were indignant with Jesus that
"his disciples did not follow the traditions of the elders," namely,
the accepted customs of the Scribes.

A. Büchler shows that, up to the age of the Amoraim, the rite of
"washing of hands" was not widespread among the nation, that it
only applied to the ceremony of eating the offering (אכילת תרומה) and

---

[34] See Mark viii. 22-23.
[35] John xii. 21.
[36] See F. Buhl, Handbuch der Geographie des Alten Palästina, Freiburg,
1896, p. 242.
[37] Mark vi. 45; $\dot{\epsilon}\omega s$ $\alpha\dot{\upsilon}\tau\dot{o}s$ $\dot{\alpha}\pi o\lambda\dot{\upsilon}\epsilon\iota$ $\tau\dot{o}\nu$ $\check{o}\chi\lambda o\nu$ (so that he sent the people
away).
[38] Matt. xi. 20-22; Luke x. 13-16.
[39] On this, see above, p. 260 ff. Dalman, op. cit. pp. 109-110 suggests that
the form $\Gamma\epsilon\nu\eta\sigma\alpha\rho\dot{\epsilon}\tau$ which occurs neither in the Talmud nor in Josephus,
was made on the analogy of Nazareth (נצרת). But it may be that this is
the feminine adjectival form הארץ הניניסרית, and that the lowland was
thus called by the people in Hebrew or Aramaic. The more correct reading
as given in Nestle is ($\dot{\epsilon}\pi\dot{\iota}$ $\tau\dot{\eta}\nu$ $\gamma\tilde{\eta}\nu$ $\tilde{\eta}\lambda\theta o\nu$ $\epsilon\dot{\iota}s$ $\Gamma\epsilon\nu\nu\eta\sigma\alpha\rho\dot{\epsilon}\tau$).

was practised by the Pharisaic Priests alone.[40] But it is difficult to place all three Synoptics so late, or to suppose that all or even some of Jesus' disciples were priests. Jesus denounced heavily this indignation of the Pharisees. He calls them "hypocrites" and their piety "a law of men that has been learned" (after Isaiah xxix.13, quoted in Mark according to the Septuagint version). Instead of defending himself he alleges against them that "they have forsaken the commandments of God to hold to the tradition of men." He gives as an example the fact that Moses said: "Honour thy father and thy mother," but the Pharisees argue that if a man say: "Korban (that is, a gift)[41] is that by which thou shouldest have profited by me," then he may no longer benefit his father or mother therewith and observe the divine law as given in the Ten Commandments.

Jesus (or the authors of the Gospel) knew that oaths were introduced by the formula "Korban," and we read in the first section of the *Talmud* tractate *Nedarim*, "Oath formulæ are קרבן, נזיר, and שבועה"; [42] and we read later that *"Konem, Koneah* and *Kones* are but other names for Korban."[43] The *Mishna* and *Talmud* make far more use of the word *"Konem"* than of *"Korban,"* either because they were written long after *"Korbans"* (sacrifices) came to an end, or because they had some scruples against using a word with such sacred associations. We still find such discussions as the following: "Korban, whole-offering (עולה), meal-offering (מנחה), sin-offering (חטאת), thank-offering (תודה), which I eat to thee" (i.e. that of thine which I eat is forbidden as a Korban)—such is forbidden; but R. Yehudah permits. *"Ha-Korban, k'Korban, Korban* which I eat to thee"—such is forbidden; but R. Yehudah permits. *"L'Korban,* I do not eat to thee"—R. Meir forbids.[44] We also find: *"Korban,* I do not eat to thee, *Korban* that I eat to thee. It is not *Korban,* I do not eat to thee"—such is permitted.[45] *Korban* is also used in the *Tosefta* in many places with the sense of oath or vow.[46] Of interest as explaining Jesus' argument is the following Mishnah: "He saw them (certain men) eating figs, and said: It is *Korban* for you (i.e. his father and brother and certain others). The School of Shammai say, They (the father and brother) were permitted, but not the

---

[40] A. Büchler, *Der Galiläische Am-Haarez des zweiten Jahrhunderts,* Wien, 1906, pp. 114, 126-130. See also his *Die Priester und der Cultus,* Wien, 1895, pp. 82-3. The question is more accurately explained by H. P. Chajes, *Rivista Israelitica,* I (1904) p. 50.

[41] The word is given in Mark vii, 11, in its Hebrew form, Κορβᾶν together with its explanation in Greek ὅ ἐστι δῶρον. Josephus, *Contra Apionem* I 22, explains *"Korban"* in exactly the same way; but see *Wars* IX iv. where the Temple treasury is likewise called *"Korban"* κορβανᾶς cf. *J.Q.R.* XIX 615-659.

[42] *Nedarim* I 1.

[43] *Ned.* I 2.

[44] *Ned.* I 4.

[45] *Ned.* II 2.

[46] *T. Ned.* I 1-3; II 3; IV 5.

others; the School of Hillel say, All were permitted." [47] Hence the father and brother (and therefore, of course, the mother) were not included within the scope of the "Korban" oath even according to the stricter interpretations of the Shammai School.

But there is another, more explicit, *Mishnah,* with a direct bearing on the charge brought by Jesus (or the Evangelists): R. Eliezer says: They open a way for a man (if he have vowed by "Korban" or "Konem," so that he shall not assume the vows too lightly) because of the honour due to his father and mother. The Sages forbid. R. Tzadok says: Before they open a way for a man, because of the honour due to his father and mother, they open a way for him because of the honour due to God (for God ordered men to beware of vows); and consequently there can be no vows (since they were not generally pleasing to God).

The Sages agree with R. Eliezer that when the matter is one between a man and his father and mother ("*e.g.,* when a man, by a vow, deprives his father of his property"—so R. Obadiah of Bertinora; "when he vows things required by his father and mother"—so Rabbi Gershom, "the Light of the Exile"), they open a door for the honour due to his father and mother. [48]

Thus both R. Eliezer and the Sages as a whole are agreed that if a man makes a vow that harmfully affects his father and mother, "they open a door for him," that he may be able to give them the honour required in the Law of Moses, and so they release him from his vow. This is quite contrary to the charge brought by Jesus. There are three possible explanations of the difference: the rule in the time of Jesus may have been otherwise, or Jesus may have been bringing an unjustifiable charge against the Pharisees, or else the authors of the Gospels had heard something about the rules concerning vows among contemporary *Tannaim* (R. Eliezer lived immediately after the Destruction), and confused permission with prohibition.

However this may be, Jesus' remarks on this occasion were over-severe. He turned to all the people, saying, with the strongest emphasis: [49] "Hear me all of you and understand: there is nothing from without the man that going into him can defile him: but the things which proceed out of the man are those that defile the man. If any man hath ears to hear, let him hear." [50] The solemn introduction ("Hear me all of you and understand") and the still more solemn conclusion "If any man hath ears to hear, let him hear," which Jesus always employs when he lays down something new or something not generally known), plainly show that he referred on this oc-

[47] *Ned.* II 2.
[48] *Ned.* IX 1. Cf. J. Mann, *Oaths and Vows in the Synoptic Gospels* (A. J. Th. 1917, XXI 260-274).
[49] Mark vii. 14-16.
[50] Matt. xv. 11 (see Dalman, *op. cit.* p. 120).

casion to something most important for Judaism as a whole, and not merely for the Pharisees alone.

He dared not explain the subject before the crowd; but to his disciples he explained that what enter a man are the various foods, which themselves cannot defile a man (Jesus' words are primitively plain: "Because it goeth not into his heart but into his belly, and goeth out into the draught which maketh all foods clean"); whereas what issue from a man are the bad qualities—"deceit, envyings, love of gain, wickedness, blasphemy, pride, foolishness, evil deeds, adultery, fornication, murder, theft, and gluttony"—which are the things which defile the man.[51] Thus Jesus would abrogate not only fasting, and decry the value of washing of hands in the "tradition of the elders" or in current traditional teaching, but would even permit (though he does this warily and only by hints) the foods forbidden in the Law of Moses.

The breach between Jesus and the Pharisees was complete.

[51] Mark vii. 17-23; Matt. xv. 12-20.

FIFTH BOOK

JESUS REVEALS HIMSELF AS MESSIAH

I. JESUS IN THE BORDERS OF TYRE AND SIDON AND IN DECAPOLIS

The strong expressions used by Jesus against the Pharisees show him again as very different from the "tender" and "placable" person depicted by Christians ("The Lamb of God;" "as a sheep before her shearers is dumb"). He was a combatant preacher and spoke as harshly to the Pharisees as ever Jeremiah did to the priests. In his preaching he was thus akin to the Prophets, while in his parables he was more akin to the *Haggadist* Pharisees. But despite this, the Pharisees could not forgive his attitude to the tradition of the elders and to the rules affecting the Sabbath and forbidden foods. The spirit of the age made them look upon his miraculous healing as the work of Satan: he "had Beelzebub" and by an unclean spirit he drove out unclean spirits; therefore he was a sorcerer, a false prophet, a beguiler and one who led men astray (as the *Talmud* describes him), and it was a religious duty to put him to death. He was compelled to escape.

After the dispute about the washing of hands, Jesus, as Mark expresses it, "arose from thence (from 'the land of Genesareth') and went to the borders of Tyre and Sidon, and when he came to a house he did not wish to be made known to any man." [1] Shortly before this, Jesus had ordered his disciples not to go "by the way of the Gentiles," and now, suddenly, he himself goes to the gentile Tyre and Sidon. [2] The reason was that he was escaping from his enemies, and this supposition is supported by the words, "And he did not wish to be made known to any man" (οὐδένα ἤθελε γνῶναι).

It would be an over-emphasis to treat this foreign sojourn as an

[1] Mark vii. 24 (cf. Matt. xv. 21).
[2] The statement in Mark v. 1 that Jesus was in the land of the Gadarenes or Geresenes even earlier than this, is, even if it is historical, certainly misplaced. Theodor Reinach (*Revue des Etudes Juives*, XLVII 177) holds that the name "Legion" given to the unclean spirit, and the swine into which the unclean spirits entered, arose from an ignorant confusion with the "Tenth Legion," stationed in Palestine 70-135 C.E., on whose standard was depicted a wild boar. This would then be a late accretion; and so Jesus was not in the Decapolis till after the dispute about washing of hands.

entire period within Jesus' ministry and, like Oscar Holtzmann, devote a special section to it.[3] It certainly, however, constitutes a withdrawal from his customary haunts and an effort to avoid the minions of Herod Antipas, who, as Jesus knew, had shown himself capable of putting John the Baptist to death.

An impression is unconsciously formed that the Evangelists make Jesus depart to the borders of Tyre and Sidon from fear of the Pharisees and Antipas, just because the Prophet Elijah went to Sarepta of Sidon from fear of Ahab and Jezebel and the Prophets of Baal;[4] but in this case we have not an attempt by the Evangelists to approximate Jesus to Elijah; Jesus himself imitated Elijah in that he was in the same plight—persecuted by both the civil and the religious authorities.

Jesus went north, accompanied by the Twelve and a few of his decreasing number of followers, including a few women, to a place no longer counted within the bounds of the Land of Israel. Many Jews lived there[5] but the Evangelists record but one act of Jesus—done for the sake of a foreign woman. A Canaanitish woman[6] begged him to drive out a devil from her little daughter. But his answer was so brusque and chauvinistic that if any other Jewish teacher of the time had said such a thing Christians would never have forgiven Judaism for it: "It is not right to take the bread from the children and cast it to the little dogs" (οὐ καλόν ἐστι λαβεῖν τὸν ἄρτον τῶν τέκνων καὶ βαλεῖν τοῖς κυναρίοις).[7] According to Matthew, Jesus added, "I was not sent except to the lost sheep of the house of Israel"[8]—the same remark which he made to the Apostles when he sent them out to the cities of Israel alone. Only after the stranger had cast herself down before him, saying: "Yea, Lord, but even the little dogs eat under the table the fragments of the children's bread," did Jesus tell her that the devil was gone out of her daughter, "and she went away unto her house, and found the child laid upon the bed," i.e., passive after an attack of frenzy.

This is the first and only time when Jesus (and even then, against his will) dealt with strangers. Other such accounts (i.e. that of the foreign centurion in Capernaum who was "a friend of Israel" and built them a synagogue[9] and especially that of the Samaritan woman)[10] are lacking in Mark and therefore unhistorical. Jesus, in all his sayings and doings, was an utter Jew: he regarded himself as sent to the Jews alone, and he regarded his people as the "chosen people" since they were the "sons of God." Therefore it was not

---

[3] *Leben Jesu,* Tübingen, 1901, pp. 233-270.
[4] Cf. Luke iv. 25-26 and 1 Kings xvii. 8-24.
[5] See J. Klausner, *Biy'mê Bayith Sheni,* p. 45.
[6] For details see H. P. Chajes, *Markus-Studien,* pp. 43-44.
[7] Mark vii. 27.
[8] Matt. xv. 24.
[9] Matt. viii. 5-13; Luke vii. 1-9.
[10] John iv. 4-42.

right to throw away "the children's bread" to non-Jews, who were little dogs and not children.

Were it not for this rough answer (which the Evangelists had no reason to invent) it might have been supposed that this Canaanitish woman in the borders of Tyre and Sidon was but an imitation of the foreign widow (Canaanite) of Sarepta of Sidon. The Gospels were, however, written at a time when the disciples of Jesus included many non-Jews, and when no one would have put in Jesus' mouth so harsh a sentiment. The episode must, therefore, have been historical.

After leaving his native town and the scenes of his early ministry, Jesus was filled with indignation against those places which had finally rejected him after he had taught and healed there; he speaks bitterly: "Woe unto thee, Chorasin, Woe unto thee, Bethsaida! For if the mighty works (the miracles) which were wrought in you had been done in Tyre and Sidon (where he was now living), they would have repented in sackcloth and ashes! But I say unto you (the disciples), that in the day of judgment it shall be more tolerable for Tyre and Sidon than for you (Chorazin and Bethsaida). And thou, Capernaum, that wast exalted to heaven, shalt go down to Sheol. For if the mighty works had been done in Sodom which were done in thee, it would have remained until this day. But I say unto you, that on the day of judgment it shall be more tolerable for the land of Sodom than for thee." [11]

Such bitterness shows clearly that his condition was becoming worse; he saw no progress in his work: he is indignant and curses. Such words have in them something of the severity and the arraignments of an Isaiah or an Ezekiel: they show not the least trace of that peculiar "tenderness" and "unconditional forgiveness." Jesus was a Jew, educated on the severe indictments of the Prophets, and at times he follows their lead: he is by no means that type which the Christians have depicted for themselves—one who forgives all, who, when offended, offends not again.

This may have been the time when Jesus taught the parable of those bidden to the feast or wedding. The important guests who had been invited did not come; therefore the wayfarers, the poor and indigent, the blind and the lame, evil and good alike, were summoned.[12] In other words: the Pharisees and Scribes, the pick of the nation, those nearest the kingdom of heaven, refused to come; therefore Jesus was forced to gather around him the publicans and sinners and harlots.

From Tyre and Sidon, Jesus returned to the Sea of Galilee; but this time he does not come back to Capernaum and the district west of the lake, but to the east of Jordan: he traverses the region of "The Ten Cities," or Decapolis.[13] These cities were all inhabited by non-

[11] Matt. xi. 20, 24; Luke x. 13-15.
[12] Matt. xxii. 1-14; Luke xiv. 16-24.
[13] Mark vii. 31.

Jews, and all (except Beth-Shean) in Transjordania; their names (from north to south) were: (1) Hyppos (Susitha), (2) Gadara, (3) Abilene (not Abel beth Ma'kha), (4) Raphon or Raphana (near Ashteroth-Karnaim), (5) Kanatha (the modern Qanawat), (6) Scythopolis (Beth Shean), (7) Pella (Pehal), (8) Dion, (9) Gerasa, (10) Philadelphia (Rabbath b'ne Ammon).[14]

At this time Jesus may have visited Gadara or Gerasa, more probably Gadara, the modern Um-Kais, one of the most important towns of the Decapolis and noted for its hot-water curative springs (דנדר המתך), often referred to in Josephus and the *Talmul;* [14a] it is recorded that Jesus here performed the miracle of driving out devils "whose name was Legion, because they were many," from a man suffering from "delirium tremens."

In the same place comes the account of the swine into which the unclean spirits entered and which fell into the water and were drowned. Swine would be natural in a town inhabited mainly by non-Jews; but, as we have already hinted,[15] the story may be only a later legend. One feature, however, is of interest: in the borders of Tyre and Sidon, and in Gadara (or Gerasa), Jesus did not find it necessary to forbid his wonders to be made public.

At Gadara (unless the episode is unhistorical) he commands him who had been healed of the "Legion" of unclean spirits "to return to his home and family and tell them all the great things which God had done for him." [16] In a foreign country where, though there might be many Jews, the main population was constituted of Greeks and Syrians, he is not afraid that the Pharisees will investigate his doings, nor is he afraid by reason of the crowds of believers; none the less he is afraid, even there, to enter the cities themselves. It was certainly then that there escaped from him that sad, heart-rending saying (which Byron has metaphorically applied to the whole race of Israel), "The foxes [17] have holes and the birds have nests, but the Son of man hath no place to lay his head." [18] No saying could be more pathetically apt or more human. . . .

Nor could Jesus find any respite in the Decapolis and he did not long remain there; for what could he, a Jew to his finger-tips, do there among the Gentiles? What interest had foreigners in the Gospel of the Messiah, or in the kingdom of heaven (which was to contain none

[14] Contrary to the evidence of Pliny and the view of Schürer, we exclude the distant Damascus from the Ten Cities; see Schürer, II⁴ 148-195.

[14a] *Shab.* 109a; *Erubin* 61a; *Sanh.* 108a; *Meg.* 6a; *Rosh ha-Shana* 23b (where possibly Gador and not Gadara is meant); *T. Rosh ha-Shana* II (1) 2; *T. Erubin* VI (V) 13 (end of section); *J. Erubin* V 7 (XXII end of p. 4); *J. Kiddushin* III 14; *J. Shabbath* III 1; *J. Ab. Zar.* V 15 (near end of section).

[15] See above, p. 293, n. 2.

[16] Mark v. 19.

[17] According to the Hebrew proverb, "no fox dies in its den" (*Kethuboth* 71b; *Nedarim* 81b; *J. Kethuboth* VII 3).

[18] Matt. viii. 20; Luke ix. 59.

but those proselytes who should "press forward" in the Days of the Messiah)? From there he goes to "the regions of Dalmanutha," [19] or "the border of Magadan" (or, according to another reading, "Magdala").[20] As for Dalmanutha, Furrer [21] thinks it lies north of Capernaum on the way to Migdal, the modern Minin; while Joseph Schwartz reads "Talmanutha" from "Talimon." [22] There is more truth in Dalman's theory that "Dalmanutha" is a corruption of "Migdal Nunaia" (the name given to Magdala), or of "[ar'a] Magdalayatha" (the Magdalene land).[23]

Jesus no longer enters this town of the "valley of Genesar" but remains outside in its purlieus (εἰς τὰ μέρη according to Mark, εἰς τὰ ὅρια according to Matthew). In the town were to be found Pharisees who demanded a sign from him, and this he would not give them. He feared to put his powers to the proof in their presence. Jesus held that signs were not essential: the men of Nineveh repented through the preaching of Jonah, and Jonah wrought no signs before them. This refusal to offer a sign in proof of his claim to be a prophet or the forerunner of the Messiah, gave the Scribes a weapon whereby to decry Jesus' value; and the officials of Herod also began to look upon him as a deceiver and beguiler.

Consequently Jesus warns his disciples: "See that ye beware of the leaven of the Pharisees and of the leaven of the Herodians" [24]— i.e., of the evil men among these two parties (cf. the *Talmudic* expression: "Who is the thwarter? the leaven that is in the dough and the servitude inflicted by the Gentile powers").[25] Matthew who failed to see a reference to an actual event, here writes: [26] "Of the leaven of the Pharisees and Sadducees," and assumes that both Pharisees and Sadducees demanded a sign; [27] Luke speaks only of the leaven of the Pharisees.[28] The disciples misunderstood the reference and thought that Jesus spoke simply about bread ("dough" and "leaven"), whereupon Jesus reproved them for their obtuseness.

It proved necessary to escape from the sphere of influence of the Pharisees and Herod Antipas, and once more we find Jesus crossing over from Antipas' into Philip's territory. He reaches Bethsaida (Julias) a second time (though this account may only be a further reference to the first visit)[29] and after staying there (apparently in the Jewish quarter near the recently Hellenised town) he removed

[19] Mark viii. 10.
[20] Matt. xv. 39.
[21] Quoted by P. W. Schmidt, *Die Geschichte Jesu, erläutert* (II) 1904, p. 314.
[22] *T'buoth ha-aretz*, ed. Luncz, p. 228 (see *J. Demai* II 1).
[23] Dalman, *op. cit.* p. 116.
[24] Mark viii. 15.
[25] *Berachoth* 17a.
[26] Matt. xvi. 7.
[27] Matt. xvi. 1.
[28] Luke xii. 1.
[29] Compare Mark viii. 22-26 and Mark vi. 45.

further north, to the second greatest city in Philip's Tetrarchy, "the villages of Cæsarea Philippi." [30] It should be observed that Jesus does not enter the city itself, but remains with his disciples in "the villages" near by. Cæsarea Philippi is the present Banyas, the Pamias of the *Talmud*, the Greek Πανείας, and the ancient Baal-Gad, the northern boundary of Palestine, where the Jordan leaves "the cave of Pamias." [31] Philip rebuilt it in honour of Augustus, and, to distinguish it from the Cæsarea in Judæa, built by Herod his father (the *Talmudic* "Cæsarea, daughter of Edem").[32] and, later, made the capital of the Roman Procurator, it was called "Cæsarea of Philip," Cæsarea Philippi. In the *Talmud* it is still called Pamias, Apamæa, or Aspamiya, and sometimes Cæsarion, to distinguish it from Cæsarea.[33] Here occurred the event which, next to the Baptism by John the Baptist, is probably the most important in the history of Jesus and Christianity.

[30] Mark viii. 27.
[31] *Bekhoroth* 55a; *Baba Bathra* 74b.
[32] *Meg.* 6a; *Lam. R.* on *Hayu tzareha l'rosh.*
[33] *Targum Yerushalmi* "Bamidbar," 34, 14; *Sukka* 27b בקיסרי ...בגליל העליון *Mechilta*, "Beshallah," § *Amalek*, 2 (ed. Friedmann 55b); בקסריון העליון... ואמרו לה בקיסריון במחלת קיסריון שהוא מת חת לפמיים (cf. "*T'buoth ha-aretz*," 239, 505-7; Derenbourg, *Massa Eretz Yisrael*, p. 134 n. 5).

II. AT CÆSAREA PHILIPPI: JESUS REVEALS HIMSELF TO HIS DISCIPLES AS THE MESSIAH

The "Son of man" was a homeless wayfarer in a foreign land. No longer is he surrounded, as in Lower Galilee, with crowds of enthusiastic believers and admirers within reach of his native town. No longer are miracles performed by him or for him. He cannot overcome or convert his enemies. What power has he left? How can his disciples continue to believe in him? Despair begins to steal into their hearts. Even he, too, has lost the old buoyancy. Do his disciples still believe in him? and, if so, what kind of a belief is theirs? He had often remarked their obtuseness: were these the stones with which he must build, and the foundations on which he must establish the kingdom of heaven?

These gloomy thoughts oppressed him as he stood there at the foot of snowcapped Hermon, in those picturesque surroundings close to the half-Gentile town of the Herodian ruler, in one of the northernmost villages of Palestine; and he turns to his disciples with the question:

"What do men say of me? Who do men say that I am?"

The disciples reply: "John the Baptist. Some say, Elijah; and others, One of the prophets."

And Jesus' teaching and manner of life did, in great measure, conform with that of John the Baptist, or Elijah whom John had imitated, or with that of a prophet like Isaiah or Jeremiah who had rebuked the nation and preached goodness and righteousness.

Jesus asks further: "But ye yourselves, who do ye say that I am?"

Whereupon Simon the fisherman, the first of the disciples both in time and worth, comes forward and says: "Thou art the Messiah!"

Such is Mark's brief account.[1] To "the Messiah" Matthew adds the words, "the son of the living God,"[2] but Luke writes simply "the Messiah of God."[3] "The living God" is quite an Hebraic expression, and to term the Messiah "son of the living God" is justifiable from the verse in the Psalm: "Thou art my son: this day have I begotten thee,"[4] since, a few verses earlier, it is said, "Against the Lord and against his anointed (his Messiah)."[5] But the words are lacking in Mark and Luke.

Matthew then adds: "And Jesus answered and said unto him,

[1] Mark viii. 27-9.
[2] Matt. xvi. 6.
[3] Luke ix. 20.
[4] Ps. 2. 7.
[5] Ps. 2. 2.

Blessed art thou, Simon bar Jonah, for flesh and blood hath not revealed this to thee, but my Father in heaven. And I say unto thee, *Thou art Peter* ("*rock*" in Greek; Aramaic *Kepha*), and the gates of hell shall not prevail against thee (the words "and on this rock I will build my Church" are absent in the early version of the Gospel used by Ephrem Syrus, a patristic writer of the fourth century); and I will give to thee the keys of the kingdom of heaven, and whatsoever thou shalt bind (forbid) on earth shall be bound in heaven, and whatsoever thou shalt loose (permit) on earth shall be loosed in heaven." [6]

Whereupon Simon bar Jonah was ever afterwards called "Kephas" (Aramaic for "stone"), or, in Greek, "Petros" (rock). All this is, however, lacking in Mark and Luke. The subsequent verses, where Jesus calls Peter "Satan," also contradict what is given in Matthew. But even in Mark's brief version there is a certain solemnity showing that apostolic circles retained the strong impression which the recognition of the messianic claims at Cæsarea Philippi made both upon Jesus and the disciples.

A great event clearly happened then. Jesus was deeply affected to find that, even in his present evil plight, his disciples had not despaired and that, despite their obtuseness, some of them recognized him as the Messiah. It may have been then that, in his happiness, Jesus uttered those wonderful words: "I thank thee, O Father, Lord of heaven and earth, that thou hast hidden these things from the wise and prudent and hast revealed them to babes (in understanding)." [7] The three Synoptics are, however, unanimous in recording that Jesus forbade his disciples to tell any one what they had learned: place and time were yet unsuitable.

They are also unanimous in saying that immediately after this episode Jesus began to teach his disciples that "the son of man must needs suffer many things," and that the elders and chief priests and scribes would reject him and that he should be killed and after three days rise again. [8]

And it is most probable that, immediately after his disciples' recognition of his messianic claims, he spoke of the sufferings which he must undergo. To deny this would make the whole history of Christianity incomprehensible. If, after the crucifixion, the disciples believed in a suffering Messiah, then Jesus must, while still alive, have spoken of such sufferings: (a) he had seen the fate of John the Baptist; (b) he was, at the time, persecuted and suffering in a foreign land; (c) the coming of the Messiah was impossible without "the pangs of the Messiah." It is true that the "pangs of the Messiah" are not, in the *Talmud,* explained as sufferings affecting the

---

[6] Matt. xvi. 17-19.
[7] Matt. xi. 25; Luke x. 21; see the saying of the early *Amora,* R. Yochanan: Since the Temple was destroyed prophecy was taken from the prophets and given to the foolish and to babes (*B. Bathra* 12b). Cf., Ed. Meyer, *op. cit.* I 280-91.
[8] Mark viii. 31; Matt. xvi. 21; Luke ix. 22.

Messiah himself, but as the sufferings of the messianic age: [9] but this "Son of man" who found himself persecuted by the Pharisees and Herodians and who did not expect to realize his claims by victorious warfare, must have begun to imagine that, before his victory, such sufferings must befall him, himself. And these sufferings must come about in Jerusalem. He says that "the elders and chief priests and scribes would reject him," and where were these except in Jerusalem? Therefore after Peter had confirmed Jesus' own belief and hope, Jesus announces that he would now go, as the Messiah, to Jerusalem.

No other place was better fitted for the Messiah's revelation, nor was any other time better fitted than the feast of Passover, the feast of the national Redemption (and, therefore, the feast of the Messiah), when tens and hundreds of thousands of people flocked to Jerusalem.

This Jesus certainly divulged to his disciples, *but no more than this*. To say that he told his disciples that "he should be killed and after three days rise again," is to go beyond the bounds of probability. Some Christian scholars hold that "after three days" signifies "after a short time," following the Scriptural verse. He shall revive us after two days, and on the third day he shall raise us up and we shall live before him.[10] But the Gospels nowhere quote such a passage in explanation of this "prophecy;" and, again, it would be a coincidence, amounting to a miracle, had he spoken of the death and revival after three days on the basis of Scripture, and then been actually killed and, after three days, been found, by his disciples, to have risen again.

Furthermore, as we shall see, Jesus feared the prospect of death; and if he foresaw this as early as Cæsarea Philippi and, in the intervening weeks or even months, had become accustomed to the prospect, why did such "human frailty" attack him suddenly? Or why were the disciples so alarmed at the crucifixion escaping in every direction? Mark felt the difficulty and points out that "they did not understand the matter (Jesus' death and resurrection) and feared to ask him."[11] Yet Jesus reverted to the subject several times afterwards, and how could they have forgotten it at the time of the arrest and crucifixion?

The whole idea of a Messiah who should be put to death was one which, in Jesus' time, was impossible of comprehension both to the Jews and to Jesus himself. Isaiah liii was then interpreted in its literal sense as referring to the nation of Israel and not to a human Messiah. "Messiah ben Joseph who should be put to death"[12] was a conception which, as the present writer has elsewhere shown,[13] came

[9] J. Klausner, *Die messianischen Vorstellungen*, pp. 46-49.
[10] Hosea vi. 2.
[11] Mark ix. 32.
[12] *Sukka* 52a.
[13] Klausner, *op. cit.* 86-103.

into being not till after Bar Kokhbah. We must, therefore, conclude that the words "and shall be killed and rise again after three days" (καὶ ἀποκτανθῆναι καὶ μετὰ τρεῖς ἡμέρας ἀναστῆναι) are a later addition by Jesus' disciples, who told or wrote his story after his shameful death was itself a convincing proof of his messianic claims; but for the conviction that Jesus *foresaw* his dreadful death, no Jewish disciples could have accepted a "crucified Messiah," a "curse of God that was hanged."

At Cæsarea Philippi, therefore, Jesus told his disciples that he was about to go to Jerusalem where he should suffer greatly but would, in the end, be victorious and be recognized by the crowds of people who had come to celebrate the Passover, as the Messiah. Simon Peter disliked this: he took Jesus aside and began to reprove him for thinking of such a procedure. If Jesus and his disciples had been so persecuted and had run such danger in Galilee, how could he dare to go to Jerusalem, the centre of civil and religious authority, where the danger which threatened them, simple Galilæans, was seven times greater!

But Jesus, totally wrapped up in his great idea, feared these beguiling persuasions of his favourite disciple, the more so because they were but reasonable; he forcibly turned away from him and, in the presence of the others, said: "Get thee behind me, Satan! For thou carest not for the things of God, but for the things of men." That is to say, Peter had more respect for ordinary things than for the great messianic destiny which God had in store for Jesus and his followers. He emphasizes to his disciples that they, too, must suffer because of him, but that to lose their life for his sake and the Gospel's was to save it, "for what shall it profit a man if he gain the whole world and lose his soul?"

The words recorded at this stage: "let him deny himself and take up his cross," [14] must be regarded as a later addition: crucifixion was not a Jewish mode of death, and Jesus, the Galilæan, could not have used such a figure of speech since Galilee did not then possess a Roman Procurator and Jewish legal processes were still in force there. Peter hinted to Jesus that in Jerusalem, the simple Galilæans —Jesus and his followers and disciples—would furnish a subject of derision to the Jerusalem city-folk. Jesus replies: "Whosoever shall be ashamed of me and of my words in this adulterous and sinful generation, the Son of man also shall be ashamed of him when he cometh in the glory of his Father with the holy angels."

And this coming of the Son of man is now no longer a thing of the distant future: "Verily I say unto you, that there be some here of them that stand by, which shall in no wise taste of death till they see the kingdom of God come with power." [15] Such is the consoling recompense for the sufferings which the disciples will be called upon

[14] Mark viii. 34.
[15] Mark viii. 33; ix. 1.

to endure for the Son of man's sake: he is now manifested to them as the Messiah himself, ranking with the holy angels, and bringing about the "end" in their days. And so long as even one of Jesus' generation survived, this mystic belief persisted in Christianity.

Conviction such as this stirred the ardour of the more intimate of his disciples. Jesus' vision, a supernatural vision, of a Messiah soon to come, brought visions to them also.

Peter, and James and John the sons of Zebedee, three enthusiasts, including the two "sons of thunder," saw Jesus in a new guise three days later when he went up with them to the summit of a high mountain (hardly Tabor, according to the groundless Christian tradition,[16] but Hermon, which is comparatively near to Cæsarea Philippi, and whose summit is covered with perpetual snow). He was transfigured before them and his garments became "glistering," exceeding white—like the snow which was on Hermon. As the Messiah he became for them very different from what he was as a Pharisaic "Rab" or "Galilæan itinerant."

In their daylight vision they seemed to see Moses and Elijah speaking with him. Peter's imagination led him to propose that they set up "three tabernacles," one for Jesus, one for Moses, and one for Elijah. Obviously, to the simple Galilæan Jew, Jesus was no more than the successor of Moses and Elijah: Moses was the great Lawgiver and greatest of the prophets, Elijah was the great wonderworker and the forerunner of the Messiah, and Jesus was the Messiah who was to come and promulgate the Law of Moses throughout the world by the aid of miracles, like to the deeds of Elijah. . . .

On this occasion, too, Jesus warns his three disciples that they tell no man what they had witnessed;[17] only in Jerusalem was his final revelation, in its entirety, to be made before the people. To the hesitation of the disciples—since before the Messiah could appear, Elijah, the forerunner, must first come—he replies that Elijah had already come, in the likeness of John the Baptist.[18]

All was ready, therefore, for the Messiah's revelation; but it must be done in Jerusalem, the Holy City, where the greatest publicity was possible, and not in an out-of-the-way corner such as Upper Galilee.

---

[16] See Dalman, *op. cit.* pp. 176-169, 176, who suggests that the high mountain is Tel Abu'l-Nada (1257 metres), or Tel Abu'l Hanzir, or Tel el-Ahmar (1238 metres), all of them near Cæsarea Philippi (*op. cit.* 176-179).
[17] Mark ix. 9.
[18] Mark ix. 11-13; Matt. xvii. 13.

III. THE JOURNEY TO JERUSALEM: AT JERICHO

Jesus and his disciples then began the journey to Jerusalem. From Cæsarea Philippi they went to Lower Galilee, either to allow the disciples to bid farewell to their kinsfolk or sell their possessions, or because the easiest route to Jerusalem was by way of Lower Galilee. Here again Mark states that Jesus did not wish to be made known to anyone.[1] They come to Capernaum for the last time, and there, as a good Jew, Jesus pays the half-shekel to the Temple fund. This was shortly before Passover, in the month Adar, and, according to the *Mishna*, "On the first of Adar they call for the shekels," "on the fifteenth of the month the money-changers (required owing to the various current coinages) dwelt in the town, and on the twenty-fifth, they took their place in the Temple."[2] It was, then, about the middle of the month Adar, when Palestine is at its best, when the rains are over and flowers are everywhere.

Jesus does not consider that he and his followers are bound to pay the half-shekel: the Messiah and his disciples are the sons of God and therefore need pay no taxes; but he does not wish, in his present plight, to arouse opposition ("to be a stumbling-block unto them"), and so, "for the sake of peace," he bids his disciples pay the tax.[3]

While in Capernaum he hears the Twelve disputing among themselves which of them shall be greatest in the kingdom of heaven? Whereupon Jesus takes a little child, embraces him and says, This child and whosoever is simple as a child and demeans himself as a child, the same shall be greatest in the kingdom of heaven. This is paralleled by the *Baraita:* "Little ones receive the presence of the Shekinah."[4] The greatest shall not be the ruler, as among the great ones of this world, but the one who is servant of all: the first shall be last.

And he reproves the disciples for striving after honour; if *they* are at fault on whom can he rely for the spreading of his teaching? Are not they now the salt of the earth? The purpose of salt is to preserve from decay, but if the salt itself lose its savour how can decay be stayed? So far be it from them to seek for honour.

[1] Mark ix. 30.
[2] *M. Shek.* I 1 and 3.
[3] Matt. xvii. 24-27.
[4] *Tractate Kallah Rabbati* §2 *Baraita* 8; cf. *Ekha R.* on *Wa-yetze mi-bath Tzion* (ed. Buber 70); *Midrash* Ps. 22, 32, ed. Buber 99 (and n. 164). Cf. also "See that ye despise not one of these little ones, for I say unto you that their angels in heaven see always the face of my Father in heaven" (Matt. xviii. 10).

Yet he promises them the greatest honour of all: "Verily I say unto you, Ye which have followed after me, in the new creation (παλιγγενεσία, "the new world" of the apocalyptic literature and the Hebrew *Midrashim*), when the Son of man shall sit on his throne of glory, ye too shall sit on twelve thrones judging the twelve tribes of Israel. And every man that hath forsaken houses and brethren and sisters and father and mother and wife and children and fields for my sake shall receive a hundred-fold (ἑκατονταπλασίονα λήψεται) and shall inherit eternal life." [5]

The ideal of Jesus is not, therefore, solely spiritual: it is a truly Jewish messianic ideal, material and worldly. This point we will touch upon later. In spite of Jesus' reproofs, the disciples continue to seek their own honour and glory: James and John, the sons of Zebedee, ask of him that, after he shall sit on "his throne of glory" as Son of man, he grant them to sit the one on his right hand and the other on his left. Matthew is ashamed to report this of the chief Apostles and records that it was their mother who asked this honour for her sons.[6]

But Jesus warns them that before he comes in his great glory he must drink the cup of affliction: are they also able to drink it? They say that they are able. Whereupon he continues: "To sit on my right hand and on my left is not mine to give, but it is for them for whom it hath been prepared of my Father." [7] Jesus does not look upon himself as all-powerful: the Jewish Messiah is also "a man of the sons of men" (such is the expression of Trypho the Jew in the *Dialogue* of Justin Martyr).[8] In the messianic age the true redeemer and the final power is God himself: the Messiah is but his most important medium.

According to Luke,[9] Jesus attempted to reach Jerusalem by way of Samaria (what the *Talmud* describes as the "interrupting strip of the Cuthites").[10] The Pharisees, who still considered him a Pharisaic "Rab," warned him [11] against Herod Antipas, but he no longer fears "that fox," [12] since he is merely passing through his territory and would soon have left it. He determines to go by way of Samaria, which was no longer in the possession of Herod but under the Roman Procurator who controlled it after Archelaus was sent in exile.

Since the Samaritans were enemies of the Jews it was doubtful whether they would permit a large company of Galilæans to pass through them, therefore Jesus despatched the bolder James and John

---

[5] Matt. xix. 28-29.
[6] Matt. xx. 20.
[7] So Matt. xx. 23.
[8] *Dialogus cum Tryphone Judæo*, beginning of §49.
[9] Luke ix. 51-3.
[10] *Hagiga 25a*; cf. J. *Hagiga* III 4; *Ekha R.* on "*Gadar ba'adi*"; *Scholion* to *Meg. Taanith* III.
[11] Luke xiii. 31-3.
[12] Luke xiii. 32.

to find whether the route were passable. But the Samaritans would not allow them to pass through and Jesus and his disciples went "unto the borders of Judæa beyond Jordan," [13] i.e., east through the Jordan Valley. This valley is referred to in the *Mishna* in conjunction with "Upper Galilee" and "Lower Galilee," and the "mountain and plain" in Judæa. [14] The party would pass through the forests near the Jordan, the Arabic "Zur," known as "The Pride of the Jordan" because of the luxurious growth of white poplars, tamarisks, large castors, liquorice and mallow trees. [15]

Here was no danger: the district was but sparsely populated owing to the heat prevalent during nine months in the year. People from the neighbouring towns and villages came to see this "wonderworker." They brought children with them that they might be blessed by the Saint, but the disciples rebuked those who brought the children: the Messiah must not be troubled. Jesus, however, was indignant: "Suffer little children to come unto me and forbid them not, for of such is the kingdom of God. Verily I say unto you: Whosoever shall not receive the kingdom of God as a little child, he shall in no wise enter therein. And he took them in his arms and blessed them." [16]

Here is a further characteristic, both attractive and significant, to be added to what has already been told about "the greatest in the kingdom of heaven." [17] Similarly in the *Talmud* we find: "Touch not my Messiahs" [18]—i.e. my anointed ones, the children at school. [19] We have already referred to a similar *Baraita*, "Children receive the presence of the Shekinah." [20]

As Jesus drew nearer to Jerusalem the nervousness, already remarked in Peter, became greater among the disciples; according to Mark: "And it came to pass when they were in the way, going up to Jerusalem, and Jesus was going before them, they were amazed; and they that followed were afraid." [21] They were afraid of the great city with its Roman and Jewish authorities, its Scribes, and its aristocratic priests. But Jesus encouraged them and led the way: the great day of his public manifestation as Messiah before the myriads of pilgrims, was drawing nearer and nearer.

Jesus crossed the Jordan and came to Jericho where a large crowd gathered. Luke [22] has preserved an account of the wealthy Zacchæus, the chief tax-gatherer (ἀρχιτελώνης). He was a man of short stature

---

[13] Mark x. 1.
[14] *Shebiith*, IX 2.
[15] Dalman, *op. cit.* 76-77.
[16] Mark x. 13-16; Matt. xix. 13-15; Luke xviii. 15-17.
[17] See above, p. 304.
[18] Ps. cv. 15; I Chron. xvi. 22.
[19] *Shabb.* 119b.
[20] *Tractate Kallah Rabbati* §2 *Baraita* 8.
[21] Mark x. 32.
[22] Luke xix, 1-10.

and in order to see Jesus climbed up a sycamore tree. Jesus recognized him (and therefore must have known him previously) and asked to be allowed to spend the night at his house (most probably because he hoped to be out of danger as the guest of such a rich and important person). The onlookers were indignant that Jesus should choose to be the guest of a sinner (as was every tax-gatherer). Whereupon Zacchæus vowed repentance and that he would give the half of his wealth to the poor and restore fourfold what he had wrongly exacted. Jesus rejoiced, declaring "that he, the tax-gatherer, was also a son of Abraham."

Characteristic and outstanding though this story is, it is lacking in Mark and Matthew. On the other hand, all three Synoptists [23] record an episode which serves, in a way, as an introduction to the revelation of the Messiah. On the road from Jericho to Jerusalem, Bartimæus υἰὸς Τιμαίου, or, in Hebrew, בן טימי), a blind beggar who had been told that "Jesus of Nazareth" was passing (such is the story as told in Mark and Luke, but in Matthew "Jesus of Nazareth" is lacking, and there are two beggars, not one), cried out: "Jesus, Son of David, have mercy on me!" This is the first occasion that Jesus is hailed by the title "Son of David," the most customary title of the Messiah.[24] Many of Jesus' circle would have silenced him, for Jesus was not yet publicly manifested as the Messiah, and excepting the disciples, all still regarded him as a Pharisaic "Rab" or, at most, a prophet. But the blind man persisted in crying out, "Son of David, have mercy on me!"

Jesus, however, approved: this was the prelude to his manifestation. Therefore he calls the blind man to him and comforts him; and this, with the Evangelists, was changed into a miracle: Jesus healed the man of his blindness. What, however, we may infer from the story is, that Jesus, having prepared himself to declare himself in Jerusalem publicly as the Messiah, saw in the blind beggar the forerunner of the coming revelation.

[23] Mark x. 46-52; Matt. xx. 29-34; Luke xviii. 35-43.
[24] J. Klausner, *Die Messianischen Vorstellungen*, p. 67; see also pp. 39-44.

IV. IN BETHPHAGE: JESUS REVEALS HIMSELF
PUBLICLY AS MESSIAH

Five days before Passover, on the second day of a week of which the sixth day was the eve of Passover as well as of Sabbath, Jesus and the Twelve drew near to Jerusalem. He reached the outermost quarter of Jerusalem, Bethphage, often referred to in the *Talmud* in the expression "Outside the wall of Bethphage," meaning entirely outside of Jerusalem.[1] Some suppose that Bethphage is the modern "Et-Tur" on the top of the Mount of Olives, wrongly called "Tur Malka" by the Jews.[2] More probably it is the extreme district of the city itself which could only doubtfully be included within the bounds of Jerusalem.[3] "Bethphage" is generally translated "House of Figs," from the verse התאנה חנטה פגיה, "the fig-tree hath ripened her figs,"[4] and the *Mishna* passage פגה בוחל, וצמל,[5] three names of the fig in its various degrees of maturity; פגה indicates an unripe fig as opposed to the בוחל, which is a fig already filled with juice but not quite ripe, and as opposed to the צמל which has become too ripe; there is the further distinction of the בכורה, the firstfruits of which are ready in June, and the תאנה, which ripens in August, and the פגה, the fig as it first appears on the tree. Since, however, the word is almost always written with an aleph (בית פאגי and not פגי) Dalman holds that פאגי is not connected with פגה,[6] but is the Latin *pagus*, a district; hence Bethphage would mean "house of the district," i.e. the boundary house of Jerusalem.[7] Yet despite the occurrence of פגן in the *Midrash*, we never find, in the entire *Talmudic* and *Midrashic* literature, the word פאגום or פאני in the suggested sense. It is preferable, therefore, to follow the older explanation that "Bethphage" means "the house of figs," a place where the פגים, unripe figs (or, perhaps, "wild figs") were plentiful.

[1] *Menahoth* XI 2; 78b; *Pesahim* 63b, 91a; *Baba Metzia* 90a; *Sanh.* 14b; *Sota* 45a; *T. Menahoth* VIII 18; *T. Pesahim* VIII 8; *Sifre* to Numbers, 151 (ed. Friedmann 55a); *Sifre Zutta*, "Naso" §17, ed. Horowitz, p. 245. See also S. Klein in Schwartz' *Jubilee Volume*, Vienna, 1917, p. 396 n. 2.
[2] See A. Neubauer, *La Géographie du Talmud*, Paris, 1868, p. 149.
[3] Against Neubauer see Dalman, *op. cit.* pp. 215-217; against his view that Bethphage was outside the wall, see *Baba Metzia* 99a ("within the wall of Bethphage"); *T. Menahoth* VIII 18, and *Sifre Zutta*, l.c.
[4] Song of Songs, ii. 13.
[5] *Nidda* V 7.
[6] Plural פניה, פנים in the Old Testament and פנים in the *Mishnah* (*Shebiith* VII 4).
[7] Dalman, *op. cit.* 217.

It may be that this name induced the Evangelists (or their sources, the disciples of Jesus) to recount here the miracle of the withered fig-tree.[8] Near Bethphage was the village of Bethany (Beth-Aniya or Beth-Th'ena), the present El'azariya (in memory of the miracle of the raising of Lazarus [Eliezer]). In spite of the dissension of Dalman[9] and Klein[10] (in whose opinion Bethany is Beth-Th'ena, while the Beth-Hine of *T. Shebüith* VII 14, *Erubin* 28b, *Pesahim* 53a is apparently near 'Anin, east of Cæsarea) it is probable that Βηθανία is "Beth-Hini" or "Bethoani" (Beth-Aniya), "Beth-Anya," mentioned in the *Talmud* precisely in a place where reference is also made to "ripe and unripe figs."[11] In any case it is difficult to agree with the view that the "booths of the House of Annas" is the Beth-Anya of the Gospels, though "The booths of the house of Hino" once occurs for "The Booths of the house of Annas."[12]

However this may be, Jesus and his disciples stopped at Bethphage; two of them were sent to a village in front to procure an ass's colt on which no man had yet ridden, such as was befitting the Messiah (for "on his throne no stranger shall sit"; and the "red heifer" must also be such as had not borne the yoke).

The point is clear: Jesus was minded to enter Jerusalem as the Messiah. The poor, persecuted Galilæan "Rab" could not enter the Holy City, which was ruled over by strangers, in the capacity of conquerer; he chooses, therefore, to enter it "poor and riding on an ass," thereby fulfilling the Scripture:[13]

"Rejoice greatly, O daughter of Zion: Shout, O daughter of Jerusalem:
Behold thy king cometh unto thee: He is just and having salvation:
Lowly and riding upon an ass: and upon a colt, the foal of an ass."

The verse is quite in accord with Jesus' mental and social condition: he had come to Jerusalem as the King-Messiah, and he was a *Tzaddiq*, a "just one," for he did not preach war and conquest but repentance and good works; and he "had salvation"—from his persecutors in Galilee; and he was "poor" (meek), to all appearances a simple Galilæan. Hence he did not, like a hero and man of war, ride upon a horse, but "upon an ass, and upon a colt, the foal of an ass."

On the colt being brought, Jesus' many followers used their garments in place of a saddle (as did the officers of Jehu when they

[8] See above, pp. 268 ff.
[9] *Op. cit.* 214 n. 4.
[10] In Schwartz' *Jubilee Volume*, p. 296 n. 2 and p. 398.
[11] *Hulin* 53a; *Pesahim* 53a; *Erubin* 28b; *T. Shebüith* VII 14. For the variants see *Arukh ha-Shalem* II 70-71 *s.v.* "Bethoane," "Beth Aniya"; cf. also *J. Ma'aseroth* IV 6; Derenbourg, *op. cit.* pp. 244-246; Klein, *M.G.W.J.* 1910, 18-22; *J.Q.R.* New series, II 545.
[12] *Baba Metzia* 88a (where also fig-trees have previously been referred to); *J. Peah* I 6; *Sifre* to Deut. 105 (ed. Friedmann 95b). See also Dalman, *op. cit.* 214. n. 4, and on the point as a whole pp. 211-214.
[13] Zech. ix. 9.

made him king of Israel).[14] Surrounded by his disciples and followers and the many onlookers, Jesus mounted upon the ass. As they went, they spread garments before him, as before kings, and many cut down branches of trees (or green grass) and spread them on the path, and cried before him: "Hosanna! Blessed is he that cometh in the name of the Lord! Hosanna in the highest!" (The last two words are quoted by Jerome from the Gospel to the Hebrews in the form "*Osanna barrama*," Heb. הושענא ברמה.) According to Mark they also cried: "Blessed be the kingdom of David our father;"[15] not "David *his* father" but "David *our* father" (*i.e.*, the father of the children of Israel)—the kingdom of the Messiah.

According to Matthew, they cried: "Hosanna to the Son of David."[16] Thus the populace, like the beggar on the way from Jericho, looked upon him as the Messianic king. We shall soon see that not all the people, nor even the majority, regarded Jesus as the son of David, and, what is more, even Jesus did not consider it essential that the Messiah should be of the house of David.

According to Matthew: "When he entered Jerusalem all the city was stirred, saying, Who is this? And the multitudes said, This is the prophet, Jesus, from Nazareth of Galilee."[17] Therefore, for most of the crowd he was neither the Messiah nor the son of David, but only a Galilæan prophet. But attention was drawn to Jesus. Owing to the fact that at the Feast of Tabernacles the Jews used to call out "Hosanna!" when they beat with the willow-boughs and took up the palm-branches (at certain stages of the popular ceremonies which mark the festival), the author of the Fourth Gospel[18] adds the further detail that the people met Jesus with palm-branches. Hence the widespread Christian custom, on the Sunday before Easter, of carrying palm-branches in warmer countries and, in colder countries (where no palms are to be found), willows—though this Jewish custom belongs not to Passover but to Tabernacles. However this may be, this Monday before Passover was a great event in the life of Jesus: there occurred near Jerusalem, almost at its gates, something which compelled attention. Before crowds of people, at the gates of the Holy City, Jerusalem, Jesus publicly revealed himself as the Messiah. All was now in readiness for proclaiming his Messiahship within Jerusalem itself.

[14] 2 Kings ix. 13.
[15] Mark xi. 10.
[16] Matt. xxi. 9.
[17] Matt. xxi. 10-11.
[18] John xii. 13.

SIXTH BOOK

JESUS IN JERUSALEM

I. THE CLEANSING OF THE TEMPLE

Jesus, at last, entered Jerusalem itself—probably after midday. Luke tells us that when Jesus "drew near and beheld the city he wept over it" and over the bitter fate that was to befall it.[1] This was certainly not his first visit to Jerusalem. Although the religious duty, "three times a year shall every male appear [in Jerusalem]," [2] was not scrupulously observed, it is difficult to suppose that so orthodox a Galilæan as Jesus had not once fulfilled the duty before he was thirty years of age. Yet notwithstanding what is recorded to the contrary in Luke and the Fourth Gospel, Jesus had never before visited Jerusalem with any degree of display, or surrounded by disciples and followers. It may well be that the wonderful vision of the Holy City, beloved by every Jew, as it suddenly appeared to his sight among the surrounding, imposing mountains, brought tears to his eyes.

He went at once to the Temple. This was the first duty of every Jew, from no matter what country, when he came to the Feast of the Passover; we have a parallel in the visit to the "Wailing Wall" at the present day. He watched what went on in the Temple, and he did this, as we shall shortly see, in no spirit of mere curiosity. "When evening drew nigh he went with the Twelve to Bethany." [3] He felt that both he and his disciples would incur danger by spending the night in Jerusalem. He was aware that he had many enemies and that it was perilous for one who had quarrelled with the Pharisees and proclaimed himself Messiah to stay for the night in a great city like Jerusalem, the centre of Roman and Jewish authority; therefore throughout his visit, and until the "Last Supper," he followed the programme of his first day: "every day he was teaching in the Temple; and every night he went out and lodged in the mount that is called the Mount of Olives." [4]

According to Matthew and Mark he stayed in Bethany at the house of Simon the Leper. It is somewhat strange that Jesus should

[1] Luke xix. 41-44.
[2] Ex. xxiii. 17; Deut. xvi. 16. Cf. *Hagiga* I 1.
[3] Mark xi. 11.
[4] Luke xxi. 37; this supports Neubauer's theory that "Beth-Anya" was on the Mount of Olives, though Luke's account may not be absolutely exact.

sit at the same table as a leper, and that a leper should live in an inhabited village like Bethany, and not "without the camp." H. P. Chajes [5] may be correct in surmising that the original Hebrew Gospel spoke of שמעון הצנוע , "Simon the Lowly" (perhaps an Essene), and that this was turned into שמעון הצרוע , "Simon the Leper." While Jesus sat at meat, there came in a woman bearing a cruse of spikenard (.or, perhaps, rose-water, assuming an original מי ורדים or שמן ורד in Hebrew instead of מי נרדים), pure and precious; this she poured over his head. Those sitting by were indignant and rebuked the woman: the valuable scent was worth three hundred dinars which might have been distributed among the poor; but Jesus said, "Suffer her to do so! she hath wrought a good work on me; for ye have the poor always with you and whensoever ye will ye can do them good: but me ye have not always" (the words, "she hath anointed my body aforehand for the burying," must be a later addition, since they do not fit in well with the reference to the poor).

The messianic king must be "anointed"(משוח) in fact. Besides, Jesus was, after all, a Jew, and did not always abstain from the world and its joys. Already we have seen him oppose fasting since he regarded himself as the bridegroom and his followers as the "children of the bridechamber." [6]

Luke, who omits this episode, tells another story of a woman. When Jesus was at meat in the house of "Simon the Pharisee" (here no mention is made of the "leper"—the original "Simon the Essene" is become a Pharisee. since neither the *Talmud* nor the Gospels mention the Essenes as a special sect), a "woman that was a sinner," *i.e.*, a harlot, came and anointed his feet with myrrh, moistened his feet with her tears, dried them with her hair and kissed them. And Jesus told her that her many sins were forgiven "because she loved much" [7] —a story of moving pathos and precious beauty. Yet the uncourteous remarks of Jesus to his host, Simon,[8] lead us to suppose that we have here only a parable that has been converted into an actual event.

The night before the third day of the week was spent in Bethany, and on the third day they went to Jerusalem, where Jesus did a great deed, the greatest *public* deed which he performed during his lifetime. When he determined to manifest himself as the Messiah he must have had some plan of action. There is no reason to suppose that, like contemporary false Messiahs, he wished to arouse a revolt against Rome. Had such been the case he would have met the same fate as they, and with his execution by the Romans his ideal would have perished. Yet we cannot suppose that he expected to be recognized as Messiah without achieving something great. Most Christian scholars conclude that Jesus deliberately went up to Jerusalem to die, and that this premeditated death was "his greatest work."

[5] *Markus-Studien*, pp. 74-5.
[6] P. 274.
[7] Luke vii. 36-59.
[8] Luke vii. 44-46.

This, however, is quite improbable. His prayer in Gethsemane and the behaviour of his disciples at his arrest and crucifixion are proof positive that the calamity was not expected. What form, then, did Jesus imagine that popular recognition of his claims would take, and how was the kingdom of heaven to be realized through him?

There is but one answer to this fundamental problem. In Jerusalem, the greatest and most holy city of his people, and at the feast of Passover, the "Day of Redemption," "the Salvation of the soul" (see the "Blessing of R. Akiba," *Pesahim* X 6), when Jewish pilgrims from all the corners of the earth flocked to Jerusalem—there and then Jesus would proclaim his call to repentance and good works, announcing that the Messiah was come . . . and that *he* was the Messiah, and that the forerunner, Elijah, had already come in the person of John the Baptist. His words were to produce the requisite effect: all people would repent. Then would come difficult times, the days of "the pangs of the Messiah," which would befall Messiah and people alike. But God would bring to pass signs and wonders: Rome would be overthrown "and that without hands," [9] by help from on high; and Jesus should be the "Son of man," "the Son of man coming with the clouds of heaven," who was to sit on the right hand of God, and, with his twelve disciples, judge the twelve tribes of Israel.

With our Western, twentieth-century education it is hard for us to grasp and believe in such an idea; but for Jesus, a son of the Orient, nineteen hundred years ago, for Jesus the visionary and steadfast believer in God, the idea was no more impossible of belief than it was for the author of the Book of Daniel or the *Book of Enoch.*

Still, to bring men to repentance, to draw all eyes to the Messiah and to the kingdom of heaven, which was bound up with the manifestation of the Messiah, Jesus must achieve some great deed, some great *public* deed, performed with the utmost display and gaining the utmost renown. It must be a public-religious deed; it might not be a political action since Jesus was neither willing nor competent to declare war against Rome: he had seen the fate of John the Baptist and the end of the many political rebels. And what public-religious deed could better secure publicity than some great deed in the Temple, the most sacred of places, which now, in the days immediately before the Passover, was crammed with Jews from every part of the world?

Jesus resolves, therefore, to purify the Temple. There were things which called for such purifying. Besides the "Holy of Holies," only the inner courts into which none but the priests and Levites might enter, were actually "holy;" the outer courts, the halls and chambers and galleries, were accessible to all Jews. So orthodox a Christian scholar as Dalman is forced to admit that "there is nowhere any mention that the priests trafficked with sacrificial ani-

[9] Dan. ii. 34; IV *Esdras* xiii. 2-13. See Klausner, *Ha-Ra'yon ha-Meshihi b'Yisrael,* Pt. II (Jerusalem, 1921), p. 65.

mals." [10]   The solemn warnings against entering even the "Temple-Mount with sticks or bags or dusty feet" and against spitting there,[11] to which the *Tosefta* adds a warning against entering "with coins tied up in handkerchiefs" [12] (the Jerusalem *Talmud* says "our Rabbis took off their shoes under the outer gate of the Temple-Mount")[13] —all this excludes any idea that the Pharisees permitted any trafficking in animals or money-changing in the Temple or even in the outer courts (since, according to the *Tosefta*, it was forbidden to bring money even within the Temple-Mount).

The fact is that, according to the *Talmud*,[14] the booths for the sale of pigeons and doves were not in the Temple at all, but in "the hill of anointing," *i.e.*, the Mount of Olives.[15] But in Jesus' time the Saducee-Bœthuseans controlled the Temple, and they may not have treated the outer court as too holy to permit of the sale of doves and pigeons or of money-changing for the purchase of seals for the various Temple offerings;[16] and such may have been allowed in the Herodian basilica to the south of the outer court, the site of the present Mosque el-Aksa.

The price of doves varied from time to time as is apparent from a passage in the *Mishna* [17] describing how Rabban Shimeon ben Gamaliel, soon after the time of Jesus, protested against the dearness of the *kinim* (bird offerings).   The Romans allowed only small copper coins to be minted in Palestine and the silver and gold coins of the time were stamped with the figure of the Emperor, making their use impossible in the Temple; and Jewish pilgrims from foreign parts brought all manner of coinage. For these two reasons, money-changers were necessary near the Temple. It was inevitable. Even to this day there are Jews who sell "Aliyoth" (the privilege of reading the blessings before and after the reading of the Law or the Prophets in the synagogues), and Christians who sell candles in their churches; though such behaviour arouses indignation in the truly devout.

The people of Jerusalem must have accustomed themselves to the Temple trading: townsfolk do not, as a rule, excite themselves over such matters. But for those coming from outlying towns and villages it was a subject for indignation: and Jesus, above all, was provoked to anger. He recalled Jeremiah's bitter reproach: "Is this

[10] Dalman, *op. cit.* 236-7.
[11] *Berachoth* IX 5.
[12] *T. Ber.* VII 19.
[13] *J. Pes.* VII 11 (35*b*).
[14] *J. Taan.* IV 8.
[15] Derenbourg, *op. cit.* II 244-6, n. 8, suggests that these are the "booths of the house of Annas" mentioned previously (p. 309). He supposes that it was the bridge over the Kidron which connected the Temple with the Mount of Anointing which was considered within the Temple bounds, since the Red Heifer was burnt there (*Para* III 6; *Midd.* II 4); there were "four booths of dealers in *Taharoth*"—pigeons and doves (*J. Taan.* IV 8).
[16] Dalman, *op. cit., l.c.*
[17] *Kerithoth* I 7.

house, which is called by my name, become a den of robbers in your eyes?" [18]

On the third day, in the morning, Jesus and his disciples and many followers, came to Jerusalem; they entered the Temple and there Jesus, with the help of his followers and some of the people, drove out the traders from the Temple-Mount, threw down the tables of the money-changers (from these "tables" comes the *Talmudic* שלחני and the Greek τραπεζίτης, as the title of the money-changers), and the seats of those who sold doves, and "suffered no man to carry any vessel through the Temple." [19]

In other words, he forbade what the *Mishna* also forbade: "they may not make it (the Temple) a short-cut." [20] Here, too, and here most of all, do we miss Jesus "the gentle," "the meek," which Christianity has endeavoured to portray. What Jesus does he does by sheer force; the Fourth Gospel records that, on this occasion, he wielded a "scourge of cords." [21] In contradiction to his familiar law [22] which Tolstoy made the foundation of his teaching, Jesus "resisted evil" in active and violent fashion. He taught the people that hitherto the Temple had suffered profanation: "Is it not written, My house shall be called the house of prayer for all people? but ye have made it a den of thieves." [23]

Both the act and the sentiment gained the approbation of the people; but the priests were enraged. The Levitic "porters," the Temple attendants under the charge of the "Segens" (lieutenants) headed by the "Segen" of the Priests (an official who ranked close to the High Priest) [24]—these dared offer no resistance owing to the crowd present; even the Roman garrison stationed in the "Baris," the Tower of Antonius (or rather in the Palace of Herod, the tower of Phasael), was unable to interfere. The struggle lasted but a few minutes. There must have been many such outbursts in the stormy days preceding the annual celebration of Passover: with the myriads of pilgrims it was impossible to avoid quarrels and even acts of violence; we can well understand why the Roman Procurator used to come up from Cæsarea to Jerusalem especially to be present for the feast of the Passover.

The act of Jesus drew popular notice and also the notice of the priests and the Scribes. They could not, however, examine into the matter until evening. But Jesus again, as was his custom, "went forth out of the city" [25]—presumably to Bethany—out of reach of those

[18] Jer. vii. 11.
[19] Mark xi. 15-16.
[20] *Berachoth* IX 8; *T. Berachoth* VII 19 (ed. Zuckermandel, p. 17, n. to line 2).
[21] John ii. 15.
[22] Matt. v. 39.
[23] Mark xi. 17.
[24] For details, see Schürer, *op. cit.* II⁴, 320-322, 328-331.
[25] Mark xi. 19.

in authority. Jesus and his disciples were satisfied with what they had accomplished in, or near, the Temple: they had aroused popular indignation against their leaders, they had won popular approval and created an impression.

II. THE DISPUTES IN THE TEMPLE-COURT

The next day Jesus and his disciples returned to Jerusalem and, as usual, entered the Temple. The "chief priests" (*i.e.*, the "Segens," or those "on duty") and scribes and elders turned and asked him; by what authority he had so acted on the previous day. Jesus answered: By the same authority with which John the Baptist acted, viz. the authority of the people who followed him. Then, in a parable closely modelled on Isaiah's, "I will sing to my beloved a song of my love touching his vineyard"[1] (which served as a common model for the parables of the Pharisees), Jesus explained that, as Messiah, what he did he did by right, and that it was forbidden to kill him.

Such is the main point of the parable which the Evangelists have modified in their own fashion: otherwise there would be no point in the two verses which follow.[2] Jesus goes on to explain: as for your marvelling that the Messiah should come in the person of a simple Galilæan carpenter-builder, "have ye not read in the Scriptures: The stone which the *builders* refused is become the headstone in the corner; this was from the Lord and it is marvellous in our eyes."[3]

Priests and scribes were indignant at the parable and at the importance which the Galilæan carpenter was attributing to himself. They were minded to arrest him, but, fearing the people, left him alone and went their way. His remarks left it clear that he had set himself up to be the Messiah. If so—he was Israel's saviour from slavery to the Romans and "Edomites." This was a matter affecting not only the Pharisees, but the "Herodians," whom we saw, on an earlier occasion, combining with the Pharisees where their authority was affected.

Since they might not take hold of him and arrest him, the two parties endeavoured, at least, to "take hold of him" in his speech (ἵνα αὐτὸν ἀγρεύσωσι λόγῳ), and so damage his popularity or have him destroyed as a rebel and conspirator. The mass of people thirsted for redemption, for freedom from the bonds of the Roman Emperor. If Jesus was the Messiah he must needs be the enemy of the Emperor. So they turn to him quietly, respecting his *amour propre*. So far he had proved that he feared nothing, neither the Temple authorities when he drove out the money-changers and the traffickers, nor the most honoured of the nation when he attacked

[1] Isa. v. 1-7.
[2] Cf. Mark xii. 1-11.
[3] Mark xii. 1-10; cf. Ps. cxviii. 21-22.

the Scribes and Pharisees; therefore let him now declare, without any fear or respect of persons, whether they should pay tribute to Cæsar.

Jesus saw that it would be dangerous to say that tribute should not be paid: he would have been promptly arrested as a rebel. He asks them to bring him a dinar. The dinar was a Roman silver coin, stamped with the figure of Cæsar and inscribed with Latin characters telling the name of the Emperor.

Jesus asks: "Whose image and superscription are these?"

They answer: "Cæsar's."

So Jesus replies: "Give unto Cæsar the things which are Cæsar's, and unto God the things which are God's."

It was a clever rejoinder: he did not oppose the payment of tribute and so was no rebel against the Government; and he distinguished "the things which are Cæsar's" from "the things which are God's," thereby hinting that, for him, the foreign Emperor was the antithesis of God.

But the answer convinced the people that Jesus was not thei· redeemer, and that he was not come to free them from the Roman · Edomite yoke. He thus lost some of his popularity. All that the Gospels say is that his examiners "were amazed at him." [4] Yet when we notice that the people *supported* him when he entered Jerusalem as the Messiah and purified the Temple, but did nothing to save him three days later when he was crucified—the change is hard to explain unless we assume that his answer about the tribute money proved to the people that not from this Galilæan Messiah could they hope for national freedom and political redemption.

Thus in Jerusalem, too, the position of Jesus grew worse: the majority of the people were against him, the Pharisees opposed him and the Herodians were his enemies. Only the Sadducees remained: an enemy of the Pharisees might be their friend. The messianic belief was, with Jesus as well as the Pharisees, bound up with the belief in the resurrection from the dead, which the Sadducees denied. The Sadducees turn, therefore, to Jesus with the riddle (which seems to have been a commonplace at the time and intended as a gibe against the Pharisees): "If a man die without children, his eldest brother must marry the widow. Now a man died who had seven brothers. The eldest surviving brother first married the widow, but he died without issue; then the next brother married her and he, too, died childless. The same happened to the third and to all the other brothers. When all the brothers come to life again at the resurrection of the dead, whose wife will she be? One must admit in answer that the resurrection of the dead is mere imagination." Jesus, however, gives the Sadducees the answer which any Pharisee would have given: "Men, when they rise from the dead, neither marry nor are given

[4] Mark xii. 17; Matt. xxii. 22; Luke xx. 25.

in marriage, but are as the angels of God." [5]   We find the same view in the *Talmud*: "The world to come consists not in eating and drinking, but the righteous sit with crowns on their heads and enjoy the brightness of the Shekinah," [6] "like the ministering angels." [7] And Jesus continues with a most typical Pharisaic exposition: "God spake to Moses from the bush, saying, I am the God of Abraham and the God of Isaac and the God of Jacob: God is not the God of the dead but the God of the living; therefore there must be a resurrection of the dead in the world to come by which resurrection Abraham, Isaac and Jacob shall come to life." [8]

The *Talmud* is full of this type of Scriptural support, and we find one *Tanna*, with almost the same "exposition," proving that the resurrection of the dead is taught in the Law: "It is written, 'And I also kept my covenant with them (Abraham, Isaac and Jacob) to give them the land of Canaan;' " [9] it says not "to you" but "to them;" therefore we must deduce the resurrection of the dead from the Law [10] —i.e. Abraham, Isaac and Jacob shall come to life again and to them shall be given the land of Canaan in the world to come.

How far, even to the last, Jesus remained a true Pharisaic Jew is to be seen from another episode.   When one of the Scribes put the question, "Which is the first of all the commandments?"   Jesus answered, "Hear, O Israel, the Lord our God, the Lord, is one, and thou shalt love the Lord thy God with all thy heart and with all thy soul and with all thy might:" that is the first commandment, and the second is like unto it, namely, "Thou shalt love thy neighbour as thyself."   The Scribe supports Jesus: "Rabbi, thou hast well said, for God is one and there is none beside him, and to love him with all the heart ("and with all the mind" is an addition not in the Old Testament) and with all the strength, and to love his neighbour as himself, is much more than all whole burnt offerings and sacrifices."   And Jesus turns to him with the remark, "Thou art not far from the kingdom of God." [11]

Jesus is thus still a Pharisee, and he finds himself in agreement with a Scribe.   Still more, the answer of Jesus is so like that of Hillel to would-be proselytes that it is difficult to suppose that only once and only casually did Jesus speak well of the Pharisees.   The fact is that Jesus, more than once, stood on the side of the Pharisees, but the Evangelists (who flourished during the struggle between Christianity and Pharisaic Judaism) only preserved isolated passages in favour of the Pharisees, and (according to Chwolsohn) often

---

[5] Mark xii. 25.
[6] *Berachoth* 17a; *Kallah Rabbati* II.
[7] This addition is found in *Aboth d'R. Nathan*, I 8 (ed. Schechter, vers. I end of p. 3a).
[8] Mark xii. 26-7.
[9] Ex. vi. 4.
[10] *Sanh.* 90b.
[11] Mark xii. 28-34.

changed "Scribes and Sadducees" to "Scribes and Pharisees," because, by the time of writing, the Sadducees were no longer important.

The Gospels preserve yet another typical Pharisaic exposition given by Jesus during his visit to Jerusalem—an exposition which has a great value.

Jesus had already declared himself Messiah. But the Messiah was to be the *Son of David*, whereas Jesus was a Galilæan and the son of Joseph the carpenter! How could he be Messiah?

To evade this serious difficulty Jesus must find a passage of Scripture according to which the Messiah need not necessarily be the Son of David; and like an expert Pharisee he finds it. In the Psalter is "A Psalm of David" which Jesus, like every Jew of the time, accepted without question as written by David and referring to the Messiah. The Psalm runs: "The Lord said unto my Lord, Sit on my right hand until I make thine enemies thy footstool." Jesus asks: If David himself calleth him (the Messiah) "Lord," how then can he be his son?[12] The Messiah need not, therefore, be the son of David, and may be the son of Joseph the Galilæan, from the out-of-the-way village of Nazareth.

That the Pharisees admitted the principle that the Messiah need *not* be the son of David only (though "Son of David" has come to be the regular title of the Messiah in the *Talmud*) is obvious from the fact that Bar Kokhbah was accepted as Messiah by R. Akiba, in spite of the fact that it is nowhere claimed for Bar Kokhbah that he was of the house of David. What, however, arouses surprise is that, while Mark quotes the exposition as proof that Jesus need not be of the house of David, Matthew and Luke also quote it,[13] although they adduce the genealogy of Jesus, tracing his descent from the house of David through his father Joseph, who was not his father at all, since, according to them, he was born of the Holy Spirit. Thus naïve were the ancients with their traditions. Modern students can hardly trust to their writings for the same accuracy and consistency called for in modern historical writings.

Although in all these disputes Jesus had argued wholly like a Pharisee he now turns and attacks the Pharisees in the strongest fashion. This fact in itself is not a cause for surprise. When a man comes to attack others of his own nation he invariably does so in the most violent terms: "Ah! sinful nation, a people laden with

---

[12] Mark xii. 35-37. The *Midrash* (*Tanhuma*, Ps. 18, end of 29, ed. Buber, p. 79) also gives a messianic interpretation of Ps. cx.: "In the time to come God will seat the King-Messiah on his right hand, as it is written, The Lord said to my Lord, Sit on my right hand (Ps. cx. 1); and Abraham on his left hand. And the face of Abraham darkened and he said, Shall one of my progeny sit on the right hand and I on the left? But God comforted him, saying, Thy progeny will be on my right hand, and I will be on thy right hand (so to speak), as it is written 'The Lord on thy right hand'" (Ps. cx. 5).

[13] Matt. xxii. 41-47; Luke xx. 41-44.

iniquity, a seed of evil-doers, children that deal corruptly, they have forsaken the Lord, they have despised the Holy One of Israel"—thus does Isaiah (i. 4) harangue the whole nation because part of them have done wrong. Similarly, when a member of a sect finds fault with others of his sect his abuse knows no limit and he is looked upon by the rest as the worst enemy of the sect. And such men, however good their intentions, certainly wrong their nation or sect by their generalizations.

And so it was with Jesus and the Pharisees. The powerful arraignment of Matthew xxiii is no more than a collection of isolated sayings gathered together in the same way as the "Sermon on the Mount" (Matt. v-vii); but Mark and Luke also tell how Jesus bitterly attacked the Pharisees in Jerusalem. He warned the people against "the Scribes who love to go about in long 'shawls' (*tallithoth*), to receive salutations in the market-places, to occupy the chief seats in the synagogues and sit in the chief seats at feasts; who swallow up widow's houses and make long prayers and let themselves be seen of all men." [14]

The collected denunciatory passages in Matthew contain much that is piercing and cutting in the extreme: "blind leaders of the blind;" "those which strain out the gnat and swallow the camel;" "ye cleanse the outside of the cup and platter, but within they are full of extortion and excess;" "ye are like unto whited sepulchres, [15] which outwardly appear beautiful, but inwardly are full of dead men's bones and of all uncleanness." [16]

Much of this criticism was certainly justified. "The cleansing of vessels was a matter more serious than the shedding of blood" [17] (though this remark is aimed by the *Tanna*, R. Zadoq, in criticism of specific acts of certain priests in connexion with an occurrence in R. Zadoq's presence); and the Elder Shammai took vast pains over the question of vetches in the Second Tithe. [18] The *Talmud*, also, finds cause for blame in "the seven kinds of Pharisees," and speaks of "the plague of Pharisees . . . who advise orphans to deprive the widow of her maintenance." [19] Yet Jesus (or the Gospels) errs by unfair generalization, by attributing to all Pharisees the defects of the few. Many of the Pharisees and their leaders acted exactly in accordance with Jesus' views: "Woe unto you, Scribes and Pharisees,

[14] Mark xii. 38-40; Luke xx. 45-47.

[15] The opposite of Rabban Yochanan ben Zakkai's remark, praising R. Eliezer ben Hyrcanus by calling him "a whitened well" (בור סוד), *Aboth* II 8.

[16] Matt. xxiii. 24-28.

[17] *Yoma* 23a; *T. Yom Kippur* I 12; but cf. *J. Yoma* II end of 2 (where "in blame" is expressly stated) and *Sifre* to Numbers, §161 ed. Friedmann 62b, ed. Horowitz, p. 222.

[18] *Ma'aser Sheni* II 4; *Eduyoth* I 8; cf. *Eduyoth* V 3, recording a dispute between the *Shammaites* and the *Hillelites* on the tithing of black cummin.

[19] *J. Sota* III 4. See above, pp. 213 ff.

hypocrites, for ye tithe mint and anise and cummin and leave undone the weightier matters of the Law, judgment and mercy and faith: but *these ye ought to have done and not to have left the other undone.*" [20] The entire Pharisaic teaching was to instil the observance of the laws affecting the relations between God and man, while not leaving undone those laws affecting the relations between man and man. Jesus, however, by his generalizations and abuse, provoked the indignation of the Pharisees and their followers.

Pharisees and Sadducees alike resented Jesus' attitude towards the Temple. One of his disciples, unused to such splendour, grew enthusiastic at the sight of the huge, massive stones of the Temple, the surviving fragments of which still astonish people to this day; and said to Jesus, "Master, behold what manner of stones and what manner of buildings!" But Jesus answered, "Seest thou these great buildings? there shall not be left here one stone upon another, which shall not be thrown down." [21]

To the same time may be attributed the saying, "I will pull down this temple, the work of men's hands, and after three days I will build another temple, not the work of men's hands." [22] According to Mark [23] this was the false evidence alleged against Jesus; according to the Fourth Gospel [24] Jesus uttered the remark with a spiritual significance at the time of the cleansing of the Temple; and in the Acts of the Apostles Stephen is accused of saying, "Jesus of Nazareth shall destroy this place (the Temple)." [25]

As Jesus sat on the Mount of Olives, facing the Temple, with Peter, James and John, the three leading and most favoured disciples, they asked, "When shall these things be?" He gives in reply a description of "the pangs of the Messiah" which he (or the author of the Gospel) calls "the beginning of woes" (ἀρχαὶ ὠδίνων). The description is very like that of the "pangs of the Messiah" in various *Talmudic Baraitas*—wars and rumours of wars (ἀκοὰς πολέμων), nation rising against nation and kingdom against kingdom, earthquakes, famines and tumults.[26] A *Talmudic Baraita* speaking of "the week when the Son of David comes" [27] speaks also of famines, wars and "noises" (קולות, rumours of wars).

Jesus next speaks of the afflictions which will befall those who believe in the Messiah, and the entire generation of "the days of the Messiah." [28] The majority of scholars incline to the opinion that

[20] Matt. xxiii. 23.
[21] Mark xiii. 2.
[22] Mark xiv. 58.
[23] Mark xiii. 57.
[24] John ii. 19.
[25] Acts vi. 14, and cf. Husband, *op. cit.* 190-3, who considers the charge justified.
[26] Mark xiii. 3-8.
[27] *Sanh.* 97a; *Derek Eretz Zutta,* beginning of X.
[28] Mark xiii. 9-27.

these nineteen verses are an apocalyptic document not earlier than the Destruction of the Temple; this apocalyptic character is plainly shown by the words, "Let him that readeth understand." [29] The section contains many details derived from the Old Testament and from the apocryphal writings concerning the "pangs of the Messiah"—"the sun shall be darkened and the moon shall not give forth its light, the stars shall fall from their courses and the hosts of heaven shall totter," "brother shall betray brother to death, and the father his son, and children shall rise against their parents;" and in the end "God shall gather together his chosen from the four winds, from the ends of earth to the ends of the heavens."

This apocalypse also recalls the *Mishna* (or, rather, the *Baraita*) at the close of *Sota*, about the "footsteps of the Messiah." [30] Another interesting point is that, in addition to clear descriptions of the persecutions which Jesus' disciples suffered and the statement that the Gospel must first be preached "to all nations," [31] there are also very obvious traces of primitive Judaistic Christianity (Nazarenism). Reference is made to "the flight of the men of Judæa to the mountains" (as happened to the Nazarenes at the time of the Destruction, when they fled to Pella, beyond Jordan, a city of the Decapolis), and when Mark writes, "Only pray that your flight be not in the winter," [32] Matthew adds, "nor on the Sabbath." [33] This shows that though the "Apocalypse" is much later than Jesus, it is still Nazarene, *i.e.,* Jewish Christian. It was impossible in Jesus' mouth: Jesus only foresaw the "pangs of the Messiah" without which there could be no "Days of the Messiah," and he saw the kingdom of heaven "nigh, even at the doors," and that "this generation should not pass away till all these things come to pass;" "but of the time of the coming of that day and that hour, no man knoweth, not even the angels of heaven, nor *the son* (*i.e.,* the Son of man), but only the Father." The disciples must, therefore, prepare themselves to meet the great day, the day of redemption, which was to come, as the *Talmud* also declares, "without the knowledge of men." [34]

[29] Mark xiii. 14.
[30] For a detailed treatment see Klausner, *Ha-Ra'yon ha-Meshihi be'Yisrael,* pts. I and II, *Die Messianischen Vorstellungen,* pp. 47-52.
[31] Mark xiii. 9-13.
[32] Mark xiii. 18.
[33] Matt. xxiv. 20.
[34] *Sanh.* 97a.

III. JUDAS ISCARIOT: THE LAST SUPPER

The selfsame day, the fourth day of the week ("two days before the feast of Passover, and the feast of unleavened bread")[1] the Sadducees and "chief priests" and scribes took council "how they might take him with subtilty, and kill him: for they said, Not during the feast, lest haply there shall be a tumult of the people." So, at least, records Mark.[2] Therefore they postponed the arrest of Jesus until after the feast. But meanwhile something happened which hastened Jesus' arrest and death.

Among the Twelve, otherwise all Galilæans, was one from Judæa, from the town of Kriyoth.[3] This disciple, Judas Iscariot, was at first as devoted a follower of Jesus as the best of the disciples since he was chosen to be one of the twelve Apostles who should preach the kingdom of heaven. Gradually his enthusiasm cooled and he began to look askance at his master's words and deeds.

He was gradually convinced that Jesus was not always successful in healing the sick; that Jesus feared his enemies and persecutors, and sought to escape and evade them; that there were marked contradictions in Jesus' teaching. One time he taught the observance of the Law in its minutest detail, ordaining the offering of sacrifices and submitting to priestly examination, and so forth; while at other times he permitted forbidden foods, paid little respect to Sabbath observance and the washing of hands, and hinted that "the new wine must be put in new bottles." One time he deferred to public opinion and paid the Temple half-shekel, and refused to countenance or discountenance the payment of tribute to Cæsar; while another time he inveighs against the Temple and the best of the nation and the nation's rulers. One time he says, "Whosoever is not against us is for us," and another time, "Every one who is not with me is against me." One time he ordains, "Strive not against evil," while another time he himself rises up against the traffickers and money-changers in the Temple and takes the law into his own hands. One time he says that a man must give all his goods to the poor, and another time he allows himself to be anointed with oil of myrrh, worth three hundred dinars.

What was more, this "Messiah" neither would nor could deliver his nation, yet he arrogated to himself the rôle of "the Son of man coming with the clouds of heaven," asserting that he should sit at the right hand of God in the Day of Judgment, daring to say of the

[1] Mark xiv. 1.   [3] See above, p. 285.
[2] Mark xiv. 1-2.

324

Temple, the most sacred place in the world, that not one stone of it should remain upon another and, actually, that he would destroy it and in its place raise up another after three days!

Judas Iscariot became convinced that here was a false Messiah or a false prophet, erring and making to err, a beguiler and one who led astray, one whom the Law commanded to be killed, one to whom the Law forbade pity or compassion or forgiveness. Till such time as Jesus divulged his messianic claims to the disciples at Cæsarea Philippi, Judas had not thought to find in Jesus more than might be found in any Pharisaic Rabbi or, at the most, in a Jewish prophet. But after this revelation to the disciples at Cæsarea, and to the entire people at Jerusalem, Judas expected that in the Holy City, the centre of the religion and the race, Jesus would demonstrate his claims by mighty works, that he would destroy the Romans and bring the Pharisees and Sadducees to naught; then all would acknowledge his messianic claims and all would see him in his pomp and majesty as the "final saviour."

But what, in fact, did Judas see? No miracles (Matthew alone [4] tells how Jesus healed the blind and lame in the Temple, matters unknown to Mark), no mighty deeds, no one is subdued by him, the mighty Messiah escapes nightly to Bethany; except for "bold" remarks against the tradition of the elders and vain arrogance, Jesus reveals no plan by which he will effect the redemption. Was it not, then, a "religious duty" to deliver up such a "deceiver" to the government and so fulfil the law: Thou shalt exterminate the evil from thy midst? [5]

This must have been Judas Iscariot's train of reasoning. The Gospels all say that he received payment for betraying his lord and Messiah; Matthew tells the exact amount, [6] "thirty pieces of silver"— a number obviously derived from the passage in Zechariah. [7] Yet it is hard to think that one who came to Jesus from afar and who followed him closely and proved himself of such merit that Jesus made him a leading disciple and sent him to preach the kingdom of heaven—that such a one as this could sell his master for gain. This could not have been the psychological cause for his action; rather was it the desperation which Judas endured because of his very proximity to Jesus and his knowledge of the human frailties of Jesus.

Judas was an educated Judæan with a keen intellect but a cold and calculating heart, accustomed to criticise and scrutinise; his knowledge of the frailties blinded him to the many virtues of Jesus, virtues which at first had so impressed him and aroused his enthusiasm. It was otherwise with the other disciples, all alike uneducated Galilæans, dull of intellect but warm-hearted; for them the virtues covered up all the defects, and till the hour of danger they remained faithful to their master, and when the short interval of doubt was

---

[4] Matt. xxi. 14.
[5] Deut. xiii. 2-12.
[6] Matt. xxvi. 15.
[7] Zech. xi. 12-13.

past they returned to his holy memory and so cherished the knowledge of his words and deeds that they survive to this day.

On the fifth day of the week (or in Mark's words, "on the first day of unleavened bread when they sacrificed the Passover")[8] it was necessary to prepare for the Passover. The first day of the feast of unleavened bread (15th Nisan) fell that year (30 C.E.) on the Sabbath, therefore the Feast of Passover (14th Nisan) fell on the eve of the Sabbath. Astronomical calculations make the 15th of Nisan fall on a Friday in the year 30, and it was not till the year 33 that the 14th fell on a Friday. But we have no certain knowledge of the arrangement of the years among the Jews in Jesus' time, during the time when there was Bœthusean-Sadducæan control of the Temple. An error of a day was easily possible before the Jews finally fixed the system of calculating the New Moon.

According to the ruling which was newly promulgated by the Pharisees in Hillel's time, the Passover was regarded as a *public* sacrifice; if, therefore, the 15th of Nisan fell on a Sabbath and the 14th on the eve of Sabbath, the Passover was sacrificed on the eve of Sabbath (the 14th of Nisan) at the moment "between the two days" (בין הערבים), even if this profaned the Sabbath; they used to argue that, like every public sacrifice, "the Passover abrogates the Sabbath rules." According, however, to an earlier ruling, which held good among the priestly party almost to the close of the period of the Second Temple, the Passover was regarded as a *private* sacrifice and one which might not abrogate the Sabbath rules; if, therefore, the 14th of Nisan fell on the eve of Sabbath, they sacrificed on the 13th instead of the 14th, so as not to profane the Sabbath (since they must sacrifice בין הערבים,[9] "in the evening at the moment of sunset.")[10] Hence Jesus and his disciples celebrated Passover on the Thursday, the 13th of Nisan, and during the ensuing night of the 14th of Nisan (the night before Friday) they had to celebrate the "Seder," the Passover meal, with its unleavened bread and bitter herbs,[11] instead of on the night of the 15th Nisan.[12]

Galilæans followed the stricter rulings dealing with the eve of Passover: "In Judæa they worked on Passover eve till midday; but in Galilee they did not work at all on the eve:" according to the Shammai school no work may be done even during the night before the eve.[13] Since the disciples were, most of them, Galilæans, they bestirred themselves and on the morning of Thursday asked Jesus

[8] Mark xiv. 12.
[9] Numbers ix. 11.
[10] Deut. xvi. 5-6.
[11] Num. ix. 11; Ex. xii. 8.
[12] For details see D. Chwolsohn, *Das letzte Passamahl Christi und der Tag seines Todes*, 2 Aufl. Leipzig, 1908, pp. 10-13, 20-44 (for the opposite view, see pp. 54-55, and the added supplementary notes in the 2nd edition).
[13] *Pesahim* IV 5; cf. IV 1.

where they were to eat the Passover and prepare the "Seder." This might not be done in Bethany since the rule was that in Jerusalem alone were the ceremonies to be performed.[14] Furthermore the Passover "could be consumed only in the night" and "only by them for whom it had been prepared."[15]

For privacy's sake, Jesus had already made the necessary arrangements with a simple Jerusalem water-carrier[16] in whose upper chamber everything was made ready for Jesus and the disciples. All, apparently, was done in secret for the same reason which compelled Jesus to lodge outside the city during that week—fear of his persecutors; and but for Judas Iscariot, Jesus and the Twelve would not have been discovered.

In the evening Jesus "and the Twelve" (including Judas Iscariot) came to the upper chamber, "and they sat down and did eat" according to the Jewish Passover rule.[17] From this state post-Pauline Christianity begins to elaborate the various episodes. After betraying Jesus, Judas Iscariot sat with him at table. Was it conceivable that Jesus the wonder-worker, Jesus the Messiah, Jesus the Son of God, was unaware of the treachery? Such is the problem raised by the uncritical belief in Jesus the Messiah.

The only possible answer was that Jesus knew of the treachery from the beginning, indicated Judas as the traitor[18] and actually referred to him as such by name.[19] Yet again, since the rest of the Twelve, and even Peter their leader, were terrified at the time of the arrest and escaped in every direction, was it possible that Jesus the wonder-worker, Jesus the Messiah, Jesus the Son of God, did not foresee this also? Again uncritical belief makes a like answer: Jesus prophesied to Peter that the same night before the cock should crow twice, he, Peter, should deny him thrice;[20] and so, of course, did it happen exactly.

Jesus broke the bread ("Mazzoth," the unleavened bread, "the bread of affliction"), gave it to the disciples[21] and said to them that they should take and eat it, for "this is my body;" he also gave them to drink from his cup, saying, "this is my blood, the blood of the new covenant, which is shed for many;"[22] and he may have added: "for the forgiveness of sins,"[23] and also: "Do this in remembrance

---

[14] Deut. xvi. 5-7; cf. *Pesahim* VII .9 (and the explanation of *Tos'photh Yom Tob*).

[15] *Zebahim* V 8.

[16] Cf. Matt. xxvi. 18, with Mark xiv. 13-15.

[17] Mark xiv. 18.

[18] Following Mark xiv. 18-21.

[19] So Matt. xxvi. 25.

[20] Mark xiv. 30.

[21] On the breaking of bread and "the cup of blessing" and the "Seder" as a whole, see Dalman, *op. cit.* 201-204, 254-255; *Jesus-Jeschua*, Leipzig, 1922, pp. 80-166.

[22] Mark xiv. 22-24.

[23] Matt. xxvi. 28.

of me," [24] though this last occurs in neither Mark nor Matthew.

This was the origin of the rite of the "Lord's Supper" and the mystical theory of "Transubstantiation" (the conversion of the bread into the body of the Messiah, and the conversion of the wine into his blood), which induced the heathen of those days to believe that the Christians used blood for their Passover. And when, in their turn, the heathen became Christians they accused the Jews, on the basis of this Christian belief, of kneading their unleavened bread in Christian blood. But the rite arose much later than the time of Jesus.

He, as an observant Jew, celebrated the Passover "Seder" on the night before the 14th of Nisan, since the 14th fell on the eve of the Sabbath and it was therefore not possible to kill the victim and roast it at the moment of sunset. Hillel's ruling, that the Passover was a public sacrifice abrogating the Sabbath laws, did not yet hold good among the priests who had charge over the sacrifices. [25]

Scripture says of the Passover: "With unleavened bread and bitter herbs shall they eat it;" therefore Jesus also ate unleavened bread with the Passover, and this is the "bread" which the Gospels refer to. He said over it the prescribed liturgical blessings ("Blessed art thou, O Lord our God! King of the universe; who bringest forth bread from the earth." "Blessed art thou, O Lord our God! King of the universe, who has sanctified us with thy commandments, and commanded us to eat unleavened bread"); he "brake it" (the usual Jewish way with the bread and "Mazzoth," which then, as with the Arabs today, was not cut with a knife; the verb has been preserved in the Gospels (ἔχλασε), and gave it to his disciples, and they all ate it as they sat. [26] Jesus and the Twelve "dipped" into the dish, [27] and drank the first of the four cups, which he had blessed (εὐχαριστήσαε) and given them all to drink (as is also the custom of the Jews today).

According to the Law they would eat bitter herbs, and these brought to Jesus' mind the "pangs of the Messiah;" they may also have drunk the four cups, following the usage laid down in the Mishna, [28] which would seem to be fairly old. Finally they sang the Hallel (ὑμνήσαντες), [29] likewise an ancient use [30] and one which gave rise to an early proverb: "The Passover is like an olive, and the Hallel splits the roofs" (the point being, to make much ado about

[24] Luke xxii. 19.
[25] T. Pesahim IV 1-2 (for other references and variant readings see Chwolsohn, op. cit. l.c.); cf. the arguments of R. Eliezer, R. Yehoshua and R. Akiba as to what extent the Passover sacrifices abrogated the Sabbath, M. Pesahim VI 1-3; Pesahim 70b; Sifre on Numbers §65 (ed. Friedmann 17a; ed. Horowitz, p. 61); Sifre Zutta, "B'ha'alothekha," 2-3 (ed. Horowitz, pp. 257-8).
[26] Mark xiv. 15-18.
[27] Mark xiv. 20.
[28] Pesahim X 1-4, 7.
[29] Mark xiv. 26.
[30] Pesahim X 5-7.

nothing).[31] All was in line with the religious practices of the Jews.

Jesus may have urged the disciples to remember this solemn meal (the most ceremonious of all meals among the Jews), the first "Seder" which he had celebrated in Jerusalem in their company.[32] He may have said: "Verily I say unto you, I shall in no wise drink of the fruit of the vine till that day when I shall drink it new in the kingdom of God," [33] since he considered the kingdom of heaven as very near, and the disciples, still less the authors of the Gospels, would not have attributed such a material sentiment to Jesus at a later stage.

But it is quite impossible to admit that Jesus would have said to his disciples that they should eat of his body and drink of his blood, "the blood of the new covenant which was shed for many." The drinking of blood, even if it was meant symbolically, could only have aroused horror in the minds of such simple Galilæan Jews; and had he expected to die within a short space of time he would not have been so disturbed when death proved imminent.

[31] *J. Pes.* VI 1; *Pes.* 85*b* gives the same proverb as a saying of Amora, in the form: כזיתא פסחא והלילא בקע אגרא: the proverb also occurs in *Cant. R*, "*Yonathi b'hag-we ha-sela,*" but in a corrupt form פסחא כביתא והלילא מתברא אברייאה (אגרייאה) (טיתא for).

[32] Eduard Meyer, *Ursprung und Anfänge des Christentums*, 1921, I 177, concludes with Wellhausen that we have here not the Passover "Seder," but an ordinary meal, the last meal which Jesus ate with his disciples, not with unleavened bread and the paschal lamb, but ordinary wheaten bread and meat and rape-seed; and so he falls into the gross error: "as is well known the *Hallel* follows the end of a meal," as though the Jews sang the *Hallel* after every meal and not only after the passover-night "Seder"! A great scholar who so often attacks Jews and Judaism (see II 32, 129, 146, 256, 281 and elsewhere) ought to know more of Judaism.

[33] Mark xiv. 25. The reference is probably to the wine "stored up" for the messianic age from the days of Creation (*Berach.* 34*b*).

IV. GETHSEMANE: THE GREAT TRAGEDY

Jesus did not *know* that death was imminent; but the *fear* of death was upon him. From his first day in Jerusalem he feared arrest by the authorities. This alone explains why every night he went to Bethany, and why he made secret arrangements with a mere water-carrier to celebrate the "Seder" in his upper room. After the "Seder" he could not, as on the other nights, return to Bethany. The verse, "And thou shalt boil it and eat it (the Passover lamb) in the place which the Lord thy God shall choose, and thou shalt return in the morning to thy tents," [1] was interpreted to mean that the Passover compelled the spending of the night in Jerusalem itself; [2] one might not even "eat" in Jerusalem and spend the night in Beth-phage; [3] though one might change places within Jerusalem: "they may eat in one place and spend the night in another." [4]

Therefore immediately after Jesus and the disciples had sung the *Hallel* they went to the Mount of Olives, the furthermost district within the limits of Jerusalem. Jesus felt depressed: he felt that he had failed in Jerusalem: he had made many powerful enemies but not many friends. He did not even trust his disciples. He found them too simple: they had not entered into the spirit of his teaching and of his ideas, and showed nothing beyond a blind veneration. They quarrelled for the honour of sitting first in the kingdom of heaven, they were afraid of the inevitable persecutions and sufferings.

They were narrow-minded—attaching importance to mere oil of myrrh, when the "Messiah," the anointed one, must needs be "anointed." He felt, too, that his enemies, the Pharisees and Saddu-cees, lay in wait for his life. Hence his deep depression.

The tragedy opened. Jesus went away to a garden called Geth-semane. [5] He parted from his disciples, telling them that he was going

[1] Deut. xvi. 17.
[2] *Sifre* to Deut. 134, ed. Friedmann 101b; *Pes.* 98b; *Hag.* 17a; *Rosh ha-Sh.* 5a (beginning).
[3] *Sifre* to Numbers, 151, ed. Friedmann 55a.
[4] *T. Pes.* VIII 17.
[5] Aramaic נַת־שְׁמָנֵי, Greek (Γεθσημ:νῆ, Γεθσεμανεῖ, etc). The name is strange: for pressing olives a בֵּית הַבַּד, press (Arabic מַעֲצָרָה, also בַּד,

with doubled "d" as in Hebrew) was used; the גַּת, vat, was used for grapes, and we find the word "gath" used only twice in *Talmudic* literature in connexion with olives (*Peah* VII 1; *T. Terumoth* III 6); but we find "Ge-shemanim" in the Old Testament (Isa. xxviii. 1), and, a fact hitherto unnoticed, the *Talmud* tells us that Abba Shaul called the "hall of wine and oil" in the Temple by the name "Beth-Shemanaya" (*T. Yom Kippur* I 3 ed. Zuckermandel p. 180). The present writer would suggest that the name נֵית שמני was originally written with the first vowel "e" and not "a," and to pray, and took with him only Peter and James and John, his favourite disciples. According to Mark, "he began to be greatly amazed and sore troubled (ἐκθαμβεῖσθαι καὶ ἀδημονεῖν), and he saith unto them (the three disciples), My soul is exceedingly sorrowful even unto death: abide ye here, and watch." [6] On this night he was afraid to be alone in the city that was full of enemies. It is all very human and very tragic, and very different from what the Gospels wish to convey as to Jesus' foreknowledge of what awaited him, as well as from what most Christian scholars try to prove—that Jesus, knowingly, went up to Jerusalem to die.

Jesus had no foreknowledge of his impending death. He did not know that he would soon be arrested and put to death. But he did know that his enemies among the Pharisees and Sadducees were many and powerful while his own followers were few and his disciples weak: "their spirit was willing, but the flesh was weak." Therefore the fear of death crept over him.

Luke preserves the curious fact that Jesus told his disciples to sell their garments and buy swords; they replied, "Lord, here are two swords," and he said to them, "It is enough." [7] He seemed to imagine that he needed *armed* protection against his enemies. The other Gospels omit this; but Luke could hardly have added it himself if he had not found it in old and reliable records. Jesus, therefore, prepared himself and his disciples for armed opposition in the time of need. There is also a covert hint that Jesus promised his disciples that he would leave Jerusalem (naturally in secret) "and go before them to Galilee." [8] The words "after I am risen from the dead," were necessarily added by the Evangelist, since the next day Jesus was crucified.

This hint shows that Jesus did not anticipate his imminent death. Yet he dreaded sufferings and persecution and like everyone of delicate susceptibilities he had a deeply disturbing premonition of impending trouble: "My soul is bitter even unto death." He went a little way apart from his disciples, fell on his face, and prayed that "if it were possible" (an obvious addition by the Evangelist) "the hour might pass away from him," or, in the common Hebrew idiom, "an evil hour which was speedily coming upon him." [9]

is derived either from "Ge-Shemanim" or the name "Beth-Shemanaya" (the Greek *beta* having been changed to the following letter in the Greek alphabet, *gamma*). Dalman's theory (*op. cit.* p. 257) that the name is נת הסימנים "the vat of signs," will not bear criticism.

[6] Mark xiv. 33-34.
[7] Luke xxii. 36, 38.
[8] Mark xiv. 28. That these words are lacking in some of the earliest MSS. only confirms the obvious fact that at an early stage this statement proved a difficulty to the Christians.
[9] See *J. Berachoth* V 1 (most versions of *Babli Berachoth* 17a lack the word "hours") and the prayer before taking out the Scroll of the Law at the three great Feasts; cf. also (*Sanh.* 102a): "a time fitted for troubles— a time fitted for good."

The disciples must have heard in the distance (for none would afterwards have invented such words, so contradictory to the Christian belief) as Jesus prayed, "Abba, Father! (a Hebrew-Aramaic diminutive of affection, reproduced in the Greek, ('Αββᾶ ὁ πατήρ) all things are possible unto thee; remove this cup from me" (the following words, "but not what I will, but what thou wilt," are an addition by the Evangelist, who could not think that a prayer of the Messiah could be refused, or that the Messiah need plead to God like a child appealing to its parents). His prayer is wonderful in its brevity and truly human!

Meanwhile the three disciples slept: they were tired after their Passover preparations and had eaten and drunk heavily (the flesh of the Passover lamb and the "four cups"). Jesus found them sleeping. He was chiefly indignant with Peter, his favourite and foremost disciple, and reproves him sadly: "Simon, sleepest thou? couldest not thou have watched with me one hour?"

Then he turns to the three, saying, "Watch and pray, lest ye too enter into temptation" (i.e. ye, too, may be arrested as my disciples), "for the spirit is willing (to withstand temptation), but the flesh is weak." [10] There is both tender indignation and kindly forgiveness: man, in spite of all his good-will to subdue his weakness, is weak, "flesh and blood," as he is typically termed in Hebrew. Jesus turns away and prays a second time to be saved from ill.

He returns to them and finds them still sleeping . . . and when he awakened them "their eyes were very heavy and they wist not what to answer him." [11] So he allows them to sleep: he could not rely on them. . . .

The whole story bears the hallmark of human truth: only a few details are dubious. It must have been transmitted to the Evangelists (or their sources) direct from Peter, James or John, with such simplicity and conviction that even the ideas or tendencies of Pauline times could not obscure their memories. The sorrow and sufferings of the solitary Son of man, profound as they are, leave on every sympathetic heart, be it the heart of the believer or unbeliever, such an impression as may never be wiped out.

[10] Mark xiv. 35-38; Matt. xxvi. 36-41.
[11] Mark xiv. 10; Matt. xxvi. 42-48. Luke (xxii. 39-46) abbreviates, but gives the verse: "and being in an agony he prayed more earnestly: and his sweat became as it were great drops of blood falling down upon the ground."

SEVENTH BOOK

THE TRIAL AND CRUCIFIXION OF JESUS

I. THE ARREST IN THE GARDEN OF GETHSEMANE

A voluminous literature has grown round the subject of Jesus' trial.[1] Most writers see in it a perversion of justice, especially the trial before the Sanhedrin, and nothing more than a "judicial murder."[2] The first attempt by a Jew to justify the condemnation of Jesus came from Joseph Salvador, the enthusiastic nationalist and forerunner of Zionism, an attempt which, besides literary onslaughts from all sides, subjected him to French prosecution.[3] It is true that if we compare the judicial procedure detailed in the *Mishna* and *Tosefta* of the *Tractate Sanhedrin*, with what we learn, particularly in Mark and Matthew, of the trial of Jesus, we are bound to conclude that the Sanhedrin broke every prescribed law of procedure. Jewish apologists have, therefore, been forced to lay the blame on a Sadducæan Sanhedrin[4] or else to cast doubt on the Gospel narratives, and to show that Pontius Pilate, the cruel Roman Procurator, was alone responsible for Jesus' death, since at that time the right to conduct criminal trials had been taken from the Jews, and crucifixion was not a Jewish but a Roman death penalty.[5]

But a truer view is gradually beginning to prevail. From numerous papyri discovered in Egypt, dating from the Roman period, and containing records of important trials conducted by or under the supervision of the Roman Government,[6] it transpires that the Roman Governors (who conducted all important trials) used to entrust preliminary investigations to the local Egyptian government.[7] This

[1] Given at the end of W. R. Husband's *The Prosecution of Jesus*, Princeton, 1916.
[2] The most violent and prejudiced is G. Rosadi, *Il Processo di Gesù*, Florence, 1904. See H. P. Chajes' criticism in "Note Marginali," *Rivista Israelitica*, I (1904), 41-57, 105-106.
[3] J. Salvador, *Histoire des institutions de Moise et du peuple hébreu*, Paris, 1828; *Jesus Christ et sa doctrine*, Paris, 1838, II 520-570.
[4] Emphasized by D. Chwolsohn, *Das letzte Passamahl*, pp. 118-125.
[5] See L. Philippsohn, *Haben die Juden wirklich Jesus gekreuzigt?* Bonn, 1866; E. G. Hirsch, *The Crucifixion from the Jewish Point of View*, Chicago, 1892.
[6] See Wilcken, *Griechische Ostraka aus Aegypten und Nubien*, I-II, Leipzig, 1899; Wenger, *Rechtshistorische Papyrusstudien*, Graz, 1902; Mitteis-Wilcken, *Grundzüge und Chrestomathie der Papyruskunde*, II Leipzig, 1912.
[7] Husband, *op. cit.* pp. 137, 181.

affords a basis for assuming that the Jerusalem Sanhedrin, also, possessed the right to make such preliminary investigation, in order to submit the results to the Roman Procurator.

Such procedure was natural: without it, it was not possible to know whether the culprit were liable to scourging or imprisonment or death, or whether he were innocent. Only after legal enquiry had shown that some capital crime (and especially insurrection or robbery)[8] was involved, was the whole conduct of the trial handed over to the Roman Governor. There is no parallel to support the normally accepted view that the Sanhedrin might conduct the actual trial and even pass sentence of death, but might not carry out the sentence.[9] On the contrary, there is a *Baraita* to the effect that, "forty years before the Destruction of the Temple (and therefore probably before the time of Jesus' trial) the trial of capital cases was taken away from Israel,'[10] and according to the Fourth Gospel: "It is not lawful for us (the Jews) to put any man to death."[11] Mark,[12] and the genuine part of Josephus' paragraph about Jesus (of which the bulk is spurious),[13] assert that Jesus was delivered "to the Gentiles" or "to Pilate" by the "chiefs of the priests and the scribes" or by "the principal men among us." These statements are all of them comprehensible if we assume that the Sanhedrin only carried out a preliminary enquiry and, when the charge was proved against Jesus, delivered him to Pilate, who alone conducted the trial proper and passed sentence. Thus we see why the procedure of the "trial" as conducted by the Sanhedrin does not conform with the details of procedure laid down in the *Mishna;* it was *not* a trial but only a preliminary judicial investigation, and, as such, it was altogether fair and legal.[14]

It is gradually being recognized,[15] however, that the *real* reason why the *Mishna* rules are at variance with the system in vogue in the time of Jesus, is that, between the two periods (the time of Jesus and the time of Rabbi Yehuda ha-Nasi) there intervened two hundred years and many and great changes.[16] We have already pointed out the fact that, in the time of Jesus, the Temple and all local government was in the hands of the Sadducæan-Bœthusean priests; hence

---

[8] T. Juster, *Les Juifs dans l'Empire Romain,* Paris, 1914, II 139-149.

[9] Husband, pp. 102-136. But cf. Juster, *l.c.*

[10] *J. Sanh.* I 1; VII 2; *Shab.* 15a.

[11] John xviii. 31.

[12] Mark x. 33.

[13] *Ant.* XVIII iii 3; see above, pp. 55 ff.

[14] Husband, pp. 182-208.

[15] The view was urged as early as 1913 by the present writer in *He-Atid* (Vol. V end), pp. 89-91.

[16] See H. Danby, "The Bearing of the Rabbinical Criminal Code on the Jewish Trial Narratives in the Gospels," *Journal of Theological Studies,* 1919, XXI 51-76; see also his *Tractate Sanhedrin, Mishna and Tosefta,* London, 1919, pp. ix-xii.

"the chiefs of the priests and the Scribes and the elders" mentioned in the Gospels were, almost entirely, Sadducees.

The Sadducees as well as the Pharisees had their "elders" and "Scribes;" but since the "Scribes" preceded the *Tannaim,* and since, when the Gospels were written, the Sadducees had lost power and importance, the Gospels use (in place of כהניא־ספריא, "priests-scribes"), the terms "Scribes and Pharisees" in the same breath, as though they were synonymous terms.[17] Bearing these points in mind we shall better comprehend the arrest and trial of Jesus, which culminated in his shameful and cruel death.

When, after the "Seder," Jesus and the Twelve went to the Mount of Olives and Judas Iscariot saw where Jesus proposed to conceal himself, Judas at once reported the place to the High Priest or the local Jewish authorities. Therefore during the time when Jesus was praying earnestly, reproving his disciples, and encouraging them to watch at their master's side in the hour of danger, Judas Iscariot approached, and "with him a great multitude with swords and staves" sent by "the chief priests (the "Seganim") and the Scribes and the elders"—who were mostly of the Sadducæan party.

The Pharisees, hitherto Jesus' main opponents, cease now to play a prominent part; their place is taken by the Sadducees and the priestly class whom Jesus had irritated by the "cleansing of the Temple" and by his reply concerning the Law of Moses and the resurrection of the dead. The Pharisees objected to Jesus' behaviour —his disparagement of many ceremonial laws, his contempt of the words of the "sages" and his consorting with publicans and ignorant folk and doubtful women. They considered his miracles sorcery and his messianic claims effrontery. Yet for all that, *he was one of themselves:* his convinced belief in the Day of Judgment and the resurrection of the dead, the messianic age and the kingdom of heaven, was a distinctively Pharisaic belief; he taught nothing which, by the rules of the Pharisees, rendered him criminally guilty.

Although there was not yet in existence the *Tractate Sanhedrin,* with its humane rules of legal procedure, which made the death penalty impossible except in the rarest cases and only retained the penalty lest some principle of the *Torah* be abrogated—even so it is inconceivable that the disciples of Hillel and Shammai could condemn anyone to death for scoffing at the words of the wise, or for disparaging certain of the ceremonial laws, or even for alleging himself to be the Messiah.[18]

[17] A. Büchler, *Die Priester und der Cultus im letzten Jahrzehnt des Jerusalemischen Tempels,* Vienna, 1895, pp. 84-88; Chwolsohn, p. 113.

[18] This is proved by the fact that during the reign of John Hyrcanus (or Alexander Jannæus) the Pharisees did not condemn to death Eliezer (or Yehuda ben Gedidiah) who had defamed the king's (or prince's) mother and the High Priest, but were content to scourge and imprison him. This brought it about that John (or Jannæus) deserted the Pharisees in favour of the Sadducees (*Ant.* XIII x 5-6; *Kiddushin* 66a).

The trial of Jesus was not in accordance with the spirit of the Pharisees, but of the Sadducees and Bœthuseans (then the majority in the Sanhedrin), to which party the High Priest, the president of the Sanhedrin, belonged (descendants of the house of Hillel did not become presidents of the Sanhedrin till after the Destruction).

As "practical politicians" the Sadducees could not calmly suffer a Galilæan visionary to proclaim himself Messiah and incite the people to riot within the Temple area, and to abuse the national leaders—particularly the Sadducees. They knew how easy it would be, during the feast of Passover, for a prophet and wonder-worker to stir the people to revolt against the Romans: the Galilæans (from whom emanated the Zealots) were specially to be distrusted. It is probable that, at that very time, there had happened some rising in Jerusalem led by a certain Barabbas, leading to the death of many.[19]

The High-Priestly party, the supreme Jerusalem Jewish authority, did not, like all shortsighted officials, enquire into the case very deeply, nor could they discriminate between a Messiah who was only a teacher and a Messiah who was a political rebel. To them Jesus seemed as great a danger to the peace of the city during Passover as was Barabbas. They must get rid of him—before the feast if possible; and though they had regarded this as not feasible owing to the likelihood of provoking an uproar.

Judas Iscariot gave them their opportunity. He informed them secretly where Jesus had gone after the "Seder," and when none would be with him except his weary disciples. Judas had nothing against his fellow-disciples (whom he looked upon as led astray by Jesus), and in order that none of them should be arrested in place of Jesus, he himself accompanied the Jewish police and their officer (the "Segen") and indicated Jesus by turning towards him and saluting him with "Rabbi! Rabbi!" The Gospels give many supplementary details, few of which are true. According to Mark, Judas kissed Jesus to signify that it was he who was to be arrested:[20] according to Matthew, Jesus replied with "Friend, wherefore art thou come?"[21] and, according to Luke, he said, "Judas, betrayest thou the Son of man with a kiss?"[22]—all of which are imaginary additions.

We have seen that Luke alone preserves the account of how Jesus wished the disciples to secure swords and found that they already had two; yet all the Gospels record that, at the moment of Jesus' arrest one of the disciples (Mark writes "One of those who stood by him;" and Matthew, "One of the men that were with Jesus") drew his sword and cut off the ear of one of the police ("a servant of the High Priest").

Mark[23] adds nothing beyond this, but Matthew preserves a tradi-

[19] Mark xv. 7; see below, p. 347, Wendland's theory.
[20] Mark xv. 44-45.
[21] Matt. xxvi. 50.
[22] Luke xxii. 48.
[23] Mark xiv. 47.

tion to the effect that Jesus rebuked him who used the sword, ordering him to return it to its sheath, "for all they that take the sword shall perish by the sword," explaining that if he wished, he could appeal to his Father "and he shall even now send me more than twelve legions of angels," but "how then should the scriptures be fulfilled that thus it must be?" [24] Luke adds further that Jesus touched the wounded ear and healed it: [25] Jesus did not wish acts of violence to be done for his sake in his presence.

Thus the story grew from Gospel to Gospel. But we may take as historical the unsuccessful attempt to oppose the arrest by force and Jesus' remark, "Are ye come out as against a robber with swords and staves to seize me? I was daily with you in the temple teaching and ye took me not," [26] though the following "but this is done that the scriptures might be fulfilled" is a later accretion.

It is interesting to note that the *Talmud* also complains of the "staves" and "clubs" of the Bœthusean High Priests, including all the infamous High Priests (among them the Annas of the Gospels) from the time of Herod onwards. It preserves a short street-ballad written about them, the first line of which mentions their "clubs" and the last their "staves;" we find reference to their secret denouncements, written or by word of mouth, and to their hard "fist," and complaints of their servants and their staves:

"Woe is me, for the house of Bœthus: woe is me, for their club!

"Woe is me, for the house of Annas: woe is me, for their whisperings!

"Woe is me, for the house of Kathros (Kantheras): woe is me, for their pen!

"Woe is me, for the house of Ishmael (ben Phiabi): woe is me for their fist!

"For they are the High Priests, and their sons the treasurers: their sons-in-law are Temple-officers, and their servants beat the people with their staves." [27]

There could scarcely be a more dreadful and hateful picture of the High Priests and their families. Their outstanding features were their "clubs" (something like an English policeman's truncheon), staves, fists and secret denouncements. *These* were those who ordered Jesus' arrest and who conducted his preliminary examination. The *Talmud* hates them and regards them as the enemies of the people, whom "they beat with their staves." The Gospels, which are as full as the *Talmud* of suppressed hate against them, try to depict them as the

[24] Matt. xxvi. 51-54.
[25] Luke xxii. 49-51.
[26] Mark xiv. 48.
[27] *Pesahim* 57a; *T. Menahoth* XIII 21. The two closing lines may not belong to the song.

agents of the Jewish people and so blame the entire people for their acts. "Hatred spoils sound judgment."

After the attempt at armed resistance had failed to do more than wound one of the police, the disciples were seized with fear and fled, leaving Jesus by himself. So great was the alarm that one of Jesus' followers, a young man (νεανίσκος) roused from sleep fled naked as he was (it is already warm in Palestine by Passover, and it was the custom to sleep naked),[28] wrapping a sheet round him; when the police seized hold of him he left the sheet in their hands and escaped.[29] This is so vivid a detail that it is unlikely that it was invented later. This young man is supposed (though for no real reason) to have been John-Mark, the disciple of Peter; to him is attributed the detailed knowledge of the prayer of Jesus; he heard it before going to sleep and afterwards recorded it in his Gospel.

[28] As is apparent from the *Mishna, Kiddushin* IV 12; cf. *Sukkah* 10b.
[29] Mark xiv. 50-52.

II. THE TRIAL

From Gethsemane on the Mount of Olives, the police took Jesus to the High Priest. In the time of the great rebellion the house of the High Priest, Annas, was, according to Josephus, in the Upper City;[1] but we do not know if this was the house allocated to all the High Priests or merely Annas' private residence. Josephus tells us[1a] that the "Council" βουλή, *i.e.*, the Sanhedrin) was below the Temple, near the bridge leading to the Upper City, and thus on the site of the present "Mehkemeh."[2] The *Talmud,* however, says plainly, "Forty years before the Destruction, the Sanhedrin left (the Chamber of Hewn Stone) and took its abode in the Booths (בחנויות)."[3] In another place the *Talmud* refers to ten changes in the meeting-place of the Sanhedrin, the first being "from the Chamber of Hewn Stone to the Booth"(חנות, or Booths,חנויות).[4] We have seen that the "Booths of the House of Annas" (which Derenbourg regards as identical with this same "Booth" or "Booths") were in the "Hill of Anointing,"[5] and the time (forty years before the Destruction) fits in with the time of Jesus, since "forty years" is just a round number. Therefore the place ("the hill of anointing") was quite near to Gethsemane.

The High Priest at the time was of the house of Annas, whose secret denunciations are complained about in the popular song. Jesus, therefore, may have been brought as a prisoner to the "Booths of the house of Annas" close by, to the nearest available place for trial (or preliminary examination). There may, also, have been a temporary prison there, for we find, in Jeremiah, "booths" (חנויות) mentioned together with a dungeon (בית הבור).[6]

The High Priest's name was Joseph, the son of Caiaphas (יוסף בן הקייף, Greek Καϊάφας, Aramaic קייפא):[7] the *Talmud* refers to "the family of the house of Kaiapha,"[8] sometimes corrupted to "Beth Kophai"[9] and even "Beth Neqiphi."[10] He was appointed by

[1] *Wars* II xvii 6.
[1a] *Wars* II xvii 6; VI vi 3.
[2] See Dalman, *op. cit.* p. 264, who concludes that it is impossible to fix the exact site where the Jews condemned Jesus.
[3] *Shab.* 15a (end); *Ab. Zar.* 8b (end).
[4] *Rosh ha-Sh.* 31a (end); for the variants, see *'Arukh he-Shalem*, III 400 (under חנות).
[5] *Op. cit.* n. 8 in *appendix*, p. 244-246. See above, p. 309 and 314.
[6] Jer. xxxvii. 15.
[7] Derenbourg, *op. cit.* p. 112, n. 2.
[8] *T. Yebam.* I 10.
[9] *Yeb.* 15b.
[10] *J. Yebam.* I 6; see "Sh'ir" in *Ha-Maggid* XVIII 17 (reprinted in Luncz's

the Procurator Valerius Gratus, remained in office under Pontius Pilate, and was finally deposed by Vitellius after the latter had deposed Pontius Pilate.[11] That he continued High Priest for nearly eighteen years (c.18-36 C.E.), whereas his predecessors in the time of Gratus each held office for barely a year, proves that he was a wily diplomatist and knew how to conduct himself towards people and Roman governor alike.

Such a man might well dread a new "Messiah," and, as a whole, the Sadducees had no sympathy for messianic ideas owing to their disturbing effect on political conditions. They were especially opposed to the post-Biblical form of the messianic idea. When Kaiaphas heard that a new Messiah had appeared in Jerusalem, and that he was from *Galilee* (a district ripe for insurrection), he feared for the consequences and ordered him to be arrested and brought to him, or to the "Booths of the house of Annas."

The Fourth Gospel [12] describes Kaiaphas as the son-in-law of Annas, son of Seth ("Αννας or "Αννας; according to Josephus "Ανανος) who had been appointed by Quirinius and deposed by Valerius Gratus (6-15 C.E.), and states that Jesus, previous to being sent to Kaiaphas, was brought before Annas (the doyen of the High Priests, five of whose sons had risen to high-priestly rank) and first examined by him. There is nothing improbable in this: a High Priest who had held the office only for a day retained the title and also sat in the Sanhedrin.[13] But the other Gospels make no mention of this examination before Annas.

According to Mark [14] and Matthew[15] the Sanhedrin held a session that same night, which was illegal since capital cases could be tried by day only.[16] But, as we have seen, the Sanhedrin was mainly composed of Sadducees and the Sadducees may have recognized no such rule. Furthermore we have assumed that this was not a trial proper, but only a preliminary investigation for which there was no rule that its work should be carried out by day only. These explanations are, however, uncalled for, since Luke knows nothing whatever of a night session: according to him there was but one session of the Sanhedrin, and that in the morning.[17]

But the Sadducees themselves would not have conducted even a

Ha-Me'ammer, II 559-560) ; Büchler's objections (*Die Priester und der Cultus*, pp. 85-87) are groundless since the High Priests are explicitly referred to.

[11] *Ant.* XVIII ii 2, and iv 3.

[12] John xviii. 13-24.

[13] *Ant.* IV xviii 2; *Horayoth* III 4; *Megillah* I 9; *Makkoth* II 6; *T. Yoma* I 4; Acts of the Apostles iv. 6. See also Büchler, *Priester u. Cultus*, p. 26; Schürer, *op. cit.* II⁴ 274-5; Ed. Meyer, *op. cit.* I 50.

[14] Mark xiv. 54.

[15] Matt. xxvi. 57.

[16] *Sanh.* IV 11.

[17] Luke xxii. 54, 66.

simple judicial enquiry either on the night of Passover or on the first day of Passover ("the feast of unleavened bread") ; the *Mishna* lays it down that capital cases may not be judged on the eve of a Sabbath or on the eve of a Festival, to avoid delay should the case not be finished that day, and all trials were forbidden on a Sabbath or Festival.[18]

We must, therefore, follow the Fourth Gospel (which is supported by a *Talmudic Baraita*) [19] and suppose that Jesus was crucified on the eve of the Sabbath and on the eve of Passover, and not (according to the Synoptic Gospels) on the Passover itself which fell on the eve of the Sabbath. We thus escape the impossible supposition that the Sanhedrin examined Jesus during the night of a Festival or (according to Luke) on the first day of the Feast of Unleavened Bread.

In one respect Luke is more accurate than Mark or Matthew : Jesus was not tried at all by night ; he was only imprisoned in the "Booths," to await trial, during the remaining hours of that night of the Last Supper and the agony in the Garden of Gethsemane. Not till the next morning, the eve of Passover, did the members of the Sanhedrin assemble. They were, most of them, Sadducees and Bœthuseans and so had no regard for the rule (which did not, perhaps, come into force until a later date) that cases might not be tried on the eves of Sabbaths or Festivals.[20] In any case, this was only a preliminary enquiry and was concerned with a matter of public danger.

They summoned witnesses against Jesus. According to Mark [21] their evidence did not agree. It is, however, more probable (since Jesus had, before large numbers of people, said things that were not lawful) that their evidence did not prove anything serious enough to render him liable to death.[22] The incident of the "cleansing of the Temple" would certainly be brought up again. The Evangelists do not, however, make any further mention of it since it was an act of unauthorised violence and, from a purely legal point of view, it was the priests who were in the right. But it was not enough to justify a sentence of death : the Temple itself was not affected, and it was not a case of profaning what was sacred.

At last there came two witnesses (according to the Gospels they were "false witnesses") who testified : "We heard him say, I will destroy this temple that is made with hands and in three days I will build another made without hands." [23] Mark,[24] though not Mat-

[18] *Sanh.* IV 1 (end) ; *Sifre* on Deut. §221 (ed. Friedmann 114b) ; *Mechilta Va-yaqhel* 1, ed. Friedmann 105a : *Sanh.* 35b.
[19] *Sanh.* 44a; see above, p. 27, n. 28.
[20] *Betzah* V 2, T. *Betzah* I 2.
[21] Mark xiv. 56.
[22] Such is the implication of Matthew xxvi. 59-60.
[23] Mark xiv. 58; Matt. xxvi. 61.
[24] Mark xiv. 59.

thew,[25] adds: "and not even so did their witness agree together." We saw how the Fourth Gospel confirmed this charge and how the same charge was brought against Stephen.[26]

Throughout the entire enquiry Jesus remained silent. At the moment such silence was best suited to his frame of mind. Jesus did not resemble in his preaching those other rebel-messiahs of the time, and it was difficult to get at the truth as to his real character. The High Priest therefore put the direct question to Jesus himself: "Art thou the Messiah?" Mark [27] here adds the words, "the Son of the Blessed." This is not a Hebrew expression and must be a later addition: it is scarcely an abbreviation of the habitual "the Holy One, blessed be he." Matthew records the question in more solemn form: "I adjure thee by the living God that thou tell us whether thou be the Messiah, the son of God!"

The oath is possible, but the words "Son of God" (which become a separate question in Luke)[28] from the mouth of a Jewish High Priest, and particularly from a Sadducee, are inconceivable.

Jesus was convinced of his messiahship: of this there is no doubt; were it not so he would have been nothing more than a mere deceiver and imposter—and such men do not make history: they do not found new religions which persist for two thousand years and hold sway among five hundred millions of civilised people. When this challenge came from the High Priest, a challenge which he had already answered affirmatively at Cæsarea Philippi and Bethphage, it was impossible but that the soul and feelings of Jesus—a mystic, a dreamer and an enthusiast—should be stirred to their depths. There is no doubt that he returned a positive answer.

According to Mark's version, he answered:[29] "I am he;" and according to Matthew:[30] "Thou sayest" derived from the answer of Jesus to Pilate); then, according to all the Synoptic Gospels, Jesus added: "And ye shall see the Son of Man sitting at the right hand of Power and coming with the clouds of heaven."[31] Could his enthusiastic belief in himself have led him to such lengths as to make use of this startling reference to himself? With an oriental possessed of such a conviction, it was by no means impossible. The two expressions "Son of man" (frequently on his lips) and "at the right hand of power" ($\dot{\epsilon}\varkappa$ $\delta\epsilon\xi\iota\tilde{\omega}\nu$ $\tau\tilde{\eta}\varsigma$ $\delta\upsilon\nu\acute{\alpha}\mu\epsilon\omega\varsigma$, a peculiar Hebrew

[25] Matt. xxvi. 61.
[26] See above, p. 322.
[27] Mark xiv. 61; Matt. xxvi. 63.
[28] Luke xxii. 66-70.
[29] Mark xiv. 62.
[30] Matt. xxvi. 64.
[31] Mark xiv. 62; Matt. xxvi. 64; Luke xxii. 70 ("the power of God"—an attempt to explain the unusual expression which in his time was not understood by non-Jews).

expression for the Deity),[32] show that the answer is perfectly in accord with Jesus' spirit and manner of speech.

To the High Priest the answer was sheer blasphemy—a Galilæan carpenter styling himself "Son of man" in the sense of the Book of Daniel and saying that he should sit on the right hand of God and come "with the clouds of heaven"! The High Priest rent his garments—the custom of the judge who heard blasphemous words.[33] According to the ruling of the *Mishna*,[34] Jesus was not worthy of death since "the blasphemer is not guilty till he have expressly pronounced the *Name;*" and Jesus, like a scrupulous Jew, said "Power" instead of "Yahweh." We have, however, already pointed out, (a) that this was a court of law mainly composed of Sadducees whose president, the High Priest, was a Bœthusean; and (b) that, even in Jesus' time, the Pharisees had not yet laid down the rules of procedure in the precise form which they receive in the *Mishna*.

Thus, for example, as opposed to what the *Mishna* decrees touching the mode of death by burning (thrusting a burning wick down the throat of the condemned), R. Eliezer ben R. Zadok, records how, during the Second Temple period, they burnt a priest's daughter, guilty of adultery, with bundles of faggots.[35] To this it was answered, "The court in those days was not skilled"—showing that many of the prescriptions of the *Mishna* (whose criminal law reached an unexampled degree of humanitarianism) were not in vogue prior to the Destruction, and that even the Pharisees had not then attained their later level of humanitarianism, still less the Sadducees. Josephus lays great emphasis on the fact that the Sadducees were "more cruel and harsh than any of the Jews in applying the laws," [36] which must mean, primarily, that they were more cruel and harsh than the Pharisees.

After rending his garments, the Bœthusean High Priest turned to the members of the Sanhedrin and asked: "What further need have we of witnesses? Ye have heard the blasphemy: what think ye?" And the Gospels add: "And they all condemned him to be worthy of death." [37] But since there had not been actual blasphemy it is difficult to believe that, even in the opinion of the Sadducees, Jesus was worthy of death. The Pharisees, at least, who were in the Sanhedrin would not declare him liable to death since they would see in his words nothing more than a rash fantasy (חוצפא כלפי שמיא,

---

[32] "From the mouth of Power" (מפי הגבורה), *Baba Metzia* 58b; *Shabb.* 88b; *Horayoth* 8a; *Makk.* 24a; *Megillah* 31b; *J. Sanh.* X 1 (p. 28 end of a); *Ex. R.* §33; see also *Shabb.* 87a; *Ex. R.* §24 *Cant. R.* on *Zoth Qomathekh.*
[33] *Sanh.* VI 5.
[34] *Ibid.*
[35] *Sanh.* VI 2; *J. Sanh.* VII 2; *T. Sanh.* IX 11.
[36] *Ant.* XX ix 1.
[37] Mark xiv. 64; Matt. xxvi. 65-66; Luke makes no mention of the death sentence; in his account of the judicial enquiry there is only a charge of general wrong-doing.

"impertinence against heaven"). He had not "pronounced the Name" and he had not beguiled others into worshipping other gods.

At this stage there begins a long series of statements by the Evangelists, having as their object to make *all the Jews*—leaders, priests, scribes, and the entire Jewish populace—responsible for the death and torture of Jesus. Therefore they emphasize the fact that not even one of the members of the Sanhedrin took the part of Jesus, though there was certainly one of them, Joseph of Arimathæa, who was not opposed to Jesus. To pile up the Jewish guilt all the Synoptists record how, even in the presence of the judges, the servants or attendants (the judges too, according to Mark and Matthew)[38] spat in the face of Jesus, covered his eyes and struck him with their fists, and said, "Prophesy unto us: who is he that struck thee?"—and they buffeted him on the cheek.

All of this (despite the "fist" of the High Priests spoken of in the street-ballad) would be impossible in the house of the High Priest and in the presence of the Sanhedrin. But we shall soon hear worse charges than these.

But who was present during the trial and heard what the witnesses said, the challenge of the High Priest and Jesus' answer? According to all three Synoptists it was Simon Peter (the Fourth Gospel reports that the disciple John was also with him), who came into the court of the High Priest together with the guards and sat with the attendants, warming himself by the fire during the cold night. In Jerusalem the warm spring nights grow cold towards the later hours. One of the High Priest's female servants (or the gatekeeper) identified him as having consorted "with Jesus of Nazareth," but Peter denied it and pretended that he did not know of what she was speaking; and when other bystanders recognized him owing to his Galilæan dialect, he swore that he did not know Jesus.

Legend declares that this painful but quite human incident was foretold by Jesus, with the detail of a threefold denial before cockcrow, so making the event not so unseemly. There is no reason to doubt the story as a whole. Peter finally recalled to mind his beloved lord and Messiah and all his intimate friendship: he was seized with remorse at having denied him, and wept bitterly.[39] It is all human, excessively human: the story has a peculiarly sad, attractive beauty, and does not spare the disciple.

The Law enacted[40] that the blasphemer, the false prophet, the beguiler and seducer, were to be stoned. It was also held that "everyone that is stoned is also hanged," and all alike held that the blasphemer who had been stoned was (after death by stoning) also hanged.[41] The *Mishna* goes into detail: "How do they hang him?

---

[38] Mark xiv. 65; Matt. xxvi. 67.
[39] Mark xiv. 66-72; Matt. xxvi. 69, 75; Luke xxii. 55-63.
[40] Deut. xiii. 7-12; xvii. 2-7.
[41] *Sanh.* VI 4.

They fix a beam in the ground and a piece of wood branches from it (R. Obadiah of Bertenora explains: "Like a peg coming out of the beam near the top") and the two hands are fastened together, and so they hang him." [42]

This is very like the form of the Roman cross which was not of the present conventional shape, but resembled the Latin and Greek capital T. The hanged victim suffered no pain since the hanging or crucifixion only took place after death had resulted from stoning; and the hanging only served to impress the onlookers during the body's short time of exposure: "They took it down at once, for if they suffered it to stay till night-time a negative commandment would thereby be broken, for it is written: [43] His corpse shall not remain [תלין , lit. spend the night] on the tree, but thou shalt surely bury it, for a curse of God is that which is hanged." [44] This verse proved a "stumbling-block" to Christianity and Paul found difficulty in suitably expounding it.

We have seen that at that time the Jews could not pass sentence of death, at least not in a case affecting a Messiah, *i.e.*, a political question. Since, therefore, it was the eve of Passover and the eve of Sabbath, the High Priest and leaders of the Sanhedrin hastened to give up Jesus to Pilate, the Procurator, in order that the case could be finished while it was still day, and so avoid the delay which would occur through the seven days of Passover (or to avoid political outbreaks at a time when Galilæan Zealots were in Jerusalem in large numbers).

It is certain that the priests did not see in Jesus anything more than an ordinary rebel: they did not recognize his special spiritual nature; what they did they did, in all simplicity, in order to save the people from the cruel vengeance of Pilate, who was on the watch for some possible excuse to demonstrate the power of Rome and the nugatory nature of Jewish autonomy in any matter of political importance.[45]

They, therefore, bound Jesus (from which it is to be presumed that he was not bound during the judicial enquiry) and brought him to Pilate. Certain of the priestly party went with him and explained to Pilate that the Sanhedrin had condemned Jesus for assuming the rôle of Messiah, *i.e.* King of the Jews: such was all the meaning that "Messiah" would convey to Pilate the Roman.

When Pilate came to Jerusalem to be present during the time of Passover he did not live in the Citadel of Antonia, but, according to

---

[42] *Sanh.* VI 4; *Sifre* on Deut. §221, ed. Friedmann 114b.
[43] Deut. xxi. 23.
[44] *Sanh. l.c.; T. Sanh.* IX 6-7. See *Sifre, l.c.:* "Could they hang him alive as did the Gentile powers? Scripture says: And he shall be slain"; see also *Sanh.* 46b.
[45] Ed. Meyer, *op. cit.* I 164-165, II 451, admits the political danger threatening people and country from Jesus' presence, even if at first there was no idea of rebellion.

the evidence of Josephus, in the Palace of Herod (one of the three towers, one of which survives under the title of "Tower of David," though it is really the "Tower of Phasael") where was a "garrison" or large barracks.[46]　Jesus was tried before Pilate in a place called the Prætorium (the Fourth Gospel calls Pilate's judgment-seat by the Aramaic term "Gabbatha," (Γαββαθᾶ, Λιθόστρωτος), in Greek meaning "stone pavement").[47]

The Procurator asked, "Art thou the king of the Jews?"　According to all three Synoptists Jesus answered, "Thou hast said" (Σὺ εἶπας).　Such an answer was characteristic of Jesus who was given to brief, pointed and enigmatic remarks.　The *Talmud* and *Midrash*[48] use the same answer, "Ye say" (אמריתון אתון, *i.e.*, but not I), when it is unsafe or unseemly to say the truth.　Thus, Jesus' answer: what else could he answer to the foreign tyrant?　He said not the least word more and this silence astonished Pilate.[49]　Jesus' speech and his argument with Pilate, given in detail by the Fourth Gospel, cannot be accepted as historical.[50]　The words attributed to Jesus: "My kingdom is not of this world," [51] however suited to and characteristic of *Christianity,* are quite impossible from Jesus the Jew.

The Evangelists elaborate the unhistorical element still further. According to Luke,[52] Pilate said that he found no fault in Jesus, and on hearing that Jesus was a Galilæan sent him to Herod Antipas, who was present in Jerusalem for the feast; and although Pilate and Antipas had been enemies they became friends again that day. Antipas welcomed this opportunity of seeing Jesus and asked for a sign from him, but Jesus remained silent.　Antipas treated him with mockery, decked him with a scarlet robe and sent him back to Pilate. Again Pilate declared that he found no fault in him, as neither did Herod; therefore he, Pilate, was minded to scourge him, only, and let him go.　Mark and Matthew are ignorant of this episode; nor was it possible for Pilate simply to scourge Jesus and liberate him, since scourging was an essential and inseparable part of the crucifixion sentence.[53]

[46] Dalman, *op. cit.* pp. 268-272.

[47] John xix. 13. H. M. Michlin (*Doar ha-Yom*, 1921, n. 274) suggests that "Gabatha" is corrupted from "Gazitha," the Fourth Gospel wrongly supposing that Pilate sat in judgment in the "Hall of Hewn Stone."

[48] *J. Kelaim* IX 4; *Eccles. R.* on *Tobhah Hokhmah 'im nahalah; Kethuboth,* 104a; *T. Kelim: Baba Kama* I 6

[49] Mark xv. 1-5; Matt. xxvii. 1-14.

[50] John xviii. 28-38.

[51] John xviii. 30.

[52] Luke xxiii. 4-16.

[53] Such is the conclusion of Husband, *op. cit.* pp. 273-4; but Josephus (*Wars* VI v 3) says that the leading people delivered up Yeshu Ben Hannan, who had prophesied evil things against Jerusalem, to the Governor Albinus, who scourged him cruelly and set him free, after that it was proved that he was mad.　The Chiliarch wished to do the same thing to Paul (Acts xxii. 24-25).

Matthew, again, relates that when Pilate was sitting in judgment his wife sent to him, saying, "Have thou nothing to do with this righteous man, for I have suffered much because of him this night in a dream." [54] Both Mark and Luke lack this incident; such a remark from a Roman matron, the wife of the Procurator, is quite unlikely.

But all four Gospels are unanimous in relating how, at every festival, Pilate used to liberate to the Jews any one prisoner whom they desired. On the present occasion another rebel, a Zealot, Barabbas by name, who had committed murder, was waiting to be crucified. Pilate wished to liberate the "King of the Jews," Jesus, since he knew "that only from envy had the chief priests betrayed him" (but how did he know it?). The chief priests (as though they did not have more urgent business on the eve of Passover and the eve of Sabbath) incited the people to demand that Barabbas, and none other, be set free.

And this the people did. On Pilate's asking: "And what, then, do ye wish that I shall do to him whom ye (and not Pilate, or even Jesus himself) call King of the Jews?" they cried out, "Crucify him!" and when the "compassionate" Pilate asked, "Why? what evil hath he done?" they continued to cry out, "Crucify him!" Then the helpless Pilate was "compelled" to do the people's will and to free Barabbas. Jesus he scourged and gave up to be crucified.[55]

To Mark's account Matthew [55a] adds that Pilate "took water and washed his hands in the presence of the people, and said: I am innocent of the blood of this righteous man, see ye to it. And all the people answered and said: His blood be upon us and upon our children!" Neither Mark nor Luke records this last point. Washing the hands as a sign that those hands are free of blood is a specifically Jewish custom used in the ceremony of "the heifer whose neck is to be broken;" [56] and how could a Roman official perform it? A more important point, however, is the fact that the right to free a criminal after condemnation belonged only to the Emperor,[57] and it is, on the whole, most unlikely that in all his four books Josephus found no opportunity of mentioning such a noteworthy custom as that of liberating a prisoner before the Passover.

In view of these difficulties Wendland supposes that the entire story about Barabbas is drawn from the account given by Philo of Alexandria about the crucifixion of a certain *Carabbas*, whose name, by the interchange of *c* and *b*, has been converted into Barabbas.[58]

Furthermore, all that we learn of Pilate from the writings of

[54] Matt. xxvii. 19.
[55] Mark xv. 6-16.
[55a] Matt. xxvii. 24-25.
[56] Deut. xxi. 6-9.
[57] See Husband, *op. cit.* p. 270.
[58] "Hermes," 1898, p. 178; see also G. Friedlander, *The Jewish Sources of the Sermon on the Mount*, London, 1911, pp. xi-xii.

Josephus and Philo proves that he was a "man of blood," cruel and tyrannical, to whom the killing of a single Galilæan Jew was no more than the killing of a fly, and who was always ready to provoke the Jews in every possible way; [59] while here he is suddenly turned into a tender, pacific being, sparing of bloodshed and anxious to save a "just man perishing through his righteousness"—all of which is particularly unlikely after he had learnt that the condemned man called himself the Messiah (which for him could only mean the "king of the Jews"), a fact which the condemned man, by his enthusiastic conviction, had in part confirmed.

The truth of the matter is that all the stories of Pilate's opposition to the crucifixion of Jesus are wholly unhistorical, emanating from the end of the first Christian century, when large numbers of Gentiles had embraced Christianity and it had become clear to Paul that the future of Christianity depended upon the Gentiles and not upon the Jews, who "remained steadfast in their unbelief" and would not recognize "the curse of God that was hanged."

Also, the Roman empire was then all-powerful and it was impolitic to irritate it; whereas the Jews were feeble, poor and persecuted. Therefore the Evangelists found it better not to place the blame for the murder of Jesus upon the powerful Romans, who were "near to the way of truth," but to place it upon the heads of the perverse Jews, who were then (immediately after the Second Destruction) dirt under the feet of their Gentile conquerors.

A few only of the priestly caste had condemned Jesus to death and given him up to Pilate, primarily because of their dread of this same Pilate, and only incidentally because of their annoyance at the "cleansing of the Temple," and because Jesus mocked "at the words of the wise," and spoke ill of the Temple; and, what was more serious, because of his blasphemy in thinking himself "the Son of man coming with the clouds of heaven," who should sit at the right hand of God.

Through fear of the Roman tyrant, those who were then the chief men among the Jews delivered up Jesus to this tyrant. No Jews took any further part in the actual trial and crucifixion: Pilate, the "man of blood" was responsible for the rest. The Jews, *as a nation,* were far less guilty of the death of Jesus than the Greeks, as a nation, were guilty of the death of Socrates; but who now would think of avenging the blood of Socrates the Greek upon his countrymen, the present Greek race? Yet these nineteen hundred years past the world has gone on avenging the blood of Jesus the Jew upon his countrymen, the Jews, who have already paid the penalty, and still go on paying the penalty in rivers and torrents of blood.

[59] See Philo, *Delegation to Caius* §38; *Ant.* XVIII iii 1, iv 1; *Wars* II ix 2. See above, pp. 163 ff.

III. THE CRUCIFIXION

Crucifixion is the most terrible and cruel death which man has ever devised for taking vengeance on his fellow man. Cicero [1] describes it as *crudelissimum teterrimumque supplicium* (the most cruel and horrifying death), and Tacitus [2] refers to it as *supplicium servile* (a despicable death). It came from Persia where, apparently it arose out of the desire not to suffer the condemned victim to defile the earth, which was sacrosanct to Ahura Mazda (Ormuzd); thence it passed to Carthage and so to the Romans, who employed it as a punishment for rebels, renegade slaves and the lowest types of criminal. Josephus, [3] an eye-witness, tells how that "joy of human kind," Titus (who read Josephus' work), crucified so many Jewish captives and fugitives during the siege of Jerusalem, that there was not sufficient room for the crosses nor sufficient crosses for the condemned!

Crucifixion was, therefore, a penalty characteristic of the Romans. It is true that Josephus [4] relates how Alexander Jannæus commanded eight-hundred rebel Pharisees to be crucified (ἀνασταυροῦν); but he points out that this was an act of barbarous cruelty in which Alexander was imitating Gentile usage. And it is also possible that the punishment was not crucifixion but hanging, and that Josephus was drawing from a foreign source which exaggerated the incident (800 crucified and 8000 exiled are round numbers open to suspicion) and so copied the term customary among Greeks and Romans.

On the other hand, it is well known that the Roman officials frequently crucified Jews: Varus on one occasion crucified two thousand, [5] and Quadratus and Felix crucified many others. [6] But to say that the *Jews* crucified Jesus or that they were even responsible for his death by crucifixion, is grossly untrue. At the worst, only a section of the aristocratic Sadducees had some part in his arrest and preliminary examination and in handing him over to Pilate. [7] But with Judæa in its then grievous plight, anyone claiming to be the Messiah could not fail to bring disaster on nation and country alike: "prac-

[1] *In Verrem*, V 64.
[2] *Annales*, IV 3, 11.
[3] *Wars* V xi 1.
[4] *Ant.* XIII xiv 2.
[5] *Ant.* XIII xvii 10; *Wars* II v 2 (end).
[6] *Wars* II xii 6, xv 2.
[7] L. Philippsohn, *Haben die Juden wirklich Jesum gekreuzigt?* Bonn, 1866; E. G. Hirsch, *Crucifixion from the Jewish Point of View*, Chicago, 1892.

tical politicians" like the Sadducees must needs take into account such a national danger.[8]

There was no real justice in the case: neither the Sanhedrin nor Pilate probed deeply enough to discover that Jesus was no rebel; and a Sadducæan court of law would not pay scrupulous regard to the fact whether or not Jesus was a "blasphemer," or "false prophet," or an inciter to idolatry, in the Biblical or *Mishnaic* sense. But when or where *has* ideal justice prevailed!

Of the two charges which the Sanhedrin brought against Jesus— blasphemy and Messianic pretensions—Pilate took account of the second only. Jesus was the "King-Messiah" and so, from Pilate's standpoint (since he could have no notion of the spiritual side to the Hebrew messianic idea), he was "king of the Jews." This was treason against the Roman Emperor for which the *Lex Juliana* knew but one punishment—death;[9] and the prescribed death of rebel traitors was—crucifixion.[10]

Scourging always preceded crucifixion: so Josephus twice informs us.[11] This was a horrible punishment, reducing the naked body to strips of raw flesh, and inflamed and bleeding weals. And when afterwards the victim's hands were nailed to the crosspiece and his feet tied (or nailed) to the base of the beam, leaving the sufferer unable to drive away the gnats and flies which settled on his naked body and on his wounds, and unable to abstain from publicly fulfilling natural needs—nothing could have been more horrible and appalling. None but the Romans, whose cruelty surpassed that of ravening beasts, could have made choice of this revolting means of death: it never could have been devised by the Jews, by the Pharisees (whose axiom was, "choose for him an easy death"), nor by their harsher contemporaries, the Sadducees.[12]

After the scourging Jesus was handed over to the Roman soldiers. The Gospels describe how the coarse Roman soldiers ridiculed him: they dressed him in purple and put on him a crown woven of *akkabith* (Arabic *'akkub, Gundelia Tournefortii*)[13] or "Jewish thorn" (ἀκάνθινον στέφανον);[14] it was not "a crown of thorns," since the in-

---

[8] Husband (*op. cit.* 182-233), a Christian scholar, admits that neither the Sanhedrin's judicial enquiry nor Pilate's sentence was contrary to the law; and we have already mentioned that Ed. Meyer (*op. cit.* I 164-5) recognized that Jesus' appearance was a political danger, and that those who gave him up to Pilate feared an actual revolution and did not merely take this opportunity of getting rid of a dangerous religious rival (see also, *op. cit.* II 451).

[9] Husband, 231-2.

[10] Suetonius, *Vespasianus*, §IV; *Claudius*, §XXV.

[11] *Wars* II xiv 9; V xi 1; see also *Titus Livius*, XXXIV 26.

[12] *T. Sanh.* IX ii; *Sanh.* 45a, 52a; *Sota* 8b; *Pesahim* 75a; *Kethuboth* 37b; *B. Qama* 51a.

[13] Dalman, *op. cit.* 210-211; he thinks it possible that it was the common Palestine thorn, which has round flowers and a thick bluish calyx.

[14] So A. Mazié of Jerusalem explains the Hebrew name "Akanthus" (which the Septuagint renders by ἀκανθαι a common ornament in the Galilæan synagogues (see his *Sokah Yehudith* in *Qobetz ha-Hebrah ha-*

tention was not to pierce his head with thorns but to scoff at him in his character of "king," decked with a "crown." They mockingly saluted him: "Hail! King of the Jews," beat him on the head with a reed (the royal sceptre), spat in his face and bowed the knee and prostrated themselves before him. After this mockery they removed the purple raiment, replaced it by his own clothes and led him away to be crucified.[15]

There is no doubt that the rough Roman soldiery were capable of such cruel horseplay and thought it fitting to make a mock of the whole Jewish nation in the person of the "king of the Jews,"[16] though it is questionable whether the facts were as the Gospels report: the time was too limited, and the strict Roman discipline would certainly not allow the soldiers to do more than obey orders—especially in the case of an important political prisoner.

The Romans, in their cruelty, usually insisted that those "which went forth to be crucified"[17] should carry on their shoulder the cross on which they were about to die[18]—yet another considered piece of cruelty. But Jesus' strength, after the long night and the scourging, failed him completely: like most of the "Rabbis" he was probably thin and emaciated. So when the soldiers who escorted Jesus encountered Simon of Cyrene (Cyrenaica in Africa), a resident of Jerusalem (whose sons Alexander and Rufus seem later to have joined the Christians),[19] "coming from the country" (a detail showing that this was not a feast-day, although it is not said whether he was working or only walking), they compelled him to carry the cross. From Pilate's Prætorium in the Phasael Tower, they went to Golgotha (so-called because it was a *skull*-shaped hill, not because it was the place of execution and filled with human skulls). General Gordon placed the site near the "Cave of Jeremiah," a hundred yards north-west of Herod's gate, on the mound known to the Jews as "The Place of Stoning,"[20] near the so-called "Garden Tomb."

There are difficulties in the way of identifying the site of the Church of the Holy Sepulchre with the actual site of the crucifixion, for a place of execution, still more a burial place, could not possibly exist *within* the city, owing to the regulations affecting clean and unclean. Thus we learn that "they do not suffer the dead to remain

Ibrith la'haqirath Eretz Yisrael w'atiqotheha I 40-42; an illustration of the "Jewish thorn" is given on p. 39).

[15] Mark xv. 17-20.

[16] See *Wars*, V x 1.

[17] An expression found in the *Midrash;* see *Sifre* on Deut. §308, ed. Friedmann 133b; *Mechilta, Yithro, "Ba-hodesh"* §86, ed. Friedmann 68b, *Midrash Tehillim (Shoher tob)* 45, 8, ed. Buber, p. 270; *Esther R.* (beginning) and elsewhere.

[18] Also referred to in the *Midrash:* "Like one who bears his cross on his shoulder" *(Gen. R.* §56); *Midrash Sekhcl Tob, "Breshith,"* 22, 6, ed. Buber, p. 61; *Pesikta Rabbati* 31, ed. Friedmann, 143b.

[19] Acts xix. 33; Romans xvi. 13.

[20] *Sanh.* VI 1; *T. Sanh.* IX 5-6.

in Jerusalem nor do they leave therein the bones of men . . . nor build there sepulchres, except only the tombs of the house of David and the tomb of Hulda the Prophetess;" [21] and, still more definitely,[22] "they do not bury the dead therein." [23]

Dalman,[24] however, holds that Golgotha was on the present site of the Holy Sepulchre, and that, at the end of the period of the Second Temple, it stood by the mainroad. He considers that גילגלתא is גל-גועתה, "The mound of Goa" a place south of Jerusalem.[25] The latter theory is, however, improbable, and the former theory arises from an attempt to justify accepted tradition. According to an ancient *Baraita*, "when a man is going out to be killed they suffer him to drink a grain of frankincense in a cup of wine to deaden his senses . . . wealthy women of Jerusalem used to contribute these things and bring them." [26] Mark points to the same custom when he says, "And they gave him wine to drink mingled with myrrh (ἐσμυρνισμένον οἶνον), but he received it not." [27]

Owing to this compassion which the "wealthy women of Jerusalem" used to show for the condemned, a tradition has developed in Luke to the effect that there went after Jesus "a multitude of women weeping and bewailing him," and Jesus is made to address a whole discourse to "the daughters of Jerusalem," which, for one in his condition, is inconceivable." [28]

Equally inconceivable is the noble saying which Luke attributes to Jesus: "Father, forgive them, for they know not what they do." [29] This has become classical; it comes fittingly from the mouth of Jesus —but not in such terrible circumstances; it is lacking both in Mark and Matthew.

The further incidents related by all three Synoptists—that the soldiers divided Jesus' garments among themselves by lot, that two thieves were crucified together with him, the one on the right and the other on the left, that the two thieves (so Matthew)[30] joined with the priests and scribes and passers-by in reviling Jesus (though according to Luke [31] one only of the thieves reviled Jesus while the second, "the penitent thief," spoke kindly with him and asked that

---

[21] *T. Negaim* VI 2; see *B. Qama* 82b.

[22] *Ab. d'R. Nathan,* ed. Schechter, version II, 39, 54a; see also version I, 35, 52b.

[23] On this subject see the additional section in Krauss's *Qadmoniyoth ha-Talmud* (the Hebrew version, Odessa, 1914) I 92-113, replying to the views of A. Büchler, *REJ,* LXII 30-50, LXIII 201-215.

[24] See his article, *Golgotha und das Grab Christi* (*Palästina-Jahrbuch,* 1913, IX 98-122) and his *Orte und Wege Jesu,* pp. 276-305.

[25] Jer. xxxi. 38.

[26] *Sanh.* 43a; *Abel Rabbati* (*Semahoth*) II 9.

[27] Mark xv. 23.

[28] Luke xxiii. 27-31.

[29] Luke xxiii. 34.

[30] Matt. xxvii. 44.

[31] Luke xxiii. 39-43.

Jesus remember him when he came "into his kingdom," receiving the promise: "This day shalt thou be with me in Paradise") and that one of the soldiers stretched up to him a reed bearing a sponge filled with vinegar (Matthew [32] has "vinegar mingled with myrrh")—these are everyone incidents introduced to fulfil certain passages from the Psalms; [33] "They parted my garments among them and on my vesture they cast lots" . . . "they gave me gall to eat and vinegar to drink;" and a verse in Isaiah: [34] "Because he poured out his soul unto death and was numbered with the transgressors: yet he bare the sin of many and made intercession for the transgressors."

On the cross-beam (*patibulum*) above, was an inscription written, according to Luke and the Fourth Gospel, in three languages, Hebrew (or Aramaic), Greek and Latin—"The King of the Jews" (so Mark); "This is Jesus, King of the Jews" (so Matthew); "This is the King of the Jews" (so Luke); or, according to the Fourth Gospel, "Jesus of Nazareth, King of the Jews." The words "King of the Jews" are common to all the Gospels. The inference is clear that Jesus was crucified as "King-Messiah," which, for non-Jews, could only mean "King of the Jews."

This renders untenable any hypothesis to the effect that Jesus never declared himself as Messiah even at the last, and that he remained no more than a Pharisaic "Rab," an "apocalyptic prophet," or a "forerunner of the Messiah." He was delivered up to Pilate as a false Messiah, and as such he was crucified by Pilate. The sly tyrant could not resist the pleasure of gibing at the Jewish nation by means of an inscription above the cross: Behold how we, the Romans, inflict the most ignominious of deaths on this so-called King of the Jews!

By eastern reckoning the crucifixion began at "the third hour" of the day, *i.e.*, nine o'clock in the morning; it was continued until "the ninth hour," *i.e.*, three in the afternoon. Death by crucifixion did not usually follow so quickly: from many quarters we learn that death sometimes did not follow till after two days or more. It serves to show that Jesus was very feeble. The horrible physical sufferings were beyond his power of endurance; and the spiritual sufferings were hardly less than the physical.

The Messiah crucified! the "Son of Man" hanged (and so become "a curse of God") by uncircumcised heathen—and yet no help from on high! The great and gracious God, Father of all men, his own heavenly Father, especially near to him, his beloved Son and Messiah —his heavenly Father came not to his help nor released him from his agony nor saved him by a miracle! The dream of his life had vanished: his life's work had perished! The thought was unbearable . . . in his terrible anguish of heart he summoned up all his remaining

---

[32] Matt. xxvii. 48 (in the best versions).
[33] Ps. xxii. 19; lxix. 22.
[34] Isa. liii. 12.

strength and cried out, in his mother-tongue, in the language of the book he loved most: "My God, my God, why hast thou forsaken me?" Matthew and Mark [35] preserve in Greek transliteration the very words almost in their Hebrew-Aramaic pronunciation: "Eloi, Eloi, lama sabachthani?" [36] It has been remarked (by Wilhelm Brandt) that a man suffering terrible tortures on the cross "does not affect quotations;" and, that the single verse from the Psalm from which the cry was drawn, served as the source of the legend about the soldiers casting lots for his garments. Jesus, however, was so permeated with the spirit of the Scriptures that he both began (at his baptism) and ended (at his crucifixion) his career with quotations from the Scriptures. It is, on the whole, unlikely that the Church would have put such a verse in the mouth of Jesus if he had not uttered it: the verse is at variance with the Christian belief concerning Jesus and his sufferings. Both Mark and Matthew relate that those standing around the cross thought, as they heard Jesus pronounce *Elohi* or *Eli,* that he was calling for *Elijah;* but they said, "Let be, let us see if Elijah will come and take him down."

Luke, however, who did not find the verse in keeping with Jesus, the Son of God, replaced it with another, more suitable verse: [37] "Father, into thy hands I commend my spirit." The Fourth Gospel makes no mention of any appeal to God: that would be out of keeping with the nature of the *Logos.*

At last, overcome by his sufferings, Jesus cried out with a loud voice . . . and gave up the ghost. When he died there were standing some distance away, Mary Magdalen, Mary the mother of James the Less and of Joses, Salome, and other women followers who had accompanied him from Galilee. The menfolk among the disciples were afraid to stand near the cross lest they be suspected of having been among the associates of the crucified Jesus.

The women had no such fear: no one in the East would pay any regard to a woman-disciple. We can imagine what they thought and what they suffered, and what was the state of mind of all Jesus' disciples and followers. Their dream of a kingdom where they should sit on twelve thrones judging the twelve tribes of Israel, had come to naught; the dreamer-king, the king-Messiah . . . was "hanged: a curse of God;" he had died an ignominious death at the hands of the Gentiles. . . .

The hour was late and "it was the eve of the Sabbath" (so Mark and Luke); [38] it was also the eve of Passover. It was necessary, therefore, to hasten the burial of the crucified Jesus. The custom in Persia, Carthage and Rome was to leave the body on the cross, food for the fowls of the air. It is doubtful whether even the

[35] Mark xv. 34; Matt. xxvii. 46.   [37] Luke xxiii. 46.
[36] Ps. xxii. 2.   [38] Mark xv. 42; Luke xxiii. 54.

Romans followed this custom in Judæa; [39] they gave some respect to the *Torah* injunction: "His body shall not remain all night," especially when, as in this case, a person of importance intervened. One of the elders of the Sanhedrin, Joseph of Arimathæa, who, according to the Gospels,[40] "also himself was looking for the kingdom of God," approached Pilate (probably at the request of the disciples) and asked for the body of Jesus. Pilate was surprised that he was so soon dead and desired that the death be confirmed by the centurion who supervised the crucifixion. The centurion confirmed the death and Pilate gave the body to Joseph of Arimathæa, who was, it would seem, an important person in Jerusalem.

Joseph bought the grave-clothes, wrapped up the body and placed it in a tomb hewn in the rock, a tomb similar to many which remain to the present day. According to the *Mishna* rule [41] those put to death by order of the court were not buried in private tombs but in tombs specially set apart by the court; but Jesus was executed not by the Jewish court, but by the Roman authorities,[42] and this was, furthermore, a case of emergency. At the mouth of the tomb a heavy stone was rolled, such as we find now with many Palestinian cave-tombs (*e.g.*, the "Tombs of the Kings," מערת מלכי־בית־חדייב, by the Jews wrongly styled מערת כלבא שבוע). And so the burial ended.[43] Here ends the life of Jesus, and here begins the history of Christianity.

[39] See *Wars* IV v. 2.
[40] So Mark (xv. 43) and Luke (xxiii. 50-51). According to Matthew (xxvii. 57) he was "one of Jesus' disciples," a fact difficult to believe.
[41] *Sanh.* VI 5.
[42] "Those killed by the Roman authority—no privilege is withheld from them" (*Abel Rabbati,* or *Semahoth,* II 11).
[43] *Mo'ed Qatan 27a; Shabbath* 152b. Important in this connexion is the *Baraita:* "It happened to one in Beth Dagan in Judæa who died on the eve of Passover, that they went and buried him, and men went in and tied a rope about the rolling stone; from the outside the men pulled and the women went in and buried him; and the men went and performed the rites for the Eve of Passover" (*T. Ahiloth* III 9; *Sifre Zutta, Hukkath* XX 16, ed. Horowitz, *Kobetz ma'asê Tannaim,* Leipzig, 1917, III 313).

IV. THE ACCOUNT OF THE RESURRECTION

The tragedy had an "epilogue:" Christianity would, otherwise, never have been possible.

The two Marys (also, according to Luke,[1] Johanna the wife of Chuza the Steward) followed Joseph of Arimathæa to find where was the tomb; the tender feelings of these ardent women could not rest: duties still remained to be fulfilled to the poor crucified body of their lord and master. They looked upon the tomb from a distance, thinking that the moment the Sabbath was over they would purchase aromatic spices and anoint the wounded body. This seems to have been the Jewish custom: "they may anoint and unwrap the dead on the Sabbath."[2] By this means they thought to show their love for the dead.

It was impossible to carry out this plan on the Sabbath: there was the difficulty of rolling away the stone, which would have constituted work on the Sabbath, and buying or selling was not done on a Sabbath or festival (therefore Luke says that they prepared the spices on the Sabbath eve).[3] Therefore they came to the tomb early on the first day of the week (according to Mark[4] the two Marys were accompanied by Salome, or, according to Luke, by Johanna).

They feared they might not be able to roll away the stone, but, to their amazement, they found it already rolled away and the tomb empty. A young man arrayed in white (an angel) was sitting by, and he said to them: "Jesus is risen; he is not here . . . go, tell his disciples and Peter. He goeth before you into Galilee: there shall ye see him, as he said unto you."

The women were startled beyond measure: "for trembling and astonishment (τρόμος καὶ ἔκστασις) had come upon them." They escaped hurriedly "and said nothing to any one; for they were afraid." Such is Mark's version, and, with slight variants, that of Matthew and Luke also. From this point (from xvi. 9 to the end of the chapter) Mark has what is only a later addition: just as Mark says little of the wonders attendant on Jesus' birth, so he has nothing marvellous to tell in his account of Jesus' resurrection.

Matthew,[5] however, relates how Mary Magdalene and the other Mary ran "with great joy" to tell the disciples that the tomb was empty and that an angel had appeared to them, and that on the way they had seen Jesus himself, who repeated to them the words of the

[1] Luke xxiv. 10.
[2] *Shabb.* XXIII 5.
[3] Luke xxiii. 54-56.

[4] Mark xvi. 1.
[5] Matt. xxviii. 8.

angel. In explanation of the empty tomb Matthew tells a whole story, occurring in no other Gospel, of how "the chief priests and Pharisees" informed Pilate on the Sabbath that Jesus, "that deceiver," while he was yet alive had said, After three days I shall rise again. They proposed to Pilate that a guard be set over the tomb and that the opening of the tomb be sealed with their seal, lest the disciples "come and steal him away and say unto the people, He is risen from the dead; and the last error be worse than the first."

To this Pilate had consented. On the first day of the week "some of the guard came into the city and told unto the chief priests all the things that were come to pass. And when they were assembled with the elders and had taken counsel, they gave large money unto the soldiers, saying, Say ye, His disciples came by night and stole him away while we slept. And if this come to the governor's ears, we will persuade him, and rid you of care. So they took the money and did as they were taught: and this saying was spread abroad among the Jews, and continueth until this day." [6]

The *Tol'doth Yeshu* actually gives such a report, and, however late we place Matthew, the report must be early. Some Christian scholars have supposed that the Jews removed the body by night and buried it in some unknown place, in order that the rock-hewn tomb might not become a holy place. Such a fear as that, however, was not likely to arise at that time; "a crucified Messiah," "a curse of God that was hanged," was such a repellent idea to the Jews that they could never have supposed that anyone existed who would venerate the tomb. It is equally difficult to suppose that the disciples themselves would steal the body: during the first few days they were too terrified by the frightful death of their Messiah. Had they done so during the night, intending to announce the following day that Jesus had come to life again, we should then have been forced to admit that their belief in the days that followed was utter trickery and fraud.

That is impossible: *deliberate imposture* is not the substance out of which the religion of millions of mankind is created. We must assume that the owner of the tomb, Joseph of Arimathæa, thought it unfitting that one who had been crucified should remain in his own ancestral tomb. Matthew alone tells us that the tomb was new, hewn out of the rock specially for Jesus the Messiah (just as the ass's colt on which Jesus rode was one on which none other had ever sat). Joseph of Arimathæa, therefore, secretly removed the body at the close of Sabbath and buried it in an unknown grave; and since he was, according to the Gospels, "one of the disciples of Jesus," or "one who was looking for the kingdom of God," there was some measure of truth in the report spread by the Jews, though it was, in the main, only the malicious invention of enemies unable to explain the "miracle."

[6] Matt. xxvii. 62-66; and xxviii. 11-15.

The fact of the women going to anoint the body is proof that neither they nor the other disciples expected the resurrection, and that Jesus had not told them beforehand that he would rise again. Mark, the oldest of the Gospels, says that the women were *afraid* to say that they had found the tomb empty and that an angel had appeared to them. It should also be remembered that one of those who saw the angel was Mary Magdalene "from whom Jesus cast out seven devils." [7] *i.e.*, a woman who had suffered from hysterics to the verge of madness. [8] In the end she could not restrain herself and told what she had seen.

Then the Apostles, with Peter at their head, remembered Jesus' words, that "he would go before them to Galilee." Judas Iscariot, of course, had left them. Matthew [9] reports that he repented his treachery, returned the thirty pieces of silver, and, like Ahitophel, hanged himself. Another account tells how he did not commit suicide but died a horrible death "at the hands of heaven." [10]

The other disciples went to Galilee, "unto the mountain where Jesus had appointed them;" [11] Jesus had, therefore, appointed a pre-arranged meeting place (of course, during his lifetime), telling them that now, as distinct from the time when he had sent them forth from Capernaum as his Apostles, they would need purse and wallet and even a sword. [12]

After his death, and after the women had, at last, related the vision which they had seen, first Peter and then the other disciples also saw Jesus in a vision (as did Paul later), when they went to the appointed mountain in Galilee. The discourse of Jesus, given at the end of Matthew, is very late and replete with the Pauline spirit. Luke (together with the Fourth Gospel) knows nothing of the appearances in Galilee; but he tells how Peter hastened to the tomb and found there only the grave-clothes.

He gives also an attractive account of how two of the disciples went from Jerusalem to Emmaus and met on the way one who explained and proved to them from the Law of Moses and the Prophets that the sufferings of Jesus were a mark of his messiahship; and when they reached Emmaus and their new companion had, at their request, gone with them to their home to take food, they perceived by the breaking of the bread that this was Jesus: and he straightway vanished.

Jesus appeared again to the disciples and "they were amazed and supposed that they had seen a spirit," but he asked them to feel his hands and his feet, "for a spirit hath not flesh and bones." He ate with them "a piece of broiled fish" and even "led them outside the city to Bethany." [13]

[7] Luke viii. 2.
[8] Cf. Matt. xii. 45.
[9] Matt. xxvii. 3-10.
[10] Acts i. 18.
[11] Matt. xxviii. 16.
[12] Luke xxii. 35-38.
[13] Luke xxiv. 12 to end.

The Fourth Gospel [14] adds further similar incidents, chiefly the story about "Thomas (Didymus) the unbelieving," who had declared that he would not believe "except I shall see in his hands the print of the nails and put my finger into the print of the nails." [15] This shows that even among the Apostles were some who at first were not convinced of Jesus' resurrection; Matthew explicitly says, "But some doubted." [16]

Here again it is impossible to suppose that there was any conscious deception: the nineteen hundred years' faith of millions is not founded on deception. There can be no question but that some of the ardent Galilæans saw their lord and Messiah in a vision. That the vision was spiritual and not material is evident from the way Paul compares his own vision with those seen by Peter and James and the other apostles.[17] As to his own vision we know from the description in the Acts of the Apostles [18] and from his own account [19] that what he saw was no vision of flesh and blood but a vision "born of the light," "an heavenly vision (οὐράνιος ὀπτασία), in which God "had revealed in me his Son" (ἀποκαλύψαι τὸν υἱὸν αὐτοῦ ἐν ἐμοί).[20] Consequently the vision seen by the disciples, a vision which Paul deliberately compares with his own, was a spiritual vision and no more. This vision became the basis of Christianity: it was treated as faithful proof of the Resurrection of Jesus, of his Messiahship, and of the near approach of the kingdom of heaven. But for this vision the memory of Jesus might have been wholly forgotten or preserved only in a collection of lofty ethical precepts and miracle stories.

Could the bulk of the Jewish nation found its belief on such a corner-stone?

[14] John xx. and the added ch. xxi.
[15] John xx. 24, 29.
[16] Matt. xxviii. 17.
[17] 1 Corinthians xv. 5-8.
[18] Acts ix. 3.
[19] Acts xxvi. 19.
[20] Galatians i. 16. Cf. J. Klausner, *Historia Israelith* IV 81-84.

EIGHTH BOOK

THE TEACHING OF JESUS

I. GENERAL NOTE

Jesus was not a philosopher who devised a new theoretical system of thought. Like the Hebrew Prophets, and like the Jewish sages from *Talmud* times till the close of the Spanish period, he put forward religious and ethical ideas which closely concerned the conduct of ordinary, daily life; and he did this whenever the occasion warranted it. Something might happen: Jesus utilizes the opportunity to draw some religious or moral lesson. Only rarely did he practise instruction for instruction's sake and piece together thoughts, sayings and proverbs, unconnected with any specific incident, like the "Proverbs of Ben Sira" or the incidental homilies given in the *Talmud* and *Midrash*.

Mark, for example, gives scarcely any sayings except those bound up with specific events. Yet there existed, prior to the Gospel of Matthew, a collection of sayings (*Logia*) which this Gospel transmits, in longer or shorter selections, as items of independent interest (*e.g.*, the Sermon on the Mount, and the harangue against the Pharisees). Luke follows in part the usage of Mark, and in part the usage of Matthew. It follows from this that where we have treated the life of Jesus in detail in the course of the present work, we have, necessarily, introduced the bulk of his teaching as well.

It is not necessary, therefore, to include in the present section *all* that Jesus taught: it will be enough to make a brief study of the principles of the teaching already given and to supplement it with points not hitherto dealt with. It need, then, be no matter of surprise if our treatment of Jesus' teaching appears scanty as compared with the detailed biography, or if it repeats many matters already touched upon. This is inevitable in view of the nature of the subject and of Jesus' manner of instruction, and the same fact has compelled most of those who have written on the life of Jesus to dovetail the teaching into the life, and not allot to it a special section.

The aim of this book (which is not only to give the life of Jesus but also to explain why his teaching has not proved acceptable to the nation from which he sprang) necessitates a special section devoted to this teaching; but this need not be lengthy after our minute treatment of the life which has included most of the teaching. It is.

unfortunately, impossible in this section to keep within the limits of pure, objective scholarship (as has been the aim in the preceding pages); argument and theorizing is inevitable—not from love of argument but from the very nature of the case.

II. THE JEWISHNESS OF JESUS

Despite the animus which Julius Wellhausen usually showed in treating of Pharisaic, *Tannaitic* and even Prophetic Judaism, he was responsible for the following bold estimate: *"Jesus was not a Christian: he was a Jew.* He did not preach a new faith, but taught men to do the will of God; and, in his opinion, as also in that of the Jews, the will of God was to be found in the Law of Moses and in the other books of Scripture." [1] How could it have been otherwise? Jesus derived his entire knowledge and point of view from the Scriptures and from a few, at most, of the Palestinian *apocryphal* and *pseudepigraphical* writings and from the Palestinian *Haggada* and *Midrash* in the primitive form in which they were then current among the Jews. *Christianity*, it must always be remembered, is the result of a combination of Jewish religion and Greek philosophy; it cannot be understood without a knowledge of Jewish-Greek (Alexandrine) literature and of contemporary Græco-Roman culture.

Jesus of Nazareth, however, was a product of Palestine alone, a product of Judaism unaffected by any foreign admixture. There were many Gentiles in Galilee, but Jesus was in no way influenced by them. In his days Galilee was the stronghold of the most enthusiastic Jewish patriotism. Jesus spoke Aramaic and there is no hint that he knew Greek—none of his sayings shows any clear mark of Greek literary influence. Without any exception he is wholly explainable by the scriptural and Pharisaic Judaism of his time.

Although our present Gospels, even the earliest of them, were composed at a time when the Christian Church was replete with religious ideas derived from the neighbouring races, the fact nevertheless emerges that Jesus never even dreamed of being a Prophet or a Messiah to the non-Jews. He has the same national pride and aloofness (*Thou hast chosen us*)[2] for which many Christians now and in the Middle Ages have blamed the Jews. Jesus commands the leper whom he cleansed to show himself to the priest and bring the offering to the Temple as Moses ordained.[3] He also enjoins that a man should bring the offering due from him, but that if he have offended his fellow he may not offer his gift until he first become reconciled.[4]

[1] *Einleitung in die drei ersten Evangelien*, Berlin, 1905, p. 113.
[2] See the *Authorised* [Jewish] *Daily Prayer Book*, ed. Singer, London, 1908, p. 4: "Blessed art thou, O Lord our God, King of the universe, who hast chosen us from all nations."
[3] Mark i. 44; Matt. viii. 4; Luke v. 4.
[4] Matt. v. 23-4.

He does not oppose fasting and prayer: he only requires that it be done without pride or display.[5] When he opposes divorce in general and his disciples ask, "Why did Moses command them to give the woman a bill of divorcement and put her away?"—he did not reply that he was come to take aught away from the Law of Moses, but, "Because of the hardness of your heart Moses wrote you this commandment"[6] (precisely as Maimonides interpreted the sacrificial system). He keeps the ceremonial laws like an observing Jew: he wears "fringes;"[7] he goes up to Jerusalem to keep the feast of Unleavened Bread, he celebrates the "Seder," blesses the bread and the unleavened cakes and breaks them and says the blessing over the wine; he dips the various herbs into the *haroseth*, drinks the "four cups" of wine and concludes with the *Hallel*.

It was against his *disciples* that the complaint was made that they did not strictly observe the Sabbath and despised the washing of hands: he himself appears to have been observant in these matters. When he sends out the disciples to preach the coming of the Messiah and the near approach of the kingdom of heaven, he tells them: "Go not the way of the *Gentiles*, neither enter into any city of the Samaritans; but go unto the lost sheep of the house of Israel."[8]

Once only does he heal a non-Jew—the daughter of the Canaanitish woman;[9] but to the Canaanitish woman he uses such harsh words that the ears of the most chauvinistic Jew must burn at them: "It is wrong to take the children's bread and throw it to the little dogs"—adding, according to Matthew,[10] words which he elsewhere addresses to the Apostles: "I was not sent except to the lost sheep of the house of Israel." "As a Gentile and as a publican" is with him the strongest term of contempt,[11] and he speaks of the Gentiles as not praying but as using "vain repetitions" ("babbling").[12] So "chauvinistic" was Jesus the Jew!

So far was Jesus from teaching the dogma which later arose—that he was the Son of God and one of the three Persons in the Godhead—that when someone hailed him as "Good master," Jesus replied, "Why callest thou me good? There is none good save one: God."[13] Matthew alone perceived the contradiction between this and the

[5] Matt. vi. 5-7, 16-18.
[6] Mark x. 5; Matt. xix. 8.
[7] The woman with the issue of blood takes hold of the "kraspedon" (hem) of his garment (Mark vi. 56; Matt. ix. 20; Luke viii. 44), but in Aramaic and Greek "kraspedon" is a stereotyped rendering of both "tsitsith" and "kanaf" (see Kohut, *Arukh ha-Shalem*, IV 364, s.v. "Kraspeda").
[8] Matt. x. 5-6.
[9] Mark vii. 24-30. The healing of the centurion's servant at Capernaum (Matt. viii. 5-13; Luke vii. 2-10) does not occur in Mark and is therefore of dubious authenticity.
[10] Matt. xv. 24.
[11] Matt. xviii. 17.
[12] Matt. vi. 7.
[13] Mark x. 18; Luke xvii. 19.

Christian doctrine of his own time: he changed the question and answer to: "Master, what good thing shall I do? . . . and he said unto him, Why askest thou me concerning what is good? There is none good save one: God." The end of the answer does not here correspond with the beginning.

When the same man asks how he shall inherit eternal life, Jesus answers: "Thou knowest the commandments: Thou shalt not commit adultery, Thou shalt not kill, Thou shalt not steal, Thou shalt not bear false witness, Thou shalt not defraud, and, Honour thy father and thy mother."

It is noticeable that Jesus here omits the commandments dealing with man's duty to God (the first four of the Ten Commandments) and introduces a further one dealing with man's duty to his neighbour: Thou shalt not defraud (unless this represents the last commandment, Thou shalt not covet). When the enquirer replies: "All these things have I done from my youth up," Jesus "looked upon him and loved him" [14] —in other words, the outlook of Jesus conformed with that of the most observant of his fellow Jews and was based on the Law.

Yet again, one of the *Scribes* asked Jesus: "What is the first of all the commandments?" and Jesus replies: "Hear, O Israel, the Lord our God, the Lord, is one: and thou shalt love the Lord thy God with all thy heart and with all thy soul . . . this is the first commandment, and the second is like unto it: Thou shalt love thy neighbour as thyself. There is no commandment greater than these."

Thus Jesus gives virtually the same answer as Hillel and Rabbi Akiba to a similar question. The Scribe replies to Jesus: "Of a truth, master, thou sayest well, for God is one and there is none else save he; and to love him with all the heart and with all the soul . . . and to love thy neighbour as thyself is greater than all the burnt offerings and sacrifices." Whereupon Jesus said to him—to the Scribe whom the Gospels treat, together with the Pharisee, as the very symbol of hypocrisy and cant—"Thou art not far from the kingdom of heaven." [15]

The Scribes and Pharisees were not, therefore, so very far removed from Jesus' standards, although he attacked them *generally* (though not nearly to the same extent as we find recorded in the Gospels); and even the great attack on the Pharisees (which Matthew, chapter xxiii, compiled out of isolated sayings, uttered at various times and on various occasions, which, however justifiable in so far as they apply to the worst of the Pharisees, referred to in the *Talmud* as the "Pharisaic plague," are unjustifiable as applied to the Pharisees in general)—even that attack Jesus prefaces by the fine words: "The Scribes and Pharisees sit in Moses' seat (*i.e.,* continue

[14] Mark x. 17-21.
[15] Mark xii. 18-34.

the teaching of Moses and adapt it to present needs) ; [16] all things therefore whatsoever they bid you, these do and observe: but do not ye after their works; for they say, and do not." [17]

The last words can be applied to the best of religious bodies and to the best of people. The *Talmud* also severely condemns those "who require what is good but do not practise it;" [18] "Seemly are the words when they come from the mouth of them which practise them; some there be which require what is good and also practise it: Ben Azzai requires what is good but does not practise it." [19] It was even complained against Tolstoy, the moral giant of our generation, that he "required good" in the way of abolition of property, but did not "practise the good," in that he lived on his own country estate. Yet this did not render his teaching valueless. Is there any system of teaching in the world (that of Christianity first and foremost) which in course of time is not corrupted by its adherents and does not, to a large extent, deteriorate into a condition of "requiring good but not practising it?"

But the *positive* attitude of Jesus towards Judaism, both Prophetic and Pharisaic, is made clear in the famous passage from the so-called "Sermon on the Mount" (which, as has already been explained, is really a collection of isolated sayings which are, in Mark and Luke, distributed throughout the entire Gospel, but in Matthew artificially collected into a single discourse) : "Think not that I came to destroy the Law or the Prophets: I came not to destroy but to fulfil; [20] for verily I say unto you, Till heaven and earth pass away, one jot or one tittle [21] shall in no wise pass away from the law till all things be accomplished. [22] Whosoever therefore shall break one of these least commandments and shall teach men so, shall be called least in the kingdom of heaven: but whosoever shall do and teach them, he shall be called great in the kingdom of heaven." [23]

Then follow the words which are an *addition* to the Law of Moses and the Prophets: "Except your righteousness shall exceed the righteousness of the scribes and Pharisees, ye shall in no wise enter

---

[16] S. Krauss (*The Emperor Hadrian: the first explorer of Palestine, Ha-Shiloach*, XXXIX p. 430) supposes that in the synagogues there actually was a "Seat of Moses" upon which the Scribes and Pharisees used to sit; and this theory receives apparent confirmation from the seat which Dr. N. Slouschz discovered in his excavation of the synagogue at Tiberias. See *Qobetz ha-Hebhra l'haqirat Eretz-Yisrael*, Vol. I, Tel Aviv, 1921, p. 30.

[17] Matt. xxiii. 2-3.

[18] *Hagiga* 14a (R. Yochanan ben Zakkai) ; *Yebamoth* 63b.

[19] *T. Yebamoth* VIII 4 (near end).

[20] Almost the same phrase occurs in Aramaic in the *Talmud* (see above, p. 45 ff.) : "I came not to lessen the Law of Moses nor [but] to add to the Law of Moses" (*Shabb.* 116b).

[21] *Menahoth* 29a, 34a; cf. *Ex. R.* §6; *Lev. R.* §19; *Cant. R.* on *Rosho kethem paz.*

[22] Cf. Luke xvi. 17.

[23] Matt. v. 17-19.

into the kingdom of heaven." [24]   Jesus' displeasure is directed only against those who regard the ceremonial laws as of greater importance than the moral laws: he is far from annulling the former: "Woe unto you Pharisees! for ye tithe mint and rue and every herb and pass over judgment and the love of God: but these ought ye to have done, and not to leave the other undone." [25]   This verse (also occurring in Matthew with slight differences) [26] proves in the strongest possible fashion that never did Jesus think of annulling the Law (or even the ceremonial laws which it contained) and setting up a new law of his own.

But not only from the Gospels is it manifest that Jesus remained a Jew in his positive attitude to the Law generally: there is other tangible and irrefutable evidence.   It is only necessary to read carefully the "Acts of the Apostles" to be convinced that all the Apostles observed the ceremonial laws, visited the Temple, there paid their vows, and generally conducted themselves as true Jews.   Simon Peter, the "rock" of the society which Jesus created (see above, p. 300ff), long resisted the permitting of forbidden foods and the reception of non-Jews into the first body of Christians; Paul opposed his opinion, calling the stricter "Judæo-Christians" "false brethren;" [27] while James, the "brother of the Lord," who did not join the Apostles until after the crucifixion, and who remained a Jew and an orthodox believer in the Jewish religion, changing but one element in it (in place of a *future* Messiah he believed that the Messiah had already come in the person of Jesus)—this same James writes in the Epistle attributed to him (which Joseph Halevy has said might have been written by a *Tanna*): "For whosoever shall keep the whole law, and yet stumble in one point, he is become guilty of all" [28]—thus advocating a severer standard than did the Pharisees.

It is likewise apparent that the earliest Christians, generally, considered that the Gospel of the kingdom of heaven was to be preached for the benefit of the Jews alone: during the first seventeen years after the Crucifixion they made no attempt to spread the teaching of Jesus among the Gentiles. [29]   If, in truth, Jesus had said: "Many shall come from the east and from the west and shall sit with the children of Abraham, Isaac and Jacob in the kingdom of heaven, but the children of the kingdom (the Jews) shall be cast out in outer darkness: there shall be weeping and gnashing of teeth" [30] —it is inconceivable that for seventeen years nothing should have been done to evangelize the Gentiles, or that Paul should have been compelled to contend with Simon Peter and James, the brother of the Lord, on

[24] Matt. v. 20-28.
[25] Luke xi. 42.
[26] Matt. xxiii. 23.
[27] Acts x. 11 and 16; Galatians, ch. ii and elsewhere.
[28] Epistle of James ii. 10.
[29] Galatians i. 13; ii. 10.
[30] Matt. viii. 11-12.

the question of abolishing the ceremonial law and of baptising the uncircumcised.

Jesus was a Jew and a Jew he remained till his last breath. His one idea was to implant within his nation the idea of the coming of the Messiah and, by repentance and good works, hasten the "end." [31]

[31] See B. Jacob, *Jesu Stellung zum Mosaischen Gesetz*, Göttingen, 1893.

III. POINTS OF OPPOSITION BETWEEN JUDAISM AND THE TEACHING OF JESUS

Ex nihilo nihil fit: had not Jesus' teaching contained a kernel of opposition to Judaism, Paul could never *in the name of Jesus* have set aside the ceremonial laws, and broken through the barriers of national Judaism. There can be no doubt that in Jesus Paul found justifying support. In detailing the life of Jesus we have already come across various opposing points of view between the teaching of Jesus and that of the Pharisees (the latter representing traditional and also Scriptural Judaism).

Jesus eats and drinks with publicans and sinners, thereby disregarding ritual separatism and the principles of clean and unclean even to the extent to which they were accepted by the "sages" at the close of the Second Temple period. Jesus, on the Sabbath, heals diseases which are not dangerous. Jesus justifies his disciples when they pluck ears of corn on the Sabbath, thereby lightly esteeming the laws of Sabbath observance.

Jesus attaches little importance to the "washing of hands," and, in the subsequent argument, permits the eating of forbidden foods. Jesus, unlike the Pharisees and the disciples of John, does not fast often, and in answer to protests points out the impossibility of combining the old and the new: "No man seweth a piece of new cloth on an old garment, else that which should fill it up taketh from it, the new from the old, and a worse rent is made; and no man putteth new wine into old wine-skins, else the wine will burst the skins, and the wine perisheth and the skins: but they put new wine into fresh wine-skins." [1]

In other words, whatever change there is must be fundamental and not gradual or partial—not as with the Pharisees, who used to read forced new interpretations into the old Scriptures, changes never intended, in order that such new explanations demanded by daily life might not seem to set aside any principle in the Law. In the opinion of Jesus, such cautious changes, such combining of the old and the new, are nothing more than sewing patch upon patch, patching up an old, out-worn garment which can no longer adhere to the new patches and will, in the end, tear away completely: New matter must take on a completely new form.

As opposed to the *Tannaim* who taught, "Look not at the vessel but at what is contained therein: a new vessel may be full of old

[1] Mark ii. 21-22.

wine," [2] Jesus taught that new wine must be contained in a new
bottle. Matthew [3] preserves a noteworthy passage to the same effect.
After likening the kingdom of heaven to treasure hidden in a field,
and telling how, when a man knew of it, he sells all that he has and
buys that field; or to a merchant in search of fine pearls who, when
he has found a pearl of great price, sells all that he has and buys
that pearl; and, finally, to a fishing-net which, spread in the sea,
brings up fish of many kinds of which the bad are thrown aside and
the good gathered into vessels—after these simple metaphors Jesus
asks his hearers: "Do ye understand these things?" and they answer,
"Yea, Lord;" whereupon he utters these weighty words: "Therefore
every scribe who hath been made a disciple to the kingdom of heaven
(μαθητευθεὶς εἰς τὴν βασιλεία τῶν οὐρανῶν) is like unto a man that is
a householder, which bringeth forth out of his treasure things new
and old." [4]

The point is clear. The Scribes and Pharisees also believe in the
kingdom of heaven. But in it they are no more than householders:
they are not strong enough to clear away the old for the sake of the
new, but overlay the one with the other, the useless and the useful
together—just like a householder with his store of possessions. But
Jesus, the *king* in the kingdom of heaven, the King-Messiah, is
minded to separate the new from the old: the new he would gather
into his vessels and the rest he would cast aside.

We saw above how, when one asked Jesus how to attain eternal
life, Jesus enumerates six only of the Ten Commandments, precisely those which embody plain, human, ethical principles, but makes
no mention of the four which comprise the known ceremonial religious duties (the first four of the Ten Commandments). [5] Not
without reason was there attributed to Jesus the apocryphal saying
according to which, on seeing a man working on the Sabbath, he
said: "If thou knowest what thou doest thou art blessed, but
if thou knowest not thou art accursed and a transgressor of the
Law." [6]

Such is the subconscious attitude of Jesus towards traditional
Judaism. It is instinctive rather than conscious: by his parables
and by certain acts of his disciples which he leaves unrebuked, sometimes also by his own doings (such as healing on the Sabbath when
the disease was not dangerous), by that juxtaposition of "It was
said to you of old time (in the written or oral Law)" and "But I
say unto you," and, above all, by his indiscriminate attack on the
Pharisees—by these means he so decries the value of the ceremonial

[2] *Aboth* IV 20.
[3] Matt. xiii. 44-52.
[4] Matt. xiii. 52.
[5] See above, p. 365 ff.
[6] Added in Codex Bezae to Luke vi. 4; see A. Resch, *Agrapha*, 2 Aufl.,
Leipzig, 1906, pp. 45-48; B. Pick, *Paralibomena*, Chicago, 1908, pp. 61-62;
and see above, p. 69.

laws as to make them of secondary importance compared to the moral laws, and *almost* to nullify them.

But only "almost:" Jesus never carried his teaching to its final conclusion. He himself observed the ceremonial laws (though not with the scrupulousness and pedantry of the Pharisees) till the last night of his life. Such a final conclusion—the abolition of the ceremonial laws and the consequent opening of the doors to the uncircumcised Gentiles—it was left for another, a Pharisee also, to reach—namely, Saul of Tarsus after he was become Paul the Apostle. But had not Jesus lent some support towards this negative attitude to the ceremonial law and to the body of traditional belief transmitted, generation by generation, from Moses to the Pharisees, Paul would never have supported himself on Jesus in his efforts to overcome the "Christian-Judaism" founded by Simon Peter and James the brother of the Lord.

But Judaism could not agree with such an attitude. For the Jews their religion was more than simple belief and more than simple moral guidance: it was a *way of life*—all life was embraced in their religion. A people does not endure on a foundation of general human faith and morality; it needs a "practical religiousness," a ceremonial form of religion which shall embody religious ideas and also crown every-day life with a halo of sanctity.

Jesus did not give any new ceremonial law to replace the old (except, perhaps, the brief form of prayer, "Our Father, which art in heaven . . ."), and so he taught no new national ways of life in spite of abolishing, or hinting at the abolition of the old ways. By this very fact he raised the nation out of its national confines: for is there not but one moral law for all nations alike? The Prophets, too, found cause for indignation in that the commandments had become a "law of men which could be taught," and that the external, ceremonial laws, such as sacrifices, were made the first principle, and righteousness, judgment and mercy matters of secondary importance. Yet the Prophets could insist on the observance of the ceremonial laws when they served to fulfil a national-religious need (*e.g.*, the Sabbath in Jeremiah and "Second Isaiah," and circumcision in Ezekiel). Furthermore, even in their stern reprobation we feel a strong air of *nationalist, Jewish* history in its close connexion with the great events of universal human history. Hence the Prophets brought it to pass that other nations "were joined unto the house of Jacob" (as actually happened from the time of the Babylonian Exile till the time of Jesus and the conversion of the royal house of Adiabene). The Pharisees and the *Tannaim*—even the earliest of them—did, indeed, "pile up the measure" of the ceremonial laws, and they so overlaid the original nucleus with a multiplicity of detail and minutiæ as unwittingly to obscure the divine purpose of these laws.

This habit Jesus rightly opposes: but he fails to see the *national* aspect of the ceremonial laws. He never actually sets them aside, but he adopts towards them an attitude as to outworn scraps in the new "messianic garment," and depreciates their religious and moral worth; he does not recognize the connexion which exists between national and human history, and he entirely lacks the wider political perspective shown by the Prophets, whose sweeping vision embraced kingdoms and nations the world over. Hence, all unwittingly, he brought it to pass that part of the "House of Jacob" was swallowed up by those other nations who, at the first, had joined themselves to that part. . . .

The problem is a very wide one and turns on fundamental principles.

All arts and sciences have their root in religion. From religion there developed the early stages of mathematics and indirectly astronomy, music as well as poetry, history in connexion with drama. In course of time the Greeks succeeded in separating art and science from religion and the Romans and European nations followed their example; but with the oriental nations—the Egyptians, the Assyrians and Babylonians, Tyre and Sidon—arts and sciences remained inseparable from religion.

In the East the learned were found only among the priests and higher officials (who also came from the priestly caste). The Jews, likewise, did not succeed in creating sciences and arts independent of religion. In one thing only did they differ from other orientals —they wrested religion from the monopoly of priests and placed its development and exegesis in the hands of laymen; thus they made religion more democratic and, in general, more nationalistic.

We have seen [7] that the "Scribe" (and his successor the *Tanna*) was not only a "Rab" and teacher, but also a lawyer, a judge, a notary (in matters of divorces and contracts), a law-maker, a physician (expert in questions touching the fitness of cattle for food, and menses), a botanist, an agriculturalist (in matters of tithes and mixed crops), and so forth. Similarly Jewish religious literature touches on such topics as algebra, surveying, medicine and astronomy (*e.g.*, in the *Book of Enoch*), zoology and botany, law and politics, history and geography, (*e.g.*, in the *Book of Jubilees*).

These did not approach the status of "science" in the Greek or in the modern sense, but they served as a substitute. They served to widen the horizon, increase the interests in life and enlarge material and spiritual culture. They preserved the national life from concentrating on a confined circle of ethico-religious ideas, and gave it a wider, more vital and more universal scope. As to the excessive meticulousness, reaching to such an extremity of far-fetched definition, hair-splitting, sophistry and casuistry, usually alleged against the *Tannaim*—this lay in the nature of the case: in the wish to embrace the whole of life in all its incidental forms

[7] See above p. 224.

(casûs), the Jewish "sages" were forced to concern themselves even with abnormal and unseemly cases.

For this Jesus, sometimes rightly, found fault with them; but they were right in their fundamental principle, namely, in their desire to bring religion and life together into a higher synthesis, to make religion life, and sanctify life with the sanctity of religion. This does not fit in with the needs of the present time, a time of narrow specialization in the sciences, when politics and culture are kept apart from religion. But in those early days, and in that Eastern world saturated with simple and all-embracing faith, this association of science and art with religion was a great boon to the nation: religion escaped the danger of exclusiveness and one-sidedness, and national life, the danger of stagnation and dryness. If it be a fact that Christianity has endured throughout nineteen hundred and twenty years and attracted thousands of millions of believers, it is equally a fact that *Talmudic* Judaism endures, alive and active, capable of rising superior to the most difficult conditions that human imagination can conceive, and that it possesses the ability of taking a lead in every new movement, both itself creating new things and also absorbing and digesting the best and newest things of others' creation— and this, too, throughout a period of some eighteen hundred and fifty years.

What did Jesus do?

Had he come and said: Instead of religion alone, I give you here science and art as national possessions independent of religion; instead of scripture commentaries—learning and poetry, likewise independent of religion; instead of ceremonial laws—grown so oppressive as to crush the warmer religious feelings—a practical and theoretical secular culture, national and humanistic. Had Jesus come with such a Gospel his name would have endured as a blessing among his nation.

But he did not come and enlarge his nation's knowledge, and art, and culture, but to abolish even such culture as it possessed, bound up with religion, a culture which the Scribes and Pharisees (unlike the Prophets who, though they ignored it in their wider political purview, did not annul it) seized upon and held tightly, as though it were the single anchor of safety left to the nation—a nation not minded to be only a religious community, but a real nation, possessed of a land, a state and authority in every sense.

Civil power!—that is naught: "Give unto Cæsar that which is Cæsar's, and unto God that which is God's;" it is not worth while to fight against the political oppression of Rome, for the political freedom of the nation. What does it matter if you *do* pay tribute to Cæsar, if only you are at peace with the Lord your God!

Civil justice, state efforts at reform of debased social conditions, would be impossible when one must "resist not evil" and when, if struck on the left cheek, the only response is to stretch out the right cheek also! How can the state endure if Jesus requires that a man "swear not at all (ὅλως)"?[8] What culture can there be in the world when Jesus ordains that man shall share all his goods with the poor and teaches that "it is easier for a camel to go through the eye of a needle than for a rich man to enter the kingdom of heaven?"[9] Even family life must break down for one who would be a true disciple of Jesus, since the Messiah accounts praiseworthy those "which make themselves eunuchs for the kingdom of heaven's sake."[10]

How can family affairs be righted if Jesus forbids the divorce of the wife on any ground whatsoever[11] ["save only for fornication"[12] —conforming with the School of Shammai: "except he have found in her a matter of lewdness"[13]—being only a later interpolation]? What interest has he in labour, in culture, in economic or political achievements, who recommends us to be as "the lilies of the field which toil not neither do they spin" but whose apparel is more glorious than that of king Solomon, or like the ravens whose mother birds are careless of their young, but the Holy One, blessed be He, supplies them with food without their labour or care (a thought drawn from, "Who giveth food to the cattle and to the ravens that call upon him,"[14] and paralleled by the *Talmudic* passage,[15] "I have never seen a gazelle a fruit gatherer, a lion a porter, or a fox a shop-keeper [nor a wolf a jar-seller] but they get their food without care)"?

In all this Jesus is the most Jewish of Jews, more Jewish than Simeon ben Shetah, more Jewish even than Hillel. Yet nothing is more dangerous to national Judaism than this *exaggerated* Judaism; it is the ruin of national culture, the national state, and national life. Where there is no call for the enactment of laws, for justice, for national statecraft, where belief in God and the practice of an extreme and one-sided ethic is in itself enough—there we have the negation of national life and of the national state.

To take one example: Jesus said, "Judge not that ye be not judged."[16] This recurs with greater emphasis in Luke and becomes a lofty ethical rule.[17] In the same Gospel occurs this brief incident: "And one of the people said to Jesus, Master, speak, I pray thee,

---

[8] Matt. v. 34.
[9] The many far fetched explanations of "the eye of a needle" and "the camel" ("small door of courtyard" or "rope") are uncalled for in view of the *Talmudic* expression "the elephant that enters the eye of a needle," *Berachoth* 55b; *Bab. Metz.* 38b.
[10] Matt. xix. 12.
[11] Mark x. 9, 12.
[12] Matt. v. 32.
[13] *Gitt.* IX 19 (end).
[14] Ps. cxlvii. 9.
[15] *Qidd.* 2b; *T. Qidd.* V 15, ed. Zuckermandel, p. 343, note on line 13.
[16] Matt. vii. 1.
[17] Luke vi. 37.

unto my brother that he divide the inheritance with me. And Jesus said unto him: Man, who made me a judge or a divider over you?"[18] Jesus thus disregards justice generally, even when it is a case of natural civil interest, free of any ill motive; he thus ignores anything concerned with material civilisation: in this sense he does not belong to civilisation.

Many scholars have concluded that the Gospel of Luke is akin in spirit to the Ebionites, the earliest Christian heresy, and that consequently whatever Luke contains that is not contained in Matthew has been revised in a "Communist-Ebionite" spirit.[19] But had not the teaching of Jesus contained a clear communist tendency, community of goods would never have been the first step taken by the first Christian brotherhood,[20] nor would James, the brother of the Lord, the first head of this brotherhood, have been so pronounced an Ebionite and ascetic.

Again, Clement of Alexandria[21] also tells us that this tendency towards the abolition of private property and abstention from material pleasures was closely connected with the beginnings of Christianity, and that those who held such views regarded Jesus as their teacher and exemplar.

Yet again, the beatitude in Luke, "Blessed are ye poor, for yours is the kingdom of heaven," is the natural form, and corresponds with the later, "Blessed are ye that hunger," and the corresponding "Woes:" "Woe unto you that are rich, for ye have received your consolation; and woe unto you that are filled, for ye shall hunger;"[22] whereas, on the contrary, the forms, "Blessed are the poor in spirit (עניי הרוח or עניים ברוח in the sense 'thirst after the Spirit,' πτωχοὶ τῷ πνεύματι)" and "Blessed are they that hunger and thirst after righteousness"[23] are by no means natural. They are artificial expressions which Matthew fashioned after Christianity had absorbed many adherents from the non-Jewish world and some from the richer classes.

The parable of the rich man and Lazarus, occurring only in Luke[23a] is not, therefore, an addition by Luke, but it has been omitted by Matthew (such parables and sayings are on the whole rare in Mark) for his own purpose. In this parable the rich man commits no wrong: he inherits Gehenna simply and solely because he was rich and derived pleasure from this world; and the poor man, Lazarus, sits "in the bosom" of our "father Abraham" (a common Hebrew figure of speech)[23b] not because he is righteous nor because

[18] Luke xii. 13-14.
[19] On the Gospel of Luke and its character, see Ed. Meyer, *op. cit.* I 1-51.
[20] Acts iv. 32, 36.
[21] *Stromata* III 6.
[22] Luke vi. 20-25.
[23] Matt. v. 4 and 7.
[23a] Luke xvi. 19-31.
[23b] 49 *Qidd.* 72b; *Pesiqta Rabbati* §43 (ed. Friedmann 180b); see

he had done good, but simply and solely because he was poor and had had no joy in this world.

There is certainly no systematic teaching of communism, for Jesus, in the selfsame Gospel, promises his disciples [24] that "there is no man that hath left house, or wife, or brethren, or parents, or children, for the kingdom of God's sake, who shall not receive manifold more *in this time,* and in the world to come eternal life." There is no conviction here that private property will disappear, together with poverty, from this earth: at Bethany Jesus plainly says, "The poor ye have always with you." [25] This negative attitude to property arises, rather, from the non-political and non-cultural standpoint which was apparent in the beginnings of Christianity in the Ebionite-Communistic movement.

This negative attitude led the Jacobins, during the French Revolution, to hail Jesus as "le bon sansculotte," and the Bolshevists to style him "the great communist;" though it is very doubtful whether Jesus, who opposed the struggle against evil, would have consented to the terrible murders during the great French, and the still greater Russian Revolution. But it is unquestionable that throughout his entire teaching there is nothing that can serve to the upkeep of the state or serve towards the maintenance of order in the existing world.

The Judaism of that time, however, had no other aim than to save the tiny nation, the guardian of great ideals, from sinking into the broad sea of heathen culture and enable it, slowly and gradually, to realize the moral teaching of the Prophets in *civil life* and in the *present world* of the Jewish state and nation.

Hence the nation as a whole could only see in such public ideals as those of Jesus, an abnormal and even dangerous phantasy; the majority, who followed the Pharisees and Scribes (*Tannaim*), the leaders of the popular party in the nation, could *on no account* accept Jesus' teaching. This teaching Jesus had imbibed from the breast of Prophetic and, to a certain extent, Pharisaic Judaism; yet it became, on one hand, the negation of everything that had vitalized Judaism; and, on the other hand, it brought Judaism to such an extreme that it became, in a sense, *non-Judaism.* Hence the strange sight:—Judaism brought forth Christianity in its first form (the teaching of Jesus), but it thrust aside its daughter when it saw that she would slay the mother with a deadly kiss.

also A. Geiger, *Elieser u. Lazarus bei Lucas u. Johannes* (*Jüdische Zeitschrift,* 1868, VI 196-201); H. P. Chajes, *Adda bar Ahaba e Rabbi* (*Rivista Israelitica,* 1907, IV 137-139); and see also W. Bacher's notes and the reply of Chajes, *op. cit.* 1907, IV 175-182; R.E.J. 1907, LIV 138 n. 1); cf. *Abel Rabbati (Semahoth)* §8: "When R. Ishmael wept when he was going out to be killed, R. Shimeon said to him, Thou art but two steps from the bosom of the righteous ones, and dost thou weep!"

[24] Luke xviii. 29-30.
[25] Mark xiv. 7; Matt. xxvi. 11.

IV. JESUS' IDEA OF GOD

That Jesus never regarded himself as God is most obvious from his reply when hailed as "Good master:" "Why callest thou me good? There is none good but one, God." [1] When the disciples would know the exact time of the coming of the kingdom of heaven, he tells them: That day and that hour no man knoweth, not even the angels of heaven, nor the Son, but the Father only. [2] Jesus is thus not omniscient: he and the Father are not equal in knowledge. When we remember that, in the Garden of Gethsemane, he begs the Father to let the cup pass from him; and that, during the crucifixion, he cries out: My God, my God, why hast thou forsaken me!—it is perfectly manifest that in no sense did he look upon himself as God. Like every Pharisaic Jew he believed in the absolute unity of God, and he turned to God in time of trouble.

Nor did he regard himself as Son of God in the later Trinitarian sense; for a Jew to believe such a thing during the period of the Second Temple is quite inconceivable: it is wholly contradictory to the belief in the absolute unity.

Jesus may have made great use of the terms "Father," "My Father," "My heavenly Father," and perhaps also "Son;" but the last is no more than the Biblical "Israel is my first-born" [3]—other nations are sons of God, but Israel is God's first-born. We likewise find: "Ye are sons of the Lord your God." [4] "I have said, Ye are gods, and ye are all sons of the Highest," [5] "And God shall call thee, Son;" [6] "I will exalt the Lord, (saying) Thou art my Father," [7] "Beloved are Israel, for they are called 'Sons of the Highest;'" [8] and, most noteworthy, the striking passage: "Even if they are foolish, even if they transgress, even if they are full of blemishes, they are still called 'Sons.'" [9]

The phrase "Our Father, who art in heaven" is so common in the *Talmudic* literature as to render quotation superfluous for those

[1] Mark x. 18; Luke xviii. 19; on Matthew's version, see above, p. 364.
[2] Matt. xxiv. 36.
[3] Ex. iv. 22.
[4] Deut. xiv. 1.
[5] Ps. 82, 6.
[6] *Ben Sira* 4, 10.
[7] *Ben Sira* 51, 10. In *Fourth Esdras,* a wholly Pharisaic production, the Messiah is called "My Son" (7, 28-29; 13, vv. 25, 34, 37, 52; 14, 9). See Klausner, *Ha-Ra'yon ha-Meshihi* II 64.
[8] *Aboth* III 3.
[9] *Sifre* on Deut. §308 (ed. Friedmann, 133a and b).

with some knowledge of Hebrew.[10] Less common, however, is the use of the singular pronoun, "*My* heavenly Father," though it is somewhat frequent in such expressions as: "What shall I do, when my heavenly Father hath so commanded me?"[11] or "These buffetings have made me to love my heavenly Father;"[12] and we also find the "diminutive of affection:" "Abba who is in heaven," "Since I have done the will of Abba who is in heaven."[13] Jesus undoubtedly used the term "Abba who is in heaven" mainly in the same sense in which it is used in the *Talmudic* literature: God is a merciful father, father of all created things, and like a father he is indulgent and forgiving, good and beneficent to all, from the flowers of the field and fowls of the air, to the sinful wrongdoer, in whose death God finds no pleasure, but only in his repentance.

In this also Jesus is a genuine Jew.

Jesus, however, makes far more use of such expressions as "Father," "My Father," "My Father in heaven," than do the Pharisees and *Tannaim;* and often when he employs it, it receives an *excessive* emphasis. The reason is plain. From the day when he was baptised by John, Jesus looked upon himself as the Messiah, and as the Messiah he was closer to God than was any other human being. On the one hand, as Messiah he is "the Son of man coming with the clouds of heaven" and "drawing near to the Ancient of days;"[14] thus, literally, he is near to the Godhead.

On the other hand, it is he, the Messiah, who is spoken of in the Psalms: "Thou art my son, this day have I begotten thee."[15] In Jesus' time it was never doubted that these words referred to the Messiah, for earlier the Psalm says definitely: "And the rulers take counsel together against the Lord and against his *anointed.*"[16] The Messiah is, therefore, the nearest to God: God is his father in a closer sense than to the rest of mankind.

It was this excessive emphasis which made Kaiaphas, the High Priest, rend his clothes at the trial of Jesus, though Jesus did not then call himself "Son of God;" it was enough that he did not deny that he was the Messiah who was to come "with the clouds of heaven" and "be brought near to the ancient of days" and sit at his right hand ("at the right hand of Power"). Such words were more terrible in the ears of this Sadducæan High Priest, for whom the Messiah was only a great earthly king, than they were to a Pharisee, whose idea of the Messiah was more spiritual.

Arising out of this *exaggerated* sense of nearness to God is Jesus'

---

[10] See, *e.g., Yoma* VIII 9; *Sota* IX 15 (*Baraita*); *Aboth* V 20, etc.

[11] *Sifra* on Levit. "*Qedoshim*" (end), 20, 26 (ed. Weiss 93b).

[12] *Mechilta*, "*Behodesh*," *Yithro*, §6 (end), ed. Friedmann 68b); *Midrash Tehillim* ("*Shoher Tob*") XII 5 (end) (ed. Buber 55a).

[13] *Lev. R.* §32 (a little before "My Father who is in heaven").

[14] Dan. vii. 13.

[15] Ps. ii. 7.

[16] Ps. ii. 2.

constant emphasis and insistence in "But I say unto you," as opposed to "them of old time," *i.e.*, the Law of Moses, the Prophets, and also the Pharisees.[17] A danger lurked in this exaggeration: it unwittingly confused Jesus' pure monotheism; it gave the impression that there was one man in the world with whom God was exceptionately intimate and for whom God bore especial love. Judaism knows this "God-nearness" in connexion with the *Tzaddiq* (the leader among the eighteenth and nineteenth century *Hasidim*) ; but such nearness was shared by many *Tzaddiqim,* and not claimed by one alone.

This preference of *one* man over the rest of mankind showed a species of favouritism on the part of God, which might induce (and after the time of Paul did, in fact, induce) a more or less idolatrous belief in Jesus as the "Paraclete," the advocate for man before God. Such a conception of the messianic title "son of God," signifying that he is nearest to God of all men (a fundamentally Jewish conception), Judaism was unable to accept. Jesus' own teaching is poles apart from the Trinitarian dogma; but it contained the germ which, fostered by gentilic Christians, developed into the doctrine of the Trinity.

There was yet another element in Jesus' idea of God which Judaism could not accept.

Jesus tells his disciples that they must love their enemies as well as their friends, since their "Father in heaven makes his sun to rise on the evil and on the good, and sends his rain upon the righteous and upon the ungodly."[18] Here it is no case of Jesus' justifying himself against the Pharisees who blamed him for eating with publicans and sinners—"they that are whole need not the physician but they that are sick;" the "sick" are no longer under consideration: both publicans and sinners are "whole" in the sight of God: sinners and non-sinners, evil and good, ungodly and righteous, all alike are of the same worth in God's sight. It follows, therefore, that God is not *absolute righteousness,* but *the good* before whom is no evil ("There is none *good* save one, and he—is God"). He is not the God of justice, in spite of his Day of Judgment: in other words, *he is not the God of History.*

With this, Jesus introduces something new into the idea of God. The *Talmud* also tells how "the rain falls equally for the righteous and for the sinful;[19] as to the sun's rising upon both good and evil (a thought also occurring in Seneca)[20] the *Talmud* relates a remarkable story concerning Alexander the Great and the King of Katsia:[21] when Alexander said to the king of Katsia that in his

[17] See Ahad ha-Am, Collected Works, IV 42-44.
[18] Matt. v. 45.
[19] *Taanith 7a.*
[20] *De beneficiis,* IV 26, 1.
[21] *Gen. R.* §33; *Lev. R.* §27; *J. Baba Metzia* II 6; *Tanhuma,* "Emor," §9 (ed. Buber p. 88 f.) ; *Pesiqta d'R. Kahana,* §9 ("*Shor o keseb*"), ed. Buber,

country they would have put to death those two scrupulous men (who had both refused the ownership of certain hidden treasure since they did not, at the time of buying the land where the treasure was found, know of its existence) and confiscated the treasure, the African king asked Alexander: Does the sun rise in your country? and are there lean cattle in it? When Alexander answered in the affirmative, the other remarked: Then the sun rises in your country through the merit of the lean cattle; you wicked rulers are not worthy of it.

Such is the Jewish conception of God: the wicked are not worthy that God's sun should rise upon them.[22] Not that Judaism does not also rate highly the repentant sinners; none say more about the value of repentance than do the authorities of the *Talmud;* it is they who said, "Where the repentant stand, the wholly righteous do not (*i.e.* are not worthy to) stand." [23] But the unrepentant *destroy the world,* they break down the *moral* order, and therefore destroy the *natural* order too. If there is no righteousness in the world, it is not worth while that this world, with its sun and moon and stars and fixed laws of nature, should continue (hence the "Flood").

God is good; but he also requires justice. He is "merciful and compassionate, long-suffering and of great kindness;" but, none the less, "he will by no means acquit the guilty." It is for this reason that the Jews acclaim their God, in the same breath, "Our Father; our King:" he is not only "Father of mercies" but "King of Judgment," the God of the social order, the God of the nation, the God of history. Jesus' idea of God is the very reverse. However lofty a conception it may represent for the *individual* moral conscience, it stands for ruin and catastrophe for the *general* conscience, for the public, social, national and universal conscience, that conscience for which "Weltgeschichte ist Weltgericht;" and such an idea of God Judaism could by no means accept.

pp. 4-5. It is noteworthy that this story of a Greek character is repeated throughout the Jewish *Midrashic* literature but is not found at all in Greek literature; it was not in accordance with the Greek spirit.

[22] See Joseph Klausner, *Torath ha-Middoth ha-Q'dumah b'Yisrael,* Vol. I Odessa, 1918, p. 57.

[23] *Berachoth* 34*b;* Sanh. 99a.

V. THE ETHICAL TEACHING OF JESUS

The main strength of Jesus lay in his ethical teaching. If we omitted the miracles and a few mystical sayings which tend to deify the Son of man, and preserved only the moral precepts and parables, the Gospels would count as one of the most wonderful collections of ethical teaching in the world. These sayings and parables are to be found chiefly in Matthew and are mainly grouped together in what is called "The Sermon on the Mount." [1] Such sayings are comparatively few in Mark, and those which occur in Luke and are lacking in Mark and Matthew, are open to suspicion as emanating from a period later than Jesus. An attempt will here be made to give the moral principles as we find them in Matthew, using in addition what is common to Mark and Luke, [2] but drawing, in the main, from the Sermon on the Mount.

The "blessed," they whose "reward is great in heaven," are the poor, they that hunger and thirst, the meek, the mourners, the merciful, the pure in heart, the peace-makers, the persecuted, and those who are reviled and blasphemed. A man may not be angry with his brother; [3] he may not call his fellow "rascal" or "fool." Before making a religious offering a man should be reconciled with any whom he may have offended. He who looks on a woman and lusts after her, commits adultery in his heart. He who divorces his wife (and marries another) commits adultery, and a divorced woman who is married to another also commits adultery; for "whom God hath joined together let not man put asunder." Better is it not to marry at all. [4]

"If thy right eye" or "thy right hand offend thee," "pull out thine eye" and "cut off thine hand: it is better that one of thy members perish than that thy whole body go down to Gehenna." [5] It is forbidden to swear any oath, even on the truth. It is forbidden to fight

[1] Matt. chh. v-vii.
[2] No treatment of the ethics of Jesus along the lines of objective scholarship yet exists in any language. The best is Ehrhardt, *Der Grundcharacter der Ethik Jesu*, Freiburg, 1895. Christian apologetic works containing unbiassed treatment are: E. Grimm, *Die Ethik Jesu*, 2 Aufl. Leipzig, 1917; F. Peabody, *Jésus-Christ et la question morale* (trad. H. Anet), Paris, 1909; H. Monnier, *La Mission historique de Jésus*, Paris, 1906.
[3] The words "without a cause" are added in the Syriac text translated by A. Merx, *Die 4 kanon. Evv. nach ihrem ältesten bekannten Texte*, Berlin, 1897, p. 9.
[4] Matt. viii. 21-22; also xix. 3-10.
[5] Matt. v. 29-30, and more explicitly Matt. xviii. 8-9.

against evil, and "whosoever smiteth thee on thy right cheek, turn to him the other also. And if any . . . would take away thy coat let him have thy cloke also. . . . Give to him that asketh thee, and from him that would borrow of thee turn not thou away." "Love your enemies and pray for them that persecute you . . . for if ye love them that love you, what reward have ye? Do not even the publicans the same? . . . Ye therefore shall be perfect as your heavenly Father is perfect."

Almsgiving should be in secret so that the left hand may not know what the right hand is doing: "When thou doest alms sound not a trumpet before thee . . . in the synagogues and in the streets." Display in prayer is likewise forbidden, or "much speaking as do the Gentiles;" but prayer should be brief, in secret, behind closed doors.

When men pray they must forgive the sins which others have committed against them, that God may forgive them that pray, the sins which they have committed against God. Not once only, nor seven times only, must a man forgive his neighbour who has sinned against him—but seventy times seven.[6] When a man fasts he must not make display of the fact nor change his appearance that men may know that he is fasting; it is enough that his heavenly Father alone knows it. Therefore Jesus, contrary to the accepted Pharisaic usage,[7] allows washing and anointing during a period of fasting.[8]

One should lay up treasure in heaven, by means of almsgiving and good works, and not on earth where "moth and rust doth corrupt and thieves break through and steal." "The lamp of the body is the eye: if therefore thine eye be single, thy whole body is full of light; . . . if the light that is in thee be darkness, how great is the darkness!"

No man can serve two masters, God and Mammon (the world). So let him take no thought for the morrow: "sufficient unto the day is the evil thereof." "Consider the lilies of the field, how they grow; they toil not, neither do they spin, . . . yet Solomon in all his glory was not arrayed like one of these; but if God doth so clothe the grass of the field which to-day is, and to-morrow is cast into the oven, shall he not much more clothe you, O ye of little faith?"

"Judge not, that ye be not judged. For with what measure ye mete it shall be measured unto you." Let not a man look on the mote that is in his brother's eye and ignore the beam that is in his own eye. "All things whatsoever ye would that men should do unto you, even so do ye also unto them: for this is the law and the prophets." To enter into the kingdom of heaven it is not enough to call Jesus, "Lord, lord!" Rather let a man do the will of his heavenly Father.

[6] Cf. Matt. vi. 14-15 with xviii. 21-35.
[7] During an ordinary fast the *Mishnah,* too, permits washing and anointing (*Taanith* I 4 and 5); but both are forbidden during exceptional fasts (*Taanith* I 6) and on the Day of Atonement (*Yoma* VIII 1).
[8] Matt. vi. 16-18

Such are the ethical principles contained in the "Sermon of the Mount." The other ethical injunctions, which may with scarcely any doubt be accepted as genuine, can be summarized as follows:

He that would follow after Jesus may not even go to bury his father: "Let the dead bury their dead." [9] He that loves father, mother or son or daughter more than Jesus, is not worthy of him,[10] "for he that findeth his soul shall lose it, and he that loseth his soul for Jesus's sake shall find it." [11] "Everyone that doeth the will of my heavenly Father, he is my brother and sister and mother." [12] "Be ye hated of all men for my name's sake." [13] "Fear not them that can kill the body but are not able to kill the soul; but rather fear him which is able to destroy both soul and body in hell," [14] for "what shall it profit a man if he gain the whole world and lose his soul?" [15] "Man is lord of the Sabbath" and "It is lawful to do good on the Sabbath," and therefore it is permitted to pluck ears of corn on the Sabbath and, on the Sabbath, to heal even in cases where life is not endangered.

"Every idle word that men shall speak, they shall give account thereof in the day of judgment." [16] Foolish vows do not bind a man, and unwashen hands do not defile him; what defile a man are evil thoughts and evil deeds—murder, theft, violence, adultery, false-witness and blasphemy.[17] Let none despise or offend children or the innocent or the ignorant, or even sinners; for if a man have a hundred sheep and lose one of them, when he have found the one "he rejoiceth over it more than over the ninety and nine which have not gone astray." [18]

"The first shall be last and the last shall be first."

It is like a king who made a marriage feast for his son and invited the chief people of the city and they did not come; then said he to his servant; Since these came not, summon from the market place and from the way side the wicked and the maimed, that they may fill the places of the guests.[19] "If thy brother sin against thee" reprove him, and if he hearken unto thee, well; if he hearken not, warn him in the presence of two or three witnesses, "and if he refuse to hear them, tell it unto the church (*ekklesia*), and if he refuse to hear the church also, let him be unto thee as the Gentile and the publican." [20]

[9] Matt. viii. 21-22.
[10] Matt. x. 37. A stronger form is given in Luke xiv. 26.
[11] Matt. x. 39.
[12] Matt. xii. 50.
[13] Matt. x. 22.
[14] Matt. x. 28.
[15] Matt. xvi. 26.
[16] Matt. xii. 36.
[17] Matt. xv. 1-20.
[18] Matt. xviii. 1-14.
[19] Matt. xx. 16; xxii. 1-14.
[20] Matt. xviii. 15-17.

The greatest commandment is, "Thou shalt love the Lord thy God with all thy heart and with all thy soul," and the second is like unto it, "Thou shalt love thy neighbour as thyself: on these two hang all the Law and the Prophets." [21] He that would win everlasting life and follow after Jesus, must not only keep the commandments— Thou shalt not kill, Thou shalt not commit adultery, Thou shalt not steal, Thou shalt not bear false witness, Thou shalt honour thy father and thy mother, and Thou shalt love thy neighbour as thyself —but he must also sell all that he has and give to the poor, for "it is easier for a camel to go through the eye of a needle than for a rich man to enter the kingdom of heaven." [22]

In the kingdom of heaven the great ones will not be like the great ones in this world whom *others* serve; but *they* shall serve others as does the Son of man.[23] The sin of the Scribes and Pharisees is twofold: What is of primary importance they make secondary, and what is secondary they make of primary importance; and they pay more regard to the letter of Scripture than to the spirit.[24] He who performs a good work for the humblest of creatures is as though he performed a good work for Jesus' sake.[25] They who take up the sword shall perish by the sword.[26]

The two mites that the widow gives to the Temple treasury are of more worth than the rich offering of the wealthy man: the latter gives of his superfluity, but she out of her lack.[27] Let him who feels himself free from sin throw the first stone at the harlot.[28] "It is better to give than to receive." [29]

These are the underlying principles of Jesus' ethical teaching.[30] Not all of these sayings may have been uttered by Jesus, but they are all in accordance with his spirit and they are all of distinct originality. Yet, with Geiger and Graetz, we can aver, without laying ourselves open to the charge of subjectivity and without any desire to argue in defence of Judaism, that *throughout the Gospels there is not one item of ethical teaching which can not be paralleled either in the Old Testament, the Apocrypha, or in the Talmudic and Midrashic literature of the period near to the time of Jesus.*[31]

[21] Matt. xxii. 35-40.
[22] Matt. xix. 16-26.
[23] Matt. xx. 45-48.
[24] Matt. xxiii (the entire chapter).
[25] Matt. xxv. 34-45; cf. x. 42 (end).
[26] Matt. xxvi. 52.
[27] Mark xii. 41-44; Luke xxi. 1-4.
[28] An apocryphal saying, included in the Fourth Gospel, viii. 7, and, in certain versions, in Luke xxi. 38; but actually belonging to Mark xii. 18 or xii. 35.
[29] Acts xx. 35 (Paul in the name of Jesus).
[30] They are collected in a Hebrew translation in *Dibhrē Yeshua*, Leipzig, 1898, a supplement to the two works of A. Resch, *Aussercanonische Paralleltexte zu den Evangelien*, Theile 1-5, 1893-1897, and *Agrapha* 2. Aufl., 1906; and also separately in *Dibhrē Yeshua*: Τὰ λόγια 'Ιησοῦ 1898.
[31] See above, pp. 110 and 114.

Furthermore, sayings similar to those in the Gospels, though found in literature later than the time of Jesus, must have been current orally among the Jews many scores of years before they were fixed in writing in the *Mishna, Talmud* or *Midrash,* because there are no grounds whatever for assuming that the Gospels influenced the authorities of the *Talmud* and *Midrash.* There are ethical sayings attributed to Jesus which recur word for word in *Talmud* or *Midrash.* For example, the saying, "With what measure ye mete it shall be measured unto you," in the Sermon on the Mount [32] occurs in exactly the same form in the *Mishna* (במדה שאדם מודד בה מודדין לו). [33] The parable of the mote and the beam, in the same chapter,[34] is uttered by the early *Tanna* and enemy of the *Gillayonim* and *Books of the Minim,* R. Tarphon: "If he (the reprover) say to him, Take the mote from thine eyes (or, according to another reading, Thy teeth), the other replies, Take the beam from thine eyes." [35] Sufficient for the day is the evil thereof,[36] is a typical *Talmudic* expression.[37]

The bulk of the rest of the sayings are to be found in the *Talmud* in a slightly different shape. For example, the saying, "He who looks on a woman to lust after her hath already committed adultery with her in his heart," [38] is found in the *Talmud* in the form, "He who deliberately looks on a woman is as though he had connexion with her;" [39] or, stated by the early *Amora,* R. Shimeon ben Lakish, "For thou mayest not say that everyone that committeth adultery with his body is called an adulterer; he that committeth adultery with his eyes is also to be called an adulterer." [40]

Jesus' saying, "It is better that one of thy members perish than that thy whole body go down to hell," [41] is also uttered by R. Tarphon, "Better that his belly burst that he go not down to the pit of destruction." [42] As to the forbidding of oaths, the *Talmud* requires "a righteous yea and a righteous nay," [43] and R. Eliezer says, "Yea is an oath and nay is an oath." [44] As a parallel to the requirement that almsgiving should be in secret, and that the left hand shall not know what the right hand does,[45] we have the saying of the early *Tanna,* R. Eliezer: "He who giveth alms in secret is greater than Moses our master;" [46] and that that is the most excellent form of almsgiving when "he gives and knows not to whom he gives, or takes and knows not from whom he takes," [47] while "he who ostentatiously gives alms to the poor—for this, God will bring him to judgment." [48] The Greek translators have probably made a mistake in the passage

[32] Matt. vii. 2.
[33] *Sota* I 7.
[34] Matt. vii. 3-5.
[35] *Baba Bathra* 15b; *Arakhin* 17b.
[36] Matt. vi. 38.
[37] *Berakhoth* 9b.
[38] Matt. v. 28.
[39] *Massekheth Kallah.*
[40] *Lev. R.* §23.

[41] Matt. v. 29-30; xviii. 8, 9.
[42] *Nidda* 13b.
[43] *Baba Bathra* 49b; *J. Shebi'ith* X 9.
[44] *Shebuoth* 36a.
[45] Matt. vi. 3.
[46] *Baba Bathra* 9b.
[47] *Ibid.* 10b (beginning).
[48] *Hagiga* 5a.

where Jesus is made to forbid "the blowing of a trumpet" (when giving alms) in the streets and synagogues; [49] the original reference may have been to the שופר של צדקה, the horn-shaped receptacle for alms, which stood in the Temple and synagogues, and, possibly, in the streets also.[50]

As a parallel to the "treasure in heaven" where "neither moth nor rust doth corrupt nor thieves break through and steal," we may quote the *Talmudic Baraita:* "It happened with Monobaz that he squandered his wealth and the wealth of his fathers (in alms) during a time of famine. His brethren and his father's house gathered around him and said: Thy fathers laid up treasure and added to their fathers' store, and dost thou waste it all! He answered: My fathers laid up treasure below; I have laid it up above. My fathers laid up treasure where the hand (of man) controlleth it; but I have laid it up where no hand controlleth it. . . . My fathers laid up treasure of Mammon; I have laid up treasure of souls. . . . My fathers laid up treasure for this world; I have laid up treasure for the world to come." [51] Here we have Jesus' ideas repeated almost word for word. Again, those "who are anxious for the morrow" Jesus calls "of little faith," [52] exactly as does the early *Tanna,* R. Eliezer ben Hyrcanus: "R. Eliezer the Great said, He who has a morsel of bread in his vessel and yet says, What shall I eat to-morrow? is of those of little faith (מקטני אמנה):" [53] and in the same way R. Eliezer Modai says: "He who created the day, created also food for the day. Thus R. Eliezer Modai used to say, He who hath ought to eat to-day and says, What shall I eat to-morrow, such a one is lacking in faith" (מחוסרי אמנה).[54]

Within the Sermon on the Mount is to be found the "Lord's Prayer," perhaps the single religious ceremony or institution (except for the appointment of the "Twelve" Apostles, or disciples) which Jesus authorized during his lifetime. He requires of his disciples and followers that "they use not vain repetitions as to the Gentiles, who say in their heart, that they shall be heard by their much speaking." [55] The same thing was said by the author of Ecclesiastes: "For God is in heaven, and thou upon earth: therefore let thy words be few." [57]

Like a real Jew, Jesus regards the prayers of the heathen as "vain repetition," "babbling." He therefore composed this brief prayer: "Our Father which art in heaven, Hallowed be thy name. Thy kingdom come. Thy will be done, as in heaven, so on earth.

[49] Matt. vi. 2.
[50] *Shek.* VI 1; *Erubin* 32a; *Gittin* 60b; *Pes.* 90b.
[51] *Baba Bathra* 11a.
[52] Matt. vi. 30-34.
[53] *Sota* 48b.
[54] *Mechilta,* Exodus, *"Way'hi b'shallach,"* §2 (ed. Friedmann 47b).
[55] Matt. vi. 7.
[56] Eccles. v. 1-2.

Give us this day our daily bread (the *Gospel to the Hebrews* reads, "our bread for to-morrow"). And forgive us our debts as we also have forgiven our debtors. And bring us not into temptation, but deliver us from the evil one." [57]

It is a remarkable prayer, universal in its appeal, earnest, brief and full of devotion. Every single clause in it is, however, to be found in Jewish prayers and sayings in the *Talmud*. "Our Father which art in heaven" is a Jewish expression found in many prayers; one ancient prayer, said on Mondays and Thursdays before returning the Scroll of the Law to the Ark, begins four times with the introductory clause: "May it be thy will, O our Father which art in heaven." [58] "May thy name be hallowed and may thy kingdom come" occurs in the "*Kaddish*," so widespread among the Jews, and containing many very ancient elements: "Exalted and sanctified be his great name in the world which he created according to his will, and may he bring about his kingdom (or 'rule in his kingdom')" [59]

"Thy will be done, as in heaven, so on earth" occurs in the "Short Prayer" (precisely as with Jesus) of the early *Tanna* already referred to, R. Eliezer: "What is the short prayer? R. Eliezer said: Do thy will in heaven, and on earth give comfort to them that fear thee, and do what is right in thy sight." [60] The phrase "Give us this day our daily bread" is found not only in the Old Testament ("Give me the bread that is needful for me") [61] but also in a variant of R. Eliezer's "Short Prayer": "May it be thy will, O our God, to give to every one his needs and to every being sufficient for his lack." [62] "Forgive us our debts" is the Sixth Blessing in the "Shemoneh-Esreh" prayer; and in Ben Sira we also find, "Forgive thy neighbour's sin and then, when thou prayest, thy sins will be forgiven; man cherisheth anger against man, and doth he seek healing (or, forgiveness) from the Lord?" [63] Finally, the clause "bring us not into temptation" comes in a *Talmudic* prayer: "Lead us not into sin or iniquity or temptation," [64] a prayer that has been included among the "First Blessings" of the Book of Prayer used throughout Jewry to the present day.

We see, therefore, that the "Lord's Prayer" can be divided up

[57] Matt. vi. 9-12; Luke xi. 1-4. We disagree with some modern scholars who would regard this prayer, also, as late; in such a case virtually nothing at all would be left to Jesus: and from nothing we cannot get anything but nothing.

[58] *Siddur Rab Amram Gaon*, ed. Frumkin, Jerusalem, 1912, p. 158.

[59] See Zvi Karl, *Ha-Kaddish, Ha-Shiloach*, XXXV 45.

[60] *T. Berachoth* III 11; *Berachoth* 29*b*; cf. "Peace among men," Luke ii. 14.

[61] Prov. xxx. 8.

[62] *T. Berachoth* III 11; *Berachoth* 29*b*.

[63] *Ben Sira* 28, 2-5; cf. in *Talmud, Rosh ha-Shana* 17*a* and *b*; *Yoma* 23*a*, 87*b*; *Meg.* 28*a*; *J. Baba Qama* VIII 10.

[64] *Berachoth* 60*b*; cf. "He will never lead men into temptation," *Sanh.* 107*a*.

into separate elements every one of which is Hebraic in form and occurs in either the Old Testament or the *Talmud*. The same applies to virtually everything which Jesus uttered. If we remember that Hillel also said that the commandment, "Thou shalt love thy neighbour as thyself," or the ethical law, "What is hateful to thyself do not unto thy neighbour," was the whole Law and the rest but commentary;[65] and that the *Talmud* says: "They who are insulted yet insult not again, who hear themselves reproached yet answer not again, who act out of love and rejoice in afflictions . . . of them Scripture says, They that love him are as the going forth of the sun in his might;"[66] and that Scripture enjoins that a man restore his enemy's ox or his ass and "help the ass of his enemy when it croucheth under its burden—"[67]: then how much more should he aid his enemy himself; and that God compels Jonah the Prophet to save Nineveh, the city of his enemies who have destroyed (or were about to destroy) his native country; and that it is said in a *Midrash*, "How doth it affect the Holy One, blessed be he, whether a man slay a beast according to *Halakha* or not, and eat it? doth it profit Him or harm Him? or how doth it affect Him whether a man eat food unclean or clean? . . . the commandments were not given save as a means to purify mankind;"[68] and the wonderful saying, "Almsgiving and good works outweigh all the commandments in the Law;"[69]—if we call to mind all these high ethical ideals (and there are very many more like them) we are inevitably led to the conclusion that Jesus scarcely introduced any ethical teaching which was fundamentally foreign to Judaism.[70] So extraordinary is the similarity that it might

[65] *Shab.* 31a.
[66] Judges vi. 31; *Yoma* 23a; *Shab.* 88b; *Gitt.* 36b.
[67] Ex. 23. 4-5.
[68] *Tanhuma, Shemini*, 12 (ed. Buber p. 30); *Gen. R.* §44 (beginning); *Lev. R.* §13.
[69] *T. Peah* IV 19.
[70] The book giving *all* the Hebrew passages illustrating the Synoptic Gospels is Shack-Billerbeck, *Kommentar zum Neuen Testament aus Talmud und Midrasch*, Vol. I-II, München, 1922-4. The following give important material: J. Eshelbacher, *Ha-Yahaduth u-mahuth ha-Natzriyuth* (Hebrew translation, ed. Ha-Zeman, Wilna, 1911); B. Balzac, *Torath ha-Adam*, vol. 2, Warsaw, 1910; F. N. Nork (S. Korn), *Rabbinische Quellen und Parallelen zu Neutestamentlischen Schriften*, Leipzig, 1839; A. Wünsche, *Neue Beiträge zur Erläuterung der Evangelien aus Talmud und Midrasch*, Göttingen, 1878; G. Friedlander, *The Jewish Sources of the Sermon on the Mount*, London, 1911; H. P. Chajes, *Rivista Israelitica*, 1904 (I) 41-57; 105-6; 214-225; 1906 (III) 83-96; 1907 (IV) 52-58; 132-136, 209-213 and elsewhere; H. P. Chajes, *Ben Stada* (*Ha-Goren*, IV 33-37). See also "Ahad ha-Am," *Al sh'te ha-S'ippim* (Collected works, IV 38-58); G. Dalman, *Christentum und Judentum*, Leipzig, 1898; H. G. Enelow, *A Jewish View of Jesus*, New York, 1920; Z'eb Markon, *Ha-Talmud w'ha-Natzruth* (*Ha-Shiloach* XXXIII 20-32, 170-176, 469-481). See also L. Bäck, *Das Wesen des Judentums*, 3. Aufl. Frankfort a. M., 1923; M. Güdemann, *Jüdische Apologetik*, Glogau, 1906; *Die Grundlagen der Jüdischen Ethik* (*Die Lehren des Judentums nach den Quellen*, herausgegeben vom Verband der Deutschen Juden) bearbeitet von S. Bernfeld, Th. I-II,

almost seem as though the Gospels were composed simply and solely out of matter contained in the *Talmud* and *Midrash*.

But there is a new thing in the Gospels. Jesus, who concerned himself with neither *Halakha* nor the secular knowledge requisite for *Halakha,* nor (except to a limited extent) with scriptural exposition—Jesus gathered together and, so to speak, condensed and concentrated ethical teachings in such a fashion as to make them more prominent than in the *Talmudic Haggada* and the *Midrashim,* where they are interspersed among more commonplace discussions and worthless matter. Even in the Old Testament, and particularly in the Pentateuch, where moral teaching is so prominent, and so purged and so lofty, this teaching is yet mingled with ceremonial laws or matters of civil and communal interest which also include ideas of vengeance and harshest reproval.

Although there is, in the *Mishna,* an entire tractate devoted exclusively to ethical teaching, viz., *Pirke Aboth,* it is but a compilation drawing on the sayings of many scores of *Tannaim* and even (in the supplementary sixth chapter, *"Kinyan Torah"*) of *Amoraim;* but the ethical teachings of the Gospel, on the contrary, came from one man only, and are, every one, stamped with the same peculiar hall-mark. A man like Jesus, for whom the ethical ideal was everything, was something hitherto unheard of in the Judaism of the day. "Jesus ben Sira" lived at least two hundred years earlier. Hillel the Elder reached an ethical standard no lower than that of Jesus; but while Jesus left behind him (taking no count of the recorded miracles) almost nothing but ethical sayings and hortatory parables, Hillel was equally, if not more, interested in *Halakha.*

Everything, from leprosy signs, *Nidda* and *Halla,* to lending on usury, comes within the scope of Hillel's teaching. He introduces amendments in civil law and marriage disputes (the *Prozbol, Batē Homah* [Lev. xxv. 31], the drafting of the marriage-settlement, and the like). He sits in the Sanhedrin. Not only is he teacher and Rabbi, but he likewise serves his nation as judge, lawgiver and administrator.

In Jesus there is nothing of this. In its place there is a far greater preoccupation in questions of ethics, and the laying down of virtually nothing but ethical rules (not, as with Hillel, religious and legal injunctions too). Hillel was all for peace and quietness and the avoiding of quarrels, and was prepared to compromise with his opponents to this end (as in the matter of Ordination on a Feast Day).[70a] Jesus, on the contrary, was, as the preacher of a moral standard, a man of contention, saying harsh things of the Pharisees and Sadducæan priests, opposing by force the traffickers in the Temple, and even suffering martyrdom for his opinions.

Berlin, 1920-1921; Irsael Abrahams, *Studies in Pharisaism and the Gospels,* First Series, Cambridge, 1917; Second Series, Cambridge, 1924.
    [70a] *Betza* 20a.

In this he is more like Jeremiah than Hillel, but while Jeremiah intervenes in the *political life* of his nation, contending not only with priests and the popular teachers, but also with *kings* and *princes*, prophesying not only against Judah and Jerusalem, but also against the Gentiles and foreign powers, and the whole of the then known world, enfolding them all in his all-embracing grip, and scrutinizing them with the acute vision of the eagle—Jesus, on the contrary, confines his exhortations within the limits of Palestine and against the Pharisees and priests of Jerusalem; as for the rest. . . . "Give unto Cæsar the things that are Cæsar's, and to God the things that are God.'s."

Thus, his ethical teaching, apparently goes beyond that of *Pirkē Aboth* and of other *Talmudic* and *Midrashic* literature. It is not lost in a sea of legal prescriptions and items of secular information. From among the overwhelming mass accumulated by the Scribes and Pharisees Jesus sought out for himself the "one pearl." But we have already pointed out that, in the interest of Judaism (and, therefore, of humanity as a whole through the medium of Judaism) this is not an advantage but a drawback.

Judaism is not only religion and it is not only ethics: it is the sum-total of all the needs of the nation, placed on a religious basis. It is a national world-outlook with an ethico-religious basis.

Thus like life itself, Judaism has its heights and its depths, and this is its glory. Judaism is a national life, a life which the national religion and human ethical principles (the ultimate object of every religion) embrace without engulfing. Jesus came and thrust aside all the requirements of the national life; it was not that he set them apart and relegated them to their separate sphere in the life of the nation: he ignored them completely; in their stead he set up nothing but an ethico-religious system bound up with his conception of the Godhead.

In the self-same moment he both annulled *Judaism* as the *life-force* of the Jewish nation, and also the nation itself as a nation. For a religion which possesses only a certain conception of God and a morality acceptable to *all* mankind, does not belong to any special nation, and, consciously or unconsciously, breaks down the barriers of nationality. This inevitably brought it to pass that his people, Israel, rejected him. In its deeper consciousness the nation felt that then, more than at any other time, they must not be swallowed up in the great cauldron of nations in the Roman Empire, which were decaying for lack of God and of social morality.

Israel's Prophets had taught that man was created in the image of God; they had proclaimed their message to all nations and kingdoms and looked forward to a time when they would all call on the name of the Lord and worship him with one accord.

Israel's spiritual leaders, the Scribes and Pharisees, also looked for the time when "all creatures should fall down before one God" and all be made "one society (a League of Nations) to do his will with a perfect heart." [70b] And the people knew, if once they compromised their nationality, that that ideal would be left with none to uphold it, and that the vision would never be fulfilled. Religion would be turned to mere visionariness, and morality would be torn and severed from life; while the manner of life of the Gentiles who were not yet capable of realizing such an ethical standard nor of being raised to the heights of the great ideal, would remain more barbarous and unholy than before.

Two thousand years of non-Jewish Christianity have proved that the Jewish people did not err. Both the instinct for national self-preservation and the cleaving to the great humanitarian ideal, emphatically demanded that Judaism reject this ethical teaching, severed, as it became, from the national life: the breach which, all unintentionally, Jesus would have made in the defences of Judaism, must needs have brought this Judaism to an end.

Yet another cause brought about this rejection: the "self-abnegation" taught by Jesus.

It is difficult to suppose that Jesus was, like John the Baptist, an ascetic. We have seen [71] how the Pharisees and the disciples of John reproved Jesus for not fasting like them, and for sitting at meat with publicans and sinners; and we have seen how he used to defend himself on the grounds that he is "the bridegroom" (and "the bridegroom is like unto a king," [72] and he, Jesus, is the "King-Messiah"), while his disciples are the "children of the bride-chamber," and neither "bridegroom" nor "children of the bridechamber" fast during the seven days of the wedding-feast. Jesus is not, therefore, the complete ascetic; he was, frequently, not averse to the pleasures of life (e.g. when the woman at Bethany poured the cruse of spikenard over his head). [73]

Yet after he had failed to arouse a great, popular movement, and after he had realized the severe opposition to his life-work, and also, perhaps, after he had begun to be persecuted by the Herodians and Pharisees, he began to adopt a "negative" attitude towards the life of this present world.

Like all who have become immersed in ethics and nothing else, he became a "pessimist;" life, the life as it is lived in this world, is valueless; nothing is to be gained by resisting evil or fighting against Roman oppression ("Give unto Cæsar the things that are Cæsar's"). Let possessions be divided amongst the poor; no rich man can be worthy of the "days of the Messiah" ("It is easier for a camel to go through the eye of a needle than for a rich man to enter

---

[70b] The *Shemoneh-Esreh* Prayer for New Year and the Day of Atonement.
[71] See above, p. 274.
[72] *Pirke d'R. Eliezer*, §16 (end).
[73] Mark xiv. 2-9; Matt. xxvi. 6-13.

the kingdom of heaven"). Let swearing be forbidden altogether, even swearing by the truth. It is preferable not to marry at all. It is forbidden to divorce a wife even though it be impossible to live with her owing to her unfaithfulness. For the sake of the kingdom of heaven, let a man forsake father and mother, brother and sister, wife and children. Let him desist from all litigation, even when it is a legal matter affecting inheritance.

Let him stretch out the left cheek to one who strikes him on the right cheek, and let him give his cloak to the one who would take away his coat. Let him take no thought for the morrow, nor amass wealth or material for the furthering of culture. He need not labour for the sake of food or raiment, but let him be like the "lilies of the field" or the "fowls of the air" which labour not, but receive everything from God.

As ethical rules for the individual, these may stand for the highest form of morality. We find similar sentiments in isolated sayings from the *Tannaim* and mediæval Jewish thinkers. On the theoretical side Judaism possesses everything that is to be found in Christianity. Judaism has also its ascetic tendencies—the Essenes, systems of thought such as are to be found in works like "The Duties of the Heart," the "Testament of R. Yehudah the Pious;" and a lofty individualistic morality has been a feature in Judaism from the time of Ezekiel ("The soul that sinneth it shall die") till the time of Hillel ("If I am not for myself, who will be for me?" and "If I am here, all is here").

But as a sole and self-sufficient national code of teaching, Judaism could by no means agree to it. The most ascetic remark to be found in the *Mishna* is that of R. Jacob (the teacher of R. Yehudah ha-Nasi): "This world is as it were an ante-chamber to the world to come;" [74] yet the same R. Jacob also says: "Better is a single hour of repentance and good works in this world than all the life of the world to come." [75] Thus *this* world is the main thing, and the moral life is to be realised *here*. The same thing happened with Jesus' ethical teaching as happened with his teaching concerning God. Jesus made himself neither God nor the Son of God, and, in his view of the Godhead, he remained a true Jew; yet by over-emphasis of the divine Fatherhood in relation to himself, he caused Paul and his contemporaries to attribute to him a conception which was both foreign to his own mind and little removed from idolatry.

So too with regard to his ethical teaching.

Judaism also knows the ideal of love for the enemy, and exemplifies it in the law dealing with an enemy's ox or ass and in the ethical teaching of the *Book of Jonah;* but Judaism never emphasized it to such a degree that it ultimately became too high an ideal for ordinary mankind, and even too high for the man of more than average moral

---

[74] *Aboth* IV 16.　　　　　　　[75] *Aboth* IV 17.

calibre.[76] The same applies to the ideal of "stretching the other cheek." Judaism also praised them "who when affronted affront not again," but it never emphasized the idea unduly, for it would be difficult for human society to exist with such a basic principle. Judaism did not forbid swearing and litigation, but enjoined "a righteous yea or nay" [77] and, in the person of Hillel, laid down the principle, "Judge not thy neighbour till thou art come into his place." [78]

Everything which Jesus ever uttered of this nature is Jewish ethical teaching, too; but his *overemphasis* was *not* Judaism, and, in fact, brought about *non*-Judaism. When these extreme ethical standards are severed from the facts of daily life and taught as religious rules, while, at the same time, everyday life is conducted along completely different lines, defined in the prevailing legal codes (which are not concerned with religion) or in accordance with improved scientific knowledge (which again is not concerned with religion)—it is inevitable that such ethical standards can make their appeal only to priests and recluses and the more spiritually minded among *individuals,* whose only interest is religion; while the rest of mankind all pursue a manner of life that is wholly secular or even pagan.

Such has been the case with Christianity from the time of Constantine till the present day: the religion has stood for what is highest ethically and ideally, while the political and social life has remained at the other extreme of barbarity and paganism. The Spanish Inquisition was not thought to be incompatible with Christianity. The Inquisition was concerned with everyday life, it was political religiousness, whereas Christianity was pure religion and ethics lifted above the calls of everyday life. This, however, can never be the case when, as with Judaism, the national religion embraces every aspect of the national life, when nation and belief are inseparable; then it is impossible to use an extreme ethical standard as a foundation.

The nation desires freedom: therefore it must fight for it. As "possessor of the state" it must ensure the security of life and property and, therefore, it must resist evil. A national community of to-day cannot endure without civil legislation—therefore the community must legislate. Swearing on oath cannot always be dispensed with. The national community of today cannot exist without private property—therefore there must be private property; the point is, rather, in what manner the rich man makes use of his property.

The social system is based on the family, therefore there is no

---

[76] It is worth noticing to what extremes apologists for the ethical teaching of Jesus are reduced, *e.g.,* E. Grimm, *Die Ethik Jesu,* 2 Aufl., Leipzig, 1917, pp. 122-134, 104, in order to be convinced how contrary to nature this teaching is.

[77] *Baba Metzia* 49a; *J. Shebi'ith* X 9.

[78] *Aboth* II 4.

place for teaching "celibacy for the kingdom of heaven's sake" as the most exalted virtue in those who would fit themselves for the kingdom of heaven. As to freedom of divorce, now, nineteen hundred years after Jesus, "enlightened" Christianity the world over is fighting for it.

What room is there in the world for justice if we must extend both cheeks to our assailants and give the thief both coat and cloak? Human civilisation is wholly based on the difference between man and nature, between human society and the brute beast and vegetable world; it is, therefore, neither possible nor seemly for man to become as "the lilies of the field" or "the fowls of the air."

But when, in reality, did Christianity ever conduct itself in accordance with these ethical standards of Jesus? In the small fellowship of his disciples community of goods was practised; but even so, the system was adopted only in part and temporarily. The earliest of Jesus' disciples married; they indulged in litigation, they hated and reviled not only their enemies but all who opposed them. Did Jesus himself abide by his own teaching? Did he love the Pharisees —who were not his enemies but simply his theoretical opponents? Did he not call them "Hypocrites," "Serpents," "Offspring of vipers?" and did he not threaten that "upon them would come all the innocent blood that was shed in the land?" [79] Did he not condemn the ungodly to hell where there would be "weeping and gnashing of teeth?"

Did he not resist evil with acts of violence—by expelling the money-changers and them that sold doves in the Temple?

Did he not promise houses and fields and even judgment thrones in the future to those who followed him? When he sent out the Twelve as his messengers to the cities of Israel did he not warn them to be "subtil as serpents and simple as doves," [80] and at the same time say that, for the city which would not receive them, it "would be more tolerable for Sodom and Gomorrah in the day of judgment than for that city." [81] And did he not say to his disciples that "whosoever denied him (Jesus) before men, Jesus would deny him also before his Father in heaven?" [82] and in this is there not vengeance, bearing of malice, unforgiveness and hatred of enemies And what of those words: 'Think not that I came to bring peace upon earth: I came not to bring peace but a sword," [83] "not peace, but dissension?" [84]

And what of those harsh, definite words: "I came to cast fire on the earth, and what will I if it is already kindled!" [85] And what of his injunction "to sell the cloak and buy a sword?" [86] And what of

[79] Matt. xxiii. 35.
[80] Matt. x. 16.
[81] Matt. x. 15.
[82] Matt. x. 33.

[83] Matt. x. 34.
[84] Luke xii. 51.
[85] Luke xii. 49.
[86] Luke xxii. 36.

those cruelest of words, "Give not what is holy to the dogs and cast not your pearls before swine?" [87]

Where in all this do we find tenderness, pardon "till seventy times seven," love of the enemy and putting forth the other cheek? This is not an arraignment against Jesus: he maintained a high moral standard in all his doings, and his stern words and the expulsion of the traffickers and money-changers were in themselves a lofty moral protest; but such contradiction between precept and practice cannot but prove that this extreme ethical teaching cannot possibly be carried out in practice in everyday life, even by so exceptional a man for whom society was naught and the individual soul everything. Then how much more impossible must it be in the sphere of political and national life?

This it was left for Judaism to perceive. We have before us two facts. In the first place, "Christian morality" was embodied in daily life by—Judaism: it is Judaism, and Judaism only, which has never produced murderers and pogrom-mongers, whereas indulgence and forgiveness have become the prime feature in its being, with the result that the Jews have been made moral (not in theory but in living fact) to the verge of abject flaccidity. In the second place, monasticism is typical not of Judaism but of Christianity, in the same way as it is typical of Buddhism. Had there been no ascetic and monastic element in Jesus' teaching, monasticism would not have become a peculiarity of Roman and Orthodox Christianity.

The Protestant Reformation which abolished monasticism and the celibacy of the clergy was a reversion to Judaism. Christianity is the halfway station between Judaism and Buddhism. Pharisaic Judaism *as a whole* (as distinct from certain individual moralists, from the time of the Essenes till the time of the writer of the *Shebet Musar*, who educed from Pharisaic Judaism an extremist ethical code) was alive to the fact that the Law "was not given to the ministering angels," [88] and it endeavoured to take account of existing conditions, but to raise them and to sanctify them. It did not teach the abolition of marriage, of oaths or of property: it sought rather to bridle sexual desire, to limit the use of oaths and lessen the evils of wealth.

By embracing life as a whole Judaism rendered an extremist morality impossible; but it hallowed the secular side of life by the help of the idea of sanctity, while rendering the idea of sanctity real and strong and palpable by contact with actual reality. Judaism is an all-embracing, all-inclusive political-national social culture; therefore together with the noblest abstract ethic, it comprises both ceremonial rules of purely religious interest and entirely secular human points of view.

[87] Matt. vii. 6.
Berachoth 25b; *Yoma* 30a; *Kiddushin* 54a; *Me'ila* 14b.

Thus in the Levitical "Code of Holiness" [89] we find, side by side, "Thou shalt love thy neighbour as thyself," and rulings about "unclean foods" and the "sacrificial remnants;" "Thou shalt not take vengeance nor bear any grudge," side by side with rulings about "mixed materials" and "cross-breeding;" "The stranger that sojourneth with you shall be as the home-born among you, and thou shalt love him as thyself," side by side with rulings about "the acquired bondmaid" (Lev. xix. 20); alongside of the lofty thought, "Ye are the sons of the Lord your God," comes the ceremonial rule, "Ye shall not cut yourselves."

"Thou shalt not take vengeance nor bear any grudge" can occur in the same book in which it is written, "Remember what Amalek did unto thee," and "Harass the Midianites;" the command to help "the ass of thine enemy that is fallen under its load" does not exclude from the Law of Moses the command, "Thou shalt not leave a soul alive," and "of the foreigner shalt thou exact usury," and "of the stranger shalt thou exact it" (Deut. xv. 2—in whatever sense this is taken).

Within the same Old Testament is included the *Book of Jonah*, teaching in unrivalled fashion the duty of forgiveness to enemies and preserving the destroyer of the fatherland; and also the *Book of Esther* describing in most garish colours the vengeance wreaked on the enemy.

All such feelings and attitudes *exist* within a people and must find place in its literature: they are all human, deeply implanted in man's nature and they may not be changed in a moment at will. A proof of this is before us in the fact that even Christianity, in addition to the New Testament, *was forced to accept unchanged the whole of the Old Testament as Canonical Scripture*, a sign that the New Testament alone did not suffice.

It did not suffice because it did not embrace the whole of life, whether civil or national, communal or private, religious or ethical, theoretical or practical.

The *Talmud* also, like the Old Testament, is all-embracing and all-inclusive. The Old Testament ideal is the Prophet Jeremiah: he is a moralist, but he is also a political worker and a great fighter on his nation's behalf.

The *Talmud* ideal is Hillel the Elder; he, no less than Jesus, was a moralist of high degree, humble, a peace-maker, and a lover of his fellow men; but he was no fighter nor politician; instead his teaching embraced the whole of the social and national life. Hillel took up his position in the centre of affairs, laboured together with the community (his favourite saying was, "Do not keep yourself apart from the community"), took within his purview all the requirements of life from every possible point of view, embodied just such ethical standards as were possible in practice, and thus sanctified and raised the tone of ordinary, every-day life, and made his ethical

[89] Lev. xix.

teaching popular and widespread. He rendered it possible of practice to any man, and not merely to the chosen few who could withdraw from the affairs of everyday life.

Jesus surpassed Hillel in his ethical ideals: he changed Hillel's "Golden Rule" from the negative form ("What thou thyself hatest do not unto thy neighbour"—in which the *Book of Tobit* [90] anticipates Hillel) to the positive form ("What thou wouldest that men should do unto thee, do thou also unto them"—in which the "Letter of Aristeas" [91] anticipates Jesus), and concerned himself more with ethical teaching than did Hillel; but his teaching has not proved possible in practice.[92]

Therefore he left the course of ordinary life untouched—wicked, cruel, pagan ; and his exalted ethical ideal was relegated to a book or, at most, became a possession of monastics and recluses who lived far apart from the paths of ordinary life.

Beyond this ethical teaching Jesus gave nothing to his nation. He cared not for reforming the world or civilisation : therefore to adopt the teaching of Jesus is to remove oneself from the whole sphere of ordered national and human existence—from law, learning and civics (all three of which were absorbed into the codes of the *Tannaim-Pharisees*), from life within the State, and from wealth in virtually all its forms. How could Judaism accede to *such* an ethical ideal?—that Judaism to which the monastic ideal had ever been foreign!

The ethic of Jesus is, however, founded on the special character of his belief in the Day of Judgment and the kingdom of heaven (the "Days of the Messiah"). Only after we have understood the nature of this belief can we comprehend how Jesus the *Jew* attained to such an extreme in his ethical teaching.

[90] *Tobit* iv. 15; the Rule is also found in Philo, as quoted by Eusebius, *Praeparatio Evangelica,* VIII 7, 6; and also in what is, in the main, a Jewish work, the *Didache,* I. 2.

[91] Ed. Wendland, p. 207; see Kautzsch, *Apocryphen und Pseudepigraphen des Alten Testaments* II 22, n. a.   See the Slavonic *Enoch* LXI 1.

[92] See "Ahad ha-Am," Collected Works, IV 45-50; G. Friedlander, *The Jewish Sources of the Sermon on the Mount,* London, 1911, pp. 230-238. Maimonides, however, in his *Sefer ha-Mitzvoth, Mitzvoth 'Asēh* §206 (ed. H. Heller, Petrokoff 1914, p. 64), gives positive and negative forms together and regards them both as equally Judaism.

VI. THE DAY OF JUDGMENT AND THE KINGDOM OF HEAVEN

When dealing with the life of Jesus we saw how, at the moment of his baptism by John in the Jordan, the idea flashed upon his mind that he was the Messiah, but that he concealed the fact from his disciples until Cæsarea-Philippi, since he shrank from the danger of stirring up a political movement against Rome (cf. the Temptation immediately after the Baptism), and took the imprisonment of John the Baptist as a warning against mixing in matters of politics. But it followed, none the less, that since there was a Messiah in the world, the "kingdom of heaven was nigh," and this news Jesus, from the outset, published and proclaimed in his teaching.

What was the nature of this kingdom of heaven, and how was it to be revealed in the world?

We have already observed [1] that the "kingdom of heaven" (the usual title in Matthew) or the "kingdom of God" (usual in Mark and Luke) [2] or the "kingdom of the Almighty" (as in the "Alenu" prayer [Singer, "Authorised Prayer Book," p. 76], "When the world shall be perfected under the kingdom of the Almighty") or the "Theokrateia" of Josephus, [3] is so entirely a Hebrew form of speech as to retain in its Greek translation the original Hebrew construction (βασιλεία τῶν οὐρανῶν, with "heaven" in the plural as always in Hebrew), and that it was widely used in Israel in Jesus' time, and generally understood without further explanations.

Jesus never explained it to any extent: in the Canonical Gospels, at least, he speaks far more of its coming than of its nature. Yet he gives sufficient indication to leave it quite clear that his notion of the kingdom of heaven and all that it involved differed but little from that of his fellow Jews in the early *Tannaitic* period.

The kingdom of heaven is the sovereignty of good—worldly, material good as well as higher, spiritual good, for "there is none good but one, and that is God." [4] In those days, before the "Days of the Messiah," Israel was in evil plight, ruled over by strangers and heathen; and the world as a whole was in like plight since it was ruled over by ungodly tyrants. There prevailed sore poverty and great tribulations, and the righteous and the godly were persecuted and afflicted.

---

[1] See p. 245.
[2] That their meaning is identical is apparent from the use of ‏יראת שמים‎ and ‏שם שמים‎ as interchangeable terms for ‏יראת אלהים‎ and ‏שם ה׳‎.
[3] *Contra Apionem* II, 16.
[4] Mark x. 18; Matt. xix. 17; Luke xviii. 19.

398

All this came about because men were given up to sin: they did not practise kindness one to another nor give alms to the poor; they robbed and oppressed and lived in luxury by despoiling the poor. They did not even observe the main commandments, but profaned the Sabbath and committed other like sins. But when once men shall practise repentance, when men shall turn from their evil ways and strive to do well one towards another, to abstain from oppression and wrong, to follow after righteousness and to call upon the Lord—then shall the God of their fathers send to them Elijah the Prophet, who shall bring the glad tidings of the coming of the redeemer, the King-Messiah, who shall redeem them from all evil, overcome their foreign enslavers by "the breath of his lips," *i.e.*, by the help of God (according to the earliest and most popular forms of the belief, the Messiah will wage war with them until he defeat them utterly, and this victory will be accomplished by divine help).

Then shall the kingdom be restored to the house of Israel under the righteous sceptre of the Messiah (hence the title *"King-*Messiah"*), and God shall judge all the nations and also the tribes of Israel; and on the Judgment Day, the Messiah shall stand at the right hand of God. The transgressors who refused to repent, whether they be of the Gentiles or of Israel (though the numbers will be far greater among the Gentiles), them shall God consume in the fire of hell.

Then shall there be on the Day of Judgment a time of distress in the world, the like of which had never been known since God created the world. Dearth and famine shall wax sore, fierce and bitter wars shall wage, contempt shall increase, internal quarrels shall reach such a pitch that the son will revile his father and the daughter rise up against her mother. Whole cities shall be destroyed. The Law shall be forgotten. False prophets shall be many, and sorrow after sorrow shall come upon the world, until the few good and righteous are purified and cleansed out of the midst of the numerous godless and unrighteous.

After the stern Day of Judgment a *new world* shall come into being, and with it shall come the "messianic age," days of happiness and prosperity, both material and spiritual. At the sound of the trumpet of the Messiah (or, rather, the trumpet that hails the coming of the messianic age) there shall be a gathering together of the exiles, of all the Jews scattered to the four corners of the earth. Those Gentiles who survive the Day of Judgment shall all become proselytes and call on the name of the one and only God, and "all the nations shall be made one society to do the will of God with a perfect heart," and the righteous and the pious shall draw near to God and enjoy all manner of good.

In the Land of Israel shall be set up a glorious kingdom of the saints of the Most High, with the King-Messiah at their head. The Temple shall be rebuilt, and all nations, still persisting according to their races and states (Judaism does not envisage the abolition of nationality in the world but the brotherhood of the nations), shall stream unto the Mountain of God and serve the God of Israel together with the chosen people. The very *fruitfulness* of the land shall increase greatly and *evil beasts* shall no longer harm mankind. Sorrow shall cease with oppression and pride, slavery and inequality, and mankind shall become a kingdom of brothers, sons of one father —their Father in heaven.

Finally shall come to pass the resurrection of the dead (a thoroughly Jewish conception, arising from a combination of the foreign, Græco-Persian, idea of the survival of the soul with the Jewish idea of the messianic age). The righteous shall come to life and (according to another view) the ungodly also, after they have been purified in the fire of hell; and the righteous shall sit in the company of Abraham, Isaac and Jacob, and of Moses, the First Redeemer, and of the rest of the saints of the world, and all shall shelter under the shadow of the Messiah.

Then and only then shall come the *world to come*, wherein is neither eating nor drinking, nor fruitfulness nor begetting of children, nor trafficking nor jealousy nor strife, but "the righteous shall sit with crowns on their heads and enjoy the brightness of the Shekina." [5]

This was the ideal of the kingdom of heaven, or "the Days of the Messiah," at the time when Jesus lived; and it was this ideal which he saw in his mind when he made his great pronouncement: "The kingdom of heaven is at hand." To him also the root principle was righteousness and well-doing, abstention from revenge and the feeling of malice, from oppression and deeds of violence, from ruthlessness and lust, and the practising of good, of pardon and forgiveness, humility and piety, and, above all, the avoidance of hypocrisy and cant, *i.e.*, regarding ceremonial laws like the washing of hands, the cleansing of vessels, tithing of herbs, as the primary element of the devout life, and treating as of secondary importance only those vital commandments bearing on a man's relations with his fellow men.

But the poor and downtrodden and afflicted, the lost and strayed, the ignorant and social outcasts whom Jesus gathered around him— these he could not attract nor satisfy with spiritual promises only: he was compelled to hold out an earthly ideal also, more particularly since he, too, was addicted to the beliefs and ideas of his race and age. We have already seen how he describes the Day of Judgment in colours closely resembling those in the ancient *Baraitas* speaking of "the pangs of the Messiah" and in old Hebrew Apocalypses; thus he says: "Verily I say unto you that I shall not drink again of the fruit of

[5] This is a very brief abstract of three books by the present writer: *Ha-Ra'yon ha-Meshihi b'Yisrael*, Vol. I: *The Period of the Prophets* (Cracow, 1909); Vol. II; *The Apocryphal and Pseudepigraphical Books* (Jerusalem, 1921); Vol. III: Period of the *Tannaim* (Jerusalem, 1923), also in German, *Die Messianischen Vorstellungen des Jüdischen Volkes im Zeitalter der Tannaiten*, Berlin, 1904.

the vine till the day when I shall drink it new in the kingdom of heaven," [6] where the reference is, without doubt, to "the wine preserved in the grape from the six days of creation." [7]

To those who forsake house and fields he promises "houses and fields a hundredfold," [8] and to his disciples he says, "Therefore will I make you to inherit the kingdom of heaven . . . that ye may eat and drink of my table in my kingdom,[9] and ye shall sit on thrones and judge the twelve tribes of Israel." [10]

And, again, in different words, "In the new creation ('the new world') when the Son of man shall sit on the throne of his glory, ye too shall sit on twelve thrones judging the twelve tribes of Israel." [11]

As for the increased fruitfulness of the earth, Papias, one of the earliest Church Fathers, speaking in the name of John of Asia Minor, has left us these words of Jesus: "The days will come in which vines shall spring up, each bearing ten thousand stocks, and on each stock ten thousand branches, and on each branch ten thousand shoots, and on each shoot ten thousand bunches, and on each bunch ten thousand grapes, and each grape when pressed shall yield five and twenty measures (lit. *baths;* one *bath* = 36 litres) of wine. And when any one of the saints shall have caught hold of one grape another shall cry, 'Better grape am I: take me; by me bless the Lord.' Likewise also a grain of wheat shall cause to spring up ten thousand ears of corn, and each ear shall hold ten thousand grains, and each grain ten pounds of fine, pure flour. And so shall it be with the rest of the fruits and seeds and every herb after its kind. And all animals which shall use those foods that are got from the ground shall live in peace and concord, in all things subject to man." [12]

This description tallies in almost every detail with the corresponding description found in the *Apocalypse of Baruch*,[13] with another in an ancient *Talmudic Baraita*,[14] and still more with an expansion of this *Baraita* found in the old *Tannaitic Midrash Sifre*.[15] Later, when Christianity moved farther and farther away from Judaism, and hopes of a speedy coming of the kingdom of heaven were disappointed, such earthly and material promises were omitted from the teaching of Christianity.

---

[6] Mark xiv. 25.

[7] *Berachoth* 34b.

[8] Mark x. 20.

[9] Cf. "The Holy One, blessed be He, will prepare a banquet for the righteous from the flesh of Leviathan" (*Baba Bathra* 75a).

[10] Luke xxii. 29-30.

[11] Matt. xix. 28.

[12] See Irenæus, *Adv. Haer.* V 33.

[13] *Baruch* 29, 5-8. For a comparison of Baruch and Papias, see Klausner, *Ha-Ra'yon ha-Meshihi b'Yisrael*, II 54-56.

[14] *Kethuboth* 111b.

[15] *Sifre* on Deut. xv and xvii (ed. Friedmann 135-6). For further detail see Klausner, *Die Mess. Vorstellungen* pp. 108-112.

But there is no doubt that Jesus could never have attracted the simple and somewhat grossly minded fishermen and peasants without the promises of worldly and material happiness, and we have noticed how, even in the Canonical Gospels, he looks forward to the banquet of the Messiah, "the table of the kingdom of heaven," and the "new wine," and also "fields and houses" in the "Days of the Messiah."

Again, in the first and second centuries of the Christian era, belief in the earthly kingdom of the Messiah was very strong, and for many centuries after, Christians believed in a Millennium (Chiliasmus), which included also this material belief recorded in Papias, and kindred ideas, a belief which has some foundation in the Prophets and the subsequent Hebrew literature ("the banquet of Leviathan," "Leviathan and the wild ox," "the wine laid up since the days of Creation," and the like).

In this respect too Jesus did not differ from the rest of his people; and, furthermore, we have reason to believe that Jesus expected the kingdom to be restored to the Jews *in the political sense.* In the first verses of the Acts of the Apostles, without any preparation or warning from the context, there suddenly comes the passage: [16] "And when they (the disciples) were gathered together they asked him, Lord, dost thou at this time (ἐν τῷ χρονῷ τούτῳ) restore the kingdom to Israel?" The verse does not raise any doubt but that Jesus would restore the kingdom to Israel: it was only a question of "when."

Jesus was, therefore, truly Jewish in everything pertaining to the belief in a worldly and even a political Messiah; the only difference was that, as against the believers in a political Messiah, he supposed that only with the help of God, without the help of armed force, he should restore the kingdom of Israel to the Jews when once they should repent.

Yet despite the Judaistic character of this messianic belief, there was in it, in the form in which Jesus conceived it, a danger to the Jews.

The Jews expected the Messiah at any time. Every day there arose false Messiahs, visionary patriots, stout-hearted but feeble-handed, who passed away like a shadow once the Romans or the Herodians had made an end of them and their deeds. Sometimes the Pharisees and *Tannaim* supported them, as Rabbi Akiba supported Bar Kokhbah; but, as a rule, the Pharisees dreaded the difficult consequences of the Messianic belief in practice.[17]

Hence, in the older *Talmudic* literature, we find an ambiguous attitude towards the Messianic promises: these is a certain wariness as touching the persons of the Messiahs, but a deep and enthusiastic belief in the Messianic hope itself. When the appointed hour should strike, God would himself redeem his people by miracles and wonders,

[16] Acts i. 6.
[17] See J. M. Elbogen, *Ph'rushim* (*Otzar ha-Yahaduth,* Specimen Volume, Warsaw, 1906) pp. 93-4.

and the Messiah would be no more than an instrument of God. Jesus, from the moment of his baptism, looked upon himself as the Messiah; the Messiah was, therefore, already in the world, and so the kingdom of heaven, the kingdom of the Messiah, was likewise in existence in the world.

Jesus definitely stated that the kingdom of heaven began with John the Baptist, "for he is Elijah that was to come," "the Law and the Prophets were until John, and from that time the kingdom of God is preached." [18] The kingdom of God was, at least, already drawing near, it was "nigh, even at the door," and nothing was lacking save repentance and good works (according to R. Eliezer).[19] Jesus, therefore, with the utmost insistence, preached repentance and good works and supposed that there was no necessity for rebellion nor even any reason why, at the moment, he should reveal himself as the Messiah. The real necessity was to stir up a great popular movement of penitents and well-doers; thus the kingdom of heaven would be brought still nearer and with it the occasion of Jesus' manifestation as Messiah.

If only the people of Galilee and Judæa and beyond Jordan would wholly repent and reach the highest level of moral conduct humanly possible, so that a man should love his enemies, forgive transgressors, associate with publicans and sinners, and extend the cheek to the smiter—then would God perform a miracle and the kingdom would be restored to Israel, nature would be brought to perfection and the whole world become an earthly Paradise.

Elijah was already come in the person of John the Baptist, and now came Jesus: and it was he who should be the "Son of Man" and sit on "the right hand of Power," and with him his twelve disciples, on the Day of Judgment when God should judge the twelve tribes of Israel. This Day of Judgment and this kingdom of heaven which was bound up with it, would not long delay; but of the day or the hour none knew save God.[20] It would come suddenly: as in the days of Noah when the floods came suddenly upon the earth, so should be the coming of the Son of man;[21] the great day of the Lord would come "like a thief in the night";[22] "as the lightning that lighteneth from one part under the heaven and shineth unto the other part under heaven, so shall the Son of man be in his day."[23]

And, in real fact, the kingdom of heaven had already begun: in a certain sense it had come: "It cometh not with observation; nor shall they say, Lo here, or Lo there; for the kingdom of heaven is within

[18] Matt. xi. 12-15; Luke vii. 28; xvi. 16.
[19] *Sanh.* 97b.
[20] Mark xiii. 32. It is interesting to notice that in Acts i. 7, "the day" becomes "the times."
[21] Matt. xxiv. 37-39.
[22] Matt. xxiv. 42-44; cf. I Thess. v. 2-3.
[23] Luke xvii. 24.

you;" [24] in other words, the Messiah is already *among you*—not, as Tolstoy interpreted the saying, "within man," but among such men as acted aright. Repentance was already at work among certain of the people: therefore the kingdom of heaven had already begun in actual fact; all that was now awaited was that the *whole* people should repent and act aright (כולו זכאי—"all be free from blame" as the *Talmud* expresses it),[25] or, at least, the majority of them. Then, by the help of God and his Messiah, the kingdom of heaven should become an actuality.

But it was, even now, in process of coming into being. Some might not see it, just as ignorant folk fail to understand how, from a small acorn, grows a great oak. The kingdom of heaven is like a grain of mustard seed which grows into a great plant; or like leaven in the dough which, little though it be, leavens the whole; or like a seed which a man casts into the ground while the world sleeps, and which springs up and grows of itself.[26]

It is true that some of the seed perishes, but what falls on good ground brings forth thirty, or even sixty or a hundredfold. It is true that among the wheat may spring up tares; but after awhile the corn in the field ripens, and the wheat and the tares are separated: the wheat is gathered to the threshing floor and the tares thrown into the furnace.[27] Jesus was convinced that "this generation shall not pass away till all be fulfilled," [28] and definitely asserted: "There are some standing here that shall not taste of death till they see the kingdom of God coming with power," [29] and again to his Apostles: "Verily I say unto you, Ye shall not have gone through the cities of Israel till the Son of man be come." [30]

During the first century and until the beginning of the second, from Stephen until the last of Jesus' contemporaries, all awaited the coming of the Messiah in their days. This is the "Parousia" (the Second Coming) which filled the thoughts of Paul, and to which he looked forward to the end of his days and about which he spoke with the utmost conviction in his epistles.[31] The watch-word of the early Christians was "Maran Atha," our Lord cometh;[32] "the days are fulfilled," the world "is waxen old" [33] and drawing to a close; but little time remains before the "end" of this world, the Day of Judgment and the kingdom of heaven.

[24] Luke xvii. 20-21.
[25] *Sanh.* 98a.
[26] Mark iv. 26-32; Matt. xiii. 3-34.
[27] Matt. xiii. 3-52.
[28] Matt. xiii. 30.
[29] Mark ix. 1.
[30] Matt. x. 23.
[31] See O. Holtzmann, *War Jesu Ekstatiker?* 1903, pp. 66-69.
[32] I Cor. xvi. 22. More correctly: *Marana ta!* "Come, O our Lord!"
[33] A terrifying picture of the end of "the youth of the world" and the "consummation of life" may be found in the *Apocalypse of Baruch*, lxxxv 10 (J. Klausner, *Ha-Ra'yon ha-Meshihi b'Yisrael*, II 57).

This same conviction explains the extremist ascetic ethical system of Jesus. If this world is so soon to cease and God is to create a "new creation," a man may distribute his possessions among the poor, he may refrain from marrying, may forsake his family, may refrain from swearing and from resisting evil. Such extremist morality is accountable as a morality of "the end of the world:" it is necessarily gloomy and pessimistic. It does not, however, follow that Jesus did not regard such morality as also an end in itself—he was a Jew and brought up on the Hebrew prophetic writings. Yet had it not been for this conviction of the nearness of the "Days of the Messiah" and the "fulfilment of the days," he could not have put forward that extremist ethic and self-abnegation which he taught in many of his parables and sayings.

If the kingdom of heaven is at hand it is worth while to sell all and buy the one precious pearl—the kingdom of God. Nor need there be any scruple in receiving publicans and sinners and harlots, since the Day of Judgment would sift out the good from the evil— just as the fisherman gathers into his net good fish and bad, and only afterwards picks out the good and discards the bad.[34]

This two-fold misapprehension of Jesus—the nearness of the kingdom of heaven and his Messiahship—perpetuated his memory and created Christianity. Had not the disciples expected his second coming Christianity could never have come into being: even as a Jewish sect, comprising the disciples and Paul, it could only have persisted through a belief that Jesus was the Messiah who was to come at God's right hand in the Day of Judgment and not suffer his followers to see corruption. But for this conviction Jesus, the Pharisaic Jew, could never have taught that extremist and individualistic ethic which neither society, state nor nation could endure, however much it might be in accord with the spirit and the needs of the afflicted and the downtrodden among the Jews and the other nations during that dreadful period of world-wide servitude, when all the nations were writhing in the claws of the cruel and voracious Roman eagle. The Jews as a whole could not, however, follow after a belief based on so slight a foundation. By this belief of Jesus his kingdom did, in reality, become "not of this world." [35] Through the overstressing of the divine Fatherhood, Jesus, in the thought of the next Christian generation, became, in spite of himself, the Son of God; and, later, to those converted from paganism, he became God himself. Yet again, through the preaching of his messianic claims, after he had failed to manifest himself to the world again, in his power and glory, he became, in spite of himself, a "sacrifice," a "ransom for many." [36]

Judaism, on the other hand, is definitely "of this world:" it seeks (*cf.*, the *"Alenu"* prayer) "to amend this *world* by the kingdom of

[34] Matt. xiii. 44-52.   [36] Mark x. 45.
[35] John xviii. 36.

God" and not only isolated individuals. Judaism does not associate the Messiah with the Godhead, nor attribute to the Messiah a deciding rôle in the day of redemption: Judaism knows nothing of redemption through an intermediary or intercessor between God and man.

The Jews as a whole could not, therefore, accept Jesus; howbeit Jesus himself, being as he was a Jew, did not regard himself as God nor think of himself as a sacrificial ransom—but by his sayings and works he gave occasion for *others* so to regard him after but a short lapse of time.

At that time Pharisaic Judaism was too mature, its purpose too fixed to endure change. Its leaders were fighting for their national existence and grappling with foreign oppressors and with those semi-foreigners who sought to crush it, and with a decadent idolatry which sought to absorb it. In such days of stress and affliction, they were themselves far removed—and would remove also their fellow-Jews—from dangerous fantasies and an extremism which most of the race could not endure.

They saw at the outset what the end would be: the result of a vain vision is semi-idolatry and an extreme morality ends in demoralization; and thus it was. It is true that, for the pagan world, there was a great gain in the belief in the one God and in the prophetic ethical teaching which was perpetuated in Christianity owing to the teaching of Jesus the Jew; in such a sense as this Judaism, through the medium of Christianity, became "a light to the Gentiles."

The Jews themselves, however, could not compromise that Pharisaic teaching which had its mainspring in Judaism and developed with Judaism, which embraced all things in its daily life and realized the ethical demands and the messianic promises of the Prophets in the national life; the Jews could not compromise this for the sake of a messianic vision and an extremist ethical code which were both alike founded on a hope which was never fulfilled.[37]

The kingdom of heaven, according to Jesus, is in the present. The kingdom of heaven, according to Judaism, is to be "in the latter days." The former is to come suddenly "like a thief in the night;" the latter will be the fruit of long development and hard work. True socialism is Jewish and not Christian. How, then, could Judaism regard Jesus as the Messiah?

And so we find the correct answer to the twofold question: Why

---

[37] Even so ardent a Christian apologist as Eduard Grimm is forced to admit this: "The kingdom of heaven as it lived in the hopes of the people of Israel could not be otherwise than something actual and tangible, like other kingdoms. And Jesus himself was not far removed from such an idea. We find ourselves, therefore, in an unusual position; if the idea of the kingdom of heaven is to rule us to-day as a living power, we must inevitably spiritualize it to such an extent that the greater part of its original character is taken from it. If, however, we would preserve the historic truth, the idea will be foreign to us and will no longer occupy a central position" (*Die Ethik Jesu*, 2 Aufl., Leipzig, 1917, p. 265).

did Jesus arise among the people of Israel? and why, in spite of that, did the people of Israel repudiate his teaching? Both things were natural, and both were inevitable in the process of human history—a history which is governed by a higher reason and whose only way is truth and justice.

VII. THE CHARACTER OF JESUS AND THE SECRET OF HIS INFLUENCE

The influence of Jesus upon his disciples and followers was exceptional. In Galilee masses of people followed him: for his sake his disciples forsook all and followed him to the danger zone, to Jerusalem; they remained faithful to him both during his life and after his terrible death. Every word he spoke—even parables which they did not understand and the more enigmatic figures of speech—they treasured like a precious pearl. As time went on his spiritual image grew ever more and more exalted till, at length, it reached the measure of the divine. Never has such a thing happened to any other human creature in enlightened, historic times and among a people claiming a two thousand years old civilisation.

What is the secret of this astonishing influence?

In the opinion of the present writer the answer should be looked for in the complex nature of his personality and also in his methods of teaching.

The great man is not recognizable as such by virtues alone, but by defects which can themselves, in certain combinations, be transformed into virtues. Like every great man Jesus was a complex of many and amazing contradictions: it was these which compelled astonishment, enthusiasm and admiration.[1]

On the one hand, Jesus was humble and lowly-minded, tender and placable, and tolerant to an unprecedented degree. He says of himself that he came not to rule but to serve. In a moment of deepest sorrow he tells how that the foxes have holes and the birds have nests, but that the Son of man has nowhere to lay his head. There were things of which he knew nothing, things known only to his heavenly Father. He could not award "thrones" in the kingdom of the Messiah: this God alone could do. If a man sin against him, the Son of man, all can be forgiven—if only the man sin not against the Holy Spirit.

On the other hand, Jesus possesses a belief in his mission which verges on the extreme of self-veneration. He is the nearest to God, and the day will come when he will sit at the right hand of God. He is greater than king Solomon, greater than the prophet Jonah,

[1] On Jesus' character see J. Ninck, *Jesus als Charakter*, Leipzig, 1906; W. Bousset, *Jesus (Religionsgesch. Volksbücher*, herausg. v. F. M. Schiele), 3 Aufl. Tübingen, 1907; O. Holtzmann, *War Jesus Ekstatiker?* Tübingen u. Leipzig, 1903; F Peabody, *Jésus-Christ et la question morale*, Paris, 1909, pp. 47-80.

and greater than the Temple. John the Baptist was greater than any who had yet lived, yet Jesus was immeasurably greater than John.

So strong was Jesus' belief in himself that he came to rely upon himself more than upon any of Israel's great ones, even Moses; this characteristic is summed up in the formula: "It was said to you by them of old time . . . but I, Jesus, say unto you . . ." We must remember that nothing is more conducive to conviction in others than a man's belief in his own self: once a man believes absolutely in himself, others, too, come to believe in him almost as they would in God. And though exaggerated self-confidence can at times be repellent, yet Jesus was so often tender, gentle and humble as to mask his intense self-confidence.

Looked upon from one side, Jesus is "one of the people." His parables have a most popular appeal. They are, almost every one of them, drawn from life in the village or small town. As a rule he conducted himself as an ordinary, simple man, a Galilæan artisan. His attraction was his simplicity, his very ordinariness, his homeliness in whatever he did or said. He loved the wild flowers with their multiplicity of colouring, and the birds which could be sold two for a farthing; he liked little children to be brought to him, "for theirs is the kingdom of heaven;" the cock-crow, the hen with her chickens, the flush of the skies at evening and their overcast look in the morning—all these find place in his sayings and parables.

But looked at from another side, he is by no means an illiterate, an *"am ha-aretz:"* he is as expert in the Scriptures as the best of the Pharisees, and he is quite at home with the Pharisee's expository devices. He is saturated with the great ideas of the Prophets and the Psalms; he can employ them for his own spiritual needs, he can expound them and adapt them and supplement them. He knows also the "tradition of the elders," the rulings of the Pharisees, and the "words of the Scribes."

And this, too, had its effect on his followers. In the eyes of the simple Galilæans, the *"ammē ha-aretz,"* his women admirers, the fishermen, the peasants and the petty officials, he appeared to be a great teacher of the Law—a "Rab." The Pharisees themselves could not ignore his teaching. He could dispute with them and confute them, no matter whether the argument turned on Scriptural proofs or post-Scriptural traditions.

Without doubt this aroused enthusiasm among his disciples, for among them were also to be found students of the Law—otherwise they could never have preserved his arguments and parables and sayings, which, at times, were of a depth which the ordinary person could not have fathomed.

Again, on the one hand, Jesus is a teacher, a "Rab," of the Pharisaic school—not a "Ba'al-Halakha" (one concerned only in the more legalistic interpretations of Scripture) but a "Ba'al-Hag-

gada" (one whose interest lay rather in the popular, edifying application of Scripture). He called around him the afflicted and the
downtrodden, and he tells them how "his yoke is easy and his burden
light;" [2] he takes compassion on the simpler folk who were "like
sheep without a shepherd;" [3] and he stood aside from the three parties
of his days—the Sadducees, Pharisees and Essenes.

On the other hand, he demands that a man forsake all for his
sake, family, home and possessions, and even his very self ("let him
hate even his own soul"), for such a one only can be his disciple
and enter the kingdom of heaven and be accounted worthy of the
"Days of the Messiah." Gentleness and charm on the one side, the
extremest moral demands on the other . . . nothing can more influence and attract people to something new, no matter whether that
something be of the smallest or the gravest importance.

Yet again, one time we see Jesus indulgent and forgiving and
easily appeased; he pardons his disciples when they commit light or
grave offences; he does not play the pedant with the sinner; he
knows that "the spirit is willing but the flesh is weak." But another
time we find him utterly unbending, pedantic and passionate, protesting and reproving in the severest terms. To his most favoured
disciple, Simon Peter—whom but a little while ago he had named
an enduring "rock"—he calls out, "Get thee behind me, Satan!" He
threatens transgressors with the fire of hell, with "outer darkness,"
with "weeping and gnashing of teeth." He curses Capernaum,
Chorazin and Bethsaida. He applies the harshest possible terms of
rebuke to the Pharisees, terms which, in their general application,
are by no means justified. He is capable even of acts of violence,
of expelling the money-changers and dove-dealers from the Temple.

These two extremes, extreme kindliness of heart and the most
violent passion, show in him a character akin to that of the Prophet—
save only that he had not the wide political perspective of the
Prophets nor their gift of divine consolation to the nation. However
this may be, these two contradictory attributes are the sign of the
great man. Only such a man, mighty in forgiveness and equally
mighty in reproof, could exert so ineffaceable an influence on all
who came in contact with him.

Finally, Jesus is, on the one hand, "a man of the world." To a
great extent he has a sense of realities. His parables and sayings
prove amply that he knew life and the world as they really are. He
can avoid his enemies and persecutors when such action is necessary;
he can be evasive in his answers (*e.g.*, the payment of tribute to
Cæsar, or the authority he claimed for his action in the Temple);

---

[2] Matt. xi. 28-30.
[3] Mark vi. 34; Matt. ix. 35; xv. 32. References are not here given to
every quotation, since most of them have already been given in the earlier
portions of the book.

and sometimes he parries in argument with a delicate though crushing sarcasm, unequalled in acuteness and pungency.

On the other hand, he shows himself a most unworldly visionary in his belief in the supernatural. He considers himself the Messiah and retains this belief to the end in the face of every disappointment. He believes that he performs miracles; he believes that he will sit "on the right hand of Power;" he believes that "heaven and earth shall pass away but that his words will not pass away." [4] Even when he is awaiting his trial before the High Priest and before Pontius Pilate he is still convinced of his Messiahship in a supernatural sense. Not unreasonably did his mother and his brethren think that "he was beside himself." The simpler folk were unable to understand the source of this strange power of faith. The Scribes attributed his power to Beelzebub, while the people of Nazareth scoffed at the miracles of this carpenter and son of a carpenter, whose brothers and sisters were men and women like themselves. But with another type of men nothing exerts a greater influence on their minds than this mystic faith in one who is otherwise perfectly normal, and even promptly alert in everyday matters.

The *complete* visionary and mystic exerts an influence only upon other visionaries like himself, and his influence soon passes. The man of practical wisdom, alert in worldly matters only, merely influences the brain while leaving the heart untouched; and never in this world was anything great achieved unless the heart, deeply stirred, has played its part. Only where mystic faith is yoked with practical prudence does there follow a strong, enduring result. And of such a nature was the influence exerted by Jesus of Nazareth upon his followers, and, through them, upon succeeding generations.

Such is the secret of Jesus' influence. The contradictory traits in his character, its positive and negative aspects, his harshness and his gentleness, his clear vision combined with his cloudy visionariness —all these united to make him a force and an influence, for which history has never yet afforded a parallel.

His *method of teaching* tended to the same end. Just like the Prophet, he invested himself with the greatest authority and depended but little on the Scriptures. Like a Pharisaic "Scribe," he spoke in parables and pregnant sayings. He was a great *artist* in parable. His parables are attractive, short, popular, drawn from everyday life, full of "instruction in wise conduct" (Prov. i. 3), simple and profound at the same time—simple in form and profound in substance.

And this (even the difficulty in grasping the point of the parable) certainly served to interest the simple Galilæans who, while they could not understand the whole, instinctively felt that this attractive covering hid beneath it a kernel of great value.

Besides the parables, there are the striking proverbs of Jesus. They are short, sharp and shrewd, hitting their mark like pointed

[4] Mark xiii. 31; Matt. xxiv. 35; Luke xxi. 33.

darts, and, in the manner of homely epigrams and proverbs, impossible to be forgotten. Herein lies the secret why his disciples could preserve the bulk of his proverbs, almost unchanged, precisely as he uttered them. Almost all are stamped with the seal of one great, single personality, the seal of Jesus, and not the several seals of many and various disciples. To quote a few:

"They that are whole have no need of the physician but they that are sick."

"Let the dead bury their dead."

"Blind leaders of the blind."

"Who strain out a gnat and swallow a camel."

"Whited sepulchres."

"It is easier for the camel to go through the eye of a needle than for a rich man to enter the kingdom of heaven."

"The rich man giveth alms of his superfluity, and the widow—of her lack."

"The spirit is willing, but the flesh is weak."

"Let him that is free from sin cast the first stone."

"It is better to give than to receive."

And there are very many more of the same type. We cannot fail to recognize in them a single, remarkable personality, showing exceptional ability to grasp the innermost principle and to voice it in a short, shrewd proverb, grasping the idea in its fulness and drawing from it some conclusion which can never again be forgotten.

This device of teaching, combined with his own complex character, explains why Jesus' teaching was never forgotten, and why it became the basis of a new faith, though there is in it nothing that is new (*i.e.*, not already contained in Judaism) except its arrangement and construction. The personality of the teacher was taken and mingled with the teaching, for most of what he taught had its origin not in theory but in practical fact, arising out of some event, some chance encounter or question, for which there promptly came the apt and penetrating rejoinder.

The tragedy of the dreadful death which came upon Jesus wrongly (though in accordance with the justice of the time), added a crown of divine glory both to the personality and to the teaching. Later arose the legend of the resurrection, heightening every value, obscuring every defect and exalting every virtue—and Jesus the Jew became half-Jew, half-Gentile, and began to hold that supernatural rank which is his today among hundreds and millions of mankind.

VIII. CONCLUSION: WHAT IS JESUS TO THE JEWS?

There is no page in this volume, no step in the life-story of Jesus, and no line in his teaching on which is not stamped the seal of Prophetic and Pharisaic Judaism and the Palestine of his day, the close of the period of the Second Temple. Hence it is somewhat strange to ask, What is Jesus to the Jews? "Jesus," says Wellhausen, "was not a Christian: he was a Jew," and, as a Jew, his life-story is that of one of the prominent men of the Jews of his time, while his teaching is Jewish teaching of a kind remarkable in its truth and its imaginativeness.

"Jesus was not a Christian," but he *became* a Christian. His teaching and his history have been severed from Israel. To this day the Jews have never accepted him, while his disciples and his followers of every generation have scoffed at and persecuted the Jews and Judaism. But even so, we cannot imagine a work of any value touching upon the history of the Jews in the time of the Second Temple which does not also include the history of Jesus and an estimate of his teaching. What, therefore, does Jesus stand for in the eyes of the Jews at the present time?

From the standpoint of general humanity he is, indeed, "a light to the Gentiles." His disciples have raised the lighted torch of the Law of Israel (even though that Law has been put forward in a mutilated and incomplete form) among the heathen of the four quarters of the world. No Jew can, therefore, overlook the value of Jesus and his teaching from the point of view of universal history. This was a fact which neither Maimonides nor Yehudah ha-Levi ignored.

But from the *national Hebrew* standpoint it is more difficult to appraise the value of Jesus. In spite of the fact that he himself was undoubtedly a "nationalist" Jew by instinct and even an extreme nationalist—as we may see from his retort to the Canaanitish woman, from his depreciatory way of referring to "the heathen and the publican," from the terms "Son of Abraham," "Daughter of Abraham" (which he uses as terms of the highest possible commendation),[1] from his deep love for Jerusalem and from his devoting himself so entirely to the cause of "the lost sheep of the house of Israel"—in spite of all this, there was in him something out of which arose "non-Judaism."

What is Jesus to the *Jewish nation* at the present day?

To the Jewish nation he can be neither God nor the Son of God,

[1] Luke xix. 9; xiii. 16. Cf. "Son of Abraham our father" (*T. Hag.* II 1); "Daughter of Abraham our father" (*B. Hag. 3a*).

in the sense conveyed by belief in the Trinity. Either conception is to the Jew not only impious and blasphemous, but incomprehensible. Neither can he, to the Jewish nation, be the Messiah: the kingdom of heaven (the "Days of the Messiah") is not yet come. Neither can they regard him as a Prophet: he lacks the Prophet's political perception and the Prophet's spirit of national consolation in the political-national sense.

Neither can they regard him as a lawgiver or the founder of a new religion: he did not even desire to be such. Neither is he a "*Tanna,*" or Pharisaic rabbi: he nearly always ranged himself in opposition to the Pharisees and did not apprehend the positive side in their work, the endeavour to take within their scope the entire national life and to strengthen the national existence.

But Jesus is, for the Jewish nation, *a great teacher of morality and an artist in parable.* He is *the* moralist for whom, in the religious life, morality counts as—everything. Indeed, as a consequence of this extremist standpoint his ethical code has become simply an ideal for the isolated few, a "Zukunfts-Musik," an ideal for "the days of the Messiah," when an "end" shall have been made of this "old world," this present social order. It is no ethical code for the nations and the social order of to-day, when men are still trying to find the way to that future of the Messiah and the Prophets, and to the "kingdom of the Almighty" spoken of by the *Talmud,* an ideal which is of "this world" and which, gradually and in the course of generations, is to take shape in this world.

But in his ethical code there is a sublimity, distinctiveness and originality in form unparalleled in any other Hebrew ethical code; neither is there any parallel to the remarkable art of his parables. The shrewdness and sharpness of his proverbs and his forceful epigrams serve, in an exceptional degree, to make ethical ideas a popular possession. If ever the day should come and this ethical code be stripped of its wrappings of miracles and mysticism, the Book of the Ethics of Jesus will be one of the choicest treasures in the literature of Israel for all time.

Jerusalem,
16 Marcheswan, 1922

GENERAL INDEX

T

U

V

INDEX OF BIBLICAL AND RABBINICAL PASSAGES